10648050

WITHDRAWN
UML LIBRARIES

FOR REFERENCE

NOT TO BE TAKEN FROM THE ROOM

CAT. NO. 23 012

PRINTED
IN
U.S.A.

AMERICAN FOREIGN
RELATIONS
1977
A DOCUMENTARY RECORD

COUNCIL ON FOREIGN RELATIONS BOOKS

The Council on Foreign Relations, Inc., is a non-profit and non-partisan organization devoted to promoting improved understanding of international affairs through the free exchange of ideas. Its membership of about 1,700 persons throughout the United States is made up of individuals with special interest and experience in international affairs. The Council has no affiliation with, and receives no funding from, the United States government. The Council does not take any position on questions of foreign policy.

The Council publishes the quarterly journal, *Foreign Affairs*. In addition, from time to time, books and monographs written by members of the Council's research staff or visiting fellows, or commissioned by the Council, or written by independent authors with critical review contributed by a Council study group, are published with the designation "Council Paper on International Affairs." Any book or monograph bearing that designation is, in the judgment of the Committee on Studies of the Council's board of directors, a responsible treatment of a significant international topic worthy of presentation to the public. All statements of fact and expressions of opinion contained in Council books, monographs, and *Foreign Affairs* articles are, however, the sole responsibility of their authors.

AMERICAN FOREIGN RELATIONS 1977

A DOCUMENTARY RECORD

Continuing the Series
DOCUMENTS ON AMERICAN FOREIGN RELATIONS
THE UNITED STATES IN WORLD AFFAIRS

Edited by ELAINE P. ADAM
with an introduction by
RICHARD P. STEBBINS

A Council on Foreign Relations Book

Published by

New York University Press • New York • 1979

Copyright © 1979 by Council on Foreign Relations, Inc.

Library of Congress Catalog Card Number: 78-57941.

ISBN: 0-8147-0567-7

Manufactured in the United States of America

PREFACE

This volume offers a condensed historical narrative together with a selection of documents reflecting salient aspects of the foreign relations of the United States in 1977. Continuing the series of foreign policy surveys initiated by the Council on Foreign Relations in 1931 under the title *The United States in World Affairs*, the volume also maintains the service provided annually for more than three decades by the separate *Documents on American Foreign Relations* series, inaugurated by the World Peace Foundation in 1939 and taken over by the Council on Foreign Relations in 1952. The fusion of narrative and documentation, commenced on a trial basis with the inception of the present series in 1971, is designed to provide a single, comprehensive, and nonpartisan record of American foreign policy as it develops during the bicentennial decade and beyond.

The interests of orderly presentation have appeared to be best served by the inclusion of a faily detailed historical essay that reviews the year's main foreign policy developments and serves as introduction to the accompanying documentary material, which is presented in a parallel sequence to facilitate cross referencing between the two parts of the volume. Some readers will no doubt be satisfied to stop with the introduction; others may wish to go directly to the documents, which are presented in authoritative texts and accompanied by whatever editorial apparatus seemed necessary for independent reference use.

A key to certain abbreviations used in footnotes throughout the volume appears at the end of the Table of Contents, and organizational abbreviations and acronyms are listed and explained in the alphabetical Index. The Appendix presents a selected checklist of historical documents that are referred to in the volume. All dates refer to the year 1977 unless a different year is specifically indicated.

The editorial procedure described above admittedly involves the exercise of a substantial measure of individual judgement and demands all possible objectivity in the handling of controversial events and data. While hopeful that the volume will not be found wanting in this regard, the editors wish to emphasize that the editorial viewpoint is of necessity a personal one and in no way seeks to reflect the outlook of the Council on Foreign Relations or any of its officers and directors, members, or staff.

Among their immediate associates, the editors would note their special indebtedness to Winston Lord, President; John Temple Swing, Vice President and Secretary; Grace Darling Griffin, Publications Manager; and Janet Rigney, Librarian, of the Council on Foreign Relations; and to Despina Papazoglou, Associate Managing Editor, and other friends at NYU Press. They are also indebted to various official agencies which have provided documentary material, and to *The New York Times* for permission to reprint texts or excerpts of documents appearing in its pages. As always, the editors themselves are responsible for the choice and presentation of the documents as well as the form and content of the editorial matter.

September 5, 1978

CONTENTS

PART TWO: DOCUMENTS

KEY TO ABBREVIATED REFERENCES

(The abbreviation GPO refers to
the U.S. Government Printing Office)

"AFR": American Foreign Relations: A Documentary Record (New York: New York University Press, for the Council on Foreign Relations; annual vols., 1971-).

"Bulletin": U.S. Department of State, *The Department of State Bulletin* (Washington: GPO, weekly through 1977, monthly thereafter). Most references are to vols. 76 (Jan.-June 1977), 77 (July-Dec. 1977), and 78 (Jan.-Feb. 1978).

"Documents": Documents on American Foreign Relations (annual vols., 1939-70). Volumes prior to 1952 published by Princeton University Press for the World Peace Foundation; volumes for 1952-66 published by Harper & Row for the Council on Foreign Relations; volumes for 1967-70 published by Simon and Schuster for the Council on Foreign Relations.

"Keesings's": Keesing's Contemporary Archives (Bristol: Keesing's Publications, Ltd., weekly).

"Presidential Documents": Weekly Compilation of Presidential Documents (Washington: GPO, weekly). Most references are to vol. 12 (1976).

"Stat.": Statutes at Large of the United States (Washington: GPO, published irregularly).

"TIAS": U.S. Department of State, *United States Treaties and Other International Agreements* (Washington: GPO, published irregularly).

"UST": U.S. Department of State, *United States Treaties and Other International Agreements* (Washington: GPO, published irregularly).

"USUN Press Releases": Press releases of the U.S. Mission to the United Nations, as reprinted in the *Department of State Bulletin*.

PART I: INTRODUCING 1977

INTRODUCING 1977

NINETEEN SEVENTY-SEVEN will be remembered as the year when Georgia's Jimmy Carter became the 39th American President and concentrated the resources of American foreign policy upon the worldwide promotion of human rights. Earlier American preoccupations—the safeguarding of national security, the slowing of the strategic arms race, the defense of the dollar—were not forgotten but occasionally seemed to fade into the background as the nation's new leaders endeavored to revivify the promises inherent in the Declaration of Independence, the Bill of Rights, the United Nations Charter, and the Universal Declaration of Human Rights, adopted by the U.N. General Assembly in 1948. "One of the most popular things I've tried to do," said President Carter in a television interview near the end of his first year in office (**Document 57**), "is to express to the world our own people's commitment to basic human rights, to freedom and independence and autonomy, the worth of a human being, whether they live here or in Russia or in South America or in Uganda or China. And I doubt that there's a national leader in the world now who doesn't think about human rights every day and how his or her actions are measured against a standard that the world is beginning to demand."

This new, intensified concern with human rights was more than a mere "gimmick," a "frill" stitched onto the bipartisan foreign policy woven under earlier administrations from World War II onward. The Carter approach to world affairs quite obviously stemmed from a broader, deeply felt political conception that ultimately aimed at nothing less than the accommodation of every phase of national policy—including foreign policy—to the moral feelings and humane aspirations of the 216,000,000 living Americans. "You know," said President Carter in the course of the same television interview, "the American people are good and decent and idealistic. And I think they want their government to be good and decent and idealistic."

Such feelings had at all times played an honored role in the shaping of the American nation; yet seldom had they been given such di-

1

rect, authoritative expression as in this year that followed so closely upon the windup of the Watergate scandals, the end of the Vietnam involvement, and the Bicentennial observances of 1976. The longing to create a more humane environment, a world that would be governed by brotherly love rather than mutual hostility, lay deep in the American character; yet its expression had been balanced, at most periods of American history, by a recognition that the path to the millennium was strewn with countless obstacles, and that hostile forces always lay in wait to take advantage of any stumbling along the way. There were times in 1977 when the Carter administration, in concentrating on its ideal goals, seemed almost to ignore the obstacles and intermediate perils—even, perhaps, to incline to the facile simplifications so prevalent in the later 1960s. If the history of 1977 can hardly be read as an "Education of Jimmy Carter," it was at any rate a time of trial and error when the Carter administration repeatedly exposed its good intentions to the test of stern reality, saw many of its cherished hopes elude its grasp, and gradually, perhaps, developed a more sophisticated awareness both of the complexities of world affairs and of the differences between the ideal and the attainable.

Among the specific objectives with which the new administration entered office—aside from its determination to encourage greater respect for human rights throughout the world—were a prompt agreement with the Soviet Union on strategic arms limitation; improved safeguards against the proliferation of nuclear weapons; a reduction in conventional arms sales to other countries; a $5 billion to $7 billion cutback in defense expenditure; a phased withdrawal of American ground forces from Korea; and, at home, a restoration of integrity in government; a sharp reduction in inflation and unemployment; initiation of a national energy policy; and a reform of the welfare system, the tax system, and other currently unsatisfactory features of the domestic scene. These aims were thoroughly consistent with the underlying determination to deemphasize conflict and confrontation and restore priority to human and cooperative values in both domestic and foreign policy. Yet none of them was to prove attainable, by any but the most technical definition, in a year whose principal effect would be to demonstrate that such ambitions were as elusive as they might be laudable.

Particularly frustrating to the administration was the way in which its new concern for human rights appeared to complicate the pursuit of other foreign policy objectives. This was above all true of the relationship between the United States and the Soviet Union, a country whose illiberal, police-state practices had increasingly troubled the American conscience over the dozen years since Leonid I. Brezhnev, currently the General Secretary of the Communist Party, had supplanted Nikita S. Khrushchev as the most visible incarnation of Soviet power. Moscow's congenital disregard for human rights as understood in the West had not by any means been overlooked by President Carter's immediate predecessors, Richard M. Nixon and Gerald R. Ford, still less by Secretary of State Henry A. Kissinger, who had carried prime responsibility for the shaping and execution of American foreign policy in the critical years 1973-76. But Dr. Kissinger had insisted, with the support of his superiors and in the face of strong opposing pressures from sections of Congress and the public, that the maintenance of a stable military and diplomatic balance between the nuclear superpowers must take precedence over any idea of pressing for a reform of Soviet internal practices. The Carter administration's refusal to softpedal its own concern for human rights caused visible irritation in the Kremlin, provided a pretext if not a motive for intensified repression of Soviet dissidents, and supplemented other factors that had already delayed the completion of a critically important Strategic Arms Limitation (SALT) agreement.

Equally ambiguous were the results of the new American policy in other parts of the world. Unfavorable comment on their human rights practices, not all of it originating with the Carter administration, caused sharp reactions in several Latin American countries, leading among other things to the peremptory cancellation of a 25-year-old military aid agreement between Brazil and the United States. American pressure for the dismantling of South Africa's racially segregated "apartheid" system seemed only to intensify the rejection of basic change by the white South African government headed by Prime Minister Johannes B. Vorster. One of the year's more harrowing occurences was the agonized, humiliating death in South African police custody of Steven Biko, a relatively moderate black leader whose role and martyrdom were likened by some to that of the late Martin Luther King, Jr. in the United States.

One highly dramatic victory for the principles of democracy and individual freedom did occur early in the year when the people of India, the second most populous nation of the contemporary world, determined in a free election to set aside the nineteen-month-old dictatorship of Mrs. Indira Gandhi and restore the parliamentary regime her father, the late Prime Minister Jawaharlal Nehru, had done so much to shape. The year brought other positive-seeming developments as well: intensified negotiations looking toward majority rule in Southern Rhodesia and Namibia; completion of treaties to govern the future of the Panama Canal and the U.S.-administered Canal Zone; still more remarkable, the initiation of a top-level dialogue between Egypt and Israel about a permanent peace in the Middle East. Less gratifying was the marked deterioration of conditions in the Horn of Africa, where open warfare between Ethiopians and Somalis enabled Cuba and the Soviet Union, already established as a presence in Angola and some other African countries, to deepen their involvement with Ethiopia's Marxist, anti-American military regime.

Dismaying at a deeper emotional level were the barbarities and acts of terrorism that continued to stain the records of the decade, from the mass atrocities that seemed to be the rule in Cambodia, Uganda, and Equatorial Guinea to the assassinations of prominent political figures like President Marien N'Gouabi of Congo, President Ibrahim al-Hamdi of Yemen, and opposition chieftain Kamal Jumblatt of Lebanon. Exhausted by its brutal civil war of 1975-76, the last-named country was otherwise comparatively quiet in 1977, and the mutual slaughter carried on by Protestant and Catholic stalwarts in Northern Ireland also diminished as compared with the preceding couple of years. But a fresh upsurge of organized terrorism on the continent of Europe—to be considered later in this discussion—drove home the lesson that no country and no culture was immune to a disease that threatened, in the words of West German President Walter Scheel, to "spread like a brush fire all over the world."[1]

"A sense of general insecurity has appeared," France's Commission to Study Violence, Delinquency and Crime, headed by Justice Minister Alain Peyrefitte, concurred. "It is as if life itself has become violent. A new aggressiveness marks personal and social relations. Assaults multiply. Insults, physical abuse, kidnapping, the use of explosives have become part of the arsenal of rivalries and disputes."[2] Such manifestations, it seemed, could only spring from a sickness at the heart of Western civilization, a sickness that mocked the ethical self-assurance of political leadership. They did not in themselves invalidate President Carter's conviction that American foreign policy should reflect the "good and decent and idealistic" qualities of the American people. They did, however, reinforce the view that more than good intentions would be needed if such qualities were to hold their own amid the rough and tumble of contemporary life.

1. UNDER NEW MANAGEMENT

The Twentieth Amendment to the American Constitution, adopted early in 1933, perpetuated some confusion in the processes of government by providing that whereas a new Congress would

[1] Quoted in *New York Times,* Oct. 26, 1977.
[2] Quoted by Jonathan Kandell in same, Aug. 7, 1977.

normally assemble on the third of January, the terms of an outgoing President and Vice-President would continue until noon on the following January 20. The result of this arrangement is a period of overlap that may become especially embarrassing in years when the control of the presidency is passing from one to the other of the two great political parties. An outgoing administration from which the nation has already withdrawn its support must still make recommendations to which no one will pay much heed; while a new administration that is burning to take office must await the ritual fulfillment of its predecessor's turn before it can begin unfolding its own prescription for national salvation.

The presidential transition of 1977 proved no exception to this rule, despite the obvious determination of both outgoing and incoming administrations to make the transfer as smooth and amicable as possible. The task of formally appraising the national situation and offering a blueprint for the period ahead again devolved upon the outgoing Republican administration led by President Ford. To his Democratic successor, Jimmy (James Earl) Carter, would fall the task of reshaping the Ford proposals in line with what would surely prove to be a somewhat different conception of the national destiny.

It would, however, have been easy to exaggerate the magnitude of the change that was occuring as the Democrats prepared to resume control of the Executive Branch of government after an eight-year interval during which Republicans had occupied the White House, though Democratic majorities had continued to dominate both houses of Congress. A visitor from Mars would probably have found more similarities than differences in the outlook of the departing and incoming Chief Executives. Both were committed supporters of a democratic political system, a free enterprise economy, and prudent management of the national finances. Abroad, both professed to stand for peace and, if possible, friendship with all nations, based on a strong national defense, a healthy alliance system, and universal adherence to the humane principles set forth in the United Nations Charter. Within this broad agreement on fundamentals, there would naturally be differences of emphasis; but they would be differences of measure and interpretation rather than of basic principle.

Dr. Kissinger Steps Aside

The need to preserve and fortify this underlying consensus, especially as it related to foreign policy matters, was among the points particularly stressed by Secretary of State Kissinger in one his final pronouncements as senior member of President Ford's outgoing cabinet. Speaking at a testimonial luncheon tendered by Washington's National Press Club on January 10,[3] the Secretary of State alluded to the deep divisions of the Vietnam-Watergate era, noted the absence of established guidelines for coping with an altered world situation, and pleaded for the building of "a new foreign policy consensus similar in scope though different in content than that which sustained the post-World War II generation."

. . .As the Administrations change [Dr. Kissinger said], let us dedicate ourselves to the task of insuring that our common purposes transcend our differences. No matter how strong the foundations we have laid, the challenges confronting the next Administration will be complex, difficult, and painful. There will continue to be, as there have been in the past, many complicated choices to make; and there will continue to be intense dispute over the wisdom of the choices made and the courses that have been set. Achievement will inevitably fall short of hope and expectation, as it has in every Administration. The new Administration may avoid some of the mistakes we made; it will surely make some new ones of its own. But all of us owe those who carry the burden of responsibility the benefit of the doubt, a healthy understanding for the magnitude of their problems and compassion for the narrow range of choices available.

The State of the Union

An equal measure of good will was evident in President Ford's concluding address on the State of the Union, delivered before a Joint Session of the Congress on January 12 (**Document 1**). To President-elect Carter, the outgoing Chief Executive wished "the very best in all that is good for our country"; to the world at large, he offered a reassuring picture of a nation at peace, its confidence now fully regained as the dissension and distrust of the past decade had finally given way before the new, affirmative spirit of the recent Bicentennial. "Taken in sum," said Mr. Ford, "I can report that the state of the Union is good. There is room for improvement, as always, but today we have a more perfect Union than when my stewardship began. . . . I am proud of the part I have had in rebuilding confidence in the Presidency, confidence in our free system, and confidence in our future. Once again, Americans believe in themselves, in their leaders, and in the promise that tomorrow holds for their children."

This optimistic tone resounded throughout the President's lengthy review of the nation's foreign and domestic affairs. "This administration leaves to its successor a world in better condition than we found," he averred. "We leave, as well, a solid foundation for progress on a range of issues that are vital to the well-being of America. . . . At home, I am encouraged by the Nation's recovery from the recession and our steady return to sound economic growth. . . . We have successfully cut inflation by more than half. . . . We have created more jobs. . . . We have cut the growth of crime by nearly 90 percent. . . ."

Admittedly, there were some shadows on this record. That there were still too many Americans unemployed—7,558,000, or 7.9 percent of the labor force, at latest count—was the President's "greatest regret" on leaving office. ". . .Crime, and the fear of crime," he conceded, "remains one of the most serious problems facing our citizens." Two issues vital to the country's international position, as well as its domestic life, were also causing Mr. Ford concern in these last days of his presidential term. Not more than half of his proposals for coping with the energy crisis—an issue "absolutely vital to the defense of our country, to the strength of our economy, and to the quality of our lives"—had thus far been enacted into law; and meanwhile, he reported, the United States' dependence upon foreign oil imports, far from diminishing, had grown from 36 percent of its needs in 1973 to 46 percent, equivalent to $34 billion in annual overseas expenditure. "Such vulnerability at present or in the future is intolerable and must be ended," Mr. Ford declared. ". . . I urgently ask Congress and the new administration to move quickly on these issues."

President Ford's other anxiety had to do with the adequacy of America's preparedness for military defense at a time when the U.S.S.R., despite the far-reaching relaxation of international tensions during recent years, was plainly engaged in a long-term effort to expand its military power on a global scale. "The United States can never tolerate a shift in strategic balance against us, or even a situation where the American people or our allies believe the balance is shifting against us," Mr. Ford warned. "The United States would risk the most serious political consequences if the world came to believe that our adversaries have a decisive margin of superiority."

Defense and the Budget

It was to forestall this possibility, President Ford asserted, that his administration had reversed what he termed "the dangerous decline of the previous decade in real resources this country was devoting to national defense." This decline, he said, had lately been superseded by a "positive trend"—i.e., a rising level of real defense expenditure. Nevertheless, the outgoing Chief Executive was plainly worried by his successor's campaign promises to limit military spending and, specifically, to cut the annual defense budget by $5 billion to $7 billion. A new reversal of policy, Mr. Ford warned, would hamstring such "critical strategic programs" as the Trident missile-launching submarine, the B-1 bomber, and the M-X intercontinental ballistic missile—programs that the Ford administration considered essential to the national security, although the Carter administration had yet to signify its acceptance of the B-1 or the M-X and might even be thinking of shelving these new weapon systems in agreement with the Russians. In addition, President Ford asserted, another downturn in defense expenditure would undermine an ongoing effort to improve the nation's conventional warfare capabilities and strengthen its role as the backbone of the NATO alliance.

Much more congenial to the thinking of the outgoing President was another Carter campaign promise that called for eliminating the Federal budget deficit, currently running at a rate exceeding $50 billion a year, and balancing the budget by the fiscal year 1981. Mr. Ford's own budgetary recommendations, submitted to Congress on January 17, went even further and called for a balanced budget by fiscal year 1980. In spite of heavy emphasis on curbing the growth of government spending, the outgoing President's forecasts allowed for a continued steady growth in national defense outlays, which were estimated to increase from $100.1 billion in the ongoing, 1977 fiscal year to $112.3 billion in FY 1978, $123.8 billion in FY 1979, $136.3 billion in FY 1980, $148.2 billion in FY 1981, and $159 billion in FY 1982.[4]

These forecasts, it was explained, reflected the results of a "major Presidential review of U.S. national defense policy and military programs." Their basis was the realization that U.S. defense policy was determined to an important degree by "the challenge to American security and to peace and stability in the world posed by the expanding, worldwide military capabilities of the Soviet Union and its allies." Although the United States preferred to settle differences by negotiation and to maintain stability through treaties and other forms of international understanding, the budget document stated, it remained the official U.S. view that successful negotiation with the Soviet Union and its allies was possible only from a "position of strength." Sustained growth in the defense effort over a period of years was therefore declared "essential to fulfill the requirements of U.S. military policy and ensure American military strength relative to that of the Soviet Union in the decade ahead."[5]

[4]U.S. Executive Office of the President, Office of Management and Budget, *The Budget of the United States Government, Fiscal Year 1978* (Washington: GPO, 1977): 52.
[5]Same: 74-5.

Other Views

As already suggested, the Ford administration's settled convictions in this matter were predestined to clash with those professed by President-elect Carter and the incoming administration. Though not as yet defined with precision, the former Georgia Governor's thinking appeared to rest upon a belief that (1) defense spending was already too high and could be substantially reduced by more efficient management; and (2) the process of arms limitation by international agreement could and should be greatly expedited in order to enhance the prospects for world peace and gain permanent relief from the burdens of the arms race.

Such sanguine expectations already had evoked some skepticism on the part of experienced officials and members of Congress, some of whom had wrestled for years with the very issues the new President was now proposing to solve. Congress, under Presidents Nixon and Ford, had vigorously asserted its authority in virtually every aspect of foreign affairs; and there had already been indications that the new, Democratic-controlled 95th Congress had no intention of becoming an appendage of the Carter White House in either policy or personnel matters.

Mr. Carter's major Cabinet appointments—including those of Cyrus R. Vance as Secretary of State, Harold R. Brown as Secretary of Defense, and W. Michael Blumenthal as Secretary of the Treasury—had encountered no significant opposition in the Senate; nor had any substantial question been raised concerning his appointment of Professor Zbigniew Brzezinski as his Assistant for National Security Affairs. But the designation of Theodore E. Sorensen, a former aide to President John F. Kennedy, as Director of Central Intelligence encountered such powerful, if obscurely motivated, opposition that the nominee himself requested the withdrawal of his name three days before the inauguration. (The post of CIA director was later conferred on Admiral Stansfield Turner, who thus assumed primary responsibility for the general overhaul of the intelligence services that was thought necessary in the wake of the numerous irregularities disclosed in recent years.)

The lines were more clearly drawn in another confirmation battle that was unleashed soon afterward by the appointment of Paul C. Warnke, a former Assistant Secretary of Defense, as Director of the Arms Control and Disarmament Agency (ACDA) and chief negotiator in the Strategic Arms Limitation Talks (SALT) with the U.S.S.R. Fears were immediately expressed by Senator Henry M. Jackson and others that Mr. Warnke might prove too "soft" a negotiator and conclude a treaty unacceptable to the Senate; and there was long and acrimonious debate that ultimately descended to such minutiae as the position of commas in official documents. Mr.

Warnke's confirmation by the Senate, when finally accorded on March 9, was granted only by the unusually narrow votes of 70 to 29 in his capacity as ACDA Director and 58 to 40 as concurrent holder of the rank of Ambassador for purposes of the SALT negotiations.

Inauguration of a Modest Man

One of the coldest winters in American history provided a commentary on President Ford's warnings about the energy problem as he and his successor mounted the windswept rostrum outside the Capitol for the inauguration ceremonies on January 20. Jimmy Carter's first words as 39th President were for the man who had steered the country through the difficult months since August 1974: "For myself and for our Nation, I want to thank my predecessor for all he has done to heal our land." In other respects, Mr. Carter's Inaugural Address **(Document 2a)** was remarkable at once for its religious accent, its personal humility, and its emphasis on moral rather than military strength as the basis of national conduct. "I would hope that the nations of the world might say that we have built a lasting peace, based not on weapons of war but on international policies which reflect our most precious values." Notable among the specifics were a reaffirmation of the commitment to "basic human rights" and a reference to "our ultimate goal—the elimination of all nuclear weapons from this Earth."

The note of humility carried over into a special message from the new President to people of other nations, recorded for broadcast through the facilities of the U.S. Information Agency **(Document 2b)**. Not content with discarding the trappings of the "imperial presidency," the new Chief Executive seemed equally concerned to disavow the "arrogance of power" in America's foreign relations. "The United States alone," he pointed out, "cannot lift from the world the terrifying specter of nuclear destruction. . .cannot guarantee the basic right of every human being to be free of poverty and hunger and disease and political repression. . .cannot ensure an equitable development of the world resources or the proper safeguarding of the world's environment." But, he said, America could and would "take the lead in such efforts," guided by its desire "to shape a world order. . .more responsive to human aspirations," and confident that its friends abroad would "join us in a common effort based on mutual trust and mutual respect."

Down to Business

Some time would necessarily elapse before the nation and the world could know in just what way these laudable if rather abstract aims would be translated into concrete policy. In a sense, the process of clarification would occupy the whole of Mr. Carter's first year in office, the close of which would leave observers still not wholly certain of the ultimate tendency of U.S. foreign policy or the ultimate balance among its various components. The new administration lost no time, however, in initiating action on a variety of fronts and in providing piecemeal indication of its thinking on current problems. January 21, President Carter's first working day in office, brought a pardon for Vietnam-era draft evaders, an appeal for national cooperation in coping with "near-critical shortages" of natural gas supplies, and preparations for the departure of Vice-President Walter F. Mondale on a ten-day visit to Europe and Japan in order to dramatize the theme of "consultation and cooperation"—particularly the U.S. view that West Germany and Japan should urgently expand their economies in order to stimulate more rapid recovery throughout the industrialized world.

Other trips were in prospect. Secretary of State Vance, although he did not plan to travel on anything like the scale of his predecessor, would soon be visiting the Middle East in order to assess the prospects for reconvening the Geneva peace conference, in abeyance since December 1973. Later he would be going to Moscow with new proposals to break the deadlock in the SALT talks. Andrew Young, the new U.S. Representative to the United Nations, was about to undertake a trip to Africa, "to demonstrate our friendship for its peoples and our commitment to peaceful change toward majority rule in southern Africa."[6] Former Defense Secretary Clark M. Clifford was being dispatched as a special presidential envoy to look into the problems involving Greece, Turkey, and Cyprus in the troubled Eastern Mediterranean. The President himself, who would later claim to have set a record by meeting with 68 heads of state in the course of the year,[7] was already looking forward to a summit conference with the leaders of the principal industrial powers which would take place in London in May.

Some fragmentary indications of the administration's substantive planning were meanwhile coming to light through official declarations and informal hints in news conferences and interviews. On January 31, the President unveiled a $31.2 billion "economic stimulus" package that included a $50 per capita rebate on personal income taxes, a feature later abandoned as the need for this form of stimulation appeared to wane. On February 22 was presented a revision of President Ford's budget proposals[8] that would add ap-

---

[6]Carter broadcast, Feb. 2, in *Presidential Documents*, 13: 144.

[7]Interview, Jan. 27, 1978, in *Presidential Documents*, 14: 237.

[8]U.S. Executive Office of the President, Office of Management and Budget, *Fiscal Year 1978 Budget Revisions, February 1977* (Washington: GPO, 1977).

proximately $11 billion each to the deficits already foreseen for the two fiscal years 1977 and 1978. Its most conspicuous features were a decrease in anticipated tax revenues, an increase in various types of social expenditure, and a reduction—though not a reversal—of the increase in national defense spending projected by President Ford. Further proposals in this area, it was understood, must await another broad review of defense policy and military programs. Also included in the Carter estimates was a proposed $1 billion increase in appropriations for foreign economic and financial assistance, details of which would be presented later in the year.[9]

Other points of policy that seemed to emerge from the statements of the President and Secretary Vance included a manifest eagerness to get on with the business of disarmament, particularly in the SALT talks with the Russians; a lively (if occasionally naïve) concern for human rights, reflected among other things in an apparent belief that Moscow could have no serious objection to American cultivation of such dissident figures as Andrei D. Sakharov, the Nobel Prize-winning physicist; and a willingness to embark on new approaches to a solution of the Arab-Israeli problem, including what looked like an increased concern for the interest of the Palestine Arabs. "There has to be a homeland provided for the Palestinian refugees who have suffered for many, many years," President Carter told the citizens of Clinton, Massachusetts on March 16 in a statement that showed less than the usual regard for Israeli susceptibilities concerning the Palestinian problem.[10]

Visit to the U.N.

These and other strands were woven into a more coherent pattern in the address the President delivered on March 17 at a special meeting of United Nations members at U.N. Headquarters in New York **(Document 3)**. "I see a hopeful world," Mr. Carter emphasized, "a world dominated by increasing demands for basic freedoms, for fundamental rights, for higher standards of human existence. We are eager to take part in the shaping of that world." Each separate element of American policy, President Carter suggested, was part of what he hoped would become, for all concerned, a "prolonged and persistent effort designed first to maintain peace and to reduce the arms race; second, to build a better and a more cooperative international economic system; and third, to work with potential adversaries as well as close friends to advance the cause of human rights." In a rapid panorama encompassing the full range of U.S. foreign policy operations, the Presi-

[9]Message to Congress, Mar. 17, in *Presidential Documents*, 13: 405-7 (*Bulletin*, 76: 340-42).
[10]Document 20b.

dent revealed among other things that the United States had determined to adhere to the two U.N. human rights covenants, one dealing with economic, social and cultural rights and the other with civil and political rights,[11] which had been drawn up with U.S. encouragement but never signed by the American Government.

Affirming Human Rights

The new administration's persistent emphasis on human rights had by this time given rise to some degree of public mystification, in part because it seemed to spring from a crusading spirit remote from that of recent American administrations, in part also because there had been indications that the new human rights standard might itself be subject to certain exceptions, particularly in the case of countries that were thought especially important to American security.

So far as the Soviet Union was concerned, the Carter administration had not concealed its dismay at Moscow's apparent determination to silence those domestic dissidents who had been attempting to monitor its observance of the pledges embodied in the so-called Helsinki Final Act, the document adopted at the conclusion of the celebrated Conference on Security and Cooperation in Europe (CSCE) in 1975. Soviet authorities, in turn, were displaying an irritation at the American attitude that could hardly promote the success of Secretary Vance's efforts, recounted in the next chapter, to interest the Kremlin in far-reaching modifications of the SALT agreement currently under negotiation.

As previously noted, there was also adverse reaction in Latin America to such developments as Secretary Vance's disclosure on February 24 that the United States was reducing its aid to Argentina and Uruguay (and Ethiopia) on human rights grounds. Even stronger repercussions followed the publication of a State Department report, commissioned earlier by the Congress, that criticized the observance of human rights by numerous countries in Latin America and elsewhere.[12] Argentina, El Salvador, and Guatemala responded by rejecting further U.S. military aid; Brazil renounced its basic aid agreement with the United States; and Uruguay, already disqualified as a military aid recipient, declared that it would accept no more U.S. economic aid either.

Such castigation of "good neighbor" republics seemed all the

---

[11] Cf. below at note 204.

[12] U.S. House of Representatives, 95th Cong., 1st sess., Committee on International Relations, *Human Rights Practices in Countries Receiving U.S. Security Assistance: Report Submitted. . .by the Department of State in accordance with Sec. 502 (b) of the Foreign Assistance Act as amended* (Committee print; Washington: GPO, 1977).

more puzzling in view of the intimation by Secretary Vance and others that the Republic of Korea, together with certain other strategically placed allies whose performance in regard to human rights had also been severely criticized, would be exempt from aid reductions on human rights grounds. But if South Korea's importance to American security was really so great that its deviations from democratic standards must be overlooked, why had President Carter committed himself months earlier to withdraw the American ground troops that were helping to defend that country against an attack from the north? And why was the administration so fearful of offending the government of President Park Chung Hee at a time when that government was itself being charged with conducting a large-scale, highly improper campaign of lobbying and influence-buying within the United States?

Secretary Vance did not go into these questions in the address on "Human Rights and Foreign Policy" which he delivered at the University of Georgia School of Law in Athens, Georgia, on April 30 **(Document 4)**. He did, however, put forward a detailed philosophical justification for what he termed the administration's "resolve . . . to make the advancement of human rights a central part of our foreign policy." Affirming the consistency of this resolve with "our tradition, our international obligations, and our laws," the Secretary of State also voiced a warning against "a rigid, hubristic attempt to impose our values on others," a "doctrinaire plan of action" that would be "as damaging as indifference." "We can nourish no illusions that a call to the banner of human rights will bring sudden transformations in authoritarian societies," Mr. Vance warned. "We are embarked on a long journey. But our faith in the dignity of the individual encourages us to believe that people in every society, according to their own traditions, will in time give their own expression to this fundamental aspiration."

The Notre Dame Speech

President Carter's first official trip abroad, a six-day European visit built around an "economic summit" meeting in London, took place in the first half of May. Its highlights were a two-day meeting with the leaders of the principal industrial nations on May 7-8 **(Document 48)**; a special, quadripartite meeting with his British, French, and West German counterparts **(Document 13)**; a quick flight to Geneva for a meeting with President Hafez al-Assad of Syria; and a summit meeting of the North Atlantic Council, also held in London on May 10 **(Document 14)**.

The principal elements of the new administration's foreign policy were by this time beginning to form a recognizable design. Prominent among them, in addition to those already mentioned, were plans for an invigorated effort to achieve a viable national energy position; an intensified campaign to inhibit the spread of nuclear weapons; and an attempt to limit and eventually reduce conventional arms transfers. One remaining uncertainty, the question whether to proceed with the controversial B-1 bomber program, was due to be cleared up within the next few weeks. In the meantime, President Carter took the opportunity of a May 22 commencement address at the University of Notre Dame **(Document 5)** to present an overall view that encompassed both the intellectual and moral roots of foreign policy and its specific manifestations as developed up to that time.

Human rights, as "a fundamental tenet of our foreign policy," again held pride of place in this carefully wrought statement, in which "a belief in human freedom" was described as the ultimate unifying factor in a nation which, Mr. Carter noted, was bound together by "no common mystique of blood or soil." His topic, the President emphasized, was "the strands that connect our action overseas with our essential character as a nation. I believe we can have a foreign policy that is democratic, that is based on fundamental values, and that uses power and influence, which we have, for humane purposes. We can also have a foreign policy that the American people both support and, for a change, know about and understand."

The recent movement from authoritarian to democratic government in India, Portugal, Spain, and Greece was proof, in President Carter's eyes, that confidence in the democratic system was not misplaced. "Being confident of our own future, we are now free of that inordinate fear of communism which once led us to embrace any dictator who joined us in that fear. I'm glad that that's being changed," he said. Admittedly, the world was still divided by ideological disputes, dominated by regional conflicts, and threatened by the danger that differences of race and wealth could lead to violence or draw the major military powers into combat. "It is a new world—but America should not fear it," Mr. Carter urged. "It is a new world—and we should help to shape it. It is a new world that calls for a new American foreign policy—a policy based on constant decency in its values and on optimism in our historical vision."

Such clarion calls would have resounded even more sonorously had Mr. Carter and his administration displayed a corresponding aptitude for practical diplomacy. In fact, the process of enunciating national aims in these first months of the new administration had gone forward amidst a degree of bureaucratic confusion that had raised some doubt about its ability to move from idealistic statement to coherent action.

In contrast to the tightly centralized foreign policy machinery of the Kissinger era, the Carter administration had opted for a looser form of organization in which authority and responsibility were diffused among such talented and strong-minded individuals as Secretary of State Vance, national Security Assistant Brzezinski, Vice-President Mondale, U.N. Representative Andrew Young, and others.

The result—accentuated in some instances by a touch of verbal exuberance—was an atmosphere of cheerful confusion that was no less characteristic of the early Carter administration than were its undoubted good intentions. A lack of full rapport with the leaders of the new 95th Congress created additional hazards as the fledgling administration, still lacking the discipline that only time and experience could impose, began to address itself to the practical responsibilities awaiting it in each of the theaters of national concern.

2. CURBING THE WAR DEMONS

Peace was the ultimate human right, the foundation of all the others; and the Carter administration had emphasized from the beginning that the quest for lasting peace would have a proportionate share of its attention. It had also indicated that the search for peace would be pursued from a somewhat different angle than in the past. American policy since World War II, President Carter asserted in his Notre Dame speech **(Document 5)**, had been "guided by two principles: a belief that Soviet expansion was almost inevitable but that it must be contained, and the corresponding belief in the importance of an almost exclusive alliance among non-Communist nations on both sides of the Atlantic." "That system," Mr. Carter added, "could not last forever unchanged. Historical trends have weakened its foundation. The unifying threat of conflict with the Soviet Union has become less intensive even though the competition has become more extensive."

But though relations with the Soviet Union ranked only third in Mr. Carter's personal priority list—behind human rights, and behind the relations among the democracies—they still accounted for a broad and weighty segment of the foreign policy agenda. In the armaments field alone, the President declared at Notre Dame, "We desire a freeze on further modernization and production of weapons and a continuing, substantial reduction of strategic nuclear weapons as well. We want a comprehensive ban on all nuclear testing, a prohibition against all chemical warfare, no attack capability against space satellites, and arms limitations in the Indian Ocean." In addition, the Chief Executive noted, "we are attempting, even at the risk of some friction with our friends, to reduce the danger of nuclear proliferation and the worldwide spread of conventional weapons."

Détente and Human Rights

None of these objectives, it seemed, would have much chance of realization without the cooperation of the Soviet Union, at once the most heavily armed of foreign states and the one with greatest influence on the world politico-military scene. A shifting of the worldwide military balance over the past few years lent added weight, for some, to the arguments in favor of effective arms control agreements with the Soviet government. But though President Carter clearly desired rapid progress in this direction, and had even expressed a hope for an early meeting with General Secretary Brezhnev, this interest had in no way lessened his determination to press for an improvement in the U.S.S.R.'s observance of basic human rights as well.

> I don't want the two to be tied together [the President said]. I think the previous administration, under Secretary Kissinger, thought that there ought to be this linkage; that if you mentioned human rights or if you failed to invite Mr. [Aleksandr I.] Solzhenitsyn to the White House that you might endanger the progress of the SALT talks.
>
> I don't feel that way. I think it ought to be clear, and I have made clear directly in communication to Mr. Brezhnev and in my meeting with Ambassador [Anatoly F.] Dobrynin, that I was reserving the right to speak out strong and forcefully whenever human rights are threatened, not every instance, but when I think it is advisable. This is not intended as a public relations attack on the Soviet Union, and I would hope that their leaders could recognize the American people's deep concern about human rights.[13]

Regrettably from an American standpoint, however, the Soviet leaders' way of recognizing American concern was backhanded to say the least. Both in the Soviet Union and in Czechoslovakia and other Soviet bloc countries, repression had been intensifying for several months in response to the agitation set off by the Helsinki conference of 1975 and the prospect of a second, follow-up meeting that was scheduled to take place in Belgrade later in 1977. The advent of the Carter administration appeared to accentuate both the agitation and the repression. These were the weeks when Soviet authorities were arresting and bringing criminal charges against

---

[13]News conference, Feb. 8, in *Presidential Documents*, 13: 160.

such prominent dissidents as Yuri F. Orlov, the organizer of committees to monitor Soviet observance of the Helsinki commitments, who was charged with libeling the Soviet political system; Aleksandr I. Ginzburg, manager of a fund to aid the families of political prisoners, who was accused of anti-Soviet agitation; and Anatoly F. Shcharansky, a prominent Jewish dissident who was charged with rendering aid to a foreign state and later was unofficially accused of having worked for the American CIA—a charge decisively rejected by President Carter at his news conference on June 13.

Soviet repression, American protest, and Soviet rejoinder spun like a gigantic pinwheel through the late winter of 1977. Among the more conspicuous manifestations of the American attitude was President Carter's encouraging reply to a personal letter from physicist Sakharov invoking U.S. intercession on behalf of imprisoned and persecuted dissidents in the U.S.S.R. and Eastern Europe.[14] At Geneva, U.S. representatives made a fruitless but well-publicized attempt to bring about a formal inquiry by the U.N. Commission on Human Rights. Though these activities produced no visible improvement in the treatment of Soviet and East European dissidents, their irritating effect on Kremlin nerves was evidenced by Brezhnev himself in a speech to the Congress of Soviet Trade Unions on March 21, only a few days before the expected arrival of the new SALT negotiating party led by Secretary Vance. "We shall not tolerate interference in our internal affairs by anyone and under any pretext," the General Secretary warned. ". . .Everybody, of course, realizes how important it is that U.S.-Soviet relations will develop further. We would like these relations to be good-neighborly ones. But this requires a definite level of mutual understanding and at least a minimum of mutual tact."[15]

New Try at SALT

Such mutterings seemed not to dampen the hopes that President Carter had invested in the Vance mission. "Some people are concerned every time Brezhnev sneezes," he reassuringly observed.[16] The "central focal point" of the forthcoming negotiations in Moscow, Mr. Carter stated at his March 24 news conference, would be "arms limitations and actual reductions for a change." The United States, he made clear, was hoping to improve substantially upon the preliminary agreement negotiated at Vladivostok in 1974, by which the Soviet Union and the United States were each to be lim-

---

[14]Texts in *New York Times*, Jan. 29 and Feb. 18, 1977.
[15]*Soviet News* (London: Press Department of the Soviet Embassy), Mar. 21, 1977: 105-6 (spelling Americanized).
[16]*New York Times*, Mar. 23, 1977.

ited to a maximum of 2,400 strategic delivery vehicles (aircraft or missiles), 1,320 of which could be "MIRVed" or equipped with multiple independently targetable reentry vehicles or warheads. Nominally designed to last until 1985, the Vladivostok understandings had not even yet been translated into firm and binding agreements, mainly because of differing views as to whether certain new weapon systems—the Soviets' "Backfire" bomber and the American cruise missile—should or should not be counted within the Vladivostok ceilings.

It would have been only reasonable to expect the Carter administration to come up with some new formula to promote a resolution of this difficult issue. More startling was President Carter's disclosure that the United States would instead endeavor to bring about a basic revision of the Vladivostok agreement, one that would involve "actual substantial reductions" below the Vladivostok ceilings. The Vladivostok terms, the President explained, would be regarded simply as a "fall-back position" in case the hoped-for reductions proved unattainable.[17]

Made public before negotiations had even started, the new U.S. position as outlined by President Carter and others aroused the deepest suspicions in Moscow. From its own point of view, the U.S.S.R. had already made significant concessions at the time of the Vladivostok meeting. Not only had it accepted, for the first time, a principle of numerical parity as between the Soviet and American strategic forces; it had also agreed to exclude from the overall ceilings the forward-based theater systems that supplemented the U.S. strategic deterrent

Soviet authorities were already disturbed at the United State's insistence that Moscow's new "Backfire" bomber—but not the new American cruise missile—be counted within the Vladivostok limits. Their suspicions can only have deepened when Secretary Vance, instead of offering a solution to the existing impasse, unveiled a new, complex, and "very finely crafted" proposal which was seen by its designers as heralding "a truly creative and novel framework for our strategic relations"[18]—but which must have looked to the Soviets like a plan for depriving them of their most potent strategic weapons.

Particularly disturbing to the Russians, it would seem, was the notion that each side should undertake to constrain those elements of its strategic program that were felt to be most threatening to the

[17]*Presidential Documents*, 13: 439 and 441. Further details on the subject matter of this chapter will be found in the 17th report to Congress of the U.S. Arms Control and Disarmament Agency, transmitted March 22, 1978 and distributed under the title *Arms Control 1977* (ACDA Publication 96; Washington: GPO, 1978).
[18]Brzezinski news conference, Apr. 1, in *Bulletin*, 76: 415 and 417.

other party. What this appeared to mean in practice was that the Soviets should cut back and halt the modernization of their strategic land-based missile (ICBM) force in return for similar restraint on the American side. Instead of the Vladivostok ceilings of 2,400 strategic delivery vehicles, of which 1,320 could be MIRVed, the United States was now proposing that each side be limited to 1,800-2,000 strategic delivery vehicles, of which 1,100-1,200 could be MIRVed. Within these limits, there would also be a special ceiling of 550 on each side for the larger types of ICBM's, including the American Minuteman III and the Soviet SS-17, SS-18, and SS-19. The U.S.S.R.'s existing force of 308 of the giant SS-18 missiles, each capable of carrying up to eight to ten warheads, would actually be reduced to not more than 150; and both sides would forego the development and deployment of the coming generation of mobile ICBMs, such as the American M-X and the Soviet SS-16.

No one in the American group had expected these far-reaching proposals to be accepted outright; but neither had most of them anticipated the vehemence of the Soviet reaction, particularly when it came to cutting the cherished Soviet missile force. The Soviets' objective in the talks, President Carter inferred at his next news conference **(Document 6a),** had been simply to confirm their understanding of the Vladivostok agreement, including the right to develop the Backfire bomber and exclude the American cruise missile. Any departure from the Vladivostok principles, Soviet Foreign Minister Andrei A. Gromyko confirmed in a televised news conference, was nothing but a crude pretext for carrying on the arms race—and, he added, in an atmosphere already poisoned by the American attitude on human rights.[19]

The outcome of the three-day Moscow meeting was not entirely negative, however. A communiqué made public as the talks concluded on March 30 **(Document 6b)** revealed that the two parties intended to continue their consideration of SALT issues, were scheduling bilateral contacts and expert meetings on other disarmament matters, and planned a thorough discussion of the Mideast problem and other questions when Secretary Vance and Foreign Minister Gromyko met again in Geneva in the first half of May. According to President Carter, no fewer than eight bilateral study groups would be set up to examine such problems as the immunity from attack of satellite observation vehicles; a comprehensive nuclear test ban; demilitarization or reduced military effort in the Indian Ocean; advance notice of missile test firings; control of conventional weapons and sales; nuclear nonproliferation; elimination of radiological or chemical warfare capabilities; and mutual limitation of civil defense efforts.

[19]*Soviet News,* Apr. 5, 1977: 113-16 and 128.

"Arms control is an ongoing process," Secretary Vance confirmed as he returned to the United States on April 2. ". . .It is not for the short-winded." "We are absolutely determined," the President echoed, "without ceasing to work harmoniously with the Soviet leaders to reduce dependence upon atomic weapons. We will do everything we can to strengthen the ties of friendship and mutual trust with the Soviet leaders. . . . And I believe that the Soviets will ultimately agree with us that it is to the advantage of the Soviet people, the American people, and the rest of the world to reduce our dependence upon this destructive weapon."[20]

Resisting Nuclear Proliferation

Such optimistic statements could not allay the widespread feeling that the net effect of the Moscow meeting had been to reduce the American-Soviet relationship to its lowest level in several years. The impression that East-West détente was reaching a dead end was strengthened by the negative outcome just at this time of still another round in the three and one-half year old Vienna negotiations on Mutual and Balanced Force Reduction (MBFR) in Central Europe, a prime concern of the United States and most of its European allies that will be discussed in the next chapter.

It is true that a variety of arms control endeavors continued to go forward on either a bilateral or a multilateral basis. Already pending before the U.S. Senate were two bilateral treaties with the Soviet Union that would undoubtedly have the support of the new administration: the Threshold Test Ban (TTB) Treaty, signed in Moscow July 3, 1974, by which the two powers undertook to refrain from conducting underground nuclear weapon tests with a yield exceeding 150 kilotons; and the Treaty on Peaceful Nuclear Explosions (PNE), signed at Washington and Moscow May 28, 1976, which embodied comparable limits on nuclear explosions for peaceful purposes. Neither treaty, however, would be considered by the Senate during 1977. A third, multilateral treaty, the Environmental Warfare Convention or "Convention on the Prohibition of Military or any other Hostile Use of Environmental Modification Techniques," had been approved by the U.N. General Assembly late in 1976 and would be signed at Geneva by representatives of 34 countries—among them Secretary Vance and Foreign Minister Gromyko—on May 18, 1977.

A more immediate concern for the new American administration had been the need for further international action to inhibit the proliferation of nuclear weapon capabilities, an objective laid down but very imperfectly assured by the celebrated Nuclear Non-proliferation Treaty of 1968. Over 100 countries had by now become parties to that treaty; but there remained a number of governments that had insisted on retaining a nuclear weapons option, as well as a much larger number that were planning to rely on an expanding use of nuclear processes in meeting their peaceful energy requirements. India, in 1974, had shown how readily a peaceful nuclear energy program could become a springboard to a nuclear weapon capability.

Conscious of the significance of the Indian experience and anxious to forestall a repetition, the Ford administration had vigorously urged the need for an intensification of, and increased reliance on, the "safeguards" program of the U.N.-related International Atomic Energy Agency (IAEA). In addition, it had taken the lead in organizing an informal "Nuclear Suppliers Group" of countries involved in the export of nuclear material and technology. Under energetic prodding from his Democratic opponent, President Ford had also issued late in 1976 a comprehensive policy statement that emphasized restrictions on the production of plutonium from used nuclear fuel—the quickest means of obtaining nuclear explosives—and restraints on the transfer of reprocessing and enrichment technology and facilities.[21]

The Carter administration had lost no time in throwing its weight behind these endeavors. Vice-President Mondale, on his postinaugural trip to Europe and Japan, had made it clear to several allied governments that the United States had reservations about their current nuclear export plans. Washington, it was known, was particularly unhappy about a West German agreement to provide a uranium enrichment plant and nuclear fuel reprocessing facility to Brazil, as well as a French agreement to furnish a reprocessing facility to Pakistan.

A further step in the evolution of American policy was the issuance on April 7 of a presidential statement (Document 7a) embodying the first results of a fresh interagency review of the question. Directed, like the Ford program, at curbing "the further spread of reprocessing capabilities of the spent nuclear fuel from which explosives can be derived," the Carter initiative went beyond its predecessor in mandating (1) an indefinite postponement of the commercial reprocessing and recycling of plutonium produced in U.S. nuclear power programs, and (2) a postponement of the entry of plutonium-producing breeder reactors into commercial use. To encourage parallel action by other countries, the President sug-

---

[21]Ford policy statement, Oct. 28, 1976, in *AFR, 1976*: 193-208. The author is much indebted to a background discussion in *Europa-Archiv* (Bonn: Deutsche Gesellschaft für Auswärtige Politik), 1977: D669-72.

gested several methods of furthering their access to alternative nuclear fuels and processes.

"We are not trying to impose our will on those nations like Japan and France and Britain and Germany which already have reprocessing plants in operation," the President insisted. "They have a special need that we don't have in that their supplies of petroleum products are not available. But we hope that they will join with us—and I believe that they will—in trying to have some worldwide understanding of the extreme threat of the further proliferation of nuclear explosive capability."

As a further step to "a strong and effective non-proliferation policy," the President transmitted to Congress on April 27 the text of a proposed legislative measure, the Nuclear Non-Proliferation Policy Act of 1977, which was designed to implement the principles set forth in his earlier statement and would become the basis, some ten months later, of the Nuclear Non-Proliferation Act of 1978.[22] Its dominant purposes, the President explained in an accompanying message (Document 7b), were (1) "to establish a strong, responsible legislative framework from which we can continue strengthened efforts to halt the spread of nuclear weapons," and (2) "to reassure other nations that the United States will be a reliable supplier of nuclear fuel and equipment for those who genuinely share our desire for non-proliferation." To this end, the legislation envisaged stricter controls over nuclear exports, insistence on the application of IAEA safeguards, and incentives to compliance in such areas as uranium resource assessment, guaranteed access to nonsensitive, low enriched uranium nuclear fuel, and spent fuel storage.[23]

The need for broader understanding of the danger in existing trends was the subject of repeated representations at the President's May meeting with allied leaders in London, where the seriousness of the issue was generally acknowledged even though the President gained little support for his negative stand on breeder reactors and the reprocessing of spent fuel. His main achievement, briefly noted in an appendix to the Downing Street Summit Declaration (Document 48), was the winning of allied consent to a technical reexamination of the nuclear fuel cycle, to be initiated at a specialized conference in the autumn. This rather limited success did not diminish Mr. Carter's eagerness, "even at the risk of some friction with our friends," as he said at Notre Dame, "to reduce the danger of nuclear proliferation and the worldwide spread of nuclear weapons."

---

[22]Public Law 95-242, Mar. 10, 1978.
[23]Fact sheet, Apr. 27, in *Presidential Documents*, 13: 611-13.

Limiting Conventional Arms Transfers

Not less resolute had been the new administration's determination to curb the growing transfer of conventional arms, particularly to nonindustrial, "third world" countries. Such traffic had grown spectacularly in recent years and, by the middle of the decade, had attained an annual figure exceeding $20 billion, of which the United States alone accounted for more than half. But though even such rivals as the United States and the U.S.S.R. were roughly in agreement about the evils of nuclear proliferation, in the conventional arms field they stood as open competitors. Despite American efforts, the two governments have never managed to agree on a formula for curbing arms shipments to their respective client states in the Middle East and elsewhere. Although such Western countries as France and Britain were also heavily involved in the traffic, it was primarily the massive arms shipments flowing from the U.S.S.R. and Eastern Europe to Arab—and, more recently, African—countries that had resulted, with the counter-efforts undertaken by the United States, in swelling the trade to its existing enormous proportions.

This burgeoning traffic had been viewed with growing apprehension by those Americans in and out of Congress who believed that "arms transfers encourage local arms races, heighten regional tensions, and distort the allocation of scarce resources, especially among the less developed countries."[24] The United States, in this view—to which the Carter administration would naturally incline—had an obligation to try to reverse the trend by mutual agreement or even, if necessary, by unilateral action.

In line with this way of thinking, Congress had already shown a growing disposition to declare at least some countries ineligible either to receive U.S. military aid or to benefit by U.S. military sales credits, which had replaced grant aid as the primary mechanism for such transfers in recent years. Not only had it blacklisted certain countries whose performance in regard to human rights and other matters was judged unsatisfactory; it had also claimed the right to withhold its approval of specific arms allotments above a certain magnitude. These stipulations had not, however, led as yet to any restriction of the actual arms flow. U.S. transfers of arms and related military services over the 27-year period 1950-1976 were estimated at $110 billion, and military sales in 1976 alone had totaled over $9 billion in 68 countries, while unfilled orders for U.S. arms and services were reckoned at a further $32 billion.[25] Fis-

---

[24]U.S. Department of State, Bureau of Public Affairs, "US Conventional Arms Transfer Policy" (GIST Series, Nov. 1977).
[25]Same.

cal year 1977 arms sales through the Department of Defense, originally said to total $9.9 billion, were later reevaluated at $11.3 billion after correction of an accounting error.[26]

The Carter administration's hopes of cutting down on this traffic had been well advertised in advance and, as already noted, had found an early reflection in the trimming of certain military aid allotments for human rights reasons. In submitting his formal recommendations for international security assistance over the next two fiscal years, President Carter on March 28 again directed attention to "downward adjustments" made on human rights grounds and noted that "a comprehensive review of our policies and practices regarding both governmental and commercial arms exports" had been undertaken with a view to bringing "greater coherence, restraint and control to our arms transfer policies and practices." "Our goal," the President emphasized, "is to develop, in close consultation with the Congress, policies which respect our commitment to the security and independence of friends and allies, which reflect our common concern for the promotion of basic human rights, and which give substance to our commitment to restrain the world arms trade."[27]

The results of this review were made public in a special presidential statement released May 19 (**Document 8**). "I have concluded," said the President, "that the United States will henceforth view arms transfers as an exceptional foreign policy implement, to be used only in instances where it can be clearly demonstrated that the transfer contributes to our national security interests." Again, however, there would be important exceptions. Controls would not apply to "countries with which we have major defense treaties (NATO, Japan, Australia, and New Zealand)." In addition, Mr. Carter emphasized, "We will remain faithful to our treaty obligations and will honor our historic responsibilities to assure the security of the State of Israel." Subject to these stipulations—and to the exercise of presidential judgment in specific instances—it was stated that the dollar value of new commitments under the military sales and military assistance programs would be reduced in the next fiscal year; that the United States would "not be the first supplier to introduce into a region newly developed, advanced weapons systems which would create a new or significantly higher combat capability"; that various other practices which tended to foment the arms race would be modified or abandoned; and that the United States would continue its efforts "to promote and advance respect

---

[26]*New York Times*, Nov. 12, 1977. The ACDA report cited in note 17 sets the figure at slightly over $9.3 billion "after correction for inflation."

[27]Letter to congressional leaders, Mar. 28, in *Presidential Documents*, 13: 458-9.

for human rights in recipient countries," as well as assessing "the economic impact of arms transfers to those less-developed countries receiving U.S. assistance."

While stressing his belief that the United States could and should "take the first step" in view of its far-reaching dominance of the world arms market, the President also emphasized his understanding "that actual reductions in the worldwide traffic in arms will require multilateral cooperation." The United States, he said, expected to meet "in the immediate future . . . with other arms suppliers, including the Soviet Union, to begin discussion of possible measures for multilateral action." In addition, he pledged to "do whatever we can to encourage regional agreements among purchasers to limit arms imports." In all these endeavors, the May 19 statement would be remembered as a point of departure and would later serve as a standard of achievement.

A Framework for SALT

Dialogue with the Russians had continued even while these unilateral steps were in the making. As planned at Moscow, Soviet and American working groups had met in Geneva early in May for a discussion of problems involved in prohibiting chemical weapons and weapons of mass destruction.[28] On May 18, Secretary Vance and Foreign Minister Gromyko had met in the same city to sign the Environmental Warfare Convention and begin three days of discussion devoted to SALT and Middle Eastern issues. On the Mideast, both sides had agreed to work for a resumption of the Geneva conference in the autumn; on SALT, they had announced a narrowing of differences and a determination to continue pressing for a new agreement.[29]

The quest for a new SALT agreement was by this time beginning to acquire a certain urgency, since the original Interim Agreement on the Limitation of Strategic Offensive Arms, concluded in Moscow in 1972 and sometimes referred to as SALT I, was due to expire on October 3, 1977. At that time, according to previous plans, the Moscow pact was to have been replaced by a new agreement, informally known as SALT II, which would be based on the Vladivostok principles and remain in effect until 1985. This was the agreement that had been the primary focus of attention at the abortive Moscow meeting in March.

What he and Gromyko had now agreed upon, Secretary Vance indicated, had less to do with a resolution of the substantive differences between the two powers than with the questions of timing and

[28]*Bulletin*, 76: 634.
[29]Communiqué, May 21, in same: 633.

form involved in setting up "a common framework for the SALT II agreement."[30] This "common framework," the Secretary of State explained, was now seen as comprising no fewer than three distinct elements: (1) a treaty running until 1985; (2) a protocol, to be concluded for a three-year period, containing items thought unsuitable for inclusion in the treaty; and (3) a statement of general principles to govern the negotiation of a later, SALT III agreement. This arrangement, according to Mr. Vance, afforded a means of "blending" the various proposals under consideration, despite the fact that the content and interrelationship of the several elements had still to be agreed upon and he was uncertain whether or not an agreement could be reached before the end of 1977.[31]

Is Détente Finished?

With or without a new SALT agreement, the Carter administration was clearly not indifferent to the need for maintaining some kind of military balance with America's principal competitor for world leadership. Its views on how the balance should be maintained, however, were distinctly its own and differed markedly from those of the administrations that had preceded it. Early in the summer, the President announced two basic decisions on U.S. military policy that would profoundly affect the future course of East-West relations as well as America's relationship with its NATO allies.

Cutting through the accumulated controversies of several years, Mr. Carter revealed on June 30 that he was shelving plans for production of the B-1 bomber, long under development as a replacement for the aging fleet of B-52 bombers dating from the 1950s. The defense of the United States, the President indicated, would continue to rest upon a "strategic triad" made up of bombers, missiles, and submarines; but the bomber component of the triad would continue to consist of B-52s, modernized as necessary and with a range that would be augmented by arming them with the new cruise missile[32]—the very weapon that had so complicated the SALT negotiations.

A few days later, on July 12, Mr. Carter disclosed his position on the relatively novel issue of the so-called neutron bomb or "enhanced radiation weapon," a highly controversial device whose special merit was understood to consist in its ability to kill people while leaving physical structures intact. Its principal usefulness, its partisans believed, would be found in Europe, where Western mili-

---

[30]News conference, May 21, in same: 628.
[31]Same: 628-33.
[32]News conference, June 30, in *Presidential Documents*, 13: 951.

tary forces felt themselves at a disadvantage because of the heavy superiority in tanks enjoyed by the U.S.S.R. and its Warsaw Pact allies. Acknowledging the strongly negative emotions evoked by the weapon, President Carter gave it as his opinion that although it should be produced, a decision on its actual deployment should be postponed.[33] Later it appeared that even production was being limited for the time being to certain particularly intricate components.

One consequence of these decisions was a volley of criticism, mainly of domestic origin, directed against the President's action in canceling or deferring weapon systems the critics deemed vital to the national defense. Another consequence, paradoxically, was a further step-up in a Soviet propaganda campaign against the United States—and against President Carter personally—that had been gathering momentum for some time and had already been characterized by the President himself as "both erroneous and ill-advised."[34] With Moscow seizing upon the neutron bomb to reinforce its campaign of denunciation against U.S. policy generally, President Carter's hopes for a meeting with Brezhnev and the completion of a SALT agreement seemed farther than ever from realization.

Reluctant as they naturally were to conclude that détente was already dead, American authorities could point to a variety of ongoing contacts on disarmament and other issues, among them the opening in Geneva of trilateral talks between the U.S.S.R., the United Kingdom, and the United States about a possible treaty to ban all nuclear weapon tests. Yet the overall trend seemed anything but encouraging.

Presidents to the Rescue

Patience and perspective were needed on both sides, said President Carter in an important address on U.S.-Soviet relations, delivered July 21 at the 31st annual meeting of the Southern Legislative Conference in Charleston, South Carolina (**Document 9**). "The whole history of Soviet-American relations teaches us," the President said, "that we will be misled if we base our long-range policies on the mood of the moment, whether that mood be euphoric or grim. . . . What matters ultimately is whether we can create a relationship of cooperation that will be rooted in the national interests of both sides. We shape our own policies to accommodate a constantly changing world, and we hope the Soviets will do the same. Together we can give this change a positive direction."

[33]*New York Times*, July 13; news conference, July 12, in *Presidential Documents*, 13: 985-6.
[34]Same: 989.

Assuring the Soviet leaders once again that American concern for human rights was not "aimed specifically at them or. . .an attack on their vital interests," Mr. Carter seemed to suggest the possibility of an even broader strategic arms deal than any yet considered. The United States, he implied, could limit the cruise missiles that were causing Moscow such anxiety if the threat against which they were directed—specifically, the threat to the American deterrent from "the very large intercontinental ballistic missiles of the Soviets"—could be "controlled." Mr. Carter closed by quoting a pacific declaration from a recent speech by Brezhnev, who had lately succeeded Nikolai V. Podgorny as Chairman of the Presidium of the Supreme Soviet—roughly equivalent to President—thus becoming the U.S.S.R.'s official Chief of State as well as the head of its Communist Party apparatus.

President Carter's olive branch, which was accompanied by some apparent lessening of United States insistence on the rights of Soviet dissidents, was not overlooked in Moscow. "We are all familiar with the latest statements by U.S. President Carter," said Brezhnev at a Kremlin dinner honoring President Tito of Yugoslavia on August 16. ". . .Compared with the previous moves by the U.S. administration these statements sound positive. Well, if there is a wish to translate them into the language of practical deeds, we shall willingly look for mutually acceptable solutions."[35]

Preserving the Interim Agreement

A mutually acceptable solution for one pressing problem was found when Foreign Minister Gromyko, visiting the United States for the opening of the U.N. General Assembly, conferred with President Carter and Secretary Vance in Washington on September 23-24. Reviewing the entire range of East-West problems but focusing particularly on "the effective prevention of nuclear war and the limitation of armaments," the two sides certified in a formal communiqué **(Document 10a)** that they had made progress in bringing their positions closer together, even though there still were issues requiring agreement. In a separate statement **(Document 10b),** Messrs. Vance and Gromyko expressed their own determination to persevere and voiced satisfaction over the operation thus far of the 1972 Treaty on the Limitation of Anti-Ballistic Missile Systems, which was about to undergo a formal review by the U.S.-U.S.S.R. Standing Consultative Committee.[36]

The situation created by the now imminent expiration of the Interim Agreement on Strategic Offensive Arms (SALT I) was met by

[35]*Soviet News*, Aug. 23, 1977: 294.
[36]Cf. the committee's communiqué of Nov. 21 in *Bulletin*, 77: 856-7.

parallel statements in which the United States declared (**Document 10c**) that in order to maintain the *status quo* while SALT II negotiations were being completed, it intended to take no action inconsistent with the provisions of the agreement, or with the goals of the negotiations, provided the Soviet Union exercised similar restraint. A similar statement was issued on behalf of the U.S.S.R.[37] The limitations imposed by the 1972 agreement would thus continue to be observed until further notice. So far as the United States was concerned, Ambassador Warnke explained to the Senate Foreign Relations Committee (**Document 10d**), this declaration of intent would not affect current defense plans and would be subject to modification at any time.

Another SALT Agreement?

Still other vital matters were under discussion in these exchanges with the Soviet Foreign Minister. On September 27, Gromyko paid a second, surprise visit to the White House, this one on the heels of an address to the U.N. General Assembly in which he had lambasted the U.S. stand on human rights and had laid before the Assembly the customary, tendentiously worded Soviet proposals relating to the consolidation of détente and the avoidance of nuclear war.[38] Continuing their consultations back in New York, Messrs. Gromyko and Vance joined on October 1 in issuing a remarkable statement on the Middle East (**Document 24**)—to be discussed in a later chapter—that seemed to bring American policy in that area closer to the Soviet position than had been true for several years.

Three days later, on October 4, President Carter himself addressed the U.N. General Assembly (**Document 11**) and stated, to the general surprise and gratification, that the SALT talks had actually reached a point where "we and the Soviets are within sight of a significant agreement in limiting the total numbers of weapons and in restricting certain categories of weapons of special concern to each of us. We can also start the crucial process of curbing the relentless march of technological development which makes nuclear weapons ever more difficult to control."

Another week was to elapse before the content of this new, still tentative SALT II agreement was made known through the columns of the *New York Times*.[39] Each side, it appeared, had conceded something in the process of filling in the tripartite framework

[37] *Soviet News*, Sept. 27, 1977: 332.
[38] Same, Oct. 4, 1977: 337-44. The Soviet proposals were later withdrawn in favor of a noncontroversial declaration which was adopted by consensus as General Assembly Resolution 32/155 of Dec. 19, 1977 *(UN Monthly Chronicle*, Jan. 1978: 53 and 130-31).
[39] Richard Burt in *New York Times*, Oct. 11, 1977.

agreed upon in May. Under the proposed eight-year treaty between the two superpowers, the total number of missiles and bombers to be allowed each side would be set between 2,160 and 2,250, entailing a reduction from present levels that would amount to some 300 for the U.S.S.R. but none for the United States. Within these totals, a maximum of 1,320 vehicles could take the form either of "MIRVed" missiles (up to a total of 1,200 or 1,250) or of aircraft carrying cruise missiles. Land-based MIRVed missiles, however, were not to exceed a total of 800 on each side.

Under a separate protocol to be concluded for a three-year period, it was further reported, cruise missiles could be deployed only aboard bombers, and would be limited to a range of 1,500 miles; the Soviet "heavy" missiles that had been of such concern to the United States would not exceed 308 in number; and the deployment of mobile ballistic missiles and certain other new weapons would be prohibited. A proposed joint declaration relating to SALT III would list a number of topics, such as Soviet civil defense preparations, to be taken up in subsequent negotiations. In addition, the Soviet Union was said to contemplate a promise that it would not increase its current production rate of two Backfire bombers per month, and would not deploy those aircraft in a way that would threaten the United States.

Address to the U.N.

President Carter's U.N. address of October 4 was his second major pronouncement at the organization's New York headquarters. Unlike his speech of March 17 **(Document 3)**, which had surveyed the whole range of American foreign policy, the October 4 address **(Document 11)** was sharply focused upon "the major dimensions of peace and the role the United States intends to play in limiting and reducing all armaments, controlling nuclear technology, restricting the arms trade, and settling disputes by peaceful means."

Noteworthy among the rhetorical flourishes that characterized this address before an audience of 149 nations was the President's assurance that the United States was "willing to go as far as possible, consistent with our security interest, in limiting and reducing our nuclear weapons." "On a reciprocal basis," he said, "we are willing now to reduce them by 10 percent or 20 percent, even 50 percent. Then we will work for further reductions to a world truly free of nuclear weapons." In another passage more notable for its forensic effect than for its substantive import, the President stated: "In order to reduce the reliance of nations on nuclear weaponry, I hereby solemnly declare on behalf of the United States that we will not use nuclear weapons except in self-defense; that is, in circumstances of an actual nuclear or conventional attack on the United

States, our territories, or Armed Forces, or such an attack on our allies." This position differed little if at all from that of past administrations.

A Doubtful Prospect

At no point in his U.N. address did the President appear to minimize the obstacles along the road to his Inaugural goal, "the elimination of all nuclear weapons from this Earth." None the less, the optimistic tone of U.S. spokesmen during these early autumn weeks contrasted strongly with the discouragements of the summer. There would, however, be still further discouragements as doubtful auguries once again began to multiply in the closing weeks of the year.

One event that gave American authorities considerable satisfaction was the three-day Organizing Conference of the International Nuclear Fuel Cycle Evaluation (INFCE), agreed upon at the London summit and duly held in Washington on October 19-21 with the participation of 44 governments and international organizations. President Carter, in his welcoming remarks on the opening day **(Document 12)**, seemed intent on deglamorizing the whole issue of nuclear power. The need for atomic power for peaceful purposes had, perhaps, been "greatly exaggerated," he said. Alternative power sources should also be carefully assessed, if only for economic reasons. At the same time, the President emphasized, the United States intended to "cooperate in every possible way. . .to give our people of the world adequate power sources and, at the same time, to keep their lives from being endangered." Two areas of American cooperation that Mr. Carter particularly mentioned had to do with ensuring the availability of adequate supplies of nuclear fuel, perhaps through an international fuel bank, and providing storage for a limited amount of spent nuclear fuels.

The main achievement of this conference was the creation of eight scientific working groups to make a two-year study focused on ways of minimizing the danger of nuclear weapons proliferation "without jeopardizing energy supplies or the development of nuclear energy for peaceful purposes."[40] Though such an inquiry might represent a useful step toward international consensus on the regulation of global nuclear capabilities, the path would obviously be a long one in view of the pressure on most countries to expand atomic power development as the centerpiece of their long-term energy programs. Even in the United States, the new constraints envisaged in the pending Nuclear Non-Proliferation Act were beginning to elicit something of a "backlash" on the part of those con-

[40]Final communiqué, Oct. 21, in *Bulletin*, 77: 661-4.

cerned with the manufacture and export of nuclear facilities and equipment.

Plans to limit the export of conventional weapons were also having to be modified in several instances to meet the requirements of important customers such as Iran, and critics were already beginning to tax the Carter administration with failure to live up to its own policies.[41]

The progress of negotiations with the Russians was also giving rise to conflicting judgments, ranging from the optimism of administration spokesmen like Ambassador Warnke to the skepticism of such figures as Senator Jackson and former Deputy Secretary of Defense Paul H. Nitze, who, with Senator Jackson, had been a leading opponent of the Warnke appointment. The United States, in this latter view, had already conceded too much to the opposing power, and any treaty based on the current understandings might well fall short of Senate approval just as they had suggested earlier in the year.

The Russians, on their side, appeared to be tormented by similar misgivings. It is true that President Brezhnev, speaking on the November 2 anniversary of the Bolshevik Revolution, encouraged partisans of détente by disavowing any notion of upsetting the existing military equilibrium, proposing a simultaneous halt in the production of nuclear weapons by all states, and offering both a moratorium on peaceful nuclear explosions and "a ban on all nuclear weapon tests for a definite period."[42] The specific issue of the SALT II negotiations, however, still seemed to be causing difficulties. One possibly ominous sign was an apparent revival, after a period of quiescence, of Moscow's concern about the effect on Soviet security of the "forward-based" nuclear delivery systems maintained in Europe under the North Atlantic Treaty Organization—an element of Western defense that had been successfully excluded from the SALT negotiations during the period since Vladivostok.

3. EAST-WEST RELATIONS AND DÉTENTE IN EUROPE

The U.S.-Soviet military balance that so preoccupied the leaders of both countries was itself a part of a larger strategic configuration that encompassed both the fifteen-nation North Atlantic alliance in

[41]E.g., *New York Times*, Oct. 11, 1977, quoting a study prepared by the research division of the Library of Congress.
[42]*Soviet News*, Nov. 8, 1977: 386.

North America and Europe and the seven-member Warsaw Pact which had been organized by the U.S.S.R. as a framework for the deployment of its military power on the European continent. The European military situation was thus a deep and continuing, if sometimes tacit, concern of the American and Soviet SALT negotiators; while, conversely, the conclusion of a new SALT agreement, dealing as it presumably would with such military items as cruise missiles and medium-range bombers, could profoundly affect the relative position of the opposing military forces in Europe itself. The relationship between the forces of NATO and those of the Warsaw Pact in Central Europe had, in fact, already become the subject of separate East-West negotiations which had begun in Vienna in 1973 but had not, as yet, resulted in any agreement as to how these forces might be reduced without impairing the security of the nations involved.

European Security and Eurocommunism

The East-West relationship in Europe had other dimensions as well. Western Europe, so long regarded as a showcase of political and economic democracy and a living testimonial to the irrelevance of Communism in advanced industrial societies, had lately been exhibiting signs of weakening resistance to Communist ambitions in certain countries where Communism still represented a vital, if partially ostracized, political force. Insisting on the genuineness of their new democratic orientation as well as their independence of Soviet control, spokesmen for the new, "Eurocommunist" trend in countries like Italy, France, and Spain were now claiming a right to participate in—even, in some cases, to guide—the processes of government in their respective countries. The question of how far the Italian, French, or other Communist parties could safely be trusted with a share of power had already become an explosive theoretical issue for the Western governments. There had been indications that it might be posed on a starkly practical level in the event of a collapse of the Italian government or a leftist victory in the French elections due in 1978.

The contest between totalitarian and liberal-democratic principles in Europe had meanwhile been going forward in a wider arena in connection with the recent Conference on Security and Co-operation in Europe (CSCE), which, as already noted, had concluded at Helsinki in the summer of 1975 with the signature, by the heads of state or government of the 35 participating nations, of a Final Act detailing a variety of principles and practices that were supposed to guide their future coexistence. In return for what amounted to a promise not to upset the political and territorial *status quo* in Europe, the United States and its Western allies had insisted on the inclusion in this document not only of certain "confidence-building measures," such as advance notification of some military movements, but also of a multitude of provisions that drew their inspiration from the Western tradition of human rights and personal and political freedoms.

These latter provisions had been accepted only with the greatest reluctance by the governments of the U.S.S.R. and the Communist countries of Eastern Europe, which saw them really as a price that had to be paid for Western concessions in the political area. The fact that they had been accepted at all had, however, offered great encouragement to those citizens of Communist-ruled countries who were sensitive to values upheld by the West. Such persons tended to view the Helsinki Final Act both as a standard of performance for their governments and as a kind of international sanction for their own activities. As had happened so often in the past, however, the attempt to bring about an enlargement of the area of political and intellectual freedom under Communism had been quickly followed by massive repression and the arrest or expulsion of the most prominent leaders of the movement.[43] Conspicuous though not unique in this respect were the official crackdown on the "Charter 77" group in Czechoslovakia and, in the U.S.S.R., the arrest of such prominent human rights advocates as Messrs. Ginzburg, Orlov, and Shcharansky—actions which, as already noted, produced a distinctly chilling effect on the development of U.S.-Soviet relations under the Carter Administration.

Stalemate in Vienna

Political developments in both Eastern and Western Europe could be viewed as aspects of a gigantic contest between opposing ways of life and politics, a contest whose outcome would determine the political and social structure of Europe for a long time to come. It was a contest, moreover, in which the Communist governments held certain assets that they were clearly in no hurry to relinquish. One of these was their monopolistic control of political processes and discourse within their own countries. Another was the one-sided advantage they had achieved in building up their military forces and armaments in Central Europe, where they enjoyed what was by this time generally conceded to be a clear superiority to the NATO forces, in numbers even if not in quality. According to NATO estimates, East bloc ground force manpower in Central Europe by 1976 had exceeded that of the West—including French

[43]Details in U.S. Department of State, Bureau of Public Affairs, Office of Media Services, *Second Semiannual Report to the Commission on Security and Cooperation in Europe, December 1, 1976-June 1, 1977* (Special Report No. 34; Washington: GPO, June 1977): 5-8.

forces not under NATO command—by the significant margin of 962,000 to 791,000, with an even greater lead in aircraft and a crushing disparity in main battle tanks.[44]

This push for military superiority in the European theater seemed not to have been deterred by the convening at Vienna in 1973 of the eleven-nation Conference on Mutual Reduction of Forces and Armaments and Associated Measures in Central Europe, known in the West as MBFR for "Mutual and Balanced Force Reduction."[45] Since the very beginning of the Vienna conference, the Western allied countries—other than France, which chose not to participate—had been advocating a two-stage plan for mutual reduction of ground forces, initially by the United States and the U.S.S.R. and later by the other participants, that would end by equalizing the ground forces of both sides at a level of around 700,000. In December, 1975, the West had supplemented this proposal by a further offer involving the withdrawal by the United States, under specific conditions, of 1,000 nuclear warheads with their related delivery vehicles. The Warsaw Pact governments, however, had shown scant interest in the Western program and had insisted instead that each country's forces, conventional and nuclear, must be reduced in equal measure, thus leaving the Warsaw countries with the same proportionate advantage at the end of the process as at its beginning.

"It is evident that this Eastern approach would diminish Western security," commented the spokesman of the Western governments, Ambassador W. de Vos Van Steenwijk of the Netherlands, as still another fruitless round of talks concluded on April 15, 1977. Such an approach, the spokesman asserted, was "obviously . . . not a logical or realistic one" but would result in "gross inequities" in view of the important differences among the participants in terms of military strength, geographical situation, and forces deployed within the reduction area. The participants in the latest round, Baron de Vos noted, had not even managed to agree on the size of each other's military forces, or the reasons for their varying estimates in this regard. A more fundamental concern, he said, was "the need for the East to move away from its basic conceptual ap-

---

[44]Cf. Lothar Ruehl, "Die Wiener Verhandlungen über einen Truppenabbau in Mitteleuropa," *Europa-Archiv*, 1977: 399-408.

[45]Direct participants in the Vienna talks were seven NATO governments (Belgium, Canada, Federal Republic of Germany, Luxembourg, Netherlands, U.K., and U.S.) and four Warsaw Pact governments (Czechoslovakia, German Democratic Republic, Poland, and U.S.S.R.). Eight other governments (Denmark, Greeece, Italy, Norway, and Turkey from the West; Bulgaria, Hungary, and Romania from the East) were classed as participants "with a special status."

proach to these negotiations" and adopt a "more realistic" approach like that of the Western participants.[46]

Though Western diplomats might hesitate to pronounce a final judgment, NATO military authorities were convinced that Soviet behavior in the MBFR talks aimed simply at gaining more time to develop an already formidable military capability. "Warsaw Pact, and especially Soviet, military capabilities continue to improve at a disturbing rate," a report to NATO's top military planning bodies asserted. "This is particularly evident in the across-the-board qualitative improvements resulting from deployment of newer, more effective weapons systems and equipment and the continuing development of even more advanced systems. Improvements in command, control, communications and infrastructure, as well as increased experience from such things as extended naval and air deployments, are also contributing to this."[47]

"The forward stationing of Soviet forces in Central Europe and in the flanks," the same report stated, "ensures a considerable capability to attack on short notice; and wide ranging force improvements, especially in the ground and air arms, are greatly adding to their readiness and flexibility for employment." "Certainly," the report added, "the Soviet leaders fully recognize the dangers of initiating any form of aggression against NATO so long as NATO retains its solidarity and strong nuclear and conventional capabilities."[48] It was because of these considerations that some Western military authorities attached such importance to the production and early deployment of the neutron bomb or "enhanced radiation warhead" which was becoming such a controversial subject on both sides of the Atlantic.

An Inconclusive Summit

The need to safeguard NATO's military capabilities and prevent a threatened erosion of allied defensive strength had been among the earliest concerns of the Carter administration, whose interest in deemphasizing the military element in foreign policy did not extend to the denial of what it viewed as legitimate defense needs. Other interests linking the United States with its allies in Europe, North America, and the Pacific had contributed to the collective decision to schedule a summit conference of allied, mainly Western, leaders in London during the first half of May. The growing economic interdependence of the so-called "industrial democracies," par-

---

[46]*NATO Review*, June 1977: 31 (*Bulletin*, 76: 482-4).
[47]Report submitted May 16-17, in *NATO Review*, June 1977: 27.
[48]Same.

ticularly at a time when recovery from the 1974-75 recession continued disappointingly slow, appeared sufficient in itself to justify
another gathering of heads of state and government of the sort that
had previously taken place in Rambouillet, France, in 1975 and in
Dorado Beach, Puerto Rico, in 1976. President Carter, in addition,
was eager to expound his views on nuclear nonproliferation, some
of which—especially his negative attitude regarding plutonium extraction and breeder reactors—were known to conflict with the outlook of important allied governments.

A dinner hosted by British Prime Minister James Callaghan preceded the formal meeting of allied leaders, which took place at 10
Downing Street, the Prime Minister's official residence, on the
weekend of May 7-8. Participating were the heads of state or government of the United Kingdom, Canada, France, West Germany,
Italy, Japan, and the United States. In addition, Roy Jenkins, President of the Commission of the European Communities, was permitted to attend the second day's meeting in spite of the objections
of President Valéry Giscard d'Estaing of France, whose policy it
was to keep the Communities clearly subordinate to the constituent
national governments.

President Carter appeared to enjoy more social than official success at this first meeting with the leaders of the industrial and democratic world. An intensive canvass of international economic
problems, to be discussed in a later chapter, fell short of eliciting
the kind of commitment to accelerated expansion that the United
States had hoped to obtain from West Germany and Japan. Nor
did the President make converts to his position on nuclear nonproliferation, although no serious objection was offered to the plan to
initiate an International Nuclear Fuel Cycle Evaluation (INFCE).
Insisting that he felt no disappointment at the results achieved, Mr.
Carter voiced special satisfaction regarding the arrangements for
implementation and follow-up of the Downing Street decisions in
advance of any future summit meeting.[49]

Rejuvenating NATO

The Downing Street summit, in any case, was but one of the important events on Mr. Carter's European schedule. On Monday
morning, May 9, he met with Prime Minister Callaghan, President
Giscard d'Estaing, and Chancellor Helmut Schmidt of West Germany in a special "four-power summit" that was devoted mainly
to reviewing questions relating to Germany—particularly Berlin,
where the Communist East German government had been implementing a series of measures apparently aimed at blurring the legal

[49]News conference, London, May 8, in *Presidential Documents*, 13: 677-8.

distinction between its own territory and that of East Berlin. In a Joint Declaration **(Document 13)** that expressed satisfaction over the broad improvement in the Berlin situation since the conclusion by the occupying powers of the Quadripartite Agreement of September 3, 1971, the allied leaders cautioned against any tampering with the provisions of that agreement or with allied rights and responsibilities in Berlin and Germany as a whole.

Later on that same Monday, the President flew to Geneva for a meeting and dinner with President Hafez al-Assad of Syria, one of a series of meetings he was holding with Middle Eastern leaders with regard to a possible resumption of the Geneva peace conference. Returning to London late that evening, the President was up again on Tuesday morning to continue the round of meetings he had been holding with individual allied leaders in the intervals of formal conferences.

At 11 o'clock on this Tuesday, May 10, came one of the highlights of the trip, the opening of a special two-day meeting of the North Atlantic Council "with the participation of Heads of State and Government." This, in effect, was merely the semiannual ministerial meeting of the Atlantic alliance's fifteen-member directing body; but the participation of President Carter and of the leaders of most of the other Atlantic nations—France, as usual, being the conspicuous exception—gave its deliberations a special weight and authority.

"We will continue to make the alliance the heart of our foreign policy," Mr. Carter assured the other NATO leaders in the formal address **(Document 14a)** that followed his introduction by NATO's Secretary-General, Joseph M.A.H. Luns of the Netherlands. "We will remain a reliable and faithful ally. We will join with you to strengthen the alliance—politically, economically and militarily. We will ask for and listen to the advice of our Allies. And we will give our views in return, candidly and as friends."

East-West relations and the common defense were the principal topics of the President's remarks in this forum, and on each he proposed a thoroughgoing review directed toward improved fulfillment of alliance goals. Particularly stressed were the need for a long-term defense program for the 1980s, and for improved cooperation in development, production, and procurement of defense equipment. The next spring meeting of the Council, to be held in Washington in 1978, might, Mr. Carter suggested, again take place at summit level in order to review the recommendations to be developed along these lines.

The President's specific proposals were formally approved by the North Atlantic Council on the following day, May 11, after Mr. Carter had returned to Washington and Secretary Vance had taken his place as head of the U.S. delegation. Although the Council's formal communique (**Document 14b**) was limited to a rather bland and uninformative survey of allied concerns, a further clarification of allied intentions was to emerge when the NATO Defense Planning Committee, consisting of the Defense Ministers of the allied powers (other than France), held its own semiannual session in Brussels on May 17-18. In a directive intended for the guidance of NATO military authorities, the ministers took the unusually definite position that all member countries of the alliance should strive to increase their defense budgets by a distinct amount—specifically, by around 3 percent a year in real terms—in the interests of avoiding what might otherwise be a continued deterioration in force capabilities relative to those of the Warsaw Pact.[50] How such a target should be reconciled with the Carter administration's professed objective of cutting the American defense budget by $5 to $7 billion would be a matter for later exegesis.

A Post-Summit Survey

There had not been opportunity at the Western summit to enter fully into every matter that concerned the allied governments. The matter of Communist claims to a share of governmental authority in Italy or France remained in abeyance, and U.S. views in this regard, though obviously more lenient than those of the previous administration, continued somewhat ambiguous. The clearest indication to date of Washington's thinking had been a statement from the Department of State on April 6 which indicated that while the new administration would not attempt to intervene in the political processes of Western European countries, it was not indifferent to the issue and would be concerned if Communists were to achieve political dominance in a Western country.[51]

Another question that would remain for future consideration had to do with the position of Spain within the Western community, now that Madrid appeared to have turned its back on the totalitarian legacy of the Franco years. The United States, for one, had long favored a closer association of Spain with the defense of the West, and Secretary Vance's first engagement after the London summit was a meeting in Madrid of the new Spanish-United States Council, the policy coordinating body established under the bilateral treaty concluded in 1976. Hopes that Spain was now entering upon a period of democratic rule would be further strengthened by the outcome of the parliamentary elections of June 15—the first such general elections to be held in Spain since 1936—in which the Union of the Democratic Center, led by Prime Minister Adolfo

[50]*NATO Review,* June 1977: 26.
[51]*New York Times,* Apr. 7, 1977.

Suárez González, placed first and the moderate Spanish Socialist Workers' Party of Felipe González won second place, outpolling the Communists under Santiago Carillo—a leading "Eurocommunist" spokesman—by better than three to one.

An informative survey of allied preoccupations in the period following the London summit was offered by the Assistant Secretary of State for European Affairs, Arthur A. Hartman, in an appearance before a House International Relations subcommittee on May 23 **(Document 15)**. "A compound of continuity and change" was Mr. Hartman's condensed description of U.S. policy with respect to Europe and the Atlantic area. In it, he said, an increased emphasis "on human rights, on curbing nuclear proliferation, and on reducing arms transfers to volatile areas" was "set in a context of commitment to the Atlantic alliance; of ongoing support for European integration and the European Community; of a close relationship with our northern neighbor, Canada; of the assurance of military security vis-a-vis the Soviet Union, combined with realistic measures to reduce East-West tension; and of a determination to treat the countries of Eastern Europe as independent and sovereign entities."

Notable in Mr. Hartman's presentation was his treatment of the relations between East and West as an aspect of the more basic problem of maintaining health and viability in the Western world itself. "The ultimate challenge that is posed for us," he said, "is not so much the challenge of a foreign threat; it is a challenge within ourselves and our societies." Like President Carter at Notre Dame, Mr. Hartman appeared to have no doubt that the challenge would be mastered, and, in addition, that "we can manage the separate but related challenge that confronts us from the Eastern half of the continent."

A phase of the Eastern challenge that now was coming into increased prominence had to do with the "follow-up" provisions of the Helsinki Final Act, which had provided for a series of later meetings to review the actions taken and to appraise the general progress of security and cooperation in Europe. The first such meeting was due to be held in Belgrade in the course of 1977, and a preparatory, organizational meeting was scheduled to convene in that capital as early as June 15. The United States, Mr. Hartman indicated in his statement, would not shrink from "some fairly frank talk with the Soviets and their allies" if this should prove necessary in order to focus the discussion on fulfillment of the specific obligations undertaken at Helsinki. "We don't want to be confrontational, but we do want to be firm," he said.

Mr. Hartman also dwelt at some length on the problem of instability in the Eastern Mediterranean, where allied cooperation on what was known as NATO's eastern flank had been impaired in consequence of the continuing rift between Greece and Turkey over Cyprus and other matters. Although the United States had pledged to use its best endeavors in helping to bring about a resolution of the Cyprus problem, President Carter's periodic reports to Congress in the matter[52] made discouraging reading. The situation was to be further complicated in subsequent weeks as the result of a parliamentary election held in Turkey on June 5; the subsequent return to office of Prime Minister Süleyman Demirel, this time as head of a coalition government with strong right-wing and nationalist representation; and the death on August 2 of President Makarios of Cyprus, the most authoritative spokesman for the Greek Cypriot community in the adversities that had followed the Turkish invasion of 1974. His eventual successor was Spyros Kyprianou, a man of comparable outlook but, inevitably, less personal authority.

The Dialogue Continues

A stream of high-level visitors to the United States continued the dialogue that had commenced with Vice-President Mondale's post-inaugural trip and President Carter's participation in the London summit. Japan's Prime Minister, Takeo Fukuda, and British Prime Minister Callaghan had previously hit the Washington trail in the earliest weeks of the new administration.[53] Now it was the turn, among others, of Chancellor Schmidt of West Germany, Prime Minister Giulio Andreotti of Italy, and, a little later, Prime Minister Raymond Barre of France. On each of these occasions, a White House statement summarizing the conversations was issued in lieu of the conventional bilateral communiqué.

That there had been "small differences" between the German and American governments—and that these differences had "often become exaggerated in public accounts"—was openly acknowledged in the report on President Carter's discussions with Chancellor Schmidt on July 13-14 (**Document 16a). Possibly the most important result of their conversations was a mutual commitment "to be in direct touch with one another in the future to make sure that exaggeration does not recur"—an expedient that was to prove no more than partially successful over the coming months.

Prime Minister Andreotti, whose Christian Democratic minority government could remain in office only so long as the Communists and various minor parties abstained from voting against it,

---

[52]Reports of Feb. 11, June 22, and Aug. 25, in *Presidential Documents*, 13: 188, 899-90 and 1254-5 (*Bulletin*, 76: 243; same, 77: 138-9 and 445).
[53]For the Fukuda visit see below at note 144. Prime Minister Callaghan met with the President on March 10 (*Presidential Documents*, 13: 337-9, 342-3; partial documentation in *Bulletin*, 76: 311-13).

"described the Italian situation in its various aspects" in two wide-ranging conversations with the President on July 26-27 **(Document 16b)**. His government's attempts to cope with Italy's chronic inflation, unemployment, strikes, and violence earned a brief, *pro forma* presidential commendation that failed again to indicate how vigorously, if at all, the Carter administration would oppose inclusion of the Communists in a future Italian government.

A similar question was coming to the fore in France as the leftist alliance of Communists, Socialists, and Left Radicals prepared for the elections to the National Assembly that were expected to take place early in 1978. The prospect of a leftist government coming to office in France appeared by no means remote at this period, although it later receded as the result of new disagreements between Communists and Socialists. In the meantime, the almost equally touchy question of U.S. landing rights for the supersonic Concorde aircraft claimed priority attention in President Carter's discussions with Prime Minister Barre on September 15-16 **(Document 16c)**. Aware of the irritation caused in France by local opposition to Concorde landings, particularly at New York's John F. Kennedy Airport, the President promised an early resolution of the issue. A subsequent governmental recommendation and Supreme Court ruling paved the way for Concorde service to JFK as well as to Dulles Airport outside Washington, where Concorde flights had been initiated earlier.

New Try at Belgrade

In these and other conversations, the President took pains to explain his administration's attitude toward human rights and to make clear that while the United States had no intention of torpedoing détente, as some of its allies appeared to fear, it also would not ignore the flagrant abuses of the Helsinki principles that continued to occur in the U.S.S.R. and in some of the Eastern European countries, notably Czechoslovakia and East Germany. Controversy over these matters had meanwhile broken out afresh at the preliminary Belgrade meeting of the 35 nations that would be taking part in the formal post-Helsinki review conference. Almost from its opening session, in fact, the Belgrade meeting had found itself impaled upon the conflict between (1) the insistence of the West, particularly the United States, on a detailed examination of the human rights situation, and (2) the attempts of the U.S.S.R. and its allies to divert the discussion to other, politically innocuous aspects of European security. Not until August 5 could agreement be reached on a set of ground rules[54] which would, in effect, permit

---

[54]German text in *Europa-Archiv*, 1977: D429-34; briefer background in *Bulletin*, 77: 679-80.

the argument to continue at the formal review conference beginning October 4.

Named as head of the U.S. delegation to the main Belgrade conference was Arthur J. Goldberg, a former Democratic Cabinet officer, Supreme Court Justice, and Representative to the United Nations whose selection was evidence in itself of the importance the United States attached to this new departure in the history of East-West relations. "On instructions personally approved by the President," said a later official report **(Document 17a)**, "all delegation members are working to assure that the Belgrade discussions result in an honest and candid review of areas where progress has been made and of areas where greater efforts are needed, especially in the vital field of human rights." In an action timed to dramatize U.S. concern with all aspects of the human rights issue, President Carter chose October 5, the second day of the conference, to redeem his pledge to sign the U.N. International Covenants on Economic, Social and Cultural Rights and on Civil and Political Rights.[55]

"Let me reaffirm in the most positive terms the wholehearted commitment of the U.S. Government to the pursuit of détente," Ambassador Goldberg declared in his opening address at Belgrade **(Document 17b)**. "Let me also restate our view that a deepening of détente, a healing of the divisions in Europe, cannot be divorced from progress in humanitarian matters and human rights. Rather, it can strengthen détente and provide a firmer basis for both security and cooperation."

This, however, was a characteristically "Western" view that was emphatically not shared by the U.S.S.R. and its associates. The essential point, for them, was the relationship among governments; human rights, as understood in the West, were at most a kind of sugar coating for the "realities" of international relations. It was because of this fundamental difference that the main Belgrade conference, like the preliminary meeting, experienced such difficulty in carrying out its assigned mission, which involved reviewing the implementation of the Helsinki Final Act, considering new proposals to improve implementation, deciding on another follow-up conference in two or three years, and drafting a concluding document. Since not a single one of these tasks had been completed by the scheduled adjournment date of December 22, the meeting prepared to reconvene in mid-January in the hope of concluding its labors by mid-February of 1978. (In fact, it adjourned March 9, 1978.)

---

[55]Cf. below at note 204.

NATO Takes Stock

The stalemate in Belgrade was symptomatic of a general slowdown that seemed to extend to virtually every phase of East-West relations in these closing weeks of 1977. The MBFR negotiations in Vienna, by now in their thirteenth round, were also heading for another year-end recess as each side continued to call for "serious revision" of the other side's position.[56] The outlines of the proposed SALT II agreement, supposedly fixed in September, continued indistinct as autumn merged into winter. In Western capitals, there was grave disquiet over the growing involvement of Cuba and the U.S.S.R. in regional conflicts in the Horn of Africa.

All these disturbing trends were noted by the NATO authorities who assembled in Brussels early in December for the semiannual ministerial sessions of the Defense Planning Committee and the North Atlantic Council. Meeting at NATO headquarters on December 6-7, Defense Ministers once again "expressed their concern at the continuing momentum of the military programs of the Warsaw Pact," which they again described as "far in excess of what would be reasonably needed for defense." In spite of their professed "concern at the serious deficiencies which still remain in the defense capabilities of the Alliance," however, the ministers "agreed that, provided the necessary additional resources are made available and used effectively by all member nations, an adequate conventional posture essential to maintain the NATO Triad of strategic, theater nuclear and conventional forces is within reach."[57]

Meeting as the North Atlantic Council on December 8-9, the Foreign Ministers of the fifteen allied powers permitted themselves a slightly more optimistic assessment of the international outlook. "Ministers noted that although recent progress in East-West relations had been uneven, there had been some favorable trends," said their communiqué **(Document 18)**. "They resolved to develop these and to seek a broader pattern of cooperation with the countries of the Warsaw Pact across a wide range of international issues. For these efforts to succeed, reciprocity and restraint are required on the part of all governments concerned. A policy of détente cannot be pursued selectively."

In a general review of allied endeavors since their London meeting, the ministers also "reaffirmed their resolve to fulfill the common purposes and enhance the effectiveness of the Alliance and agreed that the work in this direction was proceeding satisfacto-

[56]The Western position is reflected in Document 18; for the Soviet position cf. *Soviet News*, Dec. 20, 1977: 441.
[57]*NATO Review*, Feb. 1978: 26-7 (spelling Americanized).

rily." They also "expressed the hope that recent developments in the Middle East, which they welcome, will lead to a just and lasting peace in the region endorsed by all directly interested parties." This was their way of hailing what was surely the most sensational and, at the moment, appeared the most promising of all the international developments of 1977.

4. FALSE DAWN IN THE MIDEAST

As in earlier years, American authorities from the President down devoted countless hours during 1977 to the attempt to foster a Middle East peace settlement that would stabilize conditions in that troubled area and establish the prerequisites for permanent coexistence between the people of Israel and those of the surrounding Arab states. Yet the seeming breakthrough toward peace that eventually occured toward the end of the year owed less to American initiative than to the longing of the Middle Eastern peoples themselves—or, at any rate, the peoples of Egypt and Israel—for something better than the state of permanent hostility they had endured for over a generation.

The Carter administration's contribution to this development—which failed, in spite of the most optimistic expectations, to reconcile the deeply conflicting aims of the Israeli and Egyptian governments—consisted for the most part in a series of novel statements and initiatives that seemed in several instances to deviate from what had been the historic trend of American Mideast policy over the preceding 30 years. By creating an impression that American policy in this area was not in all respects immutable, the United States may well have played a role in encouraging other parties to reexamine their positions and, in at least one instance, to cast off some of the inhibitions that had tied their hands in the past.

State of the Problem

The elements that would somehow have to be combined in any lasting Mideast settlement had been readily identifiable at least since the period of the Six-Day War of June 1967, when the defeated Arab states had abandoned their previous demand for Israel's total liquidation and had begun to insist instead that Israel relinquish the extensive territories it had occupied in the 1967 conflict and return to the *de facto* boundaries within which it had lived since 1949. Territorial adjustments, peaceful relations, and the future of the Palestinian Arabs were the three main issues which, it seemed clear, would have to be resolved if a "just and lasting peace" was to be attained. Two of these issues had been specifically mentioned in U.N. Security Council Resolution 242 of November 22, 1967, which had been adopted shortly after the Six-Day War and had stood thus far as the classic statement of Middle East peace principles. The third, though only obliquely mentioned in Resolution 242, had increasingly emerged as one with an importance not less critical to the prospects of further war or peace in the area.

But since the parties to the conflict had differed in the most fundamental way with respect to all of these issues, they had remained in a state of seemingly irreconcilable hostility, had fought another large-scale war in the autumn of 1973, and had strewn a thousand difficulties in the way of the peacemaking efforts that had been indefatigably carried on by the United States with varying support from other outside powers.

Procedurally, American peacemaking efforts had oscillated according to circumstances between two separate but complementary approaches: (1) promotion of a comprehensive settlement involving all of the interested Middle Eastern parties, and (2) pursuit of a "step-by-step" procedure involving the isolation and solution of one problem at a time. Secretary of State Kissinger, in the two years that followed the 1973 conflict, had achieved remarkable successes in the "step-by-step" mode by helping to bring about a two-stage military disengagement between Israel and Egypt in the Sinai Peninsula and a corresponding separation of the Israeli and Syrian forces in the Golan Heights. But further successes along these lines had not appeared likely, and the Carter administration had indicated from the first that it would attempt to revive the movement toward a "comprehensive" settlement in the framework of the Geneva Conference on the Middle East, another relic of the Kissinger era that had been organized in the aftermath of the war of 1973 and had met briefly, under American and Soviet co-chairmanship, in December of that year.

As noted earlier, Secretary Vance's first overseas mission on becoming Secretary of State was a rapid visit to the Middle East to consult the interested governments about the prospects of reactivating the Geneva conference. Returning on February 21 from a week-long tour that had taken him to Israel, Egypt, Lebanon, Jordan, Saudi Arabia, and Syria,[58] the Secretary of State reported to Congress **(Document 19)** that he had found "a common commitment to working for peace" as well as "a consensus on the desirability of reconvening the Geneva conference sometime during the second half of 1977."

In no way did the Secretary of State appear to minimize the par-

---

[58]Documentation in *Bulletin*, 76: 209-23.

ties' strongly differing views on both substantive and procedural issues—including, among others, the question of how the Palestine Liberation Organization (PLO), as the self-appointed representative of Palestinian interests, should be included in a Geneva conference in view of Israel's rejection of any dealings with that militantly hostile body. Nevertheless, the Secretary of State reported, there was a general desire for the United States to "play an active role in facilitating the search for a settlement," and each of the leaders he had talked to had accepted an invitation to meet with President Carter over the next three months to continue the exchange of views.

Defining U.S. Policy

Secretary Vance was speaking in the context of a discussion of pending legislation directed against U.S. business compliance with the economic and financial boycott of Israel sponsored by the Arab League. Expressing sympathy with the objectives of this legislation, which was later enacted in the form of amendments to the Export Administration Act,[59] the Secretary cautioned nevertheless against precipitate action that could endanger "our important political and economic interests in the Middle East." This was his way of urging Congress to avoid offending the sensibilities of the Arab states—particularly such friendly Arab countries as Saudi Arabia, on which the United States depended not only as a source of vital petroleum supplies but also as a stabilizing influence throughout the Middle East and the Persian Gulf region.

There had been other indications that the new administration might prove a shade more sensitive to Arab attitudes—and, conversely, a shade less deferential toward Israel—than its predecessors. Some minor friction with Israel had already occured in connection with the latter's sales of military equipment in Latin America, its unsuccessful effort to purchase American "concussion bombs," and its oil drilling activities in the Gulf of Suez.[60] Concerning the substance of the Mideast problem, too, the new President had not been long in office before he began to deliver a series of loosely worded comments that suggested a revulsion against stale diplomatic formulas and a persistent groping for a fresh approach.

Mr. Carter did not, for instance, appear to feel too deeply committed by the language about "secure and recognized boundaries" that figured in the above-mentioned Security Council Resolution

---

[59]Public Law 95-52, June 22, 1977; details in *Bulletin*, 77: 162-5.
[60]These and other matters are knowledgeably surveyed in Stanley Karnow, "Carter's Long Mideast Ordeal," *New York Times Magazine*, Jan. 15, 1978: 8 ff.

242. In welcoming Israeli Prime Minister Yitzhak Rabin to Washington on March 7, Mr. Carter sidestepped the U.N. formula and referred instead to Israel's need for "defensible borders" as one of the primary motivations of current diplomatic effort.[61] Asked about the significance of this language at his March 9 news conference, Mr. Carter seemed to move even further from Resolution 242 by suggesting that legal boundaries and military defense lines need not coincide at all. Israel's defense needs, he hypothesized **(Document 20a),** might also be met by some such expedient as the establishment of defense positions or demilitarized zones, possibly manned by international forces, outside the actual frontiers. Although the idea was not entirely new, the seemingly casual manner in which it was put forward accentuated the confusion and uneasiness inseparable from any variation in what had been the official line.

Another seeming deviation from the philosophy of Resolution 242 occurred on March 16 when the President undertook to answer questions from the public at a Town Meeting in Clinton, Massachusetts. Though Resolution 242 had called, among other things, for "a just settlement of the refugee problem," it had made no specific reference to the three million or so Palestinian Arabs living outside the frontiers of Israel; and the United States had hitherto stood with Israel in its resistance to any opening up of this broader Palestinian issue, in which Israelis perceived a vital threat to their national existence. President Carter, however, in asserting at Clinton that "There has to be a homeland for the Palestine refugees" **(Document 20b),** appeared to be stating that a solution of the Palestinian problem was no less essential to peace than was the recognition of Israel's right to exist and its establishment within permanent borders. What Mr. Carter was saying might be objectively true, but the very fact that he had chosen to say it was bound to cause concern in Israel in view of its deeply rooted fear of Palestinian irredentist aspirations.

Events surrounding President Carter's April meetings with President Anwar al-Sadat of Egypt[62] and King Hussein of Jordan,[63] followed on May 9 by his meeting with Syrian President Assad in Geneva,[64] did nothing to modify the impression that the United States now felt somewhat less inhibited by Israel's special concerns, although American spokesmen continued to insist that the basic U.S. commitment to Israel's survival and security was not to be called in question.

[61] *Presidential Documents*, 13: 320.
[62] Same: 485-8, 490-92 (*Bulletin*, 76: 434-6).
[63] *Presidential Documents,* 13: 598-9, 605-7 *(Bulletin,* 76: 520-23).
[64] *Presidential Documents*, 13: 688-97 (*Bulletin*, 76: 593-6).

Perceptions of the American attitude were scarcely inspiriting to the dominant Israel Labor Party, then in the midst of its campaign for the elections to the Israeli parliament, or Knesset. Hampered in addition by a series of financial scandals that had led on April 7 to the withdrawal of Prime Minister Rabin as a candidate for the post-electoral leadership, the party that had formed the core of every Israeli government since 1948 was already on the road to a humiliating defeat in the balloting on May 17. Replacing it, to the consternation of most of those who hoped for a Mideast peace, would be the right-wing Likud (Unity) bloc led by Menahem Begin, a former anti-British terrorist whose uncompromisingly nationalist views were such as to create an impression that the prospects of an accommodation between Israel and its neighbors would now be even slimmer than before.

The CENTO Council Meeting

Promotion of a durable peace between Arabs and Israelis was but one of the concerns of American policy in an area that extended, in its largest definition, from the Aegean to the Himalayas and the Indian Ocean. At one extremity, the conflict between Turkey and Greece had already led to a compromising of NATO's European mission and undermined the solidity of Turkey as a pillar of the Central Treaty Organization (CENTO), the regional defense alliance that associated Turkey, Iran, and Pakistan with Britain and the United States. At the region's opposite end, the position of Pakistan and its relation to the power balance in Southern Asia remained a source of comparable concern. Especially was this true at a moment of political upheaval when India's voters had only recently cast off the authoritarian regime of Mrs. Indira Gandhi, and when the Pakistani government led by Zulfikar Ali Bhutto was under sharp domestic challenge for allegedly rigging the parliamentary elections held March 7, 1977.

Between these flanking regions lay the oil-producing lands on either side of the Persian Gulf, where two emerging giants, Iran and Saudi Arabia, had risen to a commanding position in the world petroleum market and had also come to rank among the most eager purchasers of sophisticated American arms. Countries with interests in this region were concerned not only with the Arab-Israeli quarrel but also with the revolutionary ferment and growing Soviet activity in the Red Sea, the Indian Ocean, and the Horn of Africa. Already well established in Somalia and with another foothold in Southern Yemen at the base of the Arabian Peninsula, the U.S.S.R. now seemed to be attempting to expand its influence in Ethiopia as well. In the meantime, a recent American initiative had led to the scheduling of bilateral U.S.-Soviet talks on possible measures to moderate the military competition between the two powers in the Indian Ocean region.

Many of these matters would presumably be discussed in connection with the 24th session of the CENTO Council, which took place in Tehran on May 14-15 with Secretary Vance heading what was technically the U.S. "observer" delegation. Arriving fresh from the London summit and his stopover in Madrid, the Secretary of State prefaced his appearance at CENTO with a day or more of talks with the Shah and other Iranian representatives. At a news conference devoted largely to reaffirming the traditional cordiality of U.S.-Iranian relations,[65] Mr. Vance laid special emphasis on the U.S. concern for human rights, but did not try to relate Iran's performance in this area, which had been harshly criticized in some foreign quarters, to the question of its eligibility to buy sophisticated American military equipment such as the Airborne Warning and Control System (AWACS) and the F-16 fighter.

Newcomers to the CENTO Council, in addition to Secretary Vance himself, included also Dr. David Owen of the United Kingdom, who had become Foreign and Commonwealth Secretary on the sudden death of Anthony Crosland. Dr. Owen and Secretary Vance were already cooperating closely on African matters, as both found occasion to point out in their formal remarks to the Council on May 14. Highlighting Mr. Vance's review of current U.S. policy **(Document 21a)** was his firm assurance that the association with CENTO's member states "is important to our nation and to President Carter's Administration, as it was to our predecessors." In concluding their two-day meeting, the participating ministers released the usual somewhat perfunctory communiqué **(Document 21b)** reviewing CENTO's progress and reiterating "their determination to ensure that the Alliance continues to contribute to the peace, security and stability of the region so as to promote further the social and economic welfare of its people."

Saudi Arabia, as a nonaligned Arab state, was not a member of CENTO; but its historic friendship with the United States, so similar in many respects to the friendship between the United States and Iran, was affirmed a few days later when Crown Prince Fahd, the brother of King Khalid and the *de facto* head of the Saudi government, paid a visit to Washington at the conclusion of President Carter's round of conferences with Middle Eastern leaders. Commending the American Chief Executive for what he characterized as his enlightened views on the Palestinian question, Prince Fahd assured him that recent rumors concerning a possible new oil embargo were groundless.[66] The very existence of such rumors, how-

[65] News conference, May 13, in *Bulletin*, 76: 612-16.
[66] *Presidential Documents*, 13: 798-800, 809-12 *(Bulletin*, 76: 670-74).

ever, was a reminder of the importance, the variety, and, in some respects, the vulnerability of American interests in the region.

Begin's Beginnings

Israel had meanwhile been going through the constitutional processes involved in the formation of its first non-Labor Party government, a coalition that would be dominated by the right-wing Likud bloc but in which three portfolios were alloted to the equally conservative National Religious Party, an additional three being reserved for the Democratic Movement for Change, a moderate grouping led by Professor Yigael Yadin. A reassurance to those who had feared a Begin government would signal a turn to extremism was the familiar presence of former Defense Minister Moshe Dayan, a fixture in many previous cabinets, as nonparty Minister of Foreign Affairs.

A definitely conciliatory note could be detected in the declaration offered by Prime Minister Begin on presenting his cabinet to the Knesset on June 20. Repeating a gesture made by each of his five predecessors, the man who had been regarded by many as a symbol of Israeli intransigence declared:

> Our prime concern is the prevention of a new war in the Middle East. I call upon King Hussein, President Sadat and President Assad to meet me—either in one of our capitals or on neutral soil, in public or away from the spotlight of publicity—in order to discuss the establishment of true peace between their countries and Israel. Much blood, too much, has been shed in the region—Jewish and Arab. Let us put an end to the bloodshed that is abhorrent to us, and sit down at the negotiating table, in sincerity and seriousness.[67]

It is true that Mr. Begin did not say what contribution, if any, Israel might make to the success of any negotiations that might be brought about. In this respect, his remarks did not appear exactly propitiatory. "The Government of Israel," he declared, "will not ask any nation, be it near or far, mighty or small, to recognize our right to exist . . . . The Jewish people has an eternal, historic right to *Eretz Israel* [the land of Israel], the inheritance of our fathers, a right that is not to be disputed or undermined."[68] Such firm positions might, it seemed, be difficult to reconcile with the territorial claims of the Arab states, the stipulations of Resolution 242, or the views of the Carter administration, as recently pulled together and

[67]Quoted from *Keesing's:* 28537
[68]Same.

restated in an authoritative address by Vice-President Mondale at San Francisco **(Document 22)**.

Among the many points on which Israelis and Arabs disagreed, none was more critical or potentially more dangerous than the fate of the so-called West Bank territories, the portion of the former Palestine mandate that had been annexed by Jordan in 1949 and occupied and administered by Israel since 1967. All Arabs agreed that Israel must give up the West Bank, in compliance with what they considered the plain language of Resolution 242, irrespective of any differences among Arab countries as to what should ulti- mately be done with the territory. Rather than being returned to Jordan, a good many Arabs wanted to see the West Bank reorgan- ized as a separate Palestinian state or "entity," possibly connected with Jordan and perhaps administratively linked to the Gaza Strip, a separate territory at one time administered by Egypt. The United States, according to Vice-President Mondale, also leaned toward "the possibility of some arrangement for a Palestinian homeland or entity—preferably in association with Jordan." Prime Minister Begin, however, maintained that the West Bank territories (or Judea and Samaria, as he preferred to call them) had been allotted to the Children of Israel in Biblical times, and that their descend- ants had a right and duty to retain them despite the predominantly Arab character of their population.

Toward Reconvening Geneva

In spite of numerous grounds for disagreement, Prime Minister Begin and President Carter got on astonishingly well when the Israeli leader paid an initial visit to Washington on July 19-20. Mr. Begin went out of his way to assure the President that all issues were negotiable, and Mr. Carter took pains to reaffirm "the endur- ing American commitment to the security and well-being of Israel." According to a White House statement issued after the first meeting **(Document 23a),** the two leaders also agreed that the goal of settling the issues through negotiations would be best served "by moving rapidly toward the reconvening of the Geneva confer- ence this year." "Strong matters and differences" had still to be re- solved between the Arab and Israeli leaders, Mr. Carter subse- quently observed; but he had found all parties "eager for accom- modation," and he believed "that we've laid the groundwork now, barring some unforeseen difficulty, that will lead to the Geneva conference in October."[69]

---

[69]Remarks to reporters, July 20, in *Presidential Documents*, 13: 1049. Full docu- mentation on the Begin visit appears in same: 1035-8, 1041-6, and 1049-50 (partial documentation in *Bulletin*, 77: 201-2).

Americans were disconcerted when Israel moved soon afterward to solidify its position on the West Bank by according legal status to three of the Israeli settlements that had been established there since 1967—and whose existence had repeatedly been characterized by the United States and others as both contrary to international law and prejudicial to peace. This, however, was to be only the first of a number of Israeli moves in occupied territories over the following weeks that looked much more like preparations to stay permanently than to withdraw as part of a peace settlement.

There also remained a persistent problem about the representation, if any, to be accorded the Palestinian Arabs at a resumed peace conference. The Palestine Liberation Organization (PLO), which was headed by guerrilla leader Yasir Arafat and claimed to be the natural representative of the 1.1 million Arabs of the West Bank and the Gaza Strip, had made itself completely unacceptable to Israel—and, supposedly, to the United States—by reason of its presumed involvement in terrorist activities, its rejection of Resolution 242, and its refusal to moderate its commitment to the liquidation of Israel and the establishment of a "secular" Palestinian state in its place. Secretary Kissinger, in negotiations with Israel since 1973, had given that country what amounted to a veto over PLO participation in the peace negotiations, and had promised that the United States would neither recognize nor negotiate with the PLO so long as that body failed to recognize Israel's right to exist and to accept Security Council Resolution 242, together with a confirmatory Resolution No. 338 of October 22, 1973.[70] President Carter, speaking in somewhat less categorical terms at his July 28 news conference **(Document 23b)**, nevertheless reaffirmed the American view that Palestinian leaders who were publicly committed to the destruction of Israel would be ineligible to participate in the peace negotiations.

Secretary Vance repeatedly came up against this Palestinian issue in the course of another swing through the Middle East in early August that featured what were described as "in-depth discussion on all issues, both substantive and procedural and with each of the leaders he met." In Israel, it was later reported, the Secretary of State suggested—and Prime Minister Begin rejected—a plan to set up a temporary international administration of the West Bank and the Gaza Strip, to be followed after an interval by a referendum in which the inhabitants would determine their own future.[71]

A White House statement issued after Secretary Vance's return **(Document 23c)** reiterated the belief "that all of the [Mideast]

[70] *AFR, 1973*: 606; same, *1975*: 413-14.
[71] James T. Wooten in *New York Times*, Jan. 8, 1978. Official documentation on the Vance trip appears in *Bulletin*, 77: 329-55.

leaders desire peace and are aware of the dangers of stalemate."
"Difficult choices requiring courageous leadership face all parties
in the future," the statement conceded, adding that those concerned had been asked to detail their positions more precisely in the
hope that "a well-prepared Geneva conference" could be reconvened "this fall."

The New York Statements

Discussions looking toward a new Geneva meeting were continu-
ously complicated by other day-to-day developments relating, for
example, to the military balance between Israel and its Arab neighbors; American action on Israeli arms requests, with the concurrent
plans for sales of advanced F-15 jet aircraft to Saudi Arabia; and
the still unsettled conditions prevailing in southern Lebanon in the
wake of that country's civil war in 1975-76. Most of Lebanon had
by this time been pacified, with the aid of an inter-Arab force consisting primarily of Syrian troops; but Israel, which had insisted
that this force stay out of the region adjacent to its northern frontiers, was itself supporting Lebanese Christian elements in their
perennial rivalry with Palestinian and Lebanese Muslim forces in
the area south of the Litani River.

In none of these matters did Israel and its American supporters
appear entirely satisfied with the attitude of the Carter administration, whose attempts at "evenhandedness" were taken, perhaps
rightly, to reflect a less indulgent attitude than that of previous administrations. The feeling that American policy was tilting toward
the Arabs was not dispelled by events surrounding the President's
meetings with some of the Foreign Ministers who had come to the
United States for the opening of the U.N. General Assembly session in September. A discussion with Foreign Minister Dayan on
September 19, centering on the questions of Palestinian representation, Israeli settlements, and an Israeli draft of a comprehensive
peace treaty, proved inconclusive.[72] Similar meetings, with equally
ambiguous results, were held in the following days with the Foreign
Ministers of Egypt, Syria, and Jordan.[73]

What really brought Israeli and American Jewish dissatisfaction
to a head was the outcome of the President's and Secretary Vance's
discussions with Foreign Minister Gromyko—the same discussions
that resulted in the purported compromise regarding a new SALT
agreement. Concluding their conversations at a meeting in New

---

[72]White House statement, Sept. 19, in *Presidential Documents*, 13: 1381-2 (*Bulletin*,
77: 634-5).
[73]*Presidential Documents*, 13: 1387-8 and 1431-2 (garbled texts in *Bulletin*, 77:
635-7).

York on October 1, the Soviet Foreign Minister and the American Secretary of State joined in issuing a statement **(Document 24)** that seemed to signal an abrupt shift in American policy. Not only did it appear to restore the Russians to a central role in Middle East diplomacy, from which they had been largely excluded through the later years of the Kissinger era. On several issues of substance the statement also seemed to reflect the Soviets' overtly pro-Arab, anti-Israeli viewpoint.

Although the Soviet-American statement affirmed the intention of both governments to facilitate in every way the resumption of the work of the Geneva conference "not later than December 1977," it completely omitted any mention of the relevant U.N. resolutions. Instead, it offered an independent and, in some respects, clearly tendentious enumeration of the key issues to be resolved. Among them was listed "the resolution of the Palestinian question, including insuring the legitimate rights of the Palestinian people" —language that had found no place in Resolutions 242 or 338 and, in the context of current usage, could even be construed as pointing toward the establishment of a Palestinian state dominated by the PLO.

The outcry, in Israel and in the American Congress and the press, was immediate and vehement. In what may have been an attempt to blunt the criticism, President Carter adopted what seemed a rather more balanced view in his October 4 address to the United Nations **(Document 11)**. "Good faith negotiations," he emphasized, "will . . . require acceptance by all sides of the fundamental rights and interests of everyone involved."

In a further placatory gesture, the President worked late into the night with Foreign Minister Dayan in drafting still another joint statement, released October 5 **(Document 25a)**, in which it was expressly stated that Resolutions 242 and 338 "remain the agreed basis for the resumption of the Geneva Peace Conference"; that past U.S.-Israeli understandings and agreements on the subject remained in force; and that acceptance of the U.S.-Soviet statement—which Prime Minister Begin, for one, had flatly rejected— was "not a prerequisite for the reconvening and conduct of the Geneva Conference."

Also included in the Carter-Dayan package was a six-point U.S.-Israeli "working paper" **(Document 25b)** embodying procedural suggestions for the reconvening of the Geneva conference. Rejecting even low-level participation by members of the PLO, the Israeli Foreign Minister was equally firm in barring any mention of a "Palestinian entity" among the topics to be discussed.[74] He did,

[74]William E. Farrell in *New York Times,* Oct. 14, 1977.

however, agree on Israel's behalf to a complex procedure whereby (1) the Arab parties to the conference would be represented by "a unified Arab delegation, which will include Palestinian Arabs"; (2) negotiation and conclusion of the actual peace treaties would be undertaken by bilateral "working groups"; and (3) the "West Bank and Gaza issues" would be "discussed"—rather than "negotiated"—in a working group consisting of "Israel, Jordan, Egypt, and the Palestinian Arabs." Provisionally kept secret while the United States endeavored to win its acceptance by the Arab parties, the document quickly leaked to the press and was subsequently communicated to the Knesset by Dayan himself.

So carefully circumscribed an approach, however, had little chance of arousing the enthusiasm of the Arab governments, and even the hope of returning to Geneva by the end of 1977 now began to look increasingly tenuous. "We may be facing now the best opportunity for a permanent Middle East settlement in our lifetime," said President Carter in a November 2 address to the General Council of the World Jewish Congress **(Document 26)**. "We must not let it slip away." Negotiations, the President conceded, "will no doubt be prolonged and often very difficult. But we are in this to stay. I will personally be prepared to use the influence of the United States to help the negotiations succeed. We will not impose our will on any party, but we will constantly encourage and try to assist the process of conciliation."

"No More War"

One Middle Eastern leader with less than the usual tolerance for procedural pettifogging was President Sadat of Egypt, a country whose precarious economic situation offered special reasons for wishing the peace process accelerated if this could be done without sacrificing essential Arab interests. Acting, it is said, after diplomatic soundings through Romanian and other channels (and with some encouragement from the United States), the Egyptian leader astonished the world by offering, in the course of an address to the Egyptian People's Assembly on November 9, to travel to Jerusalem and appear in person before the Knesset in order to explain the Arab viewpoint on the issues in dispute. That viewpoint, he emphasized, would not be tailored to Israeli preferences but would continue to encompass the evacuation of the territories occupied by Israel in 1967 as well as the "rights" of the Palestinian people, including the right to set up their own state.[75]

---

[75]Detailed documentation on the Sadat initiative and related events appears in *Europa-Archiv*, 1978: D95-130. A briefer chronology of events is printed in *Bulletin*, 77: 880-81.

Scarcely less astounding than the Sadat initiative was Prime Minister Begin's prompt acceptance of his proposal—coupled, be it noted, with a firm rejection of the specific demands for which the Egyptian leader proposed to make himself the spokesman. Amid general jubilation at the prospect of a Begin-Sadat meeting, a number of sour notes were heard. Other Arab governments seemed even more horrified than had been true at the time of Sadat's acceptance of the disengagement agreements negotiated by Secretary Kissinger in 1974 and 1975. Egypt's own Foreign Minister, Ismail Fahmy, resigned with an assertion that Sadat's precipitate action had torpedoed an agreement on resuming the Geneva conference. The U.S.S.R. was characteristically denunciatory, and even the United States exhibited signs of apprehension, repeatedly warning Egyptians and Israelis against the dangers of bilateral dealings that could upset the chances for a comprehensive settlement.

Sadat's visit to the Israeli capital on the weekend of November 19-21 quite obviously marked an historical turning point on the grand scale, notwithstanding the fact that neither side gave any evidence of modifying its position on the details of a possible peace. The Egyptian's conciliatory but firm demeanor soon disabused a watching world of any notion that he might be led to "make a deal"—e.g., by "selling out" the Palestinians in order to hasten Israel's evacuation of the Egyptian-owned Sinai Peninsula. The mere acknowledgment of Israel's existence as a nation, the Egyptian leader seemed to feel, should suffice to remove the obstacles to a peace settlement compatible with Arab feelings and with the dignity of both sides.

Operating in a blaze of television publicity, Sadat and Begin spared no effort to maintain a correct and even friendly atmosphere even as they restated generalized positions that had been expounded a thousand times already. One point on which the two leaders did seem heartily to concur was the proposition that their nations' conflicting aims should not again be pursued by force of arms. "No More War" was the quintessential message of the Jerusalem meetings. On the procedural side, it was agreed that the dialogue should continue and that its ultimate objective should be the signing at Geneva of peace treaties between Israel and each of its Arab neighbors. This in itself provided a measure of the distance traveled in the ten years since the Arab governments, meeting at Khartoum in the aftermath of the Six-Day War, had resolved upon "No peace with Israel, no negotiation with Israel, no recognition of Israel and maintenance of the rights of [the] Palestinian people in their nation."

Reporting to the Egyptian Parliament on November 26, President Sadat advanced a further suggestion: the holding, even before Geneva, of a preparatory conference in Cairo in which all parties to the conflict would participate together with the United States, the U.S.S.R., and the United Nations. President Carter, in a statement hailing what he termed a "historic breakthrough in the search for a permanent, lasting peace" **(Document 27)**, announced on November 30 that the United States would definitely accept the Egyptian invitation and would be represented by Alfred L. Atherton, Jr., the Assistant Secretary of State for Near Eastern and South Asian Affairs. Israel, too, agreed to send two prominent diplomatic representatives to Cairo, and General Ensio Siilasvuo, the Coordinator of U.N. Forces in the Mideast, was present as a U.N. observer when the conference opened on December 14. The U.S.S.R., however, declined to attend, as did the other Arab parties. The more irreconcilable Arab countries, including Syria, preferred to vent their displeasure at a separate conference held in Tripoli on December 2-5 at which they condemned Sadat's "capitulation" policy and organized a pan-Arab "Front of Steadfastness and Struggle" to continue fighting for the realization of Arab aims.

American participation at Cairo, Assistant Secretary Atherton averred as the meeting began on December 14 **(Document 28)**, was proof that the event was seen in Washington both as an "historic occasion" and as "a constructive step on the road to peace." Yet none of those who had assembled in response to Sadat's invitation could fail to be aware that the really critical decisions would be made elsewhere. For the moment, the world's attention was focused not on Cairo but on Jerusalem, where Prime Minister Begin had undertaken to draw up a peace plan that would, in effect, embody Israel's answer to the demands put forward by Sadat in the name of the Arab peoples. On the nature of the Israeli reply might hinge the possibility of an accommodation between viewpoints that had hitherto appeared irreconcilable.

The Israeli "Peace Plan"

Prime Minister Begin's "peace plan," as eventually presented to the Knesset on December 28,[76] stopped far short of meeting the basic Arab demand for evacuation of the conquered territories and self-determination for the Palestinians. One part of the plan envisaged a temporary, five-year grant of administrative autonomy— but neither self-determination nor statehood—to the Palestinian Arabs of the West Bank and the Gaza Strip. The other part, which purported to enunciate principles for an Egyptian-Israeli settlement, was mainly notable for the severity with which it proposed to limit Egypt's freedom of action in its own Sinai Peninsula after the

---

[76]Text in *Europa-Archiv*, 1978: D120-24; West Bank and Gaza portions only in *New York Times*, Dec. 29, 1977.

return to Egyptian administration. Providing among other things for a demilitarization of the Sinai as a whole, it also envisaged the confinement of Egyptian troops to positions west of the Giddi and Mitla passes in the western part of the peninsula. Israeli forces, in contrast, would continue to man a defense line in central Sinai, complete with airfields and early warning stations, for a transitional period of several years. In addition, Jewish settlements established in the Sinai since 1967 would continue under Israeli administration and military protection.

President Carter was among the first to learn the details of the Begin plan when the Israeli Prime Minister paid a second visit to the United States in mid-December. Although administration specialists are said to have found the plan distinctly unpromising,[77] the President at his meetings with Begin on December 16 and 17 "expressed his appreciation for the Prime Minister's constructive approach" and hailed his determination to hold further direct talks with President Sadat.[78] According to Prime Minister Begin's later account, Mr. Carter went further, repeatedly expressing a favorable judgment of the Israeli plan and, in a concluding session, expressly stating that it constituted a fair basis for peace negotiations.[79]

Even President Sadat reacted more mildly than might have been expected when the two leaders came together for a second, "working" meeting at Ismailia, in the Suez Canal zone, on December 25-26. The Sinai problem, in fact, seems hardly to have been discussed at all, and it was only later that Sadat made known his strong objection to permitting any Israelis to remain in the Sinai after the territory was handed back to Egypt.[80] Concerning the Palestinian problem, on the other hand, the two leaders immediately found themselves in open disagreement, with Egypt calling for a Palestinian state on the West Bank and in Gaza while Israel limited itself to advocating self-rule for the Palestinian Arabs in "Judea, Samaria, and the Gaza Strip."[81] Because of this difference, plans by the two leaders to issue a joint declaration on the principles for a peace settlement had to be shelved.

A friendly atmosphere was nevertheless preserved at Ismailia, and both parties agreed that the quest for a comprehensive settlement must continue. To this end, it was decided, the Cairo confer-

---

[77]Karnow, *loc. cit.:* 60.

[78]White House statement, Dec. 17, in *Presidential Documents*, 13: 1904 (*Bulletin*, Jan. 1978: 49).

[79]Knesset address, Dec. 28, in *Europa-Archiv*, 1978: D124.

[80]Christopher S. Wren in *New York Times*, Jan. 8, 1978; Bernard Gwertzman in same, Jan. 25, 1978.

[81]Sadat statement, Dec. 26, in *New York Times*, Dec. 27, 1977; further details in *Europa-Archiv*, 1978: D125-30.

ence should be continued at a higher, ministerial level, and should be buttressed by the establishment of two new committees: a Political Committee, headed by Ministers of Foreign Affairs, which would meet in Jerusalem with the participation of the United States; and a bilateral Military Committee, to be formed by Egypt and Israel, which would be headed by the respective Ministers of Defense and would meet in Cairo.[82] The Palestinian issue would naturally be discussed by the Political Committee; the Sinai problem, it was subsequently learned, was considered to fall within the jurisdiction of the Military Committee.

Bumps on the Peace Road

President Carter's frequent bursts of candor about the Middle East continued to be the despair of Arabs and Israelis alike. Having embarked in recent weeks on what appeared to be an overtly pro-Israeli phase, the President had disappointed many in Arab circles by his coolness toward a Palestinian state as well as his unexpected declaration that the "completely negative" attitude of the PLO—as distinguished from "moderate Palestinians"—had at least temporarily excluded that group from "serious consideration" as a participant in peace discussions.[83]

The President's reaction to the Ismailia meetings occasioned still another political tempest. In his year-end television interview on December 28 **(Document 57)**, Mr. Carter particularly lauded Prime Minister Begin's "flexibility" and described his plan for Palestinian self-rule as "a long step forward." In contrast to President Sadat, the American leader repeated, it would be his personal preference that the Palestinians "not be an independent nation, but be tied in some way to the surrounding countries, making a choice, for instance, between Israel and Jordan." "My own personal opinion," the President reiterated, "is that permanent peace can best be maintained if there is not a fairly radical, new, independent nation in the heart of the Middle East area." Despite this clear-cut preference, Mr. Carter added, "we are perfectly willing to accept any reasonable solution that the parties themselves might evolve."

Such comments "embarrassed" him, made his job "very difficult," and ignored "the core and the crux of the whole problem," President Sadat complained next day.[84] Learning of the Egyptian leader's irritation, President Carter—by that time already in Warsaw at the outset of another foreign tour—hastily rearranged his itinerary and promised to meet Sadat in Aswan on January 4, 1978, at the conclusion of his scheduled stop in Saudi Arabia. It was a

[82]Same.
[83]News conference, Dec. 15, in *Presidential Documents*, 13: 1872.
[84]*New York Times*, Dec. 30, 1977.

foregone conclusion that his brief visit to the latter country, whose increasing oil wealth had vastly magnified its influence on the Arab and even the world scene, would be devoted to encouraging the Saudis' role as a force for moderation both in the Middle East and in international petroleum affairs.

A pessimist surveying the Middle East in this final week of 1977 might easily have concluded that despite the euphoria engendered by Sadat's Jerusalem visit, the fundamental differences that had once again emerged at Ismailia must surely lead to an early breakdown of negotiations and, eventually, to a renewal of Arab-Israeli hostilities. Yet only an exceptionally bold observer could have entirely discounted the psychological impact of recent events. As W. Anthony Lake, Director of the State Department's Policy Planning Staff, observed of the Jerusalem meetings: "For a moment, the people spoke, and they said they wanted peace . . . . Perhaps more than any other time in the past 30 years, real peace is conceivable. For our part, we will do all we can to help the parties find that peace."[85]

5. WHICH WAY AFRICA?

For an administration committed to a worldwide defense of human rights and fundamental freedoms, no part of the globe presented more difficult challenges than those of Africa—particularly those southern sections of the once "dark" continent where men and women of European race continued to dominate both the black majority peoples and smaller population groups of mixed or Asian background. As already noted, one of the earliest actions of the Carter administration had been the dispatch of Andrew Young, the new U.S. Representative to the United Nations and himself of black American descent, on a mission aimed not only at demonstrating America's friendship for the peoples of Africa, but also at dramatizing its "commitment to peaceful change toward majority rule in southern Africa."

In thus espousing the cause of a transition to majority—i.e., black—rule in southern Africa's remaining white-governed territories, the Carter administration was taking up approximately where its predecessor had left off. It was none other than Secretary Kissinger, on an epochal trip to Africa in the spring of 1976, who had unequivocally—if perhaps belatedly—aligned the United States with the proponents of majority rule in the breakaway British col-

[85]Houston address, Dec. 15; text from Department of State, Bureau of Public Affairs, Office of Media Services.

ony of Southern Rhodesia (Zimbabwe), in the South African-ruled territory of South West Africa (Namibia), and, by implication at least, in the Republic of South Africa, whose system of apartheid or hierarchical separation of the races represented the very antithesis of current human rights concepts. Through the waning months of the Ford administration, Secretary Kissinger had worked with the British and others to lay a diplomatic basis for an early transition to majority rule in both Rhodesia and Namibia. At the same time, he had repeatedly urged the white South African government led by Prime Minister Vorster to read the signs of the times and transform itself while there might still be hope of avoiding an explosion of racial conflict.

Soviet-Cuban Portents

That the Carter administration intended to leave no doubt about its own attitude on these matters was demonstrated, among other things, by its prompt and vigorous support for a repeal of the so-called Byrd amendment, the legislative provision which, since 1971, had permitted U.S. imports of chrome and nickel from Rhodesia in defiance of the mandatory economic sanctions decreed years earlier by the U.N. Security Council. Repeal of the Byrd amendment, repeatedly sought but never pursued with much vigor by the Nixon and Ford administrations, was finally brought about when President Carter, just eight weeks in office, signed the appropriate legislation on March 18, 1977.[86]

But despite the eagerness with which the Carter administration embraced the goals established by its predecessor, there remained a margin of uncertainty as to how far it understood or was responding to the deeper motivations of the Ford-Kissinger policy. For Secretary Kissinger had never pretended to view the problems of the African continent in purely African, or even in purely humanistic, terms. His concern, in this as in all other aspects of foreign policy, had been the changing constellation of global power relationships, particularly as they affected the relationship between the nuclear superpowers. The factor which, beyond anything else, had spurred him to immediate concern with African issues had been the sudden appearance of the U.S.S.R. as a direct participant in African affairs and a contender for major influence on the African scene.

Already possessed of an important foothold in the East African Republic of Somalia, the U.S.S.R. in 1975 had enlarged its radius of action by a sudden intrusion into the internal quarrels of Angola, a Portuguese territory, then on the verge of independence, which had become the scene of a three-way civil war among rival

[86]Public Law 95-12, Mar. 18, 1977; signature statement in *Presidential Documents*, 13: 402-3 (*Bulletin*, 76: 333-4).

national liberation movements. Large-scale Soviet arms shipments, in conjunction with an unprecedented dispatch of thousands of troops by the Cuban government of Premier Fidel Castro, had sufficed to tip the military balance in favor of the Marxist-oriented Popular Movement for the Liberation of Angola (MPLA), which had taken over the Angolan government early in 1976 while its opponents went underground to prepare for a long-term guerrilla struggle.

These developments had been viewed with the utmost seriousness by Secretary Kissinger and President Ford, who had read the Soviet-Cuban instrusion as a challenge not just to Africa but also to the United States, to the principles of détente, and to the international equilibrium they themselves had worked so hard to foster. Debarred by Congress from directly aiding the adversaries of the MPLA, they had nevertheless maintained a highly disapproving attitude toward Angola's new leftist regime and had repeatedly called attention to the dangerous implications of developments in that country, where Cuban troops and technicians had remained in large numbers even after military operations had been suspended. More than any other single factor, it was the addition of this revolutionary, Soviet-Cuban ingredient to the African mixture that had spurred American efforts to promote a settlement of the explosive issues already sputtering elsewhere in southern Africa.

The Carter administration, with its characteristic anti-"cold war" bias, initially appeared to take a more relaxed view. There was a sense, Ambassador Young suggested in a television interview preceding his confirmation by the Senate, in which the Cubans were actually bringing "a certain stability and order" to Angola. Although the State Department promptly observed that neither Ambassador Young nor Secretary Vance condoned the presence of Cuban troops in Angola,[87] it showed no great anxiety at the indications that Angola might be developing into a center for disruptive influences extending over a wider area. The United States reacted calmly to a crisis that developed early in March when the Shaba Province of Zaïre, Angola's neighbor and a favorite of past U.S. administrations, was invaded by Angola-based exiles associated with the former Republic of Katanga. In the end it was France, rather than the United States, that helped to rescue the government of President Mobutu Sese Seko by airlifting Moroccan troops to assist in crushing the intruders under a mandate from the Organization of African Unity (OAU). The United States, Ambassador Young repeated at the height of the excitement, should not "get paranoid about a few Communists—even a few thousand Com-

---

[87]Television interview, Jan. 26, and State Department statement, Feb. 2, as reported in *New York Times*, Feb. 1 and 3, 1977.

munists." He himself, he added, stood by his earlier judgment that the Cubans in Angola had contributed to "stability" in that still volatile country.[88]

As Cuban involvement in African revolutionary activities continued to expand, however, the Carter administration would gradually begin to take a less equable view of Cuban—and Soviet—behavior. Impressed by what began to look like a Soviet attempt to use the Cubans in gaining a preponderant influence throughout the Horn of Africa, official Washington would not entirely reject the view that the Russians were embarked on some nefarious African "grand design"—perhaps an attempt to develop a chain of positions along the Western oil route that led from the Red Sea and the Persian Gulf, continuing around the Cape of Good Hope and up the west coast of Africa to Europe and the United States. Success in such a venture, it was suggested, might enable the U.S.S.R. to threaten its Western adversaries with a cutoff of their vital petroleum supplies in some future crisis.

A Southern African Survey

For the moment, however, the American government was not reacting to such nightmare visions. "Our interest is not strategic," said the Assistant Secretary of State for African Affairs, William E. Schaufele, Jr., in an April 16 address before the American Academy of Political and Social Science in Philadelphia (**Document 29**). "We have consistently made clear that the United States does not wish to play a military role anywhere in Africa. It is also not based on economic interests, although we do want to see that Western Europe as well as the United States retains access to the mineral wealth of southern Africa." More than in any other region of the world, Mr. Schaufele implied, U.S. policies in southern Africa were founded on political interests—and, not least, on the concern for human rights and human dignity in Rhodesia, Namibia, and the Republic of South Africa.

Mr. Schaufele's review of the current situation in those three lands confirmed the impression that the diplomatic processes initiated by his former chief had suffered a loss of momentum even before the change of administrations. In Rhodesia, Prime Minister Ian D. Smith had agreed in September 1976 to an Anglo-American plan providing, among other things, for the establishment of a biracial government to pave the way for the introduction of a carefully qualified form of majority rule within two years. But months of negotiation at Geneva had failed to bridge the differences between the Smith regime and the various Rhodesian nationalist

[88]Same, Apr. 12, 1977.

leaders, all of whom were skeptical about the possibility of satisfactory agreement with Smith and his supporters. Particularly noticeable was the intransigent attitude of Joshua Nkomo and Robert Mugabe, the leaders of separate guerrilla opposition movements, based respectively in Zambia and in Mozambique, that had formed a loose alliance known as the Patriotic Front. Already engaged in what amounted to a state of war with the Salisbury regime, the Patriotic Front leaders showed little interest in a negotiated settlement and appeared determined to go on fighting until their adherents could take full power.

Prime Minister Smith, who did not himself appear to entertain any real hope of an agreement with the guerrilla chiefs, seemed more inclined to push for what he called an "internal solution"—in other words, a power-sharing arrangement with more moderate black leaders such as Bishop Abel Muzorewa, the head of the United African National Council, who boasted considerable domestic following but had little support among the guerrilla fighters. Assistant Secretary Schaufele, though very insistent on the importance of reaching a peaceful solution, warned his Philadelphia audience that an "internal solution" would probably be unacceptable not only to the guerrillas but also to important nationalist elements and to the neighboring "front line" African states, a group that included Angola, Botswana, Mozambique, Tanzania, and Zambia. In the American view, Mr. Schaufele stated, such a solution could not last, and even to attempt it "would inevitably lead to increased bloodshed and violence."

In Namibia, there had developed a rather similar choice between alternative roads to independence, one based on a "deal" between white rulers and moderate Africans, the other attuned to the ambitions of more militant African nationalists. A constitutional conference meeting under official auspices in Windhoek, the South West African capital, had already produced a plan for multiracial government and independence, perhaps by the end of 1978. Known also as the "Turnhalle plan" from the gymnasium in which the conference had met, it went some distance toward meeting African tribal aspirations but failed completely to recognize the claims of the territory's most active liberation movement, the South West Africa People's Organization (SWAPO). With a membership drawn mainly from the Ovambo tribal group—the territory's largest by far—SWAPO had for several years been conducting active guerrilla warfare in northern sections of the territory from bases located in Angola and Zambia.

South African maneuvers in Namibia invariably aroused the deepest suspicions at the United Nations, and the Security Council had already registered its opposition to a Windhoek-type solution by unanimously insisting, in its Resolution 385 of January 30,

1976, "that free elections under the supervision and control of the United Nations be held for the whole of Namibia as one political entity," rather than by tribal and ethnic subdivisions as contemplated in the Turnhalle plan. Even the United States, though lacking any special predilection for SWAPO, had doubted the viability of any settlement that bypassed the country's principal guerrilla movement. Secretary Kissinger, after conferring with SWAPO's leader, Sam Nujoma, had accordingly urged the convocation at a neutral site of a U.N.-sponsored conference that would encompass "all authentic national forces, including, specifically, SWAPO."[89]

But neither the Windhoek elements nor SWAPO itself had shown much enthusiasm for this concept. SWAPO, Mr. Schaufele implied in his address, wanted no competitors and held "that independence should come about only as a result of direct negotiations between itself and the South African Government." "On this issue, also,"the Assistant Secretary added, "we urge a spirit of compromise on both sides in the belief that what may be achievable in a peaceful manner will almost certainly be preferable to anything that can be won through the force of arms alone."

Concerning South Africa itself, Mr. Schaufele once again affirmed America's dedication "to the proposition that peaceful change must succeed, if only because the alternative is so unacceptable." "We have watched with dismay," he said, "the escalation of violence in South Africa, beginning with the Soweto riots last year. We are deeply concerned that unless the spiral of violence can be arrested and reversed, there will be such a polarization of forces within South Africa that peaceful change will become immeasurably more difficult than it is already. We shall employ all reasonable channels to get this message across to the South Africans and to facilitate this change to the maximum possible extent."

At the same time, the Assistant Secretary cautioned, the United States had no alternative to pursuing a "nuanced policy" toward this independent nation whose white population had been on the scene for 300 years and represented 18 percent of all the South African people. The United States, Mr. Schaufele emphasized, did not accept South Africa's institution of apartheid, and would not recognize the Transkei or any of the other nominally independent tribal "homelands" the South African government was in the process of setting up. At the same time, he said, the United States persisted in its opinion that "The problems of South Africa should . . . be solved in South Africa—not by outside powers." Reviewing a broad array of U.S. governmental and business contacts with different elements in the South African population, Mr. Schaufele professed to find enough positive trends to justify at least a hope

[89]U.N. address, Sept. 30, 1976, in *AFR, 1976:* 472.

that South Africa, like the United States itself, would gradually evolve in the direction of a more just society.

Maputo and Vienna

Though there was little in Mr. Schaufele's speech that might not have been said under the previous administration, the wheels were already beginning to spin more rapidly as international pressure on South Africa and Rhodesia was stepped up. Even before the Schaufele address, the five Western members of the Security Council— Canada, France, West Germany, the United Kingdom, and the United States—had undertaken a collective *démarche* on Namibia. On April 7, representatives of the five governments had jointly urged Prime Minister Vorster to lay aside the Windhoek plan— which, they insisted, was quite inadequate to meet the criteria for an internationally acceptable solution as laid down in Resolution 385. There followed detailed discussions with South African officials and other interested parties, among them "representatives of the front-line states, other African leaders, SWAPO, and representatives of various political groups inside Namibia." Western spokesmen did not disguise their feeling that Resolution 385 offered "a final chance for peaceful settlement," and that "an absence of progress toward an internationally acceptable solution would have serious consequences for South Africa."[90]

Far from being limited to Namibia, moreover, American concern was by this time being openly directed to the situation in South Africa itself. "We're trying as best we can to make changes in South Africa," said President Carter on May 17. ". . . . We are very eager to see, and willing to use, all the leverage that we can to bring about an end to racial discrimination in South Africa and an end to the apartheid system. . . . We're not only trying to move ourselves but we're trying to get other nations to join with us. . . . We've gone to Vorster now and given him a request—a little bit stronger than a request, saying that if you don't do something about Namibia, then we're going to take strong action against you in the United Nations."[91]

On Rhodesia, too, there was new movement dating from the time of Prime Minister Callaghan's March 10 meeting with the President. One of the results of that meeting, it was later disclosed, had been an agreement by the two governments to work together in a joint peace initiative aimed at the emergence of "an independent Zimbabwe with majority rule in 1978." On May 11, the State Department announced that Secretary Vance and Foreign Secretary

[90]Document 30.
[91]*Presidential Documents*, 13: 744-5.

Owen had been in contact on the Rhodesian situation and had decided that they now should "enter into a phase of intensive consultations with the parties" in order to pave the way for "the independence of Rhodesia under majority rule in 1978"—in other words, within the next twenty months. To this end, it was announced, a consultative group would be sent to Salisbury under a British diplomat, accompanied by a senior American representative.[92] "We offer our assistance in a supportive manner," Ambassador Young explained. "We recognize Britain's special role. We recognize that we can only be helpful if the key parties involved believe we can be of assistance."

The views of the new U.S. Representative were set forth in some detail in his address before a U.N.-sponsored gathering known as the International Conference in Support of the Peoples of Zimbabwe and Namibia, held in Maputo, Mozambique, on May 16-21 and attended by 92 nations as well as observers and nongovernmental organizations from all parts of the world. Though free of rabble-rousing overtones, Ambassador Young's review of southern African developments **(Document 30)** bespoke an unmistakable sense of urgency. "We are in a race against time regarding Namibia and Zimbabwe," he said. "The future of those two countries and the fate of their people is certain—liberation." The essential question was whether liberation should be achieved through negotiation or through armed struggle, a clearly undesirable alternative that would exact a "cruel price" from the people to be liberated. It was because the United States was certain "that the time remaining for peaceful settlement is brief," Ambassador Young declared, that it had "urgently embarked" upon the initiatives on which it was now engaged in concert with the United Kingdom and other Western governments.

Typical of the moderate tone adopted by the American representative was his proposal to the conference "to make it clear that U.N. members, as always, prefer a negotiated settlement where it can be found." This approach, however, found little echo among those delegations that preferred the more strident anticolonialism familiar from past U.N. gatherings. Speaking as representatives of all the Western members of the Security Council, the U.S. delegation at Maputo eventually went the length of offering a formal statement of reservations to the final declaration of the conference,[93] which called among other things for a mandatory arms embargo against South Africa, strengthened U.N. sanctions against the Smith regime in Rhodesia, aid to the liberation movements and front-line states, and the convening of a special

[92]*Bulletin*, 76: 609. (For the Mar. 10 agreement, cf. Document 33.).
[93]Text of declaration in *Bulletin*, 76: 59-65; U.S. statement, May 21, in same: 58-9.

General Assembly session on the Namibian question. But though unable to buy the Maputo package as a whole, the United States did join some days later in a Security Council resolution tightening sanctions against Rhodesia by prohibiting use or transfer of funds for Rhodesian offices or agencies abroad.[94] Later in the year, as will be recounted, it also joined in ordering a mandatory arms embargo against South Africa in view of that country's continued noncompliance with U.N. standards.[95]

While Ambassador Young was speaking in Maputo, Vice-President Mondale was in Vienna at the midpoint of a tour that had begun in Lisbon and Madrid and would continue to Belgrade and London. The highlight of the Vice-President's stay in Austria's capital was a meeting with South African Prime Minister Vorster, with whom he engaged in "a day and a half of very frank and candid discussions" of the central issues of contention in southern Africa. The guiding purpose of the encounter, Mr. Mondale explained **(Document 31),** had been "to convey the new policies of our Administration regarding southern Africa—specifically Rhodesia, Namibia, and South Africa itself . . . . Put most simply, the policy which the President wished me to convey was that there was need for progress on all three issues: majority rule for Rhodesia and Namibia and a progressive transformation of South African society to the same end. We believed it was particularly important to convey the depth of our convictions."

Concerning Rhodesia and Namibia, the Vice-President took away a feeling that "we registered some useful progress but the significance of this progress will depend on future developments." On Rhodesia, he said, "Prime Minister Vorster agreed to support British-American efforts to get the directly interested parties to agree to an independence constitution and the necessary transitional arrangements, including the holding of elections in which all can take part equally, so that Zimbabwe can achieve independence during 1978 and peace."

With regard to Namibia, on the other hand, the Vice-President confirmed that South Africa's acceptance of the principle of free nationwide elections continued to be qualified by its insistence on the ethnic and tribal subdivisions embodied in the unacceptable Turnhalle plan. In this regard, Mr. Mondale could express no more than a hope that further consultations would find South Africa making "the most serious effort . . . to find a solution that pro-

---

[94]Security Council Resolution 409 (1977), adopted May 27 by consensus; details in *Bulletin*, 77: 66-7.
[95]Security Council Resolution 418 (1977), unanimously adopted Nov. 4; cf. below at note 107.

vides an impartial broadly representative and internationally acceptable interim authority in Namibia.''

It was in regard to South Africa's internal system, however, that the conflict of viewpoints had been most evident. Prime Minister Vorster seemed unimpressed by the American's insistence ''that separateness and apartheid are inherently discriminatory and that that policy of apartheid cannot be acceptable to us.'' Still less did he accept the U.S. view ''that full political participation by all the citizens of South Africa . . . is essential to a healthy, stable, and secure South Africa.'' Vice-President Mondale's public acknowledgment that he was advocating nothing less than the ''one man, one vote'' principle for South Africa would later become the object of some of Vorster's heaviest sarcasm.

''I think the message is now clear to the South African Government,'' Mr. Mondale said in summing up the Vienna talks. ''They know that we believe that perpetuating an unjust system is the surest incentive to increase Soviet influence and even racial war but quite apart from that is unjustified on its own grounds. They know that we will not defend such a system and [words omitted?] in all honesty, however, I do not know what conclusions the South African Government will draw. It is my hope that it will lead to a reassessment, to a change of course which enables us to be helpful and supportive in the difficult times that change inevitably entails. But I cannot rule out the possibility that the South African Government will not change, that our paths will diverge and our policies come into conflict should the South African Government so decide. In that event we would take steps true to our beliefs and values. We hope to be able to see progress in Rhodesia, Namibia, and South Africa. But the alternative is real, much as we dislike it. For a failure to make progress will lead to a tragedy of human history.''

Trouble in the Horn

Other developments of these weeks could only heighten the feeling that the United States was in a race against time in Africa. Military operations between the Rhodesian security forces and their guerrilla foes, particularly those based in Mozambique and led by Mugabe, were expanding in scope and violence.[96] The regime of Uganda's President Idi Amin Dada continued to exhibit the ''sustained disregard for the sanctity of life and...massive violation of basic human rights'' that were to earn a formal condemnation by the Commonwealth heads of government at a June meeting in London.[97] More startling from the standpoint of regional power poli-

[96] Cf. *Bulletin*, 77: 98.
[97] Communiqué, June 15, in *Keesing's*: 28505.

tics was the sudden emergence of Ethiopia, once thought of as America's staunchest African ally, as an accredited member of the opposing camp.

The overthrow of Ethiopa's long-time ruler, the Emperor Haile Selassie, in 1974 had been among the earliest signs of the new revolutionary wave that was now sweeping Africa. Already fighting an insurrectionary movement in Eritrea, and faced with the possibility of a similar revolt in the Somali-populated Ogaden region, Ethiopia had become a center of instability in a regional structure whose other components included the Soviet-oriented Somali Republic, led by President Muhammad Siad Barre, as well as the French Territory of the Afars and the Issas, the tiny colonial remnant that was destined to become independent in mid-1977 under the name of its capital city of Djibouti.

Amid much internal turmoil, the Ethiopian military junta that had succeeded the Emperor and was headed by Brigadier General Teferi Benti had maintained a neutralist posture that Washington had found tolerable, if scarcely exhilarating. In February, 1977, however, Brigadier Teferi lost his life in a further upheaval that brought to the top a new military leader, Lieutenant Colonel Mengistu Haile Mariam, whose anti-American and pro-Soviet proclivities were as obvious as was his ruthlessness toward real or suspected enemies. The Soviet government, apparently undeterred by the congenitally bad relationship between Ethiopia and Somalia (where the U.S.S.R. already enjoyed a preferential position of some years' standing), lost no time in offering aid and support to Ethiopia's new leaders. With startling abruptness, Ethiopia began to acquire the typical appearance of a Soviet satellite, a trend that soon was causing unconcealed anxiety not only in such neighboring African countries as the Sudan and Egypt but even in Saudi Arabia and other countries of the Arabian Peninsula.

Particularly dismaying were the indications that the Cubans, too, might be moving into Ethiopia as they had previously moved into Angola. On May 25, the State Department made known that there were already 50 Cuban military advisers in Ethiopia and stated that 400 to 500 Cuban troops might also be en route to that country. Other Cuban troops in Africa by this time, according to the State Department, included no fewer than 10,000 to 15,000 in Angola as well as 1,000 in the People's Republic of the Congo and smaller numbers in the Guineas, Somalia, and Mozambique.[98] Although Ambassador Young appeared unworried by this development and expressed a hope that the Cubans might at least put a stop to the internal killing in Ethiopia, other American authorities like Vice-President Mondale were said to take a much graver view.[99]

[98]*New York Times*, May 26, 1977.
[99]Same, May 27, 1977.

Secretary of State Vance devoted some troubled sentences to the East African situation in what was to be his major address of the year on African policy, delivered July 1 before the annual convention of the National Association for the Advancement of Colored People (NAACP) at St. Louis **(Document 32)**. Referring to the increase in Soviet arms and Cuban personnel in Africa, "We cannot ignore this increase—and we oppose it," he said. "All sides should be aware that when outside powers pour substantial quantities of arms and military personnel into Africa, it greatly enhances the danger that disputes will be resolved militarily rather than through mediation by African states or by the OAU . . . . We will consider sympathetically appeals for assistance from states which are threatened by a buildup of foreign military equipment and advisers on their borders, in the Horn and elsewhere in Africa. But we hope such local arms races and the consequent danger of deepening outside involvement can be limited."

As a general proposition, Mr. Vance intimated, the United States saw no advantage in interjecting itself into regional disputes, or in emphasizing the East-West implications of every local crisis. "Our challenge," he said, "is to find ways of being supportive without becoming interventionist or intrusive." If the United States was now putting pressure on South Africa to help establish racial justice throughout the southern part of the continent, he indicated, it was acting in the awareness that "the continued denial of racial justice in southern Africa encourages the possibilities for outside intervention." The basic U.S. objective in Africa, Mr. Vance stressed, must be "to foster a prosperous and strong Africa that is at peace with itself and at peace with the world. The long-term success of our African policy will depend more on our actual assistance to African development and our ability to help Africans resolve their disputes than on maneuvers for short-term diplomatic advantage . . . . The future of Africa will be built by African hands. Our interests and our ideals will be served as we offer our own support."

The Clock Ticks Faster

The Carter Administration's policy, as revealed thus far, was earning some applause from African leaders who had previously been critical of U.S. attitudes. "In the past," said Tanzania's President Julius K. Nyerere at a White House dinner on August 4, "American power has been an impediment to Africa's liberation; now, we feel that your power can be an aid to our struggle."[100] According to President Samora Machel of Mozambique—a country closely aligned with the U.S.S.R.—this was perhaps the first time that a President of the United States was "trying genuinely to

[100]*Presidential Documents*, 13: 1180.

understand the problems of Africa."[101] Especially gratifying was the judgement of Lieutenant General Olusegun Obasanjo of Nigeria, a country that was fast emerging both as an African great power and as an American favorite. "As far as we are concerned, " the Nigerian Head of State declared at another White House dinner on October 11, "we are happy to note that for the first time a United States administration is showing signs of recognizing the necessity of placing Africa in its proper position as a major focal point in the quest for international peace and stability."[102]

Heartening as such acknowledgement might be, however, it could not compensate for the deteriorating state of affairs in two of the principal areas of American concern, the Horn of Africa and the South African Republic. Contrary to American hopes, the concepts enunciated by Secretary Vance before the NAACP evoked no favorable echo on the part of the Russians, the Cubans, or the supporters of the South African government. By intensifying the very policies to which the United States had taken exception, these governments seemed not only to be aggravating the immediate problems but to be stacking the cards against a peaceful solution in the future.

Crisis in East Africa

So far as the Horn of Africa was concerned, the Cubans and their Soviet partners could claim with some justification that their growing presence in Ethiopia was a legitimate response to the aggressive behavior of neighboring Somalia, which had chosen this moment of Ethiopian weakness to intensify its longstanding irredentist campaign directed toward Ethiopia's Ogaden region. Officially, Somalia maintained that it was merely supporting an insurgent movement within Ethiopian territory by an indigenous, ethnic Somali "liberation front." In reality, there seemed good reason to believe that Somali national troops were also engaged in the fighting that now surged back and forth around the Ethiopian towns of Diredawa, Jijiga, and Harar. The United States, at any rate, was sufficiently shocked by Somalia's behavior to rescind an earlier offer to provide that country, among others, with limited arms aid to help counter any threat from Ethiopia. The Russians and Cubans, on their side, were not slow to profit by the situation by stepping up the flow of arms and advisers to Ethiopia and further strengthening their influence in the Ethiopian government and armed forces.

Foiled in its hope of seizing the Ogaden and deeply disillusioned by the attitude of its Moscow patrons, Somalia on November 13 de-

[101]Remarks at New York luncheon, Oct. 4, reported by Kathleen Teltsch in *New York Times*, Oct. 5, 1977.
[102]*Presidential Documents*, 13: 1529.

nounced its friendship treaty with the U.S.S.R., expelled its Soviet advisers, broke relations with Cuba, and terminated Soviet use of the submarine base at Berbera, on the Indian Ocean, together with all other facilities in the country. But such a setback to Soviet interests in poor and primitive Somalia seemed only to encourage Moscow's efforts to consolidate a position in the broad and promising Ethiopian hinterland. By December, it was widely believed that Russians, Cubans, and Ethiopians were jointly preparing for a major counteroffensive in the Ogaden which might, if successful, enable them not merely to recover that territory but to extend their dominance over Somalia proper.

New Initiative on Zimbabwe

The outlook for a peaceful solution in Rhodesia, in contrast, did not appear entirely unhopeful. A new round of intensive consultations had been initiated when Secretary Vance stopped off in London on August 12 on his way back from the Middle East; and Foreign Secretary Owen, accompanied this time by Ambassador Young, had made a far-ranging tour of African capitals toward the end of that month. Included in their itinerary was a stop at Lagos, Nigeria, to take part in an 111-nation, U.N.-sponsored World Conference for Action Against Apartheid.[103] August 31, a day when Rhodesia's white electors were voting overwhelming confidence in their current political leadership, was spent in putting the finishing touches on a new plan of settlement to be presented to Prime Minister Smith in Salisbury.

The detailed Anglo-American proposals made public on September 1 **(Document 33)** amounted to a comprehensive blueprint for an "orderly and peaceful transition to independence"—to be based on a "return to legality" and on the holding of "free and impartial elections"—in the course of 1978. Among other novel features, the new plan provided for both British and U.N. participation in the settlement procedure. The existing "illegal regime" would be replaced by a transitional administration headed by a British Resident Commissioner; and there would also be a United Nations presence that would include not only a U.N. Special Representative but also a U.N. Zimbabwe Force to supervise a cease-fire, support the civil power, and maintain liaison with both the Rhodesian armed forces and the guerrilla "Liberation Armies." It was these "Liberation Forces," Dr. Owen explained, who were expected to form the nucleus of the country's future unified national army.[104] As Resident Commissioner, the British named Field Marshal Lord Carver,

---

[103]*Bulletin*, 77: 446-51.
[104]Salisbury statement, Sept. 1, in *Survey of Current Affairs* (New York: British Information Services), Sept. 1977: 340.

former Chief of the Defence Staff. Following authorization by the Security Council,[105] U.N. Secretary-General Kurt Waldheim on October 4 appointed Lieutenant General D. Prem Chand of India as his representative in the discussion of transitional arrangements.

It was a measure of the essential fairness of the Anglo-American proposals that while welcomed by some of the more moderate black leaders, they commended themselves neither to Prime Minister Smith on one side nor to Nkomo and Mugabe, the militants of the guerrilla movement, on the other. Lord Carver and General Prem Chand received scant encouragement when they visited the scene in November. Prime Minister Smith, affecting to treat the Anglo-American proposals as stillborn, put forward on November 24 a modified version of his own plan for an internal settlement that would involve the establishment of majority rule, based on adult suffrage, under conditions to be negotiated with black leaders inside the country.

Whether by accident or design, the impact of the Smith initiative was somewhat lessened by the launching of two large-scale Rhodesian military operations against guerrilla bases in Mozambique, carried out on November 23-25 with a reported death toll exceeding 1,200. Despite this inauspicious beginning, talks on the Smith plan commenced in Salisbury on December 2 with the participation of three of the more obvious candidates for a role in an internal settlement—Bishop Muzorewa of the United African National Council; the Rev. Ndabaningi Sithole, leader of a splinter group known as the African National Council; and Senator Jeremiah Chirau of the tribally based Zimbabwe United People's Organization. Prospects for a successful outcome were variously estimated. Even if the talks succeeded, there would remain a question as to whether any internal settlement could survive the almost certain condemnation not only of militant Africans but of most of the outside world.

South African Crunch

Such hopes as might still flicker in Rhodesia evoked no answering gleam from within South Africa itself, where the trend of late 1977 seemed clearly adverse to Western hopes. Far from moving to dismantle the apartheid system as had been urged so often by Ambassador Young, Secretary Vance, Vice-President Mondale, and President Carter, the Vorster government during these months appeared determined not merely to maintain and extend the system but to intensify its repression of those who dared to criticize it.

On September 12 occurred the death in prison of Steven Biko, a

---

[105]Resolution 415 (1977), adopted Sept. 29 by a vote of 13-0-1 (U.S.S.R.), with China not voting.

leading black moderate whose treatment under detention, as detailed in subsequent legal proceedings, rivaled the worst excesses imputed to totalitarian regimes outside of Africa. Reacting to vehement criticism from at home as well as abroad, the South African government on October 19 instituted a nationwide "crackdown" that involved the banning of eighteen anti-apartheid organizations, the closing of South Africa's leading black newspaper, *The World,* the jailing of its respected editor, Percy Qoboza, and the detention of nearly 50 other dissidents.

Actions of this kind had "profoundly stirred the conscience of the American people," said Richard M. Moose, the Carter administration's new Assistant Secretary of State for African Affairs, at a congressional hearing **(Document 34)**. "More serious than the individual measures," he added, "is the collective message they carry: That in South Africa there is no room for dialogue between the minority which dominates the country and genuine leaders of the majority which is forced to suffer the indignity of apartheid and the humiliation of being denied the right of political participation."

Among the effects of this development was a weakening of Western resistance to the invocation of mandatory U.N. sanctions against South Africa, a course long advocated by other African states but hitherto opposed by the West on the ground that sanctions were unjustified in law and would probably be unfruitful in practice. Even now, attempts to isolate South Africa economically seemed inadvisable to the Western governments, and three successive draft Security Council resolutions that called for different forms of economic sanctions against South Africa were defeated by the triple vetoes of Britain, France, and the United States at a meeting on October 31. All three powers did, however, support a fourth resolution that called upon South Africa to rescind the October 19 measures and abandon apartheid.[106]

In addition, the Western powers at a further meeting of the Security Council on November 4 undertook to modify their previous stand by voting for a resolution ordering an arms embargo against South Africa and thus, for the first time in the United Nations' 32-year history, invoking punitive sanctions against a U.N. member state. A legal justification for this measure was found in an assertion that, "having regard to the policies and acts of the South African Government . . . . the acquisition by South Africa of arms and related matériel constitutes a threat to the maintenance of international peace and security." In these circumstances, all states

---

[106]Resolution 417 (1977), unanimously adopted Oct. 31; details on this and the following resolution in *Bulletin*, 77: 859-66 and *UN Monthly Chronicle*, Dec. 1977: 5-14.

were instructed by the Security Council to "cease forthwith" any provision to South Africa of arms and related matériel and to take other measures to inhibit the manufacture and maintenance by South Africa of arms and military equipment, including nuclear weapons.[107]

In giving their support to this resolution, Ambassador Young and the other Western representatives insisted that they were not abandoning hope that South Africa might still amend its conduct before a catastrophe occured. The majority of white South Africans, however, still seemed impervious to Western pleas and warnings. Elections to the South African House of Assembly on November 30 brought a landslide vote of confidence in Prime Minister Vorster and his National Party. The most probable consequence, it seemed, would be a still more uncompromising application of the central principles of apartheid—coupled, perhaps, with some cosmetic modification of its more superficial manifestations.

Outlook for Namibia

Stolidly as he rejected any Western interference in South African affairs, Prime Minister Vorster appeared to be living up to his commitment to cooperate with the Western powers in putting Namibia on the road to early independence. The Windhoek conference had done its work; now it was the turn of the five-power Western "contact group" established to negotiate with the Pretoria government. The Western position as the talks continued was concisely described by the State Department's Policy Planning Director:

> On Namibia, the five Western members of the Security Council are working toward free elections on a basis of equal individual participation. We are proposing that the United Nations should play a key role in assuring that the elections will be fair and that there will be no intimidation.[108]

The principal difficulty in this connection arose from South Africa's insistence on keeping certain military forces in the territory pending elections, a stipulation that might tend to undercut its commitment to electoral freedom. Though no agreement on this point had been reached by the end of 1977, South African and outside observers were at one in predicting that Namibian independence in some form would become a reality in the following year.

[107]Resolution 418 (1977), unanimously adopted Nov. 4.
[108]Anthony Lake, Washington address, "Africa in a Global Perspective," *Bulletin*, 77: 843.

6. ACID TEST IN LATIN AMERICA

Even while it struggled to unsnarl the racial and diplomatic tangles of southern Africa, the United States was contending with an equally knotty, possibly no less fateful problem in its own hemisphere—a problem which, in the judgment of at least some close observers, could become an occasion for outright guerrilla warfare in the Americas unless it could be promptly and equitably resolved. This, of course, was the problem of the U.S.-owned Panama Canal and the U.S.-administered Canal Zone, a longstanding source of friction within the hemisphere and one that had in recent years assumed an ever more threatening aspect.

It is unnecessary to point out that the problems which centered on the ownership, management, and defense of the Panama Canal were representative of a much wider array of issues that had caused chronic division between the United States and its Latin American and Caribbean partners. As developing countries, most of the latter shared the widespread dissatisfaction over the attitude of the rich industrial nations—particularly the United States—on matters of trade, aid, and investment. As smaller and weaker members of the inter-American system, they were obsessed by questions of national sovereignty and status and viewed the United States, the hemisphere's one military and economic superpower, with strong but ambiguous feelings from which mistrust, resentment, and a certain irritability were seldom absent. As countries governed, in many though not all instances, by authoritarian regimes of one kind or another, they took a rather cynical view of Washington's moralizing about human rights and, in most instances, had tended to shrug off its preachments about the dangers emanating from Castro's Cuba.

The Carter Debut

As had been normal in recent decades, the Carter administration came to office with a firm determination to remedy what it had been denouncing as a record of neglect and mismanagement of inter-American affairs by its immediate predecessors. It was probably no accident that President José López Portillo of Mexico should be the first foreign head of state to visit Washington after President Carter's inauguration. Nor was it surprising, in light of the critical attitudes prevailing throughout Latin America, that the new Mexican leader, addressing Congress on February 17, should have urged the United States to adopt ''a sensible policy based on efficient mechanisms . . . to reduce or eliminate fundamental problems"—problems with which, Señor López asserted, "the private interests that today almost exclusively govern [the U.S.-Latin American] relationship" had signally failed to cope.[109] President Carter was a man who took such criticisms to heart. "We will put our relations with Latin America on a more constructive footing, recognizing the global character of the region's problems," he assured the United Nations on March 17 (Document 3). "We are also working to resolve in amicable negotiations the future of the Panama Canal."

As in the Middle East, the new administration seemed quite prepared to take a fresh look at some of the inhibitions of past U.S. policy in the hemisphere. Moving promptly to reopen the stalled negotiations with Panama, it also halted air surveillance of Cuba and made known its readiness to improve relations with that country in spite of reservations about the Castro government's activities in Africa. Nor did it fail to advertise its determination to apply a more rigorous standard in human rights matters, an area in which Congress had already taken the initiative by reducing or eliminating foreign aid allotments to countries of whose regimes and policies it . disapproved. Uruguay's military-dominated government, for instance, had been disqualified for U.S. military aid in 1976, while the Chilean regime headed by General Augusto Pinochet Ugarte, widely regarded as the hemisphere's worst offender in human rights matters, had itself rejected an aid allotment that had been reduced by Congress on similar grounds.

Such was the background of Secretary Vance's disclosure on February 24 that a further reduction was planned in aid allotments to Uruguay and to Argentina, now ruled by a right-wing military junta under General Jorge Rafael Videla. As noted earlier, this action was followed soon afterward by the publication of an official report to Congress on human rights observance[110] that caused sharp reactions in at least five Latin American countries whose performance was criticized. The military-backed Brazilian government headed by General Ernesto Geisel went so far as to renounce its basic military aid agreement with the United States. Argentina, El Salvador, and Guatemala announced that they were rejecting further U.S. military aid; Uruguay, already declared ineligible for military aid, now rejected U.S. economic assistance as well.[111]

These signs of irritation did not discourage President Carter from reaffirming his commitment to human rights in what was to be his maiden speech on Latin American policy, a Pan American Day address delivered on April 14 before the Permanent Council of

[109]Official English text in *New York Times*, Feb. 18, 1977.
[110]Cf. note 12 above.
[111]Details in *Keesing's*: 28343-4.

the Organization of American States (OAS) at the Pan American Union in Washington **(Document 35)**. Three basic elements, the President said, would underlie "our new approach" to Latin American and Caribbean affairs: (1) "a high regard for the individuality and the sovereignty of each Latin American and Caribbean nation"; (2) "our respect for human rights, a respect which is also so much a part of your own tradition"; and (3) "our desire to press forward on the great issues which affect the relations between the developed and the developing nations."

Particularly stressed in President Carter's remarks—as in those of earlier Presidents—was the importance of keeping in mind the uniqueness of each individual country in a region that too easily lent itself to facile generalizations. "As you know, I am a new President," he said. "I've got a lot to learn. My heart and my interest to a major degree is in Latin America. I welcome every opportunity to strengthen the ties of friendship and a sense of common purpose and close consultation with the nations and the peoples of the Caribbean and Latin America."

Small Steps with Cuba

Events in the ensuing weeks suggested that the President was indeed determined to use all opportunities for strengthening ties within the hemisphere. As one gesture among many, Secretary of the Treasury W. Michael Blumenthal confirmed an earlier U.S. promise of increased support for the Inter-American Development Bank, the hemisphere's principal regional financial institution, which was holding its annual meeting in Guatemala City. Nor did the furor over Cuba's African role discourage new expressions of good will toward that country. "I believe," said President Carter, "that there is an inclination on the part of the American people to continue to move toward a full friendship with Cuba, and I have that as an ultimate goal."[112] The President did not minimize the obstacles in the way of such a consummation. Among them, he noted, was not only Cuba's "intrusion into African affairs in a military way" but also the detention within Cuba itself of an estimated 15,000 to 20,000 political prisoners.[113] But various small steps could nevertheless be taken, he indicated, to adjust relationships and reduce friction in the interests of both countries.

One such step was a visit to Havana toward the end of April by the new Assistant Secretary of State for Inter-American Affairs, Terence A. Todman, to conclude a bilateral agreement defining the two countries' fishing rights in overlapping offshore waters.[114]

[112]Remarks to reporters, May 31, in *Presidential Documents*, 13: 835.
[113]Remarks to reporters, May 30, in same: 833.
[114]*Bulletin*, 76: 484; text of agreement in TIAS 8627.

Likewise indicative of improving relations was Cuba's continued observance of the terms of the bilateral antihijacking agreement between the two countries, which technically expired on April 15 pursuant to its denunciation by the Havana government in 1976. Of potentially wider significance was the announcement on June 3 that both governments had agreed to the opening of "interest sections" to handle diplomatic business in their respective capitals.[115] Though falling well short of a resumption of diplomatic relations, such an arrangement would be a considerable improvement over the existing situation in which all communication between the two governments was routed through the Swiss Embassy in Havana and/or the Czechoslovak Embassy in Washington. At the same time, Cuba agreed to release 10 of the 30 Americans it was holding in prison and to review the cases of the others.

Denuclearization and Human Rights

President Carter, meanwhile, had been endeavoring to strengthen the inter-American network and demonstrate U.S. good will through the acceptance of certain new treaty obligations which had not been viewed with enthusiasm by earlier U.S. administrations. At a special ceremony in the White House Rose Garden on May 26, the President affixed his signature to Additional Protocol I to the Treaty of Tlatelolco or "Treaty for the Prohibition of Nuclear Weapons in Latin America," by which the Latin American countries had undertaken back in 1967 to turn their area into a permanently nuclear-free zone. Ten years after Tlatelolco, this commitment was still only partially effective, since Cuba had refused to sign the treaty, Argentina had signed but not ratified it, and Brazil and Chile had ratified with major limiting conditions. Nevertheless the Tlatelolco pact was widely regarded as a model for denuclearization efforts on a regional scale.

Support of the Tlatelolco treaty by outside powers had also remained incomplete up to this time. Additional Protocol II to the treaty, by which the so-called "nuclear weapon" countries were invited to pledge respect for the Latin American denuclearized zone, had been accepted by the United Kingdom, the United States, France, and China, but not thus far, by the U.S.S.R.[116] Additional Protocol I **(Document 36a)**, providing for the denuclearization of dependent territories within the zone, had also been accepted by the United Kingdom and the Netherlands but not, as yet, by France or

[115]*Bulletin*, 77: 12.
[116]Details in *Documents, 1968-69*: 392-9 and *AFR, 1971*: 456-62. The protocol was signed by the U.S.S.R., with a statement, on May 18, 1978 (*Soviet News*, May 23, 1978: 180).

the United States, the other countries with responsibility for such territories.

American hesitation with regard to Additional Protocol I was officially attributed to the presence within the nuclear-free zone, as defined by the Tlatelolco treaty, of such important U.S.-controlled areas as the Canal Zone, the Guantanamo Naval Base, the Virgin Islands, and Puerto Rico. Not until the advent of the Carter Administration was it determined that acceptance of the protocol would be "in the net interest of the United States" despite the obligation to keep those areas forever free of nuclear weapons.[117] Such a commitment, President Carter suggested at the signature ceremony on May 26 (**Document 36b**), could be regarded as one step toward the "ultimate hope," defined in his Inaugural Address, "that we can eliminate completely from the Earth any dependence upon atomic weapons." Even this small step would not become effective until the protocol had been approved by the Senate and formally ratified by the President. With the critical Panama Canal issue already looming on the legislative horizon, the President was to wait for almost a year before transmitting the protocol to the Senate on May 24, 1978.[118]

A second inter-American treaty on which the Carter administrating appeared to reverse the position of its predecessors was the American Convention on Human Rights, which was signed by President Carter at a ceremony in the Pan American Union on June 1. Drawn up at an Inter-American Conference in Costa Rica in 1969, but not in force up to that time because of an insufficiency of signatures and ratifications,[119] the convention set forth the standard civil and political rights; called, in addition, for the progressive achievement of economic, social, and cultural rights; provided an expanded basis for the work of the Inter-American Commission on Human Rights; and provided for the establishment of an Inter-American Court of Human Rights with authority to consider complaints by states parties to the convention. "I believe," said President Carter, "that no one nation can shape the attitudes of the world, and that's why it's so important for us to join in with our friends and neighbors to the south to pursue as a unified group this noble commitment and endeavor."[120]

[117]U.S. Arms Control and Disarmament Agency, *Arms Control and Disarmament Agreements: Texts and History of Negotiations*, 1977 ed. (ACDA Publication 94; Washington: GPO, 1977): 57.

[118]*Presidential Documents*, 14: 961-2.

[119]Text in *Bulletin*, 77: 28-39. Signed at San José in Nov. 1969, the convention entered into force July 8, 1978 when Grenada became the eleventh country to deposit its ratification.

[120]*Presidential Documents*, 13: 838. The convention was submitted to the Senate Feb. 23, 1978 (note 204, below).

Another manifestation of the spirit of hemispheric intimacy was Mrs. Rosalynn Carter's two-week trip to the Caribbean and Central and South America, which began on May 30 and took her to Jamaica, Costa Rica, Ecuador, Peru, Brazil, Colombia, and Venezuela—a group of countries that was somewhat weighted on the democratic side but still exemplified the wide variety of political regimes in the area. Accompanied, among others, by the wife of the Secretary of State, the First Lady had announced her intention of acting as her husband's personal envoy and engaging in serious policy discussions with the leaders of the countries visited.[121] In this intention she appears to have succeeded to a remarkable degree.

Once again, the human rights issue figured prominently throughout the tour—particularly in Brazil, where the First Lady listened with evident sympathy as students and missionaries poured out complaints about the regime's highhanded conduct. Admitting that her talks with President Geisel had failed to disclose "a complete coincidence of points of view," Mrs. Carter noted that they had also touched on other subjects, such as nuclear nonproliferation, on which the two governments were not in full agreement.[122] The overall appraisal of the trip was highly positive, however. Reports from the seven countries visited had been uniformly favorable, the President asserted as his spouse returned to Andrews Air Force Base on June 12. "We're glad to have her home," he said, "with the renewed knowledge and commitment that our friends in Central and South America are very dear to us. And I believe that the problems that did exist between ourselves and a few of the countries that she visited have to a great degree been resolved, and the agenda that she has laid out in close consultation with the leaders of those nations are already being addressed."[123]

The Seventh OAS Assembly

A broader discussion of the human rights issue took place soon afterward at the seventh regular session of the General Assembly of the OAS, held June 14-22 at St. George's in the new Caribbean Commonwealth state of Grenada. The Foreign Ministers who gathered in Grenada were too well schooled in diplomatic protocol to refer in public to the charges of police brutality and other questionable practices that had been leveled against Grenada's own government and against Sir Eric M. Gairy, who held the offices of Prime Minister and Minister of External Affairs and served as President of the General Assembly session. But all participants appeared to

[121]Departure remarks, May 30, in *Presidential Documents*, 13: 832-3.
[122]*New York Times*, June 8, 1977.
[123]*Presidential Documents*, 13: 872-3.

agree upon the importance of the human rights issue—even though, as Secretary Vance wryly observed, there was "no agreement . . . as to what the answer should be."[124]

The Secretary of State was unequivocal in reminding his colleagues from the other American governments not only of the United State's commitment to respect for the individual, but of its belief that every government shared an obligation "to promote respect for human rights among all nations." "We do not ask others to emulate our particular form of democracy," he said in his opening statement (Document 37a). "The principle of political pluralism lies at the head [*sic*] of this organization. We do support the right of all people to freely participate in their government. This right is based on the conviction that the individual citizen is a subject, not an object. Policies that contradict this tenet are alien to our shared traditions."

In addition, Secretary Vance maintained, the promotion of "justice in our societies—legal, economic, and social"—offered the surest means of defeating the kind of rampant terrorism that was now raging in the hemisphere and, in the brief twelve months since the last Assembly session, had taken the lives of two American Foreign Ministers, past or present, and almost killed a third. Like Secretary Kissinger at Santiago the year before,[125] Mr. Vance urged a strengthening of the Inter-American Commission on Human Rights as the most effective vehicle for promoting human rights on a collective basis. Also like Secretary Kissinger, he called for an organizational streamlining of the OAS (lately increased to a membership of 26 through the admission of the former Dutch territory of Surinam) and a gradual reduction of the U.S. share of the organization's budget from 66 to not over 49 percent.

Though applauded by such democratic countries as Venezuela and Colombia in South America and by Mexico, Costa Rica, and the English-speaking Caribbean states, the Secretary of State's position on the human rights issue met with strenuous opposition from Argentina, Chile, Brazil, and other countries under authoritarian rule. Where Secretary Vance had called for justice as an anti-terrorist weapon, those countries tended to argue that it was precisely the prevalence of terrorism and violence that forced them to abridge the rights of the citizen.[126] Of the 25 governments represented at Grenada—all OAS members except Cuba—only 14 supported the Assembly's principal resolution on human rights (Document 37b), which was adopted on June 22 with 8 abstentions and 3 absences. Urging support for the Inter-American Commission on

[124]Homecoming remarks, June 17, in *Bulletin*, 77: 76.
[125]*AFR, 1976*: 330-36.
[126]*Keesing's*: 28529-30.

Human Rights, the resolution called upon each member state to reaffirm its commitment to human rights and its belief "that there are no circumstances which justify torture, summary conviction, or prolonged detention without trial, contrary to law."

Foreseeing the lack of unanimity on this central issue, Secretary Vance insisted nevertheless that its very prominence in the discussion could be rated a major step in advance. "There can be no doubt," he asserted as he prepared to return to the United States, "that whatever way the actual concrete steps eventuate from this meeting, the sensitivity of all the parties at this meeting has been greatly raised, and I think this is a matter of great importance and of great significance. Therefore, I feel that the fact that this has been done indicates a very important step for this organization and for the issue of human rights, not only in this area but throughout the world."[127]

The Panama Negotiations

A highlight of the Grenada meeting was the presentation by the United States and Panama of separate reports on the negotiations they had been conducting with a view to replacing the outmoded Isthmian Canal Convention of 1903—the master agreement governing the status of the Panama Canal and the U.S.-administered Canal Zone—with new arrangements more in keeping with a contemporary outlook. Initiated more than thirteen years earlier in the wake of serious disorders in the Canal Zone, the negotiations traced their origin to a joint declaration, issued under OAS auspices on April 3, 1964, in which the two parties had undertaken to restore their ruptured diplomatic relations and designate special ambassadors to seek the elimination of the causes of conflict between them and begin procedures aiming at a "just and fair agreement."[128]

Negotiations had since gone through several phases, and were currently proceeding within a set of guidelines agreed upon when Secretary Kissinger visited Panama on February 7, 1974. Embodied in a statement of principles signed by Dr. Kissinger and Juan Antonio Tack, the then Panamanian Foreign Minister,[129] these guidelines defined a kind of "partnership" concept whereby the United States and Panama would share, and Panama would gradually inherit, the rights and responsibilities hitherto exercised by the United States on a unilateral basis. The new treaty, it was agreed, would not run forever but would have a fixed termination date; and it

---

[127]News conference, June 16, in *Bulletin*, 77: 73.
[128]Joint U.S.-Panamanian declaration, Apr. 3, 1964, in *Documents, 1964*: 311.
[129]*AFR, 1974*: 50-52.

would provide for the substitution of Panamanian for U.S. jurisdiction throughout Panamanian territory. Panama would participate both in the administration of the Canal and in its operation and defense, and would be assured a "just and equitable share" of the benefits derived from Canal operation.

To translate these principles into concrete detail had proved no easy task in view of the highflown nationalist emotions prevailing both in Panama and, to an increasing degree, in the United States. While the authoritarian regime of Brigadier General Omar Torrijos Herrera called ever more vehemently for a correction of the unequal status imposed on Panama in 1903, Americans of the stamp of former Governor Ronald Reagan of California had increasingly tended to view the issue as a test of U.S. national strength and prestige. The presidential campaign of 1976, in which Governor Reagan had adopted the Canal as the centerpiece of his unsuccessful campaign for the Republican nomination, had found all candidates, including Governor Carter, insisting on the continued primacy of U.S. rights and interests both in the waterway itself and in the ten-mile-wide Canal Zone.

"I would never give up complete control or practical control of the Panama Canal Zone, but I would continue to negotiate with the Panamanians," Governor Carter had stated during his televised debate with President Ford on October 6, 1976. " . . . I believe that we could share more fully responsibilities for the Panama Canal Zone with Panama. I would be willing to continue to raise the payment for shipment of goods through the Panama Canal Zone. I might even be willing to reduce to some degree our military emplacements in the Panama Canal Zone, but I would not relinquish practical control of the Panama Canal Zone any time in the foreseeable future."[130]

Once elected President, Mr. Carter had seemingly permitted his desire for a settlement to take precedence over his earlier views about the necessity of retaining "complete control or practical control." Suggestive of his commitment to the success of the negotiations was his decision to retain the services of Ambassador at Large Ellsworth Bunker, the Nixon-Ford administration's special representative for Panama treaty negotiations, at the same time strengthening the negotiating team through the addition of Sol M. Linowitz, a leading voice in Latin American affairs in both official and private capacities.

By June of 1977, representatives of the two countries had held two further rounds of negotiations—the first on Contadora Island, Panama, and the second in Washington—and had begun a third, intensive round in Washington that was still going forward at the

---

[130]*AFR, 1976*: 528.

time of the OAS Assembly session. Discussions, Secretary Vance reported at Grenada, had focused on these issues:

— The duration of the treaty;
— The nature and functions of the administrative organization which will operate the canal during the life of the treaty;
— The status of the American and Panamanian employees of that entity;
— An identification of the lands and waters which are necessary for the successful operation of the canal; and
— Provisions to assure that the canal remains permanently secure and open to the ships of all nations on a nondiscriminatory basis.[131]

Panama's new Foreign Minister, Nicolas González Revilla, was slightly more revealing in his report to the OAS Assembly. General Torrijos had long insisted that the Canal and the Canal Zone must definitely revert to Panama not later than the end of the twentieth century; and Foreign Minister González, in listing points already agreed in principle, asserted that the projected treaty would in fact expire December 31, 1999, at which time all territories and installations of the Canal Zone, including the Canal itself, would pass into the hands of Panama in a "practical and concrete" manner.[132]

Both sides, however, had still to move with the utmost caution in view of the exacerbated state of national feeling and the recognition that any treaty they might conclude would have to win some kind of majority approval in both countries before it could enter into force. In the United States, opponents of the treaty concept, like Governor Reagan and Senator Jesse A. Helms of North Carolina, were crying "giveaway" and predicting that the administration would never succeed in mustering the two-thirds majority required for Senate advice and consent to ratification. In Panama, the dictatorial grip that General Torrijos had maintained since seizing power in 1968 appeared to be weakening as opposition to the prospective treaty merged with opposition to his regime, thus raising a question as to his ability to "sell" the arrangement to his own fellow citizens.

By July 29, President Carter was writing General Torrijos that the U.S. negotiators had made all the concessions that were possible in view of domestic constraints. "I am confident," Mr. Carter wrote, "that you understand the problems I face and the difficulties that lie ahead for me. Please be assured that I, too, am fully sensitive to the problems and difficulties that confront you."[133]

[131]*Bulletin*, 77: 72.
[132]*Peking Review*, July 22, 1977.
[133]*New York Times*, Aug. 2, 1977.

Within another fortnight, on August 10, Ambassadors Bunker and Linowitz announced that they and their Panamanian colleagues had reached "agreement in principle on the basic elements of a new treaty—and a new relationship between our countries."[134] Actually, it appeared, there would be not one but two treaties, the first relating to the control and operation of the Canal and the other to its permanent neutrality. Taken together, President Carter asserted, the treaties would provide "a foundation for a new cooperative era in our relations with all of Latin America," thus helping "to usher in a new day in hemispheric relations."[135]

Signing the Treaties

Another four weeks were required to reduce the treaties and accompanying documents to legal form, a necessary preliminary to their official signature at a ceremony scheduled to take place at the Pan American Union on September 7. The mass of documentation involved was later conveniently summarized by Secretary Vance in his formal communication to the President recommending transmittal of the treaties to the Senate for its advice and consent to ratification **(Document 38a)**.

Officially known as the Panama Canal Treaty **(Document 38b)**, the first of the two treaties met Panama's basic requirement by establishing a terminal date of December 31, 1999, for the right of the United States to operate and defend the Panama Canal. Panama, it stipulated, would participate in these activities to an increasing extent during the intervening period, and would assume full authority when the treaty expired at the end of the century. In the meantime, the Canal Zone and its government would disappear and Panama would reassume "plenary jurisdiction" over its territory, as well as receiving substantially increased payments out of Canal revenues. Panama would grant to the United States exclusive rights in the construction of any new interoceanic canal in its territory, and the United States would not negotiate with other countries about a new interoceanic canal unless Panama agreed.

In the accompanying Neutrality Treaty, or "Treaty Concerning the Permanent Neutrality and Operation of the Panama Canal" **(Document 38c)**, Panama declared that the Canal, as an international transit waterway, "shall be permanently neutral . . . . in order that both in time of peace and in time of war it shall remain secure and open to peaceful transit by the vessels of all nations on terms of entire equality, . . . so that the Canal, and therefore the Isthmus of Panama, shall not be the target of reprisals in any armed conflict between other nations of the world." To maintain

---

[134]*Bulletin*, 77: 482.
[135]Statement of Aug. 12, in *Presidential Documents*, 13: 1216-17.

the regime of neutrality thus established, the United States and Panama agreed specifically, among other things, that (1) after the termination of the Panama Canal Treaty in 1999, Panama alone should "operate the Canal and maintain military forces, defense sites and military installations within its national territory"; and (2) vessels of war and auxiliary vessels of the two countries would "be entitled to transit the Canal expeditiously." A Protocol to the Neutrality Treaty afforded an opportunity for "all States of the world" to acknowledge the regime of permanent neutrality, associate themselves with its objectives, and promise to observe and respect it.

Implementing and supplementing the two treaties—which were intended to enter into force six months after the exchange of ratifications—were a number of separate bilateral agreements and other instruments. Panama, in addition, was promised "certain loans, guarantees and credits to assist with its economic development and to strengthen its capability to contribute to the defense of the Canal." Included in this economic cooperation program, it was disclosed, were up to $200 million in Export-Import Bank credits, up to $75 million in Agency for International Development (AID) housing guarantees, and $20 million in Overseas Private Investment Corporation (OPIC) loan guarantees. Concurrently, Panama was also to receive up to $50 million in foreign military sales credits over a ten-year period.[136]

All the American states save Cuba were represented—a majority of them by their heads of state—at the signing ceremony in Washington on September 7. Prime Minister Pierre Elliott Trudeau of Canada was also present, and joined with the representatives of OAS member countries in signing a special "Declaration of Washington" (Document 38d) in which they recorded their "profound satisfaction" at this "major step toward strengthening relations among the nations of the Western Hemisphere on a basis of common interest, equality and mutual respect for the sovereignty and independence of every state." To President Carter, who made a point of conferring privately with each of the foreign guests, the treaties marked "the commitment of the United States to the belief that fairness, and not force, should lie at the heart of our dealings with the nations of the world.[137]

The Ratification Problem

Such praises could not mask the fact that the treaties were far from popular in either country. For General Torrijos, they were at

---

[136]*Bulletin*, 77: 504.
[137]Remarks at the signing ceremony, Sept. 7, in *Presidential Documents*, 13: 1297. For the President's meetings with foreign leaders see same: 1289-1321, *passim*.

best "a stone in the shoe, which Panama would have to suffer for twenty-three [more] years in order to pluck the nail from its heart."[138] Demonstrations by both Left and Right had shown that the arrangement was distasteful to Panamanians of either persuasion. Nevertheless, the treaties could not go into effect until the Panamanian public as a whole approved them in a national plebiscite.

In the United States, the outlook for acceptance by the Senate was at least equally precarious. "Public opinion is simply not ready for it," Senator Robert C. Byrd, majority leader in the upper house, had said in August. "The polls indicate that 75 per cent of the American people are opposed to 'giving up' the Canal and you are not going to get two-thirds of the Senate to ratify that treaty unless there is a substantial change in the polls."[139] With Governor Reagan and other opponents immediately taking the warpath against the new treaties, it appeared that ratification might be delayed to a point where the issue could become embroiled in the 1978 congressional elections.

"Undue delay in ratification could cause serious problems for our foreign relations and jeopardize our long-term interests in the Canal and in the Hemisphere," President Carter warned in the message of September 16 in which he urged the Senate to give the treaties its early and favorable consideration.[140] Secretary Vance, addressing the Senate Foreign Relations Committee as it began its formal hearings on the treaties ten days later (Document 39a), insisted none the less that the issues should be examined with a thoroughness commensurate with their importance. "How we respond to an issue such as these Panama Canal treaties," he said, "will help set the tone for our relations with the rest of the world for some time to come."

In this and other speeches and statements, administration spokesmen sought to allay a multitude of doubts and fears concerning the treaties' impact on security, economic, and political interests. Not without irony in this connection was the qualified praise bestowed on Panama's often criticized regime by an American administration that had hitherto appeared so fervently committed to the support of human rights and democratic freedoms. Panama, Secretary Vance and others insisted, was not indifferent to democratic values, was not subject to Communist influence, and, moreover, was by no means deficient in the technical and management skills required to operate the Canal.

[138]Quoted by R. Narayanan and Jayashri Deshpande, "The 'Big Ditch' and the 'Big Stick': Panama Parleys," *Foreign Affairs Reports* (New Delhi: Indian Council of World Affairs), 26: 196 (Sept. 1977).
[139]Same: 199.
[140]*Presidential Documents*, 13: 1379 (*Bulletin*, 77: 486).

The Carter-Torrijos Statement

Certain specific questions relating to the Neutrality Treaty occasioned so much worry in both countries as to necessitate a second visit to Washington by General Torrijos for further discussion with President Carter. In a special Joint Statement of Understanding made public on October 14 **(Document 39b)**, the two leaders made the following points:

(1) In exercising their responsibility to assure that the Canal would remain open and secure to ships of all nations, each country would, in accordance with its constitutional processes, defend the Canal against any threat to the regime of neutrality—and, consequently, would have the right "to act against any aggression or threat directed against the Canal or against the peaceful transit of vessels through the Canal."

(2) The United States would not, however, have a right of intervention in the internal affairs of Panama, and any U.S. action relative to the Canal would "never be directed against the territorial integrity or political independence of Panama."

(3) The right of expeditious transit of the Canal for U.S. and Panamanian vessels of war and auxiliary vessels meant that in case of need or emergency they could "go to the head of the line of vessels in order to transit the Canal rapidly."

Assured in this way that the United States did not intend to intervene in their internal affairs, the voters of Panama proceeded on October 23 to endorse the treaties by a margin of approximately 2 to 1. American Senators, on their side, were also somewhat reassured by this explicit recognition of the United States' residual right of military intervention, as well as the authoritative affirmation of the "head-of-the-line" principle. Despite administration prodding, however, the year was by now too far advanced and the Senate calendar too crowded to admit of a vote on ratification before the end of 1977. The acid test of the U.S. policy in the Americas was thus pushed forward into 1978, when it would clearly figure as one of the decisive events of President Carter's second year in office.

In addition to winding up a process of negotiation that had been going on since the mid-1960's, the President's first year in office had plainly introduced incalculable changes in the atmosphere of hemispheric affairs. There was, undoubtedly, a new alertness to the human rights issue, and by the end of the year there had even been signs of what might become a trend toward restoration of constitutional government in some of the countries currently ruled by military dictatorships. Economically, too, the Latin American experience in 1977 had been comparatively favorable, with an overall growth rate exceeding 5 percent in real terms.[141] Balancing these favorable developments was the disappointed hope for the return of Cuba, apparently more than ever bent on African adventures, to the circle of American friendships.

7. ASIAN INTERLUDE

One of the more permanent characteristics of American foreign policy is an underlying, rhythmic alternation between periods of special concern with Europe and the Atlantic world and times of heightened preoccupation with the life of Asia and the Pacific. Both sectors obviously make constant claims upon American attention, and the continuing competition between the schools of thought identified as "Asia first" and "Europe first" is itself a typical feature of the national outlook. Yet a primacy of concentration on one or the other side of the globe has nevertheless been evident at virtually every stage of recent American history.

The years from 1965 to 1972, for instance, were clearly identifiable as an "Asian" or "Pacific" phase, despite the Nixon administration's efforts to reduce what it considered an excessive concentration of American strength and resources in that region. With 1973, the "Year of Europe" and of the Yom Kippur War, there began a time of heightened concentration on events beyond the Atlantic, a concentration that increasingly extended to the problems of Africa as well as those of Europe and the Near East. Official pronouncements on Asia during this period, like President Ford's address at Honolulu in 1975 and Secretary Kissinger's Seattle speech in 1976,[142] were largely aimed at allaying any suspicion that the United States was losing interest in the Pacific as the pendulum swung toward the Atlantic world.

The Atlantic emphasis in U.S. policy continued through the opening year of President Carter's administration. Having insisted throughout the campaign upon the urgency of restoring what he portrayed as a gravely damaged relationship with America's traditional allies in the Atlantic community, the new Chief Executive found various ways of manifesting his interest during a postinaugural period whose dramatic highlight was the London summit meeting with other leaders of the Western world. The added presence of Japan's Prime Minister Fukuda at the Downing Street summit was

---

[141]Annual Report of the Inter-American Development Bank, as summarized in *IMF Survey*, 7: 114-15 (Apr. 17, 1978).

[142]*AFR, 1975*: 547-52; same, *1976*: 349-62.

a reminder that the Atlantic-Pacific dichotomy was anything but clear-cut, and that Japan, like the United States and the other Western powers, had interests and responsibilities transcending any regional framework. Again, however, 1977 could be regarded as basically an "off" year in America's Pacific policy, a year in which the focus of American endeavor lay elsewhere and when Asian affairs appeared at times to involve little more than a holding operation.

Developments in Southern Asia

Despite these qualifications, the scene in Asia and the Pacific countries continued to claim the attention not only of American diplomats and regional specialists but, at least intermittently, of the public at large. Especially interesting, in light of the enhanced American sensitivity to questions of human rights and democratic procedures, were the developments in the South Asian subcontinent where India and Pakistan had carried on an uneasy coexistence over the past three decades. In a remarkable display of democratic vitality, India's voters in a general election on March 16-20 repudiated the emergency rule imposed in 1975 by Mrs. Indira Gandhi and her Congress Party and opted for the untried but democratically motivated administration of the new Janata Party led by 81-year-old Morarji R. Desai. What India gained in the renewal of democratic freedoms—and, possibly, in improved relations with the United States—might be offset to some extent by a loss of economic momentum as well as a setback to the family planning campaign, which the previous administration had pressed with counterproductive zeal.

A more distressing development was the snuffing out of what had once appeared a promising democratic experiment in neighboring Pakistan. Initiated amid the ashes of the country's military defeat by India in 1971, the parliamentary regime directed and organized by Prime Minister Zulfikar Ali Bhutto could not withstand the internal storms set off by charges of governmental rigging in the general elections held March 7. Like earlier civilian regimes in Pakistan's troubled history, this latest attempt at representative government was wiped out on July 4-5 by military intervention and the establishment of another martial law regime under the Army Chief of Staff, General Zia al-Haq. Bhutto was soon afterward arrested on charges of ordering the murder of a political opponent, and new elections that had been promised for October did not take place.

Bangladesh, the third and youngest member of the subcontinental triangle, had already succumbed to military rule in 1975 and continued during 1977 under the relatively benign authoritarianism of General Ziaur Rahman, who formally assumed the presidency on April 20 with a program calling for general elections in December 1978. A more convincing, if less widely noted, exercise in democratic government occured in Sri Lanka (Ceylon), where a national election held July 21 resulted in a resounding defeat for the Left-neutralist regime of Mrs. Sirimavo Bandaranaike and the substitution of a more conservative, comparatively pro-Western cabinet headed by J.R. Jayawardene.

East Asian Kaleidoscope

Changes of comparable import were occurring in many parts of East and Southeast Asia, where the termination of the military struggle in Indochina had fostered a reassertion of other political tendencies. "I believe that the end of U.S. involvement in Indochina signals a new era in East Asia," said Richard C. Holbrooke, the new Assistant Secretary of State for East Asian and Pacific Affairs, addressing congressional committees on March 10 in an early attempt to survey the problems of the area **(Document 40).** "While tensions persist, they are confined in scope and there is no major conflict in progress. It appears that all of the major powers, at least for the present, favor a continuation of this situation. For many East Asian countries, economic prospects are better than ever before.

"There are, nevertheless, major uncertainties in the area," Mr. Holbrooke noted. "For example: Relationships among the three states of Indochina and between Indochina and neighboring Southeast Asian countries are still ambivalent and could turn for the worse as easily as go for the better. The situation on the Korean Peninsula is presently quiet, compared to the upsurge of violence last year, but it, too, is unstable. Many countries are trying to cope, internally, with the unaccustomed absence of wartime pressures and the distortions these pressures tend to cause in both economic and political life. In brief, East Asia is undergoing its own transition from an unfortunate past to an uncertain future, albeit with high hopes for what the future will hold."

Mr. Holbrooke did not dwell particularly on conditions in Indochina, where a presidential mission would soon be attempting to clarify the status of Americans missing in action in the recent conflict. In addition, the new Assistant Secretary made only passing reference to the situation in mainland China as it emerged from the upheavals that had occured in 1976 with the deaths of Chou En-lai and Mao Tse-tung and the abortive bid for power by the "Gang of Four." Nor did he go into any detail about relations with Japan, whose new Prime Minister, Takeo Fukuda, would in any case be visiting Washington within the next few days.

The State Department representative had more to say about

South Korea and the Philippines, two allied Asian states where the United States' concern for regional security had already collided with its solicitude for human rights. In both the Philippines and the Republic of Korea, fears of an American retreat from Asia after Vietnam had contributed to the establishment earlier in the decade of authoritarian regimes whose repressive conduct had for several years been causing deep concern in the United States. As Assistant Secretary Holbrooke now conceded, however, the Carter administration—like its predecessor—considered the two Asian countries too important from a security point of view to justify applying the standard congressional remedy, a cutback in military and economic assistance. These overriding security interests, the Assistant Secretary pledged, would be much in the administration's mind as it resumed negotiations with the Philippines for the continued use of military facilities in that country. Nor would the security factor be overlooked, he promised, in implementing President Carter's pre-election pledge to withdraw American ground forces from South Korea.

First Steps in Indochina

President Carter's campaign promises with regard to South Korea were already causing some embarrassment as the new administration began to grapple with the realities of international politics. Already there had been preliminary attempts to reassure the South Koreans, the Japanese, and other interested parties that the United States would avoid precipitancy or recklessness as it moved to limit its military commitment in Northeast Asia. In the meantime, the new administration was beginning to feel its way toward a variety of other objectives, among them a reconciliation with former foes in Indochina, reaffirmation of friendship with Japan, and normalization of relations with the People's Republic of China.

Liquidation of the residues of bad feeling left over from the war in Vietnam had been among the cardinal purposes of an administration whose first official act was the announcement of a comprehensive program aimed at regularizing the status of American draft evaders and deserters from the Vietnam years. Action on another front—a clarification of the status of Americans missing in action in Indochina, and, where possible, recovery of the remains of those who had died—was instituted in February with the naming of a special Presidential Commission, headed by Leonard Woodcock of the United Auto Workers, to travel to Vietnam and Laos, establish contact with the governments of those countries, enlist their aid in accounting for the missing and returning recoverable remains, and ascertain their views on other matters affecting mutual relations.

On a five-day visit in mid-March, the Woodcock commission

was received with unaccustomed signs of good will in both the newly unified "Socialist Republic of Vietnam" and the newly reorganized "Lao People's Democratic Republic." (An attempt to establish contact with the xenophobic Communist regime in Cambodia—officially, "Democratic Kampuchea"—was rebuffed.) Though not notably successful in terms of its primary mission,[143] the commission gained an impression that both the Vietnamese and the Lao leaders were "clearly interested in establishing a new and friendlier relationship with the United States." Undisguisedly eager for U.S. aid in repairing the ravages of war, they seemed to have abandoned their previous tactic of making such aid a condition for progress in other matters. In accepting the commission's report, President Carter revealed on March 23 that he had agreed to a Vietnamese proposal to hold a new round of diplomatic talks in Paris with a view to normalizing relations between the two countries.[144]

A Visitor from Japan

Earlier that week, a two-day visit from Japan's Prime Minister Fukuda had provided opportunity to examine a range of mutual concerns in advance of the London summit planned for May. After a period of rare tranquility during the later months of the Ford administration, U.S.-Japanese relations were already beginning to reflect the influence of new or recurring problems. Among them were the phenomenal inroads currently being made by Japanese exports in U.S. and other world markets; the resultant growth of Japan's trade and payments surplus, and the continued appreciation of its currency on foreign exchange markets; the pressure being exerted by the United States for stimulative economic measures aimed at speedier world recovery; and the reluctance of Japan, as a country without significant fossil fuel resources, to associate itself with President Carter's opposition to plutonium as a nuclear power source.

Such matters were touched but lightly in the official communiqué released as the Fukuda visit reached its end on March 22 **(Document 41)**. In nuclear as in economic and political matters, emphasis was directed almost exclusively to the abstract need for the two

[143]Twelve bodies, eleven of them American servicemen and the twelfth mistakenly identified as such, were turned over to the commission by the Vietnamese. Concerning the 2,456 Americans who had failed to return from the war in Indochina—including 758 still listed as missing in action or prisoners of war—the commission concluded that none were currently alive in Vietnam or Laos and that, as a practical matter, "it is probable that no accounting will ever be possible for most of the Americans lost in Indochina." The commission's report is printed in full in *Bulletin*, 76: 366-74.

[144]*Presidential Documents*, 13: 434 (*Bulletin*, 76: 363-4).

countries to recognize one another's problems, devise good policies to meet them, preserve their "relationship of free and candid dialogue and mutual trust," and "maintain close contact on all matters of mutual concern." Concerning the projected troop withdrawals from Korea, President Carter emphasized that the United States "would proceed in ways which will not endanger the peace on the Peninsula." Concerning Japan itself, he pledged American support for the objective of making Japan a permanent member of the U.N. Security Council—a step that seemed comparatively remote at a time when China and the U.S.S.R., whose consent would obviously be needed, had not even concluded peace treaties with their World War II antagonist.

Normalization with China?

Normalization of relations with the People's Republic of China (P.R.C.), an objective originally laid down by the Nixon administration as far back as 1972, had proved an extremely slow-moving process, not only because of the historical and cultural differences between the two peoples but also because their governments held strongly opposing views about the problem of Taiwan and about the old-established government of the Republic of China, a long-standing U.S. ally and a special favorite of American conservatives, which was still ensconced in Taiwan and still claimed to be the legitimate government of all China. The Shanghai communiqué of 1972, which served as the basic charter of U.S.-P.R.C. relations, had recorded acquiescence in the thesis that Taiwan was a part of China; in addition, it had intimated that the American military presence on Taiwan would be progressively reduced as a contribution to a peaceful settlement of the Taiwan question by the Chinese themselves. Although American troop strength on the island had since been considerably reduced, the United States had shown no haste to accept the Communists' specific conditions for normal relations, which had been crystallized in a threefold demand that the United States break diplomatic relations with the government of the Republic of China, denounce its 1954 mutual security treaty with that government, and withdraw the 1,200 or so U.S. troops that still remained on Taiwan.

President Carter took a relaxed view of this matter when a participant at his May 12 news conference, observing that the Shanghai communiqué was now five years old, inquired whether he had established a target date for full recognition of the P.R.C. "It's very difficult for me to set a target date," the President responded, "because this is a two-way negotiation." Discussions relating to reciprocal financial claims had already been taking place, he noted, and there had been meetings with Huang Chen, the head of the Chinese Liaison Office in Washington. He himself, the President revealed, had decided to designate Leonard Woodcock as head of the vacant U.S. Liaison Office in Peking. Insisting that he "would like to see progress made toward normalization of relationships," Mr. Carter noted that there obviously still remained one major obstacle in "the relationship we've always had with Taiwan." "We don't want to see the Taiwanese people punished or attacked," he said. "And if we can resolve the major difficulty, I would move expeditiously to normalizing relationships with China. But I can't put a time limit on it."[145]

Friction with Korea

As for Korea, statements by the President and others during the early months of 1977 seemed primarily directed to affirming the validity of his campaign promise on the one hand and, at the same time, assuring the Koreans and the world that South Korea was not about to be left defenseless. "I think that the time period [for withdrawal of U.S. ground forces] as I described in the campaign months, a 4- or 5-year time period, is appropriate," Mr. Carter told his March 9 news conference. "The schedule for withdrawal of American ground troops would have to be worked out very carefully with the South Korean Government. It would also have to be done with the full understanding and, perhaps, participation of Japan." In addition, the President stated, "I would want to leave in place in South Korea, adequate ground forces owned by and controlled by the South Korean Government to protect themselves against any intrusion from North Korea. I would envision a continuation of American air cover for South Korea over a long period of time. But these are the basic elements, and I'm very determined that over a period of time . . . our ground troops would be withdrawn."[146]

Even with these qualifications, the withdrawal plan had scant appeal for the government of President Park Chung Hee or, for that matter, for American military authorities in Korea. In May, the Chief of Staff of U.S. Forces in South Korea, General John K. Singlaub, was quoted as stating that withdrawal of ground forces on the suggested schedule would actually "lead to war" by emboldening Communist North Korea to attack a weakened South Korea.[147] This comment, voiced at a time when high-level U.S. military and diplomatic envoys were awaited in Seoul for talks on the

[145] *Presidential Documents*, 13: 708.
[146] Same, 13: 330.
[147] *Washington Post*, May 19, as quoted in *New York Times*, May 20, 1977.

withdrawal plan, was felt in Washington to be incompatible with established policy and led directly to General Singlaub's assignment to a post outside Korea. "A decision has been made," President Carter told his May 26 news conference **(Document 42)**. "President Park has been informed, and we will work very closely with the South Koreans for an orderly transition, leaving the ground troops of the Republic of Korea strong enough to defend themselves and leaving our own commitment to them sure."

A Bird's-eye View

Most elements of the new Far Eastern policy had been fitted into place by June 29, when Secretary Vance appeared before the Asia Society in New York to deliver the year's major address on the affairs of Asia and the Pacific **(Document 43)**. "I should like," the Secretary of State declared, "to advance the basic proposition that our prospects for sustaining and developing effective relationships with the countries of East Asia are more promising than at any time since World War II. The fundamental challenges facing the Administration are to consolidate the positive developments of the past few years—the emergence of an even closer partnership with Japan, a promising 'opening' with China, the growing prosperity of the Pacific Basin economy, the emerging cohesion of the ASEAN [Association of Southeast Asian Nations] grouping—and to prevent or mitigate adverse trends which could strain the presently favorable regional environment. High stakes hang on our ability to meet this challenge, for our interests in Asia are enduring, and they are substantial."

Both adverse trends and favorable developments came in for passing mention in Mr. Vance's regional survey. Reviving economic tensions with Japan, centering on that country's mounting export surplus and gingerly approach to economic expansion, prompted another mildly worded American reference to the need for "close consultation" and "a spirit of true friendship and understanding." Observing that he would himself be visiting mainland China later in the summer, the Secretary of State reaffirmed the official commitment to "normalization" but warned that "progress may not be easy or immediately evident." Notable in his remarks about Korea was the absence of any reference to the ongoing disclosures about the Seoul government's attempts to purchase the support of U.S. congressmen and others, in some cases allegedly by outright bribery conducted through such personalities as former Ambassador Kim Dong Jo and businessman Tongsun Park.

In his comments about Southeast Asia, Secretary Vance took special note of the incipient normalization of U.S. relations with

Vietnam, whose representatives had by this time held two rounds of meetings in Paris with a U.S. delegation headed by Assistant Secretary Holbrooke. Confirming that the United States had dropped its previous opposition to Vietnam's admission to the United Nations, the Secretary indicated at the same time that Washington continued to reject the Vietnamese contention that the United States was obligated to assist in Vietnam's postwar reconstruction. Mentioned in passing was a growing international concern about the continuing outflow of refugees from Vietnam and the other countries of Indochina. In an attempt to do its share in meeting this large-scale humanitarian problem, the Carter administration would later authorize the admission to the United States of 22,000 Indochinese refugees in addition to the 150,000 admitted under the Ford administration.

From SEATO to ASEAN

Another point to which the Secretary of State refrained from directing close attention was the impending final dissolution of the South-East Asia Treaty Organization (SEATO), the five-nation regional security mechanism originally established under the South-East Asia Collective Defense Treaty or Manila Pact of 1954. The "phasing out" of SEATO, authorized by the member governments in September 1975 and formally completed June 30, 1977, eliminated a bureaucratic superstructure but left intact the mutual defense obligations of the Manila Pact itself.[148] In terms of current foreign policy, however, the United States now tended to place the emphasis on two rather different regional structures: on one side, its triangular "ANZUS" relationship with Australia and New Zealand; on the other, its growing intimacy with the five-nation Association of Southeast Asian Nations (ASEAN).

The special and enduring value of the ANZUS connection was reaffirmed at the 26th meeting of the ANZUS Council, which was held in Wellington, New Zealand, on July 27-28 with Deputy Secretary of State Warren Christopher representing the United States. In a typically frank and informal discussion devoted to both global and regional issues, the conferees confirmed their countries' broadly convergent interests, particularly "in the Asia-Pacific region and in contributing towards stability in the area." "While conscious of remaining sources of potential conflict," said their communiqué **(Document 44)**, "Ministers considered that there were reasonable prospects for continuing peace among the countries of Asia."

Among the reasons for this feeling of optimism was the promis-

---

[148]*Australian Foreign Affairs Record* (Canberra: Australian Department of Foreign Affairs), 48: 385 (July 1977).

ing condition of ASEAN—the ten-year-old association of Indonesia, Malaysia, the Philippines, Singapore, and Thailand—which was beginning to serve as an increasingly useful point of contact between the old-established Pacific powers and the non-Communist developing countries of Southeast Asia. The second summit meeting of ASEAN heads of government took place in Kuala Lumpur, Malaysia, on August 4-5, 1977, and was immediately followed by an unprecedented three days of informal discussion and formal economic talks between the ASEAN leaders and the Prime Ministers of Australia, Japan, and New Zealand. Among the results of these exchanges was a Japanese promise of significantly expanded aid to Southeast Asian development.[149]

In September, there were similar consultations in Manila between a group of ministerial representatives from the ASEAN countries and a U.S. delegation headed, in this instance, by Richard N. Cooper, Under Secretary of State for Economic Affairs. "This is the first time that the U.S. Government discussed economic issues with the ASEAN as a group," observed Philippine Foreign Secretary Carlos P. Romulo. "It was really refreshing to discuss with men conversant with the subject. . . . and whose opinions really carry weight." Arrangements were made to continue the dialogue at a technical level in preparation for a second full-dress meeting to be held in Washington in 1978.[150]

A Visit to China

Secretary Vance's visit to the People's Republic of China is usually listed among the less auspicious ventures of the Carter administration's first year. Although it may have produced some gain in mutual understanding of the obstacles to "normalization," the obstacles themselves were too substantial to be vaporized by face-to-face meetings. The Peking government, though it remained fiercely at odds with the Soviet Union and undoubtedly hoped to gain from increased trade and technological exchanges with the United States, had evidently found no reason to moderate its insistence on U.S. abandonment of the Republic of China on Taiwan. The United States, on its side, still saw no justification for trying to buy the friendship of the mainland Chinese by sacrificing this old and valued ally.

Over and above these factors, the visit of Secretary Vance occurred at a moment when the Chinese were still adjusting to a series of internal events that in effect had concluded the period of the "Cultural Revolution" begun in 1966, and, to all appearances, had

[149]Same: 402-3 (Aug. 1977) and 465-6 (Sept. 1977).
[150]*Bulletin*, 77: 595-605.

resolved the political uncertainties attendant on the deaths of Premier Chou En-lai and Party Chairman Mao Tse-tung in 1976 and the attempted seizure of power, later in that year, by the radical faction known as the "Gang of Four."

In July of 1977, the Central Committee of the Chinese Communist Party had placed its stamp of approval on the political rehabilitation of the septuagenarian Teng Hsiao-ping, a twice-purged former Chou En-lai associate who had been thrust aside in the troubles of the previous year but was currently making a comeback in his capacity as a Deputy Prime Minister in the government headed by Prime Minister and Communist Party Chairman Hua Kuo-feng. The impression that China was in the process of recommitting itself to the Chou En-lai concept of economic modernization and political moderation appeared to be confirmed when the Communist Party's Eleventh Congress, held on August 12-18, installed a party leadership in which Teng Hsiao-ping, in addition to his governmental responsibilities, was allotted a party status second only to that of Hua Kuo-feng himself.

Such changes may or may not have had an effect on Secretary Vance's talks with Hua Kuo-feng, Teng Hsiao-ping, and Foreign Minister Huang Hua, which took place in Peking on August 22-25 and adjourned, to the surprise of some observers, without the issuance of the customary formal communiqué. Since the meeting had been essentially exploratory, Mr. Vance explained at a Peking news conference **(Document 45)**, the two sides had agreed that there was no need to enshrine the proceedings in a formal record. A more cogent reason, to judge by the Secretary's cautious language, might have been the all too obvious lack of agreement on the tempo, if not the substance, of the normalization process. "Both sides," Mr. Vance noted, "clearly believe that progress and normalization of our relations in accord with the principles of the Shanghai communiqué is in our mutual interests"; but he refused to say whether there had been any progress in this regard. The most he would vouchsafe was that the meeting had been "very useful" and, from some points of view, "good" and constructive, since the two sides had not only established communication but had enhanced "our mutual understanding of our respective positions on a wide range of issues."

Even this temperate assessment was too much for the Chinese leaders. American reports of progress were unwarranted, Teng Hsiao-ping told a group of Associated Press editors and directors a few days later. In reality, he asserted, normalization efforts had been set back by Secretary Vance's visit and his failure to stand by an earlier promise allegedly made by President Ford during the latter's visit to Peking in December 1975. According to the Deputy

Prime Minister, the former President had stated at that time that once elected to a new term, he would switch American diplomatic recognition from Taipei to Peking, maintaining only unofficial and trade contacts with Taiwan as the Japanese were already doing. (President Ford later stated that this had been merely a suggestion, not a promise.) Secretary Vance, according to Teng Hsiao-ping, had offered to establish a full diplomatic mission in Peking, but had insisted at the same time on keeping at least a liaison mission in Taipei—a proposal rejected by the Chinese because of what to them appeared to be its retrogressive character.[151]

A further indication of Chinese discontent was the delay in naming a successor to Ambassador Huang Chen, who was withdrawn in November as head of the Chinese Liaison Office in Washington. The Peking leaders, it appeared, were going to be satisfied with nothing less than the withdrawal of all American recognition and support of the rival Chinese government on Taiwan; and such a reversal of historic U.S. policy still seemed remote, however flexible the Carter administration might be proving itself in other respects. Small wonder that the President himself, speaking in the immediate aftermath of the Vance mission, declared that diplomatic recognition of the P.R.C. "is undoubtedly going to be well in the future."[152]

Korean Slowdown

Stubbornly as the Chinese Communist leaders avowed their determination to "liberate" Taiwan, they carefully avoided the kind of military gestures they had employed in the 1950s, before their break with Moscow and subsequent *rapprochement* with the United States. Any current Communist threat to the peace of East Asia appeared to emanate not from the P.R.C. but rather from its independent-minded ally, the Democratic People's Republic of Korea (DPRK) ruled by Kim Il Sung. Communist North Korea, which had provoked an ugly incident involving deaths and injuries among U.S. military personnel in 1976, had never wavered in its proclaimed determination to "reunify" Korea by bringing South Korea under its sway, by force if necessary; and seldom was the world allowed to forget its bellicose temper or its willingness to challenge not only the rival government in Seoul but the United States as well.

Still another distressing incident occured on July 13, 1977, when an American cargo helicopter accidentally strayed into North Korean air space and was promptly shot down, with the loss of three

[151]Teng in *New York Times*, Sept, 7, 1977; Ford in same, Sept. 8, 1977.
[152]*Presidential Documents*, 13: 1272.

crewmen killed and a fourth captured. Both governments chose, however, to avoid sensationalizing this occurence, which was promptly smoothed over in direct negotiations. President Carter contented himself with authorizing a public statement that he "deplored the loss of life and the excessive reaction to an unarmed and inadvertent intrusion."[153]

Another effect of the incident was to accentuate the misgivings many Americans were feeling about the planned withdrawal of U.S. ground forces from the South. The administration itself had by this time resigned itself to a further slowing of the withdrawal process, and Defense Secretary Brown, completing what had become an annual security consultation with the South Korean government, revealed on July 26 that the bulk of the Second Infantry Division—the principal component of U.S. ground forces in the country—would actually remain in Korea until the very end of the withdrawal period in 1981 or 1982. Although one brigade of 6,000 men was scheduled to depart in 1978, the division's other two brigades, together with some 4,000 to 6,000 communications, logistics, and intelligence troops and 7,000 Air Force personnel, would remain for several years longer. As a further contribution to South Korean security, Secretary Brown revealed, the United States was planning a $2 billion program of military sales, credits, and gifts which would include a donation of over $500 million worth of leftover military equipment.[154]

These plans were broadly confirmed by President Carter in a subsequent request to Congress for authority to transfer U.S.-owned military equipment to the Republic of Korea. In a letter sent to congressional leaders on October 21 **(Document 46)**, the President once again explained the rationale of the withdrawal plan; underlined the need to ensure that Korean defense capabilities were not weakened, and that the withdrawal of U.S. ground forces was accomplished "in a way that will not disturb the stability that must be maintained in the region"; and asked the Congress to authorize the transfer to the Korean government, without reimbursement, of certain U.S.-owned military equipment with a depreciated value of up to $800 million, together with related services.

But now there arose a further complication in the mounting revulsion, in Congress and the country, against a regime whose agents or adherents had quite obviously been engaged upon a wholesale effort to corrupt the American political process through the subornation of American legislators. Revelations and allegations concerning the activities of Tongsun Park and others had by this time occasioned a furor rivaling the CIA and Lockheed scan-

[153]White House statement, July 16, in *Presidential Documents*, 13: 1017.
[154]Bernard Weinraub in *New York Times*, July 27, 1977.

dals of earlier years—the difference being that in this instance the inspiration for the questionable doings lay outside the United States, with Americans figuring as the corrupted rather than the corrupters. Criticism of the Seoul government, heightened by its unwillingness to assist the efforts of U.S. investigators to unravel the influence-buying scandal, had already reached a point where legislative authorization of the proposed $800 million transfer appeared extremely doubtful unless there was a drastic change of attitudes during the coming months.

Clouds Over Japan

Some other well-established American friendships were clouding over as President Carter's first year approached its end. Especially noteworthy was the situation with regard to Japan, whose relationship to the United States had so recently been hailed as virtually without problems.[155] Since Prime Minister Fukuda's visit in March, the Washington-Tokyo duet had suffered a definite loss of euphony in consequence of the continued phenomenal success of Japan's overseas trade drive and the failure of all efforts to restore a degree of balance to Japanese-American trade and monetary relationships.

Although Prime Minister Fukuda had delighted his hearers at the London summit by predicting that Japan's worrisome surplus would be converted into a deficit in 1977, experience had increasingly belied his optimistic prediction. In reality, Japanese exports for the year increased by 19.8 percent as compared with 1976; imports grew by only 9 percent; and the resultant surplus was measured at a swollen $9.75 billion—including a surplus of $7.3 billion in trade with the United States.[156] Japan's currency, meanwhile, climbed to record highs in foreign exchange markets, while the dollar sank to its lowest levels since the 1940s.

In an effort to reverse these unhealthy trends, U.S. Ambassador Mike Mansfield and others had been repeatedly urging Japan to restrain its exports and liberalize its import policies. In May, the Japanese had been persuaded to sign a so-called Orderly Marketing Agreement providing for a drastic reduction in their exports of color television sets to the United States over the next three years.[157] Yet subsequent trade talks quite failed to produce a slackening in

---

[155]*AFR, 1976*: 80-81.
[156]Preliminary figures for calendar year 1977, in *New York Times*, Jan. 21, 1978. For the fiscal year ended Mar. 31, 1978, Japan reported a record overall trade surplus of $13 billion, as well as surpluses of $8.9 billion with the U.S. and $4.6 billion with the European Communities (same, Apr. 16, 1978).
[157]*Bulletin*, 76: 684-7.

the growth of Japanese exports, and irritability increased on both sides as Japan stood firm against American pressure to revalue the yen and stonewalled rising American demands for "drastic measures" to narrow the trade gap.

Late in November, Prime Minister Fukuda reorganized his cabinet preparatory to announcing a new—but, in American eyes, still wholly inadequate—series of trade liberalization measures. Matters reached a climax in mid-December in a four-day discussion in Washington between Nobuhiko Ushiba, Japan's new Minister for External Economic Affairs, and Robert S. Strauss, President Carter's Special Representative for Trade Negotiations. Initially dismissing Japan's proposals as totally insufficient, the U.S. spokesman eventually expressed a degree of satisfaction at Tokyo's announced intention to set a 7 percent growth target for the coming year and to advance the schedule for certain tariff reductions.[158]

Even as these plans were revealed, however, the dollar was falling to a postwar low of 238 yen and rapidly losing ground against other currencies as well. Gravely as the situation affected American-Japanese relations, the problem obviously was not limited to Japan but was part of a more general malaise involving the entire world economy and America's place in it.

8. WHAT PRICE AFFLUENCE?

Seldom has a mediocre performance earned such praise as was bestowed by President Carter on the achievement of the American economy in 1977. "Last year was a good one for the United States," the Chief Executive declared in his address to Congress on the State of the Union, delivered January 19, 1978.

We reached all of our major economic goals for 1977. Four million new jobs were created—an alltime record—and the number of unemployed dropped by more than a million. Unemployment right now is the lowest it has been since 1974, and not since World War II has such a high percentage of the American people been employed.

The rate of inflation went down. There was a good growth in business profits and investments, the source of more jobs for our workers, and a higher standard of living for all our people. After taxes and inflation, there was a healthy increase in workers' wages.

[158]*New York Times*, Dec. 16, 1977.

And this year, our country will have the first $2 trillion economy in the history of the world.[159]

How Much Prosperity?

Why, if these statements were accurate—as they were—did not the mass of Americans seem more contented with their circumstances and more confident about their future? A few additional figures lend necessary shading to the President's rather light- struck picture. Economic growth, resuming early in 1975 with the formal end of the recession of the mid-1970s, had undoubtedly continued, but at a declining annual rate which had sunk from 6 percent in 1976 to 4.9 percent in 1977 and a mere 4.2 percent in the final quarter of that year. Gross national product, as measured in current dollars, had increased from $1,528.8 billion in 1975 to $1,706.5 billion in 1976 and to $1,890.1 billion in 1977, only $110 billion short of the half-trillion figure. In constant (1972) dollars, however, the 1977 GNP amounted only to a more modest $1,337.5 billion.

Consumer prices, meanwhile, had grown by 4.8 percent in 1976 and had increased by an additional 6.8 percent in 1977, although the rate of increase had slowed to a not very satisfactory 5.4 percent in the year's last two months. Although the President could rightly boast of a continued growth in employment and a further decrease in unemployment, more than 6.3 million persons—or 6.4 percent of the labor force—were still looking for work in December 1977. Peculiarly dismaying, to some observers, was the 12.7 percent unemployment rate prevailing among nonwhite workers. Others shook their heads over a year-long decline in the stock market that had shrunk the Dow Jones Industrial Average by 17.2 percent, from 1004.65 at the end of 1976 to 831.17 at the end of 1977, thus more than canceling out the gains achieved in President Ford's last year.

Petroleum and the Dollar

More clearly unsatisfactory than this mixed performance at home was a dramatic deterioration in America's international economic position as measured by the statistics of international trade, the balance of payments, and the exchange value of the dollar. It was here that the United States most visibly showed the weakening effects of the petroleum revolution of 1973-74, the fivefold increase in international oil prices decreed by the Organization of Petroleum Exporting Countries (OPEC), and the continued failure to check its

[159] *Presidential Documents*, 14: 91-2.

own vast appetite for petroleum from both domestic and foreign sources.

This was an area in which the President himself would readily admit that 1977 had been a year of colossal failure. Far from reducing its dependence on foreign oil, as urged by three successive Presidents, the nation actually increased its reliance on imported petroleum as total consumption grew by 5 percent and inventory buildups by 16 percent. Petroleum imports, at approximately 8.7 million barrels per day, supplied some 47.3 percent of 1977's domestic demand.[160] Their dollar cost, which had been held to $25 billion in 1975 and had risen to $34 billion in 1976, skyrocketed in 1977 to $44.3 billion[161] or approximately 30 percent of the nation's entire import bill.

This national thirst not only made its contribution to domestic inflation but bore much of the responsibility for America's unsatisfactory foreign trade performance in a year when exports increased by only 4.6 percent, to $120.1 billion, while imports grew in value by 22 percent to attain a towering $146.8 billion, thus swelling the resultant trade deficit, which had been measured in 1976 at an unalarming $5.9 billion, to a staggering $26.7 billion.[162] The balance-of-payments deficit on current account, held to a negligible $1.4 billion in 1976, widened to an almost unbelievable $20.2 billion, $7 billion of it during the final quarter of the year when the dollar was experiencing a daily slippage against the Japanese yen, the Swiss franc, and other hard currencies.

What Happened to Energy Policy?

These painful manifestations were not the result of official indifference to the energy problem. Ever since the Arab oil embargo and the OPEC-dictated price rises of 1973-74, American leaders had taken every opportunity to stress the disastrous nature of the nation's energy dependence and the urgent need to practice conservation, develop new energy sources, and, first and foremost, reduce the daily intake of high-priced foreign petroleum. President Nixon, President Ford, and Secretary Kissinger had sounded almost fanatical in this regard. President Carter tuned his rhetoric to a still higher pitch in a much-quoted, little-heeded television talk of April 18 **(Document 47)** in which he cited possibilities of "national

[160]American Petroleum Institute, quoted in *New York Times*, June 8, 1978.
[161]*New York Times*, Jan. 31, 1978.
[162]*Commerce America* (Washington: U.S. Department of Commerce), Feb. 13, 1978: 5-7. Revised 1977 figures, under a new reporting system introduced in 1978, are: exports, $121.1 billion; imports, $147.7 billion; deficit, $26.6 billion (same, Mar. 27, 1978: 8-9).

catastrophe" and called for actions amounting to "the moral equivalent of war, except that we will be uniting our efforts to build and not to destroy."

Addressing a joint session of Congress on April 20, Mr. Carter offered a detailed, highly complex energy program developed under the supervision of James R. Schlesinger, his principal energy adviser and later Secretary of Energy. Designed to meet all aspects of the energy problem, it focused mainly on discouraging oil and natural gas consumption through a system of taxes whose proceeds would subsequently be returned to the public in the form of credits and rebates.[163] The public, however, seemed not to be convinced that there really was an energy problem. Gasoline was freely available, and rising prices, which still remained within tolerable limits, were generally ascribed to the machinations of the international oil companies. The prevalent skepticism was heightened, if anything, by disagreement among the experts about the validity of a CIA study predicting a global petroleum shortage in the mid-1980s. Congress, in addition, was hampered both by the sheer complexity of the President's program and by significant cleavages of ideology and interest within its membership. Though widely differing energy packages were eventually enacted by the House and, much later, by the Senate, negotiations in conference dragged on beyond the year's end as the result of a number of basic differences on such technical matters as the issue of price regulation for domestically produced natural gas.

Though President Carter repeatedly identified the energy program as his primary legislative goal for 1977, he eventually was forced to recognize that it could not become law before 1978 at the earliest. In the meantime, what was frequently described as a "glut" of oil on the world market continued to undermine the sense of urgency at home, as well as casting doubt upon the fulfillment of a new austerity program adopted in October by the nineteen-nation International Energy Agency (IEA).[164]

The Downing Street Summit

Energy was but one among the preoccupations of the national leaders who gathered at 10 Downing Street, the official residence of the British Prime Minister, on May 7-8 for the third in the series of economic summit conferences that had been initiated at Rambouillet in 1975. Participants on this occasion, as already noted, were the leading statesmen of Canada, France, West Germany, Italy, Japan, the United Kingdom, and the United States; in addition, Roy Jenkins was permitted to attend the second day's session in his capacity as President of the Commission of the European Communities.

Though dominated to a considerable extent by the problems of nuclear energy and nonproliferation, the Downing Street summit did provide an opportunity for frank discussion of the state of the world economy at a time when recovery from the recession of the mid-1970s continued to lag and when inflation in most countries persisted without significant abatement. "Since 1975 the world economic situation has been improving gradually," said a general economic statement that was included as an appendix to the Joint Declaration issued at the conclusion of the meeting **(Document 48)**. "Serious problems, however, still persist in all of our countries. Our most urgent task is to create jobs while continuing to reduce inflation. Inflation is not a remedy to unemployment but one of its major causes. Progress in the fight against inflation has been uneven. The needs for adjustment between surplus and deficit countries remain large. The world has not yet fully adjusted to the depressive effects of the 1974 oil price rise."

Among the prerequisites to progress in all these matters, in the view of American and some other authorities, was the adoption by West Germany and Japan of more expansionary economic policies aimed at accelerating economic growth, stimulating imports, and promoting overall recovery, as well as ironing out disequilibria in the balance of payments and curbing the associated monetary instability. The need for such policies had been stressed by Vice-President Mondale—admittedly with limited success—on his world tour immediately after the inauguration. Thus far, however, the governments in Bonn and Tokyo had firmly rejected a line of action which, in their view, was incompatible with the continuance of the relatively moderate rates of inflation they had maintained in recent years. Chancellor Schmidt of the German Federal Republic had become as firmly identified with this cautious view as was President Carter with the expansionary approach.

Although the personal relationship between the American President and the West German Chancellor proved unexpectedly harmonious, the London summit failed to reconcile the essential issue between the two governments. Neither expansion nor stabilization, it was acknowledged, should be regarded as an end in itself; each must be pursued with an eye to its overall effect. "We commit our governments," said the Joint Declaration, "to stated economic growth targets or to stabilization policies which, taken as a whole, should provide a basis for sustained non-inflationary growth, in our own countries and worldwide and for reduction of imbalances in international payments." The targets, though not officially made public, were intended to be taken seriously, according to the American participants, who noted also that arrangements were being made to monitor the performance of the various governments as part of the preparation for another conference to be held at some time in the future.[165]

Other points of mutual concern came in for attention at a meeting whose guiding principle, it was asserted, was the determination of all participants "to respond collectively to the challenges of the future." With a careful avoidance of specifics, the conferees expressed support for the various multilateral endeavors currently going forward in the international economic area: improved financing facilities and additional resources for the International Monetary Fund (IMF); expanded trade opportunities and a new impetus for the multilateral trade negotiations known as the Tokyo Round; increased availability of nuclear energy, combined with a reduction in the risks of nuclear proliferation; and continuation of the "constructive dialogue" with developing countries that had now been going forward for more than a year in the framework of the so-called "North-South" Conference on International Economic Cooperation (CIEC).

"In our discussions we have reached substantial agreement," the Downing Street participants concluded. "Our firm purpose is now to put that agreement into action. We shall review progress on all the measures we have discussed here at Downing Street in order to maintain the momentum of recovery.

"The message of the Downing Street Summit is thus one of confidence:

—in the continuing strength of our societies and the proven democratic principles that give them vitality;
—that we are undertaking the measures needed to overcome problems and achieve a more prosperous future."

Concluding the North-South Conference

A section of the Appendix to the Downing Street Declaration was specifically devoted to the problems of the developing countries. "The world economy can only grow on a sustained and equitable basis if developing countries share in that growth," it affirmed. "Progress has been made. The industrial countries have maintained an open market system despite a deep recession. They have increased aid flows, especially to the poorer nations. Some $8 billion will be available from the IDA [International Development Association] for these nations over the next three years, as we join others in fulfilling pledges to its Fifth Replenishment. The IMF has

[165]Carter, Vance, and Blumenthal remarks, May 8, in *Presidential Documents*, 13: 676-83.

made available to developing countries, under its compensatory financing facility nearly an additional $2 billion last year. An International Fund for Agricultural Development has been created, based on common efforts by the developed [,] OPEC, and other developing nations.

"The progress and the spirit of cooperation that have emerged can serve as an excellent base for further steps," the Downing Street statement continued. "The next step will be the successful conclusion of the Conference on International Economic Cooperation and we agreed to do all in our power to achieve this."

Originally proposed by President Giscard d'Estaing in 1974 at the height of the uncertainty brought on by energy crisis, the 27-nation Conference on International Economic Cooperation (CIEC) had thus far held a single ministerial session in Paris on December 16-19, 1975. After more than a year of detailed work in specialized commissions on energy, raw materials, development, and financial affairs, it was now preparing to conclude its labors at a second ministerial-level meeting that was to be held in the French capital on May 30-June 2, 1977.

In contrast to the polemical tone that had characterized some recent encounters between developed and developing countries, the work of the CIEC had been remarkable for its relatively low-keyed, analytical approach to a wide range of developmental issues. Yet no one who had followed its deliberations could mistake the sense of grievance animating the developing countries, the revolutionary nature of their continuing demand for the establishment of a "New International Economic Order," or the unlikelihood that anything more than a small part of their aims would be accepted by the developed nations.

Secretary Vance, speaking as head of the American delegation as the conference resumed on May 30 **(Document 49a),** went out of his way to conciliate the critics of past American policy. Acknowledging the need to establish "a new international economic system" based on equity, growth, and justice, he gave assurances that the United States would actively join in efforts to this end, would favor a continuation of the dialogue in an appropriate forum, and continued to support a variety of current projects directed toward ameliorating the situation of the developing nations. Among those specifically mentioned were increases in the resources of both the International Monetary Fund and the International Bank for Reconstruction and Development (IBRD); "a special action program of $1 billion to help meet the most acute needs of the world's poorest nations"; and the creation of a common fund—"that is efficient and that works"—to help stabilize the prices of individual commodities produced by developing countries.

Neither the "Group of Nineteen," which represented developing country interests at CIEC, nor the "Group of Eight," consisting of seven developed countries plus the European Economic Community, could be wholly content with the results of their deliberations, which were set forth in some detail in an official communiqué made public following adjournment of the conference early on June 3 **(Document 49b)**. The developing country participants did not disguise their feeling that the agreed conclusions fell far short of "the objectives envisaged for a comprehensive and equitable program of action designed to establish the new international economic order." The United States, on its side, voiced disappointment at the failure to agree to a continuing dialogue on energy, a subject of transcendent importance that had not hitherto been assigned to any international forum encompassing both producer and consumer nations.[166] On the whole, however, American officials declared themselves "quite satisfied"[167] with the outcome of a conference which, to quote the official communiqué, was seen as "only one phase in the ongoing dialogue between developed and developing countries which should continue to be pursued actively in the U.N. system and other existing, appropriate bodies."[168]

Meeting of the OECD

Three weeks after the close of CIEC, Secretary Vance was back in Paris with Secretary of the Treasury Blumenthal for the annual ministerial-level meeting of the Organization for Economic Cooperation and Development (OECD), held on June 23-24 at the 24-member organization's headquarters adjoining the Bois de Boulogne. Like the Downing Street summit in May, the OECD meeting would be concerned with the entire spectrum of international economic issues, again with special emphasis upon the twofold task of promoting expansion while suppressing inflation. The question of development cooperation was another longstanding interest in an organization whose antecedents went all the way back to the Marshall Plan and the beginnings of institutionalized economic cooperation among the industrial countries of North America and Europe.

Secretaries Vance and Blumenthal divided the responsibility for expounding American views on the current state of the international economy. "We are entering a new political and economic era in the world," the Secretary of State affirmed **(Document 50a)**. "In that era North-South confrontation and northern rivalries must be

[166]News conference statement by Under Secretary of State Cooper, June 3, in *Bulletin*, 76: 649.
[167]Same.
[168]For further developments cf. below at note 202. On the commodity fund negotiations see note 22 to Document 55.

replaced by new policies based on cooperation and common action." Such policies, Mr. Vance added, would involve not only "improved economic cooperation among the industrialized nations" and "a new relationship with the developing nations," but also "increased discourse with the state trading [Communist] nations." As at CIEC, the Secretary of State drew special attention to the plight of the world's poorest peoples. "Basic human needs," he emphasized, must be a central concern of the new, evolving relationship among the nations.

Secretary Blumenthal, in his remarks on the second day of the OECD meeting,[169] focused directly on the interrelated problems of employment, growth, and stabilization—again with special insistence on the need for Germany and Japan "to achieve their growth goals and [together with Switzerland and the Netherlands] to reduce their current account surpluses." ". . . Some of our tools of economic management no longer work as they once did," the Secretary of the Treasury admitted. ". . . The tradeoff between economic activity and inflation has changed," he said, accentuating the need "to seek new programs and policies . . . in our efforts to reduce unemployment and inflation." The vital element, in Mr. Blumenthal's opinion, was "our ability to engender confidence that we will achieve sustained growth with lower unemployment and price stability and that we will maintain a strong and open monetary and trading system."

Both Secretaries voiced general satisfaction with the results of the OECD meeting, which were embodied in a lengthy communiqué together with a special declaration on relations with developing countries **(Document 50b).** Recalling the "strategy for sustained expansion" adopted by the OECD nations the year before, the participating ministers agreed that current economic growth rates left something to be desired, and intimated that a somewhat faster rate of expansion—perhaps approximating 5 percent for the OECD area as a whole—would be desirable in 1978. In addition to approving new procedures for monitoring progress under the joint strategy, the ministers came out strongly against any return to protectionist trade policies, renewed a three-year-old promise to avoid restrictive measures, and pledged their countries to pursue sound energy policies, pay special attention to youth unemployment, and increase their aid to economic development, giving special emphasis to basic human needs.

Trade Policy in the Balance

Pronouncements on international economic policy during these months invariably stressed the importance of certain activities al-

[169]*Bulletin*, 77: 109-13.

ready going forward under the aegis of the International Monetary Fund and of the General Agreement on Tariffs and Trade (GATT), two U.N.-related organizations that included both developed and developing countries and, in recent years, had evinced a mounting concern for the interests of the latter group. In a kind of tandem operation originated early in the decade, the GATT organization was sponsoring negotiations looking toward a basic reconstruction of world trade, while the IMF was providing the framework for a far-reaching reform of the international monetary system.

The operational focus of the GATT effort was the so-called Tokyo Round of Multilateral Trade Negotiations, in which between 90 and 100 countries were working toward a progressive dismantling of tariffs and other trade barriers, improvement of the framework for the conduct of world trade, and increased benefits for the trade of developing countries. After getting off to a belated start in Tokyo in 1973, the detailed trade negotiations at Geneva had dragged on longer than expected, missing their original windup date in 1975 and necessitating the adoption of a revised schedule calling for completion by the end of 1977. Tacitly acknowledging that even this latter date was not going to be met, the London Summit Declaration of May 1977 **(Document 48)** had spoken of "giving the negotiations a new impetus" with a view to making "substantive progress in key areas in 1977."

Some new impetus was in fact imparted early in July when the United States and the European Economic Community announced a broad agreement covering most of the procedural issues that had been holding up progress. A new target date of January 15, 1978 was now set—not, indeed, for the completion of the negotiations, but for the presentation of detailed proposals on industrial and agricultural tariffs, nontariff barriers, and other outstanding issues. "The total package would then be in place for final, detailed negotiations, which—give or take—should be concluded within 90 days," declared Ambassador Strauss, the President's Special Representative for Trade Negotiations. "If everything goes according to plan, we will have a GATT round of substance next spring that will cover the next decade of trade relations."[170]

One reason for the slow pace of the Tokyo Round had been the rising pressure, induced in part by recessionary conditions in the United States and other countries, for a return to some of the protectionist policies and practices associated with a bygone era. The Carter administration, while recognizing that some American industries were being hard pressed by import competition, had been exceedingly reluctant to resort to unilateral import limitation, the antithesis of the liberal U.S. trade policies traditional in recent dec-

[170]*Washington Post,* July 12, 1977, quoted in *IMF Survey,* 6: 238 (July 18, 1977).

ades. It had, however, already shown a willingness to offer some relief to selected American industries through the negotiation of so-called "Orderly Marketing Agreements," a device already widely applied in the textile and apparel field whereby exporting countries were persuaded to limit, "voluntarily," their shipments to the United States over a specified period.

A salient example of the use of this technique was Japan's reluctant agreement, noted in the preceding chapter, to restrict its shipments of color television sets to the United States. Taiwan and South Korea, at about the same period, were induced to limit their footwear exports to American destinations. In still other concessions to protectionist pressure, the administration late in 1977 was to increase duties on imported sugar and announce a system of "trigger prices" for steel imports that would result in the imposition of so-called "anti-dumping" duties whenever the price of imported steel fell below a specified level. Despite these deviations, however, American authorities continued to express a strong commitment to the principles of trade liberalization that underlay the GATT and the Tokyo Round.

Reconstructing the Monetary System

A far-reaching reorientation of the international monetary system was meanwhile going forward under the auspices of the International Monetary Fund, whose Articles of Agreement had been extensively amended in 1976 to incorporate a variety of improvements and, in particular, to accommodate the new "floating" exchange rates that had become customary in the 1970s. Though already accepted by the United States, these changes would not enter into force until they had been ratified by a specified number of other IMF members, presumably sometime early in 1978. The same was true of a projected 32.5 percent increase in the IMF quotas of member states, which, when approved, would expand the Fund's resources to a figure of 39 billion Special Drawing Rights (SDR) or over $46 billion.

While awaiting the consummation of these arrangements, the IMF had equipped itself with an important new tool in the form of a multibillion-dollar Supplementary Financing Facility—usually called the "Witteveen Facility" after the IMF Managing Director, H. Johannes Witteveen of the Netherlands—to permit expanded assistance over the next several years to member states that faced disproportionately large payments imbalances. Backed by a $10 billion pledge of support from a special *ad hoc* group that included the United States and other industrial and oil-exporting nations,[171] the Witteveen Facility was likewise expected to become operational

[171] Details in *IMF Survey*, 6: 273-6 (Sept. 5, 1977).

in 1978. Presumably it would supersede the abortive plan for a $25 billion OECD Financial Support Fund or "safety net," proposed by Secretary Kissinger in 1974 but never acted upon by the American Congress.

Continuing Foreign Aid

A more familiar responsibility had fallen to the 95th Congress in connection with the continuation of the ongoing foreign aid program for the fiscal year 1978. Two separate foreign assistance authorization bills for that year were completed in time for presidential signature at the beginning of August. One of them, the International Development and Food Assistance Act of 1977,[172] authorized $1.6 billion in new funds for foreign economic aid; the other, the International Security Assistance Act of 1977,[173] authorized a further sum of $3.2 billion which likewise included substantial allotments for economic assistance in the Near East and elsewhere. In September, Congress completed action on a third measure authorizing contributions of over $5 billion to the International Bank and its affiliated institutions and to the African and Asian Development Banks.[174] Funds to implement all of these programs in the coming fiscal year were provided in the $6.8 billion Foreign Assistance and Related Programs Appropriations Act, 1978,[175] which President Carter signed on October 31.

The principal issues in the 1977 foreign aid legislation were less concerned with the intrinsic merits of foreign aid than with the eligibility for U.S. assistance, direct or indirect, of countries that violated human rights, harbored terrorists, or otherwise incurred congressional disapproval. Continuing a line of differentiation pursued in earlier years, Congress insisted on a variety of restrictions affecting particular countries, e.g., by banning direct aid to Uganda, Cambodia, Laos, Vietnam, Mozambique, Angola, and Cuba; banning military aid to Ethiopia and Uruguay; and prohibiting military credit sales to Argentina, Brazil, El Salvador, and Guatemala.

In addition, the 1977 legislation reflected a growing congressional feeling that international development institutions like the World Bank and the International Development Association should follow the United States' example in denying aid to countries whose human rights practices failed to meet acceptable standards. This, however, was a position the Executive Branch could not possibly accept in view of the fact that such institutions were not under American control and, moreover, were legally bound to

---

[172]Public Law 95-88, Aug. 3, 1977.
[173]Public Law 95-92, Aug. 4, 1977.
[174]Public Law 95-118, Oct. 3, 1977.
[175]Public Law 95-148, Oct. 31, 1977.

decide their policy on economic rather than political grounds. In an attempt to head off crippling amendments to the foreign aid appropriation bill, President Carter did promise that U.S. representatives to the international development institutions would be instructed to vote against loans to Angola, Cambodia, Cuba, Laos, Mozambique, Uganda, and Vietnam, as well as loans for the production of sugar, palm oil, and citrus fruits for export that would injure producers in the United States. Congress nevertheless included in the Foreign Assistance Appropriations Act a "sense of the Congress" declaration to the effect that barring a presidential determination to the contrary, U.S. representatives to the institutions in question "should oppose loans and other financial or technical assistance to any country that persists in a systematic pattern of gross violations of fundamental human rights."[176]

Meeting of the Bank and Fund

Trade, monetary affairs, and economic development would all be up for consideration at the annual meeting of the Boards of Governors of the International Bank and International Monetary Fund, to be held this year in Washington on September 26-30. An even more urgent preoccupation, for many of the approximately 132 attending Finance Ministers and other delegation heads, was what appeared to be the beginning of another slowdown in the pace of recovery from the recent recession. Centering in, though not confined to, the industrial countries of Western Europe, this trend had already become sufficiently marked to prompt a limited resort to stimulative action in West Germany, Japan, and several other countries.

The United States itself, thus far in 1977, had maintained a satisfactory pace of economic expansion; but other news of the American economy was less satisfactory. Investor confidence had never fully recovered from the impact of the 1976 election, and the stock market had been steadily retreating toward a 21-month low that was achieved just before the Bank and Fund meetings. Inflation, meanwhile, had continued apace; and there had been a rapid growth in the trade deficit as imports spurted while exports increased more slowly. This experience, in turn, had accentuated the demand of some Americans for protectionist action, at the same time heightening fears that a wave of protectionism on the part of the United States and other countries could negate the objectives of the Tokyo Round and even plunge the world into a new depression.

[176]Sec. 507, Public Law 95-148. The institutions named were the International Bank for Reconstruction and Development, International Development Association, African Development Fund, Asian Development Bank, and Inter-American Development Bank.

"We meet at a time of doubt about the world's economic future," Secretary Blumenthal admitted at the outset of his remarks to the Bank and Fund meeting **(Document 51)**. "The legacy of the oil shocks of 1974, inflation, and the deep recession of 1974 and 1975 poses questions of whether our system of economic cooperation can endure." Secretary Blumenthal's basic view remained entirely positive. "The main points I want to make are these," he said:

—the world economy has begun to recover from staggering blows;
—we have in place a strategy for sustained recovery, and that strategy is working;
—and we will succeed—though success takes time—if we continue to act together and do not lose our nerve.

Managing Director Witteveen, who was planning to retire when his five-year term expired in August 1978, also took a predominantly favorable view. In analyzing present difficulties, he said, he did not wish to minimize the improvement in the general economic picture over the past year or two. "We have only to remember the gloomy outlook in 1974 to appreciate how much has been achieved," he said. "This should encourage us to tackle the remaining difficulties with determination and in a continuing spirit of international cooperation."[177] "We have been blown off course," Mr. Witteveen added, and ". . . now need to make the necessary adjustments to get back on course. . . . Clearly, our immediate task is to restore a satisfactory rate of recovery and expansion while continuing to make progress in reducing inflation."[178]

A relatively optimistic assessment of developmental trends was offered by World Bank President Robert S. McNamara. The average growth rate of developing countries, he noted, had actually increased from 3.7 percent in 1975 to 4.7 percent in 1976. Yet despite dramatic progress over the past quarter century, Mr. McNamara cautioned, there were glaring disparities in per capita income and life expectancy, not only between different developing countries but even within particular developing countries. In terms like those employed by U.S. spokesmen, the World Bank President called not merely for an acceleration of economic growth in the developing world but for channeling more of its benefits toward the "absolute poor."[179]

Applauding Mr. McNamara's emphasis and promising full U.S. cooperation, Secretary Blumenthal suggested in his own speech

[177]*IMF Survey*, 6: 316 (Oct. 10, 1977).
[178]Same: 305
[179]Same: 314.

that both the Bank and Fund pay more attention to Americans' insistence on the need for improving the lives of the poor, on the promotion of human rights, and on effective administration and realistic salary scales in international institutions. "We have a formidable agenda before us," the Secretary of the Treasury concluded, "and one that we should approach with a sense of hope and resolve. The necessary actions are difficult but the potential gains are immense. Pursuit of sound economic policies domestically and adherence to open and cooperative policies internationally will see us into a new period of economic progress and equity, worldwide."

Save the Dollar!

In spite of these and other optimistic comments, the Bank and Fund meeting was to mark a definite turn for the worse in the general economic outlook. The vague recessionary fears that had been building during the summer took on a disconcerting immediacy as both the United States and some of its OECD partners began to acknowledge the improbability of meeting the economic growth targets established only a few months earlier. Especially disturbing to all the countries concerned were the continued high level of U.S. imports, particularly petroleum imports, and the resultant widening of the trade and balance-of-payments deficits. Confidence in the American dollar was rapidly eroding as skepticism grew concerning the enactment of President Carter's much-touted energy program.

"During the fourth quarter [of 1977]," a government analyst later recorded, "the dollar depreciated sharply against most major European currencies and the Japanese yen. . . . From the end of September to the end of December, the dollar depreciated almost 14 percent against the Swiss franc; 9 percent against the German mark, Japanese yen, and British pound; 7 percent against the Dutch guilder; and 4 percent against the French franc. In contrast, the U.S. dollar appreciated 2 percent against the Canadian dollar. Measured in terms of its trade-weighted average value against both the currencies of 22 OECD and the currencies of 10 major industrial countries, the dollar declined 5 percent from the end of September to the end of December."[180]

At least a measure of order was maintained in the exchange markets during these months by stepped-up intervention on the part of foreign central banks in October and November, supplemented in November by intervention by the U.S. Federal Reserve System.[181] But U.S. authorities continued to shy away from major direct ac-

[180]Steven V. Dunaway, in *Survey of Current Business* (Washington: U.S. Department of Commerce), Mar. 1978: 41-2.
[181]Same: 43-4.

tion to support the dollar, preferring, as in the past, to assume that the trade imbalance could be corrected through appropriate action by Japan and others in conjunction with prompt adoption of the President's energy program. This quietistic attitude proved less than satisfactory to other trading nations, however. Many of the latter had begun to accuse the United States of undue complacency, while some appeared to suspect a Machiavellian policy of deliberately depressing the dollar as an aid to U.S. exports. Matching the longstanding American demand for stimulative action by Germany, Japan, and others, there was now an equally insistent demand from foreign quarters for American action to support the dollar.

President Carter offered at least a partial response to these demands in a special statement made public December 21 (**Document 52**). Less trenchant than the statements issued on comparable occasions by Presidents Eisenhower, Kennedy, Johnson, and Nixon, it did express awareness that "We have a responsibility to protect the integrity of the dollar" and that "Prompt action is needed in energy and other fields to reduce our deficits." Again directing primary attention to energy and trade, the President outlined various short-term measures to increase domestic oil production and promote exports, at the same time promising to submit in January a comprehensive program to "promote economic progress and underscore our commitment to a strong and sound U.S. economy."

Even as matters stood, Mr. Carter insisted, "The American economy and the dollar are fundamentally sound" and "recent exchange market disorders are not justified." Nevertheless, he said, "In the discharge of our responsibilities, we will, in close consultation with our friends abroad, intervene to the extent necessary to correct disorderly conditions in the exchange markets. The measures I have enumerated will deal with the root causes of these market disturbances in a more direct and fundamental way."

Coinciding with this presidential reassurance was a gratifying decision by the OPEC nations to forego a scheduled increase in the price of exported petroleum. Meeting in Venezuela at a time when oil was in abundant supply and further division threatened in their own ranks, the leading oil exporting nations opted for an avoidance of "confrontationist" tactics and contented themselves, for the time being, with reaffirming the $12.70 per barrel price established a year earlier. Such action might improve the chance that an American energy policy would be in place before the next round of price increases. Yet Congress, which had continued to take its time in this regard, was even now preparing for a month-long adjournment that would, in all probability, preclude enactment of the energy legislation before February or March of 1978 at the earliest. The nation's energy problems "will not go away between now and January 23," President Carter observed with sarcasm. "They will simply continue to get worse."[182]

9. FOREIGN POLICY IN A GLOBAL COMMUNITY

Central to the Carter administration's approach to foreign policy was its proclaimed belief in the significance of individual human beings as the foundation and *raison d'être* of all political, economic, and social structures. Endorsement of majority rule and of the "one man, one vote" principle in southern Africa, Presidential Assistant Brzezinski observed on one occasion, "reflect our fundamental view of man as a spiritual entity that transcendentally is truly equal to all others."[183] President Carter's preoccupation with human rights, Secretary Vance's solicitude for "basic human needs," expressed an underlying ethical attitude, shared in some degree by most members of the Carter administration, that was rooted in the great religions and not infrequently recalled the idealism so conspicuous in the civil rights movement of the 1960s.

A corollary of this outlook was the readiness to accept a generous measure of give and take in the relationship between the United States and other countries and international institutions. Though patriotic tradition might still insist upon the absolute priority of the nation-state and the subordination of competing interests, the Carter administration seemed less intensely committed to this outlook than had some of its recent predecessors. On the whole, it seemed to think of nation-states less as ends in themselves than as instrumentalities for harmonizing the interests of different groups of human beings. "We have already become a global community," President Carter told the United Nations Assembly on October 4 **(Document 11)**, "—but only in the sense that we face common problems and we share for good or evil a common future. . . . Power is now widely shared among many nations with different cultures and different histories and different aspirations. The question is whether we will allow our differences to defeat us or whether we will work together to realize our common hopes for peace."

Conflict or Cooperation?

This attitude was clearly not to be equated with a lack of patriotism or an abandonment of traditional national values. Indeed, it

---

[182]*Presidential Documents*, 13: 1913.
[183]Document 53.

was President Carter's contention that he had been placed in office precisely because the nation had insisted on returning to its "true" values after the aberrations of the recent past. An outward-looking foreign policy, moreover, was not a novelty in a nation that had long since shed its isolationist myopia and pooled its interests with those of other, supposedly like-minded peoples in such associations as the United Nations and NATO. Nor was there anything especially unusual about the reemergence of an idealistic view of world affairs in the country that had done so much to shape the ideology of the "free world."

It is true that many Americans had remained profoundly averse to what they considered "globaloney," and had accepted NATO's mutual security concept only because they had been assured that there was no other way of guaranteeing the safety of the United States against the dangers that might otherwise overwhelm it. Rightly or wrongly, preoccupation with the hostile forces at large in the world had remained a decisive influence on American foreign policy not only in the period after World War II but right down into the 1970s. Even foreign aid had been widely regarded less as a humanitarian obligation than as a technique for forestalling Communist takeovers in the developing world.

What was perhaps most novel in the Carter administration's approach to international affairs was its attempt to transcend this lingering obsession with foreign dangers and, instead, to enlist the support of the American people, with their friends and adversaries, in shaping what President Carter once called "a gentler, freer, more bountiful world." Whether such a shift of emphasis was realistically justified under existing world conditions would be for the future to judge. What was apparent almost immediately was that an administration actuated by such ideals would almost automatically tend—as in the Panama treaties—to take a flexible view of national security requirements and place considerable reliance on the good will of other parties. A humanistic foreign policy could hardly be based on total distrust for human motives, even those of potential adversaries.

There were, of course, important variations in the degree to which such attitudes appeared to be espoused by individual members of the Carter administration. Not many of them appeared as thoroughly imbued with the new spirit as Andrew Young, the Permanent Representative to the United Nations, whose zeal for racial justice in southern Africa appeared to reconcile him even to the sinister reality of Cuban intervention in Angola and Ethiopia. President Carter's own line was rather more cautious. "We can only improve this world if we are realistic about its complexities," he told the United Nations early in his term of office **(Document 3):**

The disagreements we face are deeply rooted, and they often raise difficult philosophical as well as territorial issues. They will not be solved easily. They will not be solved quickly. The arms race is now embedded in the very fabric of international affairs and can only be contained with the greatest difficulty. Poverty and inequality are of such monumental scope that it will take decades of deliberate and determined effort even to improve the situation substantially.

If such were President Carter's views, a practiced diplomat and lawyer like Secretary of State Vance seemed even less likely to submerge his critical instincts in a sentimental pursuit of the millennium. Secretary of Defense Brown, who bore the primary responsibility for the readiness of the defense establishment, was known to be quite skeptical of Soviet intentions, and worried audibly about the U.S.S.R.'s new heavy missiles.[184] Nor did Dr. Brzezinski seem likely to fall a prey to delusive optimism. A Polish-born professor of international relations with a background in Communist affairs, the President's National Security adviser had often taxed the previous administration with paying too little heed to third world interests. He himself, however, had been credited with highly pessimistic views about the Soviet Union and even—to the extent that such a thing was conceivable in the Carter administration—a "cold war" mentality.

Address by Dr. Brzezinski

Yet it was precisely Dr. Brzezinski who offered, in his first major speech as a member of the Carter administration, the most persuasive philosophical analysis of the attitudes that were determining its approach to world affairs. In remarks prepared for delivery before the Trilateral Commission in Bonn on October 25 **(Document 53),** the Assistant for National Security Affairs not only identified the distinctive elements in the new American diplomacy but managed to relate them to an intelligible long-range goal.

"If there is a single common theme to our efforts, it is this," Dr. Brzezinski said:

after World War II our foreign policy, by necessity, was focused primarily on issues connected with the Cold War. This gave it a sharp focus, in some cases making it easier to mobilize public opinion. A concentrated foreign policy could be supported by public emotion.

[184]*New York Times*, Sept. 16, 1977.

Today we confront a more difficult task, which calls for support based on reason. We must respond to a wider range of issues—some of which still involve the Cold War—issues stemming from a complex process of global change. A concentrated foreign policy must give way to a complex foreign policy, no longer focused on a single, dramatic task—such as the defense of the West. Instead, we must engage ourselves on the distant and difficult goal of giving shape to a world that has suddenly become politically awakened and socially restless.

Important as they were and would remain, Dr. Brzezinski insisted, East-West relations could no longer be permitted "to dominate all our perspectives"; they must, instead, be assimilated into "a broader framework of cooperation" that must also include the industrialized countries and the nations of the third world:

Today, we do not have a realistic choice between an approach centered on the Soviet Union, or cooperation with our trilateral friends, or on North-South relations. Instead, each set of issues must be approached on its own terms. A world where elements of cooperation prevail over competition entails the need to shape a wider and more cooperative global framework. We did not wish the world to be this complex; but we must deal with it in all of its complexity, even if it means having a foreign policy which cannot be reduced to a single and simplistic slogan.

Presumably because of this respect for the complexity and diversity of the real world, Dr. Brzezinski offered only a general indication of the long-range goals of the American foreign policy effort:

We are . . . seeking to create a new political and international order that is truly more participatory and genuinely more responsive to global desire for greater social justice, equity, and more opportunity for individual self-fulfillment. We believe that paying greater attention to this dimension of foreign policy is not only in our own self-interest, and indispensable to an effective working of the global economy; to us it also represents a return to some of the deepest values and historical roots of our country, while reestablishing the relevance of the West to mankind's universal condition.

"The struggle for the shape of the future," Dr. Brzezinski concluded,

has strong parallels to the experience of Western democracies in the last century and a half. And it is that experience which offers a measure of hope for a more rational and just accommodation on a vastly more complex and larger scale basis. That accommodation, which over time can acquire the character of a genuine global community, cannot be blueprinted in advance; and it will only come about through gradual changes both in the outlook and in the objective conditions of mankind. It is our confident belief that liberty and equity can indeed creatively coexist. It is our confident view of the future that democracy—in its many manifestations and with its own many stages of development—comes closest to meeting the genuinely felt needs of mankind. It is our confident judgment that our collaboration can enhance the chances that the future destiny of man is to live in a world that is creatively pluralistic.

The U.S. in the U.N.

A curious feature of the Brzezinski speech was its lack of reference to the organization that for over 30 years had most distinctively embodied the hopes of people everywhere for the kind of "global community" of which the Presidential Assistant appeared to be speaking. Whatever the reasons for Dr. Brzezinski's failure to mention the United Nations, it clearly did not signal any disregard for the world organization on the part of the Carter administration generally. Far from disregarding the United Nations, the Carter administration had given that institution new emphasis and new priority within its general foreign policy scheme.

That there had been a major change in this respect was emphasized by the Assistant Secretary of State for International Organization Affairs, Charles William Maynes, in a December 3 address to the Association of American University Women:

> We meet today in an active and fascinating period for the United Nations. After years of neglect, or indifference, toward the United Nations, our government has shown new interest and concern. In the last few months, the Administration has paid unprecedented attention to that organization. No other President has spent 2 full days at the United Nations. Secretary of State Vance went to New York and conducted bilateral discussions with some 80 foreign ministers. Secretary of Agriculture [Robert] Bergland recently led our delegation to the conference of the Food and Agriculture Organization. Secretary of Transportation [Brockman] Adams presented a major set of proposals concerning hijacking to the general conference of the International Civil Aviation Organization. The President has asked the Secretaries of other domestic agencies to play an equally active role in the work of the United Nations.

Within the General Assembly and the Security Council, there has been a burst of activity on such issues as airline hijacking; a mandatory arms embargo on South Africa; proposals to resolve the conflicts in Rhodesia, Namibia, and the Middle East; and machinery to extend the economic dialogue between the rich countries and the poor countries. In addition, there have been debates and significant resolutions on human rights, disarmament, outer space, law of the sea, restructuring of the United Nations system, and even unidentified flying objects.[185]

As always, the full, detailed record of United States participation in the United Nations would have to await the annual report by the President to the Congress, to be compiled and made public sometime after the close of the year. Among the activities that would surely be chronicled in the report for 1977—in addition to those mentioned by Assistant Secretary Maynes—would be the United Nations Water Conference held in Mar del Plata, Argentina, on March 14-25, and the United Nations Conference on Desertification held in Nairobi, Kenya, on August 29-September 9. Another outstanding event that occurred late in the summer was a special, week-long meeting of the General Assembly—technically, the Second Part of its 31st Regular Session—which took place in New York on September 13-19 and was devoted to reviewing the progress of economic development efforts in light of the outcome of the recent Paris Conference on International Economic Cooperation (CIEC).[186]

The 32nd Regular Session of the General Assembly, which opened in New York immediately afterward, will require comment later in this discussion. But meanwhile there had been other activities away from U.N. Headquarters that bore significantly upon the general aim of shaping a juster and more humane international order.

One such activity that had been carried on outside the U.N. framework had been the so-called Diplomatic Conference on the Reaffirmation and Development of International Humanitarian Law Applicable in Armed Conflicts. Initiated in Geneva in 1974 and involving over 100 states, this effort concluded June 10, 1977 following the adoption—subject to later signature and ratification—of two protocols designed to supplement the 1949 Geneva Conventions on the treatment of the wounded and sick in the field and at sea, the treatment of prisoners of war, and the treatment of civilians in time of war.[187] The first and longer of the two proto-

---

[185]*Bulletin*, Jan. 1978: 50-51.

[186]For details see *UN Monthly Chronicle*, Oct. 1977: 32-5.

[187]TIAS 3362-3365, dated at Geneva Aug. 12, 1949. (For fuller listing see Appendix.)

cols, dealing with certain requirements to be observed in international wars, embodied a significant break with the past in that its provisions were declared applicable not only to wars of the traditional kind but also to armed conflicts "in which peoples are fighting against colonial domination and alien occupation and against racist regimes in the exercise of their right of self-determination. . . ." Under this principle, nationalist guerrillas—but not mercenaries—would be entitled to the same treatment as members of conventional armed forces.[188]

Another major event of 1977 was the United States' withdrawal from membership in the International Labour Organisation (ILO), thus fulfilling a notice of intent that had been filed by Secretary Kissinger on November 6, 1975.[189] Abandonment of a 58-year-old institution which happened to be the oldest of the U.N. specialized agencies might seem a backward step on the part of a country that boasted its commitment to the ideal of "global community." But years of growing "politicization" of the ILO's work, marked by the application of a "double standard" favoring the Communist nations and increasingly evident on Mideast issues as well, had convinced the United States that the agency's traditions of due process and objectivity were being seriously if not irremediably compromised.

Hopes for a change in attitudes having been demolished by developments at the ILO's annual Conference in June 1977, President Carter had faced the unpleasant necessity of deciding whether the U.S. withdrawal should be permitted to take effect when the two-year waiting period initiated by Secretary Kissinger expired on November 5. "It is rare," said Assistant Secretary Maynes,

that any single question can produce such an intensive coalescence of foreign affairs and domestic viewpoints and pressures as this one involving the ILO did. The issue concerned the balance between benefits of membership, which were considerable, and trends in the organization, which were alarming. The President pondered this problem up until almost the final hour and then decided the United States should let its letter of withdrawal take effect. He did so, however, in the spirit that the United States will return to the ILO if its performance improves. We are

---

[188]Protocol II, dealing with internal conflicts above a certain level, afforded basic guarantees to various classes of affected persons. Texts of the two protocols, open for signature at Berne for a twelve-month period beginning Dec. 12, 1977, appear in U.N. Document A/32/144 and in *International Legal Materials*, 15: 1391-1449 (Nov. 1977).

[189]*AFR, 1975*: 418.

currently [December 1977] exploring the conditions under which we would decide to return.[190]

Setback on the Law of the Sea

In the ILO matter, a combination of Communist and third world pressures had created a situation in which the United States decided to cease participation in activities that were admittedly important to its own interests and to those of the international community. Since 1976, there had loomed the possibility that a rather similar development might occur in connection with the Third United Nations Conference on the Law of the Sea, a high-priority diplomatic gathering in which the United States and some 150 other nations had been endeavoring since 1973 to negotiate a comprehensive treaty governing the use of the oceans and their resources.

Pressures exerted upon the United States to accept arrangements it deemed contrary to its own interests had raised the tension in and around this conference to uncomfortable heights even before the 1976 election. "There are limits beyond which the United States will not go, and we are close to such limits now," Secretary Kissinger had warned as the conference concluded its Fifth Session on September 17, 1976.[191] To Ambassador at Large Elliot L. Richardson, President Carter's Special Representative for the Law of the Sea Conference, the performance of the conference's Sixth Session, held in New York from May 23 to July 15, 1977, raised a fundamental question as to "whether an agreement which accommodates the different national interests involved can be achieved through the kind of negotiations which have thus far taken place."

The principal sticking point in these negotiations, as Ambassador Richardson made clear in a press statement of July 20,[192] subsequently amplified in a report to congressional committees **(Document 54),** had to do with a divergence regarding the exploitation of the mineral resources of the deep seabed—specifically, the manganese nodules, with their freight of nickel, copper, cobalt, and manganese, that waited on the ocean bottom to be picked up by the first comer equipped to do so. Developed countries like the United States, for both commercial and strategic reasons, had insisted on the need for assured and permanent access to these resources—subject, however, to appropriate provision for the interests of the international community. Many of the developing countries, on the other hand, had preferred to advocate a wholly international form

---

[190]Address of Dec. 8, 1977, in *Bulletin,* Feb. 1978: 48. The President's decision, announced Nov. 1, is briefly recorded in *Presidential Documents*, 13: 1705-6 (*Bulletin*, 77: 912).

[191]*AFR, 1976*: 467.

[192]*Bulletin*, 77: 389-91.

of exploitation and to place severe limits on any form of national participation.

A carefully worked-out compromise, developed in informal negotiations during the 1977 session, was nullified at the last minute by the substitution of an alternative text which, in Ambassador Richardson's words, was "fundamentally unacceptable" and "totally fails to accommodate the interests of the United States." This outcome was doubly disappointing because it largely offset the progress that had been made in resolving other issues relating, for example, to a proposed 200-mile exclusive economic zone, free passage of straits, scientific research, protection of the marine environment, and peaceful settlement of disputes. Appropriate treaty language dealing with all these matters was included in a so-called Informal Composite Negotiating Text (ICNT)[193] drawn up by the President of the conference, H.S. Amerasinghe of Sri Lanka. But the language relating to seabed resource exploitation, in the American view, was worse than no language at all.

In view of the apparent remoteness of agreement on the key seabeds issue, Ambassador Richardson disclosed that he had recommended, and the President had ordered, a thorough review of the U.S. posture in advance of the next session of the conference, tentatively scheduled to take place in Geneva from March 28 through May 19, 1978. With or without a comprehensive treaty, Mr. Richardson added, the commencement of seabed mining should not be arbitrarily deferred, and it was desirable that Congress now move ahead with appropriate interim legislation.

> It is our view [he said] that U.S. legislation establishing a domestic regime for seabed mining will be needed whether there is a treaty or not—in either case, legislation will be required to regulate seabed mining in accordance with sound resource management and environmental principles; additionally, in the absence of a treaty, we will need to assure that existing international rights in the area beyond national jurisdiction are protected. . . . In our view, therefore, Congress should continue to move forward with legislation. For its part, the Administration will wish to work closely with . . . concerned committees to make the substance of the legislation consistent with our international posture.

The U.N. and the Terrorist Challenge

All of the multicolored threads of world affairs habitually came together at the annual sessions of the U.N. General Assembly. The

[193]U.N. Document A/CONF.62/WP.10, July 15, 1977; text, as corrected, in *International Legal Materials*, 15: 1108-1235 (Sept. 1977).

32nd Regular Session of this now nearly universal body convened at U.N. Headquarters in New York on Tuesday, September 20, to confront a record 131-item agenda that was to occupy it over most of the next three months. Among its initial actions were the election of Lazar Mojsov, Deputy Secretary for Foreign Affairs of Yugoslavia, as President of the session, and the admission of two new member states whose applications had already been approved by the Security Council with U.S. concurrence. With the seating of the Socialist Republic of Vietnam, successor to the former governments of North and South Vietnam, and of the new Republic of Djibouti, previously known as the French Territory of the Afars and the Issas, the membership of the world organization was increased to a total of 149.

A matter much in the minds of delegates to this Assembly was the frightening growth of terrorist activity in many parts of the world as groups of persons dissatisfied with one or another aspect of the existing order took violent means of advertising their grievances, harming their supposed enemies, and, in some cases, applying pressure for the release of imprisoned comrades. "Terrorism today," the State Department's expert had lately reported, "clearly transcends national boundaries and is a matter of international concern. . . . Between January 1968 and December 1976, there were approximately 1,150 separate international terrorist incidents. While the progression has not been even, the overall trend in the annual totals of these incidents is increasing: 1976 saw a record of 239 separate incidents"[194]—one of the most notable of which, it could be recalled, had been the hijacking of an Air France airbus to Entebbe, Uganda, and the subsequent liberation of 110 passengers and crew members by an Israeli airborne commando force.

The year 1977 had already produced its share of gruesome incidents. Among them were the killing of the President of the Congo and of the Foreign Minister of El Salvador, and the seizure by South Moluccan nationalists in the Netherlands of a train, a school, and 161 hostages in a futile political manifestation that kept the world on tenterhooks for nearly three weeks before it was snuffed out with numerous casualties by the Dutch armed forces. Notable among the terrorist incidents that had come to be of almost daily occurrence in France, Italy, and West Germany had been the activities of the so-called Baader-Meinhof gang, an ultraleftist West German group that preferred to call itself the "Red Army Faction." Thus far in 1977, the exploits of this small band had included the assassination of the Chief Prosecutor of the Federal Republic, the murder of one of West Germany's leading bank-

[194]Statement of Sept. 14 by John E. Karkashian, Acting Director, Office for Combating Terrorism, in *Bulletin*, 77: 606.

ers, and the kidnapping on September 5—with the killing of four bodyguards—of Hanns-Martin Schleyer, a nationally prominent industrialist who was still being held for ransom as the General Assembly opened.

"Violence, terrorism, assassination, undeclared wars all threaten to destroy the restraint and the moderation that must become the dominant characteristic of our age," said President Carter in his October 4 address to the Assembly **(Document 11)**. "Unless we establish a code of international behavior in which the resort to violence becomes increasingly irrelevant to the pursuit of national interests, we will crush the world's dreams for human development and the full flowering of human freedom."

In keeping with its perception of terrorism as a problem that must be dealt with at international as well as national levels, the United States had played a leading role in the elaboration of such international antiterrorist safeguards as had thus far been established, particularly in regard to aerial hijacking. "Unfortunately, there are some basic obstacles to our efforts to expand other areas of multilateral cooperation against terrorism," the State Department spokesman admitted.

Too many governments are predisposed to accept the arguments advanced by terrorist groups that the weak and the oppressed have no effective alternative to using terrorist methods as a means of seeking justice or of publicizing and advancing their cause. Other more developed countries are sometimes inhibited by political or economic considerations from taking actions which might offend governments which support or condone specific terrorist organizations. Some governments appear to be fearful that the apprehension or prosecution of terrorists will provoke new terrorist incidents in order to obtain the release of jailed comrades.[195]

This, in fact, was the kind of resistance that had stymied action on the United States' proposal of 1972 for an international convention to prevent the export of terrorism from one country to another. Although a narrower Convention on the Prevention and Punishment of Crimes Against Internationally Protected Persons, Including Diplomatic Agents,[196] had been approved in 1973 and had entered into force early in 1977, a West German proposal looking toward a convention against the taking of hostages had already occasioned so much disagreement that a 35-member U.N. drafting

[195]*Bulletin*, 77: 607.
[196]Opened for signature Dec. 28, 1973 and entered into force Feb. 20, 1977 (TIAS 8532).

committee had been unable to complete a suitable text and had recently had to ask the General Assembly to renew its mandate.

Events occurring not long after the Assembly's opening helped dissipate any complacency that might still surround this topic. On September 28, a Japanese airliner leaving Bombay was hijacked by Japanese "Red Army" terrorists who later surrendered in Algeria. October 11 brought the news that President Ibrahim al-Hamdi of the Yemen Arab Republic had been assassinated in what seemed a continuation of the intestine feuds habitual in that remote corner of the Arab world. More startling to most people was the hijacking on October 13 of a Lufthansa jet, en route from Mallorca to Frankfurt, by Arabic-speaking gunmen apparently associated with the German terrorist group that was already holding Herr Schleyer. While the plane was flown successively to Rome, Cyprus, Bahrain, Dubai, and Aden, spokesmen for the hijackers demanded the prompt release of eleven terrorists—including Andreas Baader, the leader of the group—from prisons in West Germany. Otherwise, they said, they would blow up the plane with those on board.

From Aden, where the pilot was murdered and ejected from the aircraft, the plane was flown on October 17 to Mogadishu, Somalia. In the meantime, specially trained German commandos were gathering in Turkey and Cyprus, and Somalia's President, Muhammad Siad Barre, was being persuaded to lend his government's cooperation in a rescue operation on the Entebbe pattern. Shortly before the terrorists' final deadline on October 18 (October 17 in the United States), the Bonn government was able to announce that 86 hostages—all but the murdered pilot—had been rescued at Mogadishu in a spectacular commando raid in which three of the four hijackers had perished. Later that day, Andreas Baader and two other terrorists were found dead in their prison cells in Stuttgart, West Germany—assertedly as a result of suicide, although their associates and admirers would vociferously insist they had been murdered. Next day, the body of Herr Schleyer, apparently killed after the jail deaths, was found in an abandoned car in Mulhouse in eastern France.

Even now, the General Assembly appeared to be stirred less by righteous indignation than by the threat of a worldwide, 48-hour aviation strike by the International Federation of Airline Pilots Associations, whose President, Captain Derry F. Pearce, appeared before the Assembly's Special Political Committee to denounce the U.N.'s "pathetic" record in combating hijacking. The upshot of the incident was the adoption on November 3—without a vote—of a relatively innocuous resolution that reiterated and reaffirmed past condemnations of hijacking, called on all states and the International Civil Aviation Organization to intensify their preventative efforts, and appealed for universal acceptance of existing international conventions on the subject.[197] In other actions later in the session, the Assembly authorized further work on the convention against the taking of hostages and called for further study of the underlying causes—as distinct from the prevention and repression—of terrorism.[198] The net effect of its performance was a further postponement of any serious attempt to confront the terrorist challenge.

"Consensus of the Concerned"

The consensus procedure used in adopting the antihijacking resolution exemplified a novel mode of operation that was helping to distinguish the Assembly's 32nd Regular Session from some of its more raucous predecessors. In winding up the session on December 21, Assembly President Mojsov commented on the prevalence of what he described as a "spirit of cooperation and mutual accommodation of interests, without sharp divisions and polarization." "One gets the impression," he said, "—and we hope that it is correct—that the period of blocking the solution of various problems is behind us."[199]

Ambassador Young, assessing the Assembly's achievements at the final plenary session **(Document 55),** was no less encouraged. "A more constructive and cooperative tone in the conduct of our deliberations here," a "new will to talk together about resolving our common problems," had helped, he said, to make the 32nd Session "the most constructive . . . in many years." "In this General Assembly," the U.S. Permanent Representative asserted, "we have seen a clearer consensus of the concerned emerge to replace some of the politics of frustration which seemed often to drive the work of the Assembly in the past. . . . I sense an increasing agreement that slogans lead nowhere, that purely political and tactical maneuvers in isolation from the substance not only are wasteful and damaging to this institution but they engender unproductive confrontation which inhibits progress toward solution of the crucial problems of mankind."

But even if this had been "a good Assembly" in comparison with some of its predecessors, the overall result of its endeavors was shot through with inconsistencies. In spite of signs of "a new degree of consensus" on southern African issues, Ambassador Young observed, the Assembly's resolutions on the Middle East still "tended to reflect the unhelpful rhetoric of the past rather than the refresh-

[197]Resolution 32/8, Nov. 3, 1977; text and related material in *Bulletin*, Jan. 1978: 53-5 and *UN Monthly Chronicle*, Dec. 1977: 23-6 and 81.
[198]Resolutions 32/148 and 32/147, Dec. 16, 1977; details in same, Jan. 1978: 100-101.
[199]*UN Monthly Chronicle*, Jan. 1978: 5.

ing and hopeful developments of the present." On arms control, there had been progress of a sort, since both the United States and the U.S.S.R. had for the first time supported resolutions calling for a comprehensive nuclear test ban[200] and further progress on SALT.[201] Among its other actions in this field, the Assembly determined that a contemplated special session on disarmament should be held between May 23 and June 28, 1978, and should be given a report on the projected world disarmament conference that had for several years been advocated by the Soviet Union.

The General Assembly's decisions relative to economic and social issues afforded the United States a mixture of satisfaction and disappointment. One key decision, providing in effect for continuation of the North-South "dialogue" that had recently been suspended in Paris, affirmed that "all negotiations of a global nature relating to the establishment of the new international economic order should take place within the framework of the United Nations system"—and, in addition, that a special Assembly session to assess progress in this area should be held in 1980.[202] A second important resolution, on the restructuring of the economic and social sectors of the U.N. system, provided for the appointment of a high-level Director-General for Economic Development and International Economic Cooperation to assist Secretary-General Waldheim in carrying out his responsibilities in the economic and social fields.[203]

The main event of the session with regard to human rights may well have been President Carter's action, foreshadowed in his March 17 address to the United Nations **(Document 3)**, in signing the International Covenant on Economic, Social and Cultural Rights and the International Covenant on Civil and Political Rights.[204] Originally adopted by the General Assembly in 1966, the two covenants had lately entered into force for over 40 signatory

[200]Resolution 32/78, adopted Dec. 12, 1977 by a vote of 126 (U.S., U.S.S.R.)-2 (Albania, China)-1 (France); details in same: 10.

[201]Resolution 32/87 G, adopted Dec. 12, 1977 by a vote of 134 (U.S., U.S.S.R.)-2 (Albania, China)-0; details in same: 12.

[202]Resolution 32/174, adopted Dec. 19, 1977 without vote; text and related material in same: 56 and 134.

[203]Resolution 32/197, adopted Dec. 20, 1977 without vote; details in same: 54-6.

[204]Adopted by the U.N. General Assembly Dec. 16, 1966 and entered into force respectively on Jan. 3, 1976 and Mar. 23, 1976; texts in U.S. Department of State, Bureau of Public Affairs, Office of Media Services, *Human Rights* (Selected Documents, No. 5 [Washington: GPO, 1977]): 15-29. President Carter's signature statement appears in *Presidential Documents*, 13: 1488-9 (*Bulletin*, 77: 586-7). Both covenants were transmitted to the Senate, together with the Convention on Genocide and the American Convention on Human Rights, on Feb. 23, 1978 (*Presidential Documents*, 14: 395-6).

states. They had, however, never been signed by the United States, primarily because of the doubts entertained by successive administrations about their acceptance by the Senate. In signing the two covenants at U.N. Headquarters on October 5, President Carter refrained from signing an optional protocol enabling individuals to allege violations of their civil and political rights.

Action on human rights within the General Assembly itself brought disappointment to the United States when it was decided to take no action on a longstanding proposal to appoint a U.N. Commissioner for Human Rights, "to promote and strengthen universal and effective understanding and respect for human rights and fundamental freedoms for all without distinction." A 24-power draft resolution proposing the establishment of such a post was at least temporarily shelved when the Assembly decided, by a vote of 62 to 49 with 21 abstentions, not to put the proposal to a vote until there had been an opportunity for further discussion in the Human Rights Commission.[205] Noting that "broad cosponsorship of the proposal . . . reflected support in most geographic regions," Ambassador Young suggested also that "we have taken important steps toward achievement of more awareness and agreement on action in this sensitive but critical field than we have ever had. . . ."

"If we are striking a more constructive and cooperative tone in the conduct of our deliberations here, I do not mean to suggest that we be complacent," the U.S. Representative further observed. "We have a difficult agenda facing us in the 12 months ahead"—in the Middle East, in Cyprus, in southern Africa; on human rights, arms control, and development; in economical and efficient operation of the United Nations itself. Nevertheless, the Permanent Representative reiterated, "with the consensus of the concerned that has clearly emerged at this year's General Assembly, we have begun to search for the common elements of our own interests, to stop shouting and to do more listening." And he quoted with approval the opinion of a senior official of another government who had told him, early in the session, that the U.N. seemed to be catching its "second wind."

Is This Trip Necessary?

Was the Carter administration also catching its "second wind"? And, if not, was there a prospect of its doing so in the foreseeable future? These were burning questions in late 1977, not only for Americans but for governments in every part of the world. After a brave beginning and a period of months in which most people had

[205]Details in *UN Monthly Chronicle*, Jan. 1978: 68.

been glad to give it the benefit of the doubt, America's new leadership was beginning to be judged with a severity bordering on harshness. Disappointed above all in the administration's less than dazzling record in controlling inflation and reducing unemployment, Americans were also noting signs of incoherence at various levels of government and were even beginning to question the personal competence of the Chief Executive they had elected twelve months earlier.

A significant turning point in the fortunes of the Carter administration had occured on September 21 when the President's intimate friend and adviser, Thomas Bertram (Bert) Lance, had resigned his position as Director of the Office of Management and Budget (OMB) as a result of disclosures pointing to a pattern of financial irregularities and ethical misjudgments in his career as a banker. Dismaying enough in an administration pledged to restore confidence in government, this occurrence seemed even more disheartening when viewed in the context of other developments—for which the Carter administration was clearly not responsible—suggesting that the worldwide deterioration in ethical standards and values had not ceased with Watergate. Examples that could be picked at random included the large-scale acceptance of Korean bribes and other favors by some U.S. congressmen; prevarication of some highly placed official with respect to past activites of the Central Intelligence Agency (CIA); or, to cite a foreign instance, the shady transactions and currency violations that had helped dethrone the Israel Labor Party and usher in the government of Prime Minister Begin.

It was at the height of the Lance furor, on September 23, that the White House announced President Carter's intention of undertaking a second overseas trip involving visits to eight countries in four continents during the ten-day period from November 22 to December 2: Venezuela, Brazil, Nigeria, India, Iran, France, Poland, and Belgium. Cynics were not slow to suggest that Mr. Carter was resorting to a familiar expedient of Presidents in domestic difficulty. That there was in fact an element of theatrics in the President's plan seemed doubly evident when, on November 7, he announced a postponement until after Christmas because of what he described as "the paramount importance of developing an effective energy plan this year."[206] Nor was this impression dispelled by the further announcement on December 1, with the energy legislation still hanging fire, that the trip was being divided into two parts: a first portion, with stops in Poland, Iran, India, Saudi Arabia, France, and Belgium, from December 29, 1977 to January 6, 1978; and a

[206]Speech of Nov. 8, in *Presidential Documents*, 13: 1737.

second portion, with stops in Brazil, Nigeria, and Venezuela, sometime in the spring of 1978.

Whatever the domestic factors in the President's planning, there was undoubtedly a need for something of a "tune-up" of the American foreign policy machine in the closing weeks of 1977. The stalling of Mr. Carter's energy program, in spite of White House pressure dating all the way back to the "moral equivalent of war" speech of April 18 **(Document 47),** typified the fate of various administration initiatives that seemed either to have misfired or to have become snarled in bureaucratic or diplomatic red tape, sometimes of the administration's own making. Allied governments, as the London-based International Institute for Strategic Studies (IISS) gently pointed out, were uneasy "not over the President's motives but over the implementation" of policies which often seemed uncoordinated and inconsistent."[207]

Concerning human rights in the U.S.S.R., for example, the Carter administration had begun by antagonizing the Kremlin with its open demand for the elimination of abuses; had subsequently moderated its pressure in the interest of achieving a SALT agreement; and now seemed likely to end the year with neither a SALT agreement nor an acceptable human rights situation. Nor, it seemed, was there to be any early resolution of the differences over Mutual and Balanced Force Reductions (MBFR), nuclear nonproliferation, or conventional arms transfers. America's international economic position, distorted by its huge petroleum imports, was daily going from bad to worse, amid growing friction with Japan and, to a less marked extent, with West Germany and other European partners. Normalization with China seemed to be a standstill; the Greek-Turkish-Cypriot imbroglio remained as tangled as ever; Cuba's African adventures, besides threatening to reignite the "cold war," had ruined the hope of an improvement in U.S.-Cuban relations. The law of the sea negotiations had reached an impasse, and international terrorism had scaled new heights of ghastliness.

These negative manifestations were not, of course, primarily the fault of the United States, dishearteningly as they contrasted with the euphoric expectations on which the Carter administration had ridden into office. And there were also favorable, or at least potentially favorable, trends: the signature (though not yet the ratification) of the Panama Canal treaties; intensifed negotiations on Rhodesia and Namibia; a better understanding with black African countries, and, indeed, with third world countries generally, in the United Nations and elsewhere; greater worldwide sensitivity to the

[207]Quoted in *New York Times*, May 25, 1978.

human rights issue, even where governmental practice had failed to improve. Most spectacular of all, of course, was the breakthrough in the Middle East and the incipient dialogue between Egypt and Israel—though this development, as previously explained, owed comparatively little to American influence.

The Summing Up

The Carter administration was not oblivious to criticism of its performance, and not averse to offering correction of the record. Among the efforts of the White House staff at this period was the compilation and release on December 17 of a "Summary of Domestic and National Security and Foreign Policy Accomplishments" during the administration's first year **(Document 56)** which ran, in its entirety, to over sixteen printed pages. A checklist rather than a serious evaluation, it served primarily as a reminder of the complexity of foreign affairs and of the interplay of domestic and foreign policy considerations in virtually every field.

President Carter, who personally appeared unruffled by misgivings about the state of the world and the quality of his leadership, offered his own account of 1977's accomplishments and disappointments in a wide-ranging interview with network television correspondents on December 28 **(Document 57)**. Asked how he felt about his first year in office, "I feel good about it," the President replied. "It's been an exciting and stimulating and challenging and sometimes frustrating experience for me." His biggest mistake, he suggested, had been one of "inadvertently building up expectations too high" and underestimating the time required for congressional action on controversial measures. As for the achievements:

I think that the achievements are not measured in how may bills were passed and how many bills I've signed or even my harmony with the Congress. If I have achieved anything, it's been to restore a tone to our Nation's life and attitude that most accurately exemplifies what we stand for . . .

. . . We are making slow, steady progress. We are also attempting many things simultaneously. Sometimes they get confusing because they are so voluminous and there are so many of them.

But I think having our Nation and its Government represent more accurately the hopes and dreams of the American people is a general accomplishment of which I am most proud.

Early the following morning, December 29, the President and Mrs. Carter departed on the long-planned overseas journey, accompanied among others by Secretary and Mrs. Vance and Dr. Brzezinski. Warsaw would be their first stop, and from there they would go on to observe the New Year in Tehran, continuing thereafter to India, Saudi Arabia, France, and Belgium. (A stopover in Egypt was added later.) "In all these places," Mr. Carter observed at the departure ceremony on the White House lawn,

we will be reaffirming our dedication to peace and our support of justice and of human rights.

It is a changing world, a different world, and I believe that it's also a different America whose message we will carry, an America more confident and more united, at peace with other nations and also at peace with itself, an America which is ready and able to cooperate wherever possible and to compete where necessary.

After a long period of doubt and turmoil here, we are finding our way back to the values that made us a great nation. And in this new spirit we are eager to work with all countries and all peoples in building the kind of world community that serves the individual and common needs of all.

We undertake this trip to express our own views clearly and proudly, but also to learn and to understand the opinions and the desires of others. We will try to represent our Nation and our people well, and I'll take the good will of American everywhere we go. . . .[208]

---

[208]*Presidential Documents*, 13: 1956-7. For documentation on the visits to Poland and Iran see same: 1957-76 (*Bulletin*, 78: 1-7).

PART TWO: DOCUMENTS

1. UNDER NEW MANAGEMENT

(1)   The State of the Union: Address by President Gerald R. Ford to a Joint Session of the Congress, January 12, 1977. [1]

(Excerpts)

Mr. Speaker, Mr. Vice President, [2] *Members of the 95th Congress, and distinguished guests:*

In accordance with the Constitution, I come before you once again to report on the state of the Union.

This report will be my last—maybe—[*laughter*]—but for the Union, it is only the first of such reports in our third century of independence, the close of which none of us will ever see. We can be confident, however, that 100 years from now, a freely elected President will come before a freely elected Congress chosen to renew our great Republic's pledge to the Government of the people, by the people, and for the people.

For my part, I pray the third century we are beginning will bring to all Americans, our children and their children's children, a greater measure of individual equality, opportunity, and justice, a greater abundance of spiritual and material blessings, and a higher quality of life, liberty, and the pursuit of happiness.

The state of the Union is a measurement of the many elements of which it is composed—a political union of diverse States, an economic union of varying interests, an intellectual union of common convictions, and a moral union of immutable ideals.

Taken in sum, I can report that the state of the Union is good. There is room for improvement, as always, but today we have a more perfect Union than when my stewardship began.

As a people, we discovered that our Bicentennial was much more than a celebration of the past; it became a joyous reaffirmation of

---

[1] Text from *Presidential Documents,* 13: 30-38.
[2] Speaker of the House Thomas P. O'Neill, Jr. and Vice-President Nelson A. Rockefeller.

all that it means to be Americans, a confirmation before all the world of the vitality and durability of our free institutions. I am proud to have been privileged to preside over the affairs of our Federal Government during these eventful years when we proved, as I said in my first words upon assuming office, that "our Constitution works; our great Republic is a Government of laws and not of men. Here the people rule."

The people have spoken; they have chosen a new President and a new Congress to work their will. I congratulate you—particularly the new Members—as sincerely as I did President-elect Carter. In a few days, it will be his duty to outline for you his priorities and legislative recommendations. Tonight, I will not infringe on that responsibility, but rather wish him the very best in all that is good for our country.

*　*　*

When I became President on August 9, 1974, our Nation was deeply divided and tormented. In rapid succession, the Vice President and the President had resigned in disgrace. We were still struggling with the after-effects of a long, unpopular, and bloody war in Southeast Asia. The economy was unstable and racing toward the worst recession in 40 years. People were losing jobs. The cost of living was soaring. The Congress and the Chief Executive were at loggerheads. The integrity of our constitutional process and other institutions was being questioned. For more than 15 years, domestic spending had soared as Federal programs multiplied, and the expense escalated annually. During the same period, our national security needs were steadily shortchanged. In the grave situation which prevailed in August 1974, our will to maintain our international leadership was in doubt.

I asked for your prayers and went to work.

In January 1975, I reported to the Congress that the state of the Union was not good.[3] I proposed urgent action to improve the economy and to achieve energy independence in 10 years. I reassured America's allies and sought to reduce the danger of confrontation with potential adversaries. I pledged a new direction for America.

Nineteen seventy-five was a year of difficult decisions, but Americans responded with realism, common sense, and self-discipline.

By January 1976, we were headed in a new direction, which I hold to be the right direction for a free society. It was guided by the belief that successful problemsolving requires more than Federal action alone; that it involves a full partnership among all branches

[3]*AFR, 1975:* 32.

and all levels of government, and public policies which nurture and promote the creative energies of private enterprises, institutions, and individual citizens.

A year ago, I reported that the state of the Union was better—in many ways a lot better—but still not good enough.[4]

Common sense told me to stick to the steady course we were on, to continue to restrain the inflationary growth of government, to reduce taxes as well as spending, to return local decisions to local officials, to provide for long-range sufficiency in energy and national security needs. I resisted the immense pressures of an election year to open the floodgates of Federal money and the temptation to promise more than I could deliver. I told it as it was to the American people and demonstrated to the world that in our spirited political competition, as in this chamber, Americans can disagree without being disagreeable.

Now, after 30 months as your President, I can say that while we still have a way to go, I am proud of the long way we have come together.

I am proud of the part I have had in rebuilding confidence in the Presidency, confidence in our free system, and confidence in our future. Once again, Americans believe in themselves, in their leaders, and in the promise that tomorrow holds for their children.

I am proud that today America is at peace. None of our sons are fighting and dying in battle anywhere in the world. And the chance for peace among all nations is improved by our determination to honor our vital commitments in defense of peace and freedom.

I am proud that the United States has strong defenses, strong alliances, and a sound and courageous foreign policy.

Our alliances with major partners, the great industrial democracies of Western Europe, Japan, and Canada, have never been more solid. Consultations on mutual security, defense, and East-West relations have grown closer. Collaboration has branched out into new fields such as energy, economic policy, and relations with the third world. We have used many avenues for cooperation, including summit meetings held among major allied countries. The friendship of the democracies is deeper, warmer, and more effective than at any time in 30 years.

We are maintaining stability in the strategic nuclear balance and pushing back the spectre of nuclear war. A decisive step forward was taken in the Vladivostok Accord which I negotiated with General Secretary Brezhnev—joint recognition that an equal ceiling should be placed on the number of strategic weapons on each side. With resolve and wisdom on the part of both nations, a good agreement is well within reach this year.

[4]Same, *1976:* 121.

The framework for peace in the Middle East has been built. Hopes for future progress in the Middle East were stirred by the historic agreements we reached and the trust and confidence that we formed. Thanks to American leadership, the prospects for peace in the Middle East are brighter than they have been in three decades. The Arab states and Israel continue to look to us to lead them from confrontation and war to a new era of accommodation and peace. We have no alternative but to persevere—and I am sure we will. The opportunities for a final settlement are great, and the price of failure is a return to the bloodshed and hatred that for too long have brought tragedy to all of the peoples of this area and repeatedly edged the world to the brink of war.

Our relationship with the People's Republic of China is proving its importance and its durability. We are finding more and more common ground between our two countries on basic questions of international affairs.

In my two trips to Asia as President, we have reaffirmed America's continuing vital interest in the peace and security of Asia and the Pacific Basin, established a new partnership with Japan, confirmed our dedication to the security of Korea, and reinforced our ties with the free nations of Southeast Asia.

An historic dialog has begun between industrial nations and developing nations. Most proposals on the table are the initiatives of the United States, including those on food, energy, technology, trade, investment, and commodities. We are well launched on this process of shaping positive and reliable economic relations between rich nations and poor nations over the long term.

We have made progress in trade negotiations and avoided protectionism during recession. We strengthened the international monetary system. During the past 2 years, the free world's most important economic powers have already brought about important changes that serve both developed and developing economies. The momentum already achieved must be nurtured and strengthened, for the prosperity of the rich and poor depends upon it.

In Latin America, our relations have taken on a new maturity and a sense of common enterprise.

In Africa, the quest for peace, racial justice, and economic progress is at a crucial point. The United States, in close cooperation with the United Kingdom, is actively engaged in this historic process. Will change come about by warfare and chaos and foreign intervention? Or will it come about by negotiated and fair solutions, ensuring majority rule, minority rights, and economic advance? America is committed to the side of peace and justice and to the principle that Africa should shape its own future, free of outside intervention.

American leadership has helped to stimulate new international efforts to stem the proliferation of nuclear weapons and to shape a comprehensive treaty governing the use of oceans.

I am gratified by these accomplishments. They constitute a record of broad success for America and for the peace and prosperity of all mankind. This administration leaves to its successor a world in better condition than we found. We leave, as well, a solid foundation for progress on a range of issues that are vital to the well-being of America.

What has been achieved in the field of foreign affairs and what can be accomplished by the new administration demonstrate the genius of Americans working together for the common good. It is this, our remarkable ability to work together, that has made us a unique nation. It is Congress, the President, and the people striving for a better world.

I know all patriotic Americans want this Nation's foreign policy to succeed. I urge Members of my party in this Congress to give the new President loyal support in this area. I express the hope that this new Congress will reexamine its constitutional role in international affairs.

The exclusive right to declare war, the duty to advise and consent on the part of the Senate, the power of the purse on the part of the House, are ample authority for the legislative branch and should be jealously guarded. But because we may have been too careless of these powers in the past does not justify congressional intrusion into, or obstruction of, the proper exercise of Presidential responsibilities now or in the future. There can be only one Commander in Chief. In these times, crises cannot be managed and wars cannot be waged by committee; nor can peace be pursued solely by parliamentary debate. To the ears of the world, the President speaks for the Nation. While he is, of course, ultimately accountable to the Congress, the courts, and the people, he and his emissaries must not be handicapped in advance in their relations with foreign governments, as has sometimes happened in the past.

At home, I am encouraged by the Nation's recovery from the recession and our steady return to sound economic growth. It is now continuing after the recent period of uncertainty, which is part of the price we pay for free elections.

* * *

All the basic trends are good; we are not on the brink of another recession or economic disaster. If we follow prudent policies that encourage productive investment and discourage destructive inflation, we will come out on top—and I am sure we will.

We have successfully cut inflation by more than half. When I took office, the Consumer Price Index was rising at 12.2 percent a year. During 1976, the rate of inflation was 5 percent.

We have created more jobs—over 4 million more jobs today than in the spring of 1975. Throughout this Nation today, we have over 88 million people in useful, productive jobs—more than at any other time in our Nation's history. But there are still too many Americans unemployed. This is the greatest regret that I have as I leave office.

We brought about with the Congress, after much delay, the renewal of the general revenue sharing. We expanded community development and Federal manpower programs. We began a significant urban mass transit program.

Federal programs today provide more funds for our States and local governments than ever before—$70 billion for the current fiscal year. Through these programs and others that provide aid directly to individuals, we have kept faith with our tradition of compassionate help for those who need it. As we begin our third century, we can be proud of the progress that we have made in meeting human needs for all of our citizens.

We have cut the growth of crime by nearly 90 percent. Two years ago, crime was increasing at the rate of 18 percent annually. In the first three quarters of 1976, that growth rate had been cut to 2 percent. But crime, and the fear of crime, remains one of the most serious problems facing our citizens.

We have had some successes. And there have been some disappointments. Bluntly, I must remind you that we have not made satisfactory progress toward achieving energy independence.

Energy is absolutely vital to the defense of our country, to the strength of our economy, and to the quality of our lives. Two years ago, I proposed to the Congress the first comprehensive national energy program: a specific and coordinated set of measures that would end our vulnerability to embargo, blockade, or arbitrary price increases, and would mobilize U.S. technology and resources to supply a significant share of the free world's energy after 1985.[5]

Of the major energy proposals I submitted 2 years ago, only half, belatedly, became law. In 1973, we were dependent upon foreign oil imports for 36 percent of our needs. Today, we are 40-percent dependent, and we'll pay out $34 billion for foreign oil this year. Such vulnerability at present or in the future is intolerable and must be ended.

The answer to where we stand on our national energy effort today reminds me of the old argument about whether the tank is half full or half empty. The pessimist will say we have half failed to achieve our 10-year energy goals; the optimist will say that we have half succeeded. I am always an optimist, but we must make up for lost time.

We have laid a solid foundation for completing the enormous task which confronts us. I have signed into law five major energy bills which contain significant measures for conservation, resource development, stockpiling, and standby authorities. We have moved forward to develop the naval petroleum reserves; to build a 500 million-barrel strategic petroleum stockpile; to phase out unnecessary government allocation and price controls; to develop a lasting relationship with other oil consuming nations; to improve the efficiency of energy use through conservation in automobiles, buildings, and industry; and to expand research on new technology and renewable resources such as wind power, geothermal and solar energy.

All these actions, significant as they are for the long term, are only the beginning. I recently submitted to the Congress my proposals to reorganize the Federal energy structure, and the hard choices which remain if we are serious about reducing our dependence upon foreign energy. These include programs to reverse our declining production of natural gas and increase incentives for domestic crude oil production. I proposed to minimize environmental uncertainties affecting coal development, expand nuclear power generation, and create an energy independence authority to provide government financial assistance for vital energy programs where private capital is not available.

We must explore every reasonable prospect for meeting our energy needs when our current domestic reserves of oil and natural gas begin to dwindle in the next decade. I urgently ask Congress and the new administration to move quickly on these issues. This Nation has the resources and the capability to achieve our energy goals if its Government has the will to proceed—and I think we do.

* * *

America's first goal is and always will be peace with honor. America must remain first in keeping peace in the world. We can remain first in peace only if we are never second in defense.

In presenting the state of the Union to the Congress and to the American people, I have a special obligation as Commander in Chief to report on our national defense. Our survival as a free and independent people requires, above all, strong military forces that are well-equipped and highly trained to perform their assigned mission. I am particularly gratified to report that over the past 2½ years, we have been able to reverse the dangerous decline of the previous decade in real resources this country was devoting to national defense. This was an immediate problem I faced in 1974.

The evidence was unmistakable that the Soviet Union had been steadily increasing the resources it applied to building its military strength. During this same period, the United States' real defense spending declined. In my three budgets we not only arrested that dangerous decline, but we have established the positive trend which is essential to our ability to contribute to peace and stability in the world.

The Vietnam war, both materially and psychologically, affected our overall defense posture. The dangerous antimilitary sentiment discouraged defense spending and unfairly disparaged the men and women who serve in our Armed Forces.

The challenge that now confronts this country is whether we have the national will and determination to continue this essential defense effort over the long term, as it must be continued. We can no longer afford to oscillate from year to year in so vital a matter; indeed, we have a duty to look beyond the immediate question of budgets and to examine the nature of the problem we will face over the next generation.

I am the first recent President able to address long-term, basic issues without the burden of Vietnam. The war in Indochina consumed enormous resources at the very time that the overwhelming strategic superiority we once enjoyed was disappearing. In past years, as a result of decisions by the United States, our strategic forces leveled off. Yet, the Soviet Union continued a steady, constant buildup of its own forces, committing a high percentage of its national economic effort to defense.

The United States can never tolerate a shift in strategic balance against us, or even a situation where the American people or our allies believe the balance is shifting against us. The United States would risk the most serious political consequences if the world came to believe that our adversaries have a decisive margin of superiority.

To maintain a strategic balance we must look ahead to the 1980's and beyond. The sophistication of modern weapons requires that we make decisions now if we are to ensure our security 10 years from now. Therefore, I have consistently advocated and strongly urged that we pursue three critical strategic programs: the Trident missile launching submarine; the B–1 bomber, with its superior capability to penetrate modern air defenses; and a more advanced intercontinental ballistic missile that will be better able to survive nuclear attack and deliver a devastating retaliatory strike.

In an era where the strategic nuclear forces are in rough equilibrium, the risks of conflict below the nuclear threshold may grow more perilous. A major long-term objective, therefore, is to maintain capabilities to deal with, and thereby deter, conventional challenges and crises, particularly in Europe.

We cannot rely solely on strategic forces to guarantee our security or to deter all types of aggression. We must have superior naval and marine forces to maintain freedom of the seas, strong multipurpose tactical air forces, and mobile, modern ground forces. Accordingly, I have directed a long-term effort to improve our worldwide capabilities to deal with regional crises.

I have submitted a 5-year naval building program indispensable to the Nation's maritime strategy. Because the security of Europe and the integrity of NATO remain the cornerstone of American defense policy, I have initiated a special, long-term program to ensure the capacity of the Alliance to deter or defeat aggression in Europe.

As I leave office, I can report that our national defense is effectively deterring conflict today. Our Armed Forces are capable of carrying out the variety of missions assigned to them. Programs are underway which will assure we can deter war in the years ahead. But, I also must warn that it will require a sustained effort over a period of years to maintain these capabilities. We must have the wisdom, the stamina, and the courage to prepare today for the perils of tomorrow—and I believe we will.

As I look to the future—and I assure you I intend to go on doing that for a good many years—I can say with confidence that the state of the Union is good, but we must go on making it better and better.

This gathering symbolizes the constitutional foundation which makes continued progress possible, synchronizing the skills of three independent branches of government, reserving fundamental sovereignty to the people of this great land.

It is only as the temporary representatives and servants of the people that we meet here—we bring no hereditary status or gift of infallibility and none follows us from this place. Like President Washington, like the more fortunate of his successors, I look forward to the status of private citizen with gladness and gratitude. To me, being a citizen of the United States of America is the greatest honor and privilege in this world.

*   *   *

My fellow Americans, I once asked you for your prayers, and now I give you mine: May God guide this wonderful country, its people, and those they have chosen to lead them. May our third century be illuminated by liberty and blessed with brotherhood, so that we and all who come after us may be the humble servants of thy peace. Amen.

Good night. God bless you.

(2)   Inauguration of the 39th President, January 20, 1977.

(a)   Inaugural Address of President Jimmy Carter, Delivered at the Inaugural Ceremonies at the Capitol.[6]

For myself and for our Nation, I want to thank my predecessor for all he has done to heal our land.

In this outward and physical ceremony, we attest once again to the inner and spiritual strength of our Nation. As my high school teacher, Miss Julia Coleman, used to say, "We must adjust to changing times and still hold to unchanging principles."

Here before me is the Bible used in the inauguration of our first President, in 1789, and I have just taken the oath of office on the Bible my mother gave me just a few years ago, opened to a timeless admonition from the ancient prophet Micah: "He hath showed thee, o man, what is good; and what doth the Lord require of thee, but to do justly, and to love mercy, and to walk humbly with thy God." (Micah 6:8)

This inauguration ceremony marks a new beginning, a new dedication within our government, and a new spirit among us all. A President may sense and proclaim that new spirit, but only a people can provide it.

Two centuries ago, our Nation's birth was a milestone in the long quest for freedom. But the bold and brilliant dream which excited the Founders of this Nation still awaits its consummation. I have no new dream to set forth today, but rather urge a fresh faith in the old dream.

Ours was the first society openly to define itself in terms of both spirituality and human liberty. It is that unique self-definition which has given us an exceptional appeal—but it also imposes on us a special obligation to take on those moral duties which, when assumed, seem invariably to be in our own best interests.

You have given me a great responsibility—to stay close to you, to be worthy of you, and to exemplify what you are. Let us create together a new national spirit of unity and trust. Your strength can compensate for my weakness, and your wisdom can help to minimize my mistakes.

Let us learn together and laugh together and work together and pray together, confident that in the end we will triumph together in the right.

The American dream endures. We must once again have full faith in our country—and in one another. I believe America can be better. We can be even stronger than before.

Let our recent mistakes bring a resurgent commitment to the

[6]Text from Presidential Documents, 13: 87-9.

basic principles of our Nation, for we know that if we despise our own government, we have no future. We recall in special times when we have stood briefly, but magnificently, united. In those times no prize was beyond our grasp.

But we cannot dwell upon remembered glory. We cannot afford to drift. We reject the prospect of failure or mediocrity or an inferior quality of life for any person. Our government must at the same time be both competent and compassionate.

We have already found a high degree of personal liberty, and we are now struggling to enhance equality of opportunity. Our commitment to human rights must be absolute, our laws fair, our national beauty preserved; the powerful must not persecute the weak, and human dignity must be enhanced.

We have learned that *more* is not necessarily *better*, that even our great Nation has its recognized limits, and that we can neither answer all questions nor solve all problems. We cannot afford to do everything, nor can we afford to lack boldness as we meet the future. So together, in a spirit of individual sacrifice for the common good, we must simply do our best.

Our Nation can be strong abroad only if it is strong at home. And we know that the best way to enhance freedom in other lands is to demonstrate here that our democratic system is worthy of emulation.

To be true to ourselves, we must be true to others. We will not behave in foreign places so as to violate our rules and standards here at home, for we know that the trust which our Nation earns is essential to our strength.

The world itself is now dominated by a new spirit. Peoples more numerous and more politically aware are craving, and now demanding, their place in the sun—not just for the benefit of their own physical condition, but for basic human rights.

The passion for freedom is on the rise. Tapping this new spirit, there can be no nobler nor more ambitious task for America to undertake on this day of a new beginning than to help shape a just and peaceful world that is truly humane.

We are a strong Nation, and we will maintain strength so sufficient that it need not be proven in combat—a quiet strength based not merely on the size of an arsenal, but on the nobility of ideas.

We will be ever vigilant and never vulnerable, and we will fight our wars against poverty, ignorance, and injustice, for those are the enemies against which our forces can be honorably marshalled.

We are a proudly idealistic Nation, but let no one confuse our idealism with weakness.

Because we are free, we can never be indifferent to the fate of freedom elsewhere. Our moral sense dictates a clearcut preference for those societies which share with us an abiding respect for individual human rights. We do not seek to intimidate, but it is clear that a world which others can dominate with impunity would be inhospitable to decency and a threat to the well-being of all people.

The world is still engaged in a massive armaments race designed to ensure continuing equivalent strength among potential adversaries. We pledge perseverance and wisdom in our efforts to limit the world's armaments to those necessary for each nation's own domestic safety. And we will move this year a step toward our ultimate goal—the elimination of all nuclear weapons from this Earth. We urge all other people to join us, for success can mean life instead of death.

Within us, the people of the United States, there is evident a serious and purposeful rekindling of confidence. And I join in the hope that when my time as your President has ended, people might say this about our Nation:

—that we had remembered the words of Micah and renewed our search for humility, mercy, and justice;

—that we had torn down the barriers that separated those of different race and region and religion and where there had been mistrust, built unity, with a respect for diversity;

—that we had found productive work for those able to perform it;

—that we had strengthened the American family, which is the basis of our society;

—that we had ensured respect for the law and equal treatment under the law, for the weak and the powerful, for the rich and the poor; and

—that we had enabled our people to be proud of their own government once again.

I would hope that the nations of the world might say that we had built a lasting peace, based not on weapons of war but on international policies which reflect our own most precious values.

These are not just my goals—and they will not be my accomplishments—but the affirmation of our Nation's continuing moral strength and our belief in an undiminished, ever-expanding American dream.

Thank you very much.

(b) Remarks to People of Other Nations, Recorded for Broadcast by the United States Information Agency. [7]

[7] Text from *Presidential Documents,* 13: 89-90.

I have chosen the occasion of my inauguration as President to speak not only to my own countrymen—which is traditional—but also to you, citizens of the world who did not participate in our election but who will nevertheless be affected by my decisions.

I also believe that as friends you are entitled to know how the power and influence of the United States will be exercised by its new government.

I want to assure you that the relations of the United States with the other countries and peoples of the world will be guided during my own administration by our desire to shape a world order that is more responsive to human aspirations. The United States will meet its obligation to help create a stable, just, and peaceful world order.

We will not seek to dominate nor dictate to others. As we Americans have concluded one chapter in our Nation's history and are beginning to work on another, we have, I believe, acquired a more mature perspective on the problems of the world. It is a perspective which recognizes the fact that we alone do not have all the answers to the world's problems.

The United States alone cannot lift from the world the terrifying specter of nuclear destruction. We can and will work with others to do so.

The United States alone cannot guarantee the basic right of every human being to be free of poverty and hunger and disease and political repression. We can and will cooperate with others in combating these enemies of mankind.

The United States alone cannot ensure an equitable development of the world resources or the proper safeguarding of the world's environment. But we can and will join with others in this work.

The United States can and will take the lead in such efforts.

In these endeavors we need your help, and we offer ours; we need your experience; we need your wisdom.

We need your active participation in a joint effort to move the reality of the world closer to the ideals of human freedom and dignity.

As friends, you can depend on the United States to be in the forefront of the search for world peace. You can depend on the United States to remain steadfast in its commitment to human freedom and liberty. And you can also depend on the United States to be sensitive to your own concerns and aspirations, to welcome your advice, to do its utmost to resolve international differences in a spirit of cooperation.

The problems of the world will not be easily resolved. Yet the well-being of each and every one of us—indeed our mutual survival—depends on their resolution. As President of the United States I can assure you that we intend to do our part. I ask you to join us in a common effort based on mutual trust and mutual respect.

Thank you.

(3)   Explaining United States Foreign Policy: Address by President Carter to Representatives of United Nations Member States, New York, March 17, 1977.[8]

Thank you, Mr. Secretary General.

Last night I was in Clinton, Massachusetts, at a Town Hall meeting where people of that small town decide their political and economic future.

Tonight I speak to a similar meeting where people representing nations all over the world come here to decide their political and economic future.

I am proud to be with you tonight in this house where the shared hopes of the world can find a voice. I have come here to express my own support and the continuing support of my country for the ideals of the United Nations.

We are proud that for the 32 years since its creation, the United Nations has met on American soil. And we share with you the commitments of freedom, self-government, human dignity, mutual toleration, and the peaceful resolution of disputes—which the founding principles of the United Nations and also Secretary General Kurt Waldheim so well represent.

No one nation by itself can build a world which reflects all these fine values. But the United States, my own country, has a reservoir of strength—economic strength, which we are willing to share; military strength, which we hope never to use again; and the strength of ideals, which are determined fully to maintain the backbone of our own foreign policy.

It is now 8 weeks since I became President. I have brought to office a firm commitment to a more open foreign policy. And I believe that the American people expect me to speak frankly about the policies that we intend to pursue, and it is in that spirit that I speak to you tonight about our own hopes for the future.

I see a hopeful world, a world dominated by increasing demands for basic freedoms, for fundamental rights, for higher standards of human existence. We are eager to take part in the shaping of that world.

But in seeking such a better world, we are not blind to the reality of disagreement, nor to the persisting dangers that confront us all.

[8]Text from *Presidential Documents*, 13: 397-402.

Every headline reminds us of bitter divisions, of national hostilities, of territorial conflicts, of ideological competition.

In the Middle East, peace is a quarter of a century overdue. A gathering racial conflict threatens southern Africa; new tensions are rising in the Horn of Africa. Disputes in the eastern Mediterranean remain to be resolved.

Perhaps even more ominous is the staggering arms race. The Soviet Union and the United States have accumulated thousands of nuclear weapons. Our two nations now have five times more missile warheads today than we had just 8 years ago. But we are not five times more secure. On the contrary, the arms race has only increased the risk of conflict.

We can only improve this world if we are realistic about its complexities. The disagreements that we face are deeply rooted, and they often raise difficult philosophical as well as territorial issues. They will not be solved easily. They will not be solved quickly. The arms race is now embedded in the very fabric of international affairs and can only be contained with the greatest difficulty. Poverty and inequality are of such monumental scope that it will take decades of deliberate and determined effort even to improve the situation substantially.

I stress these dangers and these difficulties because I want all of us to dedicate ourselves to a prolonged and persistent effort designed first to maintain peace and to reduce the arms race; second, to build a better and a more cooperative international economic system; and third, to work with potential adversaries as well as our close friends to advance the cause of human rights.

In seeking these goals, I realize that the United States cannot solve the problems of the world. We can sometimes help others resolve their differences, but we cannot do so by imposing our own particular solution.

In the coming months, there is important work for all of us in advancing international cooperation and economic progress in the cause of peace.

Later this spring, the leaders of several industrial nations of Europe, North America, and Japan will confer at a summit meeting in London on a broad range of issues. We must promote the health of the industrial economies. We must seek to restrain inflation and bring ways of managing our own domestic economies for the benefit of the global economy.

We must move forward with multilateral trade negotiations in Geneva.

The United States will support the efforts of our friends to strengthen the democratic institutions in Europe, and particularly in Portugal and Spain.

We will work closely with our European friends on the forthcoming Review Conference on Security and Cooperation in Europe. We want to make certain that the provisions of the Helsinki Agreement are fully implemented and that progress is made to further East-West cooperation.

In the Middle East we are doing our best to clarify areas of disagreement, to surface underlying consensus, and to help to develop mutually acceptable principles that can form a flexible framework for a just and a permanent settlement.

In southern Africa, we will work to help attain majority rule through peaceful means. We believe that such fundamental transformation can be achieved, to the advantage of both the blacks and whites who live in that region of the world. Anything less than that may bring a protracted racial war, with devastating consequences to all.

This week the Government of the United States took action to bring our country into full compliance with United Nations sanctions against the illegal regime in Rhodesia.[9] And I will sign that bill Friday in Washington.

We will put our relations with Latin America on a more constructive footing, recognizing the global character of the region's problems.

We are also working to resolve in amicable negotiations the future of the Panama Canal.

We will continue our efforts to develop further our relationships with the People's Republic of China. We recognize our parallel strategic interests in maintaining stability in Asia, and we will act in the spirit of the Shanghai Communique.

In Southeast Asia and in the Pacific, we will strengthen our association with our traditional friends, and we will seek to improve relations with our former adversaries.

We have a mission now in Vietnam seeking peaceful resolution of the differences that have separated us for so long.[10]

Throughout the world, we are ready to normalize our relationships and to seek reconciliation with all states which are ready to work with us in promoting global progress and global peace.

Above all, the search for peace requires a much more deliberate effort to contain the global arms race. Let me speak in this context, first, of the U.S.-Soviet Union relationship, and then of the wider need to contain the proliferation of arms throughout the global community.

I intend to pursue the strategic arms limitation talks between the

---

[9] Cf. Introduction at note 86.
[10] Cf. Introduction at note 143.

United States and the Soviet Union with determination and with energy.

Our Secretary of State will visit Moscow in just a few days.

SALT is extraordinarily complicated. But the basic fact is that while negotiations remain deadlocked, the arms race goes on; the security of both countries and the entire world is threatened.

My preference would be for strict controls or even a freeze on new types and new generations of weaponry and with a deep reduction in the strategic arms of both sides. Such a major step towards not only arms limitation but arms reduction would be welcomed by mankind as a giant step towards peace.

Alternatively, and perhaps much more easily, we could conclude a limited agreement based on those elements of the Vladivostok Accord on which we can find complete consensus, and set aside for prompt consideration and subsequent negotiations the more contentious issues and also the deeper reductions in nuclear weapons which I favor.

We will also explore the possibility of a total cessation of nuclear testing. While our ultimate goal is for all nuclear powers to end testing, we do not regard this as a prerequisite for the suspension of tests by the two principal nuclear powers, the Soviet Union and the United States.

We should, however, also pursue a broad, permanent multilateral agreement on this issue.

We will also seek to establish Soviet willingness to reach agreement with us on mutual military restraint in the Indian Ocean, as well as on such matters as arms exports to the troubled areas of the world.

In proposing such accommodations I remain fully aware that American-Soviet relations will continue to be highly competitive—but I believe that our competition must be balanced by cooperation in preserving peace, and thus our mutual survival.

I will seek such cooperation with the Soviet Union—earnestly, constantly, and sincerely.

However, the effort to contain the arms race is not a matter just for the United States and Soviet Union alone. There must be a wider effort to reduce the flow of weapons to all the troubled spots of this globe.

Accordingly, we will try to reach broader agreements among producer and consumer nations to limit the export of conventional arms, and we, ourselves, will take the initiative on our own because the United States has become one of the major arms suppliers of the world.

We are deeply committed to halting the proliferation of nuclear weapons. And we will undertake a new effort to reach multilateral agreements designed to provide legitimate supplies of nuclear fuels for the production of energy, while controlling the poisonous and dangerous atomic wastes.

Working with other nations represented here, we hope to advance the cause of peace. We will make a strong and a positive contribution at the upcoming Special Session on Disarmament which I understand will commence next year.

But the search for peace also means the search for justice. One of the greatest challenges before us as a nation, and therefore one of our greatest opportunities, is to participate in molding a global economic system which will bring greater prosperity to all the people of all countries.

I come from a part of the United States which is largely agrarian and which for many years did not have the advantages of adequate transportation or capital or management skills or education which were available in the industrial States of our country.

So I can sympathize with the leaders of the developing nations, and I want them to know that we will do our part.

To this end, the United States will be advancing proposals aimed at meeting the basic human needs of the developing world and helping them to increase their productive capacity. I have asked Congress to provide $7½ billion of foreign assistance in the coming year, and I will work to ensure sustained American assistance as the process of global economic development continues. I am also urging the Congress of our country to increase our contributions to the United Nations Development Program and meet in full our pledges to multilateral lending institutions, especially the International Development Association of the World Bank.

We remain committed to an open international trading system, one which does not ignore domestic concerns in the United States. We have extended duty-free treatment to many products from the developing countries. In the multilateral trade agreements in Geneva we have offered substantial trade concessions on the goods of primary interest to developing countries. And in accordance with the Tokyo Declaration, we are also examining ways to provide additional consideration for the special needs of developing countries.

The United States is willing to consider, with a positive and open attitude, the negotiation on agreements to stabilize commodity prices, including the establishment of a common funding arrangement for financing buffer stocks where they are a part of individual negotiated agreements.

I also believe that the developing countries must acquire fuller participation in the global economic decisionmaking process. Some progress has already been made in this regard by expanding participation of developing countries in the International Monetary Fund.

We must use our collective natural resources wisely and constructively. We've not always done so. Today our oceans are being plundered and defiled. With a renewed spirit of cooperation and hope we join in the Conference of the Law of the Sea in order to correct past mistakes of generations gone by and to ensure that all nations can share the bounties of the eternal oceans in the future.

We must also recognize that the world is facing serious shortages of energy. This is truly a global problem. For our part, we are determined to reduce waste and to work with others toward a fair and proper sharing of the benefits and costs of energy resources.

The search for peace and justice also means respect for human dignity. All the signatories of the U.N. Charter have pledged themselves to observe and to respect basic human rights. Thus, no member of the United Nations can claim that mistreatment of its citizens is solely its own business. Equally, no member can avoid its responsibilities to review and to speak when torture or unwarranted deprivation occurs in any part of the world.

The basic thrust of human affairs points toward a more universal demand for fundamental human rights. The United States has a historical birthright to be associated with this process.

We in the United States accept this responsibility in the fullest and the most constructive sense. Ours is a commitment, and not just a political posture. I know perhaps as well as anyone that our own ideals in the area of human rights have not always been attained in the United States, but the American people have an abiding commitment to the full realization of these ideals. And we are determined, therefore, to deal with our deficiencies quickly and openly. We have nothing to conceal.

To demonstrate this commitment, I will seek congressional approval and sign the U.N. covenants on economic, social, and cultural rights, and the covenants on civil and political rights.[11] And I will work closely with our own Congress in seeking to support the ratification not only of these two instruments but the United Nations Genocide Convention and the Treaty for the Elimination of All Forms of Racial Discrimination, as well.[12] I have just removed all restrictions on American travel abroad, and we are moving now to liberalize almost completely travel opportunities to America.

The United Nations is a global forum dedicated to the peace and well-being of every individual—no matter how weak, no matter how poor. But we have allowed its human rights machinery to be

[11] Cf. Introduction at note 204.

[12] The Convention on the Prevention and Punishment of the Crime of Genocide was submitted to the Senate May 23, 1977 (*Presidential Documents,* 13: 802-3; *Bulletin,* 76: 676); the two human rights covenants, the International Convention on the Elimination of All Forms of Racial Discrimination and the American Convention on Human Rights, were submitted to the Senate Feb. 23, 1978 (*Presidential Documents,* 14: 395-6).

ignored and sometimes politicized. There is much that can be done to strengthen it.

The Human Rights Commission should be prepared to meet more often. And all nations should be prepared to offer its fullest cooperation to the Human Rights Commission, to welcome its investigations, to work with its officials, and to act on its reports.

I would like to see the entire United Nations Human Rights Division moved back here to the central headquarters, where its activities will be in the forefront of our attention and where the attention of the press corps can stimulate us to deal honestly with this sensitive issue. The proposal made 12 years ago by the Government of Costa Rica, to establish a U.N. High Commission[er] for Human Rights, also deserves our renewed attention and our support.

Strengthened international machinery will help us to close the gap between promise and performance in protecting human rights. When gross or widespread violation takes place—contrary to international commitments—it is of concern to all. The solemn commitments of the United Nations Charter, of the United Nations Universal Declaration for Human Rights, of the Helsinki Accords, and of many other international instruments must be taken just as seriously as commercial or security agreements.

This issue is important in itself. It should not block progress on other important matters affecting the security and well-being of our people and of world peace. It is obvious that the reduction of tension, the control of nuclear arms, the achievement of harmony in the troubled areas of the world, and the provision of food, good health, and education will independently contribute to advancing the human condition.

In our relationships with other countries, these mutual concerns will be reflected in our political, our cultural, and our economic attitudes.

These then are our basic priorities as we work with other members to strengthen and to improve the United Nations.

First, we will strive for peace in the troubled areas of the world; second, we will aggressively seek to control the weaponry of war; third, we will promote a new system of international economic progress and cooperation; and fourth, we will be steadfast in our dedication to the dignity and well-being of people throughout the world.

I believe that this is a foreign policy that is consistent with my own Nation's historic values and commitments. And I believe that it is a foreign policy that is consonant with the ideals of the United Nations.

Thank you very much.

(4) *Human Rights and Foreign Policy: Address by Secretary of State Cyrus R. Vance at the University of Georgia School of Law, Athens, Georgia, April 30, 1977.* [13]

I speak today about the resolve of this Administration to make the advancement of human rights a central part of our foreign policy.

Many here today have long been advocates of human rights within our own society. And throughout our nation that struggle for civil rights continues.

In the early years of our civil rights movement, many Americans treated the issue as a "Southern" problem. They were wrong. It was and is a problem for all of us.

Now, as a nation, we must not make a comparable mistake. Protection of human rights is a challenge for *all* countries, not just for a few.

Our human rights policy must be understood in order to be effective. So today I want to set forth the substance of that policy and the results we hope to achieve.

Our concern for human rights is built upon ancient values. It looks with hope to a world in which liberty is not just a great cause, but the common condition. In the past, it may have seemed sufficient to put our name to international documents that spoke loftily of human rights. That is not enough. We will go to work, alongside other people and governments, to protect and enhance the dignity of the individual.

Let me define what we mean by "human rights."

First, there is the right to be free from governmental violation of the integrity of the person. Such violations include torture; cruel, inhuman, or degrading treatment or punishment; and arbitrary arrest or imprisonment. And they include denial of fair public trial and invasion of the home.

Second, there is the right to the fulfillment of such vital needs as food, shelter, health care, and education. We recognize that the fulfillment of this right will depend, in part, upon the stage of a nation's economic development. But we also know that this right can be violated by a government's action or inaction—for example, through corrupt official processes which divert resources to an elite at the expense of the needy or through indifference to the plight of the poor.

Third, there is the right to enjoy civil and political liberties: freedom of thought, of religion, of assembly; freedom of speech; freedom of the press; freedom of movement both within and outside one's own country; freedom to take part in government.

[13]Department of State Press Release 194; text from *Bulletin,* 76: 505-8.

Our policy is to promote all these rights. They are all recognized in the Universal Declaration of Human Rights, a basic document which the United States helped fashion and which the United Nations approved in 1948. There may be disagreement on the priorities these rights deserve. But I believe that, with work, all of these rights can become complementary and mutually reinforcing.

The philosophy of our human rights policy is revolutionary in the intellectual sense, reflecting our nation's origin and progressive values. As Archibald MacLeish wrote during our Bicentennial a year ago: ". . . the cause of human liberty is now the one great revolutionary cause. . . ."

President Carter put it this way in his speech before the United Nations:[14]

All the signatories of the United Nations Charter have pledged themselves to observe and to respect basic human rights. Thus, no member of the United Nations can claim that mistreatment of its citizens is solely its own business. Equally, no member can avoid its responsibilities to review and to speak when torture or unwarranted deprivation occurs in any part of the world.

Since 1945, international practice has confirmed that a nation's obligation to respect human rights is a matter of concern in international law.

Our obligation under the United Nations Charter is written into our own legislation. For example, our Foreign Assistance Act now reads: ". . . a principal goal of the foreign policy of the United States is to promote the increased observance of internationally recognized human rights by all countries."

In these ways, our policy is in keeping with our tradition, our international obligations, and our laws.

In pursuing a human rights policy, we must always keep in mind the limits of our power and of our wisdom. A sure formula for defeat of our goals would be a rigid, hubristic attempt to impose our values on others. A doctrinaire plan of action would be as damaging as indifference.

We must be realistic. Our country can only achieve our objectives if we shape what we do to the case at hand. In each instance, we will consider these questions as we determine whether and how to act:

1. First, we will ask ourselves, what is the nature of the case that confronts us? For example:

[14]Document 3.

What kinds of violations or deprivations are there? What is their extent?

Is there a pattern to the violations? If so, is the trend toward concern for human rights or away from it?

What is the degree of control and responsibility of the government involved?

And finally, is the government willing to permit independent outside investigation?

2. A second set of questions concerns the prospects for effective action:

Will our action be useful in promoting the overall cause of human rights?

Will it actually improve the specific conditions at hand? Or will it be likely to make things worse instead?

Is the country involved receptive to our interest and efforts?

Will others work with us, including official and private international organizations dedicated to furthering human rights?

Finally, does our sense of values and decency demand that we speak out or take action anyway, even though there is only a remote chance of making our influence felt?

3. We will ask a third set of questions in order to maintain a sense of perspective:

Have we steered away from the self-righteous and strident, remembering that our own record is not unblemished?

Have we been sensitive to genuine security interests, realizing that outbreak of armed conflict or terrorism could in itself pose a serious threat to human rights?

Have we considered *all* the rights at stake? If, for instance, we reduce aid to a government which violates the political rights of its citizens, do we not risk penalizing the hungry and poor, who bear no responsibility for the abuses of their government?

If we are determined to act, the means available range from quiet diplomacy in its many forms, through public pronouncements, to withholding of assistance. Whenever possible, we will use positive steps of encouragement and inducement. Our strong support will go to countries that are working to improve the human condition. We will always try to act in concert with other countries, through international bodies.

In the end, a decision whether and how to act in the cause of human rights is a matter for informed and careful judgment. No mechanistic formula produces an automatic answer.

It is not our purpose to intervene in the internal affairs of other countries, but as the President has emphasized, no member of the United Nations can claim that violation of internationally protected human rights is solely its own affair. It is our purpose to shape our policies in accord with our beliefs and to state them without stridency or apology when we think it is desirable to do so.

Our policy is to be applied within our own society as well as abroad. We welcome constructive criticism at the same time as we offer it.

No one should suppose that we are working in a vacuum. We place great weight on joining with others in the cause of human rights.

The U.N. system is central to this cooperative endeavor. That is why the President stressed the pursuit of human rights in his speech before the General Assembly last month. That is why he is calling for U.S. ratification of four important human rights covenants and conventions and why we are trying to strengthen the human rights machinery within the United Nations.

And that is an important reason why we have moved to comply with U.N. sanctions against Rhodesia. In one of our first acts, this Administration sought and achieved repeal of the Byrd amendment,[15] which had placed us in violation of these sanctions and thus in violation of international law. We are supporting other diplomatic efforts within the United Nations to promote basic civil and political rights in Namibia and throughout southern Africa.

Regional organizations also play a central role in promoting human rights. The President has announced that the United States will sign and seek Senate approval of the American Convention on Human Rights.[16] We will continue to work to strengthen the machinery of the Inter-American Commission on Human Rights. This will include efforts to schedule regular visits to all members of the Organization of American States, annual debates on human rights conditions, and the expansion of the inter-American educational program on human rights.

The United States is seeking increased consultation with other nations for joint programs on economic assistance and more general efforts to promote human rights. We are working to assure that our efforts reach out to all, with particular sensitivity to the problems of women.

We will meet in Belgrade later this year to review implementation of the Final Act of the Conference on Security and Cooperation in

[15]Cf. Introduction at note 86.
[16]Cf. Introduction at notes 119-120.

Europe—the so-called Helsinki conference. We will take this occasion to work for progress there on important human issues: family reunification, binational marriages, travel for personal and professional reasons, and freer access to information.

The United States looks to use of economic assistance—whether bilateral or through international financial institutions—as a means to foster basic human rights.

—We have proposed a 20 percent increase in U.S. foreign economic assistance for fiscal year 1978.

—We are expanding the program of the Agency for International Development for "New Initiatives in Human Rights" as a complement to present efforts to get the benefits of our aid to those most in need abroad.

—The programs of the United States Information Agency and the State Department's Bureau of Educational and Cultural Affairs stress support for law in society, a free press, freedom of communication, an open educational system, and respect for ethnic diversity.

This Administration's human rights policy has been framed in collaboration and consultation with Congress and private organizations. We have taken steps to assure firsthand contact, consultation, and observation when Members of Congress travel abroad to review human rights conditions.

We are implementing current laws that bring human rights considerations directly into our decisions in several international financial institutions. At the same time, we are working with the Congress to find the most effective way to fulfill our parallel commitment to international cooperation in economic development.

In accordance with human rights provisions of legislation governing our security assistance programs, we recently announced cuts in military aid to several countries.

Outside the government, there is much that can be done. We welcome the efforts of individual American citizens and private organizations—such as religious, humanitarian, and professional groups —to work for human rights with commitments of time, money, and compassion.

All these initiatives to further human rights abroad would have a hollow ring if we were not prepared to improve our own performance at home. So we have removed all restrictions on our citizens' travel abroad and are proceeding with plans to liberalize our visa policies.

We support legislation and administrative action to expand our refugee and asylum policies and to permit more victims of repressive regimes to enter the United States. During this last year, the United States spent some $475 million on assistance to refugees around the world, and we accepted 31,000 refugees for permanent resettlement in this country.

What results can we expect from all these efforts?

We may justifiably seek a rapid end to such gross violations as those cited in our law: "torture or cruel, inhuman, or degrading treatment or punishment, (or) prolonged detention without charges. . . ." Just last week our Ambassador at the United Nations, Andrew Young, suggested a series of new ways to confront the practice of torture around the world.

The promotion of other human rights is a broader challenge. The results may be slower in coming but are no less worth pursuing. And we intend to let other countries know where we stand.

We recognize that many nations of the world are organized on authoritarian rather than democratic principles—some large and powerful, others struggling to raise the lives of their people above bare subsistence levels. We can nourish no illusions that a call to the banner of human rights will bring sudden transformations in authoritarian societies.

We are embarked on a long journey. But our faith in the dignity of the individual encourages us to believe that people in every society, according to their own traditions, will in time give their own expression to this fundamental aspiration.

Our belief is strengthened by the way the Helsinki principles and the U.N. Declaration of Human Rights have found resonance in the hearts of people of many countries. Our task is to sustain this faith by our example and our encouragement.

In his inaugural address[17] three months ago, President Carter said, "Because we are free we can never be indifferent to the fate of freedom elsewhere." Again, at a meeting of the Organization of American States two weeks ago, he said, "You will find this country . . . eager to stand beside those nations which respect human rights and which promote democratic ideals."[18]

We seek these goals because they are right—and because we, too, will benefit. Our own well-being, and even our security, are enhanced in a world that shares common freedoms and in which prosperity and economic justice create the conditions for peace. And let us remember that we always risk paying a serious price when we become identified with repression.

Nations, like individuals, limit their potential when they limit their goals. The American people understand this. I am confident they will support foreign policies that reflect our traditional values. To offer less is to define America in ways we should not accept.

[17]Document 2a.
[18]Document 35.

America fought for freedom in 1776 and in two World Wars. We have offered haven to the oppressed. Millions have come to our shores in times of trouble. In time of devastation abroad, we have shared our resources.

Our encouragement and inspiration to other nations and other peoples have never been limited to the power of our military or the bounty of our economy. They have been lifted up by the message of our Revolution, the message of individual human freedom. That message has been our great national asset in times past. So it should be again.

(5)   Foreign Policy and National Character: Commencement Address by President Carter at the University of Notre Dame, Notre Dame, Indiana, May 22, 1977. [19]

Thank you very much. To Father Hesburgh [20] *and the great faculty of Notre Dame, to those who have been honored this afternoon with the degree from your great university, to the graduate and undergraduate group who I understand is the largest in the history of this great institution, friends and parents:*

Thank you for that welcome. I'm very glad to be with you. You may have started a new graduation trend which I don't deplore; that is, throwing peanuts on graduation day. [*Laughter*] The more that are used or consumed, the higher the price goes. [*Laughter*]

I really did appreciate the great honor bestowed upon me this afternoon. My other degree is blue and gold from the Navy, and I want to let you know that I do feel a kinship with those who are assembled here this afternoon. I was a little taken aback by the comment that I had brought a new accent to the White House. In the minds of many people in our country, for the first time in almost 15 years, there is no accent. [*Laughter*]

I tried to think of a story that would illustrate two points simultaneously and also be brief, which is kind of a difficult assignment. I was sitting on the Truman Balcony the other night with my good friend, Charles Kirbo, who told me about a man who was arrested and taken in to court for being drunk and for setting a bed on fire. When the judge asked him how he pled, he said, "Not guilty." He said, "I was drunk but the bed was on fire when I got in it." [*Laughter*]

I think most of the graduates can draw the parallel between that statement and what you are approaching after this graduation exercise. But there are two points to that, and I'll come to the other one in just a few minutes.

[19]Text from *Presidential Documents,* 13: 773-9.
[20]Reverend Theodore Hesburgh, President of the University of Notre Dame.

In his 25 years as president of Notre Dame, Father Hesburgh has spoken more consistently and more effectively in the support of the rights of human beings than any other person I know. His interest in the Notre Dame Center for Civil Rights has never wavered. And he played an important role in broadening the scope of the center's work—and I visited there last fall—to see this work include, now, all people in the world, as shown by last month's conference here on human rights and American foreign policy.

And that concern has been demonstrated again today in a vivid fashion by the selection of Bishop Donal Lamont, Paul Cardinal Arns, and Stephen Cardinal Kim, to receive honorary degrees. In their fight for human freedoms in Rhodesia, Brazil, and South Korea, these three religious leaders typify all that is best in their countries and in our church. I'm honored to join you in recognizing their dedication, their personal sacrifice, and their supreme courage.

Quite often, brave men like these are castigated and sometimes punished, sometimes even put to death, because they enter the realm where human rights is a struggle. And sometimes, they are blamed for the very circumstance which they helped to dramatize, but it's been there for a long time. And the flames which they seek to extinguish concern us all and are increasingly visible around the world.

Last week, I spoke in California about the domestic agenda for our Nation:[21] to provide more efficiently for the needs of our people, to demonstrate—against the dark faith of our times—that our Government can be both competent and more humane.

But I want to speak to you today about the strands that connect our actions overseas with our essential character as a nation. I believe we can have a foreign policy that is democratic, that is based on fundamental values, and that uses power and influence, which we have, for humane purposes. We can also have a foreign policy that the American people both support and, for a change, know about and understand.

I have a quiet confidence in our own political system. Because we know that democracy works, we can reject the arguments of those rulers who deny human rights to their people.

We are confident that democracy's example will be compelling, and so we seek to bring that example closer to those from whom in the past few years we have been separated and who are not yet convinced about the advantages of our kind of life.

We are confident that democratic methods are the most effective, and so we are not tempted to employ improper tactics here at home or abroad.

---

[21]Remarks to the United Auto Workers Convention, May 17, in *Presidential Documents*, 13: 724-33.

We are confident of our own strength, so we can seek substantial mutual reductions in the nuclear arms race.

And we are confident of the good sense of American people, and so we let them share in the process of making foreign policy decisions. We can thus speak with the voices of 215 million, and not just of an isolated handful.

Democracy's great recent successes—in India, Portugal, Spain, Greece—show that our confidence in this system is not misplaced. Being confident of our own future, we are now free of that inordinate fear of communism which once led us to embrace any dictator who joined us in that fear. I'm glad that that's being changed.

For too many years, we've been willing to adopt the flawed and erroneous principles and tactics of our adversaries, sometimes abandoning our own values for theirs. We've fought fire with fire, never thinking that fire is better quenched with water. This approach failed, with Vietnam the best example of its intellectual and moral poverty. But through failure, we have now found our way back to our own principles and values, and we have regained our lost confidence.

By the measure of history, our Nation's 200 years are very brief, and our rise to world eminence is briefer still. It dates from 1945 when Europe and the old international order lay in ruins. Before then America was largely on the periphery of world affairs, but since then we have inescapably been at the center of world affairs.

Our policy during this period was guided by two principles: a belief that Soviet expansion was almost inevitable but that it must be contained, and the corresponding belief in the importance of an almost exclusive alliance among non-Communist nations on both sides of the Atlantic. That system could not last forever unchanged. Historical trends have weakened its foundation. The unifying threat of conflict with the Soviet Union has become less intensive even though the competition has become more extensive.

The Vietnamese war produced a profound moral crisis sapping worldwide faith in our own policy and our system of life, a crisis of confidence made even more grave by the covert pessimism of some of our leaders.

In less than a generation, we've seen the world change dramatically. The daily lives and aspirations of most human beings have been transformed. Colonialism is nearly gone. A new sense of national identity now exists in almost 100 new countries that have been formed in the last generation. Knowledge has become more widespread; aspirations are higher. As more people have been freed from traditional constraints, more have been determined to achieve for the first time in their lives social justice.

The world is still divided by ideological disputes, dominated by regional conflicts, and threatened by danger that we will not resolve the differences of race and wealth without violence or without drawing into combat the major military powers. We can no longer separate the traditional issues of war and peace from the new global questions of justice, equity, and human rights.

It is a new world—but America should not fear it. It is a new world—and we should help to shape it. It is a new world that calls for a new American foreign policy—a policy based on constant decency in its values and on optimism in our historical vision.

We can no longer have a policy solely for the industrial nations as the foundation of global stability, but we must respond to the new reality of a politically awakening world.

We can no longer expect that the other 150 nations will follow the dictates of the powerful, but we must continue—confidently, our efforts to inspire, to persuade, and to lead.

Our policy must reflect our belief that the world can hope for more than simple survival and our belief that dignity and freedom are fundamental spiritual requirements. Our policy must shape an international system that will last longer than secret deals.

We cannot make this kind of policy by manipulation. Our policy must be open; it must be candid; it must be one of constructive global involvement, resting on five cardinal principles.

I've tried to make these premises clear to the American people since last January. Let me review what we have been doing and discuss what we intend to do.

First, we have reaffirmed America's commitment to human rights as a fundamental tenet of our foreign policy. In ancestry, religion, color, place of origin, and cultural background, we Americans are as diverse a nation as the world has ever seen. No common mystique of blood or soil unites us. What draws us together, perhaps more than anything else, is a belief in human freedom.

We want the world to know that our Nation stands for more than financial prosperity. This does not mean that we can conduct our foreign policy by rigid moral maxims. We live in a world that is imperfect and which will always be imperfect—a world that is complex and confused and which will always be complex and confused.

I understand fully the limits of moral suasion. We have no illusion that changes will come easily or soon. But I also believe that it is a mistake to undervalue the power of words and of the ideas that words embody. In our own history, that power has ranged from Thomas Paine's "Common Sense" to Martin Luther King, Jr.'s "I have a Dream."

In the life of the human spirit, words are action, much more so than many of us may realize who live in countries where freedom of expression is taken for granted. The leaders of totalitarian nations understand this very well. The proof is that words are precisely the action for which dissidents in those countries are being persecuted.

Nonetheless, we can already see dramatic, worldwide advances in the protection of the individual from the arbitrary power of the state. For us to ignore this trend would be to lose influence and moral authority in the world. To lead it will be to regain the moral stature that we once had.

The great democracies are not free because we are strong and prosperous. I believe we are strong and influential and prosperous because we are free.

Throughout the world today, in free nations and in totalitarian countries as well, there is a preoccupation with the subject of human freedom, human rights. And I believe it is incumbent on us in this country to keep that discussion, that debate, that contention alive. No other country is as well-qualified as we to set an example. We have our own shortcomings and faults, and we should strive constantly and with courage to make sure that we are legitimately proud of what we have.

Second, we've moved deliberately to reinforce the bonds among our democracies. In our recent meetings in London, we agreed to widen our economic cooperation, to promote free trade, to strengthen the world's monetary system, to seek ways of avoiding nuclear proliferation. We prepared constructive proposals for the forthcoming meetings on North-South problems of poverty, development, and global well-being, and we agreed on joint efforts to reinforce and to modernize our common defense.

You may be interested in knowing that at this NATO meeting, for the first time in more than 25 years, all members are democracies. Even more important, all of us reaffirmed our basic optimism in the future of the democratic system. Our spirit of confidence is spreading. Together, our democracies can help to shape the wider architecture of global cooperation.

Third, we've moved to engage the Soviet Union in a joint effort to halt the strategic arms race. This race is not only dangerous, it's morally deplorable. We must put an end to it.

I know it will not be easy to reach agreements. Our goal is to be fair to both sides, to produce reciprocal stability, parity, and security. We desire a freeze on further modernization and production of weapons and a continuing, substantial reduction of strategic nuclear weapons as well. We want a comprehensive ban on all nuclear testing, a prohibition against all chemical warfare, no attack capability against space satellites, and arms limitations in the Indian Ocean.

We hope that we can take joint steps with all nations toward a final agreement eliminating nuclear weapons completely from our arsenals of death. We will persist in this effort.

Now, I believe in détente with the Soviet Union. To me, it means progress toward peace. But the effects of détente should not be limited to our own two countries alone. We hope to persuade the Soviet Union that one country cannot impose its system of society upon another, either through direct military intervention or through the use of a client state's military force, as was the case with Cuban intervention in Angola.

Cooperation also implies obligation. We hope that the Soviet Union will join with us and other nations in playing a larger role in aiding the developing world, for common aid efforts will help us build a bridge of mutual confidence in one another.

Fourth, we are taking deliberate steps to improve the chances of lasting peace in the Middle East. Through wide-ranging consultation with leaders of the countries involved—Israel, Syria, Jordan, and Egypt—we have found some areas of agreement and some movement toward consensus. The negotiations must continue.

Through my own public comments, I've also tried to suggest a more flexible framework for the discussion of the three key issues which have so far been so intractable: the nature of a comprehensive peace—What is peace? What does it mean to the Israelis? What does it mean to their Arab neighbors? Secondly, the relationship between security and borders—How can the dispute over border delineations be established and settled with a feeling of security on both sides? And the issue of the Palestinian homeland.

The historic friendship that the United States has with Israel is not dependent on domestic politics in either nation; it's derived from our common respect for human freedom and from a common search for permanent peace.

We will continue to promote a settlement which all of us need. Our own policy will not be affected by changes in leadership in any of the countries in the Middle East. Therefore, we expect Israel and her neighbors to continue to be bound by United Nations Resolutions 242 and 338, which they have previously accepted.

This may be the most propitious time for a genuine settlement since the beginning of the Arab-Israeli conflict almost 30 years ago. To let this opportunity pass could mean disaster not only for the Middle East but, perhaps, for the international political and economic order as well.

And fifth, we are attempting, even at the risk of some friction with our friends, to reduce the danger of nuclear proliferation and the worldwide spread of conventional weapons.

At the recent summit, we set in motion an international effort to determine the best ways of harnessing nuclear energy for peaceful use while reducing the risks that its products will be diverted to the making of explosives.

We've already completed a comprehensive review of our own

policy on arms transfers.[22] Competition in arms sales is inimical to peace and destructive of the economic development of the poorer countries.

We will, as a matter of national policy now in our country seek to reduce the annual dollar volume of arms sales, to restrict the transfer of advanced weapons, and to reduce the extent of our coproduction arrangements about weapons with foreign states. And, just as important, we are trying to get other nations, both free and otherwise, to join us in this effort.

But all of this that I've described is just the beginning. It's a beginning aimed towards a clear goal: to create a wider framework of international cooperation suited to the new and rapidly changing historical circumstances.

We will cooperate more closely with the newly influential countries in Latin America, Africa, and Asia. We need their friendship and cooperation in a common effort as the structure of world power changes.

More than 100 years ago, Abraham Lincoln said that our Nation could not exist half slave and half free. We know a peaceful world cannot exist one-third rich and two-thirds hungry.

Most nations share our faith that in the long run, expanded and equitable trade will best help the developing countries to help themselves. But the immediate problems of hunger, disease, illiteracy, and repression are here now.

The Western democracies, the OPEC nations, and the developed Communist countries can cooperate through existing international institutions in providing more effective aid. This is an excellent alternative to war.

We have a special need for cooperation and consultation with other nations in this hemisphere—to the north and to the south. We do not need another slogan. Although these are our close friends and neighbors, our links with them are the same links of equality that we forge for the rest of the world. We will be dealing with them as part of a new, worldwide mosaic of global, regional, and bilateral relations.

It's important that we make progress toward normalizing relations with the People's Republic of China. We see the American and Chinese relationship as a central element of our global policy, and China as a key force for global peace. We wish to cooperate closely with the creative Chinese people on the problems that confront all mankind, and we hope to find a formula which can bridge some of the difficulties that still separate us.

[22]Cf. Document 8.

Finally, let me say that we are committed to a peaceful resolution of the crisis in southern Africa. The time has come for the principle of majority rule to be the basis for political order, recognizing that in a democratic system the rights of the minority must also be protected.

To be peaceful, change must come promptly. The United States is determined to work together with our European allies and with the concerned African States to shape a congenial international framework for the rapid and progressive transformation of southern African society and to help protect it from unwarranted outside interference.

Let me conclude by summarizing: Our policy is based on an historical vision of America's role. Our policy is derived from a larger view of global change. Our policy is rooted in our moral values, which never change. Our policy is reinforced by our material wealth and by our military power. Our policy is designed to serve mankind. And it is a policy that I hope will make you proud to be Americans.

Thank you.

2. CURBING THE WAR DEMONS

(6) New Try at SALT: American-Soviet Discussions in Moscow, March 28-30, 1977.

(a) News Conference Statement by President Carter, March 30, 1977.[1]

THE PRESIDENT. Good afternoon.

This has been an afternoon devoted to receiving dispatches from Moscow, and I'd like to make a report to the American people about what has occurred.

We have proposed to the Soviet leaders in the last 2 days a comprehensive package of agreements which, if concluded, will lay a permanent groundwork for a more peaceful world, an alleviation of the great threat of atomic weapons; that will maintain the political and strategic weapon capability and balance between the United States and the Soviet Union.

One of our proposals on this [*sic*] nuclear weapons talks was very brief and it was our second option. It was, in effect, to ratify the Vladivostok agreement that had already been reached.

The difference between us and the Soviet Union on this point is that the Soviets claim that Secretary Kissinger and my predecessors in the White House—Presidents Ford and, earlier, Nixon—did agree to forgo the deployment of cruise missiles. Our position is that we have never agreed to any such thing. But we asked the Soviet Union to accept an agreement on all other matters and postpone the cruise missile and the Russians' new bomber, the Backfire bomber, until continuing later discussion. They rejected that proposal.

The other one was much more far-reaching and has profound consequences that are beneficial, I think, to our own Nation and to the rest of the world. It was to have substantial reductions in the level of deployment of missile launchers and the MIRVed missiles

[1]Text from *Presidential Documents*, 13: 469-70.

below the 2400 level and the 1320 level that were established under the Vladivostok agreements—substantial reductions; secondly, to stop the development and deployment of any new weapons systems. A third point was to freeze at the present level about 550 intercontinental ballistic missiles, our Minuteman and their missiles known as the SS–17, 18, and 19.

Another was to ban the deployment of all mobile missiles, their SS–16 and others, or ours—that is under the development stage, the MX.

Another one is to have a strict limit on the deployment of the Backfire bomber and a strict limit on the range that would be permitted on cruise missiles.

Another element of the proposal was to limit the number of test firings of missiles to six firings per year of the intercontinental range and also of the medium-range missiles and to ask the Soviet Union to give us some assured mechanism by which we could distinguish between their intercontinental mobile missile, the SS–16, and their limited-range mobile missile, the SS–20.

The sum total of all this proposal was a fair, balanced, substantial reduction in the arms race which would have guaranteed, I believe, a permanent lessening of tension and a mutual benefit to both our countries. The Soviets, at least at this point, have not accepted this proposal either.

Both parties—which will be promulgated in a joint communique tomorrow—have agreed to continue the discussions the first half of May in Geneva.

You might be interested in knowing that a few other points that we proposed were to have adequate verification, an end of concealment, and the establishment of a so-called data base by which we would tell the Soviet Union the level of our own armaments at this point, and they would tell us their level of armaments at this point, so that we would have an assured, mutually agreed level of weapon capability.

I might cover just a few more things. In addition to discussing the SALT agreements in Geneva early in May, we have agreed to discuss other matters—South Africa, the upcoming possible Middle Eastern talks. And we've agreed to set up eight study groups: one, to develop an agreement whereby we might forgo the development of a capability of destroying satellite observation vehicles, so that we can have an assured way to watch the Soviets; they can have an assured way of watching us from satellites.

The second is to discuss the terms of a possible comprehensive test ban, so that we don't test in the future any more nuclear weapons. And we've also asked the Soviets to join with us in a prohibition against the testing of peaceful nuclear devices.

Another study group that has been mutually agreed to be established is to discuss the terms by which we might demilitarize or reduce the military effort in the Indian Ocean.

Another group will be set up, of experts, to discuss the terms by which we can agree on advanced notice on all missile test firings, so that perhaps 24 hours ahead of time, we would notify the Soviets when we were going to test fire one of our missiles; they would do the same for us.

Another group will be studying a way to initiate comprehensive arms control in conventional weapons and also the sale of weapons to third countries, particularly the developing nations of the world.

Another is to discuss how we might contribute, mutually, toward nonproliferation of nuclear weapon capability. Nations do need a way to produce atomic power for electricity, but we hope that the Soviets will join with us and our allies and friends in cutting down the capability of nations to use spent nuclear fuels to develop explosives.

Another item that we agreed to discuss at the Soviets' request was the termination in the capability of waging radiological or chemical warfare.

And the eighth study group that we agreed to establish is to study the means by which we could mutually agree on forgoing major efforts in civil defense. We feel that the Soviets have done a great deal on civil defense capability. We've done a less amount, but we would like for both of us to agree not to expend large sums of money on this effort.

So, the sum total of the discussions has been to lay out a firm proposal, which the Soviets have not yet responded to, on drastic reductions in nuclear capability in the future—these discussions will continue early in May—and to set up study groups to continue with the analysis of the other eight items that I described to you.

I'd be glad to answer just a few questions.[2]

(b) Joint Communiqué Issued in Moscow and Washington, March 31, 1977.[3]

On March 28–30, 1977, General Secretary of the Central Committee of the Communist Party of the Soviet Union, L. I. Brezhnev and Member of the Politbureau of the Central Committee of the Communist Party of the Soviet Union, Minister of Foreign Affairs of the USSR, A. A. Gromyko, held talks with the Secretary of State of the United States of America, Cyrus R. Vance, who was in Moscow on an official visit.

[2] For the remainder of the news conference see same: 471-3.
[3] Text from *Presidential Documents*, 13: 474-5.

In the course of the talks there was a general discussion of American-Soviet relations, as well as certain international problems of mutual interest for the US and the USSR.

Consideration of questions relevant to the completion of the new agreement on the limitation of strategic offensive arms occupied the central place in the talks. The sides have agreed to continue the consideration of these issues.

An exchange of views also took place on a number of other questions concerning the limitation of armaments and disarmament. It was agreed that bilateral contacts, including meetings of experts, would be held to discuss these matters.

The discussion of international issues included the Belgrade preparatory conference, and the situation in Cyprus and southern Africa. They reaffirmed the importance of the quadripartite agreement of September 1971. Special attention was given to the situation in the Middle East. The sides have agreed that cooperation between the US and the USSR, as co-chairmen of the Geneva Conference is essential in bringing about a just and lasting peace in the area. An understanding was reached to hold, in the first half of May, 1977, in Geneva, a meeting between the Secretary of State of the US and the Minister of Foreign Affairs of the USSR for a thorough exchange of views on the Middle East problem, including the question of resuming the work of the Geneva Conference. Some of the other issues discussed in the talks in Moscow will be reviewed at that time.[4]

The consideration of practical questions of bilateral relations produced several specific understandings.

(7)   Resisting Nuclear Proliferation: American Policy Statements, April 1977.

(a)   Nuclear Power Policy: Statement by President Carter to Reporters, April 7, 1977.[5]

(Excerpts)

THE PRESIDENT. Good morning, everybody.

I have two items to discuss with you this morning. Then I'd like to answer a few questions.

---

[4]Cf. Introduction at note 29.
[5]Text from *Presidential Documents,* 13: 502-4.

ECONOMIC STIMULUS PACKAGE

One relates to the economy and the need for continuing emphasis on the stimulation package.

* * *

NUCLEAR POWER POLICY

The second point I'd like to make before I answer questions is concerning our Nation's efforts to control the spread of nuclear explosive capability. As far back as 30 years ago, our Government made a proposal to the United Nations that there be tight international controls over nuclear fuels and particularly those that might be made into explosives.

Last year during the Presidential campaign, both I and President Ford called for strict controls over fuels to prevent the proliferation—further proliferation of nuclear explosive capability.

There is no dilemma today more difficult to address than that connected with the use of atomic power. Many countries see atomic power as their only real opportunity to deal with the dwindling supplies of oil, the increasing price of oil, and the ultimate exhaustion of both oil and natural gas.

Our country is in a little better position. We have oil supplies of our own, and we have very large reserves of coal. But even coal has its limitations. So, we will ourselves continue to use atomic power as a share of our total energy production.

The benefits of nuclear power, particularly to some foreign countries that don't have oil and coal of their own, are very practical and critical. But a serious risk is involved in the handling of nuclear fuels—the risk that component parts of this power process will be turned to providing explosives or atomic weapons.

We took an important step in reducing this risk a number of years ago by the implementation of the nonproliferation treaty which has now been signed by approximately a hundred nations. But we must go further.

We have seen recently India evolve an explosive device derived from a peaceful nuclear powerplant, and we now feel that several other nations are on the verge of becoming nuclear explosive powers.

The United States is deeply concerned about the consequences of the uncontrolled spread of this nuclear weapon capability. We can't arrest it immediately and unilaterally. We have no authority over other countries. But we believe that these risks would be vastly increased by the further spread of reprocessing capabilities of the spent nuclear fuel from which explosives can be derived.

Plutonium is especially poisonous, and, of course, enriched uranium, thorium and other chemicals or metals can be used as well.

We are now completing an extremely thorough review of our own nuclear power program. We have concluded that serious consequences can be derived from our own laxity in the handling of these materials and the spread of their use by other countries. And we believe that there is strong scientific and economic evidence that a time for a change has come.

Therefore, we will make a major change in the United States domestic nuclear energy policies and programs which I am announcing today.

We will make a concerted effort among all other countries to find better answers to the problems and risks of nuclear proliferation. And I would like to outline a few things now that we will do specifically.

First of all, we will defer indefinitely the commercial reprocessing and recycling of the plutonium produced in U.S. nuclear power programs.

From my own experience, we have concluded that a viable and adequate economic nuclear program can be maintained without such reprocessing and recycling of plutonium. The plant at Barnwell, South Carolina, for instance, will receive neither Federal encouragement nor funding from us for its completion as a reprocessing facility.

Second, we will restructure our own U.S. breeder program to give greater priority to alternative designs of the breeder other than plutonium, and to defer the date when breeder reactors would be put into commercial use.

We will continue research and development, try to shift away from plutonium, defer dependence on the breeder reactor for commercial use.

Third, we will direct funding of U.S. nuclear research and development programs to accelerate our research into alternative nuclear fuel cycles which do not involve direct access to materials that can be used for nuclear weapons.

Fourth, we will increase the U.S. capacity to produce nuclear fuels, enriched uranium in particular, to provide adequate and timely supplies of nuclear fuels to countries that need them so that they will not be required or encouraged to reprocess their own materials.

Fifth, we will propose to the Congress the necessary legislative steps to permit us to sign these supply contracts and remove the pressure for the reprocessing of nuclear fuels by other countries that do not now have this capability.

Sixth, we will continue to embargo the export of either equipment or technology that could permit uranium enrichment and chemical reprocessing.

And seventh, we will continue discussions with supplying countries and recipient countries, as well, of a wide range of international approaches and frameworks that will permit all countries to achieve their own energy needs while at the same time reducing the spread of the capability for nuclear explosive development.

Among other things—and we have discussed this with 15 or 20 national leaders already—we will explore the establishment of an international nuclear fuel cycle evaluation program so that we can share with countries that have to reprocess nuclear fuel the responsibility for curtailing the ability for the development of explosives.

One other point that ought to be made in the international negotiation field is that we have to help provide some means for the storage of spent nuclear fuel materials which are highly explosive, highly radioactive in nature.

I have been working very closely with and personally with some of the foreign leaders who are quite deeply involved in the decisions that we make. We are not trying to impose our will on those nations like Japan and France and Britain and Germany which already have reprocessing plants in operation. They have a special need that we don't have in that their supplies of petroleum products are not available.

But we hope that they will join with us—and I believe that they will—in trying to have some worldwide understanding of the extreme threat of the further proliferation of nuclear explosive capability.

I'd be glad to answer a few questions.[6]

* * *

(b) The Proposed Nuclear Non-Proliferation Act of 1977: Message from President Carter to the Congress, April 27, 1977.[7]

To the Congress of the United States:

The need to halt nuclear proliferation is one of mankind's most pressing challenges. Members of my Administration are now engaged in international discussions to find ways of controlling the spread of nuclear explosive capability without depriving any nation of the means to satisfy its energy needs. The domestic nuclear policies which I have already put forward will place our nation in a leadership position, setting a positive example for other nuclear

[6]Question and answer session with reporters appears in same: 504-6.
[7]Text from *Presidential Documents,* 13: 611.

suppliers as well as demonstrating the strength of our concern here at home for the hazards of a plutonium economy. Today I am submitting to the Congress a bill which would establish for the United States a strong and effective non-proliferation policy.

This bill relies heavily upon work which the Congress has already done, and I commend the Congress for these valuable initiatives. I look forward to working with the Congress to establish a strong, responsible legislative framework from which we can continue strengthened efforts to halt the spread of nuclear weapons.

Among our shared goals are: an increase in the effectiveness of international safeguards and controls on peaceful nuclear activities to prevent further proliferation of nuclear explosive devices, the establishment of common international sanctions to prevent such proliferation, an effort to encourage nations which have not ratified the Non-Proliferation Treaty to do so at the earliest possible date, and adoption of programs to enhance the reliability of the United States as a supplier of nuclear fuel.

This bill differs from pending proposals, however, in several respects:

1. It defines the immediate nuclear export conditions which we can reasonably ask other nations to meet while we negotiate stricter arrangements. The proposals currently before Congress would impose criteria that could force an immediate moratorium on our nuclear exports, adversely affecting certain allies whose cooperation is needed if we are to achieve our ultimate objective of non-proliferation.

2. It defines additional nuclear export conditions which will be required in new agreements for civil nuclear cooperation. In particular, we will require as a continuing condition of U.S. supply that recipients have all their nuclear activities under IAEA safeguards. I view this as an interim measure and shall make it clear to all potential recipients and to other nuclear suppliers that our first preference, and continuing objective, is universal adherence to the Non-Proliferation Treaty.

3. For the near future, it attempts to tighten the conditions for U.S. nuclear cooperation through renegotiation of existing agreements to meet the same standards as those we will require in new agreements. I believe that this approach will better meet our non-proliferation objectives than will the unilateral imposition of new export licensing conditions.

4. It increases the flexibility we need to deal with an extremely complex subject. For example, instead of requiring countries that want our nuclear exports to foreswear fuel enrichment and reprocessing for all time, it allows us to draft new agreements using incentives to encourage countries not to acquire such facilities. It also

permits me to grant exceptions when doing so would further our basic aim of non-proliferation. All new cooperation agreements would, of course, be subject to Congressional review.

This bill is intended to reassure other nations that the United States will be a reliable supplier of nuclear fuel and equipment for those who genuinely share our desire for non-proliferation. It will insure that when all statutory standards have been met, export licenses will be issued—or, if the judgment of the Executive Branch and the independent Nuclear Regulatory Commission should differ, that a workable mechanism exists for resolving the dispute.

Since I intend personally to oversee Executive Branch actions affecting non-proliferation, I do not think a substantial reorganization of the responsibility for nuclear exports within the Executive Branch is necessary. This conclusion is shared by the Nuclear Regulatory Commission.

The need for prompt action is great. Until domestic legislation is enacted, other countries will be reluctant to renegotiate their agreements with us, because they will fear that new legislation might suddenly change the terms of cooperation. If the incentives we offer them to renegotiate with us are not attractive enough, the United States could lose important existing safeguards and controls. And if our policy is too weak, we could find ourselves powerless to restrain a deadly world-wide expansion of nuclear explosive capability. I believe the legislation now submitted to you strikes the necessary balance.

JIMMY CARTER

The White House,
April 27, 1977.

(8) Curbing Conventional Arms Transfers: Statement by President Carter, May 19, 1977.[8]

The virtually unrestrained spread of conventional weaponry threatens stability in every region of the world. Total arms sales in recent years have risen to over $20 billion, and the United States accounts for more than one-half of this amount. Each year, the weapons transferred are not only more numerous but also more sophisticated and deadly. Because of the threat to world peace embodied in this spiralling arms traffic and because of the special responsibilities we bear as the largest arms seller, I believe that the United States must take steps to restrain its arms transfers.

[8] Text from *Presidential Documents,* 13: 756-7.

Therefore, shortly after my inauguration, I directed a comprehensive review of U.S. conventional arms transfer policy, including all military, political, and economic factors. After reviewing the results of this study and discussing those results with Members of Congress and foreign leaders, I have concluded that the United States will henceforth view arms transfers as an exceptional foreign policy implement, to be used only in instances where it can be clearly demonstrated that the transfer contributes to our national security interests. We will continue to utilize arms transfers to promote our security and the security of our close friends. But in the future the burden of persuasion will be on those who favor a particular arms sale, rather than those who oppose it.

To implement a policy of arms restraint, I am establishing the following set of controls, applicable to all transfers except those to countries with which we have major defense treaties (NATO, Japan, Australia, and New Zealand). We will remain faithful to our treaty obligations and will honor our historic responsibilities to assure the security of the State of Israel. These controls will be binding *unless* extraordinary circumstances necessitate a Presidential exception, *or* where I determine that countries friendly to the United States must depend on advanced weaponry to offset quantitative and other disadvantages in order to maintain a regional balance.

1. The dollar volume (in constant FY 1976 dollars) of new commitments under the Foreign Military Sales and Military Assistance Programs for weapons and weapons-related items in FY 1978 will be reduced from the FY 1977 total. Transfers which can clearly be classified as services are not covered, nor are commercial sales, which the U.S. Government monitors through the issuance of export licenses. Commercial sales are already significantly restrained by existing legislation and executive branch policy.

2. The United States will not be the first supplier to introduce into a region newly developed, advanced weapons systems which would create a new or significantly higher combat capability. Also, any commitment for sale or coproduction of such weapons is prohibited until they are operationally deployed with U.S. forces, thus removing the incentive to promote foreign sales in an effort to lower unit costs for Defense Department procurement.

3. Development or significant modification of *advanced* weapons systems *solely for export* will not be permitted.

4. Coproduction agreements for significant weapons, equipment, and major components (beyond assembly of subcomponents and the fabrication of high-turnover spare parts) are prohibited. A limited class of items will be considered for coproduction arrangements, but with restrictions on third-country exports, since these

arrangements are intended primarily for the coproducer's requirements.

5. In addition to existing requirements of the law, the United States, as a condition of sale for certain weapons, equipment, or major components, may stipulate that we will not entertain *any* requests for retransfers. By establishing at the outset that the United States will not entertain such requests, we can avoid unnecessary bilateral friction caused by later denials.

6. An amendment to the international traffic in arms regulations will be issued, requiring policy level authorization by the Department of State for actions by agents of the United States or private manufacturers which might promote the sale of arms abroad. In addition, embassies and military representatives abroad will not promote the sale of arms and the Secretary of Defense will continue his review of Government procedures, particularly procurement regulations which may provide incentives for foreign sales.

In formulating security assistance programs consistent with these controls, we will continue our efforts to promote and advance respect for human rights in recipient countries. Also, we will assess the economic impact of arms transfers to those less-developed countries receiving U.S. economic assistance.

I am initiating this policy of restraint in the full understanding that actual reductions in the worldwide traffic in arms will require multilateral cooperation. Because we dominate the world market to such a degree, I believe that the United States can and should take the first step. However, in the immediate future the United States will meet with other arms suppliers, including the Soviet Union, to begin discussion of possible measures for multilateral action. In addition, we will do whatever we can to encourage regional agreements among purchasers to limit arms imports.

(9)   United States-Soviet Relations: Address by President Carter at the 31st Annual Meeting of the Southern Legislative Conference, Charleston, July 21, 1977.[9]

(Excerpt)

*   *   *

I'm very grateful to be here as President of our country. I've learned a lot in this first 6 months. When I got to Washington and sought advice, someone said, "Just act like you're a President and

[9]Text from *Presidential Documents*, 13: 1063-9.

treat Congress like the Georgia Legislature.'' It didn't work at first. [*Laughter*]

Very quickly I realized that the Congress was treating me like I was still Governor of Georgia, but now, with the help of a great number of friends in the Congress, we've formed a kind of relationship that ought to exist between the White House and our Nation's Capitol. I think there's a genuine sense of sharing of responsibility and the burden of government, and you are a part of that circle of leaders in the State legislature and the Governors' offices, who join in with the President, the Congress, and others in making sure that our government works.

I've become even more proud of being an American. And I have become even more proud of being a southerner, too. I'm also proud to be with you today where two great rivers come together, as they say in Charleston, to form the Atlantic Ocean. This is one of our Nation's most gracious cities.

And I want to talk to you today about the hopes and problems that we as southerners and as Americans share together. I feel a special kinship with your State legislators. For 4 years I was a member of the Georgia Senate, and I still prize State government not only for the talents of those who work in it but, as Fritz Hollings says, for the closeness to the people it represents.

Our Southern States have a proud tradition of local, independent government, and now you're the heirs of that tradition. But we in the South have also felt, perhaps more directly than many others, some of the rapid changes that have taken place in this modern age. More and more our own lives are shaped by events in other cities, decisions in other States, tensions in other parts of the world.

And as Americans we cannot overlook the way that our fate is bound to that of other nations. This interdependence stretches from the health of our economy, through war and peace, to the security of our own energy supplies. It's a new world in which we cannot afford to be narrow in our vision, limited in our foresight, or selfish in our purpose.

When I took office almost exactly 6 months ago, our Nation was faced with a series of problems around the world—in southern Africa, the Middle East, in our relationships with our NATO allies, and on such tough questions as nuclear proliferation, negotiations with our former adversaries, a Panama Canal treaty, human rights, world poverty.

We have openly and publicly addressed these and other many difficult and controversial issues—some of which had been either skirted or postponed in the past.

As I pointed out in a recent press conference,[10] a period of de-

[10]News conference of July 12, in same: 993.

bate, disagreement, probing was inevitable. Our goal has not been to reach easy or transient agreements, but to find solutions that are meaningful, balanced, and lasting.

Now, a President has a responsibility to present to the people of this Nation reports and summations of complex and important matters. I feel more secure as President making decisions if I know that either the most difficult, the most complex questions that face me have been understood and debated by you and understood and debated by the Congress.

In the past I think our Nation's leaders have been guilty of making decisions in secret. And even when the decision turns out to be the right one, it makes the President, the Secretary of State speak with a weak voice when they speak alone.

Today, I want to discuss a vitally important aspect of our foreign relations, the one that may most directly shape the chances for peace for us and for our children. I would like to spell out my view of what we have done and where we are going in our relations with the Soviet Union and to reaffirm the basic principles of our national policy.

I don't have any apology for talking about foreign affairs at a southern legislative conference, because foreign affairs and those difficult decisions ought never to be made with a concept that we can abandon common sense and the sound judgment and the constructive influence of the American people.

For decades, the central problems of our foreign policy revolved around antagonism between two coalitions, one headed by the United States and the other headed by the Soviet Union.

Our national security was often defined almost exclusively in terms of military competition with the Soviet Union. This competition is still critical, because it does involve issues which could lead to war. But however important this relationship of military balance, it cannot be our sole preoccupation to the exclusion of other world issues which also concern us both.

Even if we succeed in relaxing tensions with the U.S.S.R., we could still awake one day to find that nuclear weapons have been spread to dozens of other nations who may not be as responsible as are we. Or we could struggle to limit the conventional arsenals of our two nations, to reduce the danger of war, only to undo our efforts by continuing without constraint to export armaments around the world.

As two industrial giants, we face long-term worldwide energy crises. Whatever our political differences, both of us are compelled to begin conserving world energy and developing alternatives to oil and gas.

Despite deep and continuing differences in world outlook, both of us should accept the new responsibilities imposed on us by the changing nature of international relations.

Europe and Japan rose from the rubble of war to become great economic powers. Communist parties and governments have become more widespread and more varied and, I might say, more independent from one another. Newly independent nations emerged into what has now become known as the Third World. Their role in world affairs is becoming increasingly significant.

Both the United States and the Soviet Union have learned that our countries and our people, in spite of great resources, are not all-powerful. We've learned that this world, no matter how technology has shrunk distances, is nevertheless too large and too varied to come under the sway of either one or two super powers. And what is perhaps more important of all, we have, for our part, learned, all of us, this fact, these facts in a spirit not of increasing resignation, but of increasing maturity.

I mention these familiar changes with which you are familiar because I think that to understand today's Soviet-American relationship, we must place it in perspective, both historically and in terms of the overall global scene.

The whole history of Soviet-American relations teaches us that we will be misled if we base our long-range policies on the mood of the moment, whether that mood be euphoric or grim. All of us can remember times when relations seemed especially dangerous and other times when they seemed especially bright.

We've crossed those peaks and valleys before. And we can see that, on balance, the trend in the last third of a century has been positive.

The profound differences in what our two governments believe about freedom and power and the inner lives of human beings, those differences are likely to remain; and so are other elements of competition between the United States and the Soviet Union. That competition is real and deeply rooted in the history and the values of our respective societies. But it's also true that our two countries share many important overlapping interests. Our job—my job, your job—is to explore those shared interests and use them to enlarge the areas of cooperation between us on a basis of equality and mutual respect.

As we negotiate with the Soviet Union, we will be guided by a vision of a gentler, freer, and more bountiful world. But we will have no illusions about the nature of the world as it really is. The basis for complete mutual trust between us does not yet exist. Therefore, the agreements that we reach must be anchored on each side in enlightened self-interest—what's best for us, what's best for the Soviet Union. That's why we search for areas of agreement where our real interests and those of the Soviets coincide.

We want to see the Soviets further engaged in the growing pattern of international activities designed to deal with human problems—not only because they can be of real help but because we both should be seeking for a greater stake in the creation of a constructive and peaceful world order.

When I took office, many Americans were growing disillusioned with détente—President Ford had even quit using the word, and by extension, people were concerned with the whole course of our relations with the Soviet Union. Also, and perhaps more seriously, world respect for the essential rightness of American foreign policy had been shaken by the events of a decade—Vietnam, Cambodia, CIA, Watergate. At the same time, we were beginning to regain our sense of confidence and our purpose and unity as a nation.

In this situation, I decided that it was time for honest discussions about international issues with the American people. I felt that it was urgent to restore the moral bearings of American foreign policy. And I felt that it was important to put the U.S. and Soviet relationship, in particular, on a more reciprocal, realistic, and, ultimately, more productive basis for both nations.

It's not a question of a "hard" policy or of a "soft" policy, but of a clear-eyed recognition of how most effectively to protect our own security and to create the kind of international order that I've just described. This is our goal.

We've looked at the problems in Soviet-American relations in a fresh way, and we've sought to deal with them boldly and constructively with proposals intended to produce concrete results. I'd like to point out just a few of them.

In the talks on strategic arms limitations, the SALT talks, we advanced a comprehensive proposal for genuine reductions, limitations, and a freeze on new technology which would maintain balanced strategic strength.

We have urged a complete end to all nuclear tests, and these negotiations are now underway. Agreement here could be a milestone in U.S.-Soviet relations.

We're working together toward a ban on chemical and biological warfare and the elimination of inventories of these destructive materials. We have proposed to curb the sales and transfers of conventional weapons to other countries, and we've asked France, Britain, and other countries to join with us in this effort.

We are attempting to halt the threatening proliferation of nuclear weapons among the nations of the world which don't yet have the ability to set off nuclear explosives.

We've undertaken serious negotiations on arms limitations in the Indian Ocean. We've encouraged the Soviets to sign, along with us, the Treaty of Tlatelolco, which would ban the introduction of nuclear weapons into the southern part of the Western Hemisphere.[11]

We have begun regular consultations with the Soviet leaders as cochairmen of the prospective Geneva conference to promote peace in the Middle East.

We and our allies are negotiating together with the Soviet Union and their allies in the Warsaw Pact nations to reduce the level of military forces in Europe.

We've renewed the 1972 agreement for cooperation in science and technology, and a similar agreement for cooperation in outer space.

We're seeking ways to cooperate in improving world health and in relieving world hunger.

In the strategic arms limitation talks, confirming and then building on Vladivostok accords, we need to make steady progress toward our long-term goals of genuine reductions and strict limitations, while maintaining the basic strategic balance.

We've outlined proposals incorporating significant new elements of arms control, deep reductions in the arsenals of both sides, freezing of deployment and technology, and restraining certain elements in the strategic posture of both sides that threaten to destabilize the balance which now exists.

The Vladivostok negotiations of 1974 left some issues unresolved and subject to honest differences of interpretation. Meanwhile, new developments in technology have created new concerns—the cruise missile, the very large intercontinental ballistic missiles of the Soviets.

The Soviets are worried about our cruise missiles, and we are concerned about the security of our own deterrent capability. Our cruise missiles are aimed at compensating for the growing threat to our deterrent, represented by the buildup of strategic Soviet offensive weapons forces. If these threats can be controlled, and I believe they can, then we are prepared to limit our own strategic programs. But if an agreement cannot be reached, there should be no doubt that the United States can and will do what it must to protect our security and to ensure the adequacy of our strategic posture.

Our new proposals go beyond those that have been made before. In many areas we are in fact addressing for the first time the tough, complex core of long-standing problems. We are trying for the first time to reach agreements that will not be overturned by the next technological breakthrough. We are trying, in a word, for genuine accommodation.

[11]Cf. Introduction at note 116.

But none of these proposals that I've outlined to you involves a sacrifice of security. All of them are meant to increase the security of both sides. Our view is that a SALT agreement which just reflects the lowest common denominator that can be agreed upon easily will only create an illusion of progress and, eventually, a backlash against the entire arms control process. Our view is that genuine progress in SALT will not merely stabilize competition in weapons but can also provide a basis for improvement in political relations as well.

When I say that these efforts are intended to relax tensions, I'm not speaking only of military security. I mean as well the concern among our own individual citizens, Soviet and American, that comes from the knowledge which all of you have that the leaders of our two countries have the capacity to destroy human society through misunderstandings or mistakes. If we can relax this tension by reducing the nuclear threat, not only will we make the world a safer place but we'll also free ourselves to concentrate on constructive action to give the world a better life.

We've made some progress toward our goals, but to be frank, we also hear some negative comments from the Soviet side about SALT and about our more general relations. If these comments are based on a misconception about our motives, then we will redouble our efforts to make our motives clear; but if the Soviets are merely making comments designed as propaganda to put pressure on us, let no one doubt that we will persevere.

What matters ultimately is whether we can create a relationship of cooperation that will be rooted in the national interests of both sides. We shape our own policies to accommodate a constantly changing world, and we hope the Soviets will do the same. Together we can give this change a positive direction.

Increased trade between the United States and the Soviet Union would help us both. The American-Soviet Joint Commercial Commission has resumed its meetings after a long interlude. I hope that conditions can be created that will make possible steps toward expanded trade.

In southern Africa we have pressed for Soviet and Cuban restraint. Throughout the nonaligned world, our goal is not to encourage dissension or to redivide the world into opposing ideological camps, but to expand the realm of independent, economically self-reliant nations, and to oppose attempts at new kinds of subjugation.

Part of the Soviet Union leaders' current attitude may be due to their apparent—and incorrect—belief that our concern for human rights is aimed specifically at them or is an attack on their vital interests.

There are no hidden meanings in our commitment to human rights.

We stand on what we have said on the subject of human rights. Our policy is exactly what it appears to be: the positive and sincere expression of our deepest beliefs as a people. It's addressed not to any particular people or area of the world, but to all countries equally, yes, including our own country.

And it's specifically not designed to heat up the arms race or bring back the cold war.

On the contrary, I believe that an atmosphere of peaceful cooperation is far more conducive to an increased respect for human rights than an atmosphere of belligerence or hatred or warlike confrontation. The experience of our own country this last century has proved this over and over again.

We have no illusions that the process will be quick or that change will come easily. But we are confident that if we do not abandon the struggle, the cause of personal freedom and human dignity will be enhanced in all nations of the world. We're going to do that.

In the past 6 months we've made clear our determination—both to give voice to Americans' fundamental beliefs and to obtain lasting solutions to East-West differences. If this chance to emphasize peace and cooperation instead of animosity and division is allowed to pass, it will not have been our choice.

We must always combine realism with principle. Our actions must be faithful to the essential values to which our own society is dedicated, because our faith in those values is the source of our confidence that this relationship will evolve in a more constructive direction.

I cannot forecast whether all our efforts will succeed. But there are things which give me hope, and in conclusion I would like to mention them very briefly.

This place where I now stand is one of the oldest cities in the United States. It's a beautiful town of whose culture and urban charm all Americans are proud—just as the people of the Soviet Union are justly proud of such ancient cities as Tbilisi or Novgorod, which there they lovingly preserve, as you do in Charleston, and into which they infuse a new life that makes these cities far more than just dead remnants of a glorious historical past.

Although there are deep differences in our values and ideas, we Americans and Russians belong to the same civilization whose origins stretch back hundreds of years.

Beyond all the disagreements between us—and beyond the cool calculations of mutual self-interest that our two countries bring to the negotiating table—is the invisible human reality that must bring us closer together. I mean the yearning for peace, real peace, that is in the very bones of us all.

I'm absolutely certain that the people of the Soviet Union, who have suffered so grievously in war, feel this yearning for peace. And in this they are at one with the people of the United States. It's up to all of us to help make that unspoken passion into something more than just a dream. And that responsibility falls most heavily on those like you, of course, but particularly like President Brezhnev and me, who hold in our hands the terrible power conferred on us by the modern engines of war.

Mr. Brezhnev said something very interesting recently, and I quote from his speech: "It is our belief, our firm belief," he said, "that realism in politics and the will for détente and progress will ultimately triumph, and mankind will be able to step into the 21st century in conditions of peace, stable as never before."[12]

I see no hidden meaning in that. I credit its sincerity. And I express the same hope and belief that Mr. Brezhnev expressed. With all the difficulties, all the conflicts, I believe that our planet must finally obey the Biblical injunction to "follow after the things which make for peace."

Thank you very much.

(10) Maintaining Momentum in SALT: American-Soviet Discussions in Washington, September 22-23, 1977.

(a) Joint Communiqué Issued in Washington September 24, 1977.[13]

On September 22 and 23, 1977, talks were held in Washington between Jimmy Carter, President of the United States of America, and Cyrus Vance, Secretary of State of the United States of America, and Andrei A. Gromyko, Member of the Politburo of the Central Committee of the Communist Party of the Soviet Union and Minister of Foreign Affairs of the USSR.

A useful exchange of views took place on key questions of US-Soviet relations and on several international issues of interest to both sides.

Both sides expressed their desire for a constructive and stable development of relations between the United States and the Soviet Union, building on existing treaties and agreements. To this end, both sides consider it necessary to intensify their efforts to find mutually acceptable solutions to existing problems. Both sides agreed that such efforts, which can assure progress in various spheres of

[12]Speech at Kremlin reception for heads of diplomatic missions, July 8, in *Soviet News*, July 12, 1977: 252.
[13]Department of State Press Release 434, Sept. 24, 1977; text from *Bulletin*, 77: 643-4.

US-Soviet relations, serve the interests of their peoples as well as contributing to the strengthening of peace and the lessening of international tensions.

Both sides attach particular importance to the development and implementation of further measures aimed at the effective prevention of nuclear war and the limitation of armaments, thereby contributing to progress toward real disarmament.

In their discussions, the two sides focused on issues relating to the limitation of strategic arms, particularly those pertaining to the preparation of a new agreement on the limitation of strategic offensive arms. Progress was achieved in bringing closer together the positions of the two sides. However, there are still issues requiring agreement. They have issued additional statements on this subject.

Other specific arms limitations issues which are the subject of negotiations between the US and the USSR were also discussed: negotiations for a comprehensive ban on nuclear testing; the non-proliferation of nuclear weapons; the prohibition of chemical weapons; the prohibition of radiological and other new types and systems of mass destruction weapons; and questions relating to the Indian Ocean. The two sides noted the utility of the negotiations on these issues that have so far taken place and expressed their intention of continuing their active efforts to achieve practical results.

Both sides emphasized the great importance they attach to achieving real progress in the negotiations on the mutual reduction of forces and armaments in Central Europe in accordance with the agreed principle of undiminished security for all parties. They expressed their intention to continue efforts to achieve agreement.

The two sides also expressed their intention to work for a successful and constructive Belgrade meeting of representatives of states parties to the Conference on Security and Cooperation in Europe.

Pursuant to their previous discussions, the two sides reviewed the situation in the Middle East. The US and the USSR affirmed that they will continue their determined efforts to convene the Geneva Conference by the end of this year at the latest.

> (b) *Joint Statement by Secretary of State Vance and Soviet Foreign Minister Andrei A. Gromyko, Appended to the Joint Communiqué.*[14]

In discussions between Secretary Vance and Minister Gromyko on the questions related to strategic arms, both sides—the Soviet Union and the United States of America—have reaffirmed their de-

[14]Text from *Bulletin*, 77: 644.

termination to conclude a new agreement limiting strategic offensive arms and have declared their intention to continue active negotiations with a view to completing within the near future the work on that agreement.

The United States and the Soviet Union agree that the Treaty on the Limitation of Anti-Ballistic Missile Systems, signed in Moscow in 1972 and amended in 1974, serves the security interests of both countries. They share the view that this treaty decreases the risk of nuclear war and facilitates progress in the further limitation and reduction of strategic offensive arms. Both sides also agree that the ABM treaty has operated effectively, thus demonstrating the mutual commitment of the U.S.S.R. and the U.S.A. to the goal of nuclear arms limitations and to the principle of equal security.

Accordingly, in connection with the 5-year review of the ABM treaty, the two sides reaffirm their commitment to the treaty. It is agreed that this review will be conducted in the Standing Consultative Committee after its regular fall meeting.

(c) Observance of the Interim Agreement: Statement by Secretary of State Vance, September 23, 1977.[15]

In order to maintain the status quo while SALT II negotiations are being completed, the United States declares its intention not to take any action inconsistent with the provisions of the Interim Agreement on Certain Measures With Respect to the Limitation of Strategic Offensive Arms which expires October 3, 1977, and with the goals of these ongoing negotiations provided that the Soviet Union exercises similar restraint.[16]

(d) Status of the Interim Agreement: Statement by Ambassador Paul C. Warnke, Director of the United States Arms Control and Disarmament Agency, before the Committee on Foreign Relations, United States Senate, September 26, 1977.[17]

I appreciate the opportunity to appear before the committee today to discuss the expiration of the SALT I Interim Agreement on Certain Measures With Respect to the Limitation of Strategic Offensive Arms. The 1972 Interim Agreement expires on October 3,

[15]Text from *Bulletin*, 77: 642.
[16]Cf. Introduction at note 37.
[17]Text from *Bulletin*, 77: 632-3.

and it is clear that a SALT II agreement to replace it cannot be concluded by that date.

In recent days, there has been much discussion in the press about the Administration's plans with respect to this matter. On September 23, Secretary Vance issued a statement to the effect that, in order to maintain a stable situation while the SALT II negotiations are being completed, the United States intends not to take any action inconsistent with the Interim Agreement or the goals of the ongoing negotiations, provided that the Soviet Union exercises similar restraint. The Soviets have now issued a policy statement along the lines of our statement.

It should be noted that U.S. defense plans would not cause us to exceed any of the Interim Agreement limits in the near future, while the Soviets are in a position to do so because of their active ongoing SLBM[18] construction program.

We carefully considered what action should be taken in view of the fact that the October 3 date would pass before the completion of negotiations on a new agreement. In our deliberations, we concluded, after consultation with a number of Members of both the Senate and House, that an extension of the Interim Agreement would be inappropriate for two reasons:

—First, it would have reduced the pressure on the Soviet and on us to pursue a SALT II agreement based on equal aggregates of strategic offensive arms and

—Second, it would formally reaffirm acceptance of the disparity in numbers of strategic weapons established in the Interim Agreement.

Our policy statement is exactly what it says—a declaration of present intent. It is nonbinding and nonobligatory. The Interim Agreement will expire on October 3 and will not be extended; no agreement limiting strategic offensive arms will be in force after next Monday [October 3]. The United States will be free to change the policy announced in its statement of September 23 at any time.

Because our nonbinding statement is not part of an international agreement and does not impose any obligation on the United States, we have not requested congressional approval for it. We will carefully and continually monitor Soviet activities.

If these activities or any other circumstances warrant, we will be free to take whatever actions are appropriate, irrespective of the provisions set forth in the Interim Agreement.

We will, of course, continue to consult closely with members of this committee and other Members of Congress on the progress of SALT. We hope you will support our efforts in this regard.

[18]Submarine-launched ballistic missile.

(11) *Major Dimensions of Peace: Address by President Carter at the 32nd Regular Session of the United Nations General Assembly, New York, October 4, 1977.*[19]

Mr. President,[20] *Mr. Secretary General, assembled delegates, and distinguished guests:*

Mr. President, I wish to offer first my congratulations on your election as President of the 32d General Assembly. It gives my own Government particular satisfaction to work under the leadership of a representative from Yugoslavia, a nation with which the United States enjoys close and valued relations.

We pledge our cooperation and will depend heavily on your experience and skill in guiding these discussions which we are beginning.

Mr. President, I would also like to express again the high esteem in which we hold Secretary General Waldheim. We continue to benefit greatly from our close consultations with him, and we place great trust in his leadership of this organization.

Thirty-two years ago, in the cold dawn of the Atomic Age, this organization came into being. Its first and its most urgent purpose has been to secure peace for an exhausted and ravaged world.

Present conditions in some respects appear quite hopeful, yet the assurance of peace continues to elude us. Before the end of this century, a score of nations could possess nuclear weapons. If this should happen, the world that we leave our children will mock our own hopes for peace.

The level of nuclear armaments could grow by tens of thousands, and the same situation could well occur with advanced conventional weapons. The temptation to use these weapons, for fear that someone else might do it first, would be almost irresistible.

The ever-growing trade in conventional arms subverts international commerce from a force for peace to a caterer for war.

Violence, terrorism, assassination, undeclared wars all threaten to destroy the restraint and the moderation that must become the dominant characteristic of our age.

Unless we establish a code of international behavior in which the resort to violence becomes increasingly irrelevant to the pursuit of national interests, we will crush the world's dreams for human development and the full flowering of human freedom.

We have already become a global community, but only in the sense that we face common problems and we share for good or evil a common future. In this community, power to solve the world's problems, particularly economic and political power, no longer lies solely in the hands of a few nations.

[19]Text from *Presidential Documents*, 13: 1469-77.
[20]Lazar Mojsov.

Power is now widely shared among many nations with different cultures and different histories and different aspirations. The question is whether we will allow our differences to defeat us or whether we will work together to realize our common hopes for peace.

Today I want to address the major dimensions of peace and the role the United States intends to play in limiting and reducing all armaments, controlling nuclear technology, restricting the arms trade, and settling disputes by peaceful means.

When atomic weapons were used for the first time, Winston Churchill described the power of the atom as a revelation long, mercifully withheld from man. Since then we have learned in Dürrenmatt's chilling words that "what has once been thought can never be un-thought."

If we are to have any assurance that our children are to live out their lives in a world which satisfies our hope—or that they will have a chance to live at all—we must finally come to terms with this enormous nuclear force and turn it exclusively to beneficial ends.

Peace will not be assured until the weapons of war are finally put away. While we work toward that goal, nations will want sufficient arms to preserve their security.

The United States purpose is to insure peace. It is for that reason that our military posture and our alliances will remain as strong as necessary to deter attack. However, the security of the global community cannot forever rest on a balance of terror.

In the past, war has been accepted as the ultimate arbiter of disputes among nations. But in the nuclear era we can no longer think of war as merely a continuation of diplomacy by other means. Nuclear war cannot be measured by the archaic standards of victory or defeat.

This stark reality imposes on the United States and the Soviet Union an awesome and special responsibility. The United States is engaged, along with other nations, in a broad range of negotiations. In strategic arms limitation talks, we and the Soviets are within sight of a significant agreement in limiting the total numbers of weapons and in restricting certain categories of weapons of special concern to each of us. We can also start the crucial process of curbing the relentless march of technological development which makes nuclear weapons ever more difficult to control.

We must look beyond the present and work to prevent the critical threats and instabilities of the future. In the principles of self-restraint, reciprocity, and mutual accommodation of interests, if these are observed, then the United States and the Soviet Union will not only succeed in limiting weapons but will also create a foundation of better relations in other spheres of interest.

The United States is willing to go as far as possible, consistent with our security interest, in limiting and reducing our nuclear weapons. On a reciprocal basis we are willing now to reduce them by 10 percent or 20 percent, even 50 percent. Then we will work for further reductions to a world truly free of nuclear weapons.

The United States also recognizes a threat of continued testing of nuclear explosives.

Negotiations for a comprehensive ban on nuclear explosions are now being conducted by the United States, the United Kingdom, and the Soviet Union. As in other areas where vital national security interests are engaged, agreements must be verifiable and fair. They must be seen by all the parties as serving a longer term interest that justifies the restraints of the moment.

The longer term interest in this instance is to close one more avenue of nuclear competition and thereby demonstrate to all the world that the major nuclear powers take seriously our obligations to reduce the threat of nuclear catastrophe.

My country believes that the time has come to end all explosions of nuclear devices, no matter what their claimed justification, peaceful or military, and we appreciate the efforts of other nations to reach this same goal.

During the past 9 months, I have expressed the special importance that we attach to controlling nuclear proliferation. But I fear that many do not understand why the United States feels as it does.

Why is it so important to avoid the chance that 1 or 2 or 10 other nations might acquire 1 or 2 or 10 nuclear weapons of their own?

Let me try to explain why I deeply believe that this is one of the greatest challenges that we face in the next quarter of a century.

It's a truism that nuclear weapons are a powerful deterrent. They are a deterrent because they threaten. They could be used for terrorism or blackmail as well as for war. But they threaten not just the intended enemy, they threaten every nation, combatant or noncombatant alike. That is why all of us must be concerned.

Let me be frank. The existence of nuclear weapons in the United States and the Soviet Union, in Great Britain, France, and China, is something that we cannot undo except by the painstaking process of negotiation. But the existence of these weapons does not mean that other nations need to develop their own weapons any more than it provides a reason for those of us who have them to share them with others.

Rather, it imposes two solemn obligations on the nations which have the capacity to export nuclear fuel and nuclear technology— the obligations to meet legitimate energy needs and, in doing so, to insure that nothing that we export contributes directly or indirectly to the production of nuclear explosives. That is why the supplier nations are seeking a common policy, and that is why the United

States and the Soviet Union, even as we struggle to find common ground in the SALT talks, have already moved closer toward agreement and cooperation in our efforts to limit nuclear proliferation.

I believe that the London Suppliers Group must conclude its work as it's presently constituted so that the world security will be safeguarded from the pressures of commercial competition. We have learned it is not enough to safeguard just some facilities or some materials. Full-scope, comprehensive safeguards are necessary.

Two weeks from now in our own country, more than 30 supplier and consuming nations will convene for the International Fuel Cycle Evaluation, which we proposed last spring. For the next several years experts will work together on every facet of the nuclear fuel cycle.

The scientists and the policymakers of these nations will face a tremendous challenge. We know that by the year 2000, nuclear power reactors could be producing enough plutonium to make tens of thousands of bombs every year.

I believe from my own personal knowledge of this issue that there are ways to solve the problems that we face. I believe that there are alternative fuel cycles that can be managed safely on a global basis. I hope, therefore, that the International Fuel Cycle Evaluation will have the support and the encouragement of every nation.

I've heard it said that efforts to control nuclear proliferation are futile, that the genie is already out of the bottle. I do not believe this to be true. It should not be forgotten that for 25 years the nuclear club did not expand its membership. By genuine cooperation, we can make certain that this terrible club expands no further.

Now, I've talked about the special problems of nuclear arms control and nuclear proliferation at length. Let me turn to the problem of conventional arms control, which affects potentially or directly every nation represented in this great hall. This is not a matter for the future, even the near future, but of the immediate present. Worldwide military expenditures are now in the neighborhood of $300 billion a year.

Last year the nations of the world spent more than 60 times as much—60 times as much—equipping each soldier as we spent educating each child. The industrial nations spent the most money, but the rate of growth in military spending is faster in the developing world.

While only a handful of states produce sophisticated weapons, the number of nations which seek to purchase these weapons is expanding rapidly.

The conventional arms race both causes and feeds on the threat of larger and more deadly wars. It levies an enormous burden on an already troubled world economy.

For our part, the United States has now begun to reduce its arms exports. Our aim is to reduce both the quantity and the deadliness of the weapons that we sell. We have already taken the first few steps, but we cannot go very far alone. Nations whose neighbors are purchasing large quantities of arms feel constrained to do the same. Supplier nations who practice restraint in arms sales sometimes find that they simply lose valuable commercial markets to other suppliers.

We hope to work with other supplier nations to cut back on the flow of arms and to reduce the rate at which the most advanced and sophisticated weapon technologies spread around the world. We do not expect this task to be easy or to produce instant results. But we are committed to stop the spiral of increasing sale of weapons.

Equally important, we hope that purchaser nations, individually and through regional organizations, will limit their arms imports. We are ready to provide to some nations the necessary means for legitimate self-defense, but we are also eager to work with any nation or region in order to decrease the need for more numerous, more deadly, and ever more expensive weapons.

Fourteen years ago one of my predecessors spoke in this very room under circumstances that in certain ways resembled these. It was a time, he said of comparative calm, and there was an atmosphere of rising hope about the prospect of controlling nuclear energy.[21]

The first specific step had been taken to limit the nuclear arms race—a test ban treaty signed by nearly a hundred nations.

But the succeeding years did not live up to the optimistic prospect John F. Kennedy placed before this assembly, because as a community of nations, we failed to address the deepest sources of potential conflict among us.

As we seek to establish the principles of détente among the major nuclear powers, we believe that these principles must also apply in regional conflicts.

The United States is committed to the peaceful settlement of differences. We are committed to the strengthening of the peacemaking capabilities of the United Nations and regional organizations, such as the Organization of African Unity and the Organization of American States.

The United States supports Great Britain's efforts to bring about a peaceful, rapid transition to majority rule and independence in Zimbabwe. We have joined other members of the Security Council last week and also the Secretary General in efforts to bring about independence and democratic rule in Namibia. We are pleased with the level of cooperation that we have achieved with the leaders of

---

[21]President Kennedy's address, Sept. 20, 1963, in *Documents, 1963:* 440.

the nations in the area, as well as those people who are struggling for independence.

We urge South Africa and other nations to support the proposed solution to the problems in Zimbabwe and to cooperate still more closely in providing for a smooth and prompt transition in Namibia. But it is essential that all outside nations exercise restraint in their actions in Zimbabwe and Namibia so that we can bring about this majority rule and avoid a widening war that could engulf the southern half of the African Continent.

Of all the regional conflicts in the world, none holds more menace than the Middle East. War there has already carried the world to the edge of nuclear confrontation. It has already disrupted the world economy and imposed severe hardships on the people in the developed and the developing nations alike.

So, true peace—peace embodied in binding treaties—is essential. It will be in the interest of the Israelis and the Arabs. It is in the interest of the American people. It is in the interest of the entire world.

The United Nations Security Council has provided the basis for peace in Resolutions 242 and 338, but negotiations in good faith by all parties is needed to give substance to peace.

Such good faith negotiations must be inspired by a recognition that all nations in the area—Israel and the Arab countries—have a right to exist in peace, with early establishment of economic and cultural exchange and of normal diplomatic relations. Peace must include a process in which the bitter divisions of generations, even centuries, hatreds and suspicions can be overcome. Negotiations cannot be successful if any of the parties harbor the deceitful view that peace is simply an interlude in which to prepare for war.

Good faith negotiations will also require acceptance by all sides of the fundamental rights and interests of everyone involved.

For Israel this means borders that are recognized and secure. Security arrangements are crucial to a nation that has fought for its survival in each of the last four decades. The commitment of the United States to Israel's security is unquestionable.

For the Arabs, the legitimate rights of the Palestinian people must be recognized. One of the things that binds the American people to Israel is our shared respect for human rights and the courage with which Israel has defended such rights. It is clear that a true and lasting peace in the Middle East must also respect the rights of all peoples of the area. How these rights are to be defined and implemented is, of course, for the interested parties to decide in detailed negotiations and not for us to dictate.

We do not intend to impose, from the outside, a settlement on the nations of the Middle East.

The United States has been meeting with the foreign ministers of Israel and the Arab nations involved in the search for peace. We are staying in close contact with the Soviet Union, with whom we share responsibility for reconvening the Geneva conference.

As a result of these consultations, the Soviet Union and the United States have agreed to call for the resumption of the Geneva conference before the end of this year.

While a number of procedural questions remain, if the parties continue to act in good faith, I believe that these questions can be answered.

The major powers have a special responsibility to act with restraint in areas of the world where they have competing interests, because the association of these interests with local rivalries and conflicts can lead to serious confrontation.

In the Indian Ocean area, neither we nor the Soviet Union has a large military presence, nor is there a rapidly mounting competition between us.

Restraint in the area may well begin with a mutual effort to stabilize our presence and to avoid an escalation in military competition. Then both sides can consider how our military activities in the Indian Ocean, this whole area, might be even further reduced.

The peaceful settlement of differences is, of course, essential. The United States is willing to abide by that principle, as in the case of the recently signed Panama Canal treaties.[22] Once ratified, these treaties can transform the U.S.-Panama relationship into one that permanently protects the interests and respects the sovereignty of both our countries.

We have all survived and surmounted major challenges since the United Nations was founded. But we can accelerate progress even in a world of ever-increasing diversity.

A commitment to strengthen international institutions is vital. But progress lies also in our own national policies. We can work together to form a community of peace if we accept the kind of obligations that I have suggested today.

To summarize: first, an obligation to remove the threat of nuclear weaponry, to reverse the buildup of armaments and their trade, and to conclude bilateral and multilateral arms control agreements that can bring security to all of us. In order to reduce the reliance of nations on nuclear weaponry, I hereby solemnly declare on behalf of the United States that we will not use nuclear weapons except in self-defense; that is, in circumstances of an actual nuclear or conventional attack on the United States, our territories, or Armed Forces, or such an attack on our allies.

---

[22]Documents 38-39.

In addition, we hope that initiatives by the Western nations to secure mutual and balanced force reductions in Europe will be met by equal response from the Warsaw Pact countries.

Second, an obligation to show restraint in areas of tension, to negotiate disputes and settle them peacefully, and to strengthen peacemaking capabilities of the United Nations and regional organizations.

And finally, an effort by all nations, East as well as West, North as well as South, to fulfill mankind's aspirations for human development and human freedom. It is to meet these basic demands that we build governments and seek peace.

We must share these obligations for our own mutual survival and our own mutual prosperity.

We can see a world at peace. We can work for a world without want. We can build a global community dedicated to these purposes and to human dignity.

The view that I have sketched for you today is that of only one leader in only one nation. However wealthy and powerful the United States may be, however capable of leadership, this power is increasingly only relative. The leadership increasingly is in need of being shared.

No nation has a monopoly of vision, of creativity, or of ideas. Bringing these together from many nations is our common responsibility and our common challenge. For only in these ways can the idea of a peaceful global community grow and prosper.

Thank you very much.

(12) New Ways to Peaceful Atomic Power: Remarks by President Carter at the Organizing Conference of the International Nuclear Fuel Cycle Evaluation, October 21, 1977.[23]

About 25 years ago, I was a student doing graduate work in nuclear physics and reactor technology, not too many years after the first atomic weapons had been used to destroy human beings. My study was the peaceful use of this tremendous force, working under Admiral [Hyman D.] Rickover in the development of atomic submarine powerplants.

And now we've come to a time when we can look back with a clear historic perspective at what has transpired during this quarter century. It's a great honor for us to have you leaders come from, I believe, 36 nations and 3 international organizations to think back to 1945, to remember our own President Eisenhower's proposal

[23]Text from *Presidential Documents,* 13: 1566-8.

called Atoms for Peace,[24] part of which was adopted; the later establishment of the International Atomic Energy Agency which has provided for us, so far, a very effective mechanism by which explosions could be reduced and power could be produced.

We then went into a time of at least embryonic discussions of nuclear test bans, and now we have one that still permits the testing of weapons which have the equivalent of 150,000 tons of TNT.[25] Even this has been recognized as an achievement. And, of course, we are discussing with the Soviet Union means by which we can eliminate, sometime in the future, our dependence upon atomic weapons altogether. We've lived under a threat which so far has not yet been realized, and I pray that it never shall.

In the last 32 years, there have been no people killed by the use of atomic weapons. But with the rapidly increasing price of oil and the scarcity of fuel which we have taken for granted in years gone by, there's an increasing pressure for expanding atomic power use. And commensurate with that use is also the threat of the proliferation of nuclear explosives among nations that have forgone voluntarily that opportunity up until now.

We have seen regional actions taken in the southern part of this hemisphere. The Treaty of Tlatelolco is now being ratified by the last nations,[26] we hope, to prevent the deployment of any atomic explosions—or explosives in that part of the world. We hope that this will prevail in many other parts of the world.

We've also seen progress made recently between ourselves and the Soviet Union. We are eager to see drastic reductions in the deployment of nuclear weapons. And we are now negotiating with the Soviet Union and with Great Britain for a complete elimination of the testing of atomic explosions.

At the same time, the challenge presents itself to this group and to me, as one of the world leaders, to find a means by which the consuming nations who need atomic power to produce electricity and to serve peaceful purposes—to draw a distinction between that need, which is legitimate, and the threat of the development of atomic explosions themselves.

I have a feeling that the need for atomic power itself for peaceful uses has perhaps been greatly exaggerated. And I hope that all the nations represented here and others will assess alternatives to turning to this source of power if for no other reason than because of economic considerations.

Recent studies that I have read show that we can gain the equiva-

---

[24]Address of December 8, 1953 in *Documents, 1953:* 45-52.

[25]Cf. Introduction following note 20.

[26]Cf. Introduction at note 116.

lent of a barrel of oil per day by conservation measures at very little or any cost, often zero cost or up to $3,500. North Sea oil costs capital investment about $10,000 for every barrel of oil per day derived from that source.Our own Alaskan oil will cost $20,000 in capital investment for every barrel of oil per day, or its equivalent derived at the ultimate site of use. And for the equivalent of a barrel of oil per day at the end use site for atomic power, the capital investment is between $200,000 and $300,000.

So, there's a tremendous cost even for the potential peaceful use of atomic power. Even so, we recognize that there will be a need, and we are eager to cooperate.

It's important that we understand your problems; that those nations that supply enriched uranium—ourselves, the Canadians, others—those who have major deposits of uranium ore that have presently not been exploited, like Australia, understand the need of nations that are not well blessed with uranium fuel supplies. It's important that you understand from those of us who unfortunately are nuclear weapon nations, our special commitment to reducing this threat.

I believe that in this brief session that you will have this week, followed by weeks and months of tedious, I'm sure, argumentative but productive discussions and debates, that common knowledge will benefit us all.

It's important that we combine our ingenuity, our foresight, our own experience, our research and development efforts, so that we don't duplicate the very expensive efforts to use atomic power in a useful way. And this exchange of ideas among us will be very helpful.

It's important that we know what potential nuclear fuel cycles are available to us, the quantity and the location of uranium and thorium and other nuclear fuels, the methods used for extraction, the methods used and the costs for enrichment, possible distribution systems, the proper design and use, standardization of powerplants, safety of people who live near them, proper siting considerations, the political objections to atomic powerplants themselves, the possible need for breeder reactors, the handling of spent fuel, the need or absence of a need for reprocessing the spent fuel, and international safeguards that will prevent the development of explosives.

We are eager to cooperate as a nation which is a consumer and also a supplier. We want to be sure that where there is a legitimate need and where there's a mutually agreed upon nonproliferation restraint, that there be an adequate supply of nuclear fuel.

I think an international fuel bank should be established, so that if there is a temporary breakdown in the bilateral supply of nuclear fuel, that there might be a reservoir of fuel to be supplied under those circumstances. And we'll certainly contribute our own technical ability and our own portion of the enriched uranium supplies for that purpose.

We are very eager, also, to help solve the problem of the disposal of spent nuclear fuel itself. We can't provide storage for the major portion of the world's spent fuel, but we are willing to cooperate. And when a nation demonstrates to us your need for spent nuclear fuel storage, we hope to be prepared to accept that responsibility, working closely with you.

All the costs of the nuclear fuel cycle should be accurately known, as well as possible. And there should be an openminded approach to this very controversial and very difficult subject.

I hope, as the President of our country, to learn from you, and I will welcome your advice and your counsel. I welcome your caution and, on occasion, your criticism about American policies. And I believe that we'll find a common ground on which we can work together in harmony to make sure that our people do have a better quality of life, that alternate fuel supplies are evolved in an effective and adequate way, that energy is conserved to an optimum degree, and that the threat of nuclear destruction is minimized.

I want to congratulate all of you on being willing to come here to meet together, because there has been an inclination to avoid controversy. This question is inherently controversial. The interests on occasion are highly divergent, and many of these matters have not been discussed adequately in the past.

I'm very grateful that the International Atomic Energy Agency is here because there is no conflict between this effort and the tremendous contribution that that Agency has been making and will make in the future.

We want to do everything we can to strengthen the safeguard system aleady established. And if there is a recommendation from this group that the functions of the International Atomic Energy Agency should be expanded, we will certainly be willing to contribute our own financial and other support to make that possible.

In closing, let me thank you for being willing to participate in this international discussion. I am very eager to study your own debates and derive information from you. We will cooperate in every possible way that we can to give our people of the world adequate power sources and, at the same time, to keep their lives from being endangered.

Thank you very much.

3. EAST-WEST RELATIONS AND DÉTENTE IN EUROPE

(13) Four-Power Summit in London: Declaration on Berlin, Issued by the Heads of State and Government of France, the United States, the United Kingdom, and the Federal Republic of Germany, May 9, 1977.[1]

The four heads of state and of government of France, the United States, the United Kingdom and the FRG[2] have reviewed questions relating to the situation in Germany and particularly Berlin.

The four governments expressed their satisfaction at the positive effect which the Quadripartite Agreement of 3 September 1971[3] has had on the situation in and around Berlin. They agreed that the strict observance and full implementation of the Agreement, which are indispensable to the continued improvement of the situation, are essential to the strengthening of detente, the maintenance of security and the development of cooperation throughout Europe. The governments of France, the United States and the United Kingdom noted that detente would be seriously threatened if any one of the four signatory powers to the Quadripartite Agreement were not to respect fully the undertakings confirmed by the signatory powers in the Agreement and in the Quadripartite Declaration of November 1972.[4]

The three Powers recalled that the Quadripartite Agreement was based explicitly on the fact that quadripartite rights and responsibilities and the corresponding wartime and post-war four Power agreements and decisions were not affected. They reaffirmed that this status of the special area of Berlin could not be modified unilaterally. The three Powers will continue to reject all attempts to put in question the rights and responsibilities which France, the United States, the United Kingdom and the Soviet Union retain relating to Germany as a whole and to all four sectors of Berlin.

[1] Text, as released at Geneva, from *Presidential Documents,* 13: 687.
[2] Respectively, President Giscard d'Estaing, President Carter, Prime Minister Callaghan, and Chancellor Schmidt.
[3] Excerpts in *AFR, 1971:* 166-8.
[4] Text in *AFR, 1972:* 176.

The four governments recalled that one of the essential elements in the Quadripartite Agreement is the affirmation that the ties between the Western Sectors of Berlin and the FRG should be maintained and developed in accordance with the relevant provisions of the Agreement. This conforms with the interests and wishes of the people directly concerned. In this regard, the three Powers took special note of efforts by the Federal Republic of Germany, taking into account the provisions of the Quadripartite Agreement relevant to its responsibilities for representing the interests of the Western Sectors of Berlin abroad, to enable the Western Sectors of Berlin to profit from the practical benefits of East-West relations.

The four governments pledged their cooperation in maintaining a political situation conducive to the vitality and prosperity of the Western Sectors of Berlin. The three Powers expressed their appreciation of the efforts of the Federal Republic of Germany and the Senat of Berlin to ensure that the Western Sectors remain an attractive place in which to invest and to work. They reaffirmed their commitment to the city's security, which is an indispensable prerequuisite for its economic and social development.

(14) Meeting of the North Atlantic Council, London, May 10-11, 1977.

(a) Remarks to the Council by President Carter, May 10, 1977.[5]

Introduction

Mr. President, Mr. Secretary General,[6] Excellencies, and Members of the Council:

We meet at an important time in the development of the international institutions on which our countries rely.

Here in London last week the leaders of seven nations and of the Commission of the European Communities pledged to join others in strengthening these institutions in the economic field.

Today and tomorrow this Council will discuss how to adapt the Alliance to meet the military and political challenges of the 1980's.

Taken together, these meetings should give new impetus to relations among our industrial democracies.

At the center of this effort must be strong ties between Europe

[5] Text from *Presidential Documents,* 13: 690-700. Certain interpolations in the President's as-prepared text as printed here are noted in news conference remarks, May 10, by Henry Owen, the President's Special Representative for Summit Preparations; text in same: 701.
[6] J.M.A.H. Luns (Netherlands).

and North America. In maintaining and strengthening these ties, my Administration will be guided by certain principles. Simply stated:

—We will continue to make the Alliance the heart of our foreign policy.

—We will remain a reliable and faithful ally.

—We will join with you to strengthen the Alliance— politically, economically and militarily.

—We will ask for and listen to the advice of our Allies. And we will give our views in return, candidly and as friends.

This effort rests on a strong foundation. The state of the Alliance is good. Its strategy and doctrine are solid. We derive added strength and new pride from the fact that all fifteen of our member countries are now democracies. Our Alliance is a pact for peace—*and* a pact for freedom.

The Alliance is even stronger because of solid progress toward Western European unification and the expanding role of the European Community in world affairs. The United States welcomes this development and will work closely with the Community.

Political

In the aftermath of World War II, the political imperatives were clear: to build the strength of the West and to deter Soviet aggression. Since then East-West relations have become far more complex. Managing them requires patience and skill.

Our approach to East-West relations must be guided both by a humane vision and by a sense of history. Our humane vision leads us to seek broad cooperation with Communist states for the good of mankind. Our sense of history teaches us that we and the Soviet Union will continue to compete. Yet if we manage this dual relationship properly, we can hope that cooperation will eventually overshadow competition, leading to an increasingly stable relationship between our countries and the Soviet Union.

The United States is now discussing with the Soviet Union ways to control strategic arms. By involving the Soviet Union in a continuing effort to reduce and eventually to eliminate nuclear weapons we hope not only to minimize the risks and costs of continuing arms competition but also to promote broader cooperation between our countries.

The Soviet Union has not yet accepted our proposals. But it has made clear that it wants an agreement. We will persevere in seeking an early and a genuine end to the arms race, through both a freeze on modernization of strategic weapons and substantial reductions in their number. And as we pursue this goal, we will continue to consult with you fully—not only to keep you informed but also to seek your views.

I hope that our countries can also reach agreement with the Soviet Union in limiting and reducing conventional forces. The United States strongly supports the efforts of the Alliance to gain an accord on mutual and balanced reduction of forces in Central Europe. That agreement should be based on parity in force levels through overall ceilings for the forces of NATO and the Warsaw Pact. The Soviet Union, by contrast, seeks to preserve the present conventional imbalance and to impose national force ceilings. I hope that these obstacles can be overcome. MBFR must be a means for achieving mutual security, not for gaining one-sided military advantage.

As we pursue arms control with the Soviet Union and the Warsaw Pact, we should also try to draw the nations of Eastern Europe into cooperative undertakings. Our aim is not to turn this region against the Soviet Union, but to enlarge the opportunities for all European countries to work together in meeting the challenges of modern society.

Next month delegates of 35 countries will confer in Belgrade to plan for a meeting to review progress since the Helsinki Final Act. The United States shares with you a desire to make this a useful and constructive meeting. We support a careful review of progress by *all* countries in implementing *all* parts of the Final Act. We approach these meetings in a spirit of cooperation, not of confrontation.

America's concern for human rights does not reflect a desire to impose our particular political or social arrangements on any other country. It is, rather, an expression of the most deeply felt values of the American people. We want the world to know where we stand. (We entertain no illusion that the concerns we express and the actions we take will bring rapid changes in the policies of other governments. But neither do we believe that world opinion is without effect.) We will continue to express our beliefs—not only because we must remain true to ourselves, but *also* because we are convinced that the building of a better world rests on each nation's clear expression of the values that have given meaning to its national life.

In all these tasks and others facing the Alliance, it is vital for us to work together—particularly through close consultation and cooperation with the North Atlantic Council. We do not need new institutions, only to make better use of one that has served us so well. To this end I pledge that the United States will share with the Council our views and intentions about the full range of issues affecting the Alliance.

The Council should also examine long-range problems, so as to make this consultation more effective. A special Alliance review of East-West relations, undertaken by the Council and drawing in national experts, could serve this end. Such a review might assess future trends in the Soviet Union, in Eastern Europe and in East-West relations, and analyze the implications of these trends for the Alliance. The United States is prepared to make a major contribution to this study, whose conclusions could be considered at the May 1978 NATO meeting.

Defense

Achieving our political goals depends on a credible defense and deterrent. The United States supports the existing strategy of flexible response and forward defense. We will continue to provide our share of the powerful forces adequate to fulfill this strategy. We will maintain an effective strategic deterrent, we will keep diverse and modern theatre nuclear forces in Europe, and we will maintain and improve conventional forces based here.

The threat facing the Alliance has grown steadily in recent years. The Soviet Union has achieved essential strategic nuclear equivalence. Its theatre nuclear forces have been strengthened. The Warsaw Pact's conventional forces in Europe emphasize an offensive posture. These forces are much stronger than needed for any defense purpose. Since 1965, new ground and air weapons have been introduced in most major categories: self-propelled artillery, mobile tactical missiles, mobile air defense guns, armored personnel carriers, tactical aircraft, and tanks. The pace of the Pact's buildup continues undiminished.

Let me make it clear that our first preference is for early agreement with the Soviet Union on mutual and balanced force reductions. Failing to reach this agreement, our military strength must be maintained.

The collective deterrent strength of our Alliance is effective. But it will only remain so if we work to improve it. The United States is prepared to make a major effort to this end—as Vice President Mondale told you in January—in the expectation that our Allies will do the same.

There have been real increases in allied defense spending. But difficult economic conditions set practical limits. We need to use limited resources wisely, particularly in strengthening conventional forces. To this end:

—We must combine, coordinate, and concert our national programs more effectively.

—We must find better ways to bring new technology into our armed forces.

—We must give higher priority to increasing the readiness of these forces.

To fulfill these goals, I hope our Defense Ministers, when they meet next week, will begin developing a long-term defense program to strengthen the Alliance's deterrence and defense in the 1980's. That program should help us make choices and set priorities. It should emphasize greater Alliance cooperation to ensure that our combined resources are used most effectively. It should take full advantage of work already done within the Alliance.

But plans are not enough. We must ensure that our Alliance has an adequate means for setting overall goals in defense, for measuring national performance against these goals, and for devising and carrying out joint programs. I propose that our Defense Ministers, working closely with the Secretary General, consider how best to strengthen the Alliance's ability actually to fulfill agreed programs.

After an interim report to the December 1977 meeting, I hope the Defense Ministers will submit their program to the Spring Meeting which might be held at the Summit to review their recommendations. I also hope the Defense administrators will agree next week to make high priority improvements in the capabilities of our forces over the next year.

As we strengthen our forces, we should also improve cooperation in development, production and procurement of Alliance defense equipment. The Alliance should not be weakened *militarily* by waste and overlapping. Nor should it be weakened *politically* by disputes over where to buy defense equipment.

In each of our countries, economic and political factors pose serious obstacles. None of our countries, the United States included, has been free from fault. We must make a major effort—to eliminate waste and duplication between national programs; to provide each of our countries an opportunity to develop, produce and sell competitive defense equipment; and to maintain technological excellence in all Allied combat forces. To reach these goals our countries will need to do three things:

First, the United States must be willing to promote a genuinely two-way trans-Atlantic trade in defense equipment. My Administration's decisions about the development, production and procurement of defense equipment will be taken with careful attention to the interests of all members of the Alliance. I have instructed the Secretary of Defense to seek increased opportunities to buy European defense equipment where this would mean more efficient use of Allied resources. I will work with the Congress of the United States to this end.

Second, I hope the European allies will continue to increase co-operation among themselves in defense production. I welcome the initiative taken by several of your countries in the European Program Group. A common European defense production effort would help to achieve economies of scale beyond the reach of national programs. A strengthened defense production base in Europe would enlarge the opportunities for two-way trans-Atlantic traffic in defense equipment, while adding to the overall capabilities of the Alliance.

Third, I hope that European and the North American members of the Alliance will join in exploring ways to improve cooperation in the development, production and procurement of defense equipment. This joint examination could involve the European Program Group as it gathers strength and cohesion. Some issues could be discussed in the North Atlantic Council. Whatever the forum, the United States is ready to participate in the way and at the pace that our allies wish. We are eager to join with you in trying to identify opportunities for joint development of new equipment and for increasing licensing or direct purchase of equipment that has already been developed. Together, we should look for ways to standardize our equipment and make sure it can be used by all allied forces. We should see if ways can be found to introduce into our discussions a voice that would speak for the common interests of the Alliance in offering advice about cooperation in defense equipment.

Conclusion

To conclude:

It is not enough for us to share common purposes; we must also strengthen the institutions that fulfill those purposes. We are met today to renew our dedication to one of the most important of those institutions, and to plan for actions that will help it to meet new challenges. Some of these actions can be taken in the near future. Others can be developed for review at our meeting next year at this time. I would be glad to offer Washington as the site of that meeting.

The French writer and aviator, Saint-Exupery, wrote that "the noblest task of mankind is to unite mankind." In that spirit, I am confident that we will succeed.

(b) *Communiqué Issued at the Conclusion of the Meeting.*[7]

The North Atlantic Council met in London on 10th and 11th

[7]Department of State Press Release 212, May 13; text from *Bulletin*, 76: 601-2.

May, 1977 with the participation of heads of State and Government.

The essential purpose of the Alliance is to safeguard the independence and security of its members, enabling them to promote the values of democracy and respect for human rights, individual freedom, justice and social progress, and to make possible the creation of a lasting state of peace. The Allies are firmly resolved to maintain and enhance the effectiveness of the Alliance and the ties which unite them.

Although there have been some improvements in East-West relations in recent years, elements of instability and uncertainty persist. Of particular concern is the continuing growth in the strength of offensive capabilities of the Armed Forces of the Warsaw Pact countries. In these circumstances, the Allies emphasize the need for the Alliance to maintain at an adequate level the forces required for the common defense and for deterrence. They are resolved to strengthen their mutual support efforts and cooperation.

The Allies are determined to cooperate closely in all aspects of defense production. Their aims are to achieve the most effective use of available resources and to preserve and promote the strong industrial and technological capability which is essential for the defense of the Alliance and to develop a more balanced relationship between European and North American members of the Alliance in the procurement of defense equipment. The means of deepening this cooperation should be reviewed in appropriate fora.

Leaders of states taking part in the integrated defense structure of the Alliance requested their Defense Ministers to initiate and develop a long-term program to enable NATO forces to meet the changing defense needs of the 1980s and to review the manner in which the Alliance implements its defense programs to ensure more effective follow-through.

At the same time, the Allies reaffirm their conviction that security in Europe and in the world, without which detente could not produce its beneficial effects, cannot be achieved by statements of intent, but requires concrete efforts to reduce the level of armaments through realistic measures of disarmament and arms control. They will continue to move towards this goal in a manner consistent with Allied security, while recognizing that progress also depends on a constructive attitude on the part of the Soviet Union and East European states.

The Allies warmly welcome the efforts of the United States to negotiate with the Soviet Union an agreement to limit and reduce strategic arms which takes into account Allied interests.

With respect to MBFR, the participating Allies emphasize the importance they attach to these negotiations, the goal of which is to contribute to a more stable relationship and to the strengthening of peace and security in Europe. They call for a positive response to the additional offer they made to the Warsaw Pact countries in December 1975,[8] and reaffirm their overall objective of establishing approximate parity in ground forces in the form of a common collective ceiling for ground force manpower and the reduction of the disparity in tanks, which would ensure undiminished security at a lower level of forces.

The collective security ensured by the Alliance, in addition to enhancing global stability, provides the strength and confidence that enable the member countries to persevere in their efforts to lessen the tensions between East and West and to increase progressively the areas of cooperation. In this connection the Allied leaders requested the Council in permanent session to make a fresh study of long-term trends in East-West relations and to assess their implications for the Alliance. Improvement in East-West relations will depend on the extent to which all concerned show moderation and self restraint both in Europe and in other parts of the world. With regard to Berlin and Germany as a whole, the other allies fully associated themselves with the views expressed by the heads of States and the Governments of the United States, the United Kingdom, France and the Federal Republic of Germany in their statement of 9th May, 1977, and noted in particular that the strict observance and full implementation of the Quadripartite Agreement of 3rd September, 1971 are essential to the strengthening the[9] detente, the maintenance of security and the development of cooperation throughout Europe.

The Allies stress the great importance they attach to the implementation by the CSCE signatory states of all the provisions of the Helsinki Final Act. There has been limited progress in certain fields. While welcoming this, the Allies emphasize that much still remains to be done if the potential of the Final Act is to be realized both in terms of inter-state relations and in the lives of the inhabitants of all the countries concerned. The forthcoming Belgrade meeting will provide a useful opportunity for a thorough review of the implementation of the Final Act, and for an exchange of views on ways of developing the process of detente in the future. At that meeting the Allies will work for a constructive outcome which will promote better relations between the participating States and be beneficial to all their peoples.

The Allies recognize as wholly legitimate the aspirations of people throughout the world to human rights and fundamental freedoms. They are convinced that respect for these rights and freedoms, in accordance with the commitments accepted by governments in the Charter of the United Nations and in other interna-

[8]Cf. *AFR, 1975:* 554.
[9]Other official texts omit "the."

tional documents including the Helsinki Final Act, is essential for peace, friendship and cooperation among nations.

The Allied leaders reaffirm their support for an equitable world system in which all countries, developing as well as developed, will see their best interests served and which can sustain the economic progress of all. They intend to mobilize their efforts towards the attainment of that objective, in the appropriate fora. They invite the Warsaw Pact countries to do the same.

Recognizing the vitality and vigor shown by the Alliance over the years, the Allied leaders reaffirm their determination to maintain and strengthen their close association and cohesion within the framework of the North Atlantic Treaty. On that firm foundation they will persevere in the task of building a more just and peaceful world.

(15) A Post-Summit Survey: Statement by Arthur A. Hartman, Assistant Secretary of State for European Affairs, before the Subcommittee on Europe and the Middle East of the Committee on International Relations, House of Representatives, May 23, 1977.[10]

U.S. policy toward Europe and Canada is a compound of continuity and change: Continued commitment to our traditional responsibilities and enhanced impetus to new directions necessary to meet the common challenges of the next decade.

Our increased emphasis on human rights, on curbing nuclear proliferation, and on reducing arms transfers to volatile areas is set in a context of commitment to the Atlantic alliance; of ongoing support for European integration and the European Community; of a close relationship with our northern neighbor, Canada; of the assurance of military security vis-a-vis the Soviet Union, combined with realistic measures to reduce East-West tension; and of a determination to treat the countries of Eastern Europe as independent and sovereign entities.

The three summit meetings in London this month dramatically underscored both our traditional commitments and our new directions. The unity and strength of NATO remain critical. President Carter, during the summit meetings in London two weeks ago, pledged our commitment to preserving that unity and enhancing that strength. He did so by asserting that:[11]

—We will continue to make the alliance the heart of our foreign policy.

[10]Text from *Bulletin,* 76: 635-9.
[11]Document 14a.

—We will remain a reliable and faithful ally.

—We will join with (our allies) to strengthen the alliance—politically, economically, and militarily.

—We will ask for and listen to the advice of our allies. And we will give our views in return, candidly and as friends.

The President's attendance at a NATO session on his first foreign trip demonstrates our commitment to alliance unity. Vice President Mondale's trip to Brussels to address the NATO Council only 39 hours after the inauguration underlined the same commitment.

Our commitment to join in strengthening the alliance has already been proven by the increased defense contribution to NATO in the President's first budget—over one-half billion dollars. The President has also reconfirmed our commitment to a strategy of flexible response and forward defense. To achieve the necessary strength to apply this strategy, however, all the allies must develop and modernize their forces, as well as promote efficiency by eliminating waste and duplication.

To do this, the President has proposed that NATO develop a long-term defense program for the 1980's. This program should combine, coordinate, and concert national programs; introduce new technology; and give higher priority to increasing force readiness. The NATO summit meeting enthusiastically endorsed this approach, and NATO defense ministers have already initiated follow-up work.

Finally, the President has proposed, and NATO has agreed to, a major review of East-West relations and an analysis of what these trends mean for the alliance. This study and our continuing consultations with our allies on a broad range of issues should help us forge that unity of purpose and political will that strengthens our NATO ties.

In his speech at the NATO summit, the President also expressed strong U.S. support for progress toward Western European unification and the expanding role of the European Community in world affairs and added that we will work closely with the Community. This does not mean, of course, that there will not be problems between us. In particular, it will be important to preserve the fluid transAtlantic trading relationship which has been of overall benefit both to the U.S. and to the European economies. Nor does the President's statement mean that the United States should seek to determine the character and the pace of the unification process. That is for the Europeans themselves to determine. But we are glad to give our wholehearted support to the unification process, as every U.S. Administration has done since the end of World War II.

President Carter remarked in London that for the first time all the members of the alliance are democracies. We are particularly gratified at the democratic progress in Spain and Portugal. Our continued support—and that of other friends and allies—for this progress will be necessary. The United States has taken the lead in a multilateral lending program to provide balance-of-payments assistance to the greatly strained Portuguese economy. In three weeks Spain will have its first democratic election in over four decades. Both Vice President Mondale and Secretary Vance, in their recent visits, have emphasized U.S. support for the process of democratization and for all the genuinely democratic forces in Spain.

Problems in the Eastern Mediterranean

Elsewhere in Western Europe there are serious problems affecting U.S. interests. Instability in the eastern Mediterranean is reflected in a triple problem: a Cyprus problem, an Aegean problem, and a NATO problem.

The Administration is committed to doing everything it possibly can to advance the cause of a just solution to the Cyprus problem at the earliest possible date. We recognize that the gap in positions between the two Cyprus communities remains wide after the talks in Vienna last month. We think, however, that with time, good will, and hard work a settlement can be achieved. We think it important that the negotiations continue and concentrate on the two key issues of the future governmental structure for Cyprus and the territorial aspect of the problem.

The Aegean Sea involves complex questions of international law of the sea, but also strong mutual fears and suspicions on the part of Greece and Turkey. We have urged both sides on many occasions to avoid provocative actions, pursue a path of moderation, and attempt to negotiate their differences. Talks are going on, and we hope that progress can be made on such questions as the Continental Shelf and control of the airspace in the Aegean area.

We are also anxious to strengthen our bilateral and NATO relations with both Greece and Turkey. We think this can best be done through defense cooperation agreements with both countries. In the interim, until such agreements can enter into effect, we think the security assistance program presented by the Administration for 1978 is reasonable and is in the long-term interest of both countries, the United States, and NATO.

In much of Western Europe the slowness of the economic recovery has caused major economic difficulties and exacerbated political troubles. In a large sense, only the countries themselves can deal with the root causes of these difficulties. The United States and other major industrial countries can contribute to these efforts. And the pace of our own economic recovery will have an effect on recovery in Western Europe. The seven leaders at the London economic summit recognized that in each of our countries the most urgent task is to create more jobs while continuing to reduce inflation. The United States enthusiastically subscribes to the other objectives of the economic summit: To strengthen the open international trading system and give new impetus to the Tokyo round of multilateral trade negotiations; to conserve energy and reduce our dependence on oil; and to increase the flow of aid and other real resources to developing countries.

For the last 18 months representatives of the industrialized and developing countries have been meeting at the Conference on International Economic Cooperation (CIEC) in intensive discussion of the relations between rich and poor nations. The conference will conclude with a ministerial-level meeting, beginning May 30 in Paris, where we expect the two sides will agree on a set of realistic recommendations which will foster improved relations between the industrialized and developing countries.

Priority of East-West Relations

East-West relations remain a signal priority in our European policy. The mutually reinforcing dimensions of U.S. policy toward the East remain: (1) to prevent the Soviet Union from transforming its military power into political expansion or advantage and (2) to seek to resolve conflicts and disputes through negotiation while enhancing incentives for Soviet moderation.

In SALT, the United States has a unique challenge. We know that competition with the Soviets will continue, but we must seek ways to control and especially to reduce that competition. Given the strength of our own strategic programs, and Western technological superiority, we believe that Soviet interest in accommodation with us will continue to be strong. But nothing will produce Soviet concessions which in their view would damage their security interests. Thus we must find ways to limit competition equitably.

In addition, both we and certain of our European allies are engaged in MBFR talks in Vienna, where we wish to apply the same principles of parity and where we wish to achieve a collective ceiling that does not inhibit our ability to plan our force structure within that ceiling. In Secretary Vance's discussions in Moscow we underscored the need for serious examination of force data. We indicated that this is necessary if we are to achieve the understandings necessary to promote mutual security and to avoid one-sided military advantage. The President has pledged his support for these efforts.

The major objective of NATO's deterrent is of course to convince the Soviets that any aggression would be counterproductive. But we will need to show our concern for Soviet behavior beyond the shores and borders of the European Continent. We cannot be oblivious to Soviet activities in southern Africa, the Horn, and elsewhere in the Third World. As the President said at Notre Dame yesterday,[12] "We cannot have accommodation in one part of the world and the aggravation of conflicts in another."

It is worth pointing out that, despite the new opportunities in southern Africa which Moscow has sought to exploit, in most areas the Soviet record is not particularly inspiring. The new government in India appears anxious to return to a more balanced policy of nonalignment; and Sino-Soviet relations seem to be souring anew in the wake of Soviet efforts to improve relations with the post-Mao leadership in China.

We cannot realistically seek to exclude the Soviets from a role in areas where tensions exist, such as the Middle East. It is in our interest to encourage a responsible Soviet role in helping revive the negotiation process among the parties concerned, looking toward a peace settlement in the Middle East. We should also make every effort to insulate Third World situations from East-West competition and to seek a reduction of tensions of benefit to all.

The Administration believes that Western economic engagement in the Soviet Union and Eastern Europe should be an important aspect of our policy toward the East. We see both economic and political advantages to expanding our trade ties—economic because of the export surpluses we are able to create, political because in the long run a significant East-West economic relationship should contribute to a broader lessening of tensions. In view of the growth in East-West trade and, perhaps even more important, of the large debt which the Soviets and their allies have run up with Western creditors, it would seem logical for us to take a more coordinated look at the long-term implications of our economic relations with the East. President Carter's proposal for a NATO study of East-West relations, approved in London earlier this month, should be helpful in such a process.

Continuation of CSCE Process

Let me say a word about the U.S. approach to another major multilateral negotiation now underway in the East-West context in addition to the SALT talks and MBFR—the review of implementation of the CSCE understandings reached at Helsinki.

We strongly believe that the Helsinki Final Act has initiated a process which can prove very useful for Western objectives. This is a perception which was not widely accepted at the time. The U.S. Government begins from the premise that Western unity is all-important if we are to keep CSCE consistent with our own interests.

[12]Document 5.

And we strongly favor the Western approach approved at the NATO summit that emphasizes the importance of implementation of all the obligations undertaken two years ago at Helsinki. We need to remember that the CSCE process will be a useful one only insofar as it concentrates on the importance of specific obligations. If such a concentration requires some fairly frank talk with the Soviets and their allies, we will not shrink from that. We don't want to be confrontational, but we do want to be firm.

We are fully aware of the opportunities for growing contacts with Eastern Europe, as well as the Soviet Union, that CSCE provides. We think it is only natural that the countries of Eastern Europe, so many of which have strong traditional ties with Western Europe and with the United States, should revive and expand those ties. There is some concern that increased Western contacts with the countries of Eastern Europe would be destabilizing and should therefore be kept to a minimum. I believe this concern is exaggerated. To the degree that Eastern Europe is unstable, it is unstable because of the relationship between the Eastern European countries and the Soviet Union; the West had nothing to do with defining that relationship. Our attitude will continue to be based on a determination to treat the countries of Eastern Europe as independent and sovereign and to recognize no claim to spheres of influence or to hegemony. Naturally, the process of expanding ties can only proceed at a pace which the governments of Eastern Europe are willing and able to sustain. We envisage a gradual evolutionary process, but a commitment to that process is a fundamental one for the United States.

Conditions for Progress in Human Rights

I said at the outset that the new Administration brings new directions to our policies, and this is particularly true in the human rights area. An increased priority for human rights issues can contribute to the evolution of societies in a more moderate direction without endangering Western security objectives. At the NATO summit, the allies stressed the importance of promoting respect for human rights. In our view, our human rights policy is consistent with détente and not antithetical to it; indeed, it can contribute to the détente objectives we and our allies all seek.

President Carter and Secretary Vance have made clear that we recognize the limits which are imposed upon us. As the President said yesterday, we will not conduct our foreign policy by rigid moral maxims. In many cases we are dealing with societies which have a tradition of authoritarianism that goes back many decades, even centuries. We cannot hope for changes overnight, nor should we deflect our primary objective from the essential need to moderate the international, rather than the internal, behavior of states. We do not intend to meddle in matters which can properly be considered the internal affairs of states. But at the same time, no state which has signed the U.N. Declaration on Human Rights and the Helsinki Final Act can claim that the way they treat their own citizens is entirely their internal affair.

That being said, let me emphasize our conviction that in the long run progress in human rights in Europe is best achieved in conditions of détente. We are well aware that an approach which ignores this fact would not only imperil some of our major objectives of détente but also fail to improve the condition of the very people we are trying to help.

Mr. Chairman, let me make a final point about the East-West relationship. In the end, the military balance, our ability to reduce East-West political tension, and the ultimate success of our détente policies will depend on the degree to which the West can maintain its military strength, its economic health, and its democratic values. The ultimate challenge that is posed for us is not so much the challenge of a foreign threat; it is a challenge within ourselves and our societies.

There is some pessimism in Europe about our ability to get our economies moving and to preserve the viability of our democratic systems. The summits which have just taken place in London were above all an effort to show to ourselves and to our publics and legislatures that no matter how intricate the problems that crowd about us, we have the political will and the ability to deal with them. If we can master this type of challenge, then I have every confidence that we can manage the separate but related challenge that confronts us from the Eastern half of the continent.

The final words of the seven-nation summit communique were as follows:[13]

The message of the Downing Street Summit is thus one of confidence:

—in the continuing strength of our societies and the proven democratic principles that give them vitality;

—that we are undertaking the measures needed to overcome problems and achieve a more prosperous future.

President Carter voiced that same confidence in South Bend yesterday. Let me end by recalling his words:

It is a new world, but America should not fear it. It is a new world, and we should help to shape it. It is a new world that calls

[13]Document 48.

for a new American foreign policy—a policy based on constant decency in its values and on optimism in our historical vision.

(16)   Visits of Allied Leaders to Washington, July-September 1977.

(a)   Visit of Chancellor Helmut Schmidt of the Federal Republic of Germany: White House Statement Issued at the Conclusion of the Visit, July 14, 1977.[14]

President Carter and the Chancellor of the Federal Republic of Germany, Helmut Schmidt, held three lengthy conversations during the Chancellor's official visit to Washington, July 13–15. The Chancellor came to Washington at the President's invitation, and the President hosted a White House dinner for the Chancellor and his party on July 13. The three meetings between the President and the Chancellor covered a wide range of economic, political, and security issues in which the two nations share an interest. Those discussions followed on the meetings the President and Chancellor had in May at the London Summit. In addition to the two scheduled meetings on Wednesday and Thursday mornings, the President met privately with the Chancellor for about 1 hour Wednesday night following the state dinner.

The President and the Chancellor emphasized the closeness of the consultation between their two governments and their basic agreement on major issues. They expressed the belief that the small differences between their governments in recent months have often become exaggerated in public accounts, and they committed themselves to be in direct touch with one another in the future to make sure that exaggeration does not recur.

In their first meeting, the President and the Chancellor discussed the spectrum of relations between East and West, focusing on SALT, other arms control negotiations, and the upcoming fall meeting in Belgrade of the Conference on Security and Cooperation in Europe. They also exchanged views on the situation in the Middle East and on how to move forward with international efforts to reduce the risk of nuclear proliferation, while still assuring all nations access to the nuclear energy they need. The President and the Chancellor also discussed the importance of basic human rights and its role in international affairs.

The second formal meeting between the two was devoted largely to MBFR and economic issues. The Germans presented some thoughts on MBFR, and the two sides exchanged views on how to move the negotiations forward. With regard to economic issues,

[14]Text from *Presidential Documents*, 13: 1005-6.

there was broad agreement. The Chancellor met on July 13 with Secretary Blumenthal, and the President emphasized satisfaction, in his second formal meeting with the Chancellor, at the Federal Republic's efforts to assure domestic economic growth and deal with current accounts surpluses. The two men agreed on the importance of economic stability to the political cohesion of the developed countries and to the prospects for progress in the dialog between the North and South. The President and the Chancellor also agreed on the need to move forward this year with international trade negotiations—expressing pleasure at the results of recent meetings between the President's Special Trade Representative, Robert Strauss, and the European Communities—to assure adequate international financing and to implement the commitments their countries and others undertook at the London Summit in May.

The Chancellor, who last visited the United States in July 1976 to celebrate the American Bicentennial, was accompanied by Mrs. Schmidt. His party also included leaders from German business, labor, and cultural life. At the conclusion of their last meeting, the Chancellor invited the President to visit Germany, and the President accepted in principle, indicating that he looked forward to a visit.

(b) Visit of Prime Minister Giulio Andreotti of Italy: White House Statement Issued at the Conclusion of the Visit, July 27, 1977.[15]

Italian Prime Minister Giulio Andreotti paid an official visit to Washington July 26–27 at the invitation of President Carter. He was accompanied by Foreign Minister Arnaldo Forlani. The President gave a White House dinner for the Prime Minister on July 26 and held two lengthy conversations with the Italian visitors. The talks between the President and the Prime Minister covered a wide range of political, economic, security, and cultural issues in which the two nations share an interest. These discussions were a follow-on to the meeting between the President and the Prime Minister in May at the London summit. The President and the Prime Minister expressed their intention to continue the process of close consultations between the two Governments and emphasized their basic agreement on major issues.

During their meetings, the President and the Prime Minister discussed East-West relations, focusing on SALT and other arms control negotiations; developments in Europe, with special reference to

[15]Text from *Presidential Documents,* 13: 1117-18.

the European Community; the situation in the Mediterranean and the Middle East; and the upcoming fall meeting in Belgrade of the Conference on Security and Cooperation in Europe. The President and the Prime Minister also discussed human rights and their role in international affairs, agreeing on the desirability of continuing to stress implementation of these universally accepted values as an important element in the process of détente.

The Prime Minister described the Italian situation in its various aspects. The President expressed appreciation for Italy's continued contribution to Western cooperation and Allied solidarity, and its commitment to democratic institutions.

The President and the Prime Minister discussed the economic difficulties that beset many of the industrialized democracies and pledged to work for common solutions. The two leaders agreed that the Andreotti government's economic program has moved the Italian economy toward greater stability, less inflation, and a more favorable balance of payments. They agreed on the need to persevere along the lines agreed with the IMF, as well as on the necessity of implementing the consensus reached at the London summit to adjust payments imbalances in a context of expanding trade and economic development.

The President and the Prime Minister devoted a major part of their talks to world energy problems. They affirmed their intention to enhance and reinvigorate cooperation through the International Energy Agency and, bilaterally, through the U.S.-Italy Energy Working Group to coordinate policies and assist one another in this area of great significance. In this connection, the President agreed to explore ways of meeting Italy's needs for assured supplies of natural uranium as well as financing of its nuclear power program. The two leaders discussed the special energy requirements and objectives which Italy shares with other major industrialized countries heavily dependent on imported fossil fuels. They expressed their hope that the International Nuclear Fuel Cycle Evaluation would contribute to their common objectives in the field of nuclear nonproliferation and to a satisfactory solution of the participating countries' needs for assured fuel. They also agreed to expand cooperation in energy conservation, in safe and environmentally sound operation of nuclear reactors, and in the development of new sources of energy—solar, bioconversion, geothermal, and others.

Recognizing the importance of historical ties of friendship, a common cultural heritage, and the contribution of millions of Americans of Italian descent to the intellectual, spiritual, and economic life of the United States, the President and the Prime Minister agreed that every effort should be made to increase the already significant exchanges between the two countries in the fields of education and culture.

They agreed in particular on the desirability of a new effort of reciprocal assistance, in which Italy would assist in the strengthening of Italian language and study programs in the United States, and the United States would assist in the strengthening of English language teaching and American studies programs in Italy.

The two leaders also placed high priority on a two-way expansion of student and scholarly exchange and expressed their support for efforts now underway to finance additional exchanges, through loan funds made available by the private sector in the two countries.

The President and the Prime Minister discussed other areas where future cooperation between the two countries could lead to immediate results of mutual benefit, including an agreement on defense procurement, and follow-up visits by cabinet-level officials of the two Governments in the next few months. These visits will give impetus to U.S.-Italian cooperation in the areas of defense; economic, financial, and investment relations; scientific and technological cooperation; and exchanges of information on administrative matters.

During the course of the visit, the two Governments also agreed to announce that the Chicago Symphony will perform in Milan in September 1978, in return for the participation in our Bicentennial celebration of the La Scala Opera Company. In addition, a major exhibit called "Pompeii A.D. 79" will tour the United States soon.

(c) Visit of Prime Minister Raymond Barre of France: White House Statement Issued at the Conclusion of the Visit, September 16, 1977.[16]

French Prime Minister Raymond Barre paid an official visit to Washington September 15–16 at the invitation of President Carter. The President gave a working dinner for Prime Minister Barre on September 15 and held two meetings with the Prime Minister and his party. Their talks covered the range of political, economic, and other issues of importance to the two Governments.

These issues included the Middle East, developments in southern Africa, East-West relations, security and disarmament, nuclear nonproliferation, human rights, and economic policy. The two leaders agreed that close U.S.-French consultations are important on these and other issues.

Following discussions at the seven-nation summit in London last May in which they had taken part, the President and the Prime Minister reviewed economic conditions, both worldwide and in their own countries. Prime Minister Barre noted the significant improvement in France's foreign trade account and described the

---

[16]Text from *Presidential Documents*, 13: 1363-4.

steps his government had taken to curb inflation, stimulate employment, and bring about conditions needed for sustained economic growth. President Carter reviewed the United States own economic prospects and expressed confidence that the U.S. economic recovery would continue into 1978.

President Carter emphasized the need to gain significant results in the multilateral trade negotiations in the near future. The Prime Minister stressed the importance of organized freedom of trade as a necessary condition for the orderly growth of that trade for the benefit of both developed and developing countries.

The President and the Prime Minister agreed on the importance of continued close consultation between the United States and France on international financial issues. The President said that the U.S. administration was seeking congressional authority for the United States to take part in the Supplementary Financing Facility (Witteveen facility),[17] to assure that International Monetary Fund resources are sufficient to meet current needs for official financing.

President Carter praised France's leadership in proposing and helping to sustain the North-South dialog between industrialized and developing nations. The two leaders agreed that the Conference on International Economic Cooperation, concluded last June in Paris, had produced a number of positive benefits. They committed their two Governments to continue working for a more open and just international economic system.

The President and the Prime Minister reviewed major defense and disarmament issues. President Carter affirmed the unequivocal commitment of the United States to the defense of Western Europe. He reviewed U.S. steps, in line with the program he announced at last May's London meeting of the North Atlantic Council, to strengthen American forces committed to the defense of Europe. Prime Minister Barre described France's major program to modernize and upgrade its armed forces. The two leaders agreed that these efforts and similar efforts by other allies are essential to maintain the Alliance's security into the next decade.

President Carter and Prime Minister Barre discussed current and projected disarmament talks, including SALT and the U.N. General Assembly's Special Session on Disarmament scheduled for 1978. President Carter said he is convinced that France, as a major power, can make a positive contribution both to the maintenance of allied security and to the search for a more secure and stable international order. He was most interested in Prime Minister Barre's comment on these issues and the indications given on the views that France intends to put forward in the field of disarmament.

---

[17]Cf. Introduction at note 171.

President Carter stated his appreciation for France's expressed willingness to participate in the International Fuel Cycle Evaluation, the opening conference of which is to occur next month, and noted that France's technological leadership in the field of nuclear energy makes its contribution particularly important. The President and the Prime Minister agreed that vigorous and imaginative measures are needed to develop nuclear energy while preventing any proliferation of nuclear weapons.

Prime Minister Barre explained the main features of the French energy conservation policy and stressed the vital importance of a rapid implementation of President Carter's energy program.

President Carter outlined U.S. policies on human rights. Prime Minister Barre emphasized that the concept of liberty and the rights of man will continue to inspire French foreign policy. The President and the Prime Minister discussed the Belgrade CSCE Review Conference. They agreed on the need for a thorough review of implementation of all aspects of the Helsinki Final Act, designed to promote further progress in each of these areas.

The President and the Prime Minister reviewed the situation in Africa. President Carter described U.S. steps to support the British effort to bring about a peaceful transition to majority rule in Rhodesia and expressed appreciation for French support. The two leaders agreed on the importance of progress toward social justice and majority rule in southern Africa. President Carter praised France's vital role in promoting economic development and political stability in Africa.

The two leaders also reviewed the situation in the Middle East and agreed on the importance of convening the Middle East Peace Conference.

Prime Minister Barre raised the subject of Concorde landing rights in the United States, emphasizing the importance of this issue to France. President Carter reiterated his support for a 16-month trial period for Concorde at Kennedy Airport and expressed the hope that this could be soon initiated. He also said that he would decide the future of landing rights at Dulles Airport in the very near future.

President Carter emphasized the vital importance of close cooperation between the United States and Europe. He expressed admiration for French leadership in resolving many international economic, social, political, and technological problems. Prime Minister Barre reiterated President Giscard d'Estaing's invitation to President Carter to visit France, and President Carter expressed the hope that he would soon be in a position to reply.[18]

---

[18] Cf. Introduction at note 206.

(17) Review Conference on European Security: First Part, Belgrade, October 4-December 22, 1977.

(a) Third Semiannual Report to the United States Commission on Security and Cooperation in Europe, January 1-December 1, 1977: Introduction.[19]

During this reporting period, the most significant development affecting implementation of commitments undertaken at the Conference on Security and Cooperation in Europe (CSCE) was the beginning on October 4 in Belgrade of the first CSCE follow-up meeting.

President Carter's appointment of the distinguished American jurist and diplomat, Arthur J. Goldberg, as Chairman of the US delegation and Ambassador-at-large for CSCE demonstrates the importance which the President attaches to the CSCE process and to the Belgrade meeting in particular. This meeting provides the first opportunity to conduct a full review of the understandings contained in the CSCE Final Act, signed by 35 heads of state at Helsinki in August 1975.[20] It also offers a forum to set forth clearly the President's personal commitment to a dialogue on humanitarian matters as one of the fundamental aspects of detente.

Ambassador Goldberg leads a delegation which includes all of the Congressional members of the CSCE Commission[21] as well as members of the Commission staff, a number of distinguished public members from business, academia, the labor movement and other walks of life, plus representatives of several government departments and agencies, including the Departments of State, Commerce and Defense.[22] In preparing for the Belgrade conference, the United States delegation called upon the resources of other government departments and, with the assistance of the CSCE Commission, heard the views of numerous private organizations whose interests are affected by provisions of the Final Act.

As a result, Ambassador Goldberg entered the Belgrade meeting with the broad support of the American people for his important task. On instructions approved personally by the President, all delegation members are working to assure that the Belgrade discussions result in an honest and candid review of areas where progress

[19]Text from U.S. Department of State, Bureau of Public Affairs, Office of Media Services, *Third Semiannual Report by the President to the Commission on Security and Cooperation in Europe, June 1, 1977-December 1, 1977* (Special Report No. 39; Washington: GPO, June 1977): 1-3.

[20]Text in *AFR, 1975:* 292-360.

[21]Established by Public Law 94-304, June 3, 1976.

[22]Members of the delegation are listed in Senate Report 95-773, May 2, 1978: 2.

has been made and of areas where greater efforts are needed, especially in the vital field of human rights.

The Administration shares the view expressed in the report issued by the CSCE Commission on the second anniversary of the Helsinki Summit that the Final Act offers significant potential for improvement of relations between East and West. We also agree that much of that potential is yet to be realized. The Belgrade meeting has offered a unique opportunity to give new impetus to the long-term process initiated with signature of the Final Act and to ensure that the great potential represented by this process is not left to dissipate.

The Belgrade meeting is a new venture in the history of East-West relations. It is not a negotiation as such, and it does not look toward a new agreement or to changes in the Helsinki Final Act. Its task is to conduct an exchange of views on experience gained during the past two years and to examine means of deepening cooperation in the future. The experience gained in the course of this exchange will be one of the most important results of the meeting. Based on this experience, the participants should be better able to pursue implementation both in their own countries and in their mutual relations in years to come.

The Belgrade meeting is still in progress as of December 1 and will be discussed fully in the next semiannual report.[23] However, during the first two months of discussions, Ambassador Goldberg and the United States delegation have established a position of leadership in promoting full and open discussion of the issues.

In his first address to the Belgrade meeting,[24] Ambassador Goldberg emphasized the strong US commitment to a thorough and detailed implementation review and stressed that improvement of political relations among CSCE participants could not be divorced from progress in humanitarian matters and human rights. While noting that all CSCE states should improve their implementation records, Ambassador Goldberg made clear that Eastern states have the farthest to go in fulfilling the commitments agreed upon at Helsinki. He stated that the US delegation would focus its efforts in a constructive manner on advancing what should be the noblest common goal of the Belgrade meeting: to give the process of detente a human measure and a humanitarian face.

The United States, together wtih the Western Allies and many of the neutral/nonaligned states, has since continued to pursue the

[23]Text in U.S. Department of State, Bureau of Public Affairs, Office of Public Communication, *Fourth Semiannual Report by the President to the Commission on Security and Cooperation in Europe, December 1, 1977-June 1, 1978* (Special Report No. 45; Washington: GPO, June 1978).
[24]Document 17b.

thorough and objective discussion mandated by the Final Act. We have used specific examples to illustrate areas where we believe improved implementation is needed, and we have rejected contentions that discussion of CSCE implementation can constitute interference in the internal affairs of other states. The issues raised thus far by the United States delegation span all three baskets of the Final Act and include for example:

—The repressive measures taken in some countries against human rights activists, and particularly against those individuals and groups whose activities relate solely to promoting the Final Act's goals and promises;

—The persistence of divided family cases and obstacles to the freer movement of peoples between Eastern and Western countries;

—The difficulties encountered in some Eastern countries by Western journalists and scholars seeking to engage in their professional activity;

—The difficulties encountered by national minorities and ethnic groups in seeking the rights acknowledged in Principles Seven and Eight of the Final Act, as well as continued denial in some countries of the religious freedoms endorsed by the CSCE;

—The slow progress of some countries in facilitating access to information necessary for expansion of East-West economic ties, and continued obstruction of informal contact and collaboration between Eastern and Western scientists;

—The continued jamming by a few Eastern countries of international radio broadcasts, despite the provisions of the Final Act which call for the freer exchange of information of all kinds; and

—The failure of some CSCE countries to abide by agreements in the delivery of ordinary and registered mail, despite Principle Ten of the Final Act which calls for fulfillment in good faith of obligations under international law.

While we believe that the Belgrade meeting must deal fully with all such problem issues, we realize as well that the process of implementation review is difficult and complex. The Helsinki Final Act sets forth broad commitments the fulfillment of which is primarily the responsibility of individual states, and it makes no provision for enforcement of the commitments or for agreement on how they should be construed. While all signatory states have formally accepted the commitments of the Final Act, there are real differences among them on how these commitments should be interpreted and put into practice. The United States recognizes that the CSCE is a long-term process and that the practices of many decades cannot all be changed in two years. We are therefore all the more determined to work patiently and steadfastly, for as long as may be required, to attain Helsinki's stated goals. As Secretary Vance stated in his testimony before the CSCE Commission on June 6, 1977: "The CSCE Final Act was approved by 35 heads of state and government after three years of intense negotiations. Undertakings of such gravity cannot subsequently be relaxed or overlooked."[25]

The implementation record currently being examined at Belgrade is mixed, with evidence for both optimism as well as concern. The broad principles of Basket One concerning relations among states continue to be better respected than those principles concerning relations between states and their peoples, though genuine security in Europe requires removal of the threat of arbitrary arrest or persecution no less than removal of the threat of war. The United States has always welcomed and will give serious consideration to all effective initiatives for control of the arms race, which is already the subject of a number of ongoing negotiations outside of the CSCE context. President Carter's call, made before the UN General Assembly in October,[26] for a 50 percent reduction in US and Soviet nuclear arsenals demonstrates our deep commitment to pursue not only arms limitations, but actual reductions of military forces and armaments. While we share with our Allies the belief that the CSCE is not the proper forum to address specific arms control measures, we are also confident that our serious and constructive approach at Belgrade to security issues will strengthen the climate of confidence in Europe and thereby contribute to the foundation necessary for arms reductions to take place.

In addition, however, the United States will pursue with vigor those Basket One provisions which relate to the security of individuals. By including human rights in the Final Act's Declaration of Principles, all the signatory states confirmed that respect for human rights is a legitimate subject for discussion among them, as indeed it has been at least since the UN Charter was written. We have legal and moral obligations to work for full implementation of the human rights principle and to review its past implementation at Belgrade.

In the Basket Two area, we discern some progress in economic and scientific cooperation, which reflects a positive continuation of processes begun before the Helsinki Summit. Certain problems persist, however, as for example the poor record of some countries in providing information vital to businessmen or the difficulty of private collaboration between scientists from East and West. These, also, are issues which the Belgrade meeting is examining in the hope that improvements and greater cooperation may ensue.

[25]*Bulletin*, 76: 670.
[26]Document 5.

The situation with respect to implementation of the humanitarian provisions of the Final Act is of particular concern to the many millions of people whose families and lives the East-West relationship affects. While some progress has been achieved since the Helsinki Summit, much more remains to be done. We will continue to discuss individual humanitarian cases with Eastern governments, both at Belgrade and elsewhere. Precisely because the Final Act is a balanced document that must be viewed as an integral whole, we must speak out when there are serious deficiencies in implementation of any section.

We continue to be prepared to discuss criticism of our own practices at Belgrade just as we have expected others to discuss in a constructive manner the views which we may voice about theirs. In the human rights area, we believe that the force of law and government policy in the United States is directed toward greater respect for the rights of the individual and toward the alleviation of abuses when such rights have not been fully observed. We are proud of our record, but we are also prepared to improve and do even more in all areas.

During the reporting period, for example, President Carter signed the UN covenants on human rights[27] specifically endorsed in the Final Act's Declaration of Principles. We have also taken measures, discussed in the following report, to allow travel to the United States by certain categories of people sometime excluded in the past for their political affiliation. Likewise, largely as a result of the CSCE and at the suggestion of the CSCE Commission, President Carter has agreed to appoint a panel to recommend ways of improving foreign area and language study in the United States.

The United States, with other nations, is also considering at Belgrade a number of new initiatives to enhance implementation of the Final Act by all participating states. While not in any way amending the Final Act, these undertakings should maintain momentum in the CSCE process and encourage the fulfillment of existing provisions. We are sponsoring or co-sponsoring several proposals at Belgrade which appear best-suited to these aims.

The following chapters provide a review of CSCE implementation over the past six months. The record shows some areas of progress together with some areas of inertia or even deterioration. As Ambassador Goldberg told the opening session of the Belgrade meeting, however: "In our work we will need patience, perseverence and perspective. This conference in Belgrade is one state of a dynamic process and a continuing dialogue . . . We are nearer the beginning rather than the end."

[27]Cf. Introduction at note 204.

(b) Statement by Ambassador Arthur J. Goldberg, Chairman of the United States Delegation, in Plenary Session, October 6, 1977.[28]

On behalf of the American delegation, permit me to express our sincere thanks to our hosts, the Government of Yugoslavia. We are more than grateful for the facilities and support they have so generously provided for the conduct of our work. It is particularly symbolic that this conference is held in a nation which has done so much for so long to promote security and cooperation in Europe.

Two years and two months ago the leaders of our 35 nations assembled in Helsinki to conclude—with their solemn approval—the Final Act of the Conference on Security and Cooperation in Europe (CSCE).

This week we are beginning in Belgrade a new phase of the process they initiated. We are embarking on a mutual examination of our experiences in implementing the Final Act. We are also seeking together new means of solidifying and building from the foundations laid in Helsinki.

Our task is part of a great and ancient enterprise: the search for security, the advance of cooperation in Europe. This conference is one more step toward that high goal, one part of the broader process of reducing risks of confrontation in Europe and of replacing them with opportunities for cooperation.

This meeting is both an expression and a result of considerable improvements in East-West relations. In turn, what we accomplish here in the coming months can have a direct impact on the further development of détente.

I have been designated by President Carter to speak here as the representative of the U.S. Secretary of State. I carry with me the President's deep, personal commitment to advance the goals of the Final Act and the work of which it is such an important element. He is dedicated to working constructively with all nations represented here to help fulfill the Final Act's commitment to improved European security and cooperation.

Two corollary principles make the Helsinki approach unique. One is our rule of consensus, the recognition that every nation should take part on an equal footing in decisions which affect the future of Europe. The second is also crucial: the tie, formalized by the Final Act, between the freedom and welfare of each of our nations and the freedom and welfare of each of our individual citizens.

Let me reaffirm in the most positive terms the wholehearted

[28]As-prepared text from *Bulletin*, 77: 674-9.

commitment of the U.S. Government to the pursuit of détente. Let me also restate our view that a deepening of détente, a healing of the divisions in Europe, cannot be divorced from progress in humanitarian matters and human rights. Rather, it can strengthen détente and provide a firmer basis for both security and cooperation.

The United States wants to build upon and enlarge the scope of East-West understanding, for my government is convinced that this conference in Belgrade must not be the end of the CSCE process. Rather, it must be an occasion to inject fresh momentum into that process. The true test of the work we do together lies not only in the conclusions we reach, it lies also in the higher goals we set and in the energy with which we set about meeting them.

My government will do its best to provide new impetus to the CSCE process, both here in Belgrade and in our overall policies toward Europe and the world.

—We will conduct the review of implementation on the basis of unity of all sections of the Final Act and the equal value of all the principles.

—We will make clear our intention to honor the political commitments in this document and to utilize fully the practical opportunities which it opens.

—We will discuss concrete problems of both past and future implementation.

—And we will conduct our policies in Europe fully aware of the fact that CSCE can only bear part of the burden for guarding the peace. There must also be progress in other efforts at détente; and the benefits of our efforts must be applied throughout Europe. Berlin, for example, remains a basic testing place of détente. This divided city must continue to receive the benefits of the Final Act. Berlin must prosper under the Quadripartite Agreement, free from crisis, if détente and CSCE are to succeed.

Just as the U.S. goal for Europe is one of peace, so at this conference we see[29] no confrontation. We have no desire to trade debating points. Instead, we want to exchange ideas on how better to implement the Final Act. We seek a thorough, nonpolemical, straightforward, and detailed review of implementation. And through that review, we seek to help formulate new measures which can give added concrete expression and momentum to the basic commitments of the Final Act.

General Assessment

The first obligation we all share is to conduct a candid review of

[29]Other official texts read "seek."

the promises each of us has made, the promises we have kept, and the promises we have yet to fulfill.

The assessment my country has made of the overall record of participating states over the last 26 months shows encouraging evidence of progress. But the progress displayed is not progress enough. It still falls short of the goals of the Final Act and, just as important, of the high expectations the Final Act aroused. Those expectations remain valid, and we must all be frank in judging that many of them remain unmet.

Let me comment first on what my own country has done to implement the Final Act. In general, the act codified standards which reflect American policy in dealing with other nations and with our own citizens. Nevertheless, in response to the Final Act, we have looked closely at our own behavior and—where we have the need and the means—have acted to improve our conduct. In particular, we took two steps regarding the Final Act pledge to "facilitate freer movement and contacts." First, President Carter this year removed all restrictions on travel abroad by American citizens. Second, with President Carter's support, Congress recently relaxed our visa requirements so that people wishing to visit the United States will not be excluded because of political affiliation or belief.

Moreover, in the field of human rights, President Carter on October 5 redeemed a pledge he gave last spring by signing the international covenants on human rights at the United Nations.[30] American adherence to those pacts has been a matter of personal concern to me and to many others for a decade.

The President is pledged to pursue ratification of the covenants. Meanwhile, his action yesterday is an earnest of our good faith and a proof of the positive impact the Final Act is having in the United States.

In the spheres of commercial, cultural, educational, and scientific exchanges, we have done much and have much yet to do. For example, the U.S. Government has made a special effort to inform our businessmen about provisions of the Final Act affecting their opportunities to enter and work in markets with which they have not always been sufficiently familiar. This year, we signed our first cultural, educational, and scientific cooperation agreements with Hungary and Bulgaria; and we concluded negotiations on a similar agreement with Czechoslovakia. With the Soviet Union, we renewed several scientific cooperation arrangements.

Meanwhile, in some other signatory nations, we have seen a well-intentioned and productive effort to implement the principles and provisions of the Final Act. In some nations in the East, advances have been only modest and are still far below the Final Act's stand-

---

[30]Cf. Introduction at note 204.

ards. And there are individual cases under the Final Act where forward motion has been stalled or even reversed.

Under the stimulus of the Final Act, some progress has been made in bettering relations among the participating states. The exchange of goods, knowledge, people, and ideas has expanded in some measure. Substantial obstacles do remain to travel and the flow of information between one part of Europe and another, but these have already diminished somewhat. This improvement can be seen simply in the numbers of people who have been able to leave old homes for the new ones in Europe, America, and Israel. These results mean real individual happiness, and we here must reaffirm our resolve to speed that development.

Likewise, in translating our shared political undertakings to the area of military security, the Final Act has brought another kind of exchange—promising but incomplete. Confidence-building measures, involving advance notification of maneuvers and exchange of observers have made openness a virtue in a field where secrecy was once instinctive. We have laid a foundation on which this meeting can productively build. Thus we can see some progress.

We can see it in terms of individuals and families reunited after being separated by war, accident, and history. But we must recall the many who remain apart.

We can see progress in business contacts that become business contracts. But we cannot overlook the still inadequate supply of relevant economic data on which the growth of business confidence depends.

We can see progress in books translated, performers applauded, students instructed, and scientific theories tested. But here, too, the openness and ease of contact promised at Helsinki has been only partly realized.

Thus, we cannot be satisfied with the record of implementation. The standard we have set together should be even higher, if the goals of the Final Act are to be realized.

Let me illustrate some area in which we in the United States feel old practices have not been changed sufficiently to meet the new imperatives of the Helsinki spirit.

In educational programs, it is not enough to increase the number of scholars involved; rather, a prerequisite for such an increase is improved freedom for scholars and their research. What value is there, for example, in financing a student's work abroad when for months he is denied admission to an essential archives and, when having finally been admitted one day, he is not permitted back the next—even to collect his notes?

Also, in seeking "to facilitate the freer and wider dissemination of information of all kinds," we cannot point convincingly to progress while international broadcasts are subjected to continuing interference.

Similarly, while steps have been taken to ease travel and working conditions for journalists, those advances are jeopardized when visas are made conditional on a correspondent's agreeing not to contact certain sources of information and opinion.

Finally, while real progress has been made in reuniting divided families and concluding binational marriages, satisfaction with those developments must be balanced by regret that many long-standing cases remain unresolved; that the resolution of routine cases is too often arbitrary and capricious; and that new bureaucratic obstacles are imposed on people seeking to join relatives abroad. This runs counter to the Helsinki promise "gradually to simplify" exit procedures. It is also hard to see the workings of the "positive and humanitarian spirit" when an ill and aged husband is denied, after long years of separation, the company of his nearly blind wife and their daughter.

Equally difficult to understand are broader restrictions on the right of individuals to travel or emigrate. That right is established in Article 13 of the Universal Declaration of Human Rights: "Everyone has the right to leave any country, including his own, and to return to his country." All of us have pledged in the Final Act to "act in conformity" with that Universal Declaration, and we have given specific emphasis to that promise in the Final Act's provisions on family reunification.

Human Rights and Detente

The 2 years since the Helsinki summit are particularly short when we set them against the historic divisions we are trying, through the Final Act, to bridge. Some of the deepest differences among the participating states lie in views on the status of the individual in relation to the state. The issue of human rights represents the widest gap between the ideals and practices of East and West. It is a sensitive subject on the international agenda, but one which *can* be dealt with in an understanding manner and one which *must* be discussed in order to facilitate further progress under the Final Act.

Precisely because the distance between our views on human rights is so great, we must all work to narrow the divide. This is not a simple process. In my own country, a mere 15 years ago, many Americans were denied the right to vote. But through commitment to an ideal and constant efforts to reach that ideal, this blemish on the American record was removed. Other serious blemishes remain and our efforts to remove them also remain constant. The process is inevitably a gradual one, but efforts like ours are what make progress in human rights possible under the Final Act.

In the United States, we also realize that human rights encompass economic and social rights, as well as political and civil liberties. It is our view that one set of values cannot be stressed at the expense of the other. Rather, it is the combination of these rights and the respect in which governments hold them all which offer the best promise that all can be attained.

Concern for these rights is not new either to Americans or to the other states taking part in this conference. It is enshrined in Article 1 of the Charter of the United Nations. It is enshrined in the Universal Declaration of Human Rights. And the Final Act, in Principle VII, binds all the participating states to ". . . recognize the universal significance of human rights and fundamental freedoms, respect for which is an essential factor for the peace, justice and well-being necessary to ensure the development of friendly relations and co-operation among themselves as among all States."

American policy—evolving from a history of political development with deep roots here in Europe and nurtured by the efforts of other nations—has long pursued that vision. It is explicit in our Bill of Rights. It animated the four freedoms proclaimed by President Franklin Roosevelt—freedom from want and fear, freedom of speech and religion—for which Americans last fought on this continent in the war against Fascism. It was also part of the heritage of President Kennedy when, 14 years ago, he launched a fresh initiative for world peace. He asked: ". . . is not peace, in the last analysis . . . a matter of human rights . . . ?"[31] And he proposed an ". . . agreement on a freer flow of information and people from East to West and West to East."[32]

When such an agreement was concluded in Helsinki as part of the Final Act, President Ford echoed his predecessor's words. He said: "The founders of my country did not merely say that all Americans should have these rights, but all men everywhere should have these rights."[33]

On many occasions this year, President Carter has set forth his own commitment to the continuity of American policy in the area of human rights—whether political, economic, social, or cultural. At the United Nations last March,[34] he stressed that:

> . . . the search for peace also means the search for justice . . .
> (and) the search for peace and justice means also respect for human dignity . . . I know perhaps as well as anyone that our own

[31]Address of June 10, 1963 in *Documents, 1963:* 123.
[32]Address before the U.N. General Assembly, Sept. 20, 1963 in same: 443.
[33]*AFR, 1975:* 289.
[34]Document 3.

ideals in the area of human rights have not always been attained in the United States. But the American people have an abiding commitment to the full realization of these ideals. And we are determined, therefore, to deal with our deficiencies quickly and openly.

It is in that same spirit that the U.S. delegation will speak about human rights and basic freedoms here in Belgrade. We have much to learn from that exchange of views.

Let me illustrate some of our concerns. The Principle VII guarantee of religion and belief means to us that expression of faith must not be penalized by loss of[35] reduction of educational or career opportunities. People should be free to worship without fear [of] state interference in their choice of ministers, literature, and houses of prayer.

Similarly, the "freedom of thought and conscience" we have all pledged to respect must have breathing space in which to flourish. Its expression should not be censored. Its exponents should not be imprisoned or exiled for making their thoughts known.

Moreover, the "legitimate interests" of "national minorities" in our 35 states require respect for unique cultural and linguistic heritages and active policies to preserve these traditions and achievements for future generations.

Our governments have assumed the responsibility to "promote and encourage the effective exercise" of these rights. And in Principle VII we subscribed to "the right of the individual to know and act upon his rights and duties" in the field of human rights. The response of citizens to that challenge, alone and in private or public groupings in many signatory states, has been heartening evidence of the Final Act's healthy impact on all of us. In my own country, we have benefitted by the dedication, candor, and commitment of our [joint congressional] Commission on Security and Cooperation [in] Europe. Its valuable work will be reflected in what we do here in Belgrade; and we are honored by having its members as part of our delegation.

All the more, then, we are also obliged to register vigorous disapproval of repressive measures taken in any country against individuals and private groups whose activities relate solely to promoting the Final Act's goals and promises.

Any such repression is contrary to the spirit and the letter of our common pledge. Rather, at this meeting, we should all reaffirm the valuable role to be played by individuals and organizations, in their own countries and in international associations, to help make that pledge a reality.

[35]Other official texts read "or."

Conclusion

In the coming weeks, the U.S. delegation will focus its efforts in a constructive manner on improving relations among the participating states. We are here to help to strengthen prospects for cooperation and to help move closer toward what should be the noblest common goal of this conference: to give the process of détente a human measure and a humanitarian face.

In that spirit, the U.S. delegation will consider and, as appropriate, support new measures to improve implementation of the Final Act. We see opportunities for improvement in the following areas:

—Promotion of human rights;
—Execution of confidence-building measures;
—Qualitative expansion of scientific, economic, and commercial data exchanges;
—Easing of travel for journalists and businessmen;
—Freer access to printed and broadcast information from other countries; and
—Fuller opportunities for scholars and scholarship.

This list by no means exhausts our agenda or the specific ideas the United States, with other interested states, will pursue in the coming months. There are also opportunities to promote the exchange of literature, television programs, and culture of all kinds. There are possibilities for exploring, in appropriate agencies, as the U.N. Economic Commission for Europe, the coordination of approaches to such pervasive problems as environmental pollution. And, there is great potential for expanding trade and for sharing the benefits of technology.

However, our success here will be measured not solely by words on paper but rather by what we all do both here and at home after this meeting ends. Together we must give the process of implementation direction, higher goals, and fresh momentum to insure that—when we next meet in a similar assembly—we can record even greater progress.

In our work, we will need patience, perseverance, and perspective. This conference in Belgrade is one stage of a dynamic process and a continuing dialogue. And that Helsinki process is part of an even larger effort to build more secure and humane relations among our nations and peoples.

We are nearer the beginning than the end. This conference must give the people of the signatory countries and people throughout the world a first report of first progress. It must demonstrate to them our shared commitment to go further. We owe them our best efforts and results better than those so far achieved.

(18) Meeting at Ministerial Level of the North Atlantic Council, Brussels, December 8-9, 1977: Communiqué Issued at the Conclusion of the Meeting.[36]

The North Atlantic Council met in Ministerial session in Brussels on the 8th and 9th of December, 1977.

Ministers examined developments since the Council's meeting in London last May. They reaffirmed their resolve to fulfill the common purposes and enhance the effectiveness of the Alliance and agreed that the work in this direction was proceeding satisfactorily.

Ministers emphasized that the strength, vitality and cohesion of the Alliance are drawn not only from its defense preparedness but also from the shared commitment of its peoples to the principles of democracy, respect for human rights, the rule of law and social progress and from their common desire to safeguard their freedom and independence. Ministers reaffirmed their commitment to the pursuit of détente and to the achievement of a better understanding with the countries of Eastern Europe. In these efforts they are guided by their dedication to peace and their concern for the worth of the individual. Ministers stressed that, to be significant, efforts to remove barriers within Europe should benefit the lives of individual citizens as well as relations between states. Ministers noted that although recent progress in East-West relations had been uneven, there had been some favorable trends. They resolved to develop these and to seek a broader pattern of cooperation with the countries of the Warsaw Pact across a wide range of international issues. For these efforts to succeed, reciprocity and restraint are required on the part of all governments concerned. A policy of détente cannot be pursued selectively.

Ministers considered the meeting now being held in Belgrade as a follow-up to the Helsinki Conference on Security and Cooperation in Europe. They noted that a thorough presentation of views was taking place on the degree of progress made in implementing the Final Act, but regretted that a number of specific criticisms of inadequacies in implementation had not yet received satisfactory answers. The exchange of views in Belgrade so far has confirmed that while some progress has been achieved in certain fields, much remains to be done in improving relations between states and in ensuring the rights and well-being of individuals. Ministers, recalling the importance of the commitment of all signatory governments to respect fundamental freedoms and human rights, including that of the individual to know and act upon his rights and duties in this field, affirmed their determination to pursue a dialogue on these

[36]Department of State Press Release 552, Dec. 10; text from *Bulletin,* Jan. 1978: 30-31.

matters. In addition to measures to improve implementation in other fields, Ministers considered that the scope of confidence-building measures should be broadened in accordance with the provisions of the Final Act. Recognising the long-term nature of the CSCE process, the allies will continue their efforts both during the Belgrade meeting and afterwards to ensure that a stronger impetus is given to full implementation of all provisions of the Final Act by all participating states.

Ministers expressed satisfaction at the substantial amount of work already done by the Council in permanent session on the fresh study of long-term trends in East-West relations and their implications for the Alliance requested by allied leaders at their meeting in London in May.

Ministers noted with concern that the steady growth in the military strength of the Warsaw Pact inevitably casts a shadow over the East-West relationship. Emphasizing the defensive character of the Alliance, Ministers recognized that the foundation of its security was the maintenance by the Alliance of forces sufficient in quantity and quality to deter aggression, withstand pressure or, if necessary, defend the territorial integrity of the member states. They asserted their determination to take the necessary steps to achieve this objective. In this context, Ministers reaffirmed their view that the early coming into operation of the defense cooperation agreements between allied countries will strengthen the defences of the entire Alliance in particular in the Mediterranean.

The Ministers of countries participating in the integrated defense structure of the Alliance welcomed the progress being made by those allies concerned in developing the long-term program in selected areas to enable NATO forces to meet the changing defense needs of the 1980s and the successes achieved in the program of short-term measures designed to improve the capabilities of NATO forces by the end of 1978.

Ministers took note with appreciation of reports on efforts to make more effective use of available resources for defense through increased standardization and interoperability. They welcomed initiatives to encourage the trans-Atlantic dialogue on equipment matters, to remove obstacles to the establishment of cooperative projects and to create a more balanced relationship among European and North American members of the Alliance in connection with the procurement of defense equipment.

Ministers reaffirmed their determination to strive for genuine measures of disarmament and arms control. They noted the increased activity in this field in recent months and the prospects for progress on important matters. They affirmed their intention to play a constructive role in the forthcoming United Nations special session on disarmament. They expressed the hope that 1978 would see more rapid progress in achieving concrete measures in this area.

Ministers of the participating countries reviewed the state of negotiations in Vienna on mutual and balanced force reductions (MBFR). They expressed once more their conviction that these negotiations would achieve their agreed aim of contributing to a more stable relationship and to the strengthening of peace and security in Europe only if they were to result in eliminating the existing ground force manpower disparity in Central Europe and ensuring undiminished security for all allies. These Ministers reaffirmed their position that these objectives would be achieved by their proposal to establish, in the area of reductions, approximate parity in ground forces in the form of a common collective ceiling for ground force manpower on each side and to reduce the disparity in main battle tanks. They called for a positive response to the additional offer they made to the Warsaw Pact countries in December 1975. They indicated the importance they attach to the inclusion of associated measures in an MBFR agreement. These Ministers stressed the need for a genuine data discussion as a basis for further progress in these negotiations.

Ministers discussed the recent developments in the US-USSR Strategic Arms Limitation Talks and noted with satisfaction the progress made. They expressed support for the efforts for the United States to conclude a SALT agreement which maintains and enhances strategic stability and is responsive to the security interests and concerns of the Alliance.

Ministers reviewed the developments concerning Berlin and Germany as a whole since their last meeting in May 1977. They noted with satisfaction the positive effects which the Quadripartite Agreement of September 3, 1971 continues to have in and around Berlin. The Ministers emphasized the importance of strict observation and full implementation of all the provisions of the Quadripartite Agreement, including those regarding the ties between the western sectors of Berlin and the Federal Republic of Germany and those regarding the representation abroad of the interests of the western sector of Berlin. Ministers underlined the essential connection between the situation relating to Berlin and détente, security and cooperation throughout Europe.

Ministers expressed the hope that recent developments in the Middle East, which they welcome, will lead to a just and lasting peace in the region endorsed by all directly interested parties. Ministers took note of the report on the situation in the Mediterranean prepared on their instructions. They once more emphasized the importance they attach to maintaining the balance of forces throughout the Mediterranean area. They requested the Council to continue its consultations on this subject and to report to them at their next meeting.

Ministers noted with appreciation the work of the Committee on the Challenges of Modern Society (CCMS) and the actions taken by nations to implement the CCMS recommendations and resolutions on air, inland water and marine pollution. Ministers noted that the Alliance members had resolved to deal effectively with hazardous wastes to minimize environmental damage.

The next Ministerial session of the North Atlantic Council will be held with the participation of heads of states and governments in Washington on 30th and 31st May, 1978.

4. FALSE DAWN IN THE MIDEAST

(19) Return from the Middle East: Statement by Secretary of State Vance before the Committee on International Relations, House of Representatives, March 1, 1977.[1]

(Excerpt)

* * *

Core Issues of Middle East Settlement

My appearance here follows closely on my return from the Middle East. I believe it would be appropriate to talk for a moment about our Middle East policy as a whole and about our hopes and our efforts for a peace settlement in the area.

President Carter asked me to travel to the Middle East in my first mission abroad as Secretary of State because he believes that the Middle East situation must be given very high and early priority.

My trip had several purposes:

—To demonstrate the importance the President and I attach to the achievement of a just and durable peace in the Middle East and to the maintenance of close ties between the United States and the nations I visited;

—To meet the leaders of those nations and establish the personal relationships that are so important to a diplomacy of confidence and trust; and

—To learn from them their views, so we might define more clearly areas of both agreement and disagreement and establish a base for our own diplomacy in pursuit of peace.

I am satisfied that these purposes were met. We face a long and difficult process, with no assurance of success. But this has been a good beginning, and we are determined to proceed.

[1]Text from *Bulletin,* 76: 269-70.

I was encouraged to find a number of areas of general agreement among the leaders I met:

—There is a common commitment to working for peace so that they may turn the energies of their governments to bringing the economic and social benefits of peace to their peoples.

—There is a consensus on the desirability of reconvening the Geneva conference sometime during the second half of 1977.

—Each agreed to attend such a conference without preconditions, assuming the resolution of disagreements on procedural questions.

—They would like to see the United States play an active role in facilitating the search for a settlement.

—And each leader accepted an invitation to meet with President Carter during the next three months.

This is a base on which we can build. But there are complex procedural and substantive issues that will require imagination and flexibility from us all.

While there was general agreement on what the core issues of a settlement must be, there are strongly differing views on how these issues should be resolved. These core issues are the nature of peaceful relations between Israel and her neighbors, the boundaries of peace, and the future of the Palestinians. In addition, there are sharp disagreements over whether and how the PLO should be involved in a Geneva conference.

No one can promise success. But we are committed to a serious effort at helping the nations of the Middle East find a just and lasting solution to the conflicts and tensions that have plagued them and threatened the world for nearly three decades.

Boycott Legislation and Middle East Relations

Given the inherent difficulty of this challenge, and the very high stakes we have in meeting it successfully, we believe we are bound to do what we can to enhance the chances of success by our handling of related issues.

I must also report that I did find concern in Arab capitals about the effects of legislation on commercial relations between the United States and those countries.

They also attach importance to good bilateral relations with the United States. Our shared economic and commercial interests are an important part of these relations.

The magnitude of these interests is reflected in the latest statistics on economic relations between the United States and Middle Eastern countries. Over the past four years, the Middle East market for U.S. exports has doubled in importance (from about 5 percent of total U.S. exports to nearly 10 percent of this total). During this period, our exports to the Arab countries have nearly quadrupled, to a present level of $7 billion a year. Our current exports to Israel and the Arab countries of the Middle East now total some $8.5 billion. U.S. oil imports from Arab countries now account for more than a third of total U.S. imports and more than 15 percent of total U.S. oil consumption. Reflows to the United States of petrodollars in the form of investment from the Arab states are running some $10 billion a year.

I believe that a forthright but carefully considered policy emphasizing that U.S. legislation deals—as is entirely appropriate—with U.S. commerce and the activities of U.S. persons will be understood by Arab leaders.

We have weighed carefully the risks to our important political and economic interests in the Middle East which attend further legislation directed at activities of U.S. firms related to foreign boycotts. We believe that carefully directed legislation combined with diplomatic action can protect our interests. I want to emphasize our intention to maintain close and friendly relations with the countries of the Middle East.

There is much common ground between these principles of the Administration and the objectives of the current proposals for new legislation. This Administration wants to work out with the Congress language for antiboycott legislation on which we can both agree.

I also hope it will be possible, as these hearings proceed, for the various business and other groups to reconcile their views on the provisions of some new legislation. In this respect I have received encouraging reports that the meetings between the Anti-Defamation League and the Business Roundtable have been constructive. A substantial meeting of minds by these representative groups on a set of principles on which legislation might be based will be a great help to us in our deliberations.

The other Cabinet members concerned and I would be happy to make available our experts to work with your committee staff to formulate new legislative language on which we can agree. As issues are developed for decision, I will also be happy personally to consult further with the members of this committee.

* * *

(20) Statements by President Carter, March 1977.

(a) *The Problem of Israeli Frontiers: News Conference Statements, March 9, 1977.*[2]

²Text from *Presidential Documents*, 13: 329-32 and 333.

(Excerpts)

* * *

BORDER LINES IN THE MIDDLE EAST

Q. Mr. President, there has been a lot of talk about defensible borders lately and what that means in regard to the Middle East. Could I ask you, sir, do you feel that it would be appropriate in a Middle East peace settlement for the Israelis to keep some of the occupied land they took during the 1967 war in order to have secure borders?

THE PRESIDENT. The defensible border phrase, the secure borders phrase, obviously, are just semantics. I think it's a relatively significant development in the description of possible settlement in the Middle East to talk about these things as a distinction.

The recognized borders have to be mutual. The Arab nations, the Israeli nation, has to agree on permanent and recognized borders, where sovereignty is legal as mutually agreed. Defense lines may or may not conform in the foreseeable future to those legal borders. There may be extensions of Israeli defense capability beyond the permanent and recognized borders.

I think this distinction is one that is now recognized by Israeli leaders. The definition of borders on a geographical basis is one that remains to be determined. But I think that it is important for the world to begin to see, and for the interested parties to begin to see, that there can be a distinction between the two; the ability of Israel to defend herself by international agreement or by the some-time placement of Israeli forces themselves or by monitoring stations, as has been the case in the Sinai, beyond the actual sovereignty borders as mutually agreed by Israel and her neighbors.

Q. Well, does that mean international zones between the countries?

THE PRESIDENT. International zones could very well be part of an agreement. And I think that I can see in a growing way, a step-by-step process where there might be a mutual agreement that the ultimate settlement, even including the border delineations, would be at a certain described point. In an interim state, maybe 2 years, 4 years, 8 years or more, there would be a mutual demonstration of friendship and an end to the declaration or state of war.

I think that what Israel would like to have is what we would like to have: a termination of belligerence toward Israel by her neighbors, a recognition of Israel's right to exist, the right to exist in peace, the opening up of borders with free trade, tourist travel, cultural exchange between Israel and her neighbors; in other words, a stabilization of the situation in the Middle East without a constant threat to Israel's existence by her neighbors.

This would involve substantial withdrawal of Israel's present control over territories. Now, where that withdrawal might end, I don't know. I would guess it would be some minor adjustments in the 1967 borders. But that still remains to be negotiated.

But I think this is going to be a long, tedious process. We're going to mount a major effort in our own Government in 1977, to bring the parties to Geneva. Obviously, any agreement has to be between the parties concerned. We will act as an intermediary when our good offices will serve well.

But I'm not trying to predispose our own Nation's attitudes towards what might be the ultimate details of the agreement that can mean so much to world peace.

* * *

BORDER ADJUSTMENTS IN THE MIDDLE EAST

Q. Mr. President, I'd like to try to clarify the Israeli situation, if I might. A moment ago in answering the question, you spoke of the possibility of substantial withdrawal of Israeli control over territory and then, just a few seconds later, spoke of the possibility of minor territorial concessions by the Israelis.

What is it exactly that you have in mind here? Are you really talking about some big withdrawals, or are you talking only about minor withdrawals?

THE PRESIDENT. I don't think I would use the word minor withdrawals. I think there might be minor adjustments to the 1967, pre-1967 borders. But that's a matter for Israel and her neighbors to decide between themselves.

I believe that we will know by, I'd say, the middle of May, much more clearly the positions of the interested parties. I've not yet met nor talked to the leaders in Lebanon, Syria, Jordan, Egypt—Saudi Arabia, to a lesser direct participation degree.

I will meet with all these leaders between now and the middle of May. And I don't want to try to define in any specific terms the exact delineation of borders, but I think this is obviously one of the most serious problems.

There are three basic elements: One is an ultimate commitment to complete peace in the Middle East; second, border determinations which are highly controversial and not yet been defined by either side; and, third, dealing with the Palestinian question.

And I'm not trying to act as the one to lay down an ultimate settlement. I don't know what an ultimate settlement will be. But these matters will be freely and openly debated within our own country and within the countries involved. And I think I've described as best I can my own position.

*   *   *

MIDDLE EAST BORDERS ISSUE

Q. Mr. President, I'd like to go just a little bit further in your discussion of the defensible borders issue.

If I understood you correctly, you're talking about the possibility of something like an Israeli defense line along the Jordan River and perhaps at some point on the Sinai Desert and perhaps at some point on the Golan Heights, that would be defense forces but not legal borders.

Have I understood that correctly, that your feeling is that the Israelis are going to have to have some kind of defense forces along the Jordan River and in those other places?

THE PRESIDENT. Well, you added a great deal to what I said. In the first place, I didn't mention any particular parts of the geography around Israel. And I didn't confine the defense capability to Israeli forces. These might very well be international forces. It might very well be a line that's fairly broad, say, 20 kilometers or more, where demilitarization is guaranteed on both sides. It might very well consist of outposts, electronics or, perhaps, personnel outposts as were established in the Sinai region as a result of the Egypt and Israeli agreement.

I'm not going to try to get more specific in saying what will or will not be the case. But that is a possibility that might lead to the alleviation of tension there, and it's one about which I will be discussing this matter with the representatives from the Arab countries when they come.

*   *   *

(b) A Homeland for the Palestinians: Statement at the Clinton Town Meeting, Clinton, Massachusetts, March 16, 1977.[3]

(Excerpt)

*   *   *

[3]Text from *Presidential Documents*, 13: 360-61.

Q. My name is Reverend Richard Harding, and, President Carter, it's a pleasure to welcome you to the number one everytown, USA—Clinton, Massachusetts.

I would like to ask you, Mr. President—it seems that world peace hinges greatly on the Middle East.

THE PRESIDENT. Yes.

Q. What do you personally feel must be done to establish a meaningful and a lasting peace in that area of the world? Thank you.

THE PRESIDENT. I think all of you know that there has been either war or potential war in the Middle East for the last 29 years, ever since Israel became a nation. I think one of the finest acts of the world nations that's ever occurred was to establish the State of Israel.

So, the first prerequisite of a lasting peace is the recognition of Israel by her neighbors, Israel's right to exist, Israel's right to exist permanently, Israel's right to exist in peace. That means that over a period of months or years that the borders between Israel and Syria, Israel and Lebanon, Israel and Jordan, Israel and Egypt must be opened up to travel, to tourism, to cultural exchange, to trade, so that no matter who the leaders might be in those countries, the people themselves will have formed a mutual understanding and comprehension and a sense of a common purpose to avoid the repetitious wars and death that have afflicted that region so long. That's the first prerequisite of peace.

The second one is very important and very, very difficult; and that is, the establishment of permanent borders for Israel. The Arab countries say that Israel must withdraw to the pre-1967 borderlines, Israel says that they must adjust those lines to some degree to insure their own security. That is a matter to be negotiated between the Arab countries on the one side and Israel on the other.

But borders are still a matter of great trouble and a matter of great difficulty, and there are strong differences of opinion now.

And the third ultimate requirement for peace is to deal with the Palestinian problem. The Palestinians claim up 'til this moment that Israel has no right to be there, that the land belongs to the Palestinians, and they've never yet given up their publicly professed commitment to destroy Israel. That has to be overcome.

There has to be a homeland provided for the Palestinian refugees who have suffered for many, many years. And the exact way to solve the Palestinian problem is one that first of all addresses itself right now to the Arab countries and then, secondly, to the Arab countries negotiating with Israel.

Those three major elements have got to be solved before a Middle Eastern solution can be prescribed.

I want to emphasize one more time, we offer our good offices. I think it's accurate to say that of all the nations in the world, we are the one that's most trusted, not completely, but most trusted by the Arab countries and also Israel. I guess both sides have some doubt about us. But we'll have to act kind of as a catalyst to bring about their ability to negotiate successfully with one another.

We hope that later on this year, in the latter part of this year, that we might get all of these parties to agree to come together at Geneva, to start talking to one another. They haven't done that yet. And I believe if we can get them to sit down and start talking and negotiating that we have an excellent chance to achieve peace. I can't guarantee that. It's a hope.

I hope that we will all pray that that will come to pass, because what happens in the Middle East in the future might very well cause a major war there which would quickly spread to all the other nations of the world; very possibly it could do that.

Many countries depend completely on oil from the Middle East for their life. We don't. If all oil was cut off to us from the Middle East, we could survive; but Japan imports more than 98 percent of all its energy, and other countries, like in Europe—Germany, Italy, France—are also heavily dependent on oil from the Middle East.

So, this is such a crucial area of the world that I will be devoting a major part of my own time on foreign policy between now and next fall trying to provide for a forum within which they can discuss their problems and, hopefully, let them seek out among themselves some permanent solution.

Just maybe as briefly as I could, that's the best answer I can give you to that question.

* * *

(21) The Central Treaty Organization (CENTO): 24th Meeting of the CENTO Council, Tehran, May 14-15, 1977.

(a) Statement to the Council by Secretary of State Vance, May 14, 1977.[4]

Distinguished delegates, ladies and gentlemen: It is a special pleasure for me to bring to you greetings and warm wishes from President Carter. I want in particular to express the President's

---

[4]Department of State Press Release 245, May 14; text from *Bulletin,* 76: 616-18.

deep appreciation, as well as mine and that of the members of the American delegation, to His Imperial Majesty and his government for the gracious hospitality extended to us during our visit to Tehran.

The U.S. association with the member states of CENTO is important to our nation and to President Carter's Administration, as it was to our predecessors. Personally, I look forward with anticipation to our discussions today. Our relations with each of the CENTO governments are of great importance to us. We value highly your views and your counsel. Our traditional ties of cooperation have benefited all our countries and, we believe, have positively contributed to the stability and to the security of the CENTO region.

Both now and later in our deliberations today I shall share our perception from Washington on the state of the world and the pursuit of peace.

There are some world and regional issues I would particularly like to speak about in these opening remarks.

The search for a just and lasting peace in the Middle East is one of the highest priority items on the foreign policy agenda of our country. We believe it is critically important that a meaningful beginning be made this year toward a permanent settlement of the Middle East conflict. To that end, we are working with the governments concerned to reconvene the Geneva peace conference on the Middle East in the latter part of 1977. We are also convinced, however, that the Geneva conference has to be well prepared, since failure at Geneva would bring with it serious risks of future hostilities.

Our intensive consultations with the key Middle East leaders have given us some hope for progress. In these consultations, we are seeking to clarify the positions of the parties and to identify the areas of possible agreement with respect to the basic issues that must be resolved in the final settlement; namely, the nature of peaceful relations among the parties; the question of withdrawal from occupied territories; security arrangements that will help make recognized borders secure borders; and a settlement of the problem of a homeland for the Palestinian people.

These are complex and difficult issues. Given the legacy of almost three decades of hostility, suspicion, and frustration, we do not underestimate the obstacles which must be overcome. We believe, however, that there is today in the Middle East a will for peace and a growing awareness of the grim alternatives. If all concerned keep the image of these alternatives before them, we believe that reason may prevail and that necessary compromises on all sides can be found. It should not be beyond the imagination of statesmen to devise solutions that will meet the concerns of all states and peoples in the Middle East for their security and territorial integrity, for peace and justice, and for the future prosperity and well-being of their people.

With respect to another regional area, that of Cyprus, our distinguished Foreign Minister of Turkey has already commented upon that issue, and I would merely note that we continue to follow the matters in that area with great interest and are keeping in close touch with all of the parties concerned.

Another area of great interest to all of us, as David Owen has underscored, is Africa. Recent events there have raised questions in the minds of all those who favor political, economic, and social progress for all people of that great continent. My government supports certain principles regarding the future development of Africa.

In cooperation with the countries of the region and our allies, we have worked for the early resolution of those problems preventing independence with majority rule in Rhodesia and in Namibia. We have recently announced, as David Owen has pointed out, a joint effort with the United Kingdom to expedite the process of constitutional government and peaceful transition in Rhodesia. We have also participated in a special delegation of five nations who are members of the Security Council in an effort to create an atmosphere and a process by which Namibian independence can be achieved in the near future.

In these areas and in other trouble spots, such as Zaire and the Horn of Africa, my government has operated on the principle that African problems should be resolved peacefully in an African context and in a manner acceptable to the African nations themselves. We are opposed to the use of force by external powers to bring about change in Africa.

In a large [sic] context, the United States will make positive contributions to the sense of community that is developing among nations. But we know that peaceful progress must be protected through adequate defense. We are attempting to work with the Soviet Union for a substantial reduction in strategic weapons. But we shall not in the process neglect our existing alliances and bilateral relations.

The United States will work for the peaceful resolution of disputes and for the goals of freedom, self-government, human dignity, and mutual toleration. We are determined that our foreign policy shall reflect our traditional commitments to political, social, and economic human rights; and in partnership with others, we are directing our political and economic efforts to those ends.

We are willing to share the benefits of our economic strength with others, as President Carter made plain in his address to the

United Nations.[5] We are committed to the continued improvement of the world economic system.

We are dedicated to the resolution of global problems in the areas of food, energy, environment, and trade. Whether at the United Nations, the Conference on International Economic Cooperation, or elsewhere, our hope is to work with other nations in practical ways for real solutions unencumbered by differing ideological views.

We expect our bilateral foreign assistance to exceed $7 billion this year. In addition, we have asked our Congress to authorize increases to contributions to the United Nations Development Program and to contribute very substantial funds to the various international and lending institutions, including the International Development Association.

The United States now provides for tariff-free entry into the American market of many products from developing countries. In the search for additional ways to help meet the needs of developing countries, we have decided upon other proposals such as a common fund to finance buffer stocks as part of individual commodity agreements, to participate in the special action fund, and to increase our development assistance programs.

The goal of physical well-being for people in all countries is only one aspect of justice in the broader sense. Equally important is the observance of the political and economic rights recognized in the Universal Declaration of Human Rights and in other international covenants. Encouraging these rights is central to our policy, and there is a very practical aspect to it. Each country's growth, prosperity, and stability sooner or later depend upon its ability to meet the aspirations of its people for human rights. The success of nations of the world in mastering the economic and social problems of resource limits, population growth, and environment will inevitably lead and be linked to our success in promoting individual dignity.

We have all learned there can be little security against internal dangers without strength at home founded upon economic and political justice. We have also learned that armaments can place crushing financial burdens upon us—burdens that can lessen or prevent the application of resources to social and economic development. I am confident that we can agree that our common aim is to lighten this burden through the reduction of tension and conflict throughout the world. But we shall not relax our guard unless conditions permit us to do so.

[5]Document 3.

We will work with our friends and allies, those of you present today, toward our common security, as well as for the respect and understanding among our peoples which are so basic to our mutual cooperation.

(b) Final Communiqué, May 15, 1977.[6]

TEHRAN, *May 15, 1977*—The Council of Ministers of the Central Treaty Organization (CENTO), which was inaugurated by the message of His Imperial Majesty the Shahanshah Aryamehr, read by His Excellency Mr. Amir Abbas Hoveyda, Prime Minister of Iran, held their 24th Session in Tehran on May 14–15, 1977.

The delegations were led by:

Iran—H.E. Dr. Abbas Ali Khalatbary, Minister of Foreign Affairs
Pakistan—H.E. Mr. S. Ghias Uddin Ahmad, Ambassador of Pakistan to Iran
Turkey—H.E. Mr. Ihsan Sabri Caglayangil, Minister of Foreign Affairs
United Kingdom—The Rt. Hon. David Owen, Secretary of State for Foreign and Commonwealth Affairs
United States—The Hon. Cyrus Vance, Secretary of State

Following an address by the Prime Minister of Iran, opening statements were made by leaders of the delegations and by the Secretary General of CENTO expressing their appreciation for the Shahanshah's gracious message and for the warm hospitality of the Host Government. H.E. Mr. Umit Haluk Bayulken, the Secretary General of the Central Treaty Organization, presided at the opening meeting of the Session. His Excellency Dr. A.A. Khalatbary, Minister of Foreign Affairs of Iran, presided at subsequent Council meetings.

The Council of Ministers conducted a wide-ranging and constructive review of the present international situation paying particular attention to matters of interest in the CENTO area, and noted with satisfaction the economic and social progress in the region. The Ministers pledged continued support for the Central Treaty Organization and reaffirmed the vital importance they attach to the preservation of the independence and territorial integrity of each of the Member States in the region.

During their warm and friendly discussions the Ministers explained their positions and their views regarding the problems which are of special interest and importance for their respective

[6]Text from *Bulletin,* 76: 618.

countries. The importance of peaceful and just settlement of disputes and the need to maintain vigilance in the region were reaffirmed.

The Ministers also reviewed progress towards further promoting cooperation within the Alliance in the economic and cultural fields. In reviewing the report of the Economic Committee, they directed the Committee to consider ways of expanding its work in the form of development projects with a view to strengthening and promoting economic cooperation within the Alliance. They also noted with approval the expanded cultural exchange and mass media programmes undertaken within the framework of CENTO.

The Ministers reviewed developments in the Middle East since their last meeting. They noted with satisfaction the improvement of the situation in Lebanon and paid tribute to all those who are contributing towards the solution of this problem. They agreed that the failure to achieve peace in the Middle East continues to constitute a grave threat to world peace. They reaffirmed the importance they attached to the continuation of efforts designed to achieve a settlement resulting in a just, honourable and durable peace in the Middle Eastern area as a whole.

The Council of Ministers exchanged views on developments in Europe and expressed their sincerest hopes that the Review Conference on Security and Cooperation in Europe to be held in Belgrade later this year, would lead to a further relaxation of international tension. In this context, the Ministers once again stressed that security in the CENTO region consitutes an important related element.

The Ministers noted the report of the Military Committee, and expressed satisfaction at the progress made during the past year in the improvement of cooperation among the partners in the military field.

The Ministers expressed their belief that all bilateral questions between the member countries should be discussed between the parties concerned in an atmosphere of friendships [sic] and solidarity with a view to further improving their cooperation.

The Ministers noted the progress made in countering the threat of subversion in the region and reaffirmed their resolve to continue to take the necessary measures to eliminate this threat.

In reviewing events within the CENTO region during the past year, the Ministers expressed their appreciation for the cooperation, solidarity, and friendship, demonstrated by the CENTO member countries by being among the first to come to the aid of the victims of the earthquake disaster in East Anatolia.

In concluding their review the Ministers noted with appreciation the annual report of the Secretary General, which contains many valuable recommendations. They reiterated their determination to ensure that the Alliance continues to contribute to the peace, security and stability of the region so as to promote further the social and economic welfare of its people.

The Ministers accepted the invitation of the Government of the United States to hold the next Session of the Council in Washington during April, 1978.

(22) A Framework for Middle East Peace: Address by Vice-President Walter F. Mondale before the World Affairs Council of Northern California, San Francisco, June 17, 1977.[7]

In the last several months, I've undertaken two extended foreign trips on behalf of the President to Europe and Japan. The more I travel, and the more nations I visit, the more I come to believe that the peoples of the world are not really so different—that all of us dream the same dreams for our children and that the real key to peace and cooperation in the world lies in better understanding between people. Diplomats and heads of state and elected officials must play a role, but we should never underestimate the power of ideas and education and greater understanding to break down the barriers of suspicion and fear that too often separate the nations of the world.

Your programs in the school system, on television, the lectures and seminars you hold, your model U.N. conference for students are all an important part of that effort. And I'm particularly pleased to see that you're joining together with a number of groups involved in international relations in a new World Affairs Center here in San Francisco, and I wish you every success in that venture. And so the contributions of an organization such as yours toward increased understanding in the world are really crucial, not only to the foreign policy efforts of this nation but to the search for peace.

With the words of his Inaugural Address, President Carter identified at the very outset of his Administration the guiding spirit of this nation's foreign policy:[8]

Our nation can be strong abroad only if it is strong at home, and we know that the best way to enhance freedom in other lands is to demonstrate here that our democratic system is worthy of emulation. To be true to ourselves, we must be true to others.

And he elaborated on the basic premises of our relations with other nations in his speech at Notre Dame this May:[9]

[7]Text from Bulletin, 77: 41-6.
[8]Document 2a.
[9]Document 5.

—Our policy must be rooted in our people's basic commitment to human rights.

—Our policy must be based on close cooperation with the Western industrial democracies. With them we share basic values; with them also we share a recognition that global problems cannot be solved without close cooperation among us. This was the message the President had me take to Europe and Japan in the first week of the Administration, and this was the spirit which guided the President and his colleagues at the London summit last month.

—Our policy must seek to improve relations with the Soviet Union and China. It must do so in a balanced and reciprocal way, while we maintain a strong defense.

—Our policy must recognize that the cleavage between North and South is as important as between East and West. We must reach out to the world's developing nations, seeking to narrow the gap between rich and poor.

—Finally, our policy must provide incentives for all nations to rise above ideology or narrow conceptions of self-interest and work together to resolve regional conflicts and to meet global problems that confront all people.

As an Administration, we are only five months old. However, these months have been a period of intense activity. We are committed to shaping effective policies that truly reflect America's values and objectives, and we are committed to implementing policies with other nations so as to shape a more peaceful and stable world.

One of our first tasks has been to insure that our foreign policy reflects the commitment to basic human rights that we, as Americans, share. That commitment to the inherent dignity of the individual is at the heart of the American tradition. From it flows [sic] the democratic liberties that we cherish—such as the right to worship freely; freedom of speech, of the press, of assembly, and due process of law. Those are the basic strengths of our nation.

We have survived as a free nation because we have remained committed to the defense of fundamental moral values we cherish as a people. And unless our foreign policy reflects those values it will not earn the support of the American people. Without that support, no foreign policy—no matter how brilliantly conceived—can succeed.

I believe we have restored that commitment to human rights. I am proud that the United States today stands among those who uphold human rights and human dignity in the world. I am proud that no foreign leader today has any doubt that the United States condemns torture, political imprisonment, and repression by any government, anywhere in the world. We believe that basic human rights transcend ideology. We believe all nations, regardless of political systems, must respect those rights.

Just as respect for human rights is central to our foreign policy values, so progress toward a just and lasting Middle East settlement is essential to the prospect of a more peaceful world. The President has asked me to describe what we are trying to do to achieve peace in the Middle East. We want the American people to have the fullest possible understanding of our approach, for your support is crucial to its success.

President Carter has now met with the leaders of Egypt, Syria, Jordan, and Saudi Arabia. The President met with Prime Minister Rabin of Israel, and we hope that we will soon meet with the new Prime Minister.

With the exception of the meeting with President Asad which was held in Geneva, I have participated in all of them and have sensed these leaders' great desire for peace and their longing for the benefits that peace can bring to nations too long mobilized for war. Yet at the same time, we also found deep fears and suspicions which must be overcome if peace is to be achieved in that strategic and troubled region of the world.

A genuine and lasting peace in the Middle East is of essential interest to all Americans. Conflict there carries the threat of a global confrontation and runs the risk of nuclear war. As we have seen, war in the Middle East has profound economic consequences. It can, and has, damaged the economies of the entire world. It has been a tragedy for the nations of the region. Even short of war, continued confrontation encourages radicalization and instability.

Genuine peace is needed by all parties to the conflict. The Arab nations need peace. Israel, above all, has a profound interest in peace; there is no question about that.

Israel's Survival

For almost three decades, Israel has borne the burden of constant war. More than half its entire budget is dedicated to defense. Its citizens bear the highest average tax burden in the world—more than 60 percent of their income goes for taxes.

And yet, at the same time, this valiant nation has managed to create a miracle in the desert. With ingenuity, hard work, and skill it has created a land that could be a model for economic development and for political liberty to be emulated throughout the Middle East. Democracy has thrived in Israel despite the kind of adversity that has crushed freedom in other lands.

And yet, what of the future? Is it a future in which Israel's three million people try, by force of arms alone, to hold out against the hostility and growing power of the Arab world? Or can a process of reconciliation be started—a process in which peace protects Israel's security, a peace in which the urge for revenge and recrimination is replaced by mutual recognition and respect?

America has a special responsibility and a special opportunity to help bring about this kind of peace. This comes about first of all because of our unique and profound relationship with the State of Israel since its creation more than a generation ago. Our sense of shared values and purposes means that, for Americans, the question of Israel's survival is not a political question but rather stands as a moral imperative of our foreign policy.

Key Elements for an Agreement

And yet, our special relationship with Israel has not been directed against any other country. We have been able to enjoy the friendship of much of the Arab world, where we and our close allies have important interests.

It is precisely because of our close ties with both Israel and her Arab neighbors that we are uniquely placed to promote the search for peace, to work for an improved understanding of each side's legitimate concerns, and to help them work out what we hope will be a basis for negotiation leading to a final peace in the Middle East.

When this Administration entered office on January 20, we found that the situation in the Middle East called for a new approach. The step-by-step diplomacy of our predecessors had defused the immediate tensions produced by the war of 1973. But it was also evident that it would be increasingly difficult to achieve small diplomatic concessions when the ultimate shape of a peace agreement remained obscure. At the same time, it was unlikely that an agreement on a lasting peace could be achieved at one stroke.

U.N. Security Council Resolution 242, which is supported by all the parties, provides a basis for the negotiations which are required if there is to be a settlement. But Resolution 242 does not by itself provide all that is required. We, therefore, decided to work with the parties concerned to outline the overall framework for an enduring peace. Our concept was to use this framework as the basis for a phased negotiation and implementation of specific steps toward peace.

A major impediment to this approach lay in the fact that the positions of all sides were frozen. The words and phrases used by the parties had become encrusted with the fallout of countless diplomatic battles.

We have tried to regain momentum in this process. We have encouraged Arabs and Israelis to begin thinking again seriously about the elements of peace and not to remain committed to particular words and formulations.

To this end the President has tried to describe our understanding of what the key elements of an overall framework for an agreement might be:

—A commitment to a genuine and lasting peace demonstrated by concrete acts to normalize relations among the countries of the area;
—The establishment of borders for Israel which are recognized by all and which can be kept secure;
—A fair solution to the problem of the Palestinians.

The President has set forth these elements not to dictate a peace or to impose our views but to stimulate fresh thought.

Relations Among Middle East Countries

President Carter has gone further than any of his predecessors to stress with Arab leaders the essential point that peace must mean more than merely an end to hostilities, stating as he did in Clinton, Massachusetts,[10] last March:

. . . the first prerequisite of a lasting peace is the recognition of Israel by her neighbors, Israel's right to exist, Israel's right to exist permanently, Israel's right to exist in peace. That means that over a period of months or years that the borders between Israel and Syria, Israel and Lebanon, Israel and Jordan, Israel and Egypt must be opened up to travel, to tourism, to cultural exchange, to trade, so that no matter who the leaders might be in those countries, the people themselves will have formed a mutual understanding and comprehension and a sense of a common purpose to avoid the repetitious wars and death that have afflicted that region so long. That's the first prerequisite of peace.

We have found that the Arab leaders did not insist that this kind of peace is something that only future generations could consider. Some leaders—such as King Hussein during his visit to Washington—have made clear their commitment to a "just, a lasting peace, one which would enable all the people in [the Middle East] to divert their energies and resources to build and attain a brighter future. . . ."[11]

[10]Document 20b.
[11]*Presidential Documents,* 13: 606.

So we believe that we have made some progress in getting Arab leaders to recognize Israel's right to exist and to recognize—however reluctantly—that this commitment is essential to a genuine peace; that peace must be structured in such a way that it can survive even if some leaders were to nurture aims to destroy Israel. Still, we have a long way to go. The Arabs have been insistent that Israel withdraw from the territories it occupied in the 1967 war. We have made clear our view that Israel should not be asked to withdraw unless it can secure, in return, real peace from its neighbors.

Borders and Security Arrangements

The question of withdrawal is, in essence, the question of borders. For peace to be enduring, borders must be inviolable. Nations must feel secure behind their borders. Borders must be recognized by all.

A crucial dilemma has been how to provide borders that are both secure and acceptable to all. It is understandable that Israel, having fought a war in every decade since its birth, wants borders that can be defended as easily as possible. But no borders will be secure if neighboring countries do not accept them.

The problem is that borders that might afford Israel the maximum security in military terms would not be accepted as legitimate by Israel's neighbors. Borders that Israel's neighbors would recognize, Israel has not been willing to accept as forming an adequate line of defense.

For this reason, the President has tried to separate the two issues. On the one hand, there must be recognized borders. But, in addition, there could be separate lines of defense or other measures that could enhance Israel's security. The arrangements in the Sinai and in the Golan Heights provide models of how Israel's security might be enhanced until confidence in a lasting peace can be fully developed.

We would urge all the parties to think realistically about security arrangements to reduce the fear of surprise attack, to make acts of aggression difficult if not impossible, and to limit the military forces that would confront one another in sensitive areas.

This approach recognizes the fact that there is a profound asymmetry in what the two sides in the Middle East are seeking. On the one hand, a principal Arab concern is to regain lost territory. On the other, Israel wishes peace and recognition. Territory is tangible and once ceded difficult to regain short of war. Peace, on the other hand, can be ephemeral. Peaceful intentions can change overnight unless a solid foundation of cooperation and a firm pattern of reinforcing relationships can be established to insure that all have a stake in continuing tranquillity.

We believe that separating the imperatives of security from the requirement of recognized borders is an important advance toward reconciling the differences between the two sides. It is in this way that Israel could return to approximately the borders that existed prior to the war of 1967, albeit with minor modifications as negotiated among the parties, and yet retain security lines or other arrangements that would insure Israel's safety as full confidence developed in a comprehensive peace. Thus, with borders explicitly recognized and buttressed by security measures and with the process of peace unfolding, Israel's security would be greater than it is today.

Future of the Palestinians

A further major issue is that of the future of the Palestinian people. It has been the source of continuing tragedy in the Middle East. There are two prerequisites for a lasting peace in this regard.

—First, there must be a demonstrated willingness on the part of the Palestinians to live in peace alongside Israel.
—Second, the Palestinians must be given a stake in peace so that they will turn away from the violence of the past and toward a future in which they can express their legitimate political aspirations peacefully.

Thus, if the Palestinians are willing to exist in peace and are prepared to demonstrate that willingness by recognizing Israel's right to exist in peace, the President has made clear that, in the context of a peace settlement, we believe the Palestinians should be given a chance to shed their status as homeless refugees and to partake fully of the benefits of peace in the Middle East, including the possibility of some arrangement for a Palestinian homeland or entity— preferably in association with Jordan.

How this would be accomplished and the exact character of such an entity is, of course, something that would have to be decided by the parties themselves in the course of negotiation. However, the President has suggested that the viability of this concept and the security of the region might be enhanced if this involved an association with Jordan. But I emphasize that the specifics are for the parties themselves to decide.

Necessity of Negotiating

This leads me to a further crucial aspect of our approach—the necessity of direct negotiations among the parties concerned. We cannot conceive of genuine peace existing between countries who will not talk to one another. If they are prepared for peace, the first proof is a willingness to negotiate their differences.

This is why we believe it is so important to proceed with the holding of a Geneva conference this year. That conference provides the forum for these nations to begin the working out of these problems together directly, face-to-face. We have a continuing objective to convene such a conference before the end of this year.

Underlying this entire effort to promote the process of negotiation is our determination to maintain the military security of Israel. There must be no question in anyone's mind that the United States will do what is necessary to insure the adequacy of Israel's military posture and its capacity for self-defense.

We recognize that America has a special responsiblity in this regard. In fact, in promulgating our overall policy to curb the international traffic in arms, the President specifically directed the government that we will honor our historic responsibilities to assure the security of the State of Israel. Let there be no doubt about this commitment by this Administration.

We do not intend to use our military aid as pressure on Israel. If we have differences over military aid—and we may have some—it will be on military grounds or economic grounds but not political grounds. If we have differences over diplomatic strategy—and that could happen—we will work this out on a political level. We will not alter our commitment to Israel's military security.

Let me conclude by saying that we hope the concepts I have been discussing there[12] today—concepts which the President has advanced at talks with Israeli and Arab leaders—will stimulate them to develop ideas of their own. We realize that peace cannot be imposed from the outside, and we do not intend to present the parties with a plan or a timetable or a map. Peace can only come from a genuine recognition by all parties that their interests are served by reconciliation and not by war, by faith in the future rather than bitterness over the past.

America can try to help establish the basis of trust necessary for peace. We can try to improve the atmosphere for communication. We can offer ideas, but we cannot, in the end, determine whether peace or war is the fate of the Middle East. That can only be decided by Israel and her Arab neighbors.

We believe that both sides want peace. As the President has said:[13]

This may be the most propitious time for a genuine settlement since the beginning of the Arab-Israeli conflict almost 30 years

[12]Other official texts read "here."
[13]Document 5.

ago. To let this opportunity pass could mean disaster, not only for the Middle East, but perhaps for the international political and economic order as well.

As we go forward in our mediating role, we will have to expect from time to time to have differences with both sides. But these will be differences as to tactics. Our overall objectives will be those that we believe are now shared by all sides: A permanent and enduring peace in the Middle East.

This is obviously a difficult task and there is always the possibility of failure. But it is a historic responsibility that requires the fullest possible support of the American people.

I believe we have this support. And as we go through the difficult days ahead, this support will sustain us. It will provide the strength we need to encourage all parties to put aside their fears and put trust in their hopes for a genuine and lasting Middle East peace.

John Kennedy once described the formula for peace not only in the Middle East but throughout the world, and I would like to close with his words:[14]

If we all can persevere—if we can in every land and office look beyond our own shores and ambitions—then surely the age will dawn in which the strong are just and the weak secure and the peace preserved.

(23) Toward Reconvening the Geneva Conference, July-October 1977.

(a) Meeting of President Carter and Prime Minister Menahem Begin of Israel, July 19-20, 1977: White House Statement Issued Following the First Meeting, July 19, 1977.[15]

President Carter and Israeli Prime Minister Menahem Begin met in the Cabinet Room for 2 hours. The meeting was also attended by the Vice President, Secretary of State Cyrus Vance, Assistant to the President for National Security Affairs Zbigniew Brzezinski, Assistant Secretary of State Alfred L. Atherton, Jr., United States Ambassador to Israel Samuel Lewis, and William Quandt of the National Security Council staff on the American side; and Israeli Ambassador to the United States Simcha Dinitz, Advisor to the Prime Minister Shmuel Katz, Minister of the Embassy of Israel Ha-

---

[14]Address to U.N. General Assembly, Sept. 25, 1961, in *Documents, 1961:* 484.
[15]Text from *Presidential Documents,* 13: 1037-8.

nan Bar-On, Director of the Prime Minister's Bureau Yechiel Kadishai, Political Advisor to the Prime Minister Eli Mizrachi, Military Secretary to the Prime Minister Brigadier General Ephraim Poran, and Advisor to the Prime Minister Yehuda Avner on the Israeli side.

The President began by repeating his personal pleasure at welcoming Prime Minister Begin to the White House so soon after his taking office last month. The President congratulated Mr. Begin once again on his accession to national leadership and expressed confidence that this first visit will inaugurate the close working relationship natural to the leaders of two democracies with such long-standing and deep ties of friendship. Their talks were conducted in the spirit of mutual respect common to that warm friendship between our two peoples. The President and Prime Minister agreed that their meeting and the others to follow here mark a good starting point for seeking ways toward a just and durable peace in the Middle East. They pledged their determination to achieve that peace, noting that imaginative and responsible statesmanship is essential to overcoming the challenges posed.

The meeting this morning was devoted to a thorough and searching discussion of how to move toward an overall settlement of the Arab-Israeli conflict. The President and Prime Minister each developed their ideas on the issues involved. They agreed that all the issues must be settled through negotiations between the parties based on United Nations Security Council Resolutions 242 and 338 which all the governments directly concerned have accepted. They also agreed that this goal would best be served by moving rapidly toward the reconvening of the Geneva conference this year, keeping in mind at the same time the importance of careful preparation. In this connection, they focused on the practical requirements for convening the conference, looking toward Secretary of State Vance's forthcoming trip to the area for more talks with all the leaders involved. They expressed a hope that the Prime Minister's visit will help lay the groundwork for rapid movement toward negotiations.

In the course of the talk this morning on the diplomacy of peace, the President reaffirmed the enduring American commitment to the security and well-being of Israel. He assured the Prime Minister that any differences that may occur from time to time should not be allowed to obscure America's and his personal dedication to this historic American commitment. He asked the Prime Minister to express to the people of Israel the determination of the people of the United States to help them find true peace. Discussions on how to get negotiations started between the parties will continue this afternoon in the Prime Minister's meeting with Secretary Vance. No bilateral issues were discussed at this first meeting. The President and

Prime Minister will meet again tonight at the working dinner which the President is giving at the White House, and in the Cabinet Room again tomorrow morning at 10.

(b) Palestinian Representation at a Peace Conference: News Conference Statement by President Carter, July 28, 1977.[16]

(Excerpt)

* * *

THE MIDDLE EAST

Q. I'd like to go back to the Mideast, if I may. Some people believe that in your meetings with Mr. Begin, Mr. Begin came away with sort of the best of it. They think that you rather embraced him to the extent that our leverage with Israel has now been reduced. Would you comment on that, and would you also tell us what you think now the prospects for peace versus another war are in the Mideast?

THE PRESIDENT. After I met with President Sadat and King Hussein and President Asad, there were major outcries in Israel and among the American Jewish community that I had overly embraced the Arab cause. And I think now that Mr. Begin has visited me, there's a concern we have overly embraced the Israeli cause. Obviously, when these leaders come to see me or when I go to see them, there is an effort to understand one another, to have a base of comprehension and consultation that can provide hope for the future.

Our position on the Middle East has been very carefully spelled out to the degree of specificity that I choose. We've always made it clear that, ultimately, the agreement had to be approved and mutually beneficial to the Israelis and also their Arab neighbors as well.

I think that we have a good chance to go to Geneva. There are obstacles still to be resolved. I hope that every leader involved directly in the discussions, the four major countries there, will join with us and the cochairman of the prospective conference, the Soviet Union, in restraining their statements, not being so adamant on issues, and trying to cool down the situation until all can search out common ground, and then hope to minimize the differences.

Secretary Vance will leave this weekend to visit the three Arab

[16]Text from *Presidential Documents,* 13: 1122-3.

nations plus Saudi Arabia, and then come back through Israel as well. When he returns to the United States after about a week or so, we'll have a clearer picture of the differences that still divide the countries.

I think the major stumbling block at this point is the participation in the negotiations by the Palestinian representatives. Our position has been that they ought to be represented and that we will discuss with them these elements that involve the Palestinians and other refugees at the time they forego their commitment, presently publicly espoused, that Israel should be destroyed. But until the Palestinian leaders adopt the proposition that Israel is a nation, that it will be a nation permanently, that it has a right to live in peace—until that happens, I see no way that we would advocate participation by them in the peace negotiations.

But these matters are still very fluid. What gives me hope is that I believe that all national leaders with whom I've talked genuinely want to go to Geneva to try to work out permanent peace. That's the primary basis for my optimism. But it's difficult, and past statements by these leaders when they were at war, or in the status of prospective war, have been very rigid and very adamant and sometimes abusive and filled with hatred and distrust. We're trying to get them to change from those positions of distrust to one of genuine search for peace.

I think it's accurate to say, in closing my answer, that both sides now have at least a moderate amount of confidence in us, and I've tried to take a balanced position to enhance that trust in us. If I should ever take a biased position on the part of one of the parties, then the other parties would simply forego any dependence upon us.

So, I'm very careful in my statements, privately and publicly, to be consistent, and also to be fair.

* * *

(c) Secretary Vance's Second Mideast Visit, July 31-August 11, 1977: White House Statement, August 14, 1977.[17]

(Excerpt)

Secretary Vance reported on August 14 to the President on his discussions in Egypt, Lebanon, Syria, Jordan, Saudi Arabia, and Israel, which continued the Administration's sustained search for a just and lasting peace in the Middle East. He also reported on the talks held in London concerning southern Africa.

[17]White House Press Release; text from Bulletin, 77: 355.

Secretary Vance held in-depth discussions on all issues, both substantive and procedural and with each of the leaders he met. He suggested a number of principles which might guide the negotiations and discussed with the parties their proposals on how to narrow the remaining differences. Progress was made in some areas, particularly in reaffirming Security Council Resolutions 242 and 338 as the basis for negotiations and in moving closer to a common concept of the mutual obligations of peace, although much remains to be accomplished in this respect. Major differences between Arabs and Israelis remain—on how Palestinian views can best be represented in negotiations, but also on the definition of secure and recognized borders and the nature of a Palestinian settlement.

Difficult choices requiring courageous leadership face all parties in the future. President Carter and the Secretary believe that all of the leaders desire peace and are aware of the dangers of stalemate.

The President emphasized the importance of making progress in the coming months, building on the foundations already laid. Each of the parties had been asked to provide more detailed expressions of their positions in order to accelerate the reconvening of a well-prepared Geneva conference. We remain hopeful that the conference can be reconvened this fall. In September the Secretary of State will meet in the United States with their Foreign Ministers for intensive talks to continue those held during his trip. The President will also meet with the Foreign Ministers during their upcoming visits to the United States.

The President and the Secretary of State remain determined to do all that is possible to bring about a just and lasting peace in the Middle East. With the approval of all concerned, the United States will use its influence, offer its advice, volunteer its suggestions, and work to bring the parties into fruitful negotiations. The United States will also stay in close touch with the Soviet Union as a co-chairman of the Geneva conference. Secretary Vance will meet later this week with Ambassador Dobrynin to discuss his recent Middle East trip and to hear the latest Soviet views.

* * *

(24) A Soviet-American Initiative: Joint Statement Issued by Secretary of State Vance and Foreign Minister Gromyko, New York, October 1, 1977.[18]

Having exchanged views regarding the unsafe situation which remains in the Middle East, U.S. Secretary of State Cyrus Vance and

[18]Text from *Bulletin*, 77: 639-40.

Member of the Politbureau of the Central Committee of the CPSU, Minister for Foreign Affairs of the U.S.S.R. A.A. Gromyko have the following statement to make on behalf of their countries, which are cochairmen of the Geneva Peace Conference on the Middle East:

1. Both governments are convinced that vital interests of the peoples of this area, as well as the interests of strengthening peace and international security in general, urgently dictate the necessity of achieving, as soon as possible, a just and lasting settlement of the Arab-Israeli conflict. This settlement should be comprehensive, incorporating all parties concerned and all questions.

The United States and the Soviet Union believe that, within the framework of a comprehensive settlement of the Middle East problem, all specific questions of the settlement should be resolved, including such key issues as withdrawal of Israeli Armed Forces from territories occupied in the 1967 conflict; the resolution of the Palestinian question, including insuring the legitimate rights of the Palestinian people; termination of the state of war and establishment of normal peaceful relations on the basis of mutual recognition of the principles of sovereignty, territorial integrity, and political independence.

The two governments believe that, in addition to such measures for insuring the security of the borders between Israel and the neighboring Arab states as the establishment of demilitarized zones and the agreed stationing in them of U.N. troops or observers, international guarantees of such borders as well as of the observance of the terms of the settlement can also be established should the contracting parties so desire. The United States and the Soviet Union are ready to participate in these guarantees, subject to their constitutional processes.

2. The United States and the Soviet Union believe that the only right and effective way for achieving a fundamental solution to all aspects of the Middle East problem in its entirety is negotiations within the framework of the Geneva peace conference, specially convened for these purposes, with participation in its work of the representatives of all the parties involved in the conflict including those of the Palestinian people, and legal and contractual formalization of the decisions reached at the conference.

In their capacity as cochairmen of the Geneva conference, the United States and the U.S.S.R. affirm their intention, through joint efforts and in their contacts with the parties concerned, to facilitate in every way the resumption of the work of the conference not later than December 1977. The cochairmen note that there still exist several questions of a procedural and organizational nature which remain to be agreed upon by the participants to the conference.

3. Guided by the goal of achieving a just political settlement in the Middle East and of eliminating the explosive situation in this area of the world, the United States and the U.S.S.R. appeal to all the parties in the conflict to understand the necessity for careful consideration of each other's legitimate rights and interests and to demonstrate mutual readiness to act accordingly.

(25) Agreements Between the United States and Israel, October 5, 1977.

(a) Joint Statement Issued in New York Following a Meeting Between President Carter and Foreign Minister Moshe Dayan.[19]

The U.S. and Israel agree that Security Council Resolutions 242 and 338 remain the agreed basis for the resumption of the Geneva Peace Conference and that all the understandings and agreements between them on this subject remain in force.

Proposals for removing remaining obstacles to reconvening the Geneva Conference were developed. Foreign Minister Dayan will consult his Government on the results of these discussions. Secretary Vance will discuss these proposals with the other parties to the Geneva Conference.

Acceptance of the Joint U.S.-U.S.S.R. Statement of October 1, 1977,[20] by the parties is not a prerequisite for the reconvening and conduct of the Geneva Conference.

(b) Working Paper on Geneva Conference Procedure, Made Public in Jerusalem October 13, 1977.[21]

Working paper on suggestion for the resumption of the Geneva peace conference:

1. The Arab parties will be represented by a unified Arab delegation, which will include Palestinian Arabs. After the opening sessions, the conference will split into working groups.

2. The working groups for the negotiation and conclusion of peace treaties will be formed as follows:

[19]Text from Presidential Documents, 13: 1482.
[20]Document 24.
[21]Text from New York Times, Oct. 14, 1977.

A. Egypt-Israel.

B. Jordan-Israel.

C. Syria-Israel.

D. Lebanon-Israel. (All the parties agree that Lebanon may join the conference when it so requests.)

3. The West Bank and Gaza issues will be discussed in a working group to consist of Israel, Jordan, Egypt, and the Palestinian Arabs.

4. The solution of the problem of the Arab refugees and of the Jewish refugees will be discussed in accordance with terms to be agreed upon.

5. The agreed bases for the negotiations at the Geneva peace conference on the Middle East are U.N. Security Council Resolutions 242 and 338.

6. All the initial terms of reference of the Geneva peace conference remain in force, except as may be agreed by the parties.

(26) . The Need to Persevere: Remarks by President Carter at the Meeting of the General Council of the World Jewish Congress, November 2, 1977.[22]

Chairman Phil Klutznick and President Nahum Goldmann, members of the World Jewish Congress:

As my friend Phil Klutznick pointed out, sometimes praise is not forthcoming for a Democratic President, and I want to thank you especially for that warm welcome which I haven't heard in quite a long time. Thank you very, very much for it.

I'm deeply honored to receive this medal. I accept it with a sense of gratitude because of the organization from which it comes and because of the man for whom it is named. For more than half a century, Dr. Nahum Goldmann has been a scholar and a political leader and a fighter for the rights of all people. His career is proof that a man who is outspoken and sometimes controversial can still be a brilliant and an effective statesman. As the head of this organization and many others, he has played a more significant role in world affairs than have many heads of state. He's stepping down now as president of the World Jewish Congress, but his presence will remain, for he is the kind of man whose moral authority transcends any title or any office.

[22]Text from *Presidential Documents,* 13: 1706-11.

The World Jewish Congress has always sought to promote human rights in a universal way. In this, it is faithful to the ethical traditions from which it springs, for Jewish teaching has helped to shape the consciousness of human rights that is, I believe, now growing throughout the world.

In large measure, the beginnings of the modern concept of human rights go back to the laws and the prophets of the Judeo-Christian traditions. I've been steeped in the Bible since early childhood, and I believe that anyone who reads the ancient words of the Old Testament with both sensitivity and care will find there the idea of government as something based on a voluntary covenant rather than force—the idea of equality before the law and the supremacy of law over the whims of any ruler; the idea of the dignity of the individual human being and also of the individual conscience; the idea of service to the poor and to the oppressed; the ideas of self-government and tolerance and of nations living together in peace, despite differences of belief. I know, also, the memory of Jewish persecution and especially of the holocaust lends a special quality and a heartrending sensitivity to your own commitments to human rights.

This organization has made a major contribution to ensuring that human rights became part of the charter of the United Nations as one of its three basic purposes, along with the preservation of peace and social and economic progress. The principal authors of Universal Covenant on Human Rights were Eleanor Roosevelt, an American Protestant, Charles Malik, a Lebanese Catholic, and Rene Cassin, a French Jew. Because of their work and the work of others, no government can now pretend that its mistreatment of its own citizens is merely an internal affair.

These accomplishments have helped start a process by which governments can be moved forward, exemplifying the ideals which they publicly profess. Our own actions in the field of human rights must vary according to the appropriateness and effectiveness of one kind of action or another but our judgments must be made according to a single standard, for oppression is reprehensible whether its victims are blacks in South Africa or American Indians in the Western Hemisphere or Jews in the Soviet Union or political dissidents in Chile or Czechoslovakia.

The public demonstration of our own Government's commitment to human rights is one of the major goals that my administration has set for United States foreign policy. The emphasis on human rights has raised the level of consciousness around the world and is already beginning to help overcome the crisis of spirit which recently has afflicted the nations of the West.

We are also trying to build a more cooperative international system. We are consulting more closely with our own allies, and we place special emphasis on better relations with people in South America and in Asia and in Africa. And we are searching for new areas of cooperation with the Soviet Union, especially in the area where we and the Soviets now most intensely compete—in the race for nuclear weapons.

We must halt that race. In the last few months, we've tried to work closely with the Soviets to eliminate the testing of peaceful nuclear explosives. And just in the last 24 hours, Mr. Brezhnev, President Brezhnev, has announced that the Soviets are finally coming to agree with us.[23] And we have good hopes that we might, without too much delay, realize a comprehensive test ban that would eliminate this threat from the Earth. We hope so.

But at the same time we seek cooperation, we recognize that competition is also part of international life, and we will always remain capable of defending the legitimate interests of our people. We are addressing other global problems which threaten the well-being and the security of people everywhere. They include nuclear proliferation, the excessive sales of conventional arms, food supplies and energy, and the quality of the environment. These things affect all nations of the world. And we are also seeking solutions to regional conflicts that could do incalculable damage, if not resolved.

Our efforts toward a new treaty with Panama are one example. Bringing about peaceful change in southern Africa is another. But none is more important than finding peace in the Middle East.

Sixty years ago today, November 2, 1917, the British Foreign Secretary Lord Balfour——

[At this point, the President was interrupted by demonstrators. After making the following comment on the interruption, he continued his remarks.]

One of the basic human rights that we cherish in our country is the right to speak, and I have no objection to it.

As I was saying, exactly 60 years ago today, November 2, 1917, the British Foreign Secretary, Lord Balfour, informed Lord Rothschild of his government's support for the establishment of a national home for the Jewish people in Palestine. At that time, the idea seemed visionary and few dared to believe that it could actually be translated into reality. But today Israel is a vital force, an independent and democratic Jewish state whose national existence is accepted and whose security is stronger today than ever before.

We are proud to be Israel's firm friend and closest partner, and we shall stand by Israel always.

---

[23]Cf. Introduction at note 42.

I doubt that anyone in the history of our country has traveled more than I have in my campaign for President, nor talked to more groups, nor listened to more questions, nor heard more comments. And when I say that we will always stand with Israel, I speak not only for myself as President, not only for our Government, all three of its branches, but I speak not just for American Jews but for all Americans. This is one of our deepest-felt commitments, and I have no doubt that I speak accurately for the overwhelming portion of the American people, now and forever.

Despite its great accomplishments, however, Israel has yet to realize the cherished goal of living in peace with its neighbors. Some would say that peace cannot be achieved because of the accumulated mistrust and the deep emotions which divide Israelis from Arabs. Some would say that we must realistically resign ourselves to the prospect of unending struggle and conflict in the Middle East. With such an attitude of resignation, Israel would never have been created. And with such an attitude now, peace will never be achieved. What is needed is both vision and realism so that strong leadership can transform the hostility of the past into a peaceful and constructive future.

This was a vision of the Zionist movement in the first generation after the Balfour declaration, and it can be the achievement of Israel in its second generation as an independent state.

Since becoming President, I've spent much of my time in trying to promote a peace settlement between Israel and her Arab neighbors. All Americans know that peace in the Middle East is of vital concern to our own country. We cannot merely be idle bystanders. Our friendships and our interests require that we continue to devote ourselves to the cause of peace in this most dangerous region of the world.

Earlier this year, I outlined the elements of a comprehensive peace—not in order to impose our views on the parties concerned, but rather as a way of defining some of the elements of an overall settlement which would have to be achieved through detailed negotiations.

I continue to believe that the three key issues are, first, the obligations of real peace, including the full normalization of political, economic, and cultural relations; second, the establishment of effective security measures, coupled to Israeli withdrawal from occupied territories, and agreement on final, recognized, and secure borders; and third, the resolution of the Palestinian question.

These issues are interrelated in complex ways, and for peace to be achieved that's permanent and real, all of them will have to be resolved. Recently, our diplomatic efforts have focused on establishing a framework for negotiations so that the parties themselves will become engaged in the resolution of the many substantive issues that have divided them so long. We can offer our good offices as mediators, we can make suggestions, but we cannot do the negotiating.

For serious peace talks to begin, a reconvening of the Geneva conference has become essential. All the parties have accepted the idea of comprehensive negotiations at Geneva. An agreement has already been reached on several of the important procedural arrangements. Israel has accepted, for Geneva, the idea of a unified Arab delegation, which will include Palestinians, and has agreed to discuss the future of the West Bank and the Gaza Strip with Jordan, with Egypt, and with Palestinian Arabs. This can provide the means for a Palestinian voice to be heard in the shaping of a Middle East peace, and this represents a positive and a very constructive step.

Israel has also repeated its willingness to negotiate without preconditions and has stressed that all issues are negotiable. This is an attitude that others must accept if peace talks are to succeed.

For their part, the Arab states have accepted Israel's status as a nation. They are increasingly willing to work toward peace treaties and to form individual working groups to negotiate settlement of border issues and other disputes. No longer do they refuse to sit down at the negotiating table with Israel, nor do they dispute Israel's right to live within secure and recognized borders.

That must be taken as a measure of how far we have come from the intransigent positions of the past. The procedural arrangements hammered out at the 1973 Geneva Conference can provide a good basis for a reconvened conference. Even a year ago—just think back—the notion of Israelis and Arabs engaging in face-to-face negotiations about real peace, a peace embodied in signed, binding treaties, seemed like an illusion; yet, today, such negotiations are within reach. And I'm proud of the progress that has been achieved by all nations concerned to make this dream at least possible.

But to improve the atmosphere for serious negotiations, mutual suspicions must be further reduced. One source of Arab concern about Israeli intentions has been the establishment of civilian settlements in territories currently under occupation, which we consider to be a violation of the Fourth Geneva Convention.[24] On the Arab side, much still needs to be done to remove the suspicions that exist in Israel about Arab intentions. It was not so long ago, after all, that Arab demands were often expressed in extreme and sometimes violent ways. Israel's existence was constantly called into question. The continuing refusal of the Palestinian Liberation Organization

---

[24]Convention Relative to the Protection of Civilians in Time of War, signed at Geneva Aug. 12, 1949 (6 UST 3516; TIAS 3365).

to accept U.N. Resolution 242 and Israel's right to exist, along with the resort to violence and terror by some groups, provides Israelis with tangible evidence that their worst fears may in fact be justified.

Differences naturally exist not only between Arabs and Israelis but among the Arab parties themselves. And we are actively engaged in an effort, a very difficult effort, to narrow these differences so that Geneva can be reconvened. And we've called on the other cochairman of the Geneva conference, the Soviet Union, to use its influence constructively.

We will continue to encourage a solution to the Palestinian question in a framework which does not threaten the interests of any of the concerned parties, yet respects the legitimate rights of the Palestinians. The nations involved must negotiate the settlement, but we ourselves do not prefer an independent Palestinian state on the West Bank.

Negotiations will no doubt be prolonged and often very difficult. But we are in this to stay. I will personally be prepared to use the influence of the United States to help the negotiations succeed. We will not impose our will on any party, but we will constantly encourage and try to assist the process of conciliation.

Our relations with Israel will remain strong. Since the war in 1973, we have provided $10 billion in military and economic aid to Israel, about two-thirds of which was direct grants or concessional loans. The magnitude of this assistance is unprecedented in history. It's greatly enhanced Israel's economic and military strength. Our aid will continue.

As difficult as peace through negotiations will be in the Middle East, the alternative of stalemate and war is infinitely worse. The cost of another war would be staggering in both human and economic terms. Peace, by contrast, offers great hope to the peoples of the Middle East who have already contributed so much to civilization.

Peace, which must include a permanent and secure Jewish state of Israel, has a compelling logic for the Middle East. It would begin to bring Arabs and Israelis together in creative ways to create a prosperous and a stable region. And the prospect of coexistence and cooperation would revive the spirits of those who, for so long, thought only of violence and of struggle for survival itself.

Peace would lift some of the enormous burdens of defense and uplift the people's quality of life. The idea of peace in the Middle East today is no more of a dream than was the idea of a national home for the Jews in 1917. But it will require the same dedication that made Israel a reality and has permitted it to grow and to prosper.

We may be facing now the best opportunity for a permanent Middle East peace settlement in our lifetime. We must not let it slip away. Well-meaning leaders in Israel and in the Arab nations—African, European, South American, North American, all over the world—are making an unprecedented and a concerted effort to resolve the deep-seated differences in the Middle East.

This is not a time for intemperance or partisanship; it's a time for strong and responsible leadership and a willingness to explore carefully, perhaps for the first time, the intentions of others. It's a time to use the mutual strength and the unique friendship and partnership between Israel and the United States and the influence of you and others who have a deep interest and concern to guarantee a strong and permanently free and secure Israel, at peace with her neighbors and able to contribute her tremendous human resources toward the realization of human rights and a better and more peaceful life throughout the world.

The Old Testament offers a vision of what that kind of peace might mean in its deepest sense. I leave you with these lines from the Prophet Micah—who's still one of my favorites—lines and words which no summary or paraphrase could possibly do justice. It's from the Fourth Chapter, and the first five verses:

"But in the last days it shall come to pass, that the mountain of the house of the Lord shall be established in the top of the mountains, and it shall be exalted above the hills; and people shall flow into it.

"And many nations shall come, and say, Come, and let us go up to the mountain of the Lord, and to the house of the God of Jacob; and he will teach us of his ways, and we will walk in his paths: and the law shall go forth from Zion, and the word of the Lord from Jerusalem.

"And he shall judge among many people, and rebuke strong nations afar off; and they shall beat their swords into plowshares, and their spears into pruning-hooks: nation shall not lift up a sword against nation, neither shall they learn war any more.

"But they shall sit every man under his vine and under his fig tree; and none shall make them afraid: for the mouth of the Lord of hosts hath spoken it.

"For all people will walk every one in the name of his god, but we will walk in the name of the Lord our God for ever and ever."

However we may falter, however difficult the path, it is our duty to walk together toward the fulfillment of this majestic prophesy.

Thank you very much.

(27) *"An Historic Breakthrough": News Conference Statement by President Carter, November 30, 1977.*[25]

(Excerpt)

* * *

The other comment I'd like to make is concerning the Middle East. In the last few days we have seen, I believe, an historic breakthrough in the search for a permanent, lasting peace in the Middle East because of the true leadership qualities that have been exhibited by the courage of President Sadat and the gracious reception of him in Israel by Prime Minister Begin.

This has been, already, a tremendous accomplishment. I think the importance of it is that there has been an initiation of direct, person-to-person negotiations between Israel and the major power in the Mideast among the Arab nations who are Israel's neighbors. Lebanon, Syria, Jordan have a total population of about 12 million; Egypt has a population of 36 million and has by far the greatest military force. And the fact that this strongest Arab country and the nation of Israel are now conducting direct negotiations is a major accomplishment in itself.

Two of Israel's most cherished desires have already been met. One is this face-to-face negotiation possibility, and the other one is a recognition by a major Arab leader that Israel has a right to exist. In fact, President Sadat said, "We welcome you in our midst."

The United States has been very pleased to see this reduction in distrust and a reduction in fear and a reduction in suspicion between the Arabs and the Israelis. We have played a close consultative role with both of these leaders. We have, on several instances recently, acted as intermediaries at their request. Both Prime Minister Begin and President Sadat have publicly expressed their reconfirmation that these exploratory talks are designed to lead toward a comprehensive settlement including Israel and all her neighbors.

Sunday, President Sadat called for a conference in Cairo. This is likely to be held around the 13th of December, about the middle of December. We will participate in that conference at a high level—Assistant Secretary Atherton will represent our Nation. We look on this as a very constructive step. The road toward peace has already led through Jerusalem, will now go to Cairo and ultimately, we believe, to a comprehensive consultation at Geneva.

It's not an easy thing to bring about a comprehensive peace settlement. Immediate expectations have sometimes been exaggerated. The definition of real peace—I think we've made good progress on that already. The resolution of the Palestinian question still has not

[25]Text from *Presidential Documents*, 13: 1808.

been decided. And the solution to the problem concerning borders and national security has also not been decided.

We have played, I think, a proper role. I have tried to convince, in the past, Prime Minister Begin of the good intentions of President Sadat and vice versa. When there has been no progress being made, the United States has taken the initiative. Now that progress is being made, a proper role for the United States is to support that progress and to give the credit to the strong leadership that's already been exhibited by Prime Minister Begin and President Sadat and to let our Nation be used, as called upon, to expedite the peace process.

I believe that this is a move that the whole world looks upon with great appreciation. And again, I want to express my congratulations and my appreciation to these two strong leaders for the tremendous progress already made and for their commitment to future progress.

(28) Preparatory Meeting for the Geneva Peace Conference: Statement by Alfred L. Atherton, Jr., United States Representative, Cairo, December 15, 1977.[26]

It is an honor to represent the United States on this historic occasion.

I would like first to extend congratulations to the Governments of both Egypt and Israel whose commitment to peace has made it possible for this meeting to convene. It is a particular pleasure to be sitting at this table today with friends from Egypt and Israel and with Gen. Siilasvuo [of Finland], who is present to represent Secretary General Waldheim.

In sending me here, President Carter made it clear that the U.S. Government sees the convening of this meeting in Cairo as a constructive step on the road to peace. We are ready to do whatever we can to facilitate, support, and encourage the negotiations here to prepare the way for the Geneva Middle East Peace Conference and the achievement of a comprehensive, just, and durable peace in the Middle East.

For nearly 30 years the Middle East conflict has reaped a terrible harvest of lives, resources, and energies of Arabs and Israelis alike. It is true that during this period there have been some steps forward: Security Council Resolutions 242 and 338, the convening of the Middle East Peace Conference in Geneva in 1973, and the conclusion of three limited agreements under the auspices of that conference, all testified to the increasing commitment by the parties to the search for a peaceful settlement.

[26]Department of State Press Release, Dec. 15; text from *Bulletin*, Jan. 1978: 47-8.

Yet, in spite of this progress, the remaining psychological obstacles have imposed formidable barriers, as the attempt has been made this year to take the logical next step of opening negotiations for a final peace settlement at Geneva.

The momentous events of recent weeks have fundamentally altered that situation and have provided new hope that the objective of an overall settlement embodied in peace treaties can, in fact, be achieved. With one bold stroke President Sadat has broken through the barrier and imparted new momentum toward peace. With farsightedness and statesmanship, Prime Minister Begin has responded in a manner that makes it clear that Israel, for its part, does not intend to allow this unique opportunity to be lost. These two strong and creative leaders have brought about a sea change in attitudes both in Israel and in the Arab countries, and today solutions—a month ago considered unattainable—have been suddenly brought within the realm of possibility.

Today few nations in the world would challenge the proposition that these developments have created a unique opportunity for successful negotiations leading to peace in the Middle East. The idea of peace has captured the imagination and ignited the hopes of a war-weary region. The government leaders who are charged with the responsibility, as well as the challenge, of negotiating can do so with the confidence that there is today an overwhelming public constituency in the region for peace.

All of us in this room would agree that we must not allow the momentum of these events to be lost. President Sadat has called this meeting to prepare for a reconvening of the Geneva conference, the objective of which remains the negotiation, among all the parties to the conflict, of a final peace settlement on the basis of Resolutions 242 and 338.

I must record my government's regret that others invited to this meeting have felt unable to accept the invitation to attend. Ultimately, I believe those absent will see that the process begun here is in their benefit. We are all agreed the door remains open for others to join at any time.

My government—indeed each of the governments represented here—has emphasized on numerous occasions that our objective is the negotiation of a comprehensive peace settlement. Central to my government's policy over the years is the concept that this peace can only be achieved through negotiations between the parties. Security Council Resolution 242 established the principles for those negotiations. Resolution 338, which made a convening of the conference in Geneva possible, established the process. We have always held the view that wherever and whenever the parties can start talking with one another, it is in the spirit of that mandate.

We see the discussions getting underway today in Cairo as an integral and contributory step toward a reconvening of the Geneva conference and the negotiation of a comprehensive peace. We do not agree that these proceedings are contradictory to the Geneva conference. As President Carter said:[27] "The road toward peace has already led through Jerusalem, will now go to Cairo, and ultimately, we believe, to a comprehensive consultation at Geneva."

In calling for this preparatory meeting, President Sadat has indicated two basic objectives: Making progress toward resolving the substantive problems and overcoming the remaining unresolved procedural obstacles to a Geneva conference. We believe these are realistic and obtainable goals and that valuable work can be done here. We will do everything we can to help the two negotiating parties make progress. It is for them to define in the first instance the subject matter of these discussions, but we will remain available to offer counsel, suggestions, or any other assistance the parties may feel they need.

We are opening these talks at a unique moment. All of us here must not only hope we have reached a turning point in history but also must make our contribution to insure that it will indeed prove to be a lasting turning point. The leaders of our respective governments—and our peoples—are expecting us to achieve solid results at this meeting, and we should not fail them. As President Carter recently said:[28] "We may be facing now the best opportunity for a permanent Middle East peace settlement in our lifetime. We must not let it slip by."

In closing I hope you will permit me to indulge in a brief personal reflection. For many years I have labored, on behalf of my government and with countless colleagues—some of whom have given their lives in the effort—to help our Arab and Israeli friends find a breakthrough to peace. I have shared and, I think, have acquired some understanding of the agonies both sides experience as they face decisions fateful for the future of their peoples—and, indeed, for the world. It is a great personal satisfaction to be part of these talks which hold out so much hope that the long-sought breakthrough has been achieved. The negotiation of deeply rooted differences involving vital national interests is never a smooth or easy task, and we can expect moments of discouragement. These must and can be overcome, however, if the governments we serve, and we personally, keep before us the vision we all share today of a peaceful and prosperous Middle East. My government is fully dedicated to that vision.

[27] Document 27.
[28] Document 26.

5. WHICH WAY AFRICA?

(29) "United States Relations in Southern Africa": Address by William E. Schaufele, Jr., Assistant Secretary of State for African Affairs, before the American Academy of Political and Social Science, Philadelphia, April 16, 1977.[1]

A few years ago I would not have chosen this subject to provoke discussion among a distinguished group of academic scholars. The African Continent in general, and the southern part of it in particular, excited sustained attention and debate only among a small band of specialists in academia, business circles, and the government, except in time of crisis. This has all changed radically, and there are times when I look back with some nostalgia to a more tranquil life before I became so intimately acquainted with African airline schedules and charters last year.

Probably never in the history of American diplomacy has the governmental and public interest, even absorption, in one relatively small and remote area of the world increased at such a rapid pace, from quasi-academic to substantial.

Our concern about southern Africa is quite unlike the basis for our interest in other parts of the world important to the United States, such as Europe, the Far East, and the Middle East. Our interest is not strategic. We have consistently made clear that the United States does not wish to play a military role anywhere in Africa. It is also not based on economic interests, although we do want to see that Western Europe as well as the United States retains access to the mineral wealth of southern Africa. Under the proper political circumstances I can visualize a very substantial growth in two-way trade with that part of the continent. Our recent actions with respect to the Byrd amendment[2] should make clear that we are fully capable of subordinating our economic interests to other, more vital concerns.

U.S. policies in southern Africa are essentially founded on politi-

[1]Text from *Bulletin,* 76: 464-7.
[2]Cf. Introduction at note 86.

cal interests. A significant ingredient of that interest is our concern for human rights and human dignity. Our policy toward southern Africa is guided by our ideals of liberty and equality and by our commitment to oppose racial and social injustice. We believe that the minority governments of Rhodesia, South Africa, and Namibia violate fundamental human rights as spelled out in the U.N. Declaration of Human Rights. We have spoken out on this subject forcefully and repeatedly so that there can be no mistaking our position. In conformity with our own fundamental principles as a nation, we have based our policies on the belief that the peaceful transfer of power to the black majority is not only necessary and desirable but also possible.

The foreign policy of the United States, if it is to be successful, must be firmly grounded in our own fundamental beliefs. Lacking this vital element, it would not obtain the requisite backing from our people. It is self-evident, therefore, that the United States must be engaged in southern Africa if we want to remain true to ourselves. Given the dangers involved, we cannot remain an idle spectator while the decolonization process takes place in Rhodesia and Namibia.

Similarly, I believe that our history dictates that we have a role to play with respect to the system of apartheid in South Africa. It has been a long and frequently painful process for the black and white elements of our population to work out their relationship based on the ideals of the Founding Fathers. Very substantial progress has been made in recent years in this respect, and more needs still to be done. But at least there is now hope where there once was only despair, and we are on the right road. Having come through this experience, we can, I believe, without resort to the zealotry of the converted, also contribute to the resolution of the apartheid issue. Our history as a people of many races, able to live together more or less in harmony, can be, within limits, a guide and inspiration to others.

Apartheid, of course, simply means "apartness." It enshrines the concept of separateness, without even the leavening thought of equality. The system of apartheid currently being practiced in South Africa is therefore still a considerable distance from the slightly more progressive concept finally struck down by our Supreme Court a quarter century ago. It is a measure of the distance South Africa must travel to overcome the burden of its racial heritage.

The rapid changes in Portugal brought about the decolonization of the Portuguese empire in Africa. This development of the last few years has, in turn, hastened the demise of the remaining two vestiges of the era of empire, Rhodesia and Namibia.

The policy of this Administration, and that of its predecessor, has been to try to insure that the changes which we consider inevitable for both Rhodesia and Namibia take place in a peaceful manner. There are those who believe that the transition to majority rule can come about only by force of arms. These advocates of violence believe that Ian Smith's record of procrastination in Rhodesia and South Africa's continuing important role in Namibia preclude a peaceful settlement. I strongly disagree with that view. Progress has already been made, perhaps more than we had reason to hope for only a year ago. Ian Smith has agreed to the principle of turning over power to the black majority within two years. Although negotiations broke down in Geneva over the complex questions surrounding the modalities of the transition to majority rule, I hope that talks can again be started. I am convinced there is a reasonable chance for success.

The Question of Rhodesia

We believe that the United Kingdom should continue to take the lead on the Rhodesian question since it is the sovereign power in Rhodesia. We have worked closely and well with them in the past; during February we had several intensive meetings with them in Washington to concert our policies. And Foreign Secretary Owen is currently in southern Africa to assess further the situation, on a trip planned in agreement with the United States.

It is also not an insignificant accomplishment that, in the course of working toward a peaceful settlement of southern African issues, we have strengthened our ties with the frontline states of Zambia, Tanzania, Botswana, and Mozambique. Ambassador Young, on his trip to Africa during the early days of the Carter Administration, received valuable new insights into the thinking of the African leaders on those issues of mutual concern. I want to emphasize that the frontline states continue to support the view that a peaceful solution is desirable in Rhodesia and Namibia even as armed struggle goes on. We are working closely with them to that end.

The advantages of a peaceful transition to majority rule should be manifest to all of us. The transfer of power is going to be difficult under any circumstances, and some disruption of the economic processes may be inevitable. But both Rhodesia and Namibia are potentially prosperous countries with existing structures upon which further sustained economic growth can be built. How much more desirable it would be for the black majority to inherit a country with a running economy than one so severely damaged or destroyed by prolonged strife that the immediate fruits of independence may be meager indeed.

Given the strength, on the one hand, of the Zimbabwe liberation forces, many of which are now in training camps in Mozambique and Tanzania, and the strength of the Rhodesian security forces on the other, we believe that a "solution" by combat of arms would inevitably be protracted. There would not be a quick knockout by either side. Therefore such a "solution" would be bloody and involve untold human suffering and misery, which we want to avoid if at all possible.

Prolonged violence would create a climate, moreover, conducive to intervention by forces from outside the African Continent. The frontline states have thus far successfully resisted the counsel of those contending that only armed struggle can produce success in Zimbabwe and Namibia. We cannot be sure, however, that they will always see the situation this way.

We firmly believe that African problems should be solved by the Africans themselves. Our policy has been guided by the principle that the big powers or their surrogates should not play a military role on the continent. We have seen how long it takes an outside power, once engaged in an African conflict, to withdraw its forces, and we have seen the many undesirable consequences such involvement brings in its train in terms of African stability and unity.

Following rejection of the latest British proposals in January, Ian Smith has apparently decided to attempt what he euphemistically calls an "internal solution." This involves negotiations with certain black groups and individuals, some of whom were already members of the Smith regime, to bring about majority rule. We do not believe this will lead to a solution. It ignores not only the desires of the Zimbabwe guerrilla forces and important nationalist elements but also those of the frontline states. In our view this "internal solution" cannot last; to attempt it would inevitably lead to increased bloodshed and violence.

Finally, we believe that a peaceful solution in Rhodesia and Namibia would provide a useful stimulus to orderly change in South Africa itself. Conversely, the escalation of violence in the adjoining territories could well polarize opinion in South Africa and make more difficult the achievement of any progress in the direction of racial justice in that country.

We recognize, of course, that our dedication to a peaceful, rapid, and orderly transition to majority rule needs to be backed up with concrete measures. We worked hard for the repeal of the Byrd amendment by the Congress, accomplished by a decisive margin in both Houses, placing the United States in observance with pertinent U.N. resolutions. Repeal should convince Prime Minister Smith, if he still had doubts, that he cannot count on the United States to bail him out when his policies fail. We hope now that he will give real negotiations another chance.

We intend to insure that the sanctions against Rhodesia are

strictly enforced. We will be consulting with other nations to see what can be done about tightening compliance with sanctions. We are looking into additional measures that our government might undertake to place additional pressure on Rhodesia and to convince it of the gravity of the situation.

We have provided economic assistance to the Governments of Zambia and Mozambique, in recognition of the economic losses suffered by these two countries owing to the closure of their borders with Rhodesia and the interruption of the hitherto profitable transit traffic in Rhodesian goods.

I would like to make it clear that we have no solution that we wish to impose on the various elements of the Zimbabwean political scene. We have no favorites whom we support. We will not take sides, since we believe that the Africans want to work out African solutions to African problems. We will continue to counsel maximum flexibility and readiness to compromise, maximum unity among all of the nationalist liberation forces, and a maximum effort to create the kind of atmosphere that will allow the negotiations to succeed. Both sides should come to the conclusion that their objectives can be achieved more surely and effectively by negotiation rather than by resort to arms.

The Namibian Issue

While the contentious issue of Rhodesia tends to dominate the headlines, we have not been unmindful of the need for rapid progress on the Namibian issue as well. Our policy with respect to that territory has been consistent and clear. In 1966 we voted to terminate South Africa's mandate. We have supported the finding of the International Court of Justice that South Africa's occupation was illegal.[3] We remain committed to U.N. Security Council Resolution 385[4] calling for free elections under U.N. auspices, South African withdrawal of its illegal administration, and the release of all Namibian political prisoners.

As in the case of Zimbabwe, we have cause for at least some optimism that the Namibian problem can be peacefully resolved. Some progress has been achieved. A target date of December 1978 has been set for independence, and the South Africans have fully endorsed the concept that Namibia should become independent on that date.

[3] *AFR, 1971:* 403-5.
[4] U.N. Security Council Resolution 385 (1976), adopted unanimously Jan. 30, 1976, reiterated the demand for South Africa's withdrawal of its "illegal administration" from Namibia and, among other things, declared it "imperative that free elections under the supervision and control of the United Nations be held for the whole of Namibia as one political entity." *Bulletin,* 74: 246.

A major difficulty, as we see it, has been that the present efforts to establish an interim government for Namibia have excluded the South West Africa People's Organization (SWAPO), which is recognized by the OAU and the United Nations as the sole Namibian nationalist movement. These efforts have centered on a meeting of Namibian groups in Windhoek seeking to establish an interim government to lead the country to independence. For its part, SWAPO has not wished to participate and has insisted that independence could come about only as a result of direct negotiations between itself and the South African Government. On this issue, also, we urge a spirit of compromise on both sides in the belief that what may be achievable in a peaceful manner would almost certainly be preferable to anything that can be won through the force of arms alone.

In the case of Namibia, too, it seems to us that while the positions of some of the principal contenders are far apart, good will on both sides can produce agreement. We believe that all political groups in Namibia, specifically including SWAPO, have a role to play in the process leading to independence. We consider that the United Nations should have a role to play in giving birth to an independent nation from a territory which the community of nations accepts as being under U.N. authority, at least in theory. We have proposed that an international conference on a Namibian settlement take place under U.N. aegis at a neutral site with all the concerned parties.

In support of our policy, the United States has since 1970 officially discouraged American investment in Namibia. The facilities of the Export-Import Bank are no longer available for trade with the territory. No future U.S. investments there, made on the basis of rights acquired from the South African Government following termination of the mandate, would receive U.S. Government protection against the claims of a future legitimate government in Namibia. We have urged American firms doing business in Namibia to assure that their employment practices are in conformity with the principles of the Universal Declaration of Human Rights.

Policy Toward South Africa

Our policy toward South Africa is necessarily different from our policy toward Rhodesia and Namibia.

We have had diplomatic relations with South Africa since that country became independent. In addition to our Embassy in Pretoria, we have three consulates general which keep us informed about what is going on in that country.

South Africa is not a colonial remnant. Even the leaders of black Africa do not challenge the right of the white minority to live in

South Africa. The white settlers began to cultivate the lands of South Africa 300 years ago. They are also Africans, and they have no other place to go. The problems of South Africa should therefore be solved in South Africa—not by outside powers.

Our maintenance of diplomatic relations with South Africa is by no means an indication that we accept that country's institution of apartheid. We have not minced our words in stating our unalterable opposition to apartheid and shall not do so in the future. This system is a clear violation of fundamental human rights. Last summer the United States joined a consensus in the U.N. Security Council resolution "strongly condemning" the South African Government for its role in the Soweto violence.[5] On that occasion, the acting U.S. representative called on South Africa to "take these events as a warning" and "to abandon a system which is clearly not acceptable under any standard of human rights."

As elsewhere in southern Africa we are dedicated to the proposition that peaceful change must succeed, if only because the alternative is so unacceptable. We have watched with dismay the escalation of violence in South Africa, beginning with the Soweto riots last year. We are deeply concerned that unless the spiral of violence can be arrested and reversed, there will be such a polarization of forces within South Africa that peaceful change will become immeasurably more difficult than it is already. We shall employ all reasonable channels to get this message across to the South Africans and to facilitate this change to the maximum possible extent.

It is appropriate, however, to insert here a cautionary word. Of all people, we Americans should probably be chary about providing excessive and unsolicited advice to others about how they should solve their racial problems. True, we have made impressive progress within our own country in removing the stain of injustice and discrimination based solely on race. But we must also admit that we have a considerable way to go before our achievements approach the ideals set forth in our Declaration of Independence and our Constitution.

But perhaps more important, our recent history provides testimony to the fact that change in the racial sphere came about—gradually, unevenly, perhaps even grudgingly—not because outsiders or foreigners told us what was right, but because the realization finally dawned on our people that the status quo was wrong and had to be changed for our own good. This self-realization must be given an opportunity to do its creative work in South Africa also, although I will readily agree that the time for results is limited.

It is in no one's interest if the South Africans move into an isolationist shell, closed against outside influences, there to defend

[5]Resolution 392 (1976), June 19, 1976; cf. *AFR, 1976:* 54.

themselves from all enemies foreign and domestic. Such a development would have an effect opposite from the one we wish to achieve.

Our diplomacy toward South Africa must therefore be carried out with a good deal of finesse and skill. We shall have to weigh carefully the relative merits of speaking out and of restraint.

In the circumstances I have described, the United States is necessarily pursuing a nuanced policy vis-a-vis South Africa, without compromising our principles. As I have already indicated, we have repeatedly made clear our opposition to a system under which an 18 percent minority limits the black majority economically, discriminates socially, and deprives the blacks of political rights.

As a corollary to this policy, the United States has opposed the South African Government's policy of creating a series of "bantustans," or "homelands." The Transkei was the first of these homelands to become "independent," but others are expected to be given that status by South Africa. The United States has not recognized the Transkei, and aside from South Africa, neither have other members of the United Nations. We have no intention of recognizing any of the other homelands that will be declared "independent."

In fact, the creation of these so-called states is an extension of the apartheid policy. Stripped of all euphemisms and rationalizations the concept of the homelands is unfair to the black majority. The effect of their creation is to deprive substantial elements of the black urban work force of their civil rights in South Africa and to force many urban blacks to take on citizenship of a "homeland" they have never known. The homelands were established without consulting the blacks. They are generally conglomerations of the remnants of tribal lands without contiguous borders, without the basis for economic viability, and without any basis for true political independence from South Africa.

It is worth noting that there have been some encouraging signs on the South African scene. Events of the past year have not been without their effect on the white community of South Africa. Many signs point to considerable soul-searching, even on the part of the Afrikaner community, which forms the primary political base of the ruling party. A number of leading Afrikaner intellectuals have urged that the government reconsider important elements of its policy, such as present plans for the homelands, the denial of all political rights to Africans outside the homelands, and various forms of economic discrimination.

South African businessmen, too, have begun to urge steps to improve the daily life of Africans in such areas as housing and training. In certain areas of activity which are not directly under governmental sponsorship, such as athletic and religious organizations, we detect some breakdown in previously rigid racial barriers. We have been encouraged by the actions of the Catholic Church to permit some integration of its schools and by the tolerance of this decision displayed by the South African Government. In terms of the daily life of an African in South Africa, these are small steps. But we believe they reflect that the faith of many South African whites in the possibility of maintaining indefinitely racial separation and white supremacy is being fundamentally reexamined.

The United States has adopted certain policies to demonstrate our opposition to the apartheid policy of South Africa. Since 1962 we have maintained a voluntary embargo on the sale of military equipment to South Africa. U.S. naval vessels do not call at South African ports (except for emergencies), although they regularly make courtesy calls in some black African ports.

We have redoubled our efforts to intensify our contacts with blacks in the South African population. President Carter recently invited Gathsha Buthelezi, a prominent black moderate, to the White House, underlining the Administration's interest in establishing better ties with black leadership in South Africa.

Along these same lines, we have intensified the informational activities of the U.S. Information Service in South Africa, especially among the black population. We have also expanded our exchange program, under which a cross section of the South African population, mostly blacks, visits the United States for monthlong visits. Our diplomatic and consular officers, including black Foreign Service officers, cultivate a wide range of contacts in South Africa.

Steps by U.S. Business Community

The United States has also encouraged American firms doing business in South Africa to improve working conditions for their black employees. We believe this could be a significant American contribution to the principle of social justice and provide a vehicle for promoting economic and social progress. We have been encouraged by the progress that many American firms have demonstrated in working toward the principle of equal pay for equal work, adequate pensions, improved medical and insurance benefits, and expanded opportunities for advancement based entirely on merit, rather than on the basis of race. Although there is clearly room for improvement in the performance of their labor practices, South African-based American companies have shown considerable sensitivity in dealing with their black employees. By their example they have already set in motion some of the kinds of changes that are so desperately needed.

A recent step in the right direction was the March 1, 1977, announcement by 12 major U.S. corporations with business interests in South Africa expressing support for a set of principles designed to promote equal employment rights for blacks and nonwhite minority groups.[6] These principles call for the nonsegregation of races in all dining facilities and places of work and the concept of equal pay for all employees doing equal and comparable work. We hope that these constructive steps will be emulated and expanded by other U.S. firms engaged in business in South Africa and perhaps even be adopted by the South African business community itself.

We fully recognize that American corporations genuinely desirous of wishing to institute social changes in their labor practices may fear contravening South African laws and traditional practices which discourage evolutionary changes. Moreover, many of the white unions are resistant to change. They will not countenance having a black supervisor over a white worker, and they restrict the movement of black workers into the ranks of the skilled workers despite the fact that South African industry desperately needs more skilled workers.

There is no reason why American firms cannot enter into collective bargaining agreements with black unions. Unlike the white unions, these are not officially registered. However, they are not illegal, and companies can deal with them. Several weeks ago the second largest supermarket chain in South Africa announced that it would recognize and negotiate with a black trade union. We hope this will encourage American corporations to follow suit where the existence of a black union makes this feasible.

There are those, of course, who argue that American corporations in effect have no business being in South Africa in the first place, that they are either an impediment to social change or have no real effect on change, and that their net result is to buttress the status quo elements that want apartheid to go on.

Others have come forth with opposing arguments. They claim that U.S. investment assists the economic development of South Africa, which sets in motion certain powerful currents of change that will be too powerful to withstand. Increased investment, the argument goes, helps create more jobs for blacks, inevitably some upgrading of their job skills, and this process has already resulted in new and different perceptions and attitudes that have made themselves felt on the South African political scene.

The South African blacks seem to be divided in their views on this issue. Some favor foreign, including U.S., investment while

[6]Cf. *New York Times,* Mar. 2, 1977.

others have opposed it. There is certainly no clear consensus on the question.

As a government we have stayed neutral on this issue so far. We have neither encouraged nor discouraged American investment in South Africa. This is one of many facets of our policy toward southern Africa that is currently under review.

Potential American investors have been free to decide the issue on their own, although if asked we provide them with all the information we have available. We make certain they are aware of the controversy about such investment, explain our official neutrality, note the moral and social as well as economic and political problems of working in an apartheid society, and urge that if they do invest they give priority attention to the matter of fair employment practices.

We have, however, placed some restrictions on our bilateral economic relationship. For example, we restrict the Export-Import Bank facilities in South Africa. Export-Import Bank direct loans to South African importers of U.S. products are prohibited. However, the Bank does guarantee privately financed loans as a service to U.S. exporters.

As I indicated at the outset of my remarks, there are a number of positive elements on the southern African scene. Perhaps the most promising aspect is the fact that unlike a number of African countries, Zimbabwe, Namibia, and South Africa itself have strong economic assets. Southern Africa is richly endowed with a generally favorable climate and with natural resources that the world needs. We have already announced that we stand ready to assist Zimbabwe and Namibia with training programs to promote further economic development when majority rule comes.

The rest of the African Continent has, in a relatively short time, made tremendous progress from the colonial period to independence to collectively playing a major role on the world scene. The record has inevitably been an uneven one, but there are a number of African countries where Africans and Europeans cooperate in harmony for the betterment of all. I would not suggest that the situation in southern Africa is analogous. But I do suggest that there are examples on the African Continent which give hope that political leaders can creatively build a future in which blacks and whites can coexist and prosper in peace rather than have the future imposed on them.

For the sake of Africa, and for our sake, I hope that the leadership in southern Africa will choose wisely. For our part we wish them well, and we will remain committed to doing everything in our power to insure that the outcome will be a happy one.

(30) Policy Toward Namibia and Zimbabwe: Statement by Andrew Young, United States Representative to the United Nations, before the International Conference in Support of the Peoples of Zimbabwe and Namibia, Maputo, Mozambique, May 19, 1977.[7]

I would like to thank the sponsors of the conference for enabling me and my colleagues on the American delegation to join this effort of the international community to express deeply held views about Namibia and Zimbabwe.

I congratulate Secretary General Waldheim, as well as Ambassador Salim and Ambassador Kamana[8] and through them the Committee of 24 and the U.N. Council for Namibia, for their work in organizing the conference. I would also like to thank our host, the Government of Mozambique, for its hospitality here in Maputo.

I have come to Maputo because the United States wishes to be strongly represented at this conference in support of the independence and liberation of Namibia and Zimbabwe. I have come to Maputo because one of President Carter's first acts was to demand a new and progressive policy toward Africa. And, I am here because a personal commitment to human rights requires that I be here.

I welcome this opportunity today to speak to all of you gathered here; to speak to you openly about southern Africa and the policy of my government toward the problems of Namibia and Zimbabwe. The Carter Administration wants to demonstrate by the American participation in this conference and in other ways that:

—We want it to develop, prosper, and be free;

—We very much want to associate ourselves more closely and work with Africans on a broad range of matters of mutual interest;

—We firmly believe there must be an end to the deprivation of human dignity and fundamental rights for the majority of the people of Namibia and Zimbabwe solely because of the color of their skin; and

—These last vestiges of colonialism must give way to freedom and independence based on the will of the people.

---

[7]As-prepared text from *Bulletin,* 77: 55-8.

[8]Salem Ahmed Salim, Tanzanian Representative to the U.N., and Dunstan Weston Kamana, Zambian Representative to the U.N. and Chairman, U.N. Council for Namibia.

We are in a race against time regarding Namibia and Zimbabwe. The future of those two countries and the fate of their people is certain—liberation. We are here to discuss measures that can hasten the inevitable day of freedom. We all know that among these measures will be continuing military efforts by the liberation forces. They will insist on continuing their struggle as long as fundamental political rights are denied the majority in Zimbabwe and Namibia.

The armed struggle, however, though its final outcome is inevitable, exacts a cruel price from the people of Zimbabwe and Namibia. Africa needs the leadership that will be lost in a prolonged struggle; it needs the infrastructure that will be destroyed in extended military conflict. This is why all here—whatever their views—must support efforts to press ahead with any promising approach to an early negotiated settlement. This is why one objective of this conference should be to make it clear that U.N. members, as always, prefer a negotiated settlement where it can be found.

The policies of the U.S. Government toward southern Africa reflect the Carter Administration's commitment to human rights. President Carter made it clear from the beginning that a renewed commitment to our responsibilities in the field of human rights required justice in southern Africa. But our policy in southern Africa also grows out of our policy toward Africa as a whole, a policy based on support for freedom, independence, territorial integrity, and economic development and dignity for all African nations. We believe it is in our national interest to work cooperatively with African nations on mutual economic and political concerns.

During the past several months, I have participated personally in the U.S. Government's review of the situation in southern Africa. Our conclusion is that the time remaining for peaceful settlement is brief. We therefore urgently embarked on several initiatives with the Government of the United Kingdom and several other Western governments on the Security Council. We took these initiatives on Rhodesia and Namibia because of the clear necessity of resolving these problems while time remains. Recent military tension involving the illegal Smith regime and its neighbors reveals how combustible the situation has become. The United States condemns the Rhodesian military incursions into Mozambique and Botswana and the Rhodesian threat against Zambia.

At the heart of tensions in southern Africa lies the smoldering racial crisis in South Africa itself. There as well, time is the enemy. Refusal to take daring steps now will make progress later much more painful, if not impossible. The United States will, therefore, let the South African Government know that this American Administration strongly believes that change in South Africa must begin now.

Toward this end, Vice President Mondale will be meeting in

Vienna today and tomorrow with Prime Minister Vorster of South Africa. While we are meeting in Maputo, Vice President Mondale will be conveying to Mr. Vorster all aspects of U.S. policy toward southern Africa. He will be expressing U.S. support for British Foreign Secretary Owen's initiative on Rhodesia and for the effort of the five-power contact groups to achieve a negotiated solution for Namibia consistent with Security Council Resolution 385.[9] The Vice President will underscore the need for urgent progress in Rhodesia and Namibia and for fundamental positive changes in South Africa itself in the interests of peace and stability for the entire region.[10]

Let me turn to the work of this conference. It is my strong belief that as we discuss the questions of Zimbabwe and Namibia here in Maputo, we should do so in a spirit of cooperation and with a focus on contributing to rapid solutions to the Zimbabwe and Namibia disputes which will minimize the costs in terms of human lives. This conference offers us an opportunity to explore together the ways in which we can jointly plan workable solutions. The declaration we adopt at the close of the conference should state clearly and concisely our goals and aspirations in approaching this problem. And it should keep open all roads to a negotiated settlement.

Over the past several weeks, the five Western members of the Security Council have been working together on an initiative to help find a settlement to the Namibian problem. As most of you know, the approach originated with an unprecedented joint demarche to Prime Minister Vorster of South Africa on April 7. At that meeting, Mr. Vorster was told of the necessity for a settlement in Namibia consistent with U.N. Security Council Resolution 385. It was expressed to him that an absence of progress toward an internationally acceptable solution would have serious consequences for South Africa.

From April 27 to 29 officials of the British, Canadian, French, German, and American Governments met with South African officials in Cape Town to discuss in detail the views of the West on Namibia. The discussions centered around implementation of Resolution 385 and the importance of holding free elections in Namibia under U.N. supervision. The representatives of five countries expressed their strong view that all parties to the Namibian problem should avoid any steps which would foreclose the possibility of achieving an internationally acceptable solution. The Western delegates informed the South Africans in particular that the reported plans to establish an interim government in Namibia based on the constitution developed by the Turnhalle conference would be unacceptable.

[9]Cf. note 4 to Document 29.
[10]Cf. Document 31.

Following discussions with the South Africans, including several sessions with Prime Minister Vorster, the contact group set out to discuss the points raised during the talks with the other parties to the Namibian problem. We have only just completed informing the Secretary General, representatives of the front-line states, other African leaders, SWAPO, and representatives of various political groups inside Namibia. We intend to follow up aggressively on the next stage of this process, to consolidate the points on which progress has been made, to clarify new points that have been raised, and to consult closely with all parties, particularly interested African states and SWAPO. As our host, President Samora Machel, stressed in the opening address, Security Council Resolution 385 constitutes a platform providing for a "just solution" to the Namibian conflict. We are determined to press ahead with this platform precisely because it does provide a just solution. Our initiatives with the other Western members of the Security Council are taken in that context. We will point out to South Africa that Resolution 385 offers it a final chance for peaceful settlement if it acts now.

On Zimbabwe Secretary of State Vance recently met with British Foreign Secretary David Owen to consider the Rhodesian problem in light of Secretary Owen's trip to Africa. As my colleague, Minister [of State for Foreign Affairs] Ted Rowlands, has informed you, the British Government has decided to establish a consultative group to make contact with the parties to the Rhodesian conflict which will visit the area as necessary, including Salisbury. The U.S. Government has agreed to appoint a senior U.S. official to work with the Foreign and Commonwealth Office Deputy Under Secretary John Graham, who will head the consultative group. The purpose of the group will be to engage in detailed consultation about an independence constitution for Zimbabwe, as well as the necessary transitional arrangements. We offer our assistance in a supportive manner. We recognize Britain's special role. We recognize that we can only be helpful if the key parties involved believe we can be of assistance.

We intend to work closely with all parties during this phase of intensive consultations to move forward the process leading toward majority rule in Zimbabwe. We recognize that there are serious differences of view, not only between blacks and whites, between the Smith regime and the international community, but among blacks themselves. Our hope is that as consultations proceed, these differences can be bridged and a free Zimbabwe will be a united Zimbabwe. We are not naive in thinking that unraveling a problem like the Rhodesian situation, which has been a long time in creation, will be easy. But I will pledge to you today our support and best efforts for a negotiated solution to the problem so that we may see an independent Zimbabwe under majority rule in 1978.

It is the view of my government that the diplomatic efforts on Zimbabwe and Namibia which have been launched have a chance for success. For this to happen we must be involved at every stage of U.N. discussion of Zimbabwe and Namibia. That is one reason why the United States is attending this conference.

Not all views which have been expressed here accord with U.S. policy. But let me emphasize that the goals of freedom and liberation are fundamental in the Carter Administration's approach to the issues of southern Africa. It is seeking appropriate ways to promote these goals through the aggressive pursuit of negotiated settlements. While we recognize that not all members of the United Nations will agree with every detail of the initiatives we have taken, all member nations—and this conference in particular—should be encouraged by these initiatives. We believe the final conference document should reflect this fact.

I have stressed today American support for peaceful, negotiated change in southern Africa. Our reasons involve not only our commitment to nonviolent solutions but also our realization that Africa needs peace urgently to begin the process of development as soon as possible. That is the real challenge in Africa.

We recognize that continuing armed struggle is being waged, especially in Zimbabwe. It is our hope that the fighting will be brought to an early end. We will do all in our power to end the injustices which have led to violence and bloodshed and to effect an early transition to independence in Zimbabwe and Namibia.

As you all know one of President Carter's first decisions was to press for repeal of the Byrd amendment.[11] During my last trip to Africa I informed African leaders of my confidence that the President would succeed in repealing this legislation which placed the United States in violation of Security Council resolutions regarding Rhodesia.

With the strong support of the President, the Congress has now repealed the Byrd amendment. President Carter is determined, however, to press ahead with additional measures which can help us make progress in southern Africa.

On May 17 President Carter announced that implementation of Security Council Resolution 385 on Namibia is imperative. Our efforts to secure its implementation, he noted, involve something stronger than a request. The United States is prepared to take new measures in the United Nations if we do not obtain rapid progress toward the final liberation of Namibia.[12]

[11]Cf. Introduction at note 86.
[12]Cf. Introduction at note 91.

Let me conclude by stating my desire to continue meeting with delegates to this conference and having frank and serious discussions of the issues we are considering here. We all must talk together and understand each other's views. Our goal must be to encourage change in a way that can minimize violence. In doing this, we serve our overall goal—manifesting our support for the people of Namibia and Zimbabwe and working for majority rule in southern Africa.

(31)   Discussion with South Africa: News Conference Statement by Vice-President Mondale on His Meetings with Prime Minister Johannes B. Vorster of the Republic of South Africa, Vienna, May 20, 1977.[13]

(Excerpts)

With me today are the members of our negotiating team—Tony Lake, Director of the Policy Planning Staff of the State Department; Ambassador Don McHenry [Deputy U.S. Representative to the U.N. Security Council]; David Aaron, Deputy Director of the National Security Council; and Bill Bowdler, our Ambassador to the Government of South Africa.

I have been meeting with South African Prime Minister Vorster and his government at the request of President Carter to convey the new policies of our Administration regarding southern Africa—specifically Rhodesia, Namibia, and South Africa itself. We had a day and a half of very frank and candid discussions. Both sides were aware before the meetings began of possible fundamental differences, and yet we pursued these discussions in a constructive spirit in order to improve the possibility of mutual understanding and progress. Put most simply, the policy which the President wished me to convey was that there was need for progress on all three issues: majority rule for Rhodesia and Namibia and a progressive transformation of South African society to the same end. We believed it was particularly important to convey the depth of our convictions.

There has been a transformation in American society of which we are very proud. It affects not only our domestic life but our foreign policy as well. We cannot accept, let alone defend, the governments that reject the basic principle of full human rights, economic opportunity, and political participation for all of its people regardless of race. This basic mission was accomplished during these talks. I believe our policy is clear, and I believe the South African

[13]Text from *Bulletin,* 76: 661-6.

Government now appreciates that it is deeply rooted in American experience and values. I do not know how or whether this will affect the decisions that confront South Africa, particularly in regard to its own system, but I made it clear that without evident progress that provides full political participation and an end to discrimination, the press of international events would require us to take actions based on our policy to the detriment of the constructive relations we would prefer with South Africa.

As for Rhodesia and Namibia, I believe we registered some useful progress but the significance of this progress will depend on future developments. Prime Minister Vorster agreed to support British-American efforts to get the directly interested parties to agree to an independence constitution and the necessary transitional arrangements, including the holding of elections in which all can take part equally, so that Zimbabwe can achieve independence during 1978 and peace.

Likewise every effort will be made to bring about a deescalation of violence, and it is believed that the negotiating process will be the best way to achieve this end. We believe this is an encouraging step in a positive direction. Hopefully we will work together to bring the interested parties to find a peaceful solution to the conflict in Rhodesia. The extent to which this pays off will, of course, remain to be seen as we pursue the British initiative. In this connection I made clear our support for these efforts and the closest collaboration with them.

I explained that our concept of the Zimbabwe Development Fund is different from that of the previous American Administration. Instead of being a fund aimed at buying out the white settlers in Rhodesia, we want to reorient that fund to a development fund —one that will help build a strong economy and one that will encourage the continued participation of the white population in an independent Zimbabwe. I emphasized that the United States would support a constitution for Zimbabwe that would contain guarantees of individual rights such as freedom of speech, religion, assemblage, due process of law, and an independent judiciary and that we believe these are essential to a democratic system of government.

On Namibia I made clear that we supported the efforts of the so-called contact group—which consists of the United States, West Germany, Britain, France, and Canada—in their efforts to implement Security Council Resolution 385.[14] In some respects the position of the South African Government, as reflected in the earlier talks, was encouraging. In those talks they agreed to free elections to be held on a nationwide basis for a constituent assembly which

[14]Cf. note 4 to Document 29.

would develop a national constitution for an independent Namibia. They agreed that all Namibians inside and outside the country could participate, including SWAPO. They agreed that the United Nations could be involved in the electoral process to assure that it was fair and internationally acceptable.

However, potentially important differences over the structure and character of the interim administrative authority that would run Namibia while this process takes place became much clearer in the process of our talks. South Africa wants an administrative arrangement that draws upon the structure developed at the Turnhalle conference. This structure, in the conference that proposed it, is based on ethnic and tribal lines, and as it stands it is unacceptable to us. We emphasized that any interim administrative arrangement must be impartial as to the ultimate structure of the Namibian government. Moreover, it must be broadly representative in order to be acceptable to all Namibians and to the international community.

For his part Mr. Vorster felt quite strongly that any such structure should be based on the work of the Turnhalle conference. We agreed to propose that the five-nation contact group meet with the South African Government before the end of the month in Capetown, at a time to be determined if the other members of that group agree to hear South Africa's views and the details of the proposed interim administrative authority, to see if an impartial broadly based and internationally acceptable structure can be found. We hope that it can be.

It is my view that the South African position on Namibia is involved in a positive direction in certain important respects. But unless this last issue can be satisfactorily resolved by the South African Government, fair free elections will be difficult if not impossible. I hope that the most serious effort will be made to find a solution that provides an impartial broadly representative and internationally acceptable interim authority in Namibia.

I also raised the question of political prisoners with regard to Namibia. I said that the United States believes that all political prisoners should be released. Mr. Vorster said he believes that what he called political detainees, some of which are held in other African countries, should be released. He said he would favorably consider our suggestion that all Namibian political prisoners be turned over to Namibia and that, in the event of a difference in view of whether a particular prisoner was political or criminal, a body of international jurors review the case and make a determination. This suggestion will be pursued as well when the contact group meets in Capetown.

South African prospects are much less bright for progress toward the change of course which we believe is essential to provide justice, stability, and peace in that country. We hope that South Africa will carefully review the implications of our policy and the changed circumstances which it creates. We hope that South Africans will not rely on any illusions that the United States will, in the end, intervene to save South Africa from the policies it is pursuing, for we will not do so.

I think the message is now clear to the South African Government. They know that we believe that perpetuating an unjust system is the surest incentive to increase Soviet influence and even racial war but quite apart from that is unjustified on its own grounds. They know that we will not defend such a system and in all honesty, however, I do not know what conclusions the South African Government will draw. It is my hope that it will lead to a reassessment, to a change of course which enables us to be helpful and supportive in the difficult times that change inevitably entails. But I cannot rule out the possibility that the South African Government will not change, that our paths will diverge and our policies come into conflict should the South African Government so decide. In that event we would take steps true to our beliefs and values. We hope to be able to see progress in Rhodesia, Namibia, and South Africa. But the alternative is real, much as we dislike it. For a failure to make progress will lead to a tragedy of human history.

Q. Mr. Vice President, I wonder if you would tell us if these talks, which appear indeed to have been extremely tough, what the atmosphere was, whether it was acrimonious, or whether you could tell us that it really wasn't as tough as it seemed to be?

Vice President Mondale: We were very anxious, as I indicated earlier, to conduct these talks in a constructive environment, in a nonconfrontational environment. We were anxious at the same time that this meeting be one in which we could very clearly define American policy and further make clear the depth and the permanence of our commitment to human rights as a central element in our relations with the Government of South Africa and as a policy guiding our affairs in southern Africa. The talks were candid and they were frank and I think they were nonconfrontational.

We think there may be some progress in Rhodesia. We think the statement today indicates hope. We are hopeful that the talks surrounding the details on Namibia which I mentioned will produce results that are effective and will permit the independence of Namibia within the outline and framework of U.N. Resolution 385 and that the upcoming talks in Capetown will bring about that result.

On the issue of South African policies, it is our position that separateness and apartheid are inherently discriminatory and that that policy of apartheid cannot be acceptable to us. We also are of the opinion strongly held that full political participation by all the citizens of South Africa—equal participation in the election of its national government and its political affairs—is essential to a healthy, stable, and secure South Africa.

South Africans take the view that their apartheid policies are not discriminatory. There is a basic and fundamental disagreement. They take the position that they have different nations within South Africa and that the full participation that we discussed is irrelevant. There is a fundamental and a profound disagreement. What we had hoped to do in these talks was to make it clear to the South African leadership the profound commitment that my nation has to human rights, to the elimination of discrimination, and to full political participation. We explained to them how our nation went through essentially the same dispute, and the elimination of discrimination and the achievement of full political participation has contributed enormously to the health, vitality, stability, economic growth, and social and spiritual health of our country. We are convinced that those same policies will have the same effect in other societies. That was the nature of the discussion; it was very frank, it was very candid.

* * *

Q. Mr. Vice President, could you possibly go into slightly more detail on your concept of full participation as opposed to one-man one-vote? Do you see some kind of a compromise?

Vice President Mondale: No, no. It's the same thing. Every citizen should have the right to vote and every vote should be equally weighted.

(32) "The United States and Africa—Building Positive Relations": Address by Secretary of State Vance before the Annual Convention of the National Association for the Advancement of Colored People (NAACP), St. Louis, July 1, 1977.[15]

This is a special occasion for me to meet with you and to discuss with you such an important subject: American relations with Africa.

Before I turn to our main topic, I would like to add a personal note about the man who has led this organization and who has been a voice for justice and freedom for nearly five decades. I speak of Roy Wilkins [outgoing executive director of the NAACP]—a personal friend, a man I have admired through the years.

Roy Wilkins has not finished his work. There remains an impor-

[15]Department of State Press Release 316; text from *Bulletin*, 77:165-70.

tant agenda which he helped fashion—an agenda of human rights and social justice. I know that President Carter and others in his Administration will continue to seek his help, be inspired by his strength, and strive for what he believes to be just.

While guiding the NAACP, Roy never lost sight of the importance which Africa has had for our nation. Africa matters very much to the United States. This is a fact more and more Americans are coming to understand.

You in the NAACP have recognized this fact since the first days of your organization, almost 70 years ago—in sponsoring the first Pan African Congress in 1919; in your calls, during the days of the Marshall plan, for effective assistance, as well, to Africa, the Caribbean, and other developing areas.

We in a new Administration hope that we can show similar vision as we build our policies toward Africa.

We proceed from a basic proposition: that our policies must recognize the unique identity of Africa. We can be neither right, nor effective, if we treat Africa simply as one part of the Third World, or as a testing ground of East-West competition.

African reality is incredibly diverse. But out of this diversity comes a general fact of great importance: Africa has an enormous potential—in human talent, in resources to be developed, in energy to be harnessed.

Let us consider how this is true in terms of our own national interests; for Africa's potential is tied to our own.

—The success or failure of the search for racial justice and peace in southern Africa will have profound effects among the American people. And our participation in that search is based on the values of our own society.

—The role of the African nations at the United Nations, and in other multilateral bodies, is pivotal. One-third of the U.N. member states are African.

—Africa's mineral and agricultural wealth already provides a substantial portion of our imports of such commodities as copper, cobalt, and manganese for our industries, and cocoa and coffee for our homes. And Africa supplies 38 percent of our crude petroleum imports.

—Our direct investment in sub-Saharan Africa has increased nearly sixfold over the past 15 years; our trade now is almost 12 times what it was then. And the pattern of our trade with Africa includes an even larger share for black Africa. Trade with South Africa in 1960 was 39 percent of our commerce with Africa; now, our trade with Nigeria alone is double the value of that with South Africa.

—Beyond these political and economic ties that bind our futures, there are the social and cultural links from which we have benefited greatly. Our society and culture are enriched by the heritage so many Americans find in Africa. We experience this enrichment every day—in our literature, our art, our music, and our social values.

During the past few months, as we have considered the specific policies I will discuss today, a number of broad points have emerged. They define the general nature of our approach.

First, the most effective policies toward Africa are affirmative policies. They should not be reactive to what other powers do, nor to crises as they arise. Daily headlines should not set our agenda for progress. A negative, reactive American policy that seeks only to oppose Soviet or Cuban involvement in Africa would be both dangerous and futile. Our best course is to help resolve the problems which create opportunities for external intervention.

Second, our objective must be to foster a prosperous and strong Africa that is at peace with itself and at peace with the world. The long-term success of our African policy will depend more on our actual assistance to African development and our ability to help Africans resolve their disputes than on maneuvers for short-term diplomatic advantage.

Third, our policies should recognize and encourage African nationalism. Having won independence, African nations will defend it against challenges from any source. If we try to impose American solutions for African problems, we may sow division among the Africans and undermine their ability to oppose efforts at domination by others. We will not do so.

Fourth, our policies must reflect our national values. Our deep belief in human rights—political, economic, and social—leads us to policies that support their promotion throughout Africa. This means concern for individuals whose rights are threatened anywhere on the continent. And it means making our best effort peacefully to promote racial justice in southern Africa. In this we join the many African nations who, having won their freedom, are determined that all of Africa shall be free.

Fifth, our ties with Africa are not only political, but cultural and economic as well. It is the latter two that are most enduring.

And finally, we will seek openness in our dealings with African states. We are willing to discuss any issue, African or global; to broaden our dialogue with African nations; and to try to work with them, even when we may not agree.

Only thus can we promote our views without rancor. Our renewed relations with the People's Republic of the Congo,[16] our experience at the recent conference on southern Africa in Maputo,[17] and our work with African delegations at the United Nations all demonstrate the value of this approach.

In the end, of course, our Africa policy will be judged by results, not intentions.

Assistance for Human Needs

One of Africa's principal concerns is that its basic human needs be met. Despite its vast resources, it is still one of the least developed areas of the world. Eighteen of the twenty-eight least developed countries in the world are African.

We are prepared to help.

In addition to our growing trade and investment relationships with African nations, we are committed to providing economic assistance that will directly improve the lives of those most in need. Turning this principle into practice cannot be accomplished overnight. But it must be done.

Our economic assistance to Africa is being increased from $271 million in fiscal year 1976 to a projected $450 million in fiscal year 1978. We hope that assistance from our European friends will also increase, and expect to consult with them on how we all can make the most effective contributions.

To help our aid reach rural villages, we will emphasize support for the development and sharing of appropriate technology and techniques. I have in mind such devices as small farm machinery now being manufactured in Senegal, Upper Volta, Mali, and elsewhere; hand-hydraulic palm oil presses in Nigeria; and basic agricultural extension methods that have succeeded in one nation and could be applied in another. We will also expand support for agricultural research in Africa and try to assure that our own technical assistance is appropriate to African requirements.

We also acknowledge the needs of African states for advanced techniques that will enable them to develop and process more of their own natural resources.

Our Agency for International Development, headed by Governor [John J.] Gilligan, is determined to cut down on red tape in approving assistance projects, so it can respond quickly and effectively. Greater attention will be given to projects which can be started

---

[16]An agreement in principle to restore diplomatic relations between the U.S. and the People's Republic of the Congo, which had been suspended in 1965, was announced June 6-7, 1977 *(Keesing's:* 28460).

[17]Document 30.

quickly and require minimal outside technical assistance or expensive equipment.

Men and women are more important than machines. Africa's natural resources will be developed by Africa's people. Human development is thus the key to Africa's future. While we will provide additional opportunities for Africans to study here, emphasis will be on programs of training and education in Africa.

We must also remember the importance of Africa's infrastructure. It is a vast continent, and improved transport and communications are essential to its welfare.

I am aware, as I indicate these directions for our programs, how tempting, but mistaken, it would be to design blueprints for another continent's development. We can only work effectively if we work cooperatively with African governments in behalf of *their* development priorities. Accordingly, we will seek to increase our contribution to the African Development Fund. And we are requesting from the Congress $200 million for the Sahel, to be managed in coordination with the Club du Sahel.

The long drought in the Sahel devastated the economies of some of the poorest countries in the world. Now these countries are working together to become self-sufficient in food production and to develop the ability to withstand future droughts.

In the Club du Sahel, the African states plan together for the region. The donor nations participate in the planning and determine how each can assist most effectively. They then commit the resources necessary to meet their goals. In this process, we are discovering the great value of encouraging coordination among African states; of planning with them and with other donors; and of concentrating on regional problems rather than isolated projects. For it will be essential that sensible and effective programs be planned and implemented.

America can fully support African development only if we meet the kind of commitments I have outlined. I hope that every citizen with an interest in Africa will make it clear, to the Congress and to us in the executive branch, that he or she wants those commitments met.

Promotion of Human Rights

While we address the reality of human need in Africa, we must also do what we can in behalf of human justice there.

We will be firm in our support of individual human rights. Our concern is not limited to any one region of the continent.

We must understand the diversity of African social and value systems. Gross violations of individual human dignity are no more acceptable in African terms than in ours. One of the most significant events in modern African history—and in the international effort to promote human rights—was the recent decision by Commonwealth countries to condemn the "massive violation of human rights" in Uganda.[18] Many African nations took part in this decision. Their action should be applauded.

Abuse of human rights is wrong on any grounds. It is particularly offensive when it is on the basis of race. In southern Africa, issues of race, of justice, and of self-determination have built to a crisis.

—The conflict in Rhodesia is growing. Rhodesian incursions into neighboring countries exacerbate an already dangerous situation and deserve the condemnation they have received. The choice between negotiated settlement and violent solution must be made now. The same is true for Namibia. Many lives—black and white—hang in the balance.

—The risk of increased foreign involvement is real.

—Violence within South Africa grows. There may be more time there than in Rhodesia and Namibia for people of goodwill to achieve a solution. But progress must soon be made, or goodwill could be lost.

—Crisis within the region has brought pressure for stronger action at the United Nations, and appeals to our responsibilities under its charter.

This is the reality we face. The dangers, our interests, and our values, as well as the desires of the Africans themselves, require our involvement—and our most dedicated and practical efforts.

We cannot impose solutions in southern Africa. We cannot dictate terms to any of the parties; our leverage is limited.

But we are among the few governments in the world that can talk to both white and black Africans frankly and yet with a measure of trust. We would lose our ability to be helpful if we lost that trust. It is therefore essential that our policies of encouraging justice for people of all races in southern Africa be clear to all.

After careful consideration, this Administration has decided to pursue actively solutions to all three southern African problems—Rhodesia, Namibia, and the situation within South Africa itself. These problems must be addressed together, for they are intertwined.

Some have argued that apartheid in South Africa should be ignored for the time being, in order to concentrate on achieving progress on Rhodesia and Namibia. Such a policy would be wrong and would not work.

---

[18]Cf. Introduction at note 97.

—It would be blind to the reality that the beginning of progress must be made soon within South Africa, if there is to be a possibility of peaceful solutions in the longer run;
    —It could mislead the South Africans about our real concerns;
    —It would prejudice our relations with our African friends;
    —It would do a disservice to our own beliefs; and
    —It would discourage those of all races who are working for peaceful progress within South Africa.

We believe that we can effectively influence South Africa on Rhodesia and Namibia while expressing our concerns about apartheid. Implicit in that belief is the judgment that progress in all three areas is strongly in the interest of the South African Government.

We believe that whites as well as blacks must have a future in Namibia, Zimbabwe, and South Africa. We also believe that their security lies in progress. Intransigence will only lead to greater insecurity.

We will welcome and recognize positive action by South Africa on *each* of these three issues. But the need is real for progress on *all* of them.

Let me review briefly our approach to each.

Rhodesia

We are actively supporting a British initiative to achieve a negotiated settlement of the Rhodesian crisis. In coming weeks, we will be seeking agreement on a constitution that would allow free elections, open to all parties and in which all of voting age could participate equally. These elections would establish the government of an independent Zimbabwe. Our goal is that this be accomplished during 1978.

This constitution should include a justiciable bill of rights and an independent judiciary, so that the rights of all citizens, of all races, are protected.

We also hope to lend greater assistance to the peoples of neighboring nations whose lives have been disrupted by the crisis in southern Africa.

Namibia

In Namibia a solution leading to independence is being sought through the efforts of the five Western members of the Security Council, with South Africa, the United Nations, and other interested parties, including the South West Africa People's Organization. That solution would include free elections in which the United Nations is involved, freedom for political prisoners, repeal of discriminatory laws and regulations, and the withdrawal of instruments of South African authority as the elections are held and independence achieved.

On the basis of our discussions thus far, we are encouraged by the prospects for an independent Namibia, one which will take its rightful place in the African and world community. We welcome the indications of flexibility on the part of South Africa. We are gratified by the confidence shown by many African governments in the efforts of the United States and Western associates on the Security Council. Differences remain, however, and progress will require a willingness on all sides to be openminded and forthcoming. But we will persevere.

South Africa

While pursuing these efforts for peace and justice in Namibia and Rhodesia, we have also expressed to the South African Government our firm belief in the benefits of a progressive transformation of South African society. This would mean an end to racial discrimination and the establishment of a new course toward full political participation by all South Africans.

The specific form of government through which this participation could be expressed is a matter for the people of South Africa to decide. There are many ways in which the individual rights of all citizens within South Africa could be protected. The key to the future is that South African citizens of all races now begin a dialogue on how to achieve this better future.

The South African Government's policy of establishing separate homelands for black South Africans was devised without reference to the wishes of the blacks themselves. For this reason, and because we do not believe it constitutes a fair or viable solution to South Africa's problems, we oppose this policy. We did not recognize the Transkei, and we will not recognize Bophuthatswana if its independence is proclaimed in December, as scheduled.

We deeply hope that the South African Government will play a progressive role on the three issues I have discussed. We will applaud such efforts. If there is no progress, our relations will inevitably suffer.

We cannot defend a government that is based on a system of racial domination and remain true to ourselves. For our policy toward South Africa is reinforced by change in our own society. The activities of the NAACP are a testament to the inseparability of our foreign and domestic goals. It is also entirely fitting that Andy Young, who has done so much in the struggle against our divisions at home, should now be contributing so well to the design and effectiveness of our policies abroad.

I have heard some suggest that we must support the white governments in southern Africa, come what may, since they are anti-Communist. In fact, the continued denial of racial justice in southern Africa encourages the possibilities for outside intervention.

Similarly, when such crises as the recent invasion of Zaire arise, we see no advantage in unilateral responses and emphasizing their East-West implications. We prefer to work with African nations, and with our European allies, in positive efforts to resolve such disputes. As President Carter recently said, it is best to fight fire with water.

The history of the past 15 years suggests that efforts by outside powers to dominate African nations will fail. Our challenge is to find ways of being supportive without becoming interventionist or intrusive.

We see no benefit if we interject ourselves into regional disputes. We hope that they can be resolved through the diplomatic efforts of the parties themselves in an African setting.

We are aware of the African concern that we have sometimes seemed more interested in the activities of other outside powers in Africa than in Africa itself. They know that some argue we should almost automatically respond in kind to the increase in Soviet arms and Cuban personnel in Africa.

We cannot ignore this increase—and we oppose it. All sides should be aware that when outside powers pour substantial quantities of arms and military personnel into Africa, it greatly enhances the danger that disputes will be resolved militarily rather than through mediation by African states or by the OAU.

This danger is particularly great in the Horn, where there has been an escalation of arms transfers from the outside. The current difficulties in Ethiopia, and the tensions among nations in the area, present complex diplomatic challenges. We seek friendship with all the governments of that region. We have established an embassy in the new nation of Djibouti. Its peaceful accession to independence marks a step toward stability in what remains a troubled area.

We will consider sympathetically appeals for assistance from states which are threatened by a buildup of foreign military equipment and advisers on their borders, in the Horn and elsewhere in Africa. But we hope such local arms races and the consequent dangers of deepening outside involvement can be limited.

In accordance with the policy recently announced by the President,[19] arms transfers to Africa will be an exceptional tool of our policy and will be used only after the most careful consideration.

We hope that all the major powers will join us in supporting African nationalism, rather than fragmenting it, and in concentrating on economic assistance rather than arms.

Our approach is to build positive relations with the Africans pri-

[19] Document 8.

marily through support for their political independence and economic development and through the strengthening of our economic, cultural, and social ties. Our new and positive relationships with nations like Nigeria encourage us in this course. Our efforts to build such relations may not seize the headlines. But this quiet strategy will produce long-term benefits.

Our relations will be closest with those nations whose views and actions are most congruent with ours. We will never forget or take old friends for granted. Their continuing friendship is a fundamental concern; they can rely on our support. When the territorial integrity of a friendly state is threatened, we will continue to respond to requests for appropriate assistance.

We do not insist that there is only one road to economic progress or one way of expressing the political will of a people. In so diverse a continent, we must be prepared to work with peoples and governments of distinctive and differing beliefs.

American representatives in Africa met last May to compare notes and discuss new policy ideas. They agreed that almost everywhere in the continent there is a new feeling about America—a sense of hope, a sense that we have returned to our ideals.

The future of Africa will be built with African hands. Our interests and our ideals will be served as we offer our own support. It will require the understanding and approval of this audience, and of Americans everywhere.

(33) Proposals for Zimbabwe: Text of the British White Paper Submitted to Parliament and Made Public September 1, 1977.[20]

Foreword

The British Government, with the full agreement of the United States Government and after consulting all the parties concerned, have drawn up certain proposals for the restoration of legality in Rhodesia and the settlement of the Rhodesian problem. These proposals are based on the following elements:

1. The surrender of power by the illegal regime and a return to legality.

2. An orderly and peaceful transition to independence in the course of 1978.

3. Free and impartial elections on the basis of universal adult suffrage.

---

[20]*Rhodesia: Proposals for a Settlement* (Comnd. 6919; London: HMSO, 1977); text from *Bulletin,* 77: 424-7. The annexes, not printed here, appear in same: 427-39.

4. The establishment by the British Government of a transitional administration, with the task of conducting the elections for an independent government.

5. A United Nations presence, including a United Nations force, during the transition period.

6. An Independence Constitution providing for a democratically elected government, the abolition of discrimination, the protection of individual human rights and the independence of the judiciary.

7. A Development Fund to revive the economy of the country which the United Kingdom and the United States view as predicated upon the implementation of the settlement as a whole.

A full account of the proposals is attached. The first of the Annexes to the proposals outlines the principal points of the proposed Independence Constitution; the second Annex deals with the Constitutional arrangements during the transition period; and the third Annex relates to the Development Fund. The precise provisions of the Independence Constitution will have to be elaborated in further detailed discussions with the parties and in due course will be considered at a Constitutional Conference to be held during the transition period.

It is impossible at this stage to lay down an exact timetable: but it is the intention of the British Government that elections should be held, and that Rhodesia should become independent as Zimbabwe, not later than six months after the return to legality. To achieve this it will be necessary to proceed as quickly as possible after the return to legality to the registration of voters, the delimitation of constituencies, the detailed drafting of the Constitution and its enactment under the authority of the British Parliament.

Proposals for a Settlement in Rhodesia

1. On 10 March 1977 the British and United States Governments agreed to work together on a joint peace initiative to achieve a negotiated settlement in Rhodesia. The objective was an independent Zimbabwe with majority rule in 1978.

2. To succeed, any settlement must command the support of those people of goodwill of all races and creeds who intend to live together in peace as citizens of Zimbabwe. Amongst these people there are now many conflicting interests and views. There is an atmosphere of deep distrust. The armed struggle has led to the loss of many lives and to much human suffering. The economy has been gravely weakened. But there is surely one overriding common interest, that peace should be restored and that government with the consent and in the interest of all the people should be established.

3. In April the British Foreign and Commonwealth Secretary,

Dr. Owen, toured the area and met all the parties to the problem as well as the Presidents of the five Front-Line States, the Prime Minister of South Africa and the Commissioner for External Affairs[21] of Nigeria. He set out the elements which, taken together, could in the view of the two Governments comprise a negotiated settlement, as follows:

(a) A Constitution for an independent Zimbabwe which would provide for—

(1) a democratically-elected government, with the widest possible franchise;

(2) a Bill of Rights to protect individual human rights on the basis of the Universal Declaration of Human Rights. The Bill would be "entrenched" so that amendment of it would be made subject to special legislative procedures and it would give the right to an individual who believed his rights were being infringed to seek redress through the courts;

(3) an independent judiciary.

(b) A transition period covering the surrender of power by the present regime, the installation of a neutral caretaker administration whose primary role, in addition to administering the country, would be the organisation and conduct of elections in conditions of peace and security and the preparation of the country for the transition to independence. This period, it was envisaged, would be as short as possible, and in any case not more than six months.

(c) The establishment of an internationally constituted and managed development fund (the Zimbabwe Development Fund).

4. Following that tour, Dr. Owen and the United States Secretary of State, Mr. Vance, met in London on 6 May and agreed to carry forward their consultations with the parties on the basis of these proposals. To this end they established a joint consultative group. The group met all the parties on a number of occasions in London and in Africa and carried out detailed technical discussions with them. In parallel, the Governments of interested countries have been kept informed generally of the progress of the consultations.

5. On the basis of these consultations the British Government, in full agreement with the United States Government, have now decided to put firm proposals forward, covering the three aspects of the problem described in paragraph 3 above. In doing so they emphasise that the three aspects are intimately linked and must be judged as a whole. It is impossible for every single aspect of a settlement to be acceptable to everyone. The best, if not the only, hope

[21]Joseph Garba.

for a settlement is a balanced and fair package in which, though no one may achieve all their aims, everyone can see hope for the future.

The Constitution

6. It is proposed that the Independence Constitution should provide that Zimbabwe would be a sovereign republic. Provision would be made for democratic elections on the basis of one man, one vote and one woman, one vote, for a single-chamber National Assembly. Elections would be on the basis of single-member constituencies. Detailed constitutional proposals are set out at Annex A. The proposals should not necessarily be taken as excluding alternative possibilities in certain areas which do not go to the heart of the Constitution: *e.g.* provision is made for an executive President with a Vice-President, but there might instead be a constitutional president and a Prime Minister, in which case many of the powers which it is proposed to vest in the President would be vested in the Prime Minister or would be exercised by the President on the advice of the Prime Minister.

7. Discrimination would be forbidden by a Bill of Rights protecting the rights of individuals. As described above (para. 3(a) (2)), this Bill of Rights would be entrenched in the Constitution and would be justiciable so that aggrieved individuals could enforce their rights through the courts. The Bill of Rights would permit the Government of Zimbabwe to introduce measures of land reform while guaranteeing the right to private property. The Constitution would also establish an independent judiciary and an independent Public Service Commission to ensure an efficient and nonpolitical civil service.

8. The Government of Zimbabwe would inherit the assets and debts of the Government of Southern Rhodesia and would take over past and present pensions obligations in the public sector, the rights of the pensioners being guaranteed by the Constitution. The Constitution would contain the basic provisions regulating Zimbabwe citizenship and these would be entrenched. The question whether there should be any restrictions on the possession of dual citizenship and, if so, whether there should be an extended period during which the choice would have to be made would be a matter for further discussion with the parties.[22]

9. The Commonwealth Governments in London expressed the unanimous hope that Zimbabwe would soon become a member of

[22]Any citizen of the United Kingdom and Colonies who surrenders his citizenship in order to retain or acquire the citizenship of another member of the Commonwealth is entitled to regain United Kingdom citizenship subsequently under the British Nationality Act 1964. [Footnote in original.]

the Commonwealth. The British Government will do everything to facilitate this.

The Transition

10. It is a basic premise of the British and United States Governments that the present illegal regime will surrender power so that the transitional administration may be installed peacefully. The two Governments will take such steps as seem to them appropriate to secure the transfer of power by Mr. Smith (or his successor) on a day to be agreed.

11. The British Government will place before the Security Council their proposal for the Independence Constitution (Annex A) and also their proposal for the administration of the territory of Rhodesia during the transition period leading up to independence. The latter will comprise the following elements:

(a) The appointment by the British Government, either under existing statutory powers or under new powers enacted for the purpose, of a Resident Commissioner and a Deputy. The role of the Resident Commissioner will be to administer the country, to organize and conduct the general election which, within a period not exceeding six months, will lead to independence for Zimbabwe, and to take command, as Commander-in-Chief, of all armed forces in Rhodesia, apart from the United Nations Zimbabwe Force (see below).

(b) The appointment by the Secretary-General of the United Nations, on the authority of the Security Council, of a Special Representative whose role will be to work with the Resident Commissioner and to observe that the administration of the country and the organization and conduct of the elections are fair and impartial.

(c) The establishment by resolution of the Security Council of a United Nations Zimbabwe Force whose role may include:

(1) the supervision of the cease-fire (see below);
(2) support for the civil power;
(3) liaison with the existing Rhodesian armed forces and with the forces of the Liberation Armies.

The Secretary-General will be invited to appoint a representative to enter into discussions, before the transition period, with the British Resident Commissioner designate and with all the parties with a view to establishing in detail the respective roles of all the forces in Rhodesia.

(d) The primary responsibility for the maintenance of law and order during the transition period will lie with the police forces.

They will be under the command of a Commissioner of Police who will be appointed by and responsible to the Resident Commissioner. The Special Representative of the Secretary-General of the United Nations may appoint liaison officers to the police forces.

(e) The formation, as soon as possible after the establishment of the transitional administration, of a new Zimbabwe National Army which will in due course replace all existing armed forces in Rhodesia and will be the army of the future independent State of Zimbabwe.

(f) The establishment by the Resident Commissioner of an electoral and boundary commission, with the role of carrying out the registration of voters, the delimitation of constituencies and the holding of a general election for the purposes of the Independence Constitution.

On the agreed day on which power is transferred to the transitional administration (para. 10 above), a cease-fire will come into effect within Rhodesia and measures will be taken to lift sanctions.

12. An outline of the Transitional Constitution is at Annex B.

The Zimbabwe Development Fund

13. The Zimbabwe Development Fund, jointly sponsored by the British and United States Governments, will have as a target a minimum approaching US$1,000 million and a maximum rather less than US$1,500 million to which Governments in many parts of the world will be asked to contribute. Its purpose will be to provide funds for the economic stability and development of an independent Zimbabwe through assistance to various sectors and programs such as rural development, education, health, social and economic infrastructure, and resettlement and training schemes for Africans, including those affected by the present conflict. The operations of the Fund would help to ensure that the obligations of the Zimbabwe Government under the settlement will not inhibit economic development in Zimbabwe for lack of foreign exchange and would thereby also help to reassure those who might fear that the new Government might be unable to carry out these obligations. The establishment and continued operation of the Fund are predicated upon the acceptance and implementation of the terms of the settlement as a whole. A more detailed account of the proposed Fund is at Annex C.

Conclusion

14. The British and United States Governments believe that the above proposals provide for all the citizens of the independent Zim-

babwe security, but not privilege, under the rule of law, equal political rights without discrimination, and the right to be governed by a government of their own choice. They also believe that the proposed arrangements for the transfer of power are calculated to ensure a quick, orderly and peaceful transition to independence. They have agreed to use their joint influence to the full to put the proposals into effect. But a lasting settlement cannot be imposed from outside: it is the people of Zimbabwe who must achieve their own independence. These proposals offer them a way. The two Governments urge them to seize the opportunity.

(34) New Repression in South Africa: Statement by Richard M. Moose, Assistant Secretary of State for African Affairs, before the Subcommittee on Africa of the Committee on International Relations, House of Representatives, October 26, 1977.[23]

Just a week ago today, on October 19, the Government of South Africa arbitrarily acted against a group of its citizens—black and white—in a manner which has profoundly stirred the conscience of the American people. This reaction is not confined to this country. The debate now going on in the U.N. Security Council gives a measure of the concern manifest throughout the world.

The actions in South Africa on the morning of October 19 produced this response because they reflect a blatant suppression of legitimate expression of political thought and violation of the rights of the individual. The fact that they followed on the death of black leader Steven Biko while in detention [September 12] has heightened our indignation and concern.

Let me review what took place on October 19 for certainly it will rank as a major landmark in the suppression of the aspirations of the black people of South Africa to be heard and to play a role in shaping the destiny of their own country.

—In one stroke the South African Government placed a good portion of the active and effective black leadership in preventive detention. Close to 50 such leaders now find themselves in jail.

—Major publications which the black community regarded as its own and to which blacks looked for inspiration and as outlets for their grievances and aspirations were closed. The powerful voice of Percy Qoboza [detained editor of The World, the largest newspaper for blacks in South Africa], that moderate exponent of black aspirations, momentarily fell silent.

[23]Text from *Bulletin*, 77: 897-9.

—The banning of 18 organizations working to encourage black identity and self-help has forced them to close their doors and cease their activities.

—Orders served on six white lay and church leaders who have been outspoken in their support of the cause of black rights have banished them for a period of 5 years.

—More serious than the individual measures is the collective message they carry: That in South Africa there is no room for dialogue between the minority which dominates the country and genuine leaders of the majority which is forced to suffer the indignity of apartheid and the humiliation of being denied the right of political participation.

I fear that the death of Steve Biko in detention and the South African Government's mishandling of that tragic affair, along with the bannings and detentions, are seriously diminishing what chance exists for moderation in South Africa. Those whose voices have been stilled are not extremists but persons who have been searching for peaceful ways to bring justice and harmony to their troubled land. By its actions against these courageous people, the government has once again shown its unwillingness to begin a process of real consultation with blacks, coloreds, and Indians.

This kind of dialogue among all segments of South African society is, in our view, a crucial prerequisite to any peaceful transformation and lasting social tranquility. In taking the actions that it did October 19, the South African Government has further closed channels to a process which would lead to solutions of the deep problems that beset South Africa.

By giving a clear impression that there is no remedy through moderation, rationality, and intelligent petition, the government encourages extremism. As Vice President Mondale has noted: "If present social injustice continues in any society, it will inevitably lead to growing tensions, violence, suspicion, despair, the destruction of rational dialogue, the destruction of the ability to take time to work those out carefully and with due regard for everyone."

The Administration's attitude toward apartheid and the laws which uphold that system have been expressed clearly on a number of occasions. In brief, we hold that if our relations with South Africa are not to deteriorate, it must move away from apartheid and at the same time toward a goal of full political participation by all South Africans.

We are not trying to tell South Africa what it should do. We have not prescribed particular courses of action or set forth a timetable. We have, however, made it clear that it would be increasingly difficult for the United States to maintain the relationship it has had with South Africa—a relationship we would like to see improved—

unless there are significant steps taken toward a progressive transformation of South African society.

Let me emphasize that our policy is not threatening or punitive, as some in South Africa have stated. The policy reflects fundamental American principles regarding the rights of individuals. It seeks to affirm that our relations with South Africa must be shaped by the attitude of the American people. Americans can accept neither the South African system of institutionalized discrimination based on race nor the draconian measures necessary to enforce it.

We did not lay down a threat to the South African Government. We posed it a choice. Unfortunately the choice made a week ago can only be regarded as a step backward. For that reason the Administration is considering what adjustments in our relationships are required and what responses are appropriate to make in concert with other nations. We will make our decision known very soon.

It is important that the South African Government be fully aware that Americans were deeply distressed by Steve Biko's tragic death. The Administration continues to believe, as it has stated, that there must be a full investigation into the circumstances surrounding Mr. Biko's death. The actions the government took on October 19 to detain or ban persons and organizations have also shocked the American people.

I believe it extremely important that the Congress, in reflecting the views of the American people, demonstrate to the South African Government the deep concern with which recent events are viewed. Accordingly, the Administration would fully support a resolution expressing this concern.[24] Widely supported in the House and Senate, such a resolution would represent a highly useful and effective means of communicating to the South African Government the strong opprobrium of the American people for the actions of the South African Government and our strong support for legitimate aspirations of the black, colored, and Indian peoples of South Africa.

[24]A resolution expressing concern about the recent acts of repression by the South African government (H. Con. Res. 388, 95th Cong.) was passed by the House on Oct. 31 by a vote of 347 to 54, with 5 voting "present."

6. ACID TEST IN LATIN AMERICA

(35) *"A New Approach to Policy in the Americas": Address by President Carter before the Permanent Council of the Organization of American States (OAS), Washington, April 14, 1977.*

Mr. Chairman, members of the Permanent Council, Mr. Secretary General,[2] Permanent Observers of the OAS, Chiefs of the Specialized Organizations and Agencies, members of the press, distinguished guests:

Hace tres años, tuve el honor y placer de hablar ante la Asemblea General de la OEA celebrada en mi estado de Georgia. Igaul que en Atlanta, hoy seguire el consejo de mis compañeros, que opinan— para el beneficio de buenas relaciones—seria mejor que no hablara en español hoy.

[Three years ago I had the honor and pleasure of speaking before the General Assembly of the OAS held in my State of Georgia.[3] As I did then in Atlanta, I will today follow the advice of my friends, who have the opinion that, in the interest of good relations, it would be better for me not to speak in Spanish today.]

Since I can also speak English, I will shift to that language. [*Laughter*]

That day in Atlanta, 3 years ago, I shared with you some of the thoughts that my wife and I had brought back from our visits to several of the American States. I spoke particularly for the need for constant cooperation, consultation and harmony among the nations of this hemisphere. I believe that just as strongly today as President of the United States as I did 3 years ago as Governor of Georgia.

I am delighted to be with you in this beautiful House of the Americas. For nearly three decades the OAS has stood for mutual

[1]Text from *Presidential Documents*, 13: 523-8.
[2]Alejandro Orfila (Argentina).
[3]Fourth Regular Session, Apr. 19-May 1, 1974; documentation in *AFR, 1974*: 120-31.

respect among sovereign nations, for peace, and the rule of law in this hemisphere. The OAS Charter pledges us to individual liberty and social justice. I come here now to restate our own commitment to these goals.

The challenge before us today, however, is not just to reaffirm those principles but to find ways to make them a reality. To do this, we must take account of the changes in our relationships that have taken place over the last 10 years, and we must candidly acknowledge the differences that exist among us. We must adapt our current policies and institutions to those changes so that we can pursue our goals more effectively.

As nations of the New World, we once believed that we could prosper in isolation from the Old World. But since the Second World War, in particular, all of us have taken such vital roles in the world community that isolation would now be harmful to our own best interests and to other countries. Our joining in the International Monetary Fund, the World Bank, and the General Agreement on Trade and Tariffs are all signs that we understand this. So is the United Nations Conference on Trade and Development which Raul Prebisch of Argentina made into an important forum of the developing world. Venezuela is now co-chairing[4] the Paris Conference on International Economic Cooperation. The United Nations Economic Commission for Latin America is a source of many creative ideas on development throughout the world. The leaders of many Latin American nations have been the driving force behind improving North-South negotiations.

In all these ways, the nations of Latin America were among the first in our changing world to see the importance of adapting global institutions to the new realities of our day.

The problems and the promises of our region have become as diverse as the world itself. The economies of most Latin American nations have been developing rapidly, although, of course, at different rates. Some have an impressive rate of growth. Some—a few are among the poorest in the developing world. Some have abundant energy resources; others are desperately short of energy. Some of our countries export primary products only. Some have become major exporters of advanced manufactured goods while others export little at all. Your problems of market access, technology transfer, and debt management sometimes defy regional solutions.

In addition to economic diversity, we have all developed widely varied forms and philosophies of government. This diversity has brought national pride and national strength. And as you've played more independent and important roles in world politics, we have all begun to construct more normal and more balanced and more equal relationships.

[4] With Canada.

In the light of these changes, a single United States policy toward Latin America and the Caribbean makes little sense. What we need is a wider and a more flexible approach, worked out in close consultation with you. Together, we will develop policies more suited to each nation's variety and potential. In this process, I will be particularly concerned that we not seek to divide the nations of Latin America one from another or to set Latin America apart from the rest of the world. Our own goal is to address problems in a way which will lead to productive solutions—globally, regionally, and bilaterally.

Our new approach will be based on three basic elements:

First of all is a high regard for the individuality and the sovereignty of each Latin American and Caribbean nation. We will not act abroad in ways that we would not tolerate at home in our own country.

Second is our respect for human rights, a respect which is also so much a part of your own tradition. Our values and yours require us to combat abuses of individual freedom, including those caused by political, social, and economic injustice. Our own concern for these values will naturally influence our relations with the countries of this hemisphere and throughout the world. You will find this country, the United States of America, eager to stand beside those nations which respect human rights and which promote democratic ideals.

Third is our desire to press forward on the great issues which affect the relations between the developed and the developing nations. Your economic problems are also global in character and cannot be dealt with solely on regional terms.

However, some of our own global policies are of particular interest to other American States. When major decisions are made in these areas, we will consult with you.

The United States will take a positive and an open attitude toward the negotiation of agreements to stabilize commodity prices, including the establishment of a common funding arrangement for financing buffer stocks where they are a part of individual and negotiated agreements.

We will actively pursue the multilateral trade negotiations with your governments in Geneva, Switzerland. We are committed to minimize trade restrictions, and to take into account the specific trade problems of developing countries, and to provide special and more favorable treatment where feasible and appropriate. We believe that this is in our mutual interest and that it will create important new opportunities for Latin American trade.

Our own science and technology can be useful to many of your countries. For instance, we are ready to train your technicians to use more information gathered by our own satellites, so that you can make better judgments on management of your resources and your environment. Space communications technology can also be a creative tool in helping your national television systems to promote your educational and cultural objectives.

I have asked Congress to meet in full our pledges to the Inter-American Development Bank and the other multilateral lending institutions which loan a high proportion of their capital to the relatively advanced developing countries of Latin America.

And, finally, we are directing more and more of our bilateral economic assistance to the poorer countries. We are also prepared to explore with other nations new ways of being helpful on a wide range of institutional, human development, and technological approaches which might enable them to deal more effectively with the problems of the needy. All of us have a special responsibility to help the poorest countries in the world as well as the poorest people in each of our countries.

I would like to add a word about private investment. Your governments are understandably interested in setting rules that will encourage private investors to play an important role in your development. We support your efforts and recognize that a new flexibility and adaptability are required today for foreign investment to be most useful in combining technology, capital management, and market experience to meet your development needs. We will do our part in this field to avoid differences and misunderstandings between your government and ours.

One of the most significant political trends of our time is the relationship between the developing nations of the world and the industrialized countries. We benefit from your advice and counsel, and we count on you to contribute your constructive leadership and help guide us in this North-South dialog.

We also hope to work with all nations to halt the spread of nuclear explosive capabilities. The States of Latin America took the initiative 10 years ago when you set up the first nuclear-free zone in any populated area of the world. The Treaty of Tlatelolco is a model worthy of our own admiration. For our part, the United States will sign, and I will ask the Senate to ratify, Protocol I of the Treaty, prohibiting the placement of nuclear weapons in Latin America.[5]

However, banning the spread of nuclear explosives does not require giving up the benefits of peaceful nuclear technology. We mean to work closely with all of you on new technologies to use the atom for peaceful purposes.

To slow the costly buildup of conventional arms, we are seeking global policies of restraint. We are showing restraint in our own

[5]Introduction at note 118.

policies around the world, and we will be talking to supplier nations and to prospective buyers about ways to work out a common approach. We also believe that regional agreements among producers and purchasers of arms can further such a global effort.

I spent most of this morning working on a new United States policy to reduce the sale of conventional arms around the world. Again, you in Latin America have taken the lead. The pledge of eight South American nations to limit the acquisition of offensive arms in their region is a striking example. If the eight nations can implement their pledge, their own people will not be the only ones to benefit. They will have set a standard for others throughout the world to follow.

These are challenges that face us in the future. There are also problems that plague us from the past. And we must work together to solve them.

One that addresses itself to us is the Panama Canal. In the first days of my own administration, just a few weeks ago, I directed a new approach to our negotiations with Panama on a new Canal treaty. In the light of the changes which I discussed before, the Treaty of 1903, which combines [defines] our relationship with Panama on the Canal, is no longer appropriate or effective.

I am firmly committed to negotiating in as timely a fashion as possible a new treaty which will take into account Panama's legitimate needs as a sovereign nation and our own interests and yours in the efficient operation of a neutral Canal, open on a nondiscriminatory basis to all users.

Another problem which we must in a way address together is that of Cuba. We believe that normal conduct of international affairs and particularly the negotiation of differences require communication with all countries in the world. To these ends, we are seeking to determine whether relations with Cuba can be improved on a measured and a reciprocal basis.

I am dedicated to freedom of movement between nations. I have removed restrictions on United States citizens who want to travel abroad. Today there are no restrictions imposed by our country. Today I have also removed similar travel restrictions on resident aliens in the United States.

We seek to encourage international travel, and we must take greater account of problems that transcend national borders. Drugs and international crime, including terrorism, challenge traditional concepts of diplomacy. For the well-being of our peoples, we must cooperate on these issues. With each passing year they will occupy a more and more central place in our deliberations.

I have a long-standing interest in the OAS, and I very much want to see it play an increasingly constructive role.

The General Assembly of the OAS has been an important forum

for the direct exchange of views among our governments. Such ministerial consultations are extremely useful. They allow us to apply our own collective strength to political and economic problems.

The Inter-American Commission on Human Rights has performed valuable services. It deserves increased support from all our governments. We believe deeply in the preservation and the enhancement of human rights, and the United States will work toward coordinated and multilateral action in this field. The United States will sign, and I will seek Senate approval of, the American Convention on Human Rights negotiated several years ago in Costa Rica.[6] And we will support, in cooperation with international agencies, broadened programs for aiding political refugees. I urge this organization and all its member states to take a more active role in the care, protection, and the resettlement of political refugees.

The peacekeeping function is firmly embedded in the OAS Charter. I want to encourage the Secretary General of the OAS to continue his active and effective involvement in the search for peaceable solutions to several long-standing disputes in this hemisphere. The United States will support his efforts and initiatives.

The OAS, of course, is not the only instrument of cooperation among the nations of the Americas. The Inter-American Development Bank is among the most important multilateral mechanisms for promoting development in the world today. By bringing in nations outside the Western Hemisphere, the IDB bears testimony to Latin America's growing involvement with the rest of the world.

Within this hemisphere, many of you are working toward regional and subregional integration efforts—including those in the Caribbean, in the Central American Common Market, and the Andean Pact—and we favor such efforts. They are the first steps toward Bolívar's vision of a hemisphere united.

Let me conclude by bringing up a matter that is particularly close to me because of my long interest in inter-American affairs. My wife and I have traveled and made many friends in Mexico and Brazil, the two largest and most rapidly changing countries in Latin America. And we have traveled elsewhere and made many friends in Central and South America. My wife is presently studying Spanish, along with the wife of the Secretary of State, and I have tried to keep up with my own Spanish that I learned at school. I have seen clearly how greatly our country has been blessed and enriched by the people and cultures of the Caribbean and Latin America. And we are bound together—and I see it very clearly—in culture, history, and by common purposes and ideals.

The United States actually has the fourth largest Spanish-speaking population in the world. I tried to meet many of them during

---

[6]Cf. Introduction at notes 119-120.

my campaign the last 2 years. And they gave me their support and their encouragement and their advice. The novels we read, the music we hear, the sports that we play—all reflect a growing consciousness of each other.

These intellectual, social, cultural, and educational exchanges will continue, either with or without government help. But there are steps that governments can take to speed up and enhance this process. In the months ahead, therefore, we plan to explore with your governments—individually and here in the OAS—new people-to-people programs, an increase in professional and scientific exchanges, and other ways of strengthening the ties that already link us.

The challenge we face is to awake our institutions to a changing world. We must focus our attention on the problems which face our countries and tailor each solution to its problem.

As you know, I am a new President. I've got a lot to learn. My heart and my interest to a major degree is in Latin America. I welcome every opportunity to strengthen the ties of friendship and a sense of common purpose and close consultation with the nations and the peoples of the Caribbean and Latin America.

Many of you are leaders representing your own governments. I ask for your advice and your counsel and your support as we face problems together in the future. This means a lot to our country, and it means a lot to us also to have intimate bilateral and direct relationships with you.

We look on the OAS, headquartered thankfully here in Washington, as a channel through which we might learn more and receive advice and make plans for the future.

Simón Bolívar believed that we would reach our goals only with our peoples free and our governments working in harmony. I hope that the steps that I have outlined today and the commitments that I have made will move us toward those goals of peace and freedom.

Thank you very much.

(36) Protocol I to the Treaty of Tlatelolco, Signed by the United States May 26, 1977.

(a) Additional Protocol I to the Treaty for the Prohibition of Nuclear Weapons in Latin America, Done at Mexico City February 14, 1967. [7]

(Not in force for the United States as of 1978)

[7]Text from U.S. Arms Control and Disarmament Agency, *Arms Control and Disarmament Agreements: Texts and History of Negotiations*, 1977 (ACDA Publication 94; Washington: GPO, 1977): 74.

ADDITIONAL PROTOCOL I

The undersigned Plenipotentiaries, furnished with full powers by their respective Governments,

Convinced that the Treaty for the Prohibition of Nuclear Weapons in Latin America,[8] negotiated and signed in accordance with the recommendations of the General Assembly of the United Nations in Resolution 1911 (XVIII) of 27 November 1963,[9] represents an important step towards ensuring the non-proliferation of nuclear weapons,

Aware that the non-proliferation of nuclear weapons is not an end in itself but, rather, a means of achieving general and complete disarmament at a later stage, and

Desiring to contribute, so far as lies in their power, towards ending the armaments race, especially in the field of nuclear weapons, and towards strengthening a world at peace, based on mutual respect and sovereign equality of States,

Have agreed as follows:

Article 1. To undertake to apply the statute of denuclearization in respect of warlike purposes as defined in articles 1, 3, 5 and 13 of the Treaty for the Prohibition of Nuclear Weapons in Latin America in territories for which, *de jure* or *de facto*, they are internationally responsible and which lie within the limits of the geographical zone established in that treaty.

Article 2. The duration of this Protocol shall be the same as that of the Treaty for the Prohibition of Nuclear Weapons in Latin America of which this Protocol is an annex, and the provisions regarding ratification and denunciation contained in the Treaty shall be applicable to it.

Article 3. This Protocol shall enter into force, for the States which have ratified it, on the date of the deposit of their respective instruments of ratification.

IN WITNESS WHEREOF the undersigned Plenipotentiaries, having deposited their full powers, found in good and due form, sign this Protocol on behalf of their respective Governments.

(b) Statement by President Carter on Signing the Protocol, May 26, 1977.[10]

I am very pleased this afternoon to participate in what I believe is an historical occasion. This is a ratification by the United States of

---

[8]Text in same: 63-74.
[9]Text in *Documents, 1963*: 159-60.
[10]Text from *Presidential Documents*, 13: 823.

Protocol I of the Tlatelolco Treaty, the deliberations for which were begun in November of 1964 following the Cuban missile crisis, when Brazil and 10 other Latin American countries, through the United Nations' auspices, began to evolve a commitment against the deployment or use of atomic weapons in the Latin American part of this hemisphere.

In 1971, our own country ratified Procol II[11] with the distinguished representative of our Government, Senator Hubert Humphrey, having signed that on behalf of the United States.

The ultimate hope of this commitment by all the nations involved is a complete prohibition against the ownership or deployment or use of nuclear weapons in the southern part of this hemisphere and complete international safeguards for all nuclear materials that are owned by all those countries.

So far, only two countries have not signed this treaty. One is Argentina and the other one is Cuba. France has not yet signed Protocol I, which we are signing this afternoon, and the Soviet Union has not signed Protocol II.

This is a commitment of worldwide significance. As I said in my own Inaugural Address,[12] our ultimate hope is that we can eliminate completely from the Earth any dependence upon atomic weapons, and I think it is significant and typical of our Latin American neighbors and those countries in the Caribbean that 10 years before that time they had already made this worthy commitment which sets an example for the world.

So, at this time I would like to, on behalf of the American people, to sign Protocol I of the Tlatelolco Treaty, which means that we will not deploy nuclear weapons in the Caribbean or in the Central or Southern American Continents.

We are very proud of the leadership role that the nation of Mexico has played. Tlatelolco is in the suburbs of Mexico City, and if I had my preference I would have chosen a place that has a little bit easier pronunciation but—[laughter]—I have practiced, and with the help of many people I have now learned how to say it, I believe. The Mexican Foreign Office is in Tlatelolco.

Could Senator Humphrey, come up and stand here by me, if you don't mind.

The reason for signing four documents is that they are in four languages—English, French, Spanish, and Portuguese.

[11]Text in *Documents, 1968-69*: 392-4.
[12]Document 2a.

(37) Seventh Regular Session of the General Assembly of the Organization of American States, St. George's, Grenada, June 14-22, 1977.

(a) Statement by Secretary of State Vance to the Assembly, June 14, 1977.[13]

I am delighted to join you in this informal dialogue. We are on our way to a frank, direct, and close working relationship based on the values and associations we share.

In his remarks before the Permanent Council of this organization of April 14, President Carter said:[14]

> . . . a single U.S. policy toward Latin America and the Caribbean makes little sense. What we need is a wider and a more flexible approach, worked out in close consultation with you. Together, we will develop policies more suited to each nation's variety and potential. In this process, I will be particularly concerned that we not seek to divide the nations of Latin America one from another or to set Latin America apart from the rest of the world. Our own goal is to address problems in a way which will lead to productive solutions—globally, regionally, and bilaterally.

Whatever the forum, we all recognize the special core of regional interests that brings us together here today. Our nations, for all their diversity, share historical, institutional, and personal ties.

These ties are important to us; we cannot take them for granted. Our cooperation can shape global decisions to the advantage of all our countries. In President Carter's words: "The problems and the promises of our region have become as diverse as the world itself."

Through our organization we can usefully embody that tradition of hemispheric peace, a tradition already so well advanced in the Latin American nuclear free zone. This pact has set an example to all the rest of the world, and President Carter has just strengthened my government's adherence.[15]

We are justly proud of our peacekeeping machinery, our commitment to inter-American cooperation to settle territorial disputes. And we are together in our respect for the human rights of all our peoples.

[13]Department of State Press Release 282, June 15; text from *Bulletin*, 77: 69-72.
[14]Document 35.
[15]Document 36.

Today I would like to single out two areas of regional cooperation that are of special concern to my government. These two areas are human rights and reform of the OAS. In emphasizing these two points, I do not wish to minimize the other issues before us. The hemispheric agenda is rich. The OAS can do much to strengthen our consultations, improve our cultural relations, and maintain a tradition of peace.

Of all the values which the Americas share, respect for the individual is surely the most significant. The basic constitutional documents of all our nations cite the rights of man. Nowhere are they more prominent than in the charter of this organization. In the U.N. Charter, each of our governments has accepted the obligation to promote respect for human rights among all nations.

There is no ambiguity about these obligations. A state's efforts to protect itself and secure its society cannot be exercised by denying the dignity of its individual citizens or by suppressing political dissent.

Since the last General Assembly, men who once sat among us have been victims of violent assault. We mourn the deaths of Foreign Minister Borgonovo and former Foreign Minister Letelier. And we share the relief at the narrow escape of Foreign Minister Guzzetti.[16]

If terrorism and violence in the name of dissent cannot be condoned, neither can violence that is officially sanctioned. Such action perverts the legal system that alone assures the survival of our traditions.

The surest way to defeat terrorism is to promote justice in our societies—legal, economic, and social justice. Justice that is summary undermines the future it seeks to promote. It produces only more violence, more victims, and more terrorism. Respect for the rule of law will promote justice and remove the seeds of subversion. Abandoning such respect, governments descend into the netherworld of the terrorist and lose their strongest weapon—their moral authority.

Progress toward higher universal standards of justice can also be attained by strengthening the inter-American commitment to human rights through our common action. On June 1 President Car-

[16]Foreign Minister Mauricio Borgonovo Pohl of El Salvador was found shot to death on May 11, 1977, three weeks after his kidnapping by a local "Popular Liberation Front."

Orlando Letelier, who had served successively as Foreign, Interior, and Defense Minister under the late President Allende of Chile, was killed with a companion in Washington, D.C. on Sept. 21, 1976 when a bomb exploded in his car.

Argentina's Foreign Minister, Admiral Cesar Augusto Guzzetti, was seriously wounded in an assassination attempt, presumably by left-wing guerrillas, in Buenos Aires on May 7, 1977.

ter signed the American Convention on Human Rights.[17] I believe this General Assembly should move to strengthen the Inter-American Commission on Human Rights. The Commission is elected from among the OAS member states. It serves as an independent monitor of human rights in the Americas.

My government will vote to increase the Commission's budget. The Commission needs more personnel to handle a growing caseload of complaints. With more funds, the Commission could issue more than occasional reports. It could increase its research efforts, hold more seminars, and increase the frequency of visits to every country of the hemisphere.

Several Commission reports are on our regular agenda. They have been prepared with care and independence, sometimes with full access to witnesses and records, sometimes without the cooperation of governments.

If each member state were to grant the Commission free access to national territory, this body would be able to carry out onsite investigations at times and places of its choosing. My country will grant it this facility from today. We believe that for others to do so as well would reduce misunderstandings and the dissemination of false information.

Let us work together to guide this sensitive issue into the multilateral framework we ourselves have set up and then let us use that framework to make progress.

And let there be no doubt that my government joins in dedication to international cooperation to secure economic and social rights as well as civil and political rights. We will continue to contribute to the development of poor and middle income countries, both bilaterally and multilaterally. These programs will be designed to help the poorest of our peoples.

But our cooperation in economic development must not be mocked by consistent patterns of gross violation of human rights. My government believes in the sovereignty and independence of all states. We do not ask others to emulate our particular form of democracy. The principle of political pluralism lies at the head of this organization.

We do support the right of all people to freely participate in their government. This right is based on the conviction that the individual citizen is a subject, not an object. Policies that contradict this tenet are alien to our shared traditions.

I am pleased to note the attention paid to the issue of human rights by my esteemed colleagues in statements made here today. Universal recognition of the problem is laudable, and I believe it

[17]Cf. Introduction at notes 119-120.

would be equally laudable if we all agreed to do what we can to improve the situation, individually and collectively.

As we strengthen our collective machinery for dealing with the problems of human rights, so should we also be ready to modify and bring up to date our overall organizational structure. For almost 30 years, the OAS has provided an institutional framework for inter-American cooperation. In trying to make this a more dynamic and effective organization, our representatives have been working for the last four years to come up with the draft of a new chapter.

Unfortunately this new draft does not, in our opinion, reach the goal we set. We need a charter that all member states can support without reservations, one that need not be rewritten every few years. Our charter should be flexible enough to serve well into the future.

We believe restructuring should be analyzed in a broad framework, not in piecemeal negotiations over clauses in the draft charter.

Structural reform should provide for:

—A modernized organization, free of unnecessary bureaucracy, without any hint of U.S. dominance; and

—Maximum opportunity for all American states to participate and maximum opportunity for consultations among our governments.

We need to agree upon a few important goals. President Carter, in his remarks to the Permanent Council, April 14, suggested these:

—Preserving peace and security;

—Promoting respect for human rights;

—Providing for ministerial-level consultations on major political and economic problems; and

—Expanding cultural, educational, and technical assistance.

I am happy to announce on this last point that the Carter Administration will ask our Congress to approve a contribution of $500,000 to the OAS Special Account for Culture. In addition, we are preparing a request to Congress for a further $2 million for other supporting programs.

To embody these goals, we believe, first of all, that structure and formal bureaucracy should be kept to a minimum. I do not think that the Permanent Council should be abolished—it is important to have an ongoing body with political authority to decide current issues. I suggest instead merging the existing three Councils into one.

All three have the same representatives. Time and money could be saved by making the merger official. In addition, the Secretariat should be granted greater authority to decide routine matters, thus permitting the new Council to concentrate on larger issues.

Second, informal consultations should replace much of the standing bureaucracy. Special consultations among top officials with operational responsibility should become more regular. For economic discussions, for instance, governments might send a minister of finance, trade, or industry to special OAS conferences on development or commerce. Such consultations should not be institutionalized in the OAS Charter. The General Assembly should be free to call for them as needed. Any committees required should be abolished when their work is completed.

Finally, realistic participation in our activities should reflect the diverse community of American states. Our membership policy should be universal with all independent states of the Americas free to join. My government favors the elimination of article 8 of the charter.[18] No other international organization has a similar bar to admission.

Financial obligations of member states should be realistic. We need to face two urgent tasks:

—Deciding on an appropriate U.S. assessment; and
—Deciding on appropriate contributions and roles for the smallest states.

It is an anachronism for the United States to contribute 66 percent to the assessed budget of the OAS. A balanced and healthy organization requires that no single member should pay more than 49 percent of the assessed budget.

A new system of OAS financing should be a part of overall reform. Realignment of quotas could be phased in over a period of time—as much as 5-10 years—to minimize hardship for the membership of the organization itself.

In conclusion, the United States favors a thoroughly reformed OAS structure—clear in its purpose, flexible and lean in formal machinery, vigorous in the use of informal consultation procedures, and realistically financed. We of the OAS have a heritage of which we can be justly proud. Realization of its future promise deserves nothing short of our best combined efforts.

[18]Article 8 of the OAS Charter, as amended, bars the admission to membership of former colonial areas that are subject to territorial claims by member states. Examples of such situations are Venezuela's claim to parts of Guyana and Guatemala's claim to Belize.

(b)   Promotion of Human Rights: Resolution Adopted by the Assembly, June 22, 1977.[19]

PROMOTION OF HUMAN RIGHTS

THE GENERAL ASSEMBLY,

REAFFIRMING its commitment to human dignity and freedom as expressed in the American Declaration of the Rights and Duties of Man; and

BELIEVING that effective inter-American cooperation for the integral development of the American countries of the region is basic to the promotion of full observance of human rights,

RESOLVES:

1. That the Inter-American Commission on Human Rights be commended for its efforts to promote human rights, and that its resources be increased so that it can perform its functions more effectively.

2. To recommend that the member states cooperate fully with the Commission by supplying it with the necessary documentation and taking all other measures required to facilitate the work of the Commission, including the protection from retaliation of individuals who cooperate with the Commission.

3. To instruct the Commission to organize, in cooperation with the member states, a program of consultation with governments and appropriate institutions and responsible organizations, on the observance of human rights in their countries.

4. That each member state affirms its commitment to:

a) the pursuit and achievement of human rights and undertakes to secure the termination of any such violations of human rights as may exist within its borders; and

b) the achievement of economic and social justice in its national and international relations;

and further affirms that in its pursuit of economic and social justice it will preserve human dignity and freedom, as expressed in the American Declaration of the Rights and Duties of Man, and will adhere to the rule of law.

In particular, each member state affirms its belief that there are no circumstances which justify torture, summary conviction, or prolonged detention without trial, contrary to law.

[19]AG/RES. 315 (VII-0/77), adopted by a vote of 14 in favor with 8 abstentions and 3 absences; text from OAS General Assembly, Seventh Regular Session, *Proceedings* (OAS Document OEA/Ser.P/VII-0.2; Washington: OAS, 1978), Vol. 1: 78-9.

(38) *Treaties Between the United States and Panama, Signed at Washington September 7, 1977.*

(a) *Summary of the Treaties: Letter of Submittal from Secretary of State Vance to President Carter, September 15, 1977.*[20]

DEPARTMENT OF STATE,
Washington, D.C., September 15, 1977.

The PRESIDENT,
The White House.

THE PRESIDENT: I have the honor to submit to you, with the recommendation that they be transmitted to the Senate for advice and consent to ratification, the Panama Canal Treaty[21] and the Treaty Concerning the Permanent Neutrality and Operation of the Panama Canal.[22] You signed these instruments with General Omar Torrijos Herrera, Head of Government of the Republic of Panama, at the headquarters of the Organization of American States on September 7, 1977.

These Treaties represent an important milestone in our relations with Panama and also our relations with the other countries of Latin America and the Caribbean. The Panama Canal regime established in 1903 no longer constitutes the best means to ensure the continued efficient operation and defense of the Canal.

In my view these Treaties will protect fully the United States' interests in the future operation and security of the Panama Canal. They will provide a basis for further improvement of our relations with Panama and the other nations of the Hemisphere. Moreover, the Treaties protect not only the interests of the two signatories, but also the interest of world commerce in a Canal which functions efficiently and is permanently open to vessels of all countries on a nondiscriminatory basis.

It will be recalled that negotiations with Panama looking toward a new, mutually satisfactory relationship began in 1964. Following demonstrations in Panama in January of that year and a three-month suspension of diplomatic relations, the two countries, with the cooperation of the Organization of American States, agreed on April 3, 1964, to a Joint Declaration[23] in which they undertook to seek the prompt elimination of the causes of conflict between them without limitations or preconditions of any kind. On September 24 of the following year, President Johnson and President [Marco A.

---

[20]Text from S. Ex. N, 95th Cong., 1st sess., Sept. 16, 1977: v-vii.
[21]Document 38b.
[22]Document 38c.
[23]Text in *Documents, 1964*: 311-12.

Robles] of Panama announced agreement[24] to negotiate a new treaty based on certain principles, including abrogation of the 1903 Convention, recognition of Panama's sovereignty over all its territory and provision for the possible construction of a sea-level canal. President Johnson reached the decision to negotiate with Panama after consulting with Presidents Truman and Eisenhower and other leaders of both major political parties.

Draft treaties were completed in 1967 but were not signed. In 1970 the Government of Panama formally rejected those treaties and proposed new negotiations. Additional negotiations in 1971 and 1972 failed to produce agreement. Negotiations resumed in late 1973. In February 1974, Secretary of State Kissinger initialed with Panama's Foreign Minister Tack a Joint Statement of Principles[25] to guide the negotiations, which were similar in content to those established by Presidents Johnson and Robles as guidance for the 1964–1967 negotiations. This Administration endorsed these basic concepts earlier this year, and the Treaties which Ambassadors [Ellsworth] Bunker and [Sol M.] Linowitz have negotiated and I am submitting to you reflect those principles.

Under the new Panama Canal Treaty, the United States will operate the Canal and have primary responsibility for its defense until December 31, 1999. The Treaty grants to the United States all of the rights necessary for the operation, maintenance and defense of the Canal, including the use of specific land and water areas necessary for these purposes. United States operation and maintenance of the Canal will be carried out by the Panama Canal Commission, a new United States Government agency that will replace the present Panama Canal Company and Canal Zone Government.

Panama will participate increasingly in the operation and defense of the Canal during the duration of the Treaty, and will assume responsibility for the Canal upon expiration of the Treaty.

In addition, the Panama Canal Treaty establishes basic employment policies for the Panama Canal Commission, provides for payments to the Republic of Panama out of Canal operating revenues, provides for protection of the environment and commits the two countries to study the feasibility of constructing a sea-level canal in Panama and to deal with each other regarding construction of a new interoceanic canal.

The Treaty Concerning the Permanent Neutrality and Operation of the Panama Canal will enter into force simultaneously with the Panama Canal Treaty. This Treaty establishes a regime of permanent neutrality of the Canal to ensure that the Canal, both in time of peace and time of war, "shall remain secure and open to peaceful transit by the vessels of all nations on terms of entire equality."

[24]Same, *1965*: 303-5.
[25]Text in *AFR, 1974*: 50-52.

The United States and Panama agree to maintain the regime of neutrality established in the Treaty notwithstanding the termination of any other treaties between the two countries. The Treaty does not limit in any way the measures the United States might take to ensure the maintenance of the neutrality regime. In recognition of the important contributions of the United States and Panama to the Canal, their vessels of war and auxiliary vessels shall be entitled to transit the Canal expeditiously.

The Neutrality Treaty provides for a Protocol, open to accession by all States, by which signatories would acknowledge, associate themselves with the objectives of and agree to observe and respect the regime of permanent neutrality established by that Treaty.

This report is accompanied by a summary of the terms of these Treaties.

The terms of these Treaties are implemented and supplemented by a number of separate agreements and other instruments between the United States and Panama. Additionally, arrangements have been entered into concerning continuation by United States agencies of various activities in Panama not directly related to the Canal, and efforts to provide to Panama certain loans, guaranties and credits to assist with its economic development and to strengthen its capability to contribute to the defense of the Canal. A schedule of all the above-mentioned documents accompanies this report, and the Department of State will provide copies of these documents to the Senate for its information.

I am confident you will find that these Treaties are well designed to achieve our national objectives. They provide a sound basis for the continued operation and defense of the Canal. Accordingly, I recommend that you transmit them to the Senate for its advice and consent to ratification.

Respectfully submitted.

CYRUS VANCE.

(b) The Panama Canal Treaty, Signed at Washington September 7, 1977.[26]

(Not in force as of 1978)

PANAMA CANAL TREATY

The United States of America and the Republic of Panama,
Acting in the spirit of the Joint Declaration of April 3, 1964, by

[26]Text from S. Ex. N, 95th Cong., 1st sess., Sept. 16, 1977: 8-23 (*Bulletin*, 77: 483-93). The Annex, Agreed Minute (same: 493-6), and Agreements in Implementation of Articles III and IV are omitted.

the Representatives of the Governments of the United States of America and the Republic of Panama, and of the Joint Statement of Principles of February 7, 1974, initialed by the Secretary of State of the United States of America and the Foreign Minister of the Republic of Panama, and

Acknowledging the Republic of Panama's sovereignty over its territory,

Have decided to terminate the prior Treaties pertaining to the Panama Canal and to conclude a new Treaty to serve as the basis for a new relationship between them and, accordingly, have agreed upon the following:

Article I

ABROGATION OF PRIOR TREATIES AND
ESTABLISHMENT OF A NEW RELATIONSHIP

1. Upon its entry into force, this Treaty terminates and supersedes:

(a) The Isthmian Canal Convention between the United States of America and the Republic of Panama, signed at Washington, November 18, 1903;

(b) The Treaty of Friendship and Cooperation signed at Washington, March 2, 1936, and the Treaty of Mutual Understanding and Cooperation and the related Memorandum of Understandings Reached, signed at Panama, January 25, 1955,[27] between the United States of America and the Republic of Panama;

(c) All other treaties, conventions, agreements and exchanges of notes between the United States of America and the Republic of Panama, concerning the Panama Canal which were in force prior to the entry into force of this Treaty; and

(d) Provisions concerning the Panama Canal which appear in other treaties, conventions, agreements and exchanges of notes between the United States of America and the Republic of Panama which were in force prior to the entry into force of this Treaty.

2. In accordance with the terms of this Treaty and related agreements, the Republic of Panama, as territorial sovereign, grants to the United States of America, for the duration of this Treaty, the rights necessary to regulate the transit of ships through the Panama Canal, and to manage, operate, maintain, improve, protect and de-

[27]Cf. *Documents, 1955*: 368-74.

fend the Canal. The Republic of Panama guarantees to the United States of America the peaceful use of the land and water areas which it has been granted the rights to use for such purposes pursuant to this Treaty and related agreements.

3. The Republic of Panama shall participate increasingly in the management and protection and defense of the Canal, as provided in this Treaty.

4. In view of the special relationship established by this Treaty, the United States of America and the Republic of Panama shall cooperate to assure the uninterrupted and efficient operation of the Panama Canal.

Article II

RATIFICATION, ENTRY INTO FORCE, AND TERMINATION

1. This Treaty shall be subject to ratification in accordance with the constitutional procedures of the two Parties. The instruments of ratification of this Treaty shall be exchanged at Panama at the same time as the instruments of ratification of the Treaty Concerning the Permanent Neutrality and Operation of the Panama Canal, signed this date, are exchanged. This Treaty shall enter into force, simultaneously with the Treaty Concerning the Permanent Neutrality and Operation of the Panama Canal, six calendar months from the date of the exchange of the instruments of ratification.

2. This Treaty shall terminate at noon, Panama time, December 31, 1999.

Article III

CANAL OPERATION AND MANAGEMENT

1. The Republic of Panama, as territorial sovereign, grants to the United States of America the rights to manage, operate, and maintain the Panama Canal, its complementary works, installations and equipment and to provide for the orderly transit of vessels through the Panama Canal. The United States of America accepts the grant of such rights and undertakes to exercise them in accordance with this Treaty and related agreements.

2. In carrying out the foregoing responsibilities, the United States of America may:

(a) Use for the aforementioned purposes, without cost except as provided in this Treaty, the various installations and areas (including the Panama Canal) and waters, described in the Agreement in Implementation of this Article, signed this date, as well as such other areas and installations as are made available to the United States of America under this Treaty and related agreements, and take the measures necessary to ensure sanitation of such areas;

(b) Make such improvements and alterations to the aforesaid installations and areas as it deems appropriate, consistent with the terms of this Treaty;

(c) Make and enforce all rules pertaining to the passage of vessels through the Canal and other rules with respect to navigation and maritime matters, in accordance with this Treaty and related agreements. The Republic of Panama will lend its cooperation, when necessary, in the enforcement of such rules;

(d) Establish, modify, collect and retain tolls for the use of the Panama Canal, and other charges, and establish and modify methods of their assessment;

(e) Regulate relations with employees of the United States Government;

(f) Provide supporting services to facilitate the performance of its responsibilities under this Article;

(g) Issue and enforce regulations for the effective exercise of the rights and responsibilities of the United States of America under this Treaty and related agreements. The Republic of Panama will lend its cooperation, when necessary, in the enforcement of such rules; and

(h) Exercise any other right granted under this Treaty, or otherwise agreed upon between the two Parties.

3. Pursuant to the foregoing grant of rights, the United States of America shall, in accordance with the terms of this Treaty and the provisions of United States law, carry out its responsibilities by means of a United States Government agency called the Panama Canal Commission, which shall be constituted by and in conformity with the laws of the United States of America.

(a) The Panama Canal Commission shall be supervised by a Board composed of nine members, five of whom shall be nationals of the United States of America, and four of whom shall be Panamanian nationals proposed by the Republic of Panama for appointment to such positions by the United States of America in a timely manner.

(b) Should the Republic of Panama request the United States of America to remove a Panamanian national from membership on the Board, the United States of America shall agree to such a request. In that event, the Republic of Panama shall propose another Panamanian national for appointment by the United States of America to such position in a timely manner. In case of removal of a Panamanian member of the Board at the initiative of the United States of America, both Parties will consult in advance in order to reach agreement concerning such removal, and the Republic of Panama shall propose another Panamanian national for appointment by the United States of America in his stead.

(c) The United States of America shall employ a national of the United States of America as Administrator of the Panama Canal Commission, and a Panamanian national as Deputy Administrator, through December 31, 1989. Beginning January 1, 1990, a Panamanian national shall be employed as the Administrator and a national of the United States of America shall occupy the position of Deputy Administrator. Such Panamanian nationals shall be proposed to the United States of America by the Republic of Panama for appointment to such positions by the United States of America.

(d) Should the United States of America remove the Panamanian national from his position as Deputy Administrator, or Administrator, the Republic of Panama shall propose another Panamanian national for appointment to such position by the United States of America.

4. An illustrative description of the activities the Panama Canal Commission will perform in carrying out the responsibilities and rights of the United States of America under this Article is set forth at the Annex. Also set forth in the Annex are procedures for the discontinuance or transfer of those activities performed prior to the entry into force of this Treaty by the Panama Canal Company or the Canal Zone Government which are not to be carried out by the Panama Canal Commission.

5. The Panama Canal Commission shall reimburse the Republic of Panama for the costs incurred by the Republic of Panama in providing the following public services in the Canal operating areas and in housing areas set forth in the Agreement in Implementation of Article III of this Treaty and occupied by both United States and Panamanian citizen employees of the Panama Canal Commission: police, fire protection, street maintenance, street lighting, street cleaning, traffic management and garbage collection. The Panama Canal Commission shall pay the Republic of Panama the sum of ten million United States dollars ($10,000,000) per annum for the foregoing services. It is agreed that every three years from the date that this Treaty enters into force, the costs involved in furnishing said services shall be reexamined to determine whether adjustment

of the annual payment should be made because of inflation and other relevant factors affecting the cost of such services.

6. The Republic of Panama shall be responsible for providing, in all areas comprising the former Canal Zone, services of a general jurisdictional nature such as customs and immigration, postal services, courts and licensing, in accordance with this Treaty and related agreements.

7. The United States of America and the Republic of Panama shall establish a Panama Canal Consultative Committee, composed of an equal number of high-level representatives of the United States of America and the Republic of Panama, and which may appoint such subcommittees as it may deem appropriate. This Committee shall advise the United States of America and the Republic of Panama on matters of policy affecting the Canal's operation. In view of both Parties' special interest in the continuity and efficiency of the Canal operation in the future, the Committee shall advise on matters such as general tolls policy, employment and training policies to increase the participation of Panamanian nationals in the operation of the Canal, and international policies on matters concerning the Canal. The Committee's recommendations shall be transmitted to the two Governments, which shall give such recommendations full consideration in the formulation of such policy decisions.

8. In addition to the participation of Panamanian nationals at high management levels of the Panama Canal Commission, as provided for in paragraph 3 of this Article, there shall be growing participation of Panamanian nationals at all other levels and areas of employment in the aforesaid Commission, with the objective of preparing, in an orderly and efficient fashion, for the assumption by the Republic of Panama of full responsibility for the management, operation and maintenance of the Canal upon the termination of this Treaty.

9. The use of the areas, waters and installations with respect to which the United States of America is granted rights pursuant to this Article, and the rights and legal status of United States Government agencies and employees operating in the Republic of Panama pursuant to this Article, shall be governed by the Agreement in Implementation of this Article, signed this date.

10. Upon entry into force of this Treaty, the United States Government agencies known as the Panama Canal Company and the Canal Zone Government shall cease to operate within the territory of the Republic of Panama that formerly constituted the Canal Zone.

Article IV

PROTECTION AND DEFENSE

1. The United States of America and the Republic of Panama commit themselves to protect and defend the Panama Canal. Each Party shall act, in accordance with its constitutional processes, to meet the danger resulting from an armed attack or other actions which threaten the security of the Panama Canal or of ships transiting it.

2. For the duration of this Treaty, the United States of America shall have primary responsibility to protect and defend the Canal. The rights of the United States of America to station, train, and move military forces within the Republic of Panama are described in the Agreement in Implementation of this Article, signed this date. The use of areas and installations and the legal status of the armed forces of the United States of America in the Republic of Panama shall be governed by the aforesaid Agreement.

3. In order to facilitate the participation and cooperation of the armed forces of both Parties in the protection and defense of the Canal, the United States of America and the Republic of Panama shall establish a Combined Board comprised of an equal number of senior military representatives of each Party. These representatives shall be charged by their respective governments with consulting and cooperating on all matters pertaining to the protection and defense of the Canal, and with planning for actions to be taken in concert for that purpose. Such combined protection and defense arrangements shall not inhibit the identity or lines of authority of the armed forces of the United States of America or the Republic of Panama. The Combined Board shall provide for coordination and cooperation concerning such matters as:

(a) The preparation of contingency plans for the protection and defense of the Canal based upon the cooperative efforts of the armed forces of both Parties;

(b) The planning and conduct of combined military exercises; and

(c) The conduct of United States and Panamanian military operations with respect to the protection and defense of the Canal.

4. The Combined Board shall, at five-year intervals throughout the duration of this Treaty, review the resources being made avail-

able by the two Parties for the protection and defense of the Canal. Also, the Combined Board shall make appropriate recommendations to the two Governments respecting projected requirements, the efficient utilization of available resources of the two Parties, and other matters of mutual interest with respect to the protection and defense of the Canal.

5. To the extent possible consistent with its primary responsibility for the protection and defense of the Panama Canal, the United States of America will endeavor to maintain its armed forces in the Republic of Panama in normal times at a level not in excess of that of the armed forces of the United States of America in the territory of the former Canal Zone immediately prior to the entry into force of this Treaty.

Article V

PRINCIPLE OF NON-INTERVENTION

Employees of the Panama Canal Commission, their dependents and designated contractors of the Panama Canal Commission, who are nationals of the United States of America, shall respect the laws of the Republic of Panama and shall abstain from any activity incompatible with the spirit of this Treaty. Accordingly, they shall abstain from any political activity in the Republic of Panama as well as from any intervention in the internal affairs of the Republic of Panama. The United States of America shall take all measures within its authority to ensure that the provisions of this Article are fulfilled.

Article VI

PROTECTION OF THE ENVIRONMENT

1. The United States of America and the Republic of Panama commit themselves to implement this Treaty in a manner consistent with the protection of the natural environment of the Republic of Panama. To this end, they shall consult and cooperate with each other in all appropriate ways to ensure that they shall give due regard to the protection and conservation of the environment.

2. A Joint Commission on the Environment shall be established with equal representation from the United States of America and the Republic of Panama, which shall periodically review the implementation of this Treaty and shall recommend as appropriate to the

two Governments ways to avoid or, should this not be possible, to mitigate the adverse environmental impacts which might result from their respective actions pursuant to the Treaty.

3. The United States of America and the Republic of Panama shall furnish the Joint Commission on the Environment complete information on any action taken in accordance with this Treaty which, in the judgment of both, might have a significant effect on the environment. Such information shall be made available to the Commission as far in advance of the contemplated action as possible to facilitate the study by the Commission of any potential environmental problems and to allow for consideration of the recommendation of the Commission before the contemplated action is carried out.

Article VII

FLAGS

1. The entire territory of the Republic of Panama, including the areas the use of which the Republic of Panama makes available to the United States of America pursuant to this Treaty and related agreements, shall be under the flag of the Republic of Panama, and consequently such flag always shall occupy the position of honor.

2. The flag of the United States of America may be displayed, together with the flag of the Republic of Panama, at the headquarters of the Panama Canal Commission, at the site of the Combined Board, and as provided in the Agreement in Implementation of Article IV of this Treaty.

3. The flag of the United States of America also may be displayed at other places and on some occasions, as agreed by both Parties.

Article VIII

PRIVILEGES AND IMMUNITIES

1. The installations owned or used by the agencies or instrumentalities of the United States of America operating in the Republic of Panama pursuant to this Treaty and related agreements, and their official archives and documents, shall be inviolable. The two Parties shall agree on procedures to be followed in the conduct of any criminal investigation at such locations by the Republic of Panama.

2. Agencies and instrumentalities of the Government of the

United States of America operating in the Republic of Panama pursuant to this Treaty and related agreements shall be immune from the jurisdiction of the Republic of Panama.

3. In addition to such other privileges and immunities as are afforded to employees of the United States Government and their dependents pursuant to this Treaty, the United States of America may designate up to twenty officials of the Panama Canal Commission who, along with their dependents, shall enjoy the privileges and immunities accorded to diplomatic agents and their dependents under international law and practice. The United States of America shall furnish to the Republic of Panama a list of the names of said officials and their dependents, identifying the positions they occupy in the Government of the United States of America, and shall keep such list current at all times.

Article IX

APPLICABLE LAWS AND LAW ENFORCEMENT

1. In accordance with the provisions of this Treaty and related agreements, the law of the Republic of Panama shall apply in the areas made available for the use of the United States of America pursuant to this Treaty. The law of the Republic of Panama shall be applied to matters or events which occurred in the former Canal Zone prior to the entry into force of this Treaty only to the extent specifically provided in prior treaties and agreements.

2. Natural or juridical persons who, on the date of entry into force of this Treaty, are engaged in business or non-profit activities at locations in the former Canal Zone may continue such business or activities at those locations under the same terms and conditions prevailing prior to the entry into force of this Treaty for a thirty-month transition period from its entry into force. The Republic of Panama shall maintain the same operating conditions as those applicable to the aforementioned enterprises prior to the entry into force of this Treaty in order that they may receive licenses to do business in the Republic of Panama subject to their compliance with the requirements of its law. Thereafter, such persons shall receive the same treatment under the law of the Republic of Panama as similar enterprises already established in the rest of the territory of the Republic of Panama without discrimination.

3. The rights of ownership, as recognized by the United States of America, enjoyed by natural or juridical private persons in buildings and other improvements to real property located in the former Canal Zone shall be recognized by the Republic of Panama in conformity with its laws.

4. With respect to buildings and other improvements to real property located in the Canal operating areas, housing areas or other areas subject to the licensing procedure established in Article IV of the Agreement in Implementation of Article III of this Treaty, the owners shall be authorized to continue using the land upon which their property is located in accordance with the procedures established in that Article.

5. With respect to buildings and other improvements to real property located in areas of the former Canal Zone to which the aforesaid licensing procedure is not applicable, or may cease to be applicable during the lifetime or upon termination of this Treaty, the owners may continue to use the land upon which their property is located, subject to the payment of a reasonable charge to the Republic of Panama. Should the Republic of Panama decide to sell such land, the owners of the buildings or other improvements located thereon shall be offered a first option to purchase such land at a reasonable cost. In the case of non-profit enterprises, such as churches and fraternal organizations, the cost of the purchase will be nominal in accordance with the prevailing practice in the rest of the territory of the Republic of Panama.

6. If any of the aforementioned persons are required by the Republic of Panama to discontinue their activities or vacate their property for public purposes, they shall be compensated at fair market value by the Republic of Panama.

7. The provisions of paragraphs 2–6 above shall apply to natural or juridical persons who have been engaged in business or non-profit activities at locations in the former Canal Zone for at least six months prior to the date of signature of this Treaty.

8. The Republic of Panama shall not issue, adopt or enforce any law, decrees, regulation, or international agreement or take any other action which purports to regulate or would otherwise interfere with the exercise on the part of the United States of America of any right granted under this Treaty or related agreements.

9. Vessels transiting the Canal, and cargo, passengers and crews carried on such vessels shall be exempt from any taxes, fees, or other charges by the Republic of Panama. However, in the event such vessels call at a Panamanian port, they may be assessed charges incident thereto, such as charges for services provided to the vessel. The Republic of Panama may also require the passengers and crew disembarking from such vessels to pay such taxes, fees and charges as are established under Panamanian law for persons entering its territory. Such taxes, fees and charges shall be assessed on a nondiscriminatory basis.

10. The United States of America and the Republic of Panama will cooperate in taking such steps as may from time to time be necessary to guarantee the security of the Panama Canal Commission,

its property, its employees and their dependents, and their property, the Forces of the United States of America and the members thereof, the civilian component of the United States Forces, the dependents of members of the Forces and the civilian component, and their property, and the contractors of the Panama Canal Commission and of the United States Forces, their dependents, and their property. The Republic of Panama will seek from its Legislative Branch such legislation as may be needed to carry out the foregoing purposes and to punish any offenders.

11. The Parties shall conclude an agreement whereby nationals of either State, who are sentenced by the courts of the other State, and who are not domiciled therein, may elect to serve their sentences in their State of nationality.

Article X

EMPLOYMENT WITH THE PANAMA CANAL COMMISSION

1. In exercising its rights and fulfilling its responsibilities as the employer, the United States of America shall establish employment and labor regulations which shall contain the terms, conditions and prerequisites for all categories of employees of the Panama Canal Commission. These regulations shall be provided to the Republic of Panama prior to their entry into force.

2. (a) The regulations shall establish a system of preference when hiring employees, for Panamanian applicants possessing the skills and qualifications required for employment by the Panama Canal Commission. The United States of America shall endeavor to ensure that the number of Panamanian nationals employed by the Panama Canal Commission in relation to the total number of its employees will conform to the proportion established for foreign enterprises under the law of the Republic of Panama.

(b) The terms and conditions of employment to be established will in general be no less favorable to persons already employed by the Panama Canal Company or Canal Zone Government prior to the entry into force of this Treaty, than those in effect immediately prior to that date.

3. (a) The United States of America shall establish an employment policy for the Panama Canal Commission that shall generally limit the recruitment of personnel outside the Republic of Panama to persons possessing requisite skills and qualifications which are not available in the Republic of Panama.

(b) The United States of America will establish training programs for Panamanian employees and apprentices in order to increase the number of Panamanian nationals qualified to assume positions with the Panama Canal Commission, as positions become available.

(c) Within five years from the entry into force of this Treaty, the number of United States nationals employed by the Panama Canal Commission who were previously employed by the Panama Canal Company shall be at least twenty percent less than the total number of United States nationals working for the Panama Canal Company immediately prior to the entry into force of this Treaty.

(d) The United States of America shall periodically inform the Republic of Panama, through the Coordinating Committee, established pursuant to the Agreement in Implementation of Article III of this Treaty, of available positions within the Panama Canal Commission. The Republic of Panama shall similarly provide the United States of America any information it may have as to the availability of Panamanian nationals claiming to have skills and qualifications that might be required by the Panama Canal Commission, in order that the United States of America may take this information into account.

4. The United States of America will establish qualification standards for skills, training and experience required by the Panama Canal Commission. In establishing such standards, to the extent they include a requirement for a professional license, the United States of America, without prejudice to its right to require additional professional skills and qualifications, shall recognize the professional licenses issued by the Republic of Panama.

5. The United States of America shall establish a policy for the periodic rotation, at a maximum of every five years, of United States citizen employees and other non-Panamanian employees, hired after the entry into force of this Treaty. It is recognized that certain exceptions to the said policy of rotation may be made for sound administrative reasons, such as in the case of employees holding positions requiring certain non-transferable or non-recruitable skills.

6. With regard to wages and fringe benefits, there shall be no discrimination on the basis of nationality, sex, or race. Payments by the Panama Canal Commission of additional remuneration, or the provision of other benefits, such as home leave benefits, to United States nationals employed prior to entry into force of this Treaty, or to persons of any nationality, including Panamanian nationals who are thereafter recruited outside of the Republic of Panama and who change their place of residence, shall not be considered to be discrimination for the purpose of this paragraph.

7. Persons employed by the Panama Canal Company or Canal Zone Government prior to the entry into force of this Treaty, who are displaced from their employment as a result of the discontinuance by the United States of America of certain activities pursuant

to this Treaty, will be placed by the United States of America, to the maximum extent feasible, in other appropriate jobs with the Government of the United States in accordance with United States Civil Service regulations. For such persons who are not United States nationals, placement efforts will be confined to United States Government activities located within the Republic of Panama. Likewise, persons previously employed in activities for which the Republic of Panama assumes responsibility as a result of this Treaty will be continued in their employment to the maximum extent feasible by the Republic of Panama. The Republic of Panama shall, to the maximum extent feasible, ensure that the terms and conditions of employment applicable to personnel employed in the activities for which it assumes responsibility are no less favorable than those in effect immediately prior to the entry into force of this Treaty. Non-United States nationals employed by the Panama Canal Company or Canal Zone Government prior to the entry into force of this Treaty who are involuntarily separated from their positions because of the discontinuance of an activity by reason of this Treaty, who are not entitled to an immediate annuity under the United States Civil Service Retirement System, and for whom continued employment in the Republic of Panama by the Government of the United States of America is not practicable, will be provided special job placement assistance by the Republic of Panama for employment in positions for which they may be qualified by experience and training.

8. The Parties agree to establish a system whereby the Panama Canal Commission may, if deemed mutually convenient or desirable by the two Parties, assign certain employees of the Panama Canal Commission, for a limited period of time, to assist in the operation of activities transferred to the responsibility of the Republic of Panama as a result of this Treaty or related agreements. The salaries and other costs of employment of any such persons assigned to provide such assistance shall be reimbursed to the United States of America by the Republic of Panama.

9. (a) The right of employees to negotiate collective contracts with the Panama Canal Commission is recognized. Labor relations with employees of the Panama Canal Commission shall be conducted in accordance with forms of collective bargaining established by the United States of America after consultation with employee unions.

(b) Employee unions shall have the right to affiliate with international labor organizations.

10. The United States of America will provide an appropriate early optional retirement program for all persons employed by the Panama Canal Company or Canal Zone Government immediately prior to the entry into force of this Treaty. In this regard, taking in-

to account the unique circumstances created by the provisions of this Treaty, including its duration, and their effect upon such employees, the United States of America shall, with respect to them:

(a) determine that conditions exist which invoke applicable United States law permitting early retirement annuities and apply such law for a substantial period of the duration of the Treaty;

(b) seek special legislation to provide more liberal entitlement to, and calculation of, retirement annuities than is currently provided for by law.

Article XI

PROVISIONS FOR THE TRANSITION PERIOD

The Republic of Panama shall reassume plenary jurisdiction over the former Canal Zone upon entry into force of this Treaty and in accordance with its terms.

1. In order to provide for an orderly transition to the full application of the jurisdictional arrangements established by this Treaty and related agreements, the provisions of this Article shall become applicable upon the date this Treaty enters into force, and shall remain in effect for thirty calendar months. The authority granted in this Article to the United States of America for this transition period shall supplement, and is not intended to limit, the full application and effect of the rights and authority granted to the United States of America elsewhere in this Treaty and in related agreements.

2. During this transition period, the criminal and civil laws of the United States of America shall apply concurrently with those of the Republic of Panama in certain of the areas and installations made available for the use of the United States of America pursuant to this Treaty, in accordance with the following provisions:

(a) The Republic of Panama permits the authorities of the United States of America to have the primary right to exercise criminal jurisdiction over United States citizen employees of the Panama Canal Commission and their dependents, and members of the United States Forces and civilian component and their dependents, in the following cases:

(i) for any offense committed during the transition period within such areas and installations, and

(ii) for any offense committed prior to that period in the former Canal Zone.

The Republic of Panama shall have the primary right to exercise jurisdiction over all other offenses committed by such persons, except as otherwise provided in this Treaty and related agreements or as may be otherwise agreed.

(b) Either Party may waive its primary right to exercise jurisdiction in a specific case or category of cases.

3. The United States of America shall retain the right to exercise jurisdiction in criminal cases relating to offenses committed prior to the entry into force of this Treaty in violation of the laws applicable in the former Canal Zone.

4. For the transition period, the United States of America shall retain police authority and maintain a police force in the aforementioned areas and installations. In such areas, the police authorities of the United States of America may take into custody any person not subject to their primary jurisdiction if such person is believed to have committed or to be committing any offense against applicable laws or regulations, and shall promptly transfer custody to the police authorities of the Republic of Panama. The United States of America and the Republic of Panama shall establish joint police patrols in agreed areas. Any arrests conducted by a joint patrol shall be the responsibility of the patrol member or members representing the Party having primary jurisdiction over the person or persons arrested.

5. The courts of the United States of America and related personnel, functioning in the former Canal Zone immediately prior to the entry into force of this Treaty, may continue to function during the transition period for the judicial enforcement of the jurisdiction to be exercised by the United States of America in accordance with this Article.

6. In civil cases, the civilian courts of the United States of America in the Republic of Panama shall have no jurisdiction over new cases of a private civil nature, but shall retain full jurisdiction during the transition period to dispose of any civil cases, including admiralty cases, already instituted and pending before the courts prior to the entry into force of this Treaty.

7. The laws, regulations, and administrative authority of the United States of America applicable in the former Canal Zone immediately prior to the entry into force of this Treaty shall, to the extent not inconsistent with this Treaty and related agreements, continue in force for the purpose of the exercise by the United States of America of law enforcement and judicial jurisdiction only during the transition period. The United States of America may amend, repeal or otherwise change such laws, regulations and administrative authority. The two Parties shall consult concerning procedural and substantive matters relative to the implementation of this Article, including the disposition of cases pending at the end of the

transition period and, in this respect, may enter into appropriate agreements by an exchange of notes or other instrument.

8. During this transition period, the United States of America may continue to incarcerate individuals in the areas and installations made available for the use of the United States of America by the Republic of Panama pursuant to this Treaty and related agreements, or to transfer them to penal facilities in the United States of America to serve their sentences.

Article XII

A SEA-LEVEL CANAL OR A THIRD LANE OF LOCKS

1. The United States of America and the Republic of Panama recognize that a sea-level canal may be important for international navigation in the future. Consequently, during the duration of this Treaty, both Parties commit themselves to study jointly the feasibility of a sea-level canal in the Republic of Panama, and in the event they determine that such a waterway is necessary, they shall negotiate terms, agreeable to both Parties, for its construction.

2. The United States of America and the Republic of Panama agree on the following:

(a) No new interoceanic canal shall be constructed in the territory of the Republic of Panama during the duration of this Treaty, except in accordance with the provisions of this Treaty, or as the two Parties may otherwise agree; and

(b) During the duration of this Treaty, the United States of America shall not negotiate with third States for the right to construct an interoceanic canal on any other route in the Western Hemisphere, except as the two Parties may otherwise agree.

3. The Republic of Panama grants to the United States of America the right to add a third lane of locks to the existing Panama Canal. This right may be exercised at any time during the duration of this Treaty, provided that the United States of America has delivered to the Republic of Panama copies of the plans for such construction.

4. In the event the United States of America exercises the right granted in paragraph 3 above, it may use for that purpose, in addition to the areas otherwise made available to the United States of America pursuant to this Treaty, such other areas as the two Parties may agree upon. The terms and conditions applicable to Canal operating areas made available by the Republic of Panama for the use of the United States of America pursuant to Article III of this Treaty shall apply in a similar manner to such additional areas.

5. In the construction of the aforesaid works, the United States of America shall not use nuclear excavation techniques without the previous consent of the Republic of Panama.

Article XIII

PROPERTY TRANSFER AND ECONOMIC PARTICIPATION BY
THE REPUBLIC OF PANAMA

1. Upon termination of this Treaty, the Republic of Panama shall assume total responsibility for the management, operation, and maintenance of the Panama Canal, which shall be turned over in operating condition and free of liens and debts, except as the two Parties may otherwise agree.

2. The United States of America transfers, without charge, to the Republic of Panama all right, title and interest the United States of America may have with respect to all real property, including non-removable improvements thereon, as set forth below:

(a) Upon the entry into force of this Treaty, the Panama Railroad and such property that was located in the former Canal Zone but that is not within the land and water areas the use of which is made available to the United States of America pursuant to this Treaty. However, it is agreed that the transfer on such date shall not include buildings and other facilities, except housing, the use of which is retained by the United States of America pursuant to this Treaty and related agreements, outside such areas;

(b) Such property located in an area or a portion thereof at such time as the use by the United States of America of such area or portion thereof ceases pursuant to agreement between the two Parties.

(c) Housing units made available for occupancy by members of the Armed Forces of the Republic of Panama in accordance with paragraph 5(b) of Annex B to the Agreement in Implementation of Article IV of this Treaty at such time as such units are made available to the Republic of Panama.

(d) Upon termination of this Treaty, all real property, and non-removable improvements that were used by the United States of America for the purposes of this Treaty and related agreements, and equipment related to the management, operation and maintenance of the Canal remaining in the Republic of Panama.

3. The Republic of Panama agrees to hold the United States of

America harmless with respect to any claims which may be made by third parties relating to rights, title and interest in such property.

4. The Republic of Panama shall receive, in addition, from the Panama Canal Commission a just and equitable return on the national resources which it has dedicated to the efficient management, operation, maintenance, protection and defense of the Panama Canal, in accordance with the following:

(a) An annual amount to be paid out of Canal operating revenues computed at a rate of thirty hundredths of a United States dollar ($0.30) per Panama Canal net ton, or its equivalency, for each vessel transiting the Canal, after the entry into force of this Treaty, for which tolls are charged. The rate of thirty hundredths of a United States dollar ($0.30) per Panama Canal net ton, or its equivalency, will be adjusted to reflect changes in the United States wholesale price index for total manufactured goods during biennial periods. The first adjustment shall take place five years after entry into force of this Treaty, taking into account the changes that occurred in such price index during the preceding two years. Thereafter successive adjustments shall take place at the end of each biennial period. If the United States of America should decide that another indexing method is preferable, such method shall be proposed to the Republic of Panama and applied if mutually agreed.

(b) A fixed annuity of ten million United States dollars ($10,000,000) to be paid out of Canal operating revenues. This amount shall constitute a fixed expense of the Panama Canal Commission.

(c) An annual amount of up to ten million United States dollars ($10,000,000) per year, to be paid out of Canal operating revenues to the extent that such revenues exceed expenditures of the Panama Canal Commission including amounts paid pursuant to this Treaty. In the event Canal operating revenues in any year do not produce a surplus sufficient to cover this payment, the unpaid balance shall be paid from operating surpluses in future years in a manner to be mutually agreed.

Article XIV

SETTLEMENT OF DISPUTES

In the event that any question should arise between the Parties concerning the interpretation of this Treaty or related agreements, they shall make every effort to resolve the matter through consultation in the appropriate committees established pursuant to this Treaty and related agreements, or, if appropriate, through diplomatic channels. In the event the Parties are unable to resolve a particular matter through such means, they may, in appropriate cases, agree to submit the matter to conciliation, mediation, arbitration, or such other procedure for the peaceful settlement of the dispute as they may mutually deem appropriate.

DONE at Washington, this 7th day of September, 1977, in duplicate, in the English and Spanish languages, both texts being equally authentic.

For the Republic of Panama:

OMAR TORRIJOS HERRERA,

*Head of Government of the
Republic of Panama.*

For the United States of
America:

JIMMY CARTER,

*President of the
United States of America.*

(c) Treaty Concerning the Permanent Neutrality and Operation of the Panama Canal, Signed at Washington September 7, 1977.[28]

(Not in force as of 1978)

TREATY CONCERNING THE PERMANENT NEUTRALITY AND OPERATION OF THE PANAMA CANAL

The United States of America and the Republic of Panama have agreed upon the following:

Article I

The Republic of Panama declares that the Canal, as an international transit waterway, shall be permanently neutral in accordance with the regime established in this Treaty. The same regime of neutrality shall apply to any other international waterway that may be built either partially or wholly in the territory of the Republic of Panama.

Article II

The Republic of Panama declares the neutrality of the Canal in order that both in time of peace and in time of war it shall remain

[28]Text from S. Ex. N, 95th Cong., 1st sess., Sept. 16, 1977: 31-4, 35, and 38 (*Bulletin*, 77: 496-8).

secure and open to peaceful transit by the vessels of all nations on terms of entire equality, so that there will be no discrimination against any nation, or its citizens or subjects, concerning the conditions or charges of transit, or for any other reason, and so that the Canal, and therefore the Isthmus of Panama, shall not be the target of reprisals in any armed conflict between other nations of the world. The foregoing shall be subject to the following requirements:

(a) Payment of tolls and other charges for transit and ancillary services, provided they have been fixed in conformity with the provisions of Article III (c);

(b) Compliance with applicable rules and regulations, provided such rules and regulations are applied in conformity with the provisions of Article III;

(c) The requirement that transiting vessels commit no acts of hostility while in the Canal; and

(d) Such other conditions and restrictions as are established by this Treaty.

Article III

1. For purposes of the security, efficiency and proper maintenance of the Canal the following rules shall apply:

(a) The Canal shall be operated efficiently in accordance with conditions of transit through the Canal, and rules and regulations that shall be just, equitable and reasonable, and limited to those necessary for safe navigation and efficient, sanitary operation of the Canal;

(b) Ancillary services necessary for transit through the Canal shall be provided;

(c) Tolls and other charges for transit and ancillary services shall be just, reasonable, equitable and consistent with the principles of international law;

(d) As a pre-condition of transit, vessels may be required to establish clearly the financial responsibility and guarantees for payment of reasonable and adequate indemnification, consistent with international practice and standards, for damages resulting from acts or omissions of such vessels when passing through the Canal. In the case of vessel owned or operated by a State or for which it has acknowledged responsibility, a certification by that State that it shall observe its obligations under international law to pay for damages resulting from the act or omission of such vessels when passing through the Canal shall be deemed sufficient to establish such financial responsibility;

(e) Vessels of war and auxiliary vessels of all nations shall at all times be entitled to transit the Canal, irrespective of their internal operation, means of propulsion, origin, destination or armament, without being subjected, as a condition of transit, to inspection, search or surveillance. However, such vessels may be required to certify that they have complied with all applicable health, sanitation and quarantine regulations. In addition, such vessels shall be entitled to refuse to disclose their internal operation, origin, armament, cargo or destination. However, auxiliary vessels may be required to present written assurances, certified by an official at a high level of the government of the State requesting the exemption, that they are owned or operated by that government and in this case are being used only on government noncommercial service.

2. For the purposes of this Treaty, the terms "Canal," "vessel of war," "auxiliary vessel," "internal operation," "armament" and "inspection" shall have the meanings assigned them in Annex A to this Treaty.

Article IV

The United States of America and the Republic of Panama agree to maintain the regime of neutrality established in this Treaty, which shall be maintained in order that the Canal shall remain permanently neutral, notwithstanding the termination of any other treaties entered into by the two Contracting Parties.

Article V

After the termination of the Panama Canal Treaty, only the Republic of Panama shall operate the Canal and maintain military forces, defense sites and military installations within its national territory.

Article VI

1. In recognition of the important contributions of the United States of America and of the Republic of Panama to the construction, operation, maintenance, and protection and defense of the Canal, vessels of war and auxiliary vessels of those nations shall, notwithstanding any other provisions of this Treaty, be entitled to

transit the Canal irrespective of their internal operation, means of propulsion, origin, destination, armament or cargo carried. Such vessels of war and auxiliary vessels will be entitled to transit the Canal expeditiously.

2. The United States of America, so long as it has responsibility for the operation of the Canal, may continue to provide the Republic of Colombia toll-free transit through the Canal for its troops, vessels and materials of war. Thereafter, the Republic of Panama may provide the Republic of Colombia and the Republic of Costa Rica with the right of toll-free transit.

Article VII

1. The United States of America and the Republic of Panama shall jointly sponsor a resolution in the Organization of American States opening to accession by all States of the world the Protocol to this Treaty whereby all the signatories will adhere to the objectives of this Treaty, agreeing to respect the regime of neutrality set forth herein.

2. The Organization of American States shall act as the depositary for this Treaty and related instruments.

Article VIII

This Treaty shall be subject to ratification in accordance with the constitutional procedures of the two Parties. The instruments of ratification of this Treaty shall be exchanged at Panama at the same time as the instruments of ratification of the Panama Canal Treaty, signed this date, are exchanged. This Treaty shall enter into force, simultaneously with the Panama Canal Treaty, six calendar months from the date of the exchange of the instruments of ratification.

DONE at Washington, this 7th day of September, 1977, in duplicate, in the English and Spanish languages, both texts being equally authentic.

For the Republic of Panama: For the United States of America:

OMAR TORRIJOS HERRERA,   JIMMY CARTER,

Head of Government of the   *President of the*
Republic of Panama.   *United States of America.*

ANNEX A

1. "Canal" includes the existing Panama Canal, the entrances thereto and the territorial seas of the Republic of Panama adjacent thereto, as defined on the map annexed hereto (Annex B),[29] and any other inter-oceanic waterway in which the United States of America is a participant or in which the United States of America has participated in connection with the construction or financing, that may be operated wholly or partially within the territory of the Republic of Panama, the entrances thereto and the territorial seas adjacent thereto.

2. "Vessel of war" means a ship belonging to the naval forces of a State, and bearing the external marks distinguishing warships of its nationality, under the command of an officer duly commissioned by the government and whose name appears in the Navy List, and manned by a crew which is under regular naval discipline.

3. "Auxiliary vessel" means any ship, not a vessel of war, that is owned or operated by a State and used, for the time being, exclusively on government non-commercial service.

4. "Internal operation" encompasses all machinery and propulsion systems, as well as the management and control of the vessel, including its crew. It does not include the measures necessary to transit vessels under the control of pilots while such vessels are in the Canal.

5. "Armament" means arms, ammunitions, implements of war and other equipment of a vessel which possesses characteristics appropriate for use for warlike purposes.

6. "Inspection" includes on-board examination of vessel structure, cargo, armament and internal operation. It does not include those measures strictly necessary for admeasurement, nor those measures strictly necessary to assure safe, sanitary transit and navigation, including examination of deck and visual navigation equipment, nor in the case of live cargoes, such as cattle or other livestock, that may carry communicable diseases, those measures necessary to assure that health and sanitation requirements are satisfied.

ANNEX B

PROTOCOL TO THE TREATY CONCERNING THE PERMANENT NEUTRALITY AND OPERATION OF THE PANAMA CANAL

Whereas the maintenance of the neutrality of the Panama Canal

[29]Maps appear in S. Ex. N (cited): 36-7 (*Bulletin*, 77: 499-50).

is important not only to the commerce and security of the United States of America and the Republic of Panama, but to the peace and security of the Western Hemisphere and to the interests of world commerce as well;

Whereas the regime of neutrality which the United States of America and the Republic of Panama have agreed to maintain will ensure permanent access to the Canal by vessels of all nations on the basis of entire equality;

Whereas the said regime of effective neutrality shall constitute the best protection for the Canal and shall ensure the absence of any hostile act against it;

The Contracting Parties to this Protocol have agreed upon the following:

Article I

The Contracting Parties hereby acknowledge the regime of permanent neutrality for the Canal established in the Treaty Concerning the Permanent Neutrality and Operation of the Panama Canal and associate themselves with its objectives.

Article II

The Contracting Parties agree to observe and respect the regime of permanent neutrality of the Canal in time of war as in time of peace, and to ensure that vessels of their registry strictly observe the applicable rules.

Article III

This Protocol shall be open to accession by all states of the world, and shall enter into force for each State at the time of deposit of its instrument of accession with the Secretary General of the Organization of American States.

(d) The Declaration of Washington, Signed by Representatives of the American Governments at Washington September 7, 1977.[30]

We, the Chiefs of State, Heads of Government or other representatives of the American Republics and other states present at the

[30]Text from *Bulletin*, 77: 502.

ceremony for the signature on this day of the Panama Canal Treaty establishing new arrangements for the operation, maintenance and defense of the Panama Canal until December 31st, 1999, and the Treaty concerning the permanent neutrality and operation of the Panama Canal, both concluded by the Governments of Panama and the United States of America, in accordance with the Joint Declaration between the two countries of April 3, 1964, agreed under the auspices of the Council of the OAS;

Noting that the Panama Canal Treaty is based on the recognition of the sovereignty of the Republic of Panama over the totality of its national territory;

Considering that settlement of the Panama Canal issue represents a major step toward strengthening of relations among the nations of the Western Hemisphere on a basis of common interest, equality and mutual respect for the sovereignty and independence of every state;

Recognizing the importance for hemisphere and world commerce and navigation of arrangements for assuring the continuing accessibility and neutrality of the Panama Canal;

Record our profound satisfaction at the signature by the President of the United States of America and the Chief of Government of Panama of the Panama Canal Treaty of 1977 and the Treaty Concerning the Permanent Neutrality and Operation of the Panama Canal.

DONE at Washington on September 7, 1977 in the name of:

ARGENTINA	President (Lt. Gen.) Jorge Rafael VIDELA
BAHAMAS	Prime Minister Lynden O. PINDLING
BARBADOS	Ambassador to the U.S. and OAS Oliver JACKMAN[31]
BOLIVIA	President (Maj. Gen.) Hugo BANZER Suarez
BRAZIL	Vice President Adalberto PEREIRA DOS SANTOS
CANADA	Prime Minister Pierre-Elliott TRUDEAU
CHILE	President (Maj. Gen.) Augusto PINOCHET Ugarte
COLOMBIA	President Alfonso LOPEZ Michelsen

COSTA RICA	President Daniel ODUBER Quirós
DOMINICAN REPUBLIC	President Joaquin BALAGUER
ECUADOR	President (Vice Adm.) Alfredo POVEDA Burbano
EL SALVADOR	President (Gen.) Carlos Humberto ROMERO Mena
GRENADA	Prime Minister Eric M. GAIRY
GUATEMALA	President (Brig. Gen.) Kjell LAUGERUD Garcia
GUYANA	Deputy Prime Minister Ptolemy A. REID
HAITI	Secretary of State for Foreign Affairs and Worship Edner BRUTUS
HONDURAS	President (Brig. Gen.) Juan Alberto MELGAR Castro
JAMAICA	Prime Minister Michael N. MANLEY
MEXICO	Secretary of Foreign Relations Santiago ROEL Garcia
NICARAGUA	President of Congress Cornelio H. HUECK
PARAGUAY	President (Gen.) Alfredo STROESSNER
PERU	President (Gen.) Francisco MORALES BERMUDEZ Cerrutti
SURINAM	Ambassador to the U.S. and OAS Roel F. KARAMAT
TRINIDAD AND TOBAGO	Ambassador to the U.S. and OAS Victor C. MCINTYRE
URUGUAY	President Aparacio MENDEZ Manfredini
VENEZUELA	President Carlos Andres PEREZ

---

[31]Ambassador Jackman did not sign the Declaration for Barbados on Sept. 7.

(39) Toward Ratification of the Panama Treaties.

> *(a) Meaning of the Treaties: Statement by Secretary of State Vance to the Committee on Foreign Relations, United States Senate, September 26, 1977.*[32]

Today I seek your support for new treaties governing the Panama Canal.

—First, these treaties protect and advance the national interests of both the United States and Panama.
—Second, they provide for an open, neutral, secure, and efficiently operated canal for this hemisphere and for other nations throughout the world.
—Third, they will promote constructive and positive relationships between the United States and other nations in this hemisphere.

These treaties, in my judgment, will gain us respect among other nations of the world—both large and small—because of the responsible way they resolve complex and emotional issues which have been with us for most of this century.

The treaties are a culmination of 13 years' work by four American Presidents of both major political parties and their Secretaries of State. They are the outcome of patient and skillful negotiations since 1964 by a number of dedicated political leaders, diplomats, and military men. They have been achieved because of valuable counsel and support offered by members of this committee, by representatives of American business and labor who have seen these new treaties as being in their own interest and in the larger national interest.

They are, above all, a triumph for the principle of peaceful and constructive settlement of disputes between nations. That is a principle we seek to apply in all aspects of American foreign policy.

It's quite proper that this committee, the Senate, the American people should consider carefully the content and implications of these treaties. For they should not at some later time be made the subject of partisan or divisive debate. In my opinion, they should be beyond partisanship. They should now be examined in detail by this committee and by the nation. Basic questions are being asked—and should be asked—about them. These questions express the same concerns and goals that have been on our minds during these negotiations.

[32]Department of State Press Release 433, Sept. 26; text from *Bulletin*, 77: 615-18.

—Do these treaties safeguard our national security interests in the canal?

—Do they establish a long-term basis for open and effective operation of the canal?

—Do they enhance our relationships with nations of the hemisphere?

—Do they place any new burden on the American taxpayer?

—Do American workers in the Canal Zone get a fair shake?

—And, without the treaties, what might happen?

I am satisfied in my own mind that these questions have been properly answered, thanks to the skilled and hard bargaining by our negotiators. I will discuss these questions briefly this morning.

Long-Term Operation of the Canal

The United States will control canal operations through a new U.S. Government agency—the Panama Canal Commission—to be supervised by a board composed of five Americans and four Panamanians. The commission will operate the canal until the end of this century. The present Panama Canal Company will be discontinued.

The United States will maintain responsibility for managing the canal, setting tolls, and enforcing rules of passage until the year 2000. Until the year 2000 the United States will also maintain primary responsibility for defense of the canal. After that, the United States will have responsibility to maintain the permanent neutrality of the canal to assure that it will remain open to our ships and those of all other nations on a nondiscriminatory basis.

The treaties further allow for modernization of the canal through construction of a third lane of locks and foresee the possibility of construction in Panama of a new sea-level canal. This would provide access for many modern supertankers and warships which are too large to pass through the present canal.

As to hemispheric relations, I believe the ratification and implementation of these treaties will be the single most positive action to be undertaken in recent years in our relations with Latin America. Only last month in Bogotá, the democratic governments of Venezuela, Costa Rica, Colombia, Mexico, and Jamaica issued a joint communique urging the United States and Panama to conclude the new treaties rapidly. For years, Latin American peoples and governments have viewed our negotiations with Panama over the canal as a litmus test of our intentions toward their countries.

These treaties, as negotiated, represent a fair and balanced reconciliation of the interests of the United States and Panama. They create, as has been said already this morning, a partnership under which our two countries can join in the peaceful and efficient operation of the canal. They symbolize our intentions toward the hemisphere. And they prove, once and for all, the falsity of the tired charges that we are imperialistic exploiters bent only on extracting Latin American raw materials and using the continent for our own economic interests.

National Security Aspects

As to national security aspects, representatives of the Joint Chiefs of Staff worked closely with the treaty negotiators on the security provisions and played a major role in drafting the neutrality treaty. The United States will retain all military bases and facilities—all the lands and waters—that we require for the canal's defense until the year 2000. We may keep the same force levels which we now maintain in the zone—about 9,300—and can increase them if that is necessary.

After the year 2000, as I indicated earlier, the United States will have a permanent right to maintain the canal's neutrality, including the right to defend the canal if necessary. Our warships are given the right to use the canal expeditiously. Article IV of the neutrality treaty says:[33]

The United States of America and the Republic of Panama agree to maintain the regime of neutrality established in this Treaty, which shall be maintained in order that the Canal shall remain permanently neutral, notwithstanding the termination of any other treaties entered into by the two Contracting Parties.

This means that there is no limit under the treaty on the freedom of the United States to assure permanently the canal's neutrality.

Economic Aspects

Under the treaties, Panama will receive payments which more fairly reflect the fact that it is making available its major national resource—its territory. But the treaties require no new appropriations nor do they add to the burdens of the American taxpayer.

The treaties provide that Panama will receive 30¢ per canal ton for traffic transiting the canal; a fixed annuity of $10 million per year; and an additional $10 million per year provided canal revenues permit. Panama would initially receive about $60 million per year under this formula which will apply until the year 2000. All of these payments are to be made from canal revenues. Panama will

[33]Document 38c.

thus have a strong interest in insuring unimpeded and efficient use of the canal.

We have agreed, outside the treaty, to certain arrangements which will assist the general economic development of Panama and enhance its stability. We have formally told the Panama Government that we are prepared to develop a program of loans, loan guarantees, and credits to Panama—including up to $200 million in Export-Import Bank credits over a 5-year period; up to $75 million in AID housing investment guarantees over the same period; and a loan guarantee of up to $20 million from the Overseas Private Investment Corporation. All these loans concerned require repayment. There are no grants. In addition, over a 10-year period, Panama will receive up to $50 million in foreign military sales repayment guarantees so that its armed forces can be better prepared to help defend the canal. Most of this assistance will be used to purchase American equipment. These programs will be subject to all relevant U.S. legal requirements and program criteria.

U.S. Workers in the Zone

Turning to American workers in the Canal Zone, some 3,500 American employees of the canal enterprise and their dependents live in the Canal Zone. Some have spent all their working lives there; most of these American workers will continue to be employees of the U.S. Government until their retirement. The treaties protect their basic conditions of employment. If they remain they will be free to continue living in government housing and to use the American schools and hospitals in the areas. Until the year 2000, the treaties guarantee American employees and their dependents basic civil rights, similar to those that apply in the United States, in Panamanian courts and other benefits and protections similar to those enjoyed by other U.S. Government employees overseas. The AFL-CIO, which represents both Panamanian and U.S. workers in the Canal Zone, supports these treaties.

What If the Treaties Are Rejected?

Now, what if the treaties are rejected? It would be all too easy for me to emphasize today that if 13 years of effort were lost, and these treaties were rejected, our relations with Panama would be shattered, our standing in Latin America damaged immeasurably, and the security of the canal itself placed in jeopardy.

Indeed, all of these things could and might happen if these treaties were not ratified. But that is not the major reason for supporting them. They deserve support because they are in our interest, as well as the interest of Panama.

For the people and the Government of Panama, there is the knowledge that they, eventually, will assume full jurisdiction of their own territory. There are also the economic benefits to be gained from canal revenues, from guarantees, loans, and credits— not grants—we have pledged to consider on their behalf. Panama, as a result, will be a more stable and more prosperous country.

For us, there is our knowledge that the canal will be open, neutral, secure, and efficiently operated for our benefit and for other nations in the world. We are not appropriating American taxpayers' money to accomplish this. And we will have gained the respect throughout Latin America and the world for addressing this issue peacefully and constructively. It is our interests, not foreign pressures, that led us to these treaties.

Other Questions

Let me address, very briefly, some doubts about the treaties that have been raised but can be dispelled as the facts become better known.

We are asked whether the new treaties may encourage Panama to nationalize the canal. But our new treaty rights would be no less binding than our rights under the existing treaty. Moreover, a Panama which is cooperating with us in canal management and will eventually exercise full management responsibility has no reason to seize or obstruct the canal. Any Panamanian Government will have an interest in preserving the treaties because the treaties are in the interest of Panama—as well as ourselves. These treaties, in my opinion, will reduce the chance of such an event.

It's been suggested that the new treaties could diminish our ability to maintain the neutrality of the canal. But, in fact, the Joint Chiefs of Staff are satisfied that the treaties enable us to keep the canal open indefinitely.

It has been suggested that we are paying the Panamanians to take the canal away from us. But payments to Panama will come from canal revenues, not from American taxpayers.

Finally, let me address briefly another question which has been raised—human rights in Panama. The Panamanian Government has in the past been charged with abusing civil and political rights of some of its citizens. And we have discussed this issue with that government. The closer relations between our two countries that will grow out of the new treaties will provide a more positive context in which to express such concerns, should it be necessary to do so in the future.

Already, there are encouraging signs. On September 13 Panama invited the Inter-American Human Rights Commission to send a team to investigate human rights conditions in Panama. In addition, it has invited the United Nations to send observers to its plebiscite which will be held on the new treaties next month. At the same time, the Panamanian Government has made continuing and real commitments to the economic and social rights of its citizens. Its economic development plans give priority to upgrading the housing, nutrition, health care, and education of the ordinary Panamanian citizen.

How we respond to an issue such as these Panama Canal treaties will help set the tone for our relations with the rest of the world for some time to come. Both we, and others, are under considerable pressure in our domestic economies. There is a tendency toward economic protectionism. And there is a question about the most appropriate ways to use our power in a world grown so complex.

Panama is a small country. It would be all too easy for us to lash out, in impatience and frustration, to tell Panama and Latin America—and other countries around the world—that we intend both to speak loudly and to carry a big stick and to turn away from the treaties four Presidents have sought over so long a time.

But that, in my judgment, would not be conduct appropriate to a responsible world power or consonant with the character and ideals of the American people. Any nation's foreign policy is based, in the end, not just upon its interests—and, in Panama, our interests are clear and apparent—it is also based upon the nature and will of its people.

I believe the American people want to live in peace with their neighbors; want to be strong, but to use their strength with restraint; want all peoples, everywhere, to have their own chance to better themselves and to live in self-respect. That is all part of our American tradition. That is why I am convinced that after the national debate they deserve, these treaties will be approved without reservations by the Senate with the strong support of the American people.

(b) The Carter-Torrijos Statement: Statement of Understanding Made Public by President Carter and General Omar Torrijos Herrera, Head of Government of the Republic of Panama, October 14, 1977.[34]

Under the Treaty Concerning the Permanent Neutrality and Operation of the Panama Canal (the Neutrality Treaty),[35] Panama and the United States have the responsibility to assure that the Panama Canal will remain open and secure to ships of all nations. The correct interpretation of this principle is that each of the two

---

[34] Text from *Presidential Documents*, 13: 1547.
[35] Document 38c.

countries shall, in accordance with their respective constitutional processes, defend the Canal against any threat to the regime of neutrality, and consequently shall have the right to act against any aggression or threat directed against the Canal or against the peaceful transit of vessels through the Canal.

This does not mean, nor shall it be interpreted as a right of intervention of the United States in the internal affairs of Panama. Any United States action will be directed at insuring that the Canal will remain open, secure and accessible, and it shall never be directed against the territorial integrity or political independence of Panama.

The Neutrality Treaty provides that the vessels of war and auxiliary vessels of the United States and Panama will be entitled to transit the Canal expeditiously. This is intended, and it shall so be interpreted, to assure the transit of such vessels through the Canal as quickly as possible, without any impediment, with expedited treatment, and in case of need or emergency, to go to the head of the line of vessels in order to transit the Canal rapidly.

7. ASIAN INTERLUDE

(40) *"A New Era in East Asia": Statement by Richard C. Holbrooke, Assistant Secretary of State-designate for East Asian and Pacific Affairs, before the Subcommittee on Asian and Pacific Affairs of the Committee on International Relations, House of Representatives, March 10, 1977.*[1]

I am pleased to have this opportunity to testify today on our economic and security assistance programs in East Asia and the Pacific. I greatly look forward to establishing a constructive, compatible relationship with this subcommittee and to working closely with its members.

Mr. Chairman, I believe that the end of U.S. involvement in Indochina signals a new era in East Asia. While tensions persist, they are confined in scope and there is no major conflict in progress. It appears that all of the major powers, at least for the present, favor a continuation of this situation. For many East Asian countries, economic prospects are better than ever before.

There are, nevertheless, major uncertainties in the area. For example: Relationships among the three states of Indochina and between Indochina and neighboring Southeast Asian countries are still ambivalent and could turn for the worse as easily as go for the better. The situation on the Korean Peninsula is presently quiet, compared to the upsurge of violence last year, but it, too, is unstable. Many countries are trying to cope, internally, with the unaccustomed absence of wartime pressures and the distortions these pressures tend to cause in both economic and political life. In brief, East Asia is undergoing its own transition from an unfortunate past to an uncertain future, albeit with high hopes for what the future will hold.

The changing circumstances in East Asia and our attitude toward this region obviously require us to take a fresh look at our present

[1]Text from *Bulletin*, 76: 322-6. Assistant Secretary Holbrooke's nomination was confirmed by the Senate on Mar. 23.

policies. As you know, we are considering new approaches to a number of issues, such as the reduction of our ground forces in Korea, the normalization of diplomatic relations with the People's Republic of China, the renegotiation of our use of military facilities in the Philippines, and more effective ways to improve observance of human rights. While we will need additional time to formulate fully detailed positions on these questions, several broad policy guidelines are already clear:

—The United States shall remain an Asian-Pacific power.

—We shall preserve a balanced and flexible military posture in the western Pacific.

—We shall maintain close ties to Japan.

—We shall make efforts to normalize diplomatic relations with the People's Republic of China, with due regard for the security of the people of Taiwan.

—We have already moved forward on the normalization of diplomatic relations with Vietnam, with the forthcoming departure of a Presidential Commission to Hanoi.[2]

—Our security and economic ties with our allies in New Zealand and Australia remain strong.

—We intend to phase out our ground forces in Korea, while insuring that the security of Korea is in no way threatened. Our troop withdrawal will be carried out in close consultation with the Republic of Korea and with Japan.

—The United States continues to have an interest in Southeast Asia and will play an appropriate role there. We look forward, for example, to successful negotiations with the Philippines on the use of bases there.

—The United States is dedicated to improving the world economic structure and to this end will work with both developed and developing countries in East Asia. At the same time, we will promote mutually beneficial bilateral trade and investment.

—We expect continued cooperation with the individual countries of East Asia and eagerly await the opening of economic consultations with the Association of Southeast Asian Nations (ASEAN), comprising Singapore, Malaysia, Thailand, Indonesia, and the Philippines.[3]

Purposes of Assistance Programs

I will now address the more specific question of U.S. economic and security assistance in East Asia. With regard to AID, we have

---

[2]Cf. Introduction at note 143.
[3]Cf. Introduction at note 150.

only development programs in this region.

On March 2 Secretary Vance testified before the Subcommittee on Foreign Operations of the House Appropriations Committee on our foreign assistance programs. I would like to reiterate several of the comments the Secretary made that are especially relevant to East Asia.

First, he emphasized that the United States' foreign economic assistance reflects our nation's concern for the world's poor.

Second, he noted that our own economic prosperity is intertwined with the fortunes of other nations and that we must move swiftly, in concert with developing countries, toward expanding global supplies of food, energy, and raw materials, toward coping with population growth, and toward fostering economic development.

Third, he pointed out that our selective military assistance supports the security of our friends and allies, thus providing them with greater opportunities for social and economic progress.

Finally, the Secretary set forth the Department's views on human rights, giving strong support to the observance of human rights throughout the world and favoring expression of this principle in our foreign economic assistance programs; however, no simple formula can be applied with regard to human rights violations, since economic and security goals must be taken into consideration along with our great concern for each individual's case.

In recent years, there has been greater economic growth in the East Asian region—an important market as well as significant source of such raw materials as petroleum, tin, rubber, and coconut—than in any other part of the world. Yet despite impressive progress in certain economic sectors, the nations of Southeast Asia still have far to go in their development efforts, particularly in meeting the needs of the rural and urban poor.

We feel our bilateral economic assistance efforts are truly helping the most needy elements of the Asian population as well as furthering our own policy objectives.

In our own economic assistance programs, we have tried to enhance regional cohesion. Cooperative organizations for which we provided the financial impetus several years ago are now functioning on their own with the full support of the Asians themselves. With this in mind, we are looking forward optimistically to economic consultations later this year with the Association of Southeast Asian Nations. While we hope that these talks will emphasize the desirability of fostering close and mutually beneficial trade and investment relations, we wish to hear views on other ways the United States can help ASEAN's regional cooperation.

Of course, in addition to these bilateral programs we contribute substantially to multilateral financial institutions, such as the International Bank for Reconstruction and Development (IBRD) and the Asian Development Bank (ADB). These institutions are particularly important, and I urge the subcommittee to support the Administration's request for their full funding.[4] As you know, our support encourages other donors, thus multiplying the effect of our contribution.

We propose six recipients for security assistance in fiscal year 1978: the Republic of China, Korea, Indonesia, Malaysia, the Philippines, and Thailand.

With regard to the Republic of China, we are in the process of phasing out our security assistance program and thus are proposing this year only $25 million in credits and a small sum for grant training. Korea and the Philippines will be discussed separately. In recent times Indonesia and Malaysia have emphasized economic development and have kept military spending to a minimum. However, since the Communist victories in Indochina, the Indonesians have become more concerned about their security and are making modest efforts to upgrade their own defenses. We feel our security assistance is an appropriate contribution to the preservation of the independence of these countries and to regional stability in the still-uncertain post-Vietnam period.

Thailand is a country with obvious security concerns—stemming from both hostile neighbors and an active, externally supported insurgency—and one with which we have had a longstanding security relationship. Again, we believe assistance to Thailand is an important contribution under present circumstances to regional security and an expression of continued U.S. interest in Southeast Asia.

Turning to our economic assistance programs, you will find them focused primarily on the rural poor, on those people who have not shared adequately in the relative prosperity of much of the region. Our first long-term objective is to attain a 3.5 percent growth rate in annual production of food grains by 1985. Our second goal is to slow down the population increases which often cancel out increases in food production. Moreover, we have important health and education programs which similarly are aimed at improving the quality of rural life and furthering agricultural development. I feel that this emphasis in our program reflects the needs of the recipient countries, as well as the concern for the poor expressed by Congress in assistance legislation.

Assistance to Republic of Korea

I understand you are especially interested in our assistance programs for Korea and the Philippines.

With regard to Korea, our policy decisions should be made in the

[4]Cf. Introduction at note 174.

light of our primary objective: to maintain a deterrent that will insure peace on the peninsula. Although North Korea refuses to renew the dialogue with the South which was initiated in 1972, remains intransigent on all the political issues which divide Korea, and continues to pursue its goal of reunification of the peninsula, we have determined that a phased withdrawal of American ground forces can be undertaken while still meeting our security goal. This withdrawal will be carried out on a timetable yet to be determined. In order to maintain the military balance on the peninsula and deter renewed North Korean aggression, we will maintain our air capability in Korea and will continue to assist in the strengthening of the armed forces of the Republic of Korea through a program of foreign military sales assistance. This assistance is designed to concentrate on areas where Korean capabilities need improvement.

The impressive economic development achieved by the Republic of Korea has allowed us to phase out our economic assistance, except for a proposed title I Public Law 480 program in fiscal year 1978 of $109.3 million. Similarly, Korean economic progress led to the termination of grant military assistance in fiscal year 1976, except for a small sum for the costs of delivery of previously funded materiel. The Republic of Korea has formulated its own force improvement plan, which seems to be both militarily and economically feasible. This plan calls for expenditure of approximately $5 billion for the period 1976–81, of which roughly $3.5 billion will be in foreign exchange. Most of this foreign exchange will be expended in the United States. We believe the sum proposed for credit sales—$275 million in fiscal year 1978—is appropriate in view of our mutual security interests and our desire to strengthen Korean forces as we phase out our ground troops.

As President Carter has made clear, we are deeply concerned about human rights violations in Korea. We are particularly concerned with restrictions on political activity which have led to the arrest of many Korean citizens voicing peaceful opposition to the present government. We will continue to express our concern in authoritative ways and to encourage a human rights situation consistent with normally accepted international standards.

At the same time, we believe it would be a serious mistake to cut back our longstanding assistance to the South Korean armed forces which helps these forces better cope with the formidable task of protecting their country against the threat from the north. Moreover, most South Koreans, including domestic critics of the government, strongly favor continuation of U.S.-Korean security ties and assistance. In brief, we will work for an improvement in South Korea's defensive capability while pressing vigorously for an improvement in the human rights situation.

Our Public Law 480 program in Korea is tied to an understanding we have with the Koreans on textiles. The United States has benefited from this arrangement. Cuts in this program would mostly affect agricultural development and would not, I feel, be an appropriate or effective response to the human rights issue.

Programs for the Philippines

Turning to the Philippines, it may be useful to recall that the United States has strong and unique historical ties with the Philippines as well as an important military interest in that country because of its strategic location. Our security relationship is defined in three major agreements: the 1947 Military Base Agreement, the 1951 Mutual Defense Treaty, and a Military Assistance Agreement, revised in 1953. The base agreement is currently under renegotiation. As you know, the Administration is currently studying the status of these negotiations with the Philippines. Pending the outcome of this review, it is difficult to comment concerning these negotiations; but it is clear that if agreement is reached it will include an element of compensation beyond the programs I am presenting to you today.

Our security ties with the Philippines and our military facilities there serve important U.S. national interests today, just as they did during World War II and during the war in Vietnam. They contribute significantly to the maintenance of stability in Southeast Asia and to our ability to keep vital sealanes open in the event of hostilities. Finally, our bases contribute to our ability to meet our obligations under the bilateral mutual defense pact with the Philippine Government concluded in 1951.

The Philippines views our security assistance program as evidence of continued U.S. interest in and commitment to the defense of that country and as an important factor in our contribution to the bilateral security relationship. As its contribution to a mutual security relationship, the Philippine Government grants us the use of a number of military facilities, the most important of which are Subic Bay Naval Base and Clark Air Base. Moreover, the Philippine Government is attempting to increase, with our help, its ability to meet its own defense needs.

The security assistance proposed for fiscal year 1978—$19.6 million in grant materiel, $800,000 for training, and $20 million in credit sales—represents a continuation of existing programs. These programs are aimed at improving the ability of the Philippine armed forces to defend their own country.

The United States also has important economic ties with the Philippines: over $1 billion in investment, a flourishing trade relationship, and a large resident American business community. We are currently discussing with the Philippine Government a new agreement regarding economic and commercial relations that will replace the expired Laurel-Langley Agreement.

It is clear from our political, military, and economic relationship with the Philippines that we have a continuing interest in assisting that country's economic development. In the past, U.S. aid has not only contributed to Philippine economic development but has also provided important encouragement for other foreign donors to continue and enlarge their contributions. At present, U.S. bilateral aid constitutes approximately 12 percent of the $500 million total of external assistance to the Philippines. The Japanese contribution is approximately the same, while multilateral donors such as the ADB and IBRD supply almost all of the balance. Our total proposals for fiscal year 1978 include loans of $51,190,000, grants of $11,781,000, and Public Law 480 programs totaling $34,803,000, making a grand total of $97,774,000.

We are obviously troubled by human rights abuses in the Philippines. Since the institution of martial law in 1972, there have been wide-ranging arrests and detentions without trial, in some cases for as long as four years. Recent government actions have included deportation of several foreign missionaries and newsmen, the closing down of several church radio stations and publications, and arrests of church social workers accused of improper political activity. Our concern has been communicated to the Philippine Government, along with our strong view that there should be a marked improvement in the situation.

However, we don't believe that security or economic assistance should be reduced because of the human rights problem. As I have noted, the Philippines has strategic importance, not only for our own country but also for nations friendly to the United States in the region, and thus we should continue our support.

Our economic assistance programs are clearly directed toward aiding the rural poor. Termination of these programs would not lead to an improvement in the human rights situation in the Philippines. Rather, it would most probably increase financial pressures on the government, raise doubts about our security and political relationships, and put pressures on the Philippine Government to take even more forceful domestic security measures. Given the importance of our bilateral political, security, and economic relations, we believe we will have more influence with the Philippine Government with regard to the human rights situation if we continue our assistance rather than if we reduce or terminate our programs.

We have gone through a traumatic experience in Asia in the last decade from which we have finally emerged. While this part of the world is, fortunately, less volatile and preoccupying than during the Vietnam war, we still have important interests there. The significance of Japan, a key ally, is obvious. Improved relations with the

People's Republic of China are crucial in both a global and bilateral context. We are still interested in the independence and development of our friends in Southeast Asia.

I believe the Administration's economic and security assistance proposals for fiscal year 1978 represent an appropriate contribution on the part of our government to peace, stability, and development in East Asia. Moreover, it is essential that we maintain our own credibility and sustain our old friends in the area as both we and they develop new policies to fit a new set of circumstances.

(41) Encounter with Japan: Joint Communiqué Issued in Washington on Conclusion of the Visit of Prime Minister. Takeo Fukuda, March 21-22, 1977.[5]

President Carter and Prime Minister Fukuda met in Washington March 21 and 22 for a comprehensive and fruitful exchange of views on matters of mutual interest.

They expressed satisfaction that through the meetings, a relationship of free and candid dialogue and mutual trust was established between the new leaders of the governments of the United States and Japan. They agreed that the two Governments would maintain close contact and consultation on all matters of common concern.

The President and the Prime Minister expressed their determination that the two countries, recognizing their respective responsibilities as industrialized democracies, endeavor to bring about a more peaceful and prosperous international community. To this end, they agreed that it is essential for the industrialized democracies to develop harmonized positions toward major economic issues through close consultation. They agreed further that it is important to sustain and develop dialogue and cooperation with countries whose political systems differ and which are in varying stages of economic development.

The President and the Prime Minister noted with satisfaction that the friendly and cooperative relations between the United States and Japan have continued to expand throughout diverse areas in the lives of the two peoples—not only in economic and political interchange, but in such varied fields as science and technology, medicine, education and culture. They looked forward to further collaboration on both private and governmental levels in all these areas. The President and the Prime Minister confirmed their common determination to further strengthen the partnership between their two countries, based on shared democratic values and a deep respect for individual freedom and fundamental human rights.

[5]Text from *Presidential Documents*, 13: 424-7.

The President and the Prime Minister confirmed their common recognition that the interdependence of nations requires that the industrial countries manage their economies with due consideration for global economic needs, including those of the developing nations. They agreed that economic recovery of the industrialized democracies is indispensable to the stable growth of the international economy, and that nations with large-scale economies, including the United States and Japan, while seeking to avoid recrudescent inflation, should contribute to the stimulation of the world economy in a manner commensurate with their respective situations. They agreed that both Governments would continue to consult closely to this end.

They agreed that a liberal world trading system is essential for the sound development of the world economy, and in this connection expressed their determination to seek significant early progress in the Tokyo Round of the Multilateral Trade Negotiations and to bring those negotiations to a successful conclusion as soon as possible.

They reconfirmed the need for the nations concerned, including the United States and Japan, to address constructively the issues posed in the North-South relationship. They noted the continuing seriousness of the global energy problem and reconfirmed the importance of taking further steps to conserve energy and to develop new and alternative energy sources. They agreed on the necessity of intensifed consumer country cooperation in the International Energy Agency and of continued promotion of cooperation between the oil-importing and oil-producing countries. They agreed that both Governments would continue their efforts to identify and promote positive solutions to these issues, and would endeavor to bring the Ministerial Meeting of the Conference on International Economic Cooperation to a successful conclusion.

The President and the Prime Minister welcomed the convening in London in May of the summit conference of the major industrial countries. They expressed their expectation that the conference, in a spirit of cooperation and solidarity, would serve as a forum for a constructive and creative exchange of views on problems confronting the world economy.

The President and the Prime Minister reviewed the current international situation, and reaffirmed their recognition that the maintenance of a durable peace in the Asian-Pacific region is necessary for world peace and security.

They agreed that the close cooperative relationship between the United States and Japan, joined by bonds of friendship and trust, is indispensable to a stable international political structure in the Asian-Pacific region. They noted that the Treaty of Mutual Cooperation and Security between the United States and Japan has greatly contributed to the maintenance of peace and security in the Far

East, and expressed their conviction that the firm maintenance of the Treaty serves the long-term interests of both countries.

The President reaffirmed that the United States as a Pacific nation, maintains a strong interest in the Asian-Pacific region, and will continue to play an active and constructive role there. He added that the United States will honor its security commitments and intends to retain a balanced and flexible military presence in the Western Pacific. The Prime Minister welcomed this affirmation by the United States and expressed his intention that Japan would further contribute to the stability and development of that region in various fields, including economic development.

Noting the activities of the Association of Southeast Asian Nations, the President and the Prime Minister valued highly the efforts of its member countries to strengthen their self-reliance and the resilience of the region. They also reaffirmed that the two countries are prepared to continue cooperation and assistance in support of the efforts of the ASEAN countries toward regional cohesion and development.[6]

Taking note of the situation in Indochina, they expressed the view that the peaceful and stable development of this area would be desirable for the future of Southeast Asia as a whole.

The President and the Prime Minister noted the continuing importance of the maintenance of peace and stability on the Korean Peninsula for the security of Japan and East Asia as a whole. They agreed on the desirability of continued efforts to reduce tension on the Korean Peninsula and strongly hoped for an early resumption of the dialogue between the South and the North. In connection with the intended withdrawal of United States ground forces in the Republic of Korea, the President stated that the United States, after consultation with the Republic of Korea and also with Japan, would proceed in ways which would not endanger the peace on the Peninsula. He affirmed that the United States remains committed to the defense of the Republic of Korea.

The President and the Prime Minister emphasized that, as a first step toward the most urgent task of nuclear disarmament, nuclear testing in all environments should be banned promptly. With respect to the international transfer of conventional weapons, they emphasized that measures to restrain such transfers should be considered by the international community as a matter of priority. In connection with the prevention of nuclear proliferation, the President welcomed the ratification by Japan last year of the Treaty on the Non-Proliferation of Nuclear Weapons.

The President and the Prime Minister, recognizing the important role the United Nations is playing in the contemporary world, agreed that Japan and the United States should cooperate for the

---

[6]Cf. Introduction at notes 149-150.

strengthening of that organization. In this connection, the President expressed his belief that Japan is fully qualified to become a permanent member of the Security Council of the United Nations, and stated American support for that objective. The Prime Minister expressed his appreciation for the President's statement.

The President and the Prime Minister reaffirmed that the use of nuclear energy for peaceful purposes should not lead to nuclear proliferation. In this connection, the President expressed his determination to develop United States policies which would support a more effective nonproliferation regime. The Prime Minister stated that for Japan, a party to the Non-Proliferation Treaty and a highly industrialized state heavily dependent on imported energy resources, it is essential to progress toward implementation of its program for the development and utilization of nuclear energy. The President agreed to give full consideration to Japan's position regarding its energy needs in connection with the formulation of a new nuclear policy by the United States. The President and the Prime Minister agreed on the necessity for close cooperation between the United States and Japan in developing a workable policy which will meet Japan's concerns and contribute to a more effective non-proliferation regime.

The President and the Prime Minister discussed matters concerning bilateral trade, fisheries, and civil aviation. They agreed on the importance of continued close consultation and cooperation between the two Governments to attain mutually acceptable and equitable solutions to problems pending between the United States and Japan.

The Prime Minister conveyed an invitation from the Government of Japan to President and Mrs. Carter to visit Japan. The President accepted this invitation with deep appreciation and stated that he looked forward to visiting Japan at a mutually convenient time.

(42) Withdrawal of United States Ground Forces from South Korea: News Conference Statement by President Carter, May 28, 1977.[7]

(Excerpt)

*   *   *

GENERAL SINGLAUB AND WITHDRAWAL OF U.S. GROUND
TROOPS FROM SOUTH KOREA

Q. Why did you fire General Singlaub? He claims that the of-

[7]Text from *Presidential Documents*, 13: 817. For background cf. Introduction at note 147.

ficers there have never been given a rationale on withdrawal. And
have you had any soundings from North Korea as to the possibility
of improving relations?

THE PRESIDENT. Well in the first place, General Singlaub was
not fired. General Singlaub was informed that he was not being
fired; he was not being chastised or punished. He was being transferred to a new position at an equivalent degree of responsibility
and stature.

We have, however, considered very carefully the question of our
troops to be withdrawn from South Korea, the Republic of Korea,
ground troops. This is a matter that has been considered by our
Government for years. We have been in South Korea now more
than 25 years. There has never been a policy of our Government
evolved for permanent placement of ground troops in South Korea.

In 1970 and 1971, a full division of troops was withdrawn. Many
leaders in our country and in the Republic of Korea have advocated
complete removal of ground troops from Korea.

Melvin Laird, the former Republican Secretary of Defense, is
one of those. President Park himself, the President of the Republic
of Korea, has called for the removal completely of American
troops.

The essence of the question is, is our country committed on a
permanent basis to keep troops in South Korea even if they are not
needed to maintain the stability of that peninsula? I think it is accurate to say that the time has come for a very careful, very orderly
withdrawal over a period of 4 or 5 years of ground troops, leaving
intact an adequate degree of strength in the Republic of Korea to
withstand any forseeable attack and making it clear to the North
Koreans, the Chinese, the Soviets, that our commitment to South
Korea is undeviating and is staunch.

We will leave there adequate intelligence forces, observation
forces, air forces, naval forces, and a firm, open commitment to
our defense treaty, so there need not be any doubt about potential
adversaries concerning our support of South Korea.

I think it is accurate to point out that overall strategic considerations have changed since the 1940's and early 1950's, when the
Korean question came into most prominence in the international
scene. The relationship between the Soviet Union and us, the People's Republic of China and us, and the relationship between the
People's Republic and the Soviet Union have all changed, among
other things.

South Korea, because of their own incentive and deep dedication
to progress, now has one of the most strong economies in the
world. Their growth rate last year in real terms was 15 percent.
They have massive, very healthy industry—in steel, shipbuilding,
electronics, chemical industries—to make it possible for them to

grow into a position of defending themselves.

We have also a complete confidence in the deep purpose of the South Koreans to defend their own country. Compared to the North Koreans, they have a two-to-one advantage in total population, and they have much greater access to the Western industrialized democracies for advanced equipment and for technology.

So, for all of these reasons, I think it is appropriate now for us to withdraw those troops. A decision has been made. President Park has been informed. And we will work very closely with the South Koreans for an orderly transition, leaving the ground troops of the Republic of Korea strong enough to defend themselves and leaving our own commitment to them sure.

I might say that this has been brought about by two things—our complete confidence in the Republic of Korea and its ability and a complete awareness on the part of the rest of the world that our own commitment is firm.[8]

*   *   *

(43) "America's Role in Consolidating a Peaceful Balance and Promoting Economic Growth in Asia":   Address by Secretary of State Vance before the Asia Society, New York, June 29, 1977.[9]

It is a great honor to be with you tonight. For 20 years the Asia Society has been building bridges of understanding between Asians and Americans. Much of the credit belongs to the Society's founder, John D. Rockefeller III. His interest in the cultures of Asia is enduring; his concern for Asian-American relations is profound; the contributions of the Society which he created are legion.

This evening I want to talk to you about America's role in Asia—an Asia that is at last at peace, but an Asia not without its uncertainties.

I should like to advance the basic proposition that our prospects for sustaining and developing effective relationships with the countries of East Asia are more promising than at any time since World War II. The fundamental challenges facing the Administration are to consolidate the positive developments of the past few years—the emergence of an even closer partnership with Japan, a promising "opening" with China, the growing prosperity of the Pacific Basin economy, the emerging cohesion of the ASEAN grouping—and to prevent or mitigate adverse trends which could strain the presently favorable regional environment. High stakes hang on our ability to

[8]See further Documents 43 and 46.
[9]Department of State Press Release 313; text from *Bulletin*, 77: 141-5.

meet this challenge, for our interests in Asia are enduring, and they are substantial.

I hope to leave you with these understandings:

—First, the United States is and will remain an Asian and Pacific power.

—Second, the United States will continue its key role in contributing to peace and stability in Asia and the Pacific.

—Third, the United States seeks normal and friendly relations with the countries in the area on the basis of reciprocity and mutual respect.

—Fourth, the United States will pursue mutual expansion of trade and investment across the Pacific, recognizing the growing interdependence of the economies of the United States and the region.

—Fifth, we will use our influence to improve the human condition of the peoples of Asia.

In all of this, there can be no doubt of the enduring vitality of our country's relationships with the peoples of Asia and the Pacific.

To the people of Asia I say tonight without qualification that our nation has recovered its self-confidence at home. And we have not abandoned our interest in Asia.

We are and will remain a Pacific nation, by virtue of our geography, our history, our commerce, and our interests. Roughly one-quarter of all our trade is now with East Asia and the Pacific; last year we sold $22 billion worth of our products in the region. For the last five years more of our trade has been with that region than with any other, including the European Community.

To be able to speak of peace and stability in Asia is a welcome change. But serious problems persist. Our tasks are to help consolidate the emerging peaceful balance in Asia and to promote economic growth that offers promise to its peoples.

The United States will pursue its relations with the nations of Asia with an open mind. We will continue to work closely with allies and friends. And we hope to normalize relations on a mutually constructive basis with those who have been adversaries.

The United States recognizes the importance of its continuing contribution to Asian security. We will maintain a strong military presence in the area.

Japan

Of our allies and old friends, none is more important than Japan. Our mutual security treaty is a cornerstone of peace in East

Asia. Japan's democratic institutions are firmly rooted. No people anywhere enjoy greater political freedom. Its dedication to peace is unquestioned. Twenty-five years ago, even though Japan had recovered from the devastation of war, its economic advance was just beginning. Today Japan's per capita gross national product is almost $5,000. In 1953 it was only about $700 in current value, less than that in many developing countries today.

Japan's growth has been an indispensable ingredient in the economic advance of the less developed countries in the region. Its aid has been important in contributing to the well-being of these countries; we welcome its commitment to double its assistance within the next five years.

Japan's great achievements have brought with them corresponding responsibilities. Its actions, like ours, are bound to have an impact far beyond its own borders. An enlarged Japanese market for the manufactured products of other countries would make an important contribution to a healthier world economic equilibrium, as would high rates of expansion in order to stimulate the economies of other countries.

The United States and Japan must proceed in close consultation. Above all, we must settle any issue between us in a spirit of true friendship and understanding.

People's Republic of China

Turning to China, after 25 years of confrontation, we are carrying on a constructive dialogue with the People's Republic of China.

Vast differences in culture, social systems, ideology, and foreign policy still separate our two countries. But the Chinese and American people no longer face each other with the hostility, misunderstanding, and virtually complete separation that existed for two decades.

We consider friendly relations with China to be a central part of our foreign policy. China's role in maintaining world peace is vital. A constructive relationship with China is important, not only regionally, but also for global equilibrium. Such a relationship will threaten no one. It will serve only peace.

The involvement of a fourth of mankind in the search for the solution of global issues is important.

In structuring our relationship with the Chinese, we will not enter into any agreements with others that are directed against the People's Republic of China. We recognize and respect China's strong commitments to independence, unity, and self-reliance.

Our policy toward China will continue to be guided by the principles of the Shanghai communique, and on that basis we shall seek to move toward full normalization of relations. We acknowledge the view expressed in the Shanghai communique that there is but one China. We also place importance on the peaceful settlement of the Taiwan question by the Chinese themselves.

In seven weeks, I shall be in Peking to talk with the leaders of China.[10] A broad range of world issues demands our attention. And we want to explore ways to normalize further our bilateral relationship with the People's Republic of China. Mutual and reciprocal efforts in this regard are essential.

As we prepare to go to Peking, we recognize that progress may not be easy or immediately evident. But this Administration is committed to the process, and we are approaching the talks in Peking with that in mind.

Across Asia we have close and historic ties with many other nations, and we intend to seek new ways to strengthen them.

Republic of Korea

The Republic of Korea has made good use of the opportunities provided by peace on the peninsula to become increasingly self-reliant and self-sufficient. The standard of living of its people has improved significantly over the past decade; its trade has grown enormously; its agriculture has been revolutionized.

Our security commitment to the Republic of Korea and our determination to maintain it are essential to the preservation of peace in Northeast Asia.

South Korea's growth and strength are the basis for President Carter's decision to proceed with a carefully phased withdrawal of American ground troops. This will be done in a way that will not endanger the security of South Korea. We will also seek, with the concurrence of the Congress, to strengthen South Korea's defense capabilities. Furthermore:

—Our ground troops constitute only about 5 percent of the total ground troops committed to the defense of South Korea.

—The gradual withdrawal of these troops over four to five years will be offset by the growing strength and self-confidence of the South Korean armed forces.

—Our air, naval, and other supporting elements will remain.

—We are working closely with the Koreans to help them increase their own defense capabilities.

The United States and the Republic of Korea share a strong desire to establish a durable framework for maintaining peace and stability on the peninsula.

---

[10]Cf. Document 45.

—We support the entry of North and South Korea into the United Nations without prejudice to ultimate reunification.

—We are prepared to move toward improved relations with North Korea provided North Korea's allies take steps to improve relations with South Korea.

—We have proposed negotiations to replace the existing armistice with more permanent arrangements.

—We have offered to meet for this purpose with South and North Korea and the People's Republic of China, as the parties most immediately concerned, and to explore with them the possibilities for a larger conference with Korea's other neighbors, including the Soviet Union. We will enter any negotiations over the future of the peninsula only with the participation of the Republic of Korea.

Association of Southeast Asian Nations

Ten years ago, even while war raged in Indochina, five Southeast Asian countries created a new instrument for peace—the Association of Southeast Asian Nations, or ASEAN. Our ties with one of its members, the Philippines, are rooted in our shared history. The strength of these ties is reinforced by our mutual defense treaty. Each of ASEAN's other four members—Thailand, Indonesia, Malaysia, and Singapore—is an old and valued friend.

Our economic ties with the ASEAN countries have become increasingly important. From the ASEAN area we obtain one-tenth of our crude oil imports and a much higher percentage of our rubber, tin, cocoa, bauxite, and other important raw materials. These five countries, with a population larger than all of South America, bought $3.7 billion worth of American goods in 1976.

We will maintain close bilateral relations with each ASEAN country. And we welcome the opportunity to deal with them through their organization when this is their wish. We are especially pleased that the first formal U.S.-ASEAN consultation will be held within a very few months, in Manila.[11] These talks will, we hope, form the basis for stronger American support of Southeast Asian regional efforts.

Australia and New Zealand

Close relations between the United States, Australia, and New Zealand long antedate our formal alliance in ANZUS. Only last week, the President welcomed Australian Prime Minister Malcolm Fraser to Washington.[12] In their wide-ranging talks, particular at-

---

[11]Cf. Introduction at note 150.

[12]June 22-23; documentation in *Presidential Documents*, 13: 902-3.

tention was paid to the Asian region. The contribution Australia and New Zealand make to the region is vital, and we will consult closely with them on all matters of common interest.

Socialist Republic of Vietnam

While we work with traditional friends, we have begun the process of normalizing relations with the Socialist Republic of Vietnam. Our old friends in Southeast Asia and the Pacific have been kept fully informed of our talks with the Vietnamese. They agree that the interests of all would be served by the establishment of normal relations between Vietnam and the United States.

The scars of war still exist on both sides. Both sides retain a residue of bitterness that must be overcome. But there is some progress.

—Together with the Vietnamese, we have devised a system for identifying and returning the remains of Americans missing in action in Vietnam.[13] Soon the remains of 20 more American pilots will be returned from the land where they died—some as long as a decade ago—to the land they served so honorably and so well.

—We have lifted restrictions on travel to Vietnam and taken other positive steps to assist in the process of reconciliation.

—We have offered to lift the trade embargo as we establish diplomatic relations.

—And we will no longer oppose Vietnam's membership in the United Nations. I expect to see its delegation seated there at the next General Assembly session.

These steps make clear that we seek to move forward in building a new relationship. Remembering the lessons of the past, neither side should be obsessed by them or draw the wrong conclusions. We cannot accept an interpretation of the past that imposes unfounded obligations on us.

Meanwhile, a new flow of Indochinese refugees commands the world's urgent humanitarian concern. Their numbers are growing at a rate of 1,500 a month. A few countries—including Thailand, France, Canada, Australia, and most recently Israel—have done much to help these unfortunate people. Some nations, however, have turned their backs, leaving an increasing number of refugees to perish by drowning or disease. I urge that shelter and aid be offered to these refugees, until more permanent resettlement can be arranged.

Today, as we look across the vast Pacific, we see the web of rela-

[13]Cf. Introduction at note 143.

tionships that links us together. In Korea, we see the obvious interaction of the interests of the Koreans, the Chinese, the Japanese,
the Soviets, and ourselves. Elsewhere, the web is even more intricate and complex.

Economic Progress and Problems

Peace has freed the United States and Asia to focus attention on
economic growth, which has been such a striking fact about modern Asia.

Japan's economic miracle is well known, but the remarkable economic record of other countries in Asia has received less attention.
Over the past five years, for example, the economy of the Republic
of Korea expanded by 11 percent; the economies of Singapore, Indonesia, and Malaysia by roughly 8 percent; the economy of the
Philippines by almost 7 percent.

Continuation of these gains cannot be taken for granted. We
must adopt policies to insure that economic progress is not reversed
and that the benefits are more widely spread.

President Carter's pledges at the London summit[14] are as relevant to Asia as they are to other parts of the world.

—We will continue to fight inflation.

—We will continue to seek ways of developing new energy resources and to insure stable and equitable fuel prices.

—We will resist protectionist trends and support a liberal
trading system.

—We will support the establishment of price-stabilizing commodity agreements and buffer stocks for selected commodities,
financed by producers and consumers and supported by a common fund.

In addition, our policies in Asia will be tailored to the economic
problems and opportunities of the region. The role of the Asian
Development Bank is of particular importance.

Human Needs and Rights

In the field of development, the United States has recently taken
the lead in calling for a concerted international effort to act on an
agenda of basic human needs.

In Asia and elsewhere in the developing world, our human needs
agenda must include the following essential elements which I outlined last week at the OECD ministerial meeting in Paris:[15]

[14]Document 48.
[15]Document 50.

—Development of the Third World's rural areas where the great majority of the poorest people live;

—An integrated strategy for increased food production and better nutrition in these areas;

—An emphasis on preventive medicine, family planning, and prenatal care at minimal cost;

—Expanded programs of primary and secondary education and on-the-job technical training; and

—Renewed efforts to involve women in the process of development.

To all of these efforts the United States pledges its strong support. But in many countries rapid population growth poses a threat to economic development. While pressures of population on the land are already threatening East Asia's natural environment, some East Asian countries will double their 1970 population by the end of the century. I believe the United States must help countries coping with these difficult problems.

We must be equally concerned with other aspects of human rights—the right to live under a rule of law that protects against cruel, arbitrary, and degrading treatment; to participate in government and its decisions; to voice opinions freely; to seek peaceful change.

We understand cultural differences. Our tradition stresses the individual's rights and welfare; some Asian traditions stress the rights and welfare of the group. We applaud the determination of Asian countries to preserve the ability, won at great cost, to determine their own policies and establish their own institutions.

But we believe strongly that there are new and greater opportunities for improving the human condition in the Asia I have described today—a continent at peace, the home of gifted and capable people secure in their national independence.

With vigilance and determination, with friendship and understanding, we encourage our Asian friends to grasp their opportunities to promote the human rights of their peoples.

To do so will not weaken any nation. On the contrary, strength of a deeper sort—the strength that comes from the full participation of all the people—will be the long-term result of dedication to the improvement of the human condition.

Those countries in Asia which have already embarked on this course will be the stronger for it, and we shall be able to work more closely with them.

I began tonight by speaking of the welcome promise of peace, and of peaceful change, that is taking hold across the region. I want to close by stressing my deep hope for a new sense of community in

Asia and the Pacific. We seek:

—To build on our relationships of mutual respect;
—To consolidate the fragile stability already achieved;
—To bring greater freedom and greater respect for human rights; and
—To erase the divisions that persist.

Toward this I pledge the best efforts of the Administration; for this I ask the support of our friends in Asia and of the American people.

(44) Twenty-sixth Meeting of the ANZUS Council, Wellington, New Zealand, July 27-28, 1977: Final Communiqué.[16]

The ANZUS Council held its twenty-sixth meeting in Wellington on 27 and 28 July 1977. The Minister for Foreign Affairs, the Hon. Andrew Peacock, represented Australia; the Deputy Secretary of State, the Hon. Warren Christopher, represented the United States; and the Deputy Prime Minister and Minister of Foreign Affairs, the Rt. Hon. Brian Talboys, represented New Zealand.

The Council discussions were conducted, as in previous years, in an informal atmosphere enabling Ministers to exchange views freely and gain a fuller appreciation of each country's approach to a wide range of foreign policy and defence matters. The Ministers reaffirmed the enduring value of annual Council sessions.

The frank consultations which had taken place amongst the three countries since the formation of the Alliance were a tangible expression of their close and friendly relations. This relationship was re-enforced by the three countries' common commitment to democratic institutions, the rule of law and respect for basic human rights and freedom. The ANZUS partners undertook to continue to work together to promote their shared interests in fulfilment of the purposes of the Treaty.

The Ministers recognised that the health of the economies of the three partners is of concern to each, for it affects their capacity to play the responsive and responsible role that world and regional circumstances demand of them and which is their common desire. They therefore agreed that they would consider their economic relationships and mutual problems within this larger framework.

The Ministers exchanged views on many aspects of international

---

[16]Text from *Australian Foreign Affairs Record* (Canberra; Australian Department of Foreign Affairs), 48: 410-12 (Aug. 1977).

affairs especially the sources of tension in various parts of the world and current attempts to ease these tensions.

The Council attached importance to the current Strategic Arms Limitation Talks between the United States and the USSR, and Ministers underlined the continuing need to prevent the proliferation of nuclear weapons. They renewed their call on all countries to accede to the Non-proliferation Treaty and for early conclusion of a Comprehensive Test Ban Treaty. The Council saw the forthcoming United Nations Special Session on Disarmament as an opportunity to give a new impetus to arms control negotiations and thereby to reduce world tension and the risk of international conflict.

The Council's review of world developments included consideration of the global economic situation. Ministers agreed that international access to markets and resources was a factor of continuing importance to global and regional stability. All countries were seen by the Council as having a clear responsibility to foster international economic co-operation. Ministers reiterated their commitment to maintain and if possible increase effectively and substantially the flow of assistance to the developing world and to play a constructive part in international efforts to bring about a more equitable and soundly based world economic order. This was acknowledged as a vital factor in establishing an international climate conducive to general economic and social betterment and ultimately to lasting peace. They recalled their reaffirmation at the recent Organisation for Economic Co-operation and Development (OECD) Ministerial Council meeting of the strategy for sustained economic expansion aimed at a progressive return to full employment and price stability.[17]

The Council welcomed the achievements of the Association of South East Asian Nations (ASEAN) in promoting the economic and social development of its members.[18]

Discussion of the global situation also noted developments in the Middle East and Africa. The Ministers exchanged views on the meetings between the United States and the USSR on mutual arms limitations in the Indian Ocean. They agreed that a military escalation between the U.S. and the USSR in the Indian Ocean should be avoided and that any arms limitations agreement must be balanced in its effects and consistent with the security interests of the ANZUS partners.

The Council members shared a special interest in the Asia-Pacific region and in contributing towards stability in the area. While conscious of remaining sources of potential conflict, Ministers consid-

[17]Document 50.
[18]Cf. Introduction at notes 149-150.

ered that there were reasonable prospects for continuing peace among the countries of Asia.

The Council noted that each of the ANZUS members attaches special importance to its relations with Japan and to the close consultations which they maintain with that country on the many matters of mutual interest.

The importance of the role of China as well, in regional and world affairs, was particularly noted by the Council.

The Council noted the impressive economic achievements of the Republic of Korea (ROK), the improvement of the ROK armed forces and the continuing support to be provided by the United States to safeguard the military balance on the Korean Peninsula.

The Council saw the development of friendly relations and co-operation among the countries of South-East Asia as making a tangible contribution to international stability.

The Council also welcomed the continuing growth of regional institutions in the South Pacific, and their contribution to the welfare of countries in the region. Ministers confirmed that all the ANZUS partners were keen to promote the economic development of the South Pacific and noted recent increases in development assistance to the region. Since the last Council session these questions had been the subject of a useful meeting of officials of the three countries. Council members commented that South Pacific countries could expect continued support from the ANZUS partners on a bilateral and regional basis. Ministers looked forward to co-operation with South Pacific nations in new areas such as the management and development of marine resources.

The Council members referred to the continuing program of combined exercises and training exchanges organised by the defence forces of member countries, and noted the positive contribution these made to the effectiveness of their armed forces.

The Australian and New Zealand representatives referred to the agreement reached in Canberra on 28 April between their Defence Ministers on the further development of defence co-operation between Australia and New Zealand. The Council welcomed this development as a significant practical contribution to the strengthening of the Alliance.

The Council members reaffirmed the high value each attaches to the ANZUS Alliance and to the framework which it continues to provide for maintaining the closest of relations among the ANZUS partners. In stating their concern that the Asia-Pacific region should develop in such a way as to bring peace and prosperity to the area, Ministers agreed to consult regularly on matters of common interest.

It was agreed that the next ANZUS Council meeting would be held in Washington in 1978 at a date to be decided.

(45)　A Visit to China: News Conference Remarks by Secretary of State Vance, Peking, August 25, 1977.[19]

(Excerpts)

Secretary Vance: Let me say at the outset that we are very appreciative of the kind hospitality of our Chinese hosts. You have all been witnesses to the extraordinarily gracious arrangements the Government of the People's Republic of China has provided for myself and to all of our party. As you know, I met with Chairman Hua Kuo-feng, Vice Premier Teng Hsiao-ping, and Foreign Minister Huang Hua during my 4 days in Peking. We had candid and serious talks on a wide range of international and bilateral matters. I consider the talks to have been very useful and will report in detail on them to the President upon my return.

I don't want to get into details of the talks but, as a general characterization, let me simply say the following. I believe that our talks were very important in establishing important communications between senior officials of our two governments which will continue in the future. Our talks enhanced our mutual understanding of our respective positions on a wide range of issues. As to international issues, our discussions touched on major political, economic, and strategic questions ranging across the globe. We confirmed that we share important common concerns on many subjects. As for bilateral matters we had a most useful exchange of views. Both sides clearly believe that progress and normalization of our relations in accord with the principles of the Shanghai communique is in our mutual interests. I look forward to continuing our discussions.

Now, I will be happy to take questions.

*　*　*

Q. On the question of normalization, after these talks do you feel that the Chinese have a sense of urgency about the process of normalization or do we have an indefinite amount of time for them?

Secretary Vance: I think it would be inappropriate for me to comment on behalf of the People's Republic of China. Any such questions should be addressed to them. We both have explained to each other our views in depth on the question of normalization and this, I think, has been very useful to us and appropriate.

---

[19]Department of State Press Release 407, Aug. 26; text from *Bulletin*, 77: 368-72. For the background cf. Introduction at note 151.

Q. Let me put it to you. Do you feel a sense of urgency about the process?

Secretary Vance: I don't think it is helpful to characterize the situation in terms of urgency or lack of urgency. I have a report to make to the President when I get home and I will report to him in full detail at that time. Just a minute, please. Let me say that this was an exploratory trip as I said at the outset and I think, as Chairman Hua Kuo-feng said this afternoon, that it was important that we have these exploratory discussions.

* * *

Q. After 4 days of talks, do you feel that generally, since you don't want to go into specifics, do you feel that you are any closer to resolving this major obstacle to normalization?

Secretary Vance: Again, I would repeat that these talks were exploratory. I think that they were useful talks and I think that, as a result of that, both of us clearly understand the views of each other —and that, I think, has been good and useful.

Q. Well then maybe the questions ought to be, are we further apart than before we came here? They're useful and· we're still exploring. Is there greater distance now between us and the People's Republic than there was before you came here?

Secretary Vance: The answer is no.

Q. In his toast the Foreign Minister said: "We believe that Sino-U.S. relations will surely move forward steadily as desired by both our peoples so long as both sides make sincere efforts in conformity with the principles of the Shanghai communique."[20] Do you feel that the United States is making such a sincere effort?

Secretary Vance: I do.

Q. In your toast and the Foreign Minister's toast tonight, both of you mentioned points in common.[21] Could you identify the points in common?

Secretary Vance: Again, I think it is inappropriate at this point for me to go into detail. I still have to report to the President of the United States. I think it is significant that both of us have indicated in our toasts and in other statements which we have made that we do find a number of points of common interest and I think that is the important point.

* * *

[20]*Bulletin*, 77: 367.
[21]Same.

Q. How long do you think it will be before the remaining 1,000 or so American troops are pulled out of Taiwan?

Secretary Vance: I do not wish to get into specifics on any of those kinds of questions.

Q. Did you actually discuss the mechanics of normalization in all these talks?

Secretary Vance: We discussed normalization and the details of normalization.

Q. Could you give us some idea of the nature of your discussions with the Chinese on the subject of the Soviet Union?

Secretary Vance: One of the subjects which we discussed was the Soviet Union; but let me repeat what I have said many times, namely, that our relationship with the People's Republic of China is one of the central elements of our foreign policy but that in no way jeopardizes any third country. I have said that repeatedly and I say it again.

Q. Did you reach agreement or near agreement on any of the lesser issues—bilateral issues like exchanges, trade, assets, or other such items?

Secretary Vance: We were involved in exploratory talks and we discussed the kind of issues which you have mentioned. This was but the first talk between our two governments and talks will continue in the future.

*   *   *

Q. The President said a couple of weeks ago that he thought it was possible that relations could be normalized with the People's Republic by the end of next year. Do you think after 4 days of talks that is still a possible and realistic hope?

Secretary Vance: I wouldn't want to contradict the President in any way.

*   *   *

Q. Would you say in the most general terms that you are going away from here more confident of being able to normalize relations or merely better informed on the difficulties?

Secretary Vance: I would say that I go away from here better informed. Certainly there is no question about that. I think as I leave here that the leaders of the People's Republic probably now have a better understanding of the views of our government and the people of the United States on these issues, and I hope and believe that as a part of that process we are both more understanding and thus are in a position where we have a better grasp of the problems of normalization. We both have stated that we believe it is in the interests of our two countries to proceed toward normalization. That has been the stated goal of our country. It has been stated by the President and by me and it remains our position.

* * *

Q. A technical question. Why is there no communique at the end of this meeting?
Secretary Vance: The reason is a very simple one. We talked it over. We decided that, inasmuch as this was an exploratory meeting, there was no need for a communique at this time. There had been previous meetings here during the last Administration where there were no communiques. It seemed to me that, there being no reason for it, there was no need to try and draft a communique. Our hosts agreed and we decided to proceed in that fashion. It was as simple as that.

* * *

Q. Without going into substance, are you able to say that you made, in this series of meetings, any progress toward normalization?
Secretary Vance: Let me say simply that I think this was a very useful meeting. As I have said before, it was a good meeting, a constructive meeting. I will leave it at that.

* * *

(46) Transfer of Defense Articles to the Republic of Korea: Letter from President Carter to Legislative Leaders, October 21, 1977.[22]

I am transmitting today for the consideration of the Congress legislation which will authorize the transfer of certain United States-owned defense articles to the Republic of Korea. A draft bill and a section by section analysis of its provisions are enclosed.

In the Korean War the independence and security of the Republic of Korea were preserved at a cost of 34,000 American lives and

[22]Text from *Presidential Documents*, 13: 1576-7. The letter was addressed to Speaker of the House O'Neill, President of the Senate Mondale, and Senate Majority Leader Byrd. For the background cf. Introduction at note 154.

many billions of dollars. Since then, a major objective of United States foreign policy has been the avoidance of renewed hostilities and the maintenance of peace on the Korean peninsula. Our security relationship with the Republic of Korea, which has been the cornerstone of this policy, has consisted of three principal elements—our 1954 Mutual Defense Treaty, a program of military and economic assistance, and the presence of United States Armed Forces in Korea.

Peace and stability in Northeast Asia are vital to our national interests, and stability on the Korean peninsula is essential to that goal. I am determined, therefore, to maintain our commitment to the security of the Republic of Korea. However, our security relationship is not a static one, and the specific ways in which we seek to accomplish our basic policy objectives must be evaluated in light of present circumstances.

Within this context, I have concluded that the withdrawal of U.S. ground combat forces from Korea over a four- to five-year period can be accomplished in a manner which will not endanger the security of the Republic of Korea. So long as it is conducted in a way which will assure continued peace and stability in Northeast Asia, the ground force withdrawal is a natural evolution of our ongoing security relationship. Both governments have understood that the presence of U.S. ground forces was not permanent and is related directly to the maintenance of the military balance. With appropriate assistance, such as that included in the legislation I am proposing, the Republic of Korea will be able to assume a larger share of its defense burden and assume the tasks of U.S. units being withdrawn.

I have established a tentative schedule for the withdrawal of ground combat forces: 6,000 men, including one brigade of the Second Division, will be withdrawn by the end of 1978. The remainder of the ground forces will be withdrawn incrementally with the final withdrawal taking place in 1981 or 1982. U.S. air forces will remain in Korea with a small U.S. Army element to provide communications, intelligence and logistic support to our forces and those of the ROK.

My decision to withdraw U.S. ground combat forces from Korea rests on certain basic considerations:

—Korea's impressive economic growth over the past decade and the corresponding increase in Korea's ability to defend itself;

—our continued firm determination to maintain our basic security commitment to Korea, and to retain a significant military presence there, composed mainly of air and key support units, together with the continuing presence of U.S. naval units in the area; we believe that these forces, as well as the major U.S.

forces remaining in the Western Pacific, provide a clear and visible U.S. deterrent to North Korean miscalculation;

— our assessment of the broader international context of the Korea question, particularly the pattern of interrelationships between the great powers in the area;

— our readiness, subject to Congressional consultations and approval, to take appropriate actions to assure that the ground force withdrawal does not weaken Republic of Korea defense capabilities.

The decision to withdraw ground combat forces from Korea has involved full consultations with the Korean Government. The Governments of Japan and other friendly nations in Asia have been kept fully informed, both of our withdrawal intentions and of our continuing firm commitment to Korean security. We have made it clear to both the People's Republic of China and the Soviet Union that the withdrawal decision signals no weakening of our commitment. The North Korean Government should be in no doubt about our position.

The legislation I am proposing is designed to help make certain that Korean defense capabilities are not weakened by our ground force withdrawal. It provides for the transfer of certain U.S.-owned military equipment (primarily in the custody of U.S. forces in Korea) and related services to the Korean Government, without reimbursement. We envisage at most the transfer of equipment with a depreciated value of about $800 million.

Even with this no-cost transfer, the withdrawal will require the Korean Government to devote a larger share of its financial resources, both foreign exchange and local currency, to defense. In my judgment, the transfer provided for in the draft legislation will ease the incremental fiscal burden of withdrawal on the Korean Government to an amount which can be borne without diverting excessive resources from the high priority task of economic development.

The bill provides that the President shall transmit an annual report to the Congress, through the five-year period during which the anticipated equipment transfer will take place, detailing the types, quantities and value of defense articles furnished to Korea under this Act.

The transfer of equipment to the Korean Government to be authorized by the bill will ensure that the withdrawal of U.S. ground forces is accomplished in a way that will not disturb the stability that must be maintained in the region. Since the initial phase of that withdrawal will take place in 1978, I urge the Congress to enact promptly the proposed legislation.

Sincerely,

JIMMY CARTER

8. WHAT PRICE AFFLUENCE?

(47)   The Energy Problem: Radio-Television Address by President Carter, April 18, 1977.[1]

Good evening:

Tonight I want to have an unpleasant talk with you about a problem that is unprecedented in our history. With the exception of preventing war, this is the greatest challenge that our country will face during our lifetime.

The energy crisis has not yet overwhelmed us, but it will if we do not act quickly. It's a problem that we will not be able to solve in the next few years, and it's likely to get progressively worse through the rest of this century.

We must not be selfish or timid if we hope to have a decent world for our children and our grandchildren. We simply must balance our demand for energy with our rapidly shrinking resources. By acting now we can control our future instead of letting the future control us.

Two days from now, I will present to the Congress my energy proposals.[2] Its Members will be my partners, and they have already given me a great deal of valuable advice.

Many of these proposals will be unpopular. Some will cause you to put up with inconveniences and to make sacrifices. The most important thing about these proposals is that the alternative may be a national catastrophe. Further delay can affect our strength and our power as a Nation.

Our decision about energy will test the character of the American people and the ability of the President and the Congress to govern this Nation. This difficult effort will be the moral equivalent of war, except that we will be uniting our efforts to build and not to destroy.

Now, I know that some of you may doubt that we face real ener-

[1] Text from *Presidential Documents*, 13: 560-65.
[2] Wednesday, Apr. 20; cf. Introduction at note 163.

gy shortages. The 1973 gas lines are gone and with this springtime weather, our homes are warm again. But our energy problem is worse tonight than it was in 1973 or a few weeks ago in the dead of winter. It's worse because more waste has occurred and more time has passed by without our planning for the future. And it will get worse every day until we act.

The oil and natural gas that we rely on for 75 percent of our energy are simply running out. In spite of increased effort, domestic production has been dropping steadily at about 6 percent a year. Imports have doubled in the last 5 years. Our Nation's economic and political independence is becoming increasingly vulnerable. Unless profound changes are made to lower oil consumption, we now believe that early in the 1980's the world will be demanding more oil than it can produce.

The world now uses about 60 million barrels of oil a day, and demand increases each year about 5 percent. This means that just to stay even we need the production of a new Texas every year, an Alaskan North Slope every 9 months, or a new Saudi Arabia every 3 years. Obviously, this cannot continue.

We must look back into history to understand our energy problem. Twice in the last several hundred years, there has been a transition in the way people use energy.

The first was about 200 years ago, when we changed away from wood—which had provided about 90 percent of all fuel—to coal, which was much more efficient. This change became the basis of the Industrial Revolution.

The second change took place in this century, with the growing use of oil and natural gas. They were more convenient and cheaper than coal, and the supply seemed to be almost without limit. They made possible the age of automobile and airplane travel. Nearly everyone who is alive today grew up during this period, and we have never known anything different.

Because we are now running out of gas and oil, we must prepare quickly for a third change—to strict conservation and to the renewed use of coal and to permanent renewable energy sources like solar power.

The world has not prepared for the future. During the 1950's, people used twice as much oil as during the 1940's. During the 1960's, we used twice as much as during the 1950's. And in each of those decades, more oil was consumed than in all of man's previous history combined.

World consumption of oil is still going up. If it were possible to keep it rising during the 1970's and 1980's by 5 percent a year as it has in the past, we could use up all the proven reserves of oil in the entire world by the end of the next decade.

I know that many of you have suspected that some supplies of oil and gas are being withheld from the market. You may be right, but suspicions about the oil companies cannot change the fact that we are running out of petroleum.

All of us have heard about the large oil fields on Alaska's North Slope. In a few years, when the North Slope is producing fully, its total output will be just about equal to 2 years' increase in our own Nation's energy demand.

Each new inventory of world oil reserves has been more disturbing than the last. World oil production can probably keep going up for another 6 or 8 years. But sometime in the 1980's, it can't go up any more. Demand will overtake production. We have no choice about that.

But we do have a choice about how we will spend the next few years. Each American uses the energy equivalent of 60 barrels of oil per person each year. Ours is the most wasteful nation on earth. We waste more energy than we import. With about the same standard of living, we use twice as much energy per person as do other countries like Germany, Japan, and Sweden.

One choice, of course, is to continue doing what we've been doing before. We can drift along for a few more years.

Our consumption of oil would keep going up every year. Our cars would continue to be too large and inefficient. Three-quarters of them would carry only one person—the driver—while our public transportation system continues to decline. We can delay insulating our homes, and they will continue to lose about 50 percent of their heat in waste. We can continue using scarce oil and natural gas to generate electricity and continue wasting two-thirds of their fuel value in the process.

If we do not act, then by 1985 we will be using 33 percent more energy than we use today.

We can't substantially increase our domestic production, so we would need to import twice as much oil as we do now. Supplies will be uncertain. The cost will keep going up. Six years ago, we paid $3.7 billion for imported oil. Last year we spent $36 billion for imported oil—nearly 10 times as much—and this year we may spend $45 billion.

Unless we act, we will spend more than $550 billion for imported oil by 1985—more than $2,500 for every man, woman, and child in America. Along with that money that we transport overseas, we will continue losing American jobs and become increasingly vulnerable to supply interruptions.

Now we have a choice. But if we wait, we will constantly live in fear of embargoes. We could endanger our freedom as a sovereign nation to act in foreign affairs. Within 10 years, we would not be able to import enough oil from any country, at any acceptable price.

If we wait and do not act, then our factories will not be able to keep our people on the job with reduced supplies of fuel.

Too few of our utility companies will have switched to coal, which is our most abundant energy source. We will not be ready to keep our transportation system running with smaller and more efficient cars and a better network of buses, trains, and public transportation.

We will feel mounting pressure to plunder the environment. We will have to have a crash program to build more nuclear plants, strip mine and burn more coal, and drill more offshore wells than if we begin to conserve right now.

Inflation will soar; production will go down; people will lose their jobs. Intense competition for oil will build up among nations and also among the different regions within our own country. This has already started.

If we fail to act soon, we will face an economic, social, and political crisis that will threaten our free institutions. But we still have another choice. We can begin to prepare right now. We can decide to act while there is still time. That is the concept of the energy policy that we will present on Wednesday.

Our national energy plan is based on 10 fundamental principles. The first principle is that we can have an effective and comprehensive energy policy only if the Government takes responsibility for it and if the people understand the seriousness of the challenge and are willing to make sacrifices.

The second principle is that healthy economic growth must continue. Only by saving energy can we maintain our standard of living and keep our people at work. An effective conservation program will create hundreds of thousands of new jobs.

The third principle is that we must protect the environment. Our energy problems have the same cause as our environmental problems—wasteful use of resources. Conservation helps us solve both problems at once.

The fourth principle is that we must reduce our vulnerability to potentially devastating embargoes. We can protect ourselves from uncertain supplies by reducing our demand for oil, by making the most of our abundant resources such as coal, and by developing a strategic petroleum reserve.

The fifth principle is that we must be fair. Our solutions must ask equal sacrifices from every region, every class of people, and every interest group. Industry will have to do its part to conserve just as consumers will. The energy producers deserve fair treatment, but we will not let the oil companies profiteer.

The sixth principle, and the cornerstone of our policy, is to reduce demand through conservation. Our emphasis on conservation is a clear difference between this plan and others which merely encouraged crash production efforts. Conservation is the quickest, cheapest, most practical source of energy. Conservation is the only way that we can buy a barrel of oil for about $2. It costs about $13 to waste it.

The seventh principle is that prices should generally reflect the true replacement cost of energy. We are only cheating ourselves if we make energy artificially cheap and use more than we can really afford.

The eighth principle is that Government policies must be predictable and certain. Both consumers and producers need policies they can count on so they can plan ahead. This is one reason that I'm working with the Congress to create a new Department of Energy to replace more than 50 different agencies that now have some control over energy.[3]

The ninth principle is that we must conserve the fuels that are scarcest and make the most of those that are plentiful. We can't continue to use oil and gas for 75 percent of our consumption, as we do now, when they only make up 7 percent of our domestic reserves. We need to shift to plentiful coal, while taking care to protect the environment, and to apply stricter safety standards to nuclear energy.

The tenth and last principle is that we must start now to develop the new, unconventional sources of energy that we will rely on in the next century.

Now, these 10 principles have guided the development of the policy that I will describe to you and the Congress on Wednesday night.

Our energy plan will also include a number of specific goals to measure our progress toward a stable energy system. These are the goals that we set for 1985:

—to reduce the annual growth rate in our energy demand to less than 2 percent;

—to reduce gasoline consumption by 10 percent below its current level;

—to cut in half the portion of U.S. oil which is imported—from a potential level of 16 million barrels to 6 million barrels a day;

—to establish a strategic petroleum reserve of one billion barrels, more than a 6-months supply;

—to increase our coal production by about two-thirds to more than one billion tons a year;

[3]Proposed by President Carter on Mar. 4, 1977, the Department of Energy Organization Act (Public Law 95-91) was signed into law on Aug. 4, 1977 and the Department was activated Oct. 1, 1977 with James R. Schlesinger as Secretary.

—to insulate 90 percent of American homes and all new buildings;
—to use solar energy in more than 2½ million houses.

We will monitor our progress toward these goals year-by-year. Our plan will call for strict conservation measures if we fall behind. I can't tell you that these measures will be easy, nor will they be popular. But I think most of you realize that a policy which does not ask for changes or sacrifices would not be an effective policy at this late date.

This plan is essential to protect our jobs, our environment, our standard of living, and our future. Whether this plan truly makes a difference will not be decided now here in Washington but in every town and every factory, in every home and on every highway and every farm.

I believe that this can be a positive challenge. There is something especially American in the kinds of changes that we have to make. We've always been proud, through our history, of being efficient people. We've always been proud of our ingenuity, our skill at answering questions. Now we need efficiency and ingenuity more than ever.

We've always been proud of our leadership in the world. And now we have a chance again to give the world a positive example.

We've always been proud of our vision of the future. We've always wanted to give our children and our grandchildren a world richer in possibilities than we have had ourselves. They are the ones that we must provide for now. They are the ones who will suffer most if we don't act.

I've given you some of the principles of the plan. I'm sure that each of you will find something you don't like about the specifics of our proposal. It will demand that we make sacrifices and changes in every life. To some degree, the sacrifices will be painful—but so is any meaningful sacrifice. It will lead to some higher costs and to some greater inconvenience for everyone. But the sacrifices can be gradual, realistic, and they are necessary. Above all, they will be fair. No one will gain an unfair advantage through this plan. No one will be asked to bear an unfair burden.

We will monitor the accuracy of data from the oil and natural gas companies for the first time, so that we will always know their true production, supplies, reserves, and profits. Those citizens who insist on driving large, unnecessarily powerful cars must expect to pay more for that luxury.

We can be sure that all the special interest groups in the country will attack the part of this plan that affects them directly. They will say that sacrifice is fine as long as other people do it, but that their sacrifice is unreasonable or unfair or harmful to the country. If they succeed with this approach, then the burden on the ordinary citizen, who is not organized into an interest group, would be crushing.

There should be only one test for this program—whether it will help our country. Other generations of Americans have faced and mastered great challenges. I have faith that meeting this challenge will make our own lives even richer. If you will join me so that we can work together with patriotism and courage, we will again prove that our great Nation can lead the world into an age of peace, independence, and freedom.

Thank you very much, and good night.

(48) The Downing Street Economic Summit, London, May 7-8, 1977: Joint Declaration and Appendix Issued at the Conclusion of the Meeting.[4]

In two days of intensive discussion at Downing Street we have agreed on how we can best help to promote the well-being both of our own countries and of others.

The world economy has to be seen as a whole; it involves not only co-operation among national Governments but also strengthening appropriate international organizations. We were reinforced in our awareness of the interrelationship of all the issues before us, as well as our own interdependence. We are determined to respond collectively to the challenges of the future.

—Our most urgent task is to create more jobs while continuing to reduce inflation. Inflation does not reduce unemployment. On the contrary it is one of its major causes. We are particularly concerned about the problem of unemployment among young people. We have agreed that there will be an exchange of experience and ideas on providing the young with job opportunities.

—We commit our governments to stated economic growth targets or [sic] to stabilization policies which, taken as a whole, should provide a basis for sustained non-inflationary growth, in our own countries and worldwide and for reduction of imbalances in international payments.

[4]Text from *Presidential Documents*, 13: 671-6. Participants in the meeting, held at 10 Downing Street, the official residence of the British Prime Minister, were President Carter, President Giscard d'Estaing, Prime Minister Trudeau, Chancellor Schmidt, Prime Minister Andreotti, Prime Minister Fukuda, and Prime Minister Callaghan. Roy Jenkins, President of the Commission of the European Communities, participated in the second day of the meeting.

—Improved financing facilities are needed. The International Monetary Fund must play a prominent role. We commit ourselves to seek additional resources for the IMF and support the linkage of its lending practices to the adoption of appropriate stabilization policies.

—We will provide strong political leadership to expand opportunities for trade to strengthen the open international trading system, which will increase job opportunities. We reject protectionism: it would foster unemployment, increase inflation and undermine the welfare of our peoples. We will give a new impetus to the Tokyo Round of Multilateral Trade Negotiations. Our objective is to make substantive progress in key areas in 1977. In this field structural changes in the world economy must be taken into consideration.

—We will further conserve energy and increase and diversify energy production, so that we reduce our dependence on oil. We agree on the need to increase nuclear energy to help meet the world's energy requirements. We commit ourselves to do this while reducing the risks of nuclear proliferation. We are launching an urgent study to determine how best to fulfill these purposes.

—The world economy can only grow on a sustained and equitable basis if developing countries share in that growth. We are agreed to do all in our power to achieve a successful conclusion of the CIEC and we commit ourselves to a continued constructive dialogue with developing countries. We aim to increase the flow of aid and other real resources to those countries. We invite the COMECON countries to do the same. We support multilateral institutions such as the World Bank, whose general resources should be increased sufficiently to permit its lending to rise in real terms. We stress the importance of secure private investments to foster world economic progress.

To carry out these tasks we need the assistance and cooperation of others. We will seek that cooperation in appropriate international institutions, such as the United Nations, the World Bank, the IMF, the GATT and OECD. Those among us whose countries are members of the European Economic Community intend to make their efforts within its framework.

In our discussions we have reached substantial agreement. Our firm purpose is now to put that agreement into action. We shall review progress on all the measures we have discussed here at Downing Street in order to maintain the momentum of recovery.

The message of the Downing Street Summit is thus one of confidence:

—in the continuing strength of our societies and the proven democratic principles that give them vitality;
—that we are undertaking the measures needed to overcome problems and achieve a more prosperous future.

APPENDIX TO THE INTERNATIONAL ECONOMIC SUMMIT MEETING DECLARATION

World Economic Prospects

Since 1975 the world economic situation has been improving gradually. Serious problems, however, still persist in all of our countries. Our most urgent task is to create jobs while continuing to reduce inflation. Inflation is not a remedy to unemployment but one of its major causes. Progress in the fight against inflation has been uneven. The needs for adjustment between surplus and deficit countries remain large. The world has not yet fully adjusted to the depressive effects of the 1974 oil price rise.

We commit our Governments to targets for growth and stabilization which vary from country to country but which, taken as a whole, should provide a basis for sustained non-inflationary growth worldwide.

Some of our countries have adopted reasonably expansionist growth targets for 1977. The governments of these countries will keep their policies under review, and commit themselves to adopt further policies, if needed to achieve their stated target rates and to contribute to the adjustment of payments imbalances. Others are pursuing stabilization policies designed to provide a basis for sustained growth without increasing inflationary expectations. The governments of these countries will continue to pursue those goals.

These two sets of policies are interrelated. Those of the first group of countries should help to create an environment conducive to expansion in the others without adding to inflation. Only if growth rates can be maintained in the first group and increased in the second, and inflation tackled successfully in both, can unemployment be reduced.

We are particularly concerned about the problem of unemployment among young people. Therefore we shall promote the training of young people in order to build a skilled and flexible labor force so that they can be ready to take advantage of the upturn in economic activity as it develops. All of our governments, individually or collectively, are taking appropriate measures to this end. We must learn as much as possible from each other and agree to exchange experiences and ideas.

Success in managing our domestic economies will not only

strengthen world economic growth but also contribute to success in four other main economic fields to which we now turn—balance of payments financing, trade, energy and North/South relations. Progress in these fields will in turn contribute to world economic recovery.

Balance of Payments Financing

For some years to come oil-importing nations, as a group, will be facing substantial payments deficits and importing capital from OPEC nations to finance them. The deficit for the current year could run as high as $45 billion. Only through a reduction in our dependence on imported oil and a rise in the capacity of oil-producing nations to import can that deficit be reduced.

This deficit needs to be distributed among the oil-consuming nations in a pattern compatible with their ability to attract capital on a continuing basis. The need for adjustment to this pattern remains large, and it will take much international co-operation, and determined action by surplus as well as deficit countries, if continuing progress is to be made. Strategies of adjustment in the deficit countries must include emphasis on elimination of domestic sources of inflation and improvement in international cost-price relationships. It is important that industrial countries in relatively strong payments positions should ensure continued adequate expansion of domestic demand, within prudent limits. Moreover these countries, as well as other countries in strong payments positions, should promote increased flows of long-term capital exports.

The International Monetary Fund must play a prominent role in balance of payments financing and adjustment. We therefore strongly endorse the recent agreement of the Interim Committee of the IMF to seek additional resources for that organization and to link IMF lending to the adoption of appropriate stabilization policies. These added resources will strengthen the ability of the IMF to encourage and assist member countries in adopting policies which will limit payments deficits and warrant their financing through the private markets. These resources should be used with the conditionality and flexibility required to encourage an appropriate pace of adjustment.

This IMF proposal should facilitate the maintenance of reasonable levels of economic activity and reduce the danger of resort to trade and payments restrictions. It demonstrates co-operation between oil-exporting nations, industrial nations in stronger financial positions, and the IMF. It will contribute materially to the health and progress of the world economy. In pursuit of this objective, we also reaffirm our intention to strive to increase monetary stability.

We agreed that the international monetary and financial system, in its new and agreed legal framework, should be strengthened by the early implementation of the increase in quotas. We will work towards an early agreement within the IMF on another increase in the quotas of that organization.

Trade

We are committed to providing strong political leadership for the global effort to expand opportunities for trade and to strengthen the open international trading system. Achievement of these goals is central to world economic prosperity and the effective resolution of economic problems faced by both developed and developing countries throughout the world.

Policies on [sic] protectionism foster unemployment, increase inflation and undermine the welfare of our peoples. We are therefore agreed on the need to maintain our political commitment to an open and non-discriminatory world trading system. We will seek both nationally and through the appropriate international institutions to promote solutions that create new jobs and consumer benefits through expanded trade and to avoid approaches which restrict trade.

The Tokyo Round of multilateral trade negotiations must be pursued vigorously. The continuing economic difficulties make it even more essential to achieve the objective of the Tokyo Declaration and to negotiate a comprehensive set of agreements to the maximum benefit of all. Toward this end, we will seek this year to achieve substantive progress in such key areas as:

(i) a tariff reduction plan of broadest possible application designed to achieve a substantial cut and harmonization and in certain cases the elimination of tariffs;

(ii) codes, agreements and other measures that will facilitate a significant reduction of non-tariff barriers to trade and the avoidance of new barriers in the future and that will take into account the structural changes which have taken place in the world economy;

(iii) a mutually acceptable approach to agriculture that will achieve increased expansion and stabilization of trade, and greater assurance of world food supplies.

Such progress should not remove the right of individual countries under existing international agreements to avoid significant market disruption.

While seeking to conclude comprehensive and balanced agreements on the basis of reciprocity among all industrial countries we are determined, in accordance with the aims of the Tokyo Declaration, to ensure that the agreements provide special benefits to developing countries.

We welcome the action taken by Governments to reduce counter-productive competition in officially supported export credits and propose that substantial further efforts be made this year to improve and extend the present consensus in this area.

We consider that irregular practices and improper conduct should be eliminated from international trade, banking and commerce, and we welcome the work being done toward international agreements prohibiting illicit payments.

Energy

We welcome the measures taken by a number of Governments to increase energy conservation. The increase in demand for energy and oil imports continues at a rate which places excessive pressure on the world's depleting hydrocarbon resources. We agree therefore on the need to do everything possible to strengthen our efforts still further.

We are committed to national and joint efforts to limit energy demand and to increase and diversify supplies. There will need to be greater exchanges of technology and joint research and development aimed at more efficient energy use, improved recovery and use of coal and other conventional resources, and the development of new energy sources.

Increasing reliance will have to be placed on nuclear energy to satisfy growing energy requirements and to help diversify sources of energy. This should be done with the utmost precaution with respect to the generation and dissemination of material that can be used for nuclear weapons. Our objective is to meet the world's energy needs and to make peaceful use of nuclear energy widely available, while avoiding the danger of the spread of nuclear weapons. We are also agreed that, in order to be effective, nonproliferation policies should as far as possible be acceptable to both industrialized and developing countries alike. To this end, we are undertaking a preliminary analysis to be completed within two months of the best means of advancing these objectives, including the study of terms of reference for international fuel cycle evaluation.

The oil-importing developing countries have special problems both in securing and in paying for the energy supplies needed to sustain their economic development programs. They require additional help in expanding their domestic energy production and to this end we hope the World Bank, as its resources grow, will give special emphasis to projects that serve this purpose.

We intend to do our utmost to ensure, during this transitional period, that the energy market functions harmoniously, in particular through strict conservation measures and the development of all our energy resources. We hope very much that the oil-producing countries will take these efforts into account and will make their contribution as well.

We believe that these activities are essential to enable all countries to have continuing energy supplies now and for the future at reasonable prices consistent with sustained non-inflationary economic growth, and we intend through all useful channels to concert our policies in continued consultation and cooperation with each other and with other countries.

North/South Relations

The world economy can only grow on a sustained and equitable basis if developing countries share in that growth. Progress has been made. The industrial countries have maintained an open market system despite a deep recession. They have increased aid flows, especially to poorer nations. Some $8 billion will be available from the IDA for these nations over the next three years, as we join others in fulfilling pledges to its Fifth Replenishment. The IMF has made available to developing countries, under its compensatory financing facility nearly an additional $2 billion last year. An International Fund for Agricultural Development has been created, based on common efforts by the developed[,] OPEC, and other developing nations.

The progress and the spirit of cooperation that have emerged can serve as an excellent base for further steps. The next step will be the successful conclusion of the Conference on International Economic Cooperation and we agreed to do all in our power to achieve this.

We shall work:

(i) to increase the flow of aid and other real resources from the industrial to developing countries, particularly to the 800 million people who now live in absolute poverty; and to improve the effectiveness of aid;

(ii) to facilitate developing countries' access to sources of international finance;

(iii) to support such multilateral lending institutions as the World Bank, whose lending capacity we believe will have to be increased in the years ahead to permit its lending to increase in real terms and widen in scope;

(iv) to promote the secure investment needed to foster world economic development;

(v) to secure productive results from negotiations about the stabilization of commodity prices and the creation of a Common Fund for individual buffer stock agreements and to consider problems of the stabilization of export earnings of developing countries; and

(vi) to continue to improve access in a non-disruptive way to the markets of industrial countries for the products of developing nations.

It is desirable that these actions by developed and developing countries be assessed and concerted in relation to each other and to the larger goals that our countries share. We hope that the World Bank, together with the IMF, will consult with other developed and developing countries in exploring how this could best be done.

The well-being of the developed and developing nations are bound up together. The developing countries' growing prosperity benefit industrial countries, as the latter's growth benefits developing nations. Both developed and developing nations have a mutual interest in maintaining a climate conducive to stable growth worldwide.

(49) Final Meeting at Ministerial Level of the Conference on International Economic Cooperation, Paris, May 30-June 2, 1977.

(a) Address by Secretary of State Vance to the Conference, May 30, 1977.[5]

The message I bring from my President and from the United States is this:

We believe in the purposes and objectives of this conference.

We are committed to finding solutions to problems which face no single country, but all of us.

We are under no illusion that the actions we take this week will resolve problems that have been centuries in the making.

But we know that failure is not acceptable—not acceptable to any person or any nation at this conference.

I want you to know where my country stands. In recent years I know that some have come to question the motives of my country and to believe that we, as a rich and powerful nation, can only be addressed as though we were an adversary. At this meeting, and at this moment, I want the policy of the United States to be understood.

There should be a new international economic system. In that system there must be equity; there must be growth; but above all,

[5]Department of State Press Release 244, May 31; text from Bulletin, 76: 645-8.

there must be justice. We are prepared to help build that new system.

But at the same time, we are prepared to admit that it will not be built here this week, nor will it be built without many painful adjustments, accommodations, and sacrifices by all of us present here today.

The United States will not be passive in this effort. We will not merely react. We will join with you in sharing the responsibility to lead.

As a first step, and before the business of this conference has been completed, I wish to make clear that we believe the North-South dialogue should continue. We are openminded about the appropriate forum.

The larger vision underlying CIEC is far more important than the smaller and temporary interests which sometimes divide us. It is this larger vision—the vision of a world in which common humanity and common values can override regional or national selfishness—which we must continually keep foremost in our minds.

Now let me speak about the tangible ways we can begin—here this week.

Transfer of Resources

First, the transfer of resources.

Development requires capital, technology, and managerial skills on an enormous scale. They must come from many nations, in many ways. Official development assistance will remain a significant source of support and must be increased worldwide. But private capital is also vital and will continue to offer even greater resources over a wider range of activities than official aid.

In the last two years the United States, through both private and official sources, has provided capital transfers to the developing world averaging 1 percent of our gross national product. But we know that even these transfers are no more than a beginning and that they have not always been most usefully directed.

We are joining with others in channeling billions of dollars in new resources to existing multilateral institutions—the International Development Association, the World Bank and regional banks, and the International Finance Corporation. And the poorest countries can look forward to a new source of finance to help produce food for their people—the billion-dollar International Fund for Agricultural Development.

Let me be candid. Too many of our transfers, too much of our aid, has not been intelligently directed to the purposes and priorities which will really make a difference in people's lives.

We are still learning what works in international development and what does not; what creates lasting change and what does not—and when I say we, I mean the rich and poor nations alike.

For our part, President Carter will seek from the Congress a substantial increase in the volume of our bilateral and multilateral aid programs over the coming five years. But we will also demand that this aid be more effectively planned, delivered, and administered.

The American people will support an effective aid program that is devised clearly and specifically to meet human needs. They also will insist that other rich nations, many of which have already taken the lead, also make significant contributions. And they also will expect that recipients of assistance display a proper concern for the economic, social, political, and human rights of their citizens.

We believe the industrialized Communist countries also should increase their development assistance. We are prepared to join with them in such assistance, when and where they are willing to do it.

We should agree here to support a substantial increase in the general capital of the International Bank for Reconstruction and Development. Such an increase would not only permit the World Bank to expand its normal lending in real terms, it also would enable the bank to undertake new programs in areas of growing importance—energy, resource development, and commodity diversification.

The development of local oil, coal, gas, and other energy resources in developing countries poor in energy will help ease the rising financial burden of high-priced oil imports. The United States is prepared to share in any such program of energy development.

We are ready, too, at this conference to join with other countries in a special action program of $1 billion to help meet the most acute needs of the world's poorest nations. For our part, the Carter Administration, subject to congressional approval, is prepared to devote an extra $375 million over present levels in bilateral aid for the poorest countries.

We can be counted upon to help in ways the American Congress and American people will support. That means insistence upon sound developmental criteria in use of money we contribute.

Since this conference is about poor people as much as poor countries, my government will be willing to participate in a plan to develop specific programs to alleviate the problem of absolute poverty on a global basis. Such a plan must deal with needs that directly affect the way people live their lives:

—Essential health services, particularly in rural areas;
—Increased food production and adequate nutrition;
—Basic education, also in rural areas;
—A chance for a worthwhile job, to help people provide a better life for themselves and for their children.

The United States plans to ask the members of the OECD to consider ways to achieve these objectives in the OECD's general work program. Participation of the developing countries in this process will be essential.

Private Investment

After resource transfers, there is private investment—investment that builds in a partnership that works for developing countries and investors alike. The growth plans of the world's developing economies require a level of foreign investment well beyond the capacity of official sources alone.

Private capital from abroad can contribute as substantially to the growth of the developing countries as it has to the industrialization of the United States.

But private investment can be effective only if it is truly acceptable to the host country. Each nation must decide for itself the role that private investment should play in development. Private firms, in turn, will invest where they are confident of positive and predictable treatment.

Monetary System

The nature and functioning of the monetary system are fundamental to smooth operation of the world economy. We all have a high stake in it. The issues are both technical and complex, but we are prepared to—indeed we must—discuss them together.

Many countries, including developing countries, need balance-of-payments assistance. In the last two years, we have seen major increases in balance-of-payments help for countries that need it most.

The International Monetary Fund has expanded its compensatory finance facility, provided increased credit, and established a new Trust Fund, built with profits from the sale of gold and devoted to the needs of the world's poor majority.

We in the United States will support more resources for the International Monetary Fund for balance-of-payments assistance. We strongly support both the new facility currently under discussion and an IMF quota increase adequate to meet the heavy demands on the Fund from countries in deficit.

We look forward to the agreed-upon study of the evolving role of the special drawing rights as the principal reserve asset in the international monetary system, fully recognizing the importance of this question to both developed and developing countries.

We are particularly aware of the growing volume of international indebtedness and the need for establishing orderly procedures for addressing particular cases before they reach a critical stage.

Commodities

In addition to resource transfers and capital, trade in commodities is critical, as well as our shared interests in stability of price and supply.

When commodity markets fluctuate wildly, development planning in low-income countries is disrupted or made impossible. When commodity prices rise sharply, inflation intensifies and lasts long after these prices have turned downward—hitting rich and poor countries alike. Through this conference, we have agreed on the need for common action to moderate fluctuations in commodity prices, supply, and earnings. We must work together:

—To establish agreements between producers and consumers to stabilize the prices of individual commodities, wherever the nature of the commodity and the market permit;

—To create a common fund—that is efficient and that works—to back up commodity agreements;

—To assure the adequacy of compensatory finance to help offset fluctuation in the export earnings of developing countries;

—To provide enough investment to develop new supplies of primary products adequate to meet the needs of an expanding world economy; and

—To support product improvement and diversification where specific commodities face stagnant or declining demand.

The United States will take part in all these efforts.

We belong to the coffee and tin agreements, and we strongly support an effective international sugar agreement. We are ready to join in financing reserve stocks of sugar to assure stable prices, and the Carter Administration will ask Congress for a U.S. contribution to the tin buffer stock.

We hope that agreement will soon be reached on an international system of nationally held grain reserves to enhance food security. Five years ago, world grain stocks shrunk and prices soared. Today, harvests are more plentiful. But we cannot rely on this in the future. For countries and peoples living on the margin of existence, there must be reliable and growing supplies of food.

The United States is committed to work toward additional stabilization agreements. Where it is agreed that direct governmental contributions are appropriate to finance buffer stocks, we will join producers and consumers in financing them.

Trade

Next, there is the critical effort to expand and liberalize trade. We can all be proud that we have maintained an open trading system throughout a period of extraordinary economic stress. For the developing world, this has provided continued access to the world's major markets and provided export earnings to pay for imports of capital goods, food, and raw materials. For the United States, liberal trade has offered expanded opportunities for jobs and sales from exports. Liberal trade has given us lower prices and wider choice for consumers.

This conference is not the place for detailed trade negotiations. But we in the United States pledge that, at Geneva, we shall seek areas of more favorable treatment for developing-country products.

This Administration is committed to giving new impetus to the Tokyo Round of multilateral trade negotiations. We are committed to making real progress in key areas in 1977.

Energy

The next item on our agenda is energy. All of us share an urgent need for a reliable energy supply, strict energy conservation, and a shift to new energy resources. President Carter has proposed a comprehensive domestic energy policy[6] to reduce our country's profligate use of energy, to limit American dependence on imported oil, and to speed the development of new energy technologies.

In addition, the prosperity of the world economy depends on stable energy prices and reliable supply. And equity in the world economy demands this as well. In the energy commission, the acute problems faced by developing countries which rely on imported oil have been made painfully clear.

Over the longer term, both rich and poor countries must make increased use of their own local energy resources. This conference should help find ways to transfer appropriate energy technology to the developing countries.

This conference is a beginning, and only that. Its real significance will be in what together we do now. For its part, the United States will carry out the pledges I have made today. We shall take seriously the results of this conference.

But to build on these efforts—on the commitments we have made and shall make to one another—we are charged with seeing that what is discussed here is translated into positive action that benefits nations and individual people. In the last three decades, the nations of the industrialized world have gained a far deeper awareness of the concerns, the hopes, the needs of the people in the developing world—the majority of mankind.

Our work will continue. Our success will be measured in many ways: in our agreements, in our surmounting of inevitable disagreements, and in our future dedication to a new international economic system based on equity, growth, and justice.

We commit ourselves here and now to consult and collaborate and to join in the most significant effort of our time: To bring the benefits of mankind's progress to all mankind.

(b) Final Communiqué of the Conference, June 3, 1977.[7]

The Conference on International Economic Cooperation held its final meeting in Paris, at the Ministerial level, from May 30 to June 2, 1977. Representatives of the following 27 members of the Conference took part: Algeria, Argentina, Australia, Brazil, Cameroon, Canada, Arab Republic of Egypt, European Economic Community, India, Indonesia, Iran, Iraq, Jamaica, Japan, Mexico, Nigeria, Pakistan, Peru, Saudi Arabia, Spain, Sweden, Switzerland, United States, Venezuela, Yugoslavia, Zaire and Zambia. The participants welcomed the presence of the Secretary General of the United Nations. The following observers also attended the Conference: OPEC, IEA, UNCTAD, OECD, FAO, GATT, UNDP, UNIDO, IMF, IBRD and SELA.

The Honorable Allan J. MacEachen, PC, MP, President of the Privy Council of Canada, and His Excellency Dr. Manual Perez-Guerrero, Minister of State for International Economic Affairs of Venezuela, Co-Chairmen of the Conference, presided over the Ministerial meeting. Mr. Bernard Guitton [of France] served in his capacity of Executive Secretary of the Conference.

The Ministerial representatives at the meeting recognized that during the course of its work, and within the framework established at the Ministerial meeting with which the Conference was initiated in December 1975,[8] the Conference had examined a wide variety of economic issues in the areas of energy, raw materials, development and finance. There was recognition that the issues in each of these areas are closely interrelated and that particular attention should be given to the problems of the developing countries, especially the most seriously affected among them.

The Co-Chairmen of the Commissions on Energy, Mr. Stephen Bosworth and H.E. Abdul-Haidi Taher; on Raw Materials, Their Excellencies Alfonso Arias Schreiber and Hiromichi Miyazaki; on Development, H.E. Messaoud Ait-Chaalal and Mr. Edmund Wellenstein; and on Financial Affairs, Mr. Stanley Payton and H.E. Mohammed Yeganeh presented on May 14 the final reports of the work of the four commissions, which were considered at a meeting

[7]Department of State Press Release 257, June 3; text from *Bulletin*, 76: 650-52.
[8]Communiqué of Dec. 19, 1975 in *AFR, 1975*: 590-92.

of senior officials of the Conference on May 26-28, and subsequently submitted to the Ministerial meeting.

The participants recalled their agreement that the Conference should lead to concrete proposals for an equitable and comprehensive programme for international economic cooperation including agreements, decisions, commitments and recommendations. They also recalled their agreement that action by the Conference should constitute a significant advance in international economic cooperation and make a substantial contribution to the economic development of the developing countries.

The participants were able to agree on a number of issues and measures relating to:

Energy:

1. Conclusion and recommendation on availability and supply in a commercial sense, except for purchasing power constraint.[9]

2. Recognition of the depletable nature of oil and gas. The transition from oil-based energy mix to more permanent and renewable sources of energy.

3. Conservation and increased efficiency of energy utilization.

4. Need to develop all forms of energy.

5. General conclusions and recommendations for national action and international cooperation in the energy field.

Raw Materials and Trade:

1. Establishment of a common fund with purposes, objectives and other constituent elements to be further negotiated in UNCTAD.[10]

2. Research and development and some other measures for natural products competing with synthetics.

3. Measures for international cooperation in the field of marketing and distribution of raw materials.

4. Measures to assist importing developing countries to develop and diversify their indigenous natural resources.

5. Agreement for improving generalized system of preferences [GSP] schemes: identification of areas for special and more favorable treatment for developing countries in the multilateral trade negotiations [MTN], and certain other trade questions.

---

[9]The Group of 19 considers that this item should be viewed in the context of the report of the Co-Chairmen of the Energy Commission to the Ministerial meeting and the proposal presented to the Energy Commission by the delegates of Egypt, Iran, Iraq, and Venezuela. [Footnote in original.] The proposal referred to called for protection of the purchasing power of energy and export earnings "through indexation or any other appropriate methods." Text in *International Legal Materials*, 16: 975-6 (July 1977).

[10]Cf. note 22 to Document 55.

Development:

1. Volume and quality of official development assistance.

2. Provision by developed countries of $1 billion in a special action program for individual low-income countries facing general problems of transfer of resources.

3. Food and agriculture.

4. Assistance to infrastructure development in developing countries with particular reference to Africa.

5. Several aspects of the industrialization of developing countries.

6. Industrial property, implementation of relevant UNCTAD resolutions on transfer of technology and on U.N. Conference on Science and Technology.

Finance:

1. Private foreign direct investment, except criteria for compensation, transferability of income and capital and jurisdiction and standards for settlement of disputes.

2. Developing country access to capital markets.

3. Other financial flows (monetary issues).

4. Cooperation among developing countries.

The texts agreed appear in the attached Annex which is an integral part of this document.[11]

The participants were not able to agree on other issues and measures relating to:

Energy:

1. Price of energy and purchasing power of energy export earnings.

2. Accumulated revenues from oil exports.

3. Financial assistance to bridge external payments problems of oil importing countries or oil importing developing countries.

4. Recommendations on resources within the Law of the Sea Conference.

5. Continuing consultations on energy.

Raw Materials and Trade:

1. Purchasing power of developing countries.

2. Measures related to compensatory financing.

3. Aspects of local processing and diversification.

[11]Not printed here.

4. Measures relating to interests of developing countries in: world shipping tonnage and trade; representation on commodity exchanges; a code of conduct for liner conferences, and other matters.

5. Production control and other measures concerning synthetics.

6. Investment in the field of raw materials.

7. Means for protecting the interests of developing countries which might be adversely affected by the implementation of the integrated program.

8. Relationship of the integrated program to the new international economic order.

9. Measures related to trade policies, to the institutional framework of trade, to aspects of the GSP, to the MTN, and to conditions of supply.

Development:

1. Indebtedness of developing countries.

2. Adjustment assistance measures.

3. Access to markets for manufactured and semi-manufactured products.

4. Transnational corporations.

Finance:

1. Criteria for compensation, transferability of income and capital and jurisdiction and standards for settlement of disputes.

2. Measures against inflation.

3. Financial assets of oil exporting developing countries.

The proposals made by participants or groups of participants on these matters also appear in the same Annex.

The participants from developing countries in CIEC, while recognizing that progress has been made in CIEC to meet certain proposals of developing countries, noted with regret that most of the proposals for structural changes in the international economic system and certain of the proposals for urgent actions on pressing problems have not been agreed upon.

Therefore, the Group of 19 feels that the conclusions of CIEC fall short of the objectives envisaged for a comprehensive and equitable program of action designed to establish the new international economic order.

The participants from developed countries in CIEC welcomed the spirit of cooperation in which on the whole the Conference took place and expressed their determination to maintain that spirit as the dialogue between developing and developed countries continues in other places. They regretted that it had not proved possible to reach agreement on some important areas of the dialogue such as certain aspects of energy co-operation.

The participants in the Conference think that it has contributed to a broader understanding of the international economic situation and that its intensive discussions have been useful to all participants. They agreed that CIEC was only one phase in the ongoing dialogue between developed and developing countries which should continue to be pursued actively in the U.N. system and other existing, appropriate bodies.[12]

The members of the Conference agreed to transmit the results of the Conference to the United Nations General Assembly at its resumed 31st Session and to all other relevant international bodies for their consideration and appropriate action. They further agreed to recommend that intensive consideration of outstanding problems be continued within the United Nations system and other existing, appropriate bodies.

The participants in the Conference pledged themselves to carry out in a timely and effective manner the measures for international cooperation agreed to herein. They invite the countries which did not participate in the Conference to join in this cooperative effort.

Finally, the Ministerial representatives at the Conference reiterated their appreciation to the President of the French Republic and to the Government of France for their hospitality and for their cooperation in facilitating the work of the Conference on International Economic Cooperation.

(50) *Meeting at Ministerial Level of the Council of the Organization for Economic Cooperation and Development, Paris, June 23-24, 1977.*

(a) *Intervention by Secretary of State Vance before the Meeting, June 23, 1977.*[13]

As we begin our important deliberations today, it is worth keeping in mind how far we have come over the past 30 years. Many of our nations three decades ago faced basic questions:

Could democratic forms of government survive?
Could we overcome the ravages and divisions of war and build a system of cooperation to foster prosperity and peace?

---

[12]Cf. Introduction at note 202.
[13]Department of State Press Release 301, June 23; text from *Bulletin*, 77: 105-9.

Could the industrial nations hope for any kind of constructive relationship with emerging new countries?

Did those new nations have, in turn, any real chance for survival?

If we view our problems today against problems of *that* time, and the progress we have made in resolving them, we can conclude that the future holds promise for us.

Our hope of 30 years ago and the impulse that led to the founding of the OEEC[14] and this organization was our common dedication to an ideal of human progress.

I believe that it is that hope and dedication which hold us together still. I value this meeting as an occasion to confirm the commitment of the Carter Administration to the OECD. We consider this organization unique and its role essential. It is the major forum for economic management and coordination among the industrial democracies.

That, we recognize, is a major undertaking. The challenge before us is great: not just to nourish our own well-being, but to make the world economy work better—with growth, equity, and justice for all.

We are entering a new political and economic era in the world. In that era North-South confrontation and northern rivalries must be replaced by new policies based on cooperation and common action. This will mean:

—Improved economic cooperation among the industrialized nations; and

—A new relationship with the developing nations; and

—Increasing discourse with the state trading nations.

A new relationship with the South and new discourse with the East depend, first, on the state of our own nations. We bear the main responsibility for assuring the kind of economic recovery that translates into a better life for individuals everywhere.

Economic decisions are only part of that enterprise. A fundamental dimension is political. Can we bring our shared values, traditions, and aspirations to bear on our economic problems? I believe that we can and will.

We have taken steps to confirm that resolve. Democracy has been tested—and found working. All our members today enjoy representative government. Portugal, Spain, and Greece have our support, as they strive to strengthen their democratic institutions.

[14]Organization for European Economic Cooperation, established pursuant to an address by Secretary of State George C. Marshall at Harvard University, June 5, 1947 (text in *Documents, 1947*: 9-11).

Our commitment to economic cooperation has been tried—and found unshaken. The Downing Street summit and other recent meetings of heads of government reflect significant collective endeavor. We look forward to maintaining the momentum attained at those meetings.

Let me sketch a few items, some of which Secretary Blumenthal will discuss further tomorrow.[15]

—We must assure sustained economic recovery. We should establish national targets for economic growth and objectives for stabilization, together with our OECD commitment to more rapid growth this next year.

—We must overcome both unemployment and inflation which sap our economic strength and imperil support for our political institutions. Since unemployment hits the young especially hard, the United States favors the convening of an OECD-sponsored conference on jobs for youth.

—We must reject protectionism and expand trade. We believe this ministerial should renew the OECD trade pledge and determine how best to resolve trade problems affecting our domestic industries before they become crises. We will press for substantial progress this year in the multilateral trade negotiations and advance work to prohibit improper conduct and illicit payments in international commerce.

—We must address key questions of finance. Both surplus and deficit countries must take domestic steps to bring about external adjustment. We are now engaged in efforts to increase the resources available to finance balance-of-payments deficits through the International Monetary Fund. If, contrary to our expectations, these efforts are not successful, then we should jointly examine present and projected financial facilities in the IMF and consider what should be done about the OECD Financial Support Fund.[16] Under these circumstances we would be prepared to consider all available alternatives, including the OECD fund.

—Energy, finally, is a particular challenge to the political purpose and cohesion of the industrial nations. Overdependence on imported oil underscores our political and economic vulnerability. The outlook is not good—unless we intensify efforts within and among our nations.

President Carter is firm in his determination to implement our national energy plan. He knows that we must reduce vulnerability

---

[15]Cf. Introduction at note 169.
[16]Cf. *AFR, 1976*: 93 and Introduction at note 171.

to embargo and price increases and that we must begin to adjust now to the postpetroleum age.

We must also match our domestic programs with stronger international efforts, both to conserve energy and to increase and diversify sources of supply. We must exchange vital technology and enter into joint research and development. The October ministerial of the International Energy Agency should confirm our commitment to targets for reduced dependence on imported oil.[17]

Nuclear energy is a field of special interest. The United States remains committed to the use of nuclear energy and to the system of international safeguards that maintains the critical distance between civilian and military uses of nuclear energy. However, if we are to meet both the security and energy needs of our peoples, we must find ways to maintain an effective safeguards system as we approach the plutonium generation of nuclear technology.

For that reason, we have opposed the premature entry into a plutonium economy until we have found ways to reconcile our energy and security concerns. It is in this spirit that we have suggested a study of these questions in the international nuclear fuel cycle evaluation program.

The combined challenge of these issues before the OECD—the need for sustained economic recovery, unemployment and inflation, trade, finance, and energy—has a global scope. It also affects directly the great cities of our countries. Although urban decay and social malaise preceded these problems, many have grown worse because of them. The city of the seventies too often has an inhumane face.

We need to understand better the impact from the interaction of domestic and international economic trends on the place where most of our citizens live. The United States, therefore, proposes the establishment of an ad hoc working group on urban concerns to prepare a draft action program for our consideration next year.

No pursuit of global economic welfare can be complete without reference to the nations of the East. The OECD has done a good job in undertaking factual and analytic studies of East-West economic relations. I want particularly to congratulate the Secretary General[18] for his leadership on the East-West project.

We must engage the COMECON nations in our shared economic challenges and responsibilities. They, like us, can and should help address issues in the North-South dialogue. We both have a moral and a practical interest in increasing the flow of resources and technical assistance to the developing world.

We should urge the COMECON countries to join us in seeking

[17]Cf. Introduction at note 164.
[18]Emile van Lennep (Netherlands).

genuine, apolitical solutions to problems of global economic development. To be more specific:

—They can improve the quality and increase the amount of their development assistance through both bilateral and multilateral programs.

—They can contribute to world food security by participating in arrangements sought under the auspices of the International Wheat Council.

—They can help establish equitable multilateral arrangements for commodities.

It is not enough to worry about our own welfare or seek more cooperation from the East. That limited perspective overlooks more than half of the world's population and a far greater percentage of countries. Solutions to our problems rest on the realization that our problems are linked to those of the Third World and that the aspirations of our citizens are similar to theirs. Let me be clear on two points:

First, the goals and values of our societies—economic, political, and humanitarian—cannot be achieved fully in isolation from trends in developing nations.

Second, we must understand that in relations between developing and developed nations, what one side gains is not necessarily the other side's loss.

Relations between developed and developing nations need not spawn conflict. We have concluded an era when the central question was whether to cooperate. We have begun a period in which we must develop the means and institutions for cooperation.

That is the corner we have turned at CIEC. The OECD must now take part in this new start. Together we must maintain continuing cooperation among ourselves and with our counterparts in the developing world.

We, therefore, urge the Secretary General of this organization to bring about more effective coordination of OECD efforts in North-South issues, to propose options for discussion in the U.N. Third Development Decade, and to formulate longer term strategy and initiatives of mutual benefit to the North and South.

We also recommend that this conference endorse the proposed declaration on relations with developing nations. This declaration expresses our shared political commitment to the search for more beneficial methods of cooperation. It, too, could signal a new beginning.

An important part of the declaration stresses increased attention to the basic human needs of all the peoples of the world. The old agenda for economic development and many of the old issues for negotiation are no longer enough. We need more focus on that part of the world population that lacks essential food, water, shelter, and health care, as well as employment and education. We must direct our efforts to meet more effectively the needs of the poorest peoples in the developing world.

The case for more concerted action is clear. Almost one billion people live in absolute poverty. The problem is growing. Increases in GNP for many developing countries have not meant increased benefits for the poor. For many, in fact, life is worse. Development has too often not "trickled down."

Knowledge about the development process and the ability to overcome poverty are now within our grasp. What we miss is the joint recognition by developed and developing nations that the North-South dialogue is about *human beings* and that equality of opportunity for a fuller life makes sense for *people*, not just states. Let me suggest how we might begin.

First, we must marshal a sense of our means and priorities. For that purpose, I propose that the OECD establish a special working group mandated to design a program for basic human needs. That program should profit from the work in the Development Assistance Committee and should be presented for discussion at the Executive Committee in special session by the end of this year. The program should include:

—Projections of domestic and international resources required to implement a successful approach to basic human needs;

—Proposals for sharing costs among developed and developing nations; and

—Agreement on measures needed to use those resources most effectively.

Second, we must engage the interest and expertise of the developing nations themselves. We need to share perspectives on a shared problem. No strategy for development can succeed without requisite political will within Third World nations. For that purpose, we should encourage consultations and efforts to identify the kinds of policy changes required to address basic human needs and suggest means for judging progress.

Third, we must move swiftly to expand on specific proposals for an agenda on basic human needs. It should include the following fundamental elements:

—Rural development and food production: We must give greater priority to the development of the Third World's rural areas where the great majority of the poorest people live. We must begin with an integrated strategy which emphasizes increased food production and better nutrition in these areas.

—Health: At the same time we must emphasize preventive medicine, family planning, prenatal care, and other forms of medical assistance which, with minimal cost, could mean the most for the poorest. Again, the relation to an overall strategy for rural development is key: increases in productive employment and crop yields can help make better nutrition possible and bring better health for more people.

—Education: Education deserves a similar priority. We should stress primary and secondary education and promote on-the-job technical training. The goal is to enhance the capacity for productive employment and provide a way out of absolute poverty.

Two areas, related to any human needs strategy, of import in their own right:

—Women: Although poverty strikes all, in many countries women suffer more than do men from poor health, little or no schooling, and meager diet. Their traditional roles often keep women out of the paid work force and lock them into low status. There is a direct relationship between higher education and employment opportunities for women and smaller families. High birth rates both reflect the specific situation of many women and reinforce the general cycle of poverty. Release from rural poverty may well begin with the real economic and social emancipation of women.

—Ecological disaster: Finally, a substantial part of absolute poverty stems from the toll taken over time by ecological disaster, as in the Sahel. The poor bear a disproportionate burden when overpopulation, economic underdevelopment, and ecological overstress interact. Developing nations, with two-thirds of the world's population, suffer 90 percent of disaster-related deaths.

The OECD has a unique opportunity to support emerging efforts in the United Nations and to work with developing nations on means to provide longer term alleviation of ecological disaster. Efforts at early warning and access to food reserves are among measures which address the core of basic human needs.

Obviously, attention to basic human needs is only part of a broader strategy for development. It should not supplant other important efforts at economic advancement which this organization has supported and which have contributed to economic development in the Third World. To supplant other ongoing efforts is not our purpose; we wish to add a vital dimension. If we do not do so, we run the risk of losing the support of our legislative bodies and peoples.

It is in meeting the challenge of fulfilling basic human needs that both developed and developing nations can more firmly establish their joint commitment to individual human dignity. We thus look forward to making this concern more central to the new relationship and to moving toward more specific programs for implementation by the time we meet next year.

At the beginning, I pointed to the progress we have made together. It has been a long, hard, but rewarding road we have traveled. But we have left one destination without reaching another. We are in transit to a new era of cooperation and common action.

In practical terms our journey will involve going beyond new directions for industrial democracies, new discourse with state trading nations, and new relationships with developing countries. It will take us to a firmer focus on people. It is the individual and collective hope of people, their rights and their needs, that deserve the fullest measure of our dedication.

(b) Communiqué and Declaration Issued at the Conclusion of the Meeting, June 24, 1977.[19]

1. The Council of the Organisation for Economic Co-operation and Development met at Ministerial level on 23rd June, under the Chairmanship of the Honourable Andrew Peacock, M.P., Australian Minister for Foreign Affairs, and on 24th June with the Right Honourable Phillip Lynch, M.P., Australian Treasurer, in the Chair.

Development Co-operation

2. Ministers reviewed the results of the Conference on International Economic Co-operation[20] and discussed longer-term aspects of international development co-operation. Ministers then adopted the Declaration on Relations with Developing Countries annexed to this Communiqué. They reaffirmed the importance of close collaboration and strengthened co-ordination within the OECD to assist Member Governments to prepare for specific discussions with the developing countries in the various international fora in working toward the objectives set forth in the Declaration.

Energy

3. Ministers recognised that an imbalance between world energy

---

[19]OECD Press Release A/(77)25; text from *Bulletin*, 77: 118-20.
[20]Document 49.

supply and demand, which could occur as early as the 1980s, would have severe economic, social and political repercussions in OECD countries and throughout the world. They expressed their determination to avoid that situation by stronger action to conserve energy and develop alternative sources of energy and by including sound energy policies in their overall economic policy.

Commodities

4. Ministers noted the importance of continuing discussions on commodities and endorsed the agreement reached in the CIEC to establish a Common Fund with the specific purposes, objectives and other constituent elements to be further negotiated in UNCTAD, and the willingness declared at the Conference to make all efforts for the success of the negotiations being undertaken in UNCTAD on commodities. They invited the Organisation to continue its work in the field of commodities in order to assist Member countries in these efforts, and to examine other related commodity issues.

Trade

5. Ministers agreed that, while in several respects the economic situation was different from that which prevailed at the time of the adoption of the Trade Declaration in 1974,[21] it was still characterised by exceptional difficulties and divergencies in Member countries' situations. They noted with concern that persistent high levels of unemployment and difficulties in certain sectors have increased protectionist pressures. Ministers emphasized that recourse to protectionist policies would foster unemployment, increase inflation and reduce economic welfare. They agreed that the present economic situation together with the increasing interdependence of OECD economies reinforced the need for a renewed political commitment to avoid restrictive unilateral trade and current account measures and the artificial stimulation of exports; measures of this kind tended to carry the risk of proliferation with self-defeating implications. They also agreed that such a commitment and related disciplines in the field of general economic policy were an essential element of the strategy for sustained non-inflationary economic growth in the OECD area. Indeed such growth should itself facilitate the avoidance of restrictions.

6. Member Governments[22] therefore decided to renew, for a further year, their Trade Declaration of 30th May, 1974. They agreed that full use should be made of the existing possibilities for consultation in order to find and implement multilaterally-acceptable solutions to trade problems, whether industrial or agricultural, in a

[21]Text in *AFR, 1974*: 150-51.
[22]Spain has reserved temporarily its position. [Footnote in original.]

manner which would take into account the interests of all concerned. In the case of sectoral problems, every effort should be made to identify such problems before they assume critical proportions and to proceed to consultations in their regard, taking into consideration, inter alia, structural changes in the world economy.

7. Ministers welcomed the progress achieved in multilateral cooperation concerning export credits and underlined the need for further efforts to improve and extend the consensus on guidelines for the extension of officially-supported export credits.

8. Ministers reaffirmed that it was essential to maintain an open and multilateral trading system as a basic element in the overall approach to the economic problems with which their countries were confronted and stressed the importance of giving impetus to the Multilateral Trade Negotiations with the objective of making substantive progress in key areas in 1977, and achieving agreement over the range of issues as rapidly as possible.

9. Ministers welcomed the work being done in the United Nations Economic and Social Council on corrupt practices in international commercial transactions, and expressed the hope that it would take the measures necessary with a view to reaching agreement as early as possible on appropriate means, including the negotiation of an international agreement, of combating illicit payments.

International Investment and Multinational Enterprises

10. Recalling the Declaration and the Decisions of OECD Member Governments of 21st June, 1976, on International Investment and Multinational Enterprises,[23] Ministers also welcomed the work of the United Nations Commission on Transnational Corporations on a code of conduct.

Progress Under the Strategy for Sustained Economic Expansion

11. Ministers reaffirmed the strategy for sustained expansion, aiming at a progressive return to full employment and price stability, which they adopted in June 1976.[24] The basic premise on which this strategy rests is that the steady economic growth needed to restore full employment and satisfy rising economic and social aspirations will not prove sustainable unless Member countries make further progress towards eradicating inflation. Ministers examined the progress made in implementing the strategy and reviewed the prospects for the coming year. While recognising that serious problems persisted, they welcomed the fact that some Member Governments had committed themselves to economic growth targets dur-

[23]Cf. AFR, 1976: 435 at note 11.
[24]Same: 437-9.

ing 1977 and some others to stabilization policies which were intended to provide a basis for sustained non-inflationary growth world-wide.

12. Ministers agreed that the achievement of the objectives of the strategy would be promoted by a somewhat faster rate of expansion in the OECD area as a whole in 1978 than seems likely to be achieved in 1977, although this does not apply to some countries. An overall growth rate of OECD GNP of around 5 per cent in 1978 would at this point seem desirable and consistent with the strategy. They agreed that, where necessary and appropriate, action should be taken to achieve this. This somewhat faster rate of expansion should:

—enable real progress to be made in reducing unemployment next year;

—help to stimulate the productive investment needed to provide jobs for the unemployed; and

—be compatible with a further reduction in the rate of inflation.

13. Further progress against inflation will not come about of its own accord. Determined action will be required to slow down the price/wage spiral. Some countries will need to pursue—and some to reinforce—vigorous stabilization policies. To promote better payments equilibrium, Member countries in a weak external position will hold the growth of domestic demand to a rate compatible with reducing inflation, and also follow policies to improve their competitive position, so as to attain a sustainable current-account position. Member countries in a strong external position will provide for a sustained expansion of domestic demand compatible with further reduction of inflation; they are ready to see a weakening in their current-account position and an appreciation of their currencies in response to underlying market forces.

14. Specific objectives and policies for expansion and stabilization will vary as between Member countries. But, taken together, they must provide the basis for sustained non-inflationary growth in the OECD area and the world economy as a whole. Ministers agreed on the need to strengthen procedures for monitoring progress under the strategy. To this end, they decided that Member countries would communicate their preliminary objectives for the growth of output and domestic demand and their stabilization policies for 1978 to the Organisation so that their mutual consistency and global implications can be examined, and can then provide the basis for monitoring progress during the course of next year.

15. Ministers recognised that a sustained increase in demand, while necessary, will not on its own solve the problems of unem-

ployment and lagging investment, which are due in part to structural causes and the legacy of events of recent years.

—Lagging investment now can lead to unemployment later. In countries where real wages have run ahead of productivity increases in recent years there is a need to increase the return on investment. In some countries there may be need for a greater consensus between government, labour and management on the reduced scope for increases in public and private consumption.

—In prevailing circumstances further efforts where appropriate should be made to supplement overall demand management policies by specific measures designed to increase employment, including policies which help adapt the labour force to the requirements of rapid structural and technological change.

—In the efforts to reduce unemployment, particular attention should be paid to the unemployment of young workers. Special measures have been taken in many countries and more may be needed. Ministers instructed the Organisation to strengthen its exchange of experience and to organise urgently a high-level conference for this purpose.

16. Ministers reviewed the international payments situation. They welcomed the progress being made towards a more appropriate payments position by some of the larger Member countries. While some of the smaller Member countries are also making progress in the right direction, many of them are still running unsustainably large current account deficits. Ministers underlined the need for continued efforts to arrive at a more sustainable pattern of current-account positions in the OECD area. They agreed on the need to ensure that adequate official financing facilities are available to back up appropriate stabilization programmes. In this connection they heard a statement by the Managing Director of the International Monetary Fund on the progress made in negotiating additional resources to finance balance of payments through the IMF. Many Ministers stressed the importance they attached to implementation of the OECD Financial Support Fund in addition to the IMF facility.

17. Ministers noted that present conjunctural difficulties are exacerbating longer-run structural and development problems, as well as the employment and balance-of-payments difficulties, of some Member countries. Ministers therefore agreed that the competent bodies of the Organisation dealing with the various aspects of these problems should, in a positive and coordinated way, take into consideration the means to overcome such difficulties.

18. Ministers noted with interest the recommendations contained

in the report *Towards Full Employment and Price Stability* produced by a group of experts under the chairmanship of Professor [Paul W.] McCracken and instructed the Organisation to examine both the analysis and recommendations in the Report. They agreed that, taking account of the important differences between countries, the Organisation and Member Governments should study in particular the recommendation that, over the medium term, a policy of not accommodating high rates of inflation should be built around some or all of the following elements: publicly-announced norms for the growth of the monetary aggregates; a fiscal policy geared to guidelines for public expenditure and a budget norm designed to avoid giving an inflationary stimulus; and consultative arrangements designed to clarify the kind of price and wage behaviour consistent with achieving and maintaining full employment.

19. Ministers also noted with interest the reports by the OECD Trade Union Advisory Committee on a strategy for full employment and instructed the Organisation to study and evaluate the proposals contained in them, as well as in the paper by the OECD Business and Industry Advisory Committee on non-inflationary growth.

DECLARATION ON RELATIONS WITH DEVELOPING COUNTRIES, ADOPTED BY GOVERNMENTS OF OECD-MEMBER COUNTRIES ON 23RD JUNE, 1977

1. Ministers of Member governments of the OECD meeting in Paris on 23rd June, 1977, discussed relations with developing countries and the longer-term orientation of international development co-operation.

2. Ministers affirmed that the CIEC had played a valuable role in building up a climate of dialogue between the developing and developed countries. It had provided the opportunity for a thorough global examination of the major issues involved and agreement was reached on a number of important points, although it had not been possible to reach agreement on some other important topics of mutual interest. All Member governments of the OECD, including those who did not participate in the CIEC, joined together in welcoming the agreements that were reached there. They also welcomed the intention of some OECD Member governments in addition to those who took part in the Conference, to associate themselves with a Special Action Programme announced at that Conference.

3. Looking ahead, they agreed that further efforts were needed on the part of both developed and developing countries to build a more equitable and stable international economic system, one which would create a better life for all people. These efforts will be

supported by a return to full health of the international economy which is the concern of developed and developing countries alike. Recalling their Declaration of 28th May, 1975,[25] Ministers expressed their readiness to pursue actively the on-going dialogue with developing countries in the United Nations system and in other appropriate fora and to co-operate in solving economic and social problems of common concern, thereby making it possible for the developing countries to participate increasingly in the benefits of an improved and expanding world economy. In this connection, they stressed their willingness to encourage effective international co-operation and dialogue on energy.

4. Welcoming the progress made in development co-operation on many fronts, Ministers acknowledged the necessity to continue working with developing countries towards improved and more effective development co-operation policies. They affirmed that while development co-operation concerned relations between governments its objective was the well-being of individuals; development co-operation should therefore fulfill the dual purposes of growth of incomes and meeting basic needs of individuals in all developing countries. They stressed that development policies for transfers of resources and structural changes should be clearly directed to these purposes. This was particularly necessary in order that the objectives and policy concepts of development co-operation would be better understood and supported by the peoples of industrialised and developing countries.

5. Ministers of OECD countries, donors of aid, reaffirmed the intention, as expressed by their countries in different fora, to increase effectively and substantially their official development assistance and to achieve an improved balance of their efforts in this regard. They announced their determination to direct, in co-operation with developing countries, a progressively larger share of their efforts to programmes meeting basic human needs. To realise this new orientation with respect to all developing countries, they also agreed to review the scope and direction of development assistance with a view to achieving greater volume and more efficiency in its use in an enlarged international effort.

(51) Annual Meeting of the Boards of Governors of the International Monetary Fund and the International Bank for Reconstruction and Development, Washington, September 26-30, 1977: Remarks of Secretary of the Treasury W. Michael Blumenthal to the Meeting, September 27, 1977.[26]

[25]Text in *AFR, 1975*: 226-7.
[26]Text from Department of the Treasury Press Release, June 27, 1977.

We meet at a time of doubt about the world's economic future. The legacy of the oil shocks of 1974, inflation, and the deep recession of 1974 and 1975 poses questions of whether our system of international economic cooperation can endure.

The main points I want to make are these:

—the world economy has begun to recover from staggering blows;

—we have in place a strategy for sustained recovery, and that strategy is working;

—and we will succeed—though success takes time—if we continue to act together and do not lose our nerve.

The effective functioning of the institutions that bring us together today—the Bank and the Fund—is a critical part of that cooperative effort.

The U.S. Economy

I will first report to you on the condition of the United States economy.

I am pleased that we are continuing to make solid progress. We have recorded economic growth of 7.5 percent for the first quarter and 6.2 percent for the second.

We expect to meet our target for real growth during 1977 of over 5½ percent and we expect continued strong growth in 1978.

We have reduced our unemployment rate by about one percentage point and so far this year have created more than 2 million new jobs.

Inflationary pressures are diminishing, despite the adverse effects of an unusually harsh winter. Consumer prices rose at the rate of more than 8 percent in the first half of the year. We expect the rate to decline to less than 5 percent in the second half.

We also have problems—serious ones.

Unemployment is much too high. Creating new jobs to bring it down is a top priority.

Despite our progress, inflation also remains too high. We know well how difficult it is to break the inflationary cycle.

Business investment, though increasing, is weaker than it should be.

Energy consumption and oil imports are excessive.

Our current account deficit is likely to be in the range of $16 to $20 billion.

In part, the shift in our current account position since 1975 has been caused by our heavy consumption of oil. But it is also a consequence of the comparatively high rate of economic growth in the

United States and more restrained expansion in many other countries.

We are determined to correct our problems.

The expansionary effects of new programs for public works and public service jobs will show up strongly in coming months.

We have undertaken a series of measures to keep inflation under control and to bring it down.

President Carter will soon present tax proposals that will include important new incentives to stimulate business and encourage higher productivity.

We are urging Congress to complete action on legislation which will encourage energy conservation and increase domestic energy production. That program will be an important first step. But more will have to be done to limit demand and, especially, to develop new domestic energy supplies.

We look to countries with payments surpluses to expand their economies to the maximum extent consistent with the need to combat inflation. Such moves are essential to a smoothly functioning international economic system. We are encouraged by expansionary measures decided on or implemented in recent weeks.

The Strategy of Cooperation

The international economic system is under stress because of the need to adjust to wide variations in national economic performance, high energy costs, and large imbalances in international payments positions.

A broad strategy to facilitate these adjustments has been agreed in international discussions. The guiding principle of that strategy is cooperation.

It calls for symmetrical action by both surplus and deficit countries to eliminate payments imbalances.

It calls on countries in strong payments positions to achieve adequate demand consisent with the control of inflation.

It calls on countries in payments difficulties to deploy resources more effectively so as to bring current accounts into line with sustainable financing.

One point is clear. If this strategy is to succeed, the oil-exporting countries will have to show restraint in their pricing. This is an essential element of international cooperation and is in the interest of the oil-exporting and oil-importing nations alike.

We also need to resist protectionist pressures. Most importantly, we must work for the successful completion of the Tokyo round of the GATT negotiations.

The IMF, with its key role at the center of the international economic system, must be in a position to help countries carry out the agreed strategy.

This requires *first* of all that the Fund have adequate resources.

The United States has formally consented to the increase in its quota agreed to in the Sixth Quota Review. We urge others to act promptly so that the increased quotas can be put into effect without further delay.

We welcome the new Supplementary Financing Facility to provide an additional $10 billion for nations whose financing needs are especially large. We intend to press for prompt legislative authorization of U.S. participation.

A permanent expansion of IMF resources for the longer term is also needed. We will work for agreement on an adequate increase in Fund quotas during the Seventh Quota Review.

The *second* requirement is that the fund use these resources to foster necessary adjustment. As the Supplementary Financing Facility recognizes, serious imbalances cannot be financed indefinitely. Current account positions must be brought into line with sustainable capital flows. The facility retains the central principle that IMF financing should support programs that will correct the payments problems of borrowers, not postpone their resolution.

In today's circumstances, that process will in some cases require a longer period of time. Consequently, the United States supports the provisions in the new Facility that introduce flexibility in determining the pace of adjustment.

In large measure, this comes down to a question of balance and judgment in the Fund's operations. The Fund cannot avoid its responsibilities to press for needed changes; nor, on the other hand, can it be rigid and inflexible in requiring adjustments. The course it must steer is often narrow and difficult.

I believe that, on the whole, the Fund has carried out this responsibility with skill and sensitivity. I am confident it will continue to condition the use of its resources in a reasonable and equitable manner, taking into account the needs and circumstances of individual countries as well as the particular conditions in the world economy today. It is not a matter of whether the Fund attaches conditions, but what kind. In individual cases, there will be a need to adjust the emphasis between deflationary measures and policies for the redirection of resources to productive investment and improvement of external accounts.

Third, we must bear in mind the influence of the actions of the Fund on the flow of private capital. It is inevitable and right that the private capital market will continue to play the dominant role in financing imbalances.

At the same time, banks, in their lending policies, are increasingly looking to the existence of stand-by arrangements with the Fund. These arrangements, with their stipulations about domestic economic and external adjustment policies, can considerably strengthen nations' creditworthiness.

A greater availability of information may also prove useful and feasible. The Executive Board is currently examining the question of how the system might be strengthened by greater private access to factual information produced by the Fund, on a basis that respects the confidential relationships between the Fund and its members.

I believe that in general it is important to explore possible methods to make sure that private and public flows of capital are compatible with each other. This, too, is a way of strengthening the international financial system.

The responsibility of the Fund goes beyond its operations in support of countries in payments difficulty.

The amended Articles give the Fund an important, explicit, role in overseeing the operations of the system as a whole and in exercising surveillance over the exchange rate policies of its member governments.

The principles to guide the Fund in carrying out these responsibilities reflect widely held views, and a consensus has also been reached on the procedures to be used. It is underlying economic and financial factors that should determine exchange rates. That is recognized.

I believe we all acknowledge that in carrying out these new provisions the Fund will have to approach its task cautiously. These are uncharted waters. History is by no means an adequate guide to the future. Only by experience will it be possible to test the principles we have established and to modify them where it is proven necessary. It is evident that the Fund's effectiveness in this area will depend on the genuine support of its members for the principles it develops.

I believe the Fund is in an excellent position to undertake this new role. It is now time for the member countries of the IMF to act by approving the amended Articles and bringing these provisions into effect.

Problems of Development

Establishing conditions for sustained growth and strengthening the financial adjustment processes are the most pressing intermediate-term issues facing the world economy. The critical long-term problem, however, is to assure economic growth with equity in the developing world.

President Carter spoke yesterday of the strong commitment of the United States to help in the effort to meet the basic human needs of the world's poor.[27] President McNamara gave us a picture of the magnitude of the task.[28]

Action is required by both industrial and developing countries.

The most important contribution the industrial countries can make is to achieve adequate, sustained economic growth in the context of an open international economic system. In the past year the oil-importing developing countries have improved their trade position by $8 billion as a result of the export opportunities arising from the growth in the U.S. economy. An acceleration in the economic expansion of other industrial countries would provide comparable benefits. For such benefits to be realized in the future markets must be open and protectionism resisted.

Healthy economic conditions in the industrial world will also facilitate the flow of capital to meet productive needs in the developing countries. In this connection we must review our efforts to assure adequate access to private capital markets.

In addition, specific actions must be taken to facilitate the growth of developing countries.

A substantial increase in the transfer of official capital to developing countries is necessary. The United States will do its share. The Congress has authorized over $5 billion in contributions to the international development banks and has supported a sizeable increase in bilateral assistance. We are prepared to begin formal negotiations in the Board of Directors of the World Bank leading to a general increase in its capital.

We must work together to strengthen arrangements for stabilizing earnings from raw material exports.

We must also approach the management of international indebtedness, not as a crisis, but as a short- and medium-term balance of payments problem. We can draw encouragement from the fact that the aggregate current account deficit of the oil-importing developing countries declined in 1976 as the world economy began to recover. Where individual countries face severe balance of payments problems, the new Supplementary Financing Facility will help to facilitate adjustment.

Actions by the industrial countries are only part of the story. The real payoff lies in the policies adopted by the developing countries. This is not surprising. Four-fifths of the investment capital of developing countries is mobilized from domestic savings. Domestic policies will determine not only how much savings can be mobilized in the future but also how efficiently resources are used and how effectively the developing countries can take advantage of an expanding international economic environment.

[27]Text in *Presidential Documents*, 13: 1423-5.
[28]Cf. Introduction at note 179.

The development partnership requires not only healthy global economic conditions that will enable the developing economies to grow, but also efforts by the developing countries to assure that the benefits of growth are enjoyed by their poorest citizens.

In this connection, my government strongly supports the new directions charted by the World Bank in financing social and economic development. The Bank has pioneered in designing new approaches to alleviate urban poverty and stimulate rural development. I believe the continued expansion of the activities of the World Bank Group, more than any other single action, will contribute to constructive relations between industrial and developing countries.

In supporting this expansion, the United States will urge:

—more emphasis on food production, expanding employment opportunities, and other measures to improve the lot of the world's poorest people.

—increased lending to expand energy resources in developing countries.

—using the Bank's resources to facilitate the adoption of sound economic policies in the developing countries.

I am convinced that foreign assistance will not have the support of the American people unless they perceive that it is making a real contribution to improving the lives of the poor.

My government also believes that the goals and purposes of development encompass human rights as well as freedom from economic privation and want. The United States Congress has instructed the Administration to seek international agreement on standards for human rights. We will pursue this mandate.

Looking ahead, the Bank and the Fund have a vital and expanding role to play in the international economic system. Their record entitles them to strong support and they shall have it from the United States.

I must point to a problem, however, that concerns both the Bank and the Fund. My government's continued ability to support these two institutions will depend on their efficient administration. Most importantly, we must resolve the issue of proper compensation policies for their staffs and Executive Directors.

On salaries there is need for restraint. More generally, it is essential to overhaul the entire compensation system of these institutions—as well as the systems of other international organizations—to meet today's realities. We hope that the Joint Committee set up to review the situation will enable us to move to such a new system. We must not permit this issue to threaten these great institutions.

As I conclude my comments, it is a matter of deep regret to the United States and to me personally that as the Fund crosses a threshold into a new era of operations, it will lose the valued services of its Managing Director, our trusted friend, Johannes Witteveen. He has guided the Fund with firmness, fairness, imagination, and good sense.

He deserves a large portion of the credit for the great progress the Fund has recorded in recent years, and he leaves the institution strong and fully capable of meeting its new and challenging responsibilities. I join other Governors in expressing our thanks.

We have a formidable agenda before us and one that we should approach with a sense of hope and resolve. The necessary actions are difficult but the potential gains are immense. Pursuit of sound economic policies domestically and adherence to open and cooperative policies internationally will see us into a new period of economic progress and equity, worldwide.

(52) The United States Balance of Trade and Payments: Statement by President Carter, December 21, 1977.[29]

The United States balance of trade and payments has shifted this year to a large deficit position. The two main causes appear to be large oil imports by the United States and relatively slow economic growth in Japan, Germany, and other nations.

These deficits have contributed to some disorder in the exchange markets and rapid movements in exchange rates. Heightened uncertainty and increased exchange market pressure in recent weeks have coincided with the delay in congressional action on our energy legislation. A mistaken belief that the United States is not prepared to adopt an effective energy program has been partly responsible for recent, unsettled conditions in the exchange markets. We have a responsibility to protect the integrity of the dollar. Prompt action is needed in energy and other fields to reduce our deficits.

Last April, I submitted to the Congress a comprehensive conservation and conversion program[30] to reduce our dependence on foreign oil. I am confident that the Congress will not allow this situation to continue to deteriorate through inaction. I am equally confident that the American people will fully support this critically important program. When enacted, the measures now under consideration will have increasingly beneficial effect in coming years and exert their main impact by 1985.

---

[29]Text from *Presidential Documents*, 13: 1911-13.
[30]Cf. Introduction at note 163.

The United States is currently importing petroleum at a cost of about 45 billion a year. In 1978, taking account of planned production of Alaskan oil, our oil imports will be stable, despite substantial purchases for our Strategic Petroleum Reserve. Nevertheless, it is essential that we take further steps to curtail these imports in order to reduce both our excessive dependence on imported oil and the burden on our balance of payments. The energy measures I am now proposing are designed to serve these ends.

I have instructed the Department of Energy to pursue efforts to:

—expand production of oil at the Elk Hills Naval Petroleum Reserve;

—encourage an expansion of production at Prudhoe Bay above the 1.2 million barrels a day planned for early 1978;

—maintain production of California crude at a high level;

—work with appropriate governmental and private interests in expediting provision of adequate pipeline capacity for transport of Alaskan and Californian oil east of the Rocky Mountains.

Combined with conservation measures, these efforts offer good promise.

The new measures will take effect in the period immediately ahead and serve as a bridge until the implementation of the more comprehensive legislative program begins to exert fundamental changes in our energy balance in the years ahead.

I have also instituted measures to expand U.S. exports:

—We have doubled Commodity Credit Corporation credits to support agricultural exports.

—In 1978, we will increase sharply lending activity by the Export-Import Bank, to support exports generally.

We will not engage in unfair competition for export markets; we will fully respect our understandings with other Governments regarding export credit terms. But within these understandings, there is room for a more active effort to expand our exports. Through such an effort, I believe we can achieve substantial increases in exports in 1978, as well as in subsequent years.

With these measures, the prospects for an improvement in our trade position will be good. Some of these measures will begin to take effect in 1978. When fully implemented, these measures, energy and non-energy, should produce an annual improvement in our trade position of several billion dollars and will improve the U.S. balance of payments.

There has been a great deal of public discussion in recent weeks about the large U.S. trade and payments deficits and the movement of rates in the exchange markets, mainly between the dollar and the German mark and Japanese yen. The American economy and the dollar are fundamentally sound; U.S. products on the whole are competitive. While some exchange rate adjustment has been understandable in light of economic developments in Germany, Japan, and the United States, recent exchange market disorders are not justified.

The new energy measures strike directly at a key part of the balance of trade problem. The export measures will enable us to respond effectively to expanding export opportunities. Together, the energy and export measures represent action to strengthen our balance of payments and deal with our trade deficit in a substantive way, by improving the underlying conditions upon which the value of the dollar fundamentally depends.

Furthermore, next month I shall be presenting to the Congress a comprehensive economic program designed to insure a healthy and growing economy, to increase business capital investment, to expand industrial capacity and productivity, and to maintain prudent budgetary policies while counteracting inflationary pressures. These and related measures will promote economic progress and underscore our commitment to a strong and sound U.S. economy.

In the discharge of our responsibilities, we will, in close consultation with our friends abroad, intervene to the extent necessary to counter disorderly conditions in the exchange markets. The measures I have enumerated will deal with the root causes of these market disturbances in a more direct and fundamental way.

9. FOREIGN POLICY IN A GLOBAL COMMUNITY

(53) "American Policy and Global Change": Remarks by Zbigniew Brzezinski, Assistant to the President for National Security Affairs, before the Trilateral Commission, Bonn, October 30, 1977.[1]

I want to use this opportunity to speak of American policy and of global change. In doing so, let me stress, first of all, the underlying continuity of that policy. Since 1945, the United States, with its allies, has been engaged in an effort to create a more congenial international setting for our values, for our interests, and for our future. But we have done this while the international political system has felt the pressures of two simultaneous trends: an intense ideological and power conflict, and a remarkable expansion in the scope of its participation, produced by the waning of empires and the resulting tripling in the number of nation-states. This conjunction—of conflict rooted in ideology, power, and national ambitions, with a sudden expansion in international participation—has made for extraordinary turbulence in world affairs.

Nonetheless, our basic commitments have remained unchanged from administration to administration. This is especially the case with our collective security—and our commitment to common defense remains a central and constant element in our policy. What has changed is the international context in which we have sought to maintain these commitments. The nature of that change has often presented us with enormously complex problems of analysis, and even of values. In reacting to global change, what factors should we stress and why? In an era of such rapid change, with some of that change involving values clearly in conflict with our own traditions, is it more important to preserve the status quo, or to try to shape that change in directions that preserve our interests and enhance our values? Or is it possible to do some of both?

Each administration has answered these questions somewhat differently, thereby setting for itself somewhat different priorities.

[1] Press Release of The Trilateral Commission, Oct. 25, 1977.

Today, while emphasizing the underlying continuity in American foreign policy, I wish to share with you some thoughts on how the new Carter Administration defines its objectives, and how it responds to continuing as well as to new global dilemmas.

In broad terms, the Carter Administration set for itself four basic priorities:

1. To overcome the crisis of the spirit;
2. To help shape a wider and more cooperative world system;
3. To resolve conflicts that left unresolved are not likely to be contained;
4. To engage governments and peoples in responding to new and key global dilemmas.

1. Overcoming the Crisis of the Spirit

In some regards, the crisis of the spirit in recent years has been specifically American; in a larger sense, it has been part of the broader malaise of the West; in some respects, it is related to the political awakening of mankind, which has had the effect of transforming heretofore seemingly universal Western values into an apparently parochial perspective. As a crisis of historical confidence, and of international relevance to a world that ·seemingly rejects Western values, its essence has been well expressed by Hermann Hesse writing in *Steppenwolf*: —

Human life is reduced to real suffering, to hell, only when two ages, two cultures and religions overlap. . . . There are times when a whole generation is caught in this way between two ages, two modes of life, with the consequence that it loses all power to understand itself and has no standard, no security, no simple acquiescence.

In its specific American dimension, the crisis of the spirit was stimulated by the Vietnamese War and by the constitutional and moral crisis of Watergate. In Western Europe and Japan, the very pace of the efforts to overcome the traumatic legacies of World War II may still have played a role. Raymond Aron has also recently pointed at the broader implications of this crisis: "A hedonistic civilization, so shortsighted as to devote itself only to the material satisfactions of the day, condemns itself to death when it is no longer interested in the future, and loses thereby its sustaining sense of history."

This is why the new American President put so much emphasis, as early as in his Inaugural Address,[2] on "the new spirit." Faced

[2]Document 2a.

with a world that was losing faith in America, by the widespread global phenomenon of anti-Americanism, the new Administration put high on its list of priorities the need to revive both American confidence and the spiritual relevance of the West to emerging global dilemmas. We sensed that, for far too long, the United States had been seen—often correctly—as opposed to change, committed primarily to stability for the sake of stability, preoccupied with the balance of power for the sake of the preservation of privilege. We deliberately set out to identify the United States with the notion that change is a positive phenomenon; that we believe that change can be channeled in constructive directions; and that internationally change can be made compatible with our own underlying spiritual values.

The emphasis we have put on human rights is derived from this perspective. We believe that human rights is an idea whose historic time has come. Throughout the world, because of higher literacy, better communications, and a closer sense of interdependence, people are demanding and asserting their basic rights. This phenomenon manifests itself—though in different ways and with differing priorities—in the Far East and in Southern Africa; in Latin America and in Eastern Europe and the USSR; and it has asserted itself in recent years in our own society on the racial front and it is also making itself felt in other advanced industrial democracies. We do not make the acceptance of our view of human rights a precondition for specific bilateral relationships; nor do we wish to prescribe our specific norms for other societies. But we do believe that these two words "human rights" summarize mankind's social progress; that they represent the genuine historical inevitability of our time; and that neither the United States nor the West should be ashamed of our commitment to the advancement of human rights.

In addition, the revival of popular American concern for events beyond our shores derives in part from the special emphasis that the Administration has placed on relating our foreign policy goals to deeper American values. The reawakened American concern for human rights thus not only reflects the deep convictions of the President and of most Americans; this concern has also played a significant role in overcoming widespread popular disillusion and cynicism about foreign policy, thus enabling the United States again to play a more constructive role across a broad range of international issues.

I believe it is fair to say that the crisis of the spirit in the United States is coming to an end. The changing outlook of the United States on the world today has several dimensions:

—*A revival of American optimism.* This is not the mere expectation of good fortune expressed in Bismarck's remark that "a special providence seems to look after drunks, fools, and Americans." Rather, it reflects confidence in the basic strength of our position in the world and of the moral character of that position.

—*A reawakening of American idealism.* President Carter does not shrink from affirming our basic values at home and abroad. Americans support him in that. We do not seek to impose our principles on others, but we do not intend to be silent about the things that we believe in deeply. More, by reaffirming our commitment to basic notions that man is entitled to certain basic human rights, and that the Western democratic system gives people the greatest opportunity for self-expression, we contribute to the spiritual revival of the West. A West that believes only in material consumption has a message of no relevance to the rest of the world. A West that stands for genuine liberty and self-fulfillment of the individual has a message and the necessary point of departure for a dialogue with the rest of the world about basic human needs—material, social, political, and technological.

—*A rekindling of America's commitment to reform.* The current international situation demands a creative effort to devise new habits of conduct and new institutions for dealing with regional and global problems. We accept this challenge with enthusiasm rather than resignation, recognizing that we cannot design solutions unilaterally nor engage the interests and efforts of others without patient and thorough consultations.

I believe that the last ten months have already seen a significant reduction in anti-Americanism abroad. I believe the new, and confident, American approach to world affairs, rooted in our values, is beginning to reestablish the basis for an American role that can truly be morally just and politically effective.

2. Towards a Wider and More Cooperative World System

For us, the point of departure for America's involvement in the world is our relationship with Western Europe and Japan. The bonds of interest and sentiment which link our destinies have a special character. We share a commitment to democratic procedures, civil rights, the market system, open societies. We confront the common problems of post-industrial societies. We are not merely occasional allies; we are permanent friends. If we are determined to reassert American leadership in world affairs, we conceive of it as shared leadership; no one country today can have a monopoly or even predominance of wisdom, initiative, or responsibility.

Because of this understanding and belief, we set out immediately in January to bring relations with Europe and Japan to the forefront of U.S. foreign policy. This was the symbolism—and the substance—behind Vice President Mondale's trip, beginning only 96 hours after the Inauguration. And it was the reason the President made his first foreign trip to Western Europe, whose unity we strongly favor, for the three summits with our major partners. We sought to consult on the many issues with which we are vitally concerned, first and foremost with our industrial state partners.

Our objective in this is not a pursuit of identical policies. But together we must relate our respective national security policies and our economic efforts to promote reconciliation among nations and to more effective international economic cooperation. In dealing with each other, moreover, we must acknowledge a higher standard of mutual concern than normally marks relations between sovereign states. We must accept a greater commitment to consult, and to adjust our national policies in the light of their impact on our key partners.

The economic Summit last May was a useful forum for consulting regarding our economic policy. The NATO Summit developed joint steps to enhance our collective security. Furthermore, in Presidential Directive No. 18, the President recently recommitted the United States to a policy of forward defense in Europe and to continued security of our allies in the Far East. But that commitment needs to be defined and refined in the light of changing circumstances, and both its strategic as well as tactical implications will require greater cooperation and joint reevaluation in the years ahead.

Similarly, we must jointly face the danger that the advanced world will soon confront an energy crisis of mounting proportions, and all of us—and especially the United States, must develop conservation and innovation on an increasingly urgent basis.

A secure and economically cooperative community of the advanced industrial democracies is the necessary source of stability for a broad system of international cooperation. We are aware of the pitfalls of constructing a geometric world—whether bilateral or trilateral or pentagonal—that leaves out the majority of mankind who live in the developing countries. A global structure that would ignore this reality would be inhumane, for it would reflect indifference to the hardships of others; it would be unrealistic, for we cannot ignore scores of nations with whom we are increasingly interdependent; and it would be damaging in the long run, for the problems that we neglect today will come back in a more virulent form tomorrow. We are therefore seeking to create a new political and international order that is truly more participatory and genuinely more responsive to global desire for greater social justice, equity, and more opportunity for individual self-fulfillment. We believe that paying greater attention to this dimension of foreign policy is not only in our own self-interest, and indispensable to an effective working of the global economy; to us it also represents a return to some of the deepest values and historical roots of our own country, while reestablishing the relevance of the West to mankind's universal condition.

It is in this spirit that the new Administration has sought to put our relations with Latin America and with Africa on a new plane. We have abandoned the traditional device of formulating a new slogan to encapsule U.S. relations with Latin America. Instead, we have emphasized that we respect the diversity of the Latin American nations; that we seek to relate to them on a bilateral basis in most cases, on a regional basis when useful, and on a global basis in regard to problems which are more universal. I believe that most Latin American nations respect and welcome this approach. They see in it the rejection of traditional U.S. paternalism and the beginning of more mature and normal relations, similar to those which the United States has with other nations of the world.

Regarding Africa, we have sought, and I believe successfully, to identify ourselves with the just aspirations of black Africans. We have broken with the posture of indifference and insensitivity which at times in the past characterized American attitudes toward those aspirations. In so doing, I believe that we are also making it easier for the United States, as for the West in general, to play a creative role in dealing with some international problems that today confront the African community.

In Asia, where the United States will continue to play a major role, we are encouraged by the progress made in some parts of this vast region. The emergence of ASEAN, the growing prosperity of the Pacific Basin, the constructive character of recent Japanese initiatives are welcome developments, which will cumulatively contribute to a healthier international order.

In brief, our approach to developing nations is characterized by our willingness to actively seek solutions to remaining "anti-colonialist" issues; by our engagement in the search for answers to the more structural problems of North-South relations; by our desire to collaborate closely with the increasingly influential emerging states; and by our desire to make foreign aid more responsive to the needs of the world's poorest peoples.

At the same time, a wider and more cooperative world system has to include also that part of the world which is ruled by Communist governments. One-third of mankind now lives under Communist systems, and these states have to be assimilated, to the extent that they are willing, into a wider fabric of global cooperation. The objective is thus to assimilate East-West relations into a broader framework of cooperation, rather than to concentrate on East-West relations as the decisive and dominant concern of our times.

In the 1950s, world affairs were dominated by an intense confrontation between the U.S. and the Soviet bloc. In the 1960s, world affairs were dominated by growing diversity in the Communist world and by a competitive relationship between the United States and the Soviet Union. And in the early 1970s, many foreign observers became concerned that the next era would be marked by efforts to create a U.S.-Soviet condominium. An enduring thread runs through these generalizations; whether marked by confrontation, competition, or the feared prospect of a condominium, U.S.-Soviet relations tended to dominate American foreign policy and, indeed, world affairs.

This should no longer be, or need be, the case. East-West relations, notably U.S.-Soviet relations, involve and will continue to involve elements of both competition and cooperation. We are quietly confident about our ability and determination to compete, economically, politically, and militarily. But managing a relationship that will be both competitive and cooperative cannot be permitted to dominate all our perspectives. Today, we do not have a realistic choice between an approach centered on the Soviet Union, or cooperation with our trilateral friends, or on North-South relations. Instead, each set of issues must be approached on its own terms. A world where elements of cooperation prevail over competition entails the need to shape a wider and more cooperative global framework. We did not wish the world to be this complex; but we must deal with it in all of its complexity, even if it means having a foreign policy which cannot be reduced to a single and simplistic slogan.

This is why we will seek to engage the Soviet Union in wider forms of cooperation. As President Carter said in Notre Dame University,[3] we desire a detente that will be both comprehensive and reciprocal. We desire cooperation in the Indian Ocean, in the Middle East, and in Europe, as well as on wider global issues. We also want to contain the arms race. The arms race is costly, and dangerous. We seek to reduce—and to keep reducing—the level of strategic armaments on both sides, to freeze the improvement of weaponry on both sides, and to achieve an agreement in which each side is responsive to more specific strategic concerns of the other. I believe that the next SALT agreement will, in some measure, reflect these three objectives; it will thus provide a useful basis for seeking even more ambitious limits in SALT III, perhaps also paving the way to more comprehensive security negotiations in the European context, beyond the MBFR negotiations.

No architecture for a more stable and just world order would be complete without taking into account the proper role of the People's Republic of China. We recognize not only that peace in East and Southeast Asia depends upon a constructive Sino-American relationship, but that China can help immensely in maintaining a global equilibrium as well. Mutual interest, not sentiment, brought our two countries closer together. We must continue working to make our relationship closer still. Normalization in that relationship is necessary, but even short of it both sides should find it useful to develop a closer consultative relationship, so that each side adequately understands and takes into account the legitimate global concerns of the other. In fact, a deeper consultative relationship can result in an approach to world affairs that is mutually reinforcing and increasingly cooperative.

3. Resolving Conflicts

The third major objective that we set for ourselves last January was to focus on the three major issues which in our judgment contain the greatest potential for destructive escalation.

The first of these involves the future of the Panama Canal. To most Panamanians and to many Latin Americans this issue is perceived as a vestige of U.S. colonialism, a perspective widely shared in the Third World as well. I must candidly say that the effort to obtain a new treaty which would phase out the U.S. presence in the Canal Zone, and which will permit Panama to increase its participation in the operation and defense of the Canal, while retaining for the United States ultimate security responsibility, is not a popular matter in the United States. Yet the new Administration recognizes that efforts to maintain the status quo would poison our relations with Latin America and eventually even jeopardize our ability to keep the Canal open. We are thus determined to demonstrate that the most powerful nation in the world is willing to work with one of the world's smallest nations to fashion a relationship based on partnership and mutual respect. We also hope thereby to demonstrate that watertight zones of big power predominance are an historical anachronism, a point which may have some relevance to some other parts of the world as well.

The second major issue we faced last January was in Southern Africa. There we confront the danger that racial conflict might also become before long an ideological war, with external involvement. In cooperation with the African states, we seek in Southern Africa to promote a solution based on justice. Majority rule and one man-one vote reflect our fundamental view of man as a spiritual entity that transcendentally is truly equal to all others. And we are willing to play a continuing role in solving the problems of Southern Africa, on terms acceptable to the people who live there. In Zimbabwe this means supporting a rapid transition to majority rule; in

Namibia, it means assumption of power by an African government resting on the will of the majority. We recognize also that the situation in the Republic of South Africa is much more complex and will take much more time to resolve. We know that the issue of South Africa involves a fundamental conflict of philosophy, history, and self-definition. We are anxious to help create conditions that will make accommodation to a new reality—one more in keeping with the spirit of the times—as peaceful and palatable to those most affected as is possible.

We are also determined to do our part to make certain that Africa in general does not become the terrain for ideological conflict. This is why we insist that major powers refrain from interference and from fueling conflicts, whether in Southern Africa or the African Horn. The problems of this continent are painful enough without infecting them with ideological issues derived from another age and from other continents.

The third crucial problem on which we determined to concentrate was in the Middle East. Continued conflict in that region poses a direct threat to international peace, while increasingly radicalizing Israel's neighbors. Such conflict poses a danger as much to Europe and to Japan as to the United States, not to speak of Israel itself. We also perceived that an opportunity existed to move more rapidly towards truly a genuine peace. The Israelis, who have fought so courageously for their survival and to whose survival every morally sensitive person must be committed, have often stated that territories occupied in 1967 were being held until their Arab neighbors were prepared to undertake full scale peace commitments. Our administration, therefore, building on the step-by-step arrangements attained by the previous U.S. administration, has sought to elicit and to crystallize growing Arab moderation, thereby making possible direct negotiations between the parties. We hope that a full scale conference may be convened before too long, and that in the meantime all parties will maintain a posture of moderation, bearing in mind that sometimes excessive precision on details is an enemy of accommodation.

The road ahead, however, will be extraordinarily difficult, and we recognize this fact. I believe that Europe and Japan, and indeed most of mankind, share our commitment to promoting a settlement, and in different ways they, too, can exercise a constructive influence in pleading for the necessary spirit of moderation needed to settle a conflict so pregnant with political and moral complexities.

4. Responsiveness to New Global Dilemmas

Finally, our major objective has been to join with others in increasing the level of global sensitivity to two key problems which, in our judgment, have been given inadequate attention in the past. They are nonproliferation and conventional arms transfers.

Our nuclear nonproliferation policy recognizes two needs: to help each nation to secure the energy it needs, and to stop the spread of nuclear weaponry. Thus our policy is not designed to impose artificial prohibitions on the inevitable spread of an essential technology. Rather we have to induce nations to take a fresh look at the problems of the plutonium fuel cycle, and to concentrate greater attention on the technical alternatives which we believe exist. The policy rests on a firm economic and technical base which has two key elements. First, the energy plans of many nations— particularly the developed states—are based on what we regard as inflated estimates of future energy demand. Second, we think that global reserves of uranium and thorium are much larger than was previously estimated.

Our analysis of these considerations impels us to the conclusion that the reprocessing and reuse of plutonium at this time would be premature—in the U.S. and elsewhere. Therefore, last spring, the President postponed reprocessing in the U.S. for the indefinite future, and proposed an International Nuclear Fuel Cycle Evaluation in which developed and developing states could jointly examine these and related issues in an effort to reach mutually agreed answers. I am pleased to report that last week more than 35 nations convened in Washington for the first meeting of this historic undertaking.[4]

We also wish to raise the level of awareness about the dangers involved in growing conventional arms transfers. These transfers have more than doubled over the past decade. Not only has there been a dramatic increase in the volume of arms, but those sold today are of ever increasing sophistication. While only a handful of states produce such weapons, the number of nations which seek to purchase them is increasing rapidly. The momentum continues to build, despite the enormous burden that is levied on an already faltering world economy. The tragic irony is that resources diverted from economic and social development to buy arms may undermine the very security the arms are intended to purchase.

The United States is moving to meet this global threat to the welfare of mankind. We have begun to restrain our arms exports; at the same time, realizing that we cannot deal with this global problem alone, we intend to work with other suppliers to cut back on the flow of arms and the rate at which advanced weapon technologies spread. Equally important, we hope to work with arms importers to reduce the demand for more numerous and costly weapons. While we remain ready to provide our friends with the necessary

[4]Cf. Document 12.

means for self-defense, we are determined to do what can be done to reverse the spiraling increase of arms exports.

Since the beginning of this Administration, we have been fully aware that these two problems are complex; that they will require a sophisticated strategy to be worked out over many years; and that they also may complicate relations with our friends and allies represented here. Yet none of us can afford to ignore the implications of failing to deal effectively with either nonproliferation or arms transfers; just as economic interdependence is now a new fact of life for the United States, so this political interdependence is affecting us all.

In these four areas, I have tried to indicate major issues and ideas that have influenced our approach to foreign policy this year. I do not claim that we have succeeded in reaching our goals. Some of them may not be attained during the life of this Administration. But I believe that real progress has been made:

1. Anti-Americanism has waned; there has been a revival of historical confidence *in* the United States and *about* the United States; our commitment to human rights is helping to restore genuine meaning to the word democracy, and thus the democracies' relevance to the world.

2. We have made some progress in fulfilling the Summit decisions of last May, but we need to do more, especially in regards to economic growth and the avoidance of protectionism.

We have improved somewhat the climate of North-South relations and placed our relations with Latin America and Africa on a more cooperative and mature basis.

We have also made progress in our continuing efforts to put U.S.-Soviet relations on a stable and equitable basis, without generating the extremes of public euphoria or hostility. Indeed, today we are negotiating on a wider variety of bilateral issues than probably at any previous time in U.S.-Soviet relations.

3. We have signed a just treaty with Panama and are now seeking its ratification;[5] we have engaged U.S. prestige and influence in the effort to obtain fair solutions to Southern African problems; we have made progress in obtaining Israeli and Arab willingness to negotiate on the three key issues in the Middle Eastern conflict: namely, the nature of peace, the relation between territorial and security arrangements, and the Palestinian question. I believe all the parties now realize that the U.S. is serious in its desire to promote a comprehensive peace settlement.

4. We have adopted self-imposed restraints on our arms ex-

ports through the obligation to reduce our totals from year to year; we are now engaged in negotiating self-restraint arrangements with other countries. We have also succeeded in generating genuine interest in nonproliferation, despite—and perhaps even because of—the friction that this issue initially produced.

If there is a single common theme to our efforts, it is this: after World War II our foreign policy, by necessity, was focused primarily on issues connected with the Cold War. This gave it a sharp focus, in some cases making it easier to mobilize public opinion. A concentrated foreign policy could be supported by public emotion.

Today we confront a more difficult task, which calls for support based on reason. We must respond to a wider range of issues—some of which still involve the Cold War—issues stemming from a complex process of global change. A concentrated foreign policy must give way to a complex foreign policy, no longer focused on a single, dramatic task—such as the defense of the West. Instead, we must engage ourselves on the distant and difficult goal of giving shape to a world that has suddenly become politically awakened and socially restless.

The struggle for the shape of the future thus has strong parallels to the experience of Western democracies in the last century and a half. And it is that experience which offers a measure of hope for a more rational and just accommodation on a vastly more complex and larger scale basis. That accommodation, which over time can acquire the character of a genuine global community, cannot be blueprinted in advance; and it will only come about through gradual changes both in the outlook and in the objective conditions of mankind. It is our confident belief that liberty and equity can indeed creatively coexist. It is our confident view of the future that democracy—in its many manifestations and with its own many stages of development—comes closest to meeting the genuinely felt needs of mankind. It is our confident judgment that our collaboration can enhance the chances that the future destiny of man is to live in a world that is creatively pluralistic.

Thank you.

(54) The Law of the Sea: Statement by Ambassador Elliot L. Richardson, Special Representative of the President for the Law of the Sea Conference, before Committees of the House of Representatives, October 4, 1977.[6]

[6]Text from *Bulletin*, 77: 741-6. The statement was made before the House Committee on Commerce, Science, and Transportation and the Subcommittee on Public Lands and Resources of the House Committee on Energy and Natural Resources.

(Excerpts)

I am pleased to have this opportunity to appear before you today to discuss the results of the sixth session of the Third U.N. Conference on the Law of the Sea and to present our views on the deep seabed mining legislation before your committees.

As you are aware, the last session produced mixed results. While progress was made in a number of areas, the proposed articles on deep seabed mining in the Informal Composite Negotiating Text—the ICNT—which resulted from the session were fundamentally unacceptable to the United States. The failure of this meeting of the conference to produce a text which could serve as a basis for negotiation on deep seabeds has a direct bearing on what I wish to discuss with you today—legislation to regulate deep seabed mining by U.S. citizens, in particular the bills which are presently before you.

My testimony will begin first with the conference itself, then describe our review, and finally discuss the need for and substance of deep seabed mining legislation.

Law of the Sea Conference

The sixth session of the U.N. Law of the Sea Conference was held in New York from May 23 to July 15. The first 3 weeks of formal work were devoted exclusively to deep seabed issues. At the request of a large number of delegations, ours included, the daily informal talks were held under the chairmanship of Minister Jens Evensen of Norway who acted as the working group leader for First [Seabed] Committee chairman, Paul Engo of the Cameroon. Evensen's selection was an outgrowth of his previously successful efforts to facilitate compromises in other conference committees, particularly in the Second Committee dealing with fisheries and navigation, as well as his useful efforts on seabeds at intersessional meetings in February-March.

A difficult but nonetheless good start was made during the first 21 days in moving the deep seabed negotiations away from the deadlock that was characteristic of the fifth session in the fall of 1976. As a result of this effort and following on from it, Evensen produced a number of compromise texts on the critical elements of a deep seabeds regime. These Evensen proposals were by no means acceptable from our standpoint, but the resulting texts did represent the product of an open discussion involving all of the countries represented at the conference. The Evensen texts could have been a basis for further negotiation breaking the impasse on seabed mining.

Unfortunately, however, these texts—the product of weeks of hard work—were substantially amended at the last moment by

Chairman Engo, who forwarded to the conference President a First Committee text that totally fails to accommodate the interests of the United States. This text[7] was produced in private; never discussed with a representative group of concerned nations—treating weeks of serious debate and responsible negotiation as essentially irrelevant.

Those who have followed the Law of the Sea Conference since its Caracas session in 1974[8] are well aware that the texts on deep seabed mining which have been produced at succeeding sessions have been either praised or criticized in what seems to be a flip-flop pattern. The Single Negotiating Text produced in Geneva in 1975[9] "favored" the developing countries; the Revised Single Negotiating Text from New York in 1976[10] was asserted to have "favored" the developed states. And now we have the ICNT, again "favoring" the developing countries. This conference pattern has hardly been conducive to development of agreement on a compromise approach accommodating the many different national interests involved.

As I noted on July 20,[11] among the serious points of substantive difficulty in the latest deep seabeds text and the system it would define are the following:

—It would not give the assured access under reasonable conditions that is necessary if we and others could be expected to help finance the Enterprise and to accept a "parallel system" as a basis of compromise.

—It could be read to make technology transfer by contractors a condition of access to the deep seabed—subject, at least in part, to negotiation in the pursuit of a contract.

—It could be read to give the Seabed Authority[12] the power effectively to mandate joint ventures with the Authority as a condition for access.

—It fails to set clear and reasonable limits on the financial burdens to be borne by contractors, thus throwing up an obstacle perhaps sufficient to stifle seabed development.

—It would set an artificial limit on seabed production of minerals from nodules which is not only objectionable in principle but also far more stringent than would be necessary to protect land-based producers from possible adverse effects.

—It would give the Seabed Authority extremely broad, open-

[7]Cf. at Introduction at note 193.
[8]*AFR, 1974:* 315-26.
[9]Cf. same, *1975:* 144.
[10]Cf. same, *1976:* 102.
[11]Cf. Introduction at note 192.
[12]International Seabed Resource Authority.

ended power to regulate all other mineral production from the seabed "as appropriate."

—It could be read as giving the Authority unacceptable new power to regulate scientific research in the area.

—It would fail adequately to protect minority interests in its system of governance and would, accordingly, threaten to allow the abuse of power by an anomalous "majority."

—It would allow the distribution of benefits from seabed exploitation to peoples and countries not parties to the convention.

—It would seriously prejudice the likely long-term character of the international regime by requiring that—if agreement to the contrary is not reached within 25 years—the regime automatically be converted into a "unitary" system, ruling out direct access by contractors, except to the extent that the Authority might seek their participation in joint ventures with it.

These are serious deficiencies. What is involved here is the establishment of a regime for half the Earth's surface. While today's technology points only to manganese nodules, there is no telling what lies ahead in the future. We simply cannot agree to a regime which would unnecessarily inhibit, and perhaps even prevent, deep seabed development. To do so would make a mockery of the "common heritage of mankind" and reduce to a pitiful trickle the benefits that could otherwise accrue—not only to the entrepreneurs who will risk their capital but also to mankind as a whole, in particular the developing countries.

The developing countries tell us they wish a new international economic order in which they might participate as equal partners. But what good is an order for half the Earth's surface that won't work? No one can force the investment of capital and technology. It must be induced to flow. We thus have a major interest, in addition to the resources, in the international institution we create for the deep seabed. We seek an institution which will represent a true accommodation of the interests of both developing and developed countries—a precedent for the future.

What happened at the sixth session is therefore particularly disappointing. We were prepared to agree to a compromise which would produce maximum benefits to be shared with the poorer countries while at the same time opening up the opportunity for the developing world itself to participate in the effort. Such a compromise would be a major achievement—not only for the benefits to be attained from resource exploitation as such but also as a precedent for future world institutions.

Before I close my discussion of the conference, I believe it is important to note in some detail the accomplishments and other developments at the last session. The ICNT reflects improvements on issues relating to our military, politico-military, and commercial interests in freedom of navigation and overflight. In this respect, new provisions were negotiated and incorporated into the ICNT regarding the proposed 200-mile exclusive economic zone (EEZ) which appear to safeguard traditional high seas freedoms within the EEZ except for specific resource-related rights accorded coastal states. Similarly, we were able to maintain broadly supported articles on transit through, over, and under straits over the diminishing opposition of a small number of states.

The text on protection of the marine environment is little changed from the Revised Single Negotiating Text. It contains several potentially helpful provisions on all sources of ocean pollution and a balanced system for controlling vessel source pollution. Progress was also made toward the establishment of a comprehensive system for the peaceful settlement of disputes arising from ocean uses. I do not want to leave you with the impression, however, that all the issues just mentioned have been settled to our complete satisfaction. We will continue to seek improvements at any future negotiations.

The result on marine scientific research was mixed. On the one hand, we were able to narrow the scope of the listed categories of research activities for which the coastal state can deny consent and to retain provisions on tacit consent. On the negative side, the ICNT contains a regime whereby research in the economic zone is generally subject to the consent of the coastal state. The ICNT does provide that coastal states shall grant their approval of research "in normal circumstances." This was intended to cover all situations but those involving seriously abnormal political relations. Provisions for impartial dispute settlement with regard to research are poorly stated.

I should note that the United States and a handful of other researching states were completely isolated on marine scientific research. The developing countries and some developed countries, particularly the U.S.S.R., favored complete coastal state discretionary consent authority over all marine scientific research. We made a major effort to improve the text, and I sincerely believe we were successful at least in withstanding majority pressure for an impossibly restrictive regime.

Review

Because of the serious defects of the deep seabeds section of the ICNT, I recommended to the President that we review not only the balance among all of our substantive interests but also whether an agreement which accommodates the different national interests involved can be achieved through the kind of negotiations which have thus far taken place.

This review has now begun. We expect to complete it before the end of the year. A key question will involve our posture toward the next session of the conference which is proposed for Geneva from March 28 through May 19. In determining this posture, we will take into account three essential factors:

—An assessment of the relative weight of our several interests in a comprehensive Law of the Sea treaty;
—An assessment of the likelihood of a treaty text emerging from the conference which would accommodate those interests. This assessment will obviously take into account the attitudes of other countries toward both achieving a fair and open process and making the essential compromises that are necessary if U.S. interests are to be accommodated;
—An assessment of the alternatives to any comprehensive treaty which is likely to result from the Law of the Sea Conference.

Deep Seabed Mining Legislation

Last spring, prior to the sixth session, I testified before a number of congressional committees to the effect that we did not support legislation at that time but that we would review this position in light of the results of the sixth session.[13] We believed there was a risk at that time that Administration support for legislation could adversely affect progress at that session. We were particularly concerned that the chance to obtain the good will and tone of the intersessional meeting held in Geneva in February and March under Minister Evensen's chairmanship not in any way be jeopardized. We also felt that the sixth session offered reasonable prospects of a breakthrough on deep seabed issues.

As it turned out, and as I have explained earlier in this testimony, the breakthrough did not materialize. Indeed, the session saw a serious retrogression. The issue is therefore once again posed as to whether the Administration should now support legislation which would authorize U.S. seabed miners to move forward pending agreement on an international regime.

It is our view that U.S. legislation establishing a domestic regime for seabed mining will be needed whether there is a treaty or not—in either case, legislation will be required to regulate seabed mining in accordance with sound resource management and environmental principles; additionally, in the absence of a treaty, we will need to assure that existing international rights in the area beyond national jurisdiction are protected. If there is no treaty, the issue of legisla-

---

[13]Text of statement before the House Subcommittee on Oceanography, Apr. 27, in *Bulletin*, 76: 524-7.

tion boils down to two questions—one as to its timing; the other as to its content.

As to timing, the Administration believes that if there is to be any meaning to the "common heritage of mankind," those with the technology and resources to make it a reality must move forward. In our view, therefore, Congress should continue to move forward with legislation. For its part, the Administration will wish to work closely with this committee and other concerned committees to make the substance of the legislation consistent with our international posture.

With respect to the substance of deep seabed mining legislation, I and officials of several agencies have on various occasions informed Members of Congress of Administration views. There has clearly been a good measure of responsiveness to those views on the part of you who have participated in drafting the legislation before us,[14] and I would like to express my appreciation for this. I am confident it augurs well for continuing cooperative efforts on these matters in the future.

May I briefly review the main elements of Administration policy before turning to a discussion of the bills before us. In our view, legislation:

—Should be interim in nature, providing for its own supersession by a treaty;

—Should contain provisions for harmonizing U.S. regulations with those of reciprocating states so as to avoid conflict;

—Should provide for environmental protection, sound resource management, and protection of life and property at sea;

—Should provide that seabed mining by U.S. companies produce financial benefits for the international community;

—Should address the exploratory stage of deep seabed mining in detail but treat most generally the framework for a regulatory regime for exploitation, with the date for entry into force of such a regime left open;

—Should not be specific with regard to the assignment or allocation of mining sites for exploitation;

—Should not require that processing plants be located in the United States;

—Should not offer U.S. mining companies financial protection against adverse effects of a treaty concluded subsequent to the passage of legislation and after expenditures by those companies; and

—Should assure that all provisions of the legislation leave undisturbed the concept of high seas freedoms.

[14] S. 2053 and S. 2085, 95th Cong.

These elements provide the framework within which the Administration would be able to support ocean mining legislation.

* * *

These are the general comments I would like to make on the legislation before you. Let me reiterate the Administration's appreciation for the willingness of the concerned Members of Congress to give consideration to our views with regard to deep seabed mining. Members of my staff will be giving the committees detailed drafting suggestions soon—this week, I hope.

The manner in which we proceed with seabed development has major significance for the future access to resources and for the future of world institutions and the means for establishing them. While we are reviewing our participation in the Law of the Sea Conference, we must exercise great care in moving forward alternative means of proceeding with seabed mining.

I shall look forward to continuing our close collaboration to the end that the best possible regime for deep seabed resources might be developed.

(55) 32nd Regular Session of the United Nations General Assembly, New York, September 20-December 21, 1977: Statement in Plenary Session by Ambassador Andrew Young, United States Permanent Representative to the United Nations, December 21, 1977.[15]

I am pleased to say that I believe we have achieved an important and hopeful shift in the development of the General Assembly. We are drawing to a close what has been, in many ways, the most constructive session in many years. In this General Assembly we have seen a clearer consensus of the concerned emerge to replace some of the politics of frustration which seemed often to drive the work of the Assembly in the past.

This year we all saw an obvious change of mood, a sign that all of our governments and delegates are beginning to question the value of the slogans and cliches which have governed their activities so often during the past several years. I sense an increasing agreement that slogans lead nowhere, that purely political and tactical maneuvers in isolation from the substance not only are wasteful and damaging to this institution but they engender unproductive confrontation which inhibits progress toward solution of the crucial problems of mankind.

[15]USUN Press Release 150; text from *Bulletin*, 78: 52-5 (Feb. 1978). Closing paragraphs omitted.

In short, this has been a good Assembly. It may even have been historically important because of progress on several fronts but mainly because of this new will to talk together about resolving our common problems. This is a solid record that my government values highly and a record that I intend to convey to the American people in the months ahead.

Middle East

What has this Assembly accomplished, and why did this occur?

First, let us turn to the area where the United Nations has, for 30 years, borne special responsibilities for maintaining peace and security—the Middle East. This fall we saw in President Sadat's visit to Jerusalem one of the most courageous moves in the history of modern diplomacy. His action, and the response of Prime Minister Begin, have created an unprecedented opportunity. Their visit demonstrated the profound desire for peace by peoples who have undergone the devastation of four tragic wars.

On most other issues this fall, this Assembly gave the impression of being closely conscious of, and relevant to, real events. But resolutions which were adopted in [on] the Middle East tended to reflect the unhelpful rhetoric of the past rather than the refreshing and hopeful developments of the present. There seemed a very real possibility that the world was passing the United Nations by.

In all fairness, I think that the delegates and their governments may have sometimes found it difficult, because of the swift pace of developments, to reflect in New York the dynamic new possibilities for progress in the Middle East.

Despite the unreality of some of these debates, the role of the United Nations as an institution in Middle East affairs remained important and constructive. We must all keep this in mind, as Prime Minister Begin did when he called on the Secretary General to discuss the contribution the United Nations can make to the peace process. U.N. peacekeeping efforts for many years now have helped provide the breathing space which is necessary to permit the parties concerned to hammer out the terribly difficult but essential decisions which must be taken if we are to have an enduring peace—at long last—in the Middle East.

Amidst the headlines this fall, a fact overlooked was that the Security Council renewed without controversy the mandate of the Disengagement Observer Force in the Middle East,[16] a process that in the past has been drawn-out and painful. Nor did the world or the media focus on the fact that General Assembly approval of funding for the Middle East peacekeeping efforts this year,[17] in contrast to the past, was routine and noncontroversial.

[16]Resolution 420 (1977), Nov. 30, 1977.
[17]Resolution 32/4 B and C, Dec. 2, 1977.

Nor did the public place sufficient importance on the U.N. role this fall in enabling intensive consultations to take place among the leaders of the governments principally concerned with a Middle East settlement. This included the opportunity for U.S. and Soviet foreign ministers to further their talks on this subject.

All of these developments helped prepare the way for the kind of agreements on meaningful measures which are required for the ultimate settlement we all desire in the Middle East.

Southern Africa

An important part of the new atmosphere in this General Assembly was engendered by what my government considers to be significant movement of the U.N. community toward a new degree of consensus on the common goals in the southern African issues. I am proud that my government and the people of the United States have drawn closer in association and cooperation with our African friends.

The world community is virtually unanimous in its support for the goals of liberation of the people in southern Africa. There are few who would reject the work that has been launched to guarantee freedom, independence, and self-rule for all the people of this region. My government is committed to this monumental task.

In Rhodesia we have been sharply aware of the breathing room granted the U.K.-U.S. effort by the way the General Assembly treated this problem in all its debates, in committee as well as plenary. We also understand and accept the significance of the postponement of further debate in the Security Council.

The tragic actions of the Government of South Africa this fall sparked a justifiable explosion of protest from around the world that found its expression in this Organization through the unanimous decision of the Security Council to impose mandatory sanctions on South Africa[18]—the first time sanctions under chapter VII of the charter have been imposed on a member state of the United Nations. This was a true consensus. It was an historic step forward by the United Nations in its long effort to achieve freedom and human dignity in Africa.

Economic and Social Issues

On economic and social issues, we have reached two important milestones rooted in consensus.[19] We have achieved agreement on a mechanism to oversee the continuing dialogue between the industrialized and the developing nations. Many thought we would not be

[18]Cf. Introduction at note 107.
[19]Cf. Introduction at notes 202-203.

able to come to terms on even the procedure for carrying on this dialogue—for we had failed numerous times in the past—but we were able to carry it off.

In addition, after a 2-year study on restructuring of the economic and social functions of the United Nations, we reached agreement on some highly significant changes that should clearly improve the efficiency and effectiveness of these operations and insure that the delivery of services of the U.N. agencies to the world's poor is greatly enhanced.

We have also made some progress on human rights. This was the Assembly at which the President of the United States signed the International Covenants on Economic, Social and Cultural Rights and Civil and Political Rights. It was the Assembly at which broad cosponsorship of the proposal to create the position of High Commissioner for Human Rights reflected support in most geographic regions, even though ultimate passage was not possible this year. This was also the Assembly at which delegations from a number of regions made significant human rights proposals. I think we have taken important steps toward achievement of more awareness and agreement on action in this sensitive but critical field than we have ever had. At the same time, we have much work to do.

Arms Control

One of the most encouraging things about this fall's General Assembly was the extent of agreement we reached on arms control issues.

On a comprehensive test ban, for example, the key resolution commanded very broad support—not only from the Soviet Union and the United States but also from almost all of the nonnuclear nations.

On nonproliferation, there was a genuine readiness to exchange views seriously and to develop an acceptable resolution that recognizes the broad responsibility of all nations not to contribute to proliferation.

Resolutions calling for nuclear free zones in Africa, the Middle East, and South Asia commanded strong acceptance, and my government was pleased to be able to support them. And both the United States and the Soviets were to vote for a resolution endorsing goals in the Strategic Arms Limitation Talks.

The action of this Assembly in adopting by consensus—I emphasize by consensus—a resolution on aircraft hijacking was a particularly significant achievement of this session, making the world's airways safer for peoples of all nations.

In addition, this fall negotiations in the United Nations have made substantial progress toward establishing a joint committee on

missing persons in Cyprus,[20] a positive indication that there is willingness on both sides to resolve differences through negotiation.

We have taken steps to support the important recommendations
of the International Civil Service Commission for improvements in
the staffing of the United Nations. We have expanded the U.N.
membership as we work toward the ultimate goal of universality.
We reached a consensus resolution on Guam[21] and avoided the confrontational resolutions of the past. We have even taken radical
steps to curb first-class air travel for all U.N. employees below the
level of the Secretary General himself.

Positive Assembly Record

The reasons for this quite positive record are many. I do not need
to recite them to delegates here, but I believe it is particularly important for people outside this body to focus on them.

First, I think, is the emerging agreement that the time for oppor-
tunism on many issues before the United Nations is passing. The
issues are too pressing, the dangers too great. This year's Assembly
gives us more hope that this body has taken a new and positive
course. While we clearly cannot agree on all precise policy prescrip-
tions, there is growing agreement that it is incumbent on all of us to
advance serious proposals for dealing with critical issues.

Second, there is, I believe growing agreement among members
that the developed and the developing countries have fundamental,
long-term interests that converge more often than they diverge. In
my own country, for example, changes of policy have resulted in
deeper interest in the problems of southern Africa, progress on a
Panama Canal treaty, renewed concern about human rights, and
closer relations with many countries in the developing world. There
are differences, to be sure, and some are hard to bridge. But for all
nations—large and small—it is increasingly absurd to refuse to recognize the impact we all have on one another.

On economic issues, for example, my country, which has historically been oriented toward our industrialized trading partners, now
finds that the developing nations constitute its fastest growing markets and continue to be a prime source of many of its raw materials.
So we find that all regions are of growing importance to America's
welfare and interests.

In turn, the developing countries are finding that the industrialized societies offer indispensable markets, needed capital, and vital
technical assistance. Increasingly, we have to understand jointly
that our task is not to pressure one another—both sides, after all,
are quite capable of resisting pressure—but to find a much better

[20]General Assembly Resolution 32/128, Dec. 16, 1977, adopted without vote.
[21]General Assembly Resolution 32/28, Nov. 28, 1977, adopted without vote.

process to help both sides to discern and develop their common interests in cooperation. This is why the agreement of this Assembly to an overview mechanism for the North-South dialogue is so critical.

Third—and this will be disputed by some, although I strongly believe it is true—we are moving toward a more widely shared set of common values and interests. Thirty years ago, few in the developed world cared one way or the other about economic or social conditions in the developing nations. In that period, few in the developing countries realized that internal domestic policies of the industrialized countries could have such significant impact on economic conditions in their own faraway lands. Today there is an intense international debate about the best means for achieving a new international economic order which will be more just and healthy. Two questions [*sic*] is not *whether* we should do this, but *how*.

Fourth—and the world largely ignores this—effective new forms of decisionmaking have been employed in compiling our record at this General Assembly. One is the important development of small-group techniques of reaching agreement on potentially divisive issues. So-called contact groups, consisting of representatives of the various interest groups or "friends of the chairmen" of larger committees, have been able to make important progress in informal sessions.

The other major procedural technique that deserves mention is that of consensus decisionmaking. The public tends to focus on disagreements among us, but over the past 2 years about 63% of the decisions in the General Assembly have been taken by consensus. Although important differences are sometimes inappropriately covered over by consensus decisions, in most cases the differences have been so narrowed by intensive negotiation and debate that it is not even necessary to take a vote on these issues. Consensus decisions during the current Assembly have, I believe, been even more frequent than last year.

If we are striking a more constructive and cooperative tone in the conduct of our deliberations here, I do not mean to suggest that we be complacent. We have a difficult agenda facing us in the 12 months ahead.

The Future Agenda

On the vital issues of maintaining the peace, first of all, we must keep the momentum going. Almost all of us agree that the time is right for movement. We must maintain that consensus, and this is only possible by continuing our efforts to clarify the issues and achieve agreements on the problems that threaten us all.

In the Middle East, let us build on the historic steps already taken, abandon destructive positions, and seize an unprecedented opportunity for peace. Let us set our minds, in the intersessional months ahead, to contribute our ideas, our information, and our wisdom in conducting the affairs of the United Nations to support the moves toward peace.

In Cyprus, now that the parties have moved close to agreement on one important issue—the committee on missing persons—let us in the United Nations maintain the momentum to broaden the areas of agreement and reach a lasting settlement.

In Rhodesia, the supportive consensus created here by this body has undoubtedly played a major role in bringing Ian Smith to understand that he must step down in favor of a legitimate majority government elected by the people of Zimbabwe. We continue to believe that the initiative which the United States has been pursuing in support of the United Kingdom remains the best framework for an internationally acceptable transition to majority rule. Let us continue to work together to bring about the necessary peaceful conclusion to this effort.

In Namibia, the five Western ambassadors have just completed another round of talks with the front line states, the South West Africa People's Organization, Nigeria, and South Africa. The differences between the parties have been narrowed considerably over the last several months since our contact group began functioning. But the remaining issues stubbornly resist final agreement between the parties. Let us continue to work together in pursuance of an internationally acceptable settlement which will lead to true self-determination and independence for the people of Namibia.

In South Africa itself, let us build on the new consensus—not merely on the utter unacceptability of apartheid but also on the need to convince South Africa to move in a progressive direction. The consensus of the world community is more solid and sweeping than ever before. Let us make clear that our goal is not to isolate South Africa but to encourage the kind of meaningful social change that can bring full participation by all South African citizens in their own governance and national life.

Next year we will mark the 30th anniversary of the signing of the Universal Declaration of Human Rights. Its adoption was accomplished at a very early stage of the life of this Organization. It was virtually our first priority in those days. While there has been some progress in human rights since then, we still have a long way to go. There are still far too many abuses. As we mark this significant anniversary, let us restore to high priority this Organization's concern for human rights, and let us resolve that next year's General Assembly will be a high point for constructive collective action to advance this vital cause.

Next year will also provide us with a significant opportunity for progress on arms control issues. Our Special Session on Disarmament next May and June is unprecedented. Never before has the United Nations sponsored a gathering of this magnitude on this subject. Never before have we had a chance to concentrate the attention of all nations on these life-and-death questions in this way. This is no longer a concern of only the nations of the East and West: The developing countries, the nonnuclear countries—indeed all countries—have an important stake in these discussions. Let us all pledge to work within our governments to make a major effort to bring this Special Session successfully to meaningful understandings and practical ways to enhance our disarmament goals.

This session of the Assembly was another major step in the improved economic dialogue between the developing countries and the industrialized countries. As the resumed 31st session of this Assembly ended, just prior to the opening of this one, it was clear to all that a major task would be to find a mutually acceptable framework for the continuation of a high-level overview of economic cooperation within the U.N. system. The 32d General Assembly has met this challenge; let us all work for constructive discussions in the Commitee of the Whole we have agreed upon.

For the United States, expectations will be high. If the construction of a new international economic order is to be a growing consensus and not a verbal contest, each group of countries—East and West, oil producers and consumers, industrialized, industrializing, and agricultural—must explore ways in which change can be achieved consistent with economic security for all. We know each others' needs and concerns. We have learned even more about them during this Assembly. Let us get on with the work that remains to be done.

In many areas once characterized by disagreement, we have achieved consensus. In others, we have thus far failed.

One area in which more work remains to be done relates to the negotiations for a common fund under the auspices of the U.N. Conference on Trade and Development.[22] The suspension of the negotiations in Geneva took place rather late in our session; with so much else under way, it was certainly a difficult task for all of us here in New York to provide a real impetus for their constructive resumption.

Unfortunately, we were not able to reach agreement on a resolution which would have facilitated resumption of the negotiations. As you know, we worked toward a resolution in the Second Com-

---

[22]Negotiations looking toward the establishment of a common fund for commodities, initiated at Geneva in Mar. 1977 in the framework of a U.N. Negotiating Conference on a Common Fund, were suspended early in December as the result of disagreements between developed and developing countries over the proposed fund's range of operations and capital structure.

mittee last week that would have permitted the negotiations to be resumed on a constructive basis. Regrettably, it was not possible to achieve a positive nonprejudicial statement.[23] Let us, therefore, work together to find a way to minimize polemics and to conduct a balanced and dispassionate assessment of the important issues involved. We believe that such an assessment is necessary before any further progress can be made.

Let me mention one final area that merits urgent attention next year.

The budget we have just approved is nearly a 30% increase over that of the last biennium.[24] We have approved many good programs and projects. Indeed, nearly all of them are good. But the U.N.'s resources are not unlimited. I think it is fair to say we are sponsoring too many conferences, too many special interest programs, too many "private bills" of assistance in individual countries when such steps should be reserved for only the most critical cases.

I will be the first to admit that my government has not always followed a policy of fiscal restraint itself. But the need for fiscal stringency is paramount. It applies to all of us. We need to get priorities, carefully analyze all proposals, clarify our objectives, and restrain ourselves on expenditures until we have sorted out for ourselves exactly which actions are the most pressing.

A consensus resolution of this Assembly last year expressed concern about this problem and requested the assistance of the Secretary General in identifying expenditure priorities. The U.N. system budget was $124 million in 1947. It was nearly $2.5 billion in 1976. These are significant sums which we all know can—with proper programming and management—be better used. Let us commit ourselves to this task in the coming year.

In short, we have a difficult agenda before us. The problems do not vanish with the sound of the last gavel. But with the consensus of the concerned that has clearly emerged at this year's General Assembly, we have begun to search for the common elements of our own interests, to stop shouting and to do more listening.

A senior official of another government told me early in this Assembly that the United Nations seemed to be catching its "second wind." I think that is clearly true. This emerging consensus on how to work together on world issues provides us all with a source of

---

[23]General Assembly Resolution 32/193, adopted Dec. 19, 1977 by a vote of 127-0-13 (U.S.), called upon countries which had not yet done so to take the necessary political decisions to enable the Negotiating Conference to resume its work within a clearly established negotiating framework.

[24]Appropriations totaling $985,913,300 for the two-year period 1978-79 were approved by General Assembly Resolution 32/123 A, adopted Dec. 21, 1977 by a vote of 119-9-6 (U.S.).

new hope and optimism. That is good for the United Nations. It is good for the world. It is good for the people we represent.

* * *

(56) "Administration's First-Year Accomplishments": Summary of Domestic and National Security and Foreign Policy Accomplishments, Made Public by the White House December 17, 1977.[25]

(Excerpts)

SUMMARY AND OUTLINE OF FIRST-YEAR
DOMESTIC ACCOMPLISHMENTS

* * *

OUTLINE BY TOPIC OF FIRST-YEAR
DOMESTIC ACCOMPLISHMENTS

Agriculture

1. *Food and Agriculture Act*—proposed and signed into law a comprehensive food and agriculture bill[26] which removes inequities in community programs; establishes the principle that price support loans should be kept at levels enabling American food and fiber to remain competitive in world markets; uses a cost-of-production concept to set income support levels; improves administration of the P.L. 480 (Food for Peace) program; improves the food stamp program by eliminating the purchase requirement, standardizing deduction, lowering net income eligibility limits, and (because of the elimination of the purchase requirement) making as many as 2 million persons eligible for food stamps for the first time.

2. *Grain Reserve*—initiated plan to place 30–35 million metric tons of food and feed grains in reserve during the next year.

3. *International Grain Agreement*—initiated negotiations with major grain exporting and importing nations to reach an international agreement stabilizing world grain prices.

4. *Sugar*—negotiated an international sugar agreement[27] which will protect domestic sugar producers while stabilizing world sugar prices (congressional ratification pending).

[25]Text from *Presidential Documents*, 13: 1888-1904.
[26]Public Law 95-113, Sept. 29, 1977; Carter signature statement in same, 13: 1433-5.
[27]Done at Geneva Oct. 7, 1977 and signed by the U.S. Dec. 9, 1977. Not in force as of Aug. 1978.

5. *Emergency Drought Assistance*—proposed and signed into law legislation designed to help farmers hit by the severe droughts of the past spring and summer; provided over $800 million in emergency drought assistance.

* * *

Employment

* * *

8. *Undocumented Aliens*—proposed a comprehensive program to control the presence of millions of undocumented aliens in the country.[28] The program includes a prohibition against employers' hiring undocumented aliens.

* * *

Energy

1. *National Energy Plan*—proposed the Nation's first comprehensive energy policy.[29] Bills have passed both Houses of Congress and are now in conference.

2. *Emergency Natural Gas*—proposed and signed into law a bill that permitted the President to make emergency allocations of natural gas during last winter's shortage and permitted emergency purchase of unregulated gas.

3. *Department of Energy*—proposed and signed into law a bill to combine 11 Government entities into one Cabinet-level Department of Energy.

4. *Alaska Natural Gas*—negotiated an agreement with Canada concerning a joint transportation route (the ALCAN Project) for Alaskan natural gas; secured congressional approval of the route decision.

5. *Strategic Petroleum Reserve*—undertook to expand the National Strategic Petroleum Reserve from 500 million barrels to 1 billion barrels of oil, giving the country a 10-month stockpile.

6. *Nuclear Nonproliferation*—proposed legislation to control the worldwide spread of nuclear fuels by applying uniform standards for licensing of nuclear exports, establishing criteria for the negotiation of new nuclear technology exchange agreements, and authorizing regulations for more expeditious review of nuclear export licenses;[30] passed the House.

[28]Text of the President's message, Aug. 4, in *Presidential Documents*, 13: 1170-75.
[29]Document 47.
[30]Document 12.

Environment

* * *

7. *Whaling*—ordered protection of whales within 200 miles of U.S. coast; cooperated with the International Whaling Commission on bowhead whales; and supported a 10-year, worldwide moratorium on commercial whaling.

* * *

10. *Oil Spills*—proposed legislation establishing liability for oil tanker spills and leading to the development of regulations to prevent future spills.

Government Efficiency, Reorganization, and Regulatory Reform

1. *Reorganization Authority*—proposed and signed into law legislation authorizing the President to reorganize executive agencies and departments, subject to congressional veto.

2. *Reorganizations*—completed three individual reorganizations requiring congressional assent:

—Department of Energy (legislation combining and streamlining 11 Government entities into one new major department);[31]
—Executive Office of the President (reorganization plan reducing size of Executive Office of the President by seven entities and reducing the White House staff by 28 percent, compared to the size of the staff inherited from the previous administration);
—International Communication Agency (reorganization plan combining and streamlining United States Information Agency and cultural functions of the State Department);[32]
—also completed other reorganizations not requiring congressional assent, including HEW, USDA, DOT, and the intelligence functions of CIA and DOD.[33]

* * *

[31]Note 3 to Document 47.
[32]Text of the President's message on Reorganization Plan No. 2, Oct. 11, in *Presidential Documents*, 13: 1519-25 (*Bulletin*, 77: 683-5).
[33]Text of the President's announcement, Aug. 4, in *Presidential Documents*, 13: 1175-7 (*Bulletin*, 77: 306-7).

Integrity and Openness

* * *

5. *Security Classification System*—initiated a comprehensive study of the Government's security classification system; proposed reforming the system and reducing unnecessary classification in a draft Executive order which is now being circulated for public comment.

Justice

1. *Pardon*—issued pardon for all selective service law violators from the Vietnam war period.

* * *

3. *Prisoner Exchange*—supported and signed into law legislation to implement treaties permitting the exchange of prisoners with Mexico and Canada;[34] these transfers are now taking place.

* * *

6. *Foreign Intelligence Wiretapping*—developed legislation that would, for the first time, require court warrants for foreign intelligence wiretapping done by the U.S. Government; passed Senate Judiciary Committee.

* * *

Social Services

* * *

5. *Indochina Refugees*—proposed and signed into law an extension of the Indochina Refugee Assistance Act,[35] which helps the States resettle Indochinese refugees.

* * *

Trade

1. *Color TV's*—negotiated an orderly marketing agreement to

[34]Public Law 95-144, Oct. 28; Carter signature statement in *Presidential Documents*, 13: 1673-4.
[35]Public Law 95-145, Oct. 28; Carter signature statement in same: 1672.

reduce imports of color television sets from Japan from 2.7 million in 1976 to 1.75 million annually for the next 3 years, a 35-percent reduction.[36]

2. *Shoes*—negotiated an orderly marketing agreement to reduce imports of shoes from Taiwan and South Korea from 200 million pairs in 1976 to an average of 162 million pairs during the next 4 years.[37]

3. *Anti-Boycott*—helped to develop and signed into law a bill[38] prohibiting American participation in secondary economic boycotts by foreign countries such as the Arab boycott of Israel.

4. *Steel*—announced a comprehensive program to help the domestic steel industry by establishing a "reference price system," which will curb the dumping of under-priced, imported steel.[39]

Transportation

1. *U.S.-U.K. Air Agreement*—negotiated a new air services agreement with the United Kingdom.

* * *

4. *Concorde Noise Rules*—proposed the first noise rules to govern domestic flights of the Concorde SST and any future SST's. The proposed rules would permit Concordes to use domestic airports only if they meet reasonable, nondiscriminatory noise rules set by local airport operators. New SST's would be required to meet the 1969 subsonic noise standards.

* * *

7. *International Airfares*—approved Laker Airways' application for low-cost, transatlantic service and subsequent applications from other airlines offering reduced transatlantic and advance- purchase fares.

* * *

Veterans

1. *Discharge Review*—established a discharge review program to permit upgrading of less-than-honorable discharges for Vietnam era veterans; signed a bill expanding this principle to cover all veterans.

* * *

[36]Cf. Introduction at note 157.
[37]*Presidential Documents*, 13: 908.
[38]Cf. Introduction at note 59.
[39]Cf. Introduction following note 170.

Miscellaneous

To date (12/15/77), the President has:

—sent 49 treaties and legislative messages to Congress
—signed 235 bills and allowed no bills to become law without his signature
—vetoed two bills (the ERDA authorization bill and the rabbit meat inspection bill)
—held 27 bill signing ceremonies
—held 21 national press conferences
—given 16 interviews to groups of non-Washington reporters
—given 28 individual interviews
—held 60 meetings with foreign heads of state or government
—hosted 17 state and working dinners at the White House
—received 2.3 million letters and cards.

SUMMARY OF FIRST-YEAR ACCOMPLISHMENTS IN NATIONAL SECURITY AND FOREIGN POLICY

In his commencement address at the University of Notre Dame on May 22,[40] the President outlined the objectives of his foreign policy and described "the strands that connect our actions overseas with our essential character as a nation."

He declared his belief that "we can have a foreign policy that is democratic, that is based on fundamental values, and that uses power and influence . . . for humane purposes. We can also have a foreign policy that the American people both support . . . and understand . . .

"Our policy must be open; it must be candid; it must be one of constructive global involvement, resting on five cardinal principles . . .

"First, we have reaffirmed America's commitment to human rights as a fundamental tenet of our foreign policy . . .

"Second, we have moved deliberately to reinforce the bonds among . . . democracies . . .

"Third, we have moved to engage the Soviet Union in a joint effort to halt the strategic arms race . . .

"Fourth, we are taking deliberate steps to improve the chances of lasting peace in the Middle East . . .

"And fifth, we are attempting . . . to reduce the danger of nuclear proliferation and the worldwide spread of conventional weapons . . ."

The administration, by its work in international affairs this year,

[40]Document 5.

has sought to carry out the objectives which the President set forth at Notre Dame. Among the principal accomplishments in the realm of foreign policy and national security are these:

HUMAN RIGHTS

The President has strengthened our human rights policy, and we are letting it be known clearly that the United States stands with the victims of represssion. We are also working to advance the full range of human rights, economic and social as well as civil and political. He has signed the American Convention on Human Rights, the International Covenant on Economic, Social, and Cultural Rights. Our foreign assistance programs will reflect more clearly our human rights concerns. We have encouraged several countries to permit inspection visits from the International Committee of the Red Cross. We are strongly supporting international organizations concerned with human rights, particularly the Inter-American Commission on Human Rights, whose budget was tripled this year.

NUCLEAR PROLIFERATION

The administration has developed a comprehensive policy covering domestic and export activities and has initiated an international, technical evaluation of the entire nuclear fuel cycle. The President signed Protocol I of the Treaty of Tlatelolco, which creates a nuclear weapons-free zone in Latin America.

ARMS TRANSFERS

For the first time, the United States has adopted a policy of restraining both the number and the kinds of American arms sold abroad. We have also begun to discuss restraint with other major arms suppliers.

STRATEGIC ARMS LIMITATION TALKS

At the end of the last administration, the SALT negotiations were at a stalemate. The efforts of this administration, beginning with the March proposal set forth by Secretary Vance in Moscow, have resulted in major progress in the SALT negotiations. We are now working on a comprehensive settlement consisting of a treaty to last through 1985, a 3-year protocol, and a Statement of Principles to guide the SALT III negotiations. Almost all the major issues are now resolved, and we anticipate completion of a SALT III treaty in the early part of next year.

PANAMA CANAL TREATIES

After 14 years of negotiations under four U.S. Presidents, the United States and Panama adjusted their relationship as it applies to the Panama Canal. President Carter and General Omar Torrijos signed two canal treaties on September 9 [7], 1977 which would gradually transfer responsibility for the operation and defense of a neutral canal to Panama. The treaties give the United States the permanent right to defend the Canal's neutrality.

COMPREHENSIVE TEST BAN

Negotiations are underway on a treaty banning all nuclear explosions.

NORTH-SOUTH RELATIONS

The United States image in the less-developed world and the United Nations has changed dramatically from that of an adversary to that of a potential partner. In the Security Council debate on Africa, we played a mediating role. Our arms control policies have made a favorable impression on the United Nations' annual review of disarmament issues. We played a constructive role in the Maputo and Lagos conferences. And we participated, for the first time, in an ASEAN (Association of Southeast Asian Nations) ministerial meeting. The appointment of Ambassador Andrew Young highlighted our concern for the Third World.

WESTERN EUROPE

The administration has: participated in a successful Belgrade CSCE conference (Commission [Conference] on Security and Cooperation in Europe), including a review of human rights; prepared another MBFR (mutual and balanced force reductions) proposal to advance talks; inaugurated four NATO efforts (the long-term defense program; the short-term improvements; the "two-way street" in defense purchases; the East-West study); agreed to provide a $300-million loan and forged a multination consortium to help democracy in Portugal; and secured a major IMF loan for Italy.

SOVIET UNION-EASTERN EUROPE

The administration has put the U.S.-Soviet relationship on a more reciprocal, realistic, and what we hope will be an ultimately more productive basis for both nations. The administration has improved relations with various Eastern European countries, including Yugoslavia, as a result of the Vice President's visit, and Poland, as a result of Secretary [of Commerce Juanita] Kreps' visit and the President's scheduled state visit.

ARAB-ISRAELI CONFLICT

The administration stressed the need for a comprehensive settlement which has three core elements: definition of the nature of the peace, establishment of recognized borders and security, and resolution of the Palestinian question. We have urged, with considerable success, the Arabs and the Israelis to be forthcoming on peace commitments, direct negotiations, and peace treaties. We have supported the Sadat-Begin dialog.

PEOPLE'S REPUBLIC OF CHINA

The administration has followed the Shanghai Communique in efforts toward normalization of relations, while emphasizing the mutuality of efforts necessary to complete the process. Recognizing their strategic importance, we have also continued to develop a consultative relationship with the Chinese on global affairs.

KOREA

The details of the Korean ground troop withdrawal plan have been designed to alleviate major Asian apprehensions that the United States is in the process of disengaging from the region.

VIETNAM

The administration has started the process of normalizing relations through talks in Paris and has established a mechanism to continue to try to account for our servicemen still missing in action.

AFRICA

Vice President Mondale informed Prime Minister Vorster in Vienna that U.S.-South Africa relations depended upon South Africa moving away from apartheid. With the British, we offered a plan for Rhodesian independence. We initiated a Five Power Group to negotiate toward an independent Namibia. We have restored good relations, based on mutual respect, with black African states of all political leanings.

LATIN AMERICA

The administration has developed a new global approach to Latin America and the Caribbean, one which recognizes the diversity of the region rather than one which pretends a single policy identified by a simple slogan. (This approach has been well-received in the region.) The President signed the Panama Canal treaties. Through direct negotiations with Cuba, we have concluded a fisheries agreement and established an interest section in each country. We have ratified an exchange of prisoners treaty with Mexico and negotiated one with Bolivia. We have adopted a comprehensive policy for the Caribbean and have been joined by 28 nations and 16 international institutions to establish a Caribbean Group for Cooperation in Economic Development. We have dramatically improved our relations with a number of countries, including Venezuela, Jamaica, Peru, and Mexico.

LONDON SUMMIT

With the leaders of major industrial democracies, the President reached agreement at the London Summit on a common program for international economic cooperation.

MULTILATERAL TRADE NEGOTIATIONS

The administration has reached agreement with the European Economic Community on a timetable for negotiations, breaking a long stalemate.

DEFENSE AND SECURITY

The administration has formulated a comprehensive, national defense strategy which includes an overall American posture toward the Soviet Union. The President reached a decision not to produce the B-1 bomber but to proceed with cruise missiles.

INTELLIGENCE

The administration has reorganized the intelligence agencies and has taken comprehensive steps to protect telecommunications.

INTERNATIONAL COMMUNICATIONS

The administration has established a new International Communication Agency to replace the United States Information Agency and the Bureau of Educational and Cultural Affairs in the Department of State.

DEFENSE BUDGET REDUCTION

The President met his campaign pledge to cut military spending by $5 to $7 billion. The Ford budget for fiscal year 1978 was $123 billion. The Carter budget is $117 billion, as approved by Congress.

(57) "Conversation with the President": Remarks by President Carter in an Interview with Network Television Correspondents, December 28, 1977.[41]

(Excerpts)

THE PRESIDENT. This year we have had fireside chats and television programs and telephone call-in shows and press conferences twice a month and meetings with editors from almost every State in the Nation. And I've been very pleased to stay in touch with the American people.

Tonight we have four distinguished news reporters from the four major networks in our country. And I want to welcome you here as another opportunity for me to speak to the American people with tough interrogations from those who understand our country very well.

I understand Mr. Brokaw has the first question.

THE PRESIDENT'S OVERSEAS TRIP

MR. BROKAW. Mr. President, there are a number of subjects that we want to cover tonight, including some news developments

---

[41]Text from *Presidential Documents*, 13: 1941-56. The interview was conducted by Tom Brokaw, NBC News; Bob Schieffer, CBS News; Robert MacNeil, Public Broadcasting Service: and Barbara Walters, ABC News.

that are going on even as we speak. I want to begin, however, with a question about the trip that you leave on tomorrow. It was originally postponed because you did not yet have the energy bill passed. It still has not been passed.

My question is this: Aren't you playing into the twin themes of your critics who complain that your energy bill has not been passed, that you have failed on the major domestic priority of your administration, and that your foreign policy has no real definition, because this trip seems to have no urgent theme to it?

THE PRESIDENT. Well, the only major legislation that did not pass the Congress this year and which I was expecting to pass, was energy. Speaker of the House Tip [Thomas P.] O'Neill said that it was the most productive session since the first term of Franklin Roosevelt. I'll let him be the judge of that.

The energy legislation, I think, will be the first item on the agenda when the Congress reconvenes in January. And there's no doubt that wherever I go on this trip—to Eastern Europe, to Western Europe, to the Mideast, to India—what our Nation does about energy will be a prime question.

We are the leader of the world. We are one of the major oil producers. We are the greatest consumer. And until Congress does take action on the energy proposal that I put forward last April, and which the House of Representatives passed in August, that cloud will hang over the determination and leadership qualities of our country.

So, I am disappointed about that. As far as the trip is concerned, it's carefully planned. We began working on this trip last March, and the nations that we will visit are important to us both domestically and in our foreign relations.

Poland—in Eastern Europe, a Communist government with close ties to the Soviet Union but also friendships with us, heavy trade with the Western nations, relatively willing to give people their religious freedom and other freedoms. We will have a good meeting, I think, in Poland.

We go from there to Iran, very close military ally of ours, a strong trade partner of ours with whom we share many political responsibilities.

And then we go to India, the biggest democracy in the world, one that in recent years has turned perhaps excessively toward the Soviet Union, but under the new leadership of Prime Minister Desai is moving back toward us and assuming a good role of, I would say, neutrality. And we have a strong friendship with India. It's a strong country. They are almost self-sufficient now. They have food surpluses.

We come back from there to Saudi Arabia, our major supplier of imported oil, a nation that's worked closely with us in foreign affairs in many parts of the world.

From there back to France, our historic ally, keystone in Europe. I'll have long discussions with President Giscard there and then go back to Brussels to strengthen our relationships with the European Community and with NATO.

So, every stop will be productive for us. I'll be taking the word and the good will and the sense of importance of the American people toward them in learning about those countries in the process.

But energy will be the tie that will bind us together on this trip, and I hope that this will demonstrate to the American people and to the Congress the necessity for rapid action on one of the most controversial and divisive issues that the Congress has ever faced, and that is to give our country for the first time a comprehensive energy policy.

THE MIDDLE EAST

MR. SCHIEFFER. Mr. President, I know we'll all want to get back to just how you plan to go about getting that energy policy. But while we are on foreign policy, I'd like to ask you about the Middle East. President Sadat, I think everyone agrees, made a spectacular gesture that opened up a whole new era here. Do you feel that the Israelis have as yet made a comparable gesture? Have they been flexible enough in your view?

THE PRESIDENT. Both President Sadat and Prime Minister Begin have been bold and courageous. We've been dealing with the Mideast question as a nation for decades, in a leadership role at least within the last two administrations. And we see the complexities of the questions and the obstacles to progress. When I first became President, we spelled out the basic issues: withdrawal from occupied territories, secure borders, the establishment of real peace, the recognition of Israel's right to be there, and dealing with the Palestinian question.

We are now in a role of supporter. We encourage them to continue with their fruitful negotiations. We try to resolve difficulties to give advice and counsel when we are requested to do it. This is a better role for us. In the past, we've been in the unenviable position and sometimes unpleasant position, sometimes nonproductive position as mediator among parties who wouldn't even speak to each other. So, I think that the progress that has been made in the last month and a half has been remarkable and has been much greater than I had anticipated.

And I know Sadat and Begin well and personally and favorably. If any two leaders on earth have the strength and the determination and the courage to make progress toward peace in the most difficult region that I've ever known, it is Prime Minister Begin and

President Sadat. There is no reason for us to be discouraged about it. We will help in every way we can to let their progress be fruitful. I think that President Sadat and Prime Minister Begin could have reached a fairly quick solution of just the Egyptian-Israeli problem in the Sinai region. But this is not what they want.

They both want to try to resolve the other questions: What is real peace? Will Israel be recognized as a permanent neighbor to the countries that surround them? Can the Palestinian question, the West Bank, the Gaza Strip be addressed successfully? And knowing how difficult these questions are, I have nothing but admiration for them, nothing but congratulations for them on what they have achieved so far.

MR. MACNEIL. Mr. President, you are going to see King Hussein of Jordan in Tehran. President Sadat said in an interview that was broadcast on public television last night that King Hussein had told him that he was fully behind his efforts. In public until now, King Hussein's opinion has been relatively mysterious. Do you have any information that would make you agree with Mr. Sadat, and are you going to discuss that with King Hussein and urge him to support the Sadat initiative when you see him?

THE PRESIDENT. I don't intend to put any pressure on King Hussein—I couldn't if I wanted to—to immediately begin to negotiate with Israel and Egypt as a partner. If he wants to do it, we would certainly welcome that. What I will try to learn, however, is what role Jordan is willing to play in the resolution of the Palestinian-West Bank problem, at what point he thinks it would be advisable for him to enter the negotiations personally as a government leader, and what we can do to get him to give his open support and encouragement to both Begin and Sadat as they struggle to resolve the differences between them.

I think King Hussein has indeed in his private discussions with Secretary Vance and his personal communications to me, shown a very positive attitude. And in his travels around the Middle East to visit with other leaders, some who don't encourage the talks, like President Asad, those who are very hopeful for progress, like those in Saudi Arabia, I think he's shown a constructive attitude already. But it helps me to understand on a current basis the remaining problems and in what way they can be brought in to achieve a comprehensive peace.

I think they all trust our country. Our motives are good. We've never misled them. We've been honest and as a person, as a country that carried messages from one to another. And I think that this puts us in a position to exert legitimate influence. But what we've always hoped for is direct negotiations or discussions, communications among the leaders involved with our offering good offices when we are requested to do it.

MS. WALTERS. Mr. President, the chief stumbling block right now does seem to be what we might call the right of return of the Palestinians to the West Bank and the Gaza. You have in the past come out against an independent nation per se on the West Bank, but you have also talked of the legitimate rights of the Palestinians, and you have been in favor of some kind of an entity—although people are still a little obscure about what that means—an entity perhaps linked to Jordan.

Would you, in the light of the developments now, clarify your views for us today, tell us if they have changed, and if they have not, is it because the United States has decided to be neutral on this subject?

THE PRESIDENT. Well, you've described my position very well. We do favor a homeland or an entity wherein the Palestinians can live in peace. I think Prime Minister Begin has taken a long step forward in offering to President Sadat, and indirectly to the Palestinians, self-rule.

President Sadat so far is insisting that the so-called Palestinian entity be an independent nation. My own preference is that they not be an independent nation but be tied in some way with the surrounding countries, making a choice, for instance, between Israel and Jordan.

President Sadat has not yet agreed to that position of ours. Prime Minister Begin has offered that the citizens who live in the West Bank area or the Gaza Strip be given an option to be either Israeli citizens or Jordanian citizens, to actually run for the Knesset as candidates and to vote in elections, both national, Israeli and Jordan, or local elections in the occupied territories once they are released.

But we don't have any real choice. I've expressed an opinion. But if Israel should negotiate with the surrounding countries a different solution, we would certainly support it.

But my own personal opinion is that permanent peace can best be maintained if there's not a fairly radical, new independent nation in the heart of the Middle Eastern area.

MS. WALTERS. In view of the deadlock now, however, have you tried to convince either side of your opinion? You've had conversations with both.

THE PRESIDENT. I've expressed this opinion to President Asad, to King Hussein, to President Sadat, to Crown Prince Fahd, and also to Prime Minister Begin, privately. And, of course, they have heard my statements publicly. Our preference is not to have an independent nation there, but we are perfectly willing to accept any reasonable solution that the parties themselves might evolve.

MR. SCHIEFFER. If I could just get back to the question I asked you, do I take it that you would not pass judgment in public, at least at this point, on whether the Israelis have been flexible enough in the negotiating so far? Do you think that the position that they put forward—Mr. Begin said today that there would always be Israeli troops on the West Bank and that all who wanted peace would have to know that—is that a realistic negotiating position?

THE PRESIDENT. Yes. It's certainly a realistic negotiating position.

MR. SCHIEFFER. But would Mr. Sadat ever accept that?

THE PRESIDENT. I don't know. There is a great deal of flexibility there—the number of military outposts, the length of time when this interim solution might be in effect—I think Prime Minister Begin said it would be reassessed at the end of five years—the degree of participation of the governments of Israel and Jordan in a possible administrative arrangement—all these questions could add a tone of progress or a possibility for resolution of what seems to be insurmountable obstacles.

So, I think that Prime Minister Begin already has shown a great deal of flexibility. Obviously, President Sadat and King Hussein and others would have to accept whatever proposal is put forward.

But the length of time when the interim agreement would be in effect would be negotiable and the exact relationship between the new self-rule government as far as its autonomy is concerned, its dependence upon or subservience to the Jordanians or the Israelis—all these things are still to be negotiated. So, I think there is enough flexibility at this point.

MR. MACNEIL. Could I just ask one followup on that?

THE PRESIDENT. Please.

MR. MACNEIL. Has either Egypt or Israel, or both, asked the United States formally yet to provide guarantees for any agreement that is made?

THE PRESIDENT. Well, in my private conversations with some of them, they have expressed to me that if a guarantee arrangement between ourselves and Israel should be worked out, that it would be acceptable to the Arab leaders. But we've never discussed this between ourselves and Israel in any definitive form.

My preference would be that our involvement would be minimized after an agreement has been reached. But if it became a matter of having the negotiations break down completely, our having some limited role as mutually accepted among those parties involved, then we would consider it very, very favorably.

STRATEGIC ARMS LIMITATION TALKS

MR. BROKAW. Mr. President, if we may move along in another area of foreign policy for just a moment, there now seems to be some signals coming out of Geneva, and even from friends of this administration, that we will not have a SALT agreement in 1978, or at least one will not get before the Senate. That's the word from Senator Alan Cranston,[42] who is known as a very good vote counter in the Senate. Is that your thinking as well, that we are not going to have a SALT agreement with the Russians during this next year?

THE PRESIDENT. I would be disappointed if we don't have a SALT agreement this year. We've made good progress on SALT. We started out with SALT I, the Soviets having a very heavy advantage, about a three to two ratio in their favor. President Ford and Secretary Kissinger made great progress, I think, at Vladivostok and in their subsequent negotiations, to provide the first indication of equality. And we will maintain that posture of mutual advantage between ourselves and the Soviets.

We have added a new dimension, to have tight constraints on future deployment of weapons, both quantitatively and also the quality of the weapons, and to reduce actually the number of destructive weapons permitted.

We still have some negotiating to do. But we have made good progress on SALT. We have also been pleased with the results of negotiations with the Soviet Union on the comprehensive test ban to prohibit any testing of nuclear weapons at all.

And we have made progress, also, in trying to stop a military buildup in the Indian Ocean. My guess is that President Brezhnev would be likely to want to come here to visit after those three negotiations have made some substantial progress and when there is a prospect of immediate resolution of the remaining differences.

I would never approve a SALT agreement nor present one to the Congress that didn't have an adequate degree of verification of compliance and which didn't protect the right of our own country to defend itself and to carry out our domestic and foreign policy. Whatever I put forward to the Congress will be good for our Nation.

We've had a maximum degree of involvement by the Congress. We've even had Senators in Europe at the negotiating table. And we've kept them informed as the progress is made.

---

[42]Democrat from California.

So, my guess is that 1978 will see us successful, and my guess is that when we present it to the Congress, the SALT agreement will be approved.

* * *

ADMINISTRATION PRIORITIES; PANAMA CANAL TREATY

MS. WALTERS. Mr. President, it is reported that Vice President Mondale, with you, of course, is working on a list of your top priorities for next year with the feeling perhaps that you had too many top priorities this year to give to Congress. Can you tell us what the top two or three priorities would be, and can you tell us if it would include a national health insurance program, which organized labor feels you promised to introduce this year?

THE PRESIDENT. Yes, I intend to introduce a national health program to the Congress this year, late in this session. They can't pass it this year, but it will be introduced.

Dealing with the economy, which we've just discussed, would be a top priority. Completing work on the energy package would be the first specific thing that we'll do. One of the most important is to resolve the Panama Canal Treaty question.

About 75 years ago in the middle of the night the American Secretary of State signed the Panama Canal Treaty that presently is in existence. No Panamanian has ever signed it; no Panamanian ever saw it before it was signed. It was signed by a Frenchman who benefited financially from the terms of the treaty on behalf of the Panamanians.

That treaty gave us a chance to do a tremendous job in building the Panama Canal, keeping it open for international shipping. It's helped our country a lot. It's something of which we can be proud.

Presidents Eisenhower and Kennedy recognized that the present treaty was inadequate. President Johnson started negotiations to change it. Presidents Nixon and Ford continued. And we concluded it this year.

It's one of the most difficult political questions that we'll have to deal with. It's going to take a lot of time in the Congress to pass it.

What we wanted was one that treated us and Panama fairly, and we got it. We wanted a treaty that did not put a financial burden on the American taxpayer, and we got it. We wanted treaties that would guarantee proper operation of the Panama Canal itself, for us and for foreign shipping, and we got it. We wanted treaties that would also guarantee us permanently the right to take what action we think necessary to keep the canal safe, to defend it, and to keep it open for us to use, and we got it.

We wanted treaties—two treaties there are—that would give us the right for expeditious passage in time of need or emergency, for our ships to go to the head of the line and go through the canal without delay, and we got it. We wanted treaties also that would be acceptable in the eyes of the international community, particularly in Latin America, and we got them.

So, this is what we have tried to do under four Presidents, and we have finally succeeded. And I would say that would be one of the most difficult challenges that we have politically this year. It is absolutely crucial that the Senate ratify these treaties, and I think the terms are very favorable to us and to Panama.

MR. BROKAW. You've got all that in the treaty, Mr. President. Do you have the votes in the Senate?

THE PRESIDENT. I think we will get the votes in the Senate.

MR. BROKAW. Do you not now have them?

THE PRESIDENT. I can't say for sure that we do because many Senators still haven't expressed their commitment to me or their opinion. But I was talking to President Ford this past week, who's strongly supportive of the treaties, along with Secretary Kissinger and others, and he said that in his speeches to college groups and others around the Nation, that he is getting an increasingly favorable response from the audience. I think public opinion is building up for the treaties as they know the terms of them.

MR. MACNEIL. Could we interpret this as the beginning of a new campaign on your part to get out and sell the treaty? You've been criticized for having left the ground to the opposition somewhat. Are you going to make a major effort personally to try and sell it?

THE PRESIDENT. Yes. I consider it one of my most important responsibilities.

MR. MACNEIL. And can you meet the deadline that President Torrijos has set of April, which he says is urgent, and that Panama's patience could be exhausted.

THE PRESIDENT. Well, no, I don't feel any constraint to operate under a deadline. But both Senator Byrd and I and the leaders of the Senate all hope that we can resolve that issue early in the year, certainly I think by April.

MS. WALTERS. On that—since, by the way, just to get back to my original questions—it seems that your priorities next year are very similar to your priorities this year, energy and the economy. But in October, you and President Torrijos issued a statement[43]—a joint statement to remove the doubts about the rights of the United States to defend the neutrality of the canal and also the right of ships to pass promptly through it. A number of Senators have felt

[43]Document 39b.

that they might be more comfortable with this if it were actually written into the treaty.

Would you be willing to see the treaty amended so that it would reflect this understanding, this statement between you and General Torrijos?

THE PRESIDENT. No. I think it would be good to have a signed agreement between me and President Torrijos, and he has indicated he would be glad to sign that statement that was made, and of course, I would too. I think the Senate could express an understanding that the treaty was being approved by them with the understanding that this was a proper interpretation. But to actually amend the treaty would require Panama to have another referendum on the subject, and they've already had one.

Many people in Panama think that the treaties are too favorable to the United States. And I don't think it would be fair to them after they negotiated in good faith to cause them to have a completely new referendum. I would certainly hate to have two ratification votes in the Senate, separated by several months. So, I think that the Senate can very well express its understanding of what the treaties mean. We can exchange documents with the Panamanian leader. To amend the treaties, though, I think would be inadvisable.

* * *

CRITICISM OF THE PRESIDENT

MS. WALTERS. Mr. President, it's almost the end of your first year in office, and it's almost New Year's Eve, and that's the time for people to take stock, and maybe when they take stock, they are a little more critical than they should be. However, I would like to give you a list of people who currently say that they are unhappy about you.

Labor is unhappy because they say that you are dragging your feet on the medical insurance bill and on full employment. Business has said it's unhappy; they just don't have confidence in you. The blacks are unhappy again because of full employment and the lack of it and what Robin [MacNeil] just brought out, and I talked with Vernon Jordan,[44] who had expressed his unhappiness with you last July and still feels the same way, he says. Many women are unhappy because of your stand on Federal aid to abortion, and there aren't enough women appointed to administrative posts. Striking farmers are rolling up their tractors in Plains. [*Laughter*] Who is your constituency, or to put it another way, who's happy?

[44]Executive Director of the National Association for the Advancement of Colored People.

THE PRESIDENT. Well, Barbara, I think this is inherent and almost inevitable in a free nation like ours. The news media legitimately reports the disharmony and the arguments and the debates because they are more exciting than the achievements.

It's good for us to remember at the end of this year that we live in the strongest nation on Earth—militarily the strongest, economically the strongest, politically the strongest—a nation that is a leader worldwide, that's trusted, that's making progress, dealing with the developing nations, the Western European nations, Latin America, making progress toward controlling atomic weapons.

Domestically God has blessed us with tremendous natural resources, a free enterprise system that lets people benefit from their own contributions, their own initiative.

We have so much in common. We are a nation of highly diverse people, different people, but we are one people, and we've come from almost nothing 200 years ago to this position of sustained leadership and prosperity. The standard of living in our country for even the poorest person far exceeds the average living standard in many nations of the world. We are unselfish. And I think the threat to our country is that we might, in grasping for advantage or in emphasizing differences, lose that sense of common commitment and common purpose and a common future that binds us together and makes us great.

I don't have any fear about the future. I think that when I make mistakes or when the Congress makes mistakes or when we delay in solving apparently insoluble questions, our country is so strong and so vital and the people are bound together so closely that we can prevail in any case.

And I think the expressions of dissatisfaction, although they are legitimate in many instances, are overemphasized. I think our country is much greater than that.

* * *

REFLECTIONS ON FIRST YEAR IN OFFICE

MR. SCHIEFFER. Mr. President, speaking of Abraham Lincoln, Abraham Lincoln said just toward the end of his Presidency, he said, "I must confess that events have controlled me rather than the other way around." I wonder, looking back over your first year, how do you feel about this first year?

THE PRESIDENT. I feel good about it. It's been an exciting and stimulating and challenging and sometimes frustrating experience for me.

MR. SCHIEFFER. Were you controlled by events?

THE PRESIDENT. I think—yes, I think so. I've tried to represent what the American people want me to be and what they are. I noticed one of the news commentators the other night said that when I said during the campaign that I wanted a government as good as the American people are, that it was demagoguery.

I don't think that's accurate. You know, the American people are good and decent and idealistic. And I think they want their Government to be good and decent and idealistic.

One of the most popular things that I've tried to do is to express to the world our own people's commitment to basic human rights, to freedom and independence and autonomy, the worth of a human being, whether they live here or in Russia or in South America or in Uganda or China. And I doubt that there's a national leader in the world now who doesn't think about human rights every day and how his or her actions are measured against a standard that the world is beginning to demand.

So, I think what I've tried to do is to see what is good in our Nation, in our people, in our past, and try to preserve it and to deal with changing events to the best of my ability. I've got a good Cabinet. I've had good cooperation and support from the Congress, who recognized my newness in Washington. And overall, although I see great problems ahead of us, I feel confident.

I got my staff—the National Security Council—today to give me an analysis of the world situation as it was a year ago, and the comparison doesn't look bad. I think we are trusted now where we weren't before, say in Africa, primarily because of the influence of Andrew Young. I believe that our intentions are recognized as being good. So, in all I think it's been a good year for us.

* * *

MS. WALTERS. Mr. President, can you tell us what you think has been your greatest single achievement this past year and also, even though we hear that you don't have sleepless nights—everyone makes mistakes—what you think your biggest mistake has been?

THE PRESIDENT. I think my biggest mistake has been in inadvertently building up expectations too high. I underestimated the difficulty and the time required for Congress to take actions on controversial measures. It's much easier for me to study and evolve and present legislation to the Congress than it is for them to pass it in its final form. And I've dashed some hopes and disappointed people that thought we might act quicker.

I think that the achievements are not measured in how many bills were passed and how many bills I've signed or even my harmony with the Congress. If I have achieved anything, it's been to restore a tone to our Nation's life and attitude that most accurately exemplifies what we stand for. I use the human rights issue as one example. It gratifies me to know that the nations of Africa now look to us with friendship and with trust, whereas, just a short time ago, they wouldn't permit our Secretary of State to come in their country.

It gratifies me to see a burgeoning friendship with Latin American nations and to see our NATO allies now recommitting themselves to strong military commitments. And it gratifies me to see some progress being made in relieving tensions between ourselves and the Soviet Union. We are making slow, steady progress. We are attempting many things simultaneously. Sometimes they get confusing because they are so voluminous and there are so many of them.

But I think having our Nation and its Government represent more accurately the hopes and dreams of the American people is a general accomplishment of which I am most proud.

* * *

APPENDIX:
SELECTED HISTORICAL DOCUMENTS
1945-1976

1945

Charter of the United Nations, opened for signature at San Francisco June 26, 1945 and entered into force Oct. 24, 1945 (TS 993; 59 Stat. 1031).

The IMF Articles of Agreement: Articles of Agreement of the International Monetary Fund, opened for signature at Washington Dec. 27, 1945 and entered into force on the same day (TIAS 1501; 60 Stat. 1401).

1947

The Rio Treaty: Inter-American Treaty of Reciprocal Assistance, opened for signature at Rio de Janeiro Sept. 24, 1947 and entered into force Dec. 3, 1948 (TIAS 1838; 62 Stat. 1681); text in *Documents, 1947:* 534-40.

1948

The OAS Charter: Charter of the Organization of American States, signed at Bogotá Apr. 30, 1948 and entered into force Dec. 13, 1951 (TIAS 2361; 2 UST 2394); text in *Documents, 1948:* 484-502.

The Genocide Convention: Convention on the Prevention and Punishment of the Crime of Genocide, done at Paris Dec. 9, 1948 and entered into force Jan. 12, 1951 (not in force for the U.S.); text in *Documents, 1948:* 435-8.

The Universal Declaration of Human Rights: U.N. General Assembly Resolution 217 A (III), adopted in Paris Dec. 10, 1948; text in *Documents, 1948:* 430-35.

1949

The North Atlantic Treaty, signed at Washington Apr. 4, 1949 and entered into force Aug. 24, 1949 (TIAS 1964; 63 Stat. 2241); text in *Documents, 1949:* 612-15.

The Geneva Conventions: Convention for the Amelioration of the Condition of the Wounded and Sick in Armed Forces in the Field; Convention for the Amelioration of the Condition of the Wounded, Sick and Shipwrecked Members of the Armed Forces at Sea; Convention Relative to the Treatment of Prisoners of War; Convention Relative to the Protection of Civilian Persons in Time of War; done (dated) at Geneva Aug. 12, 1949 and entered into force for the U.S. Feb. 2, 1956 (TIAS 3362, 3363, 3364, and 3365; 6 UST 3114, 3217, 3316, and 3515).

1951

The ANZUS Treaty: Tripartite Security Treaty between the Governments of Australia, New Zealand, and the United States, signed at San Francisco Sept. 1, 1951 and entered into force Apr. 29, 1952 (TIAS 2493; 3 UST 3420); text in *Documents, 1951:* 263-5.

1953

The Korean Armistice: Agreement Concerning a Military Armistice in Korea, signed at Panmunjom and entered into force July 27, 1953 (TIAS 2782; 4 UST 234); partial text in *Documents, 1953:* 289-97.

The U.S.-Korean Treaty: Mutual Defense Treaty between the U.S. and the Republic of Korea, signed at Washington Oct. 1, 1953 and entered into force Nov. 17, 1954 (TIAS 3097; 5 UST 2368); text in *Documents, 1953:* 312-13.

1954

Public Law 480: Agricultural Trade Development and Assistance Act of 1954, approved July 10, 1954 (Public Law 480, 83rd Cong.).

The Manila Pact: South-East Asia Collective Defense Treaty, signed in Manila Sept. 8, 1954 and entered into force Feb. 19, 1955 (TIAS 3170; 6 UST 81); text in *Documents, 1954:* 319-23.

1959

The Antarctic Treaty, signed at Washington Dec. 1, 1959 and entered into force June 23, 1961 (TIAS 4790; 12 UST 794); text in *Documents, 1959:* 528-35.

1960

The U.S.-Japan Security Treaty: Treaty of Mutual Cooperation and Security between the U.S. and Japan, signed at Washington Jan. 19, 1960 and entered into force June 23, 1960 (TIAS 4509; 11 UST 1632); text in *Documents, 1960:* 425-31.

1963

The "Hot Line" Agreement: U.S.-Soviet Memorandum of Understanding Regarding the Establishment of a Direct Communications Link, signed at Geneva and entered into force June 20, 1963 (TIAS 5362; 14 UST 1825); text in *Documents, 1963:* 115-16.

The Nuclear Test Ban Treaty: Treaty Banning Nuclear Weapon Tests in the Atmosphere, in Outer Space and Under Water, signed in Moscow Aug. 5, 1963 and entered into force Oct. 10, 1963 (TIAS 5433; 14 UST 1313); text in *Documents, 1963:* 130-32.

The Tokyo Convention: Convention on Offenses and Certain Other Acts Committed on Board Aircraft, done at Tokyo Sept. 14, 1963 and entered into force Dec. 4, 1969 (TIAS 6768; 20 UST 2941).

International Covenant on the Elimination of All Forms of Racial Discrimination, adopted by U.N. General Assembly Resolution 2106 A (XX) of Dec. 21, 1965 and signed by U.S. Sept. 28, 1966 but not in force for the U.S. as of 1978; text in *Documents, 1966:* 399-412.

1966

International Covenant on Economic, Social and Cultural Rights, adopted by U.N. General Assembly Resolution 2202 A (XXI) of Dec. 16, 1966 and entered into force Jan. 3, 1976; signed by the U.S. Oct. 5, 1977 but not in force for the U.S. as of 1978.

International Covenant on Civil and Political Rights, adopted by U.N. General Assembly Resolution 2202 A (XXI) of Dec. 16, 1966 and entered into force Mar. 23, 1976; signed by U.S. Oct. 5, 1977 but not in force for the U.S. as of 1978.

1967

The Outer Space Treaty: Treaty on Principles Governing the Activities of States in the Exploration and Use of Outer Space, Including the Moon and Other Celestial Bodies, signed Jan. 27, 1967 and entered into force Oct. 10, 1967 (TIAS 6347; 18 UST 2410); text in *Documents, 1966:* 391-8.

The Treaty of Tlatelolco: Treaty for the Prohibition of Nuclear Weapons in Latin America, opened for signature at Mexico City Feb. 14, 1967 and entered into force Apr. 22, 1968 (text in U.S. Arms Control and Disarmament Agency, *Documents on Disarmament, 1967:* 69-83).

Additional Protocol I: Done at Mexico City Feb. 14, 1967 and signed by U.S. May 26, 1977, but not in force for the U.S. as of 1978; text in *AFR, 1977:* Document 36a.

Additional Protocol II: Done at Mexico City Feb. 14, 1967 and entered into force for the U.S. May 12, 1971 (TIAS 7137; 22 UST 754); text in *Documents, 1968-9:* 392-4.

Protocol of Amendment to the Charter of the Organization of American States, signed at Buenos Aires Feb. 27, 1967 and entered into force Feb. 27, 1970 (TIAS 6847; 21 UST 607); summary in *Documents, 1968-9:* 399-401.

U.N. Security Council Resolution 242 (1967), enunciating principles for peace in the Middle East, adopted Nov. 22, 1967; text in *Documents, 1967:* 169-70.

1968

The Astronaut Rescue Agreement: Agreement on the Rescue of Astronauts, the Return of Astronauts, and the Return of Objects Launched into Space, signed Apr. 22, 1968 and entered into force Dec. 3, 1968 (TIAS 6599; 19 UST 7570); text in *Documents, 1967:* 392-6.

The Nuclear Nonproliferation Treaty: Treaty on the Non-Proliferation of Nuclear Weapons, signed in London, Moscow and Washington July 1, 1968 and entered into force Mar. 5, 1970 (TIAS 6839; 21 UST 483); text in *Documents, 1968-9:* 62-8.

1969

American Convention on Human Rights, opened for signature at San José Nov. 1969 and entered into force July 8, 1978; signed by U.S. June 1, 1977, but not in force for the U.S. as of 1978; text in *Bulletin,* 77: 28-39.

1970

Declaration on Friendly Relations: Declaration on Principles of International Law concerning Friendly Relations and Co-operation Among States, adopted as U.N. General Assembly Resolution 2625 (XXV), Oct. 24, 1970.

The Hague Convention: Convention for the Suppression of Unlawful Seizure of Aircraft, done at The Hague Dec. 16, 1970 and entered into force Oct. 14, 1971 (TIAS 7192; 22 UST 1641); text in *Documents, 1970:* 350-55.

1971

The Anti-Terrorist Convention: Convention to Prevent and Punish the Acts of Terrorism Taking the Form of Crimes Against Persons and Related Extortion That Are of International Significance, done at Washington Feb. 2, 1971 and entered into force Oct. 20, 1976 (TIAS 8413); text in *AFR, 1971:* 437-41.

The Seabed Arms Limitation Treaty: Treaty on the Prohibition of the Emplacement of Nuclear Weapons and Other Weapons of

Mass Destruction on the Seabed and the Ocean Floor and in the Subsoil Thereof, opened for signature Feb. 11, 1971 and entered into force May 18, 1972 (TIAS 7337; 23 UST 701); text in *Documents, 1970:* 69-73.

The Berlin Agreement: Quadripartite Agreement on Berlin Between the United States of America and Other Governments, signed at Berlin Sept. 3, 1971 and entered into force June 3, 1972 (TIAS 7551; 24 UST 283); text in *AFR, 1971:* 166-70.

The Montreal Convention: Convention for the Suppression of Unlawful Acts Against the Safety of Civil Aviation, done at Montreal Sept. 23, 1971 and entered into force Jan. 26, 1973 (TIAS 7570; 24 UST 565); text in *AFR, 1971:* 548-55.

Agreement on Measures to Reduce the Risk of Outbreak of Nuclear War Between the United States of America and the Union of Soviet Socialist Republics, signed in Washington and entered into force Sept. 30, 1971 (TIAS 7186; 22 UST 1590); text in *AFR, 1971:* 110-12.

The Second "Hot Line" Agreement: Agreement Between the United States of America and the Union of Soviet Socialist Republics on Measures to Improve the U.S.A.-U.S.S.R. Direct Communications Link, signed in Washington and entered into force Sept. 30, 1971 (TIAS 7187; 22 UST 1598); text in *AFR, 1971:* 113-14.

1972

The Shanghai Communique: Joint Statement issued at Shanghai on the conclusion of President Nixon's visit to the People's Republic of China, Feb. 27, 1972; text in *AFR, 1972:* 307-11.

The Space Liability Convention: Convention on International Liability for Damage Caused by Space Objects, done at London, Moscow, and Washington Mar. 29, 1972, and entered into force Sept. 1, 1972 (TIAS 7762; 24 UST 2389); text in *AFR, 1971:* 555-65.

The Biological Warfare Convention: Convention on the Prohibition of the Development, Production and Stockpiling of Bacteriological (Biological) and Toxin Weapons and on Their Destruction, opened for signature in London, Moscow, and Washington Apr. 10, 1972 and entered into force Mar. 26, 1975 (TIAS 8062; 26 UST 583); text in *AFR, 1971:* 90-95.

The ABM Treaty: Treaty Between the United States of America and the Union of Soviet Socialist Republics on the Limitation of Anti-Ballistic Missile Systems, signed in Moscow May 26, 1972 and entered into force Oct. 3, 1972 (TIAS 7503; 23 UST 3425); text in *AFR, 1972:* 90-95.

The Interim Agreement: Interim Agreement Between the United States of America and the Union of Soviet Socialist Republics on Certain Measures with Respect to the Limitation of Strategic Offensive Arms, signed in Moscow May 26, 1972 and entered into force Oct. 3, 1972 (TIAS 7504; 23 UST 3462); text in *AFR, 1972:* 97-101.

Declaration on the Human Environment, adopted by the U.N. Conference on the Human Environment at Stockholm June 16, 1972; text in *AFR, 1972:* 470-75.

1973

U.N. Security Council Resolution 338 (1973), calling for peace negotiations on the Middle East, adopted Oct. 22, 1973: text in *AFR, 1973:* 459.

The War Powers Act: Public Law 93-148, passed by the Senate Oct. 10 and by the House of Representatives Oct. 12, 1973 and repassed over the President's veto on Nov. 7, 1973: text in *AFR, 1973:* 484-90.

The Diplomatic Protection Convention: Convention on the Prevention and Punishment of Crimes Against Internationally Protected Persons, Including Diplomatic Agents, done at New York Dec. 14, 1973 and entered into force Feb. 20, 1977 (TIAS 8532); text in *AFR, 1973:* 586-94.

1974

Declaration on the Establishment of a New International Economic Order, adopted as U.N. General Assembly Resolution 3201 (S-VI), May 1, 1974; text in *AFR, 1974:* 103-7.

The ABM Protocol: Protocol to the Treaty on the Limitation of Anti-Ballistic Missile Systems, signed in Moscow July 3, 1974 and entered into force May 24, 1976 (TIAS 8276; 27 UST 1645); text in *AFR, 1974:* 226-8.

The Threshold Test Ban (TTB) Treaty: Treaty on the Limitation of Underground Nuclear Weapons Tests, signed in Moscow July 3, 1974 but not in force as of Sept. 1978; text in *AFR, 1974:* 229-33.

The IEA Agreement: Agreement on an International Energy Program, done at Paris Nov. 18, 1974 and entered into force Jan. 19, 1976 (TIAS 8278; 27 UST 1685); text in *AFR, 1974:* 466-90.

The Vladivostok Statement: Joint statement on the limitation of strategic offensive arms, released in Vladivostok Nov. 24, 1974; text in *AFR, 1974:* 508-9.

Charter of Economic Rights and Duties of States, adopted as U.N. General Assembly Resolution 3281 (XXIX), Dec. 12, 1974; text in *AFR, 1974:* 528-41.

1975

The Space Registration Convention: Convention on the Registration of Objects Launched into Outer Space, opened for signature at New York Jan. 14, 1975 and entered into force Sept. 15, 1976 (TIAS 8480).

Fifth International Tin Agreement, done at Geneva June 21, 1975 and entered into force June 14, 1977 (TIAS 8607).

The Helsinki Final Act: Final Act of the Conference on Security and Cooperation in Europe, signed in Helsinki Aug. 1, 1975; text in *AFR, 1975:* 292-360.

The Anti-Zionist Resolution: U.N. General Assembly Resolution 3379 (XXX), adopted Nov. 10, 1975; text in *AFR, 1975:* 507-8.

International Coffee Agreement, 1976, done at London Dec. 3, 1975 and entered into force Aug. 1, 1977 (TIAS 8683).

1976

U.S.-Spanish Treaty: Treaty of Friendship and Cooperation between the United States of America and Spain, signed at Madrid Jan. 24, 1976 and entered into force Sept. 21, 1976 (TIAS 8360); text in *AFR, 1976:* 212-15.

U.N. Security Council Resolution 385 (1976), calling for U.N.-sponsored elections in Namibia; adopted Jan. 30, 1976.

The IMF Amendment: Second Amendment of Articles of Agreement of the International Monetary Fund, approved by the IMF Board of Governors at Washington Apr. 30, 1976 and entered into force Apr. 1, 1978 (TIAS 8937).

Peaceful Nuclear Explosions (PNE) Treaty: Treaty between the United States of America and the Union of Soviet Socialist Republics on Underground Nuclear Explosions for Peaceful Purposes, signed in Washington and Moscow May 28, 1976 but not in force as of Sept. 1978; text in *AFR, 1976:* 181-6.

Environmental Modification Convention: Convention on the Prohibition of Military or Any Other Hostile Use of Environmental Modification Techniques, adopted by U.N. General Assembly Resolution 31/72 of Dec. 10, 1976 and signed at Geneva May 18, 1977 but not in force as of 1978; text in *AFR, 1976:* 188-93.

INDEX

A

ABM Treaty (signed Moscow May 26, 1972), 29

ACDA, *see* Arms Control and Disarmament Agency

Afars and Isaas, Territory of, *see* Djibouti, Republic of

Africa, 51, 62-78; and Cuban-Soviet involvement, 3-4, 45, 63-5, 72, 74-5, 80, 124; in Ford address (Jan. 12, excerpts), 148; Carter reference (New York, Mar. 17), 160; same (Notre Dame, May 22), 176; same (New York, Oct. 4), 206; Hartman reference, 225; Vance reference (Tehran, May 14), 260; Schaufele address, 290-300; Vance address (St. Louis, July 1), 310-19; in White House Summary (Dec. 17), 489-90

African Development Bank, 118; African Development Fund, Vance reference (St. Louis, July 1), 314

Agency for International Development (AID), 90; Vance reference (St. Louis, July 1), 313-14; Holbrooke reference, 380-81

AID, *see* Agency for International Development

Airline Pilot Association, International Federation of, 134

Algeria, 134

Amerasinghe, H.S., 131

American Convention on Human Rights (signed San José, Nov. 1969), 83; Vance reference (Apr. 30, Athens, Georgia), 168

Amin Dada, Idi, 71

Andreotti, Giulio, 42-3; White House statement on meeting with Carter (July 27), 229-31

Angola, 66, 118-19; Cuba-Soviet involvement, 4, 63-5, 72, 124; Carter reference (Notre Dame, May 22), 176

ANZUS, 101; Vance reference (New York, June 29), 395-6; Council meeting (Wellington, July 27-28): communiqué, 399-401

Arab-Israeli conflict, 3, 11, 30, 39, 46-50, 52-62, 140; in Ford address (Jan. 12, excerpts), 148; Carter reference (New York, Mar. 17), 160; same (Notre Dame, May 22), 176; same (New York, Oct. 4), 206-7; in NATO communiqué (Brussels, Dec. 9), 249-50; Vance statement on Middle East visit (Mar. 1, excerpt), 251-3; Carter statements on borders (Mar. 9, excerpts), 253-6; on Palestine homeland (Clinton, Mass., Mar. 16, excerpt), 256-8;

B

C

D

E

F

I

L

M

N

O

Y

Z

University of Lowell
Library